ASBESTOS:

Medical and Legal Aspects

THIRD EDITION

To David Palmer
with best wishes

ASBESTOS:

Medical and Legal Aspects

THIRD EDITION

by

Barry I. Castleman

with a contribution by
Stephen L. Berger

Prentice Hall Law & Business

Permissions, Prentice Hall Law & Business
270 Sylvan Avenue
Englewood Cliffs, N.J. 07632

Printed in the United States of America

Library of Congress Cataloging-in-Publication Data

Castleman, Barry I.
Asbestos : medical and legal aspects / by Barry I. Castleman, with a contribution by Stephen L. Berger.—3rd ed.
p. cm.
Includes bibliographical references and index.
ISBN 0-13-048414-8
1. Asbestosis. 2. Asbestos—Toxicology. 3. Asbestos industry—
Health aspects. 4. Asbestos—Law and legislation—United States.
I. Berger, Stephen L. II. Title.
RC775.A8C38 1990 90-7730
363.17'91—dc20 CIP

to Grace

Contents

Foreword xv

Preface to Third Edition xix

Acknowledgments xxi

1. The Development of Knowledge About Asbestosis 1

From Antiquity to Rediscovery 1
Case Reports in Medical Journals 6
The British Survey of Disease in Asbestos Factories .. 11
Other Events of 1930 17
1931-1935: Taking Account of Asbestosis 23
Conclusion 33

2. Cancer 39
Introduction 39
Discovery of the Cancer Threat with Asbestosis 40
Early Saranac Laboratory Cancer Tests with Asbestos 46
Additional Reports and Reviews Published in the 1940s 59
The Factory Inspectorate Report on Asbestosis and Cancer 62
The Scientific American Article 63
Dr. Wyers' Report from Cape Asbestos 63
Dr. Schepers' Visit to America 64
The Saranac Lab's Cancer Studies for the Quebec Asbestos Mining Association 67

More Reports and Reviews Linking Asbestos and Cancer 70
The Seventh Saranac Symposium 73
The Louvain Symposium 77
Other Reports in the Early 1950s 77
1955: Doll's Study and Other Events 80
Negative Opinions on Asbestos as a Cause of Cancer 84
Other Developments in 1955 87
Industry Reaction 90
The Industrial Hygiene Foundation Cancer Study ... 94
Remaining Doubters 97
National Differences in Asbestos Carcinogenicity 99
More Reports of Lung Cancer, Mesothelioma, and Other Cancers from Asbestos 101
Other Sources of Information on Asbestos and Cancer 109
Some Historical Comments of Asbestos Industry Medical Experts on Asbestos Carcinogenicity 111
Conclusion 112

3. Compensation: The Final Check-up 131

Early History of Workers' Compensation 131
Compensation for Asbestos Disease 142
Asbestos Compensation in the Early Years: Damage Suits 144
Workers' Compensation Law in Great Britain 146
Industry "Editing" of Medical Publications: Lanza's Surveys 148
The Asbestos Magazine Letters 151
Rising Tide of Compensation in the 1930s 153
Three Stories of Compensation 160
A Lobster Lunch with Vandiver Brown 160
Owens-Corning "Fiber-glass Itch Documents" 162
Saranac Compensation Reviews for Manufacturers ... 163
Published Literature on Compensability of Asbestosis Disability in Asbestos Product Users ... 165

Cancer ... 168
Workers' Compensation Claims by Insulators against Contracting Divisions of Asbestos Product Manufacturers ... 172
Lawsuits by Product Users Against Asbestos Manufacturers ... 187
Corporate Compensation Meetings at Manville ... 189
The Law Journals and Informal Consultation with Insurance Officials on Compensation Matters ... 191
Asbestosis Compensation in U.S. Navy Shipyards ... 193
The Mancuso Documents ... 194
Compensation at the Asbestos Mines in Canada ... 197
Obstacles to Workers' Compensation ... 200
Chapter Eleven ... 205
Conclusion ... 207

4. Thresholds and Standards ... 223

Social Origins and Nature of Direct Measures to Prevent Occupational Disease in the United States ... 223
Standards for Asbestos ... 237

Early British Factory Surveys and Standards ... 238
U.S. Reports Relating Degree of Exposure to Degree of Disease Risk ... 241
Plant Surveys by the U.S. Public Health Service ... 244
Asbestos Fiber Fraction of Inhaled Dust ... 250
Dust Control Measures in Germany ... 252
Unsteady Movement Toward Numerical Exposure Limits ... 254
The American Conference of Governmental Industrial Hygienists TLVs ... 257
Reaction in Other Countries to U.S. Numerical Guidelines for Asbestosis ... 260
Length of Fibers and Asbestosis ... 262

The Added Threat of Cancer 264
Criticism of the TLV and Delayed Response 266
Development of the Current U.S. Asbestos Standard 272
How many Fibers a Day is 2 Fibers per Cubic Centimeter? 275
Standards in the United Kingdom and Sweden, 1960-1970 276
Exposure to Asbestos in Insulation Work 278
Cancer from Asbestos in the Absence of Asbestosis 289
Efficacy of Current Standards and Proposals to Change Them 290
Conclusion 294

5. Asbestos Product Use **313**

The Charges: Failure to Test, Failure to Warn 314
Basic "State of the Art" Defense Arguments 316
The Published Literature on Asbestos Disease from Product Use 318
The Fleischer, Viles, Gade, and Drinker Report 329
Other Early Population Studies of Asbestosis in Insulators 332
The "Downstream" Literature 338
Unpublished Documentation 339
Epidemiology of Cancer in Asbestos Product Users 349
Conclusion 350

6. Alternatives to Asbestos Insulation **355**

Introduction 355
Patents and Government Publications 356
The Role of Asbestos 359
Magnesia Insulation 359
Calcium Silicate Insulation 363
Insulating Cements 373
Conclusion 374

Annotated List of Thermal Insulation Patents 380
Annotated List of Cement Patents 404
Annotated List of Friction Element Patents 406
Annotated List of Miscellaneous Asbestos Substitute Patents 410
Annotated List of Other Asbestos Substitute References 412

7. "Bystander" Asbestos Disease 423

Introduction 424
Earliest Recognition of the Potential for Bystander Asbestos Disease 424
Asbestosis and Cancer in Bystanders in the 1940s 427
Asbestos Air Pollution in the Community 427
A Mesothelioma Epidemic Forces the Issue of Environmental Asbestos Cancer 431
Household-Contact Asbestos Disease 432
Conclusion 436

8. Asbestos Disease in Brake Repair Workers 443

Annotated Bibliography of Health Hazards from Friction Product Manufacture and Repair 448
Brake Lining Manufacture 448
Grinding and Drilling Brake Linings—Early Papers 449
Compensation 450
Asbestos Air Pollution Hazard from Brake Wear 450
Remaining Chronology of Papers Relating to Asbestos Hazard in Brake Repair (through 1985) .. 451
Commercial Substitution of Asbestos in Friction Products 468
Control Technology for Brake and Clutch Work 473
Case Reports of Mesothelioma in Brake Repair Workers 476

9. Company Knowledge **481**

Raybestos-Manhattan, Inc. 484
Owens-Illinois (O-I) 492
Armstrong Cork 500
Fibreboard Corporation 500
Owens-Corning Fiberglas Corporation (OCF) 502
Unarco 509
Pittsburgh-Corning Corporation 511
Eagle-Picher Industries 513
United States Gypsum Company 516
Southern Textile Corporation 519
Keene Corporation 521
Union Carbide Corporation 523
W.R. Grace & Company 526
GAF Corporation 530
Companies Mining Asbestos in Quebec, Canada .. 532
Philip Carey Manufacturing Company 537
Asbestos Corporation Limited (ACL) 540
Johns-Manville Corporation 542
National Gypsum Company 549
Turner & Newall, Ltd. 554
Railroad Companies 561

10. Historical Research on Toxic Substances **569**

Introduction 569
Index Medicus 570
Computerized Indexes 571
Reviews—NIOSH Criteria Documents and other reports 571
Abstracts 576
Medical Textbooks 580
Carcinogens—See Hueper, IARC 585
Medical Conference Proceedings 591
International Labor Office Publications 593

Industry Trade Associations and Research Organizations 595
Unions 610
Engineering Journals 610
U.S. Government Documents 612
U.S. Department of Health and Human Services .. 612
U.S. Department of Labor 617
Bureau of Labor Statistics Safety Codes 626
U.S. Navy 628
U.S. Department of the Interior 630
U.S. Consumer Product Safety Commission 630
U.S. Department of Justice 630
U.S. Environmental Protection Agency 630
State and Local Government Documents 632
Government Publications in the United Kingdom 633
Archives and Collected Papers of Scientific Researchers 636
Trade Journals and the Technology Indexes 639
Patents 643
Insurance Literature 644
Encyclopedias 648
Newspaper Articles 649

11. The Legacy and the Challenge 651

Introduction 651
Mortality Estimates (U.S.) 654
Continuing Asbestos Exposure in the United States .. 657
The Economic and Social Cost of Asbestos Disease in the United States 664
Asbestos Litigation 666
Public Opinion and Public Health Policy 676
Criminal Sanctions and Personal Responsibility 683
Traditional Public Health Measures 689
Victims' Groups 690
Worldwide Proliferation of Asbestos Disease 691
The Current Expansion of Markets for Asbestos 700

The Role of the Canadian Government and other Governments in Promoting Asbestos Use 705
Conclusion 711

Appendix 1 719

The Asbestos Magazine Letters of 1935 719

Appendix 2 723

Prepared Statement of Francis H. May, Executive Vice President, Johns-Manville Corporation, November 14, 1978 724
Knowledge of a Hazard 725
Failure to Act 729
Conspiracy 733

Appendix 3 745

Correspondence with the *Journal of Occupational Medicine* about Health Risk of Asbestos in Drinking Water 745

Appendix 4 749

Chart used in trial by plaintiffs charging manufacturers with "Conspiracy of Silence" 750

Appendix 5 751

The Anthony J. Lanza Research Laboratories: New York University's Monument to Mendacity in Industrial Medicine 751

Index 757

Foreword

Barry Castleman's doctoral dissertation research demonstrates certain universal concepts on exposure and disease that were known for decades and repeatedly emphasized by Dr. Wilhelm C. Hueper, the world's foremost authority on environmental cancer.

Disease occurs wherever the exposure to the toxic or carcinogenic agent occurs, regardless of the country, the type of industry, job title, job assignment, or location of exposure. The disease will follow the trail of the exposure, and extend the chain of carcinogenic risk beyond the workplace, to the users of the products, to the general environment, the home, wherever and to whomever such exposures have occurred. It is the exposure and the nature of that exposure to asbestos that determines the risk and the diseases that subsequently result.

The disease itself provides the medical evidence that the nature of the exposure to asbestos was harmful, regardless of any description of limited or intermittent exposures or numerical designations in any regulations.

There are marked variations for each individual in the biological host response to toxic and cancer causing agents. The development of the carcinogenic risk due to asbestos or any other carcinogenic agent does not require a continuous exposure. The cancer risk does not cease when the exposure to the carcinogenic agent ceases, but rather the individual carries the increased cancer risk for the remaining years of life.

The need for and the importance of warning information about infectious, toxic, or cancer-causing chemicals has been a fundamental principle of public health for 100 years. Warnings make possible protective measures by those exposed, and provide the support for proper participation in the implementation of the protective measures required.

Historically, the identification and recognition of occupational cancers in the progress of medicine have been based primarily upon clinical epidemiology, the observations of physicians in practice. Virtually all the major observations relative to occupational cancer were first derived when a doctor saw a cluster of cases of a specific type of cancer among a group of workers in a particular occupation or industry, engaged in the manufacture or use of certain industrial materials.

For decades, the medical reports by doctors on disease and cancer pertaining to asbestos provided the essential evidence of the harmful effects of asbestos; so that proper protective measures, controls and medical surveillance by industry should not have been delayed for those who were exposed or used their products.

There has been a tremendous time lag between the already medically established diseases and the time when the compensation and other governmental agencies legally recognized such diseases. Carcinogens have existed in the environment, in the workplace, in air, soil and water without the establishment of governmental regulations for such carcinogens. The absence of a regulation does not make a cancer-causing agent safe for use or mean that a cancer risk does not exist.

The lessons of the asbestos experience, the long tragic chain of adverse medical, legal, and societal consequences, have reinforced the well recognized principle that the employer, the producer of chemical agents, has always had the inherent responsibility not to endanger the community or society. This responsibility, when ignored or slighted by management as evidenced by asbestos, as well as other carcinogenic agents, brings about an irreversible legacy of human and economic disaster in succeeding decades.

Moreover, the absence of governmental intervention and regulation in the past as well as the present, on behalf of the industrial population and the public, relative to carcinogenic agents, because of political pressures, does not in any way lessen or absolve the inherent responsibility of the initiator of the risk, the company or organization which brings about and causes the exposure to occur among workers and the public. Every manufacturer and processor of toxic and cancer-causing agents has had the responsibility to provide protective measures to the workers and to the public and all who use or are exposed to the harmful components of these products.

The mere adoption of regulations has no real meaning without the professional, industrial, and governmental resources and legal and moral determination to implement such regulations. For decades tens of thousands of industrial chemicals have been introduced into the work environment individually or in combination without prior testing for their cancer-causing effects. Unfortunately, this difficult problem of recognition of health effects has been compounded because there never has been more than a fraction of the professional personnel in industrial hygiene, toxicology and industrial medicine required to study the effects of such chemicals in the environment. Historically, the governmental effort, Federal and State, in industrial hygiene and industrial medicine in the investigation of occupational cancer as well as other toxic exposures, has been relatively insignificant.

What Dr. Hueper warned (in 1964) has been demonstrated in this book on asbestos. "Cancers of all types and causes display, even under already existing conditions, all the characteristics of an epidemic in slow motion. Through a continued, unrestrained, needless, avoidable and in part reckless increasing contamination of the human environment with chemical and physical carcinogens, and with chemicals supporting and potentiating their action, the stage is being set indeed for a future occurrence of a catastrophic epidemic, which once present cannot be effectively checked for decades with the means available nor can its course appreciably be altered once it has been set in motion."

What must be recognized is the virtual vacuum of scientific investigation over the years, of the microchemical environment of the industries throughout the country. The point is that as long as the necessary studies relative to the known and unknown hazards are not carried out, and thousands of these studies are required, the true magnitude of the scope of the health problems due to the industrial chemical environment will not be uncovered and made known to society.

Industrialization has proceeded at an ever-expanding pace for decades. But there never was the concommitant recognition of the need to determine what would happen to the industrial population and the public in terms of industrial chemical exposures. It must also be realized that studies in the absence of action to inform and protect the public will not meet the needs of society.

Thomas F. Mancuso, M.D.
June 28, 1984

Preface to the Third Edition

This is an attempt to tell the history of asbestos and public health in a comprehensive manner. However, it can only be an attempt to piece together and analyze what is revealed; it is not all that is known, still less is it all that happened. The historical background will no doubt continue to emerge, as time goes on.

It should not be too much to hope that a public good will be wrested from so much suffering, that a human-made tragedy such as this will never occur again. But dominant market forces militate against the protection of workers and the control of pollution. Society's attempts to apply laws to regulate business and protect workers, consumers, and the environment have faced entrenched opposition from the most powerful sectors of society. Can fundamental social behavior modification of vast, impersonal business enterprises be accomplished, given today's balance of power in society?

To break with the terms of the past, where the companies in an industry would even consider doing what has been done with asbestos, certain rules of society need to be changed, and others need just as badly to be preserved. One way to tell which laws cut which way is to consider what signals their existence and enforcement send to the Vandiver Browns of the world.

Those who inherit the challenge of seeing if we can do better this time and the next time around will be best prepared by a thorough understanding of the conditions that led to the asbestos disease epidemic, of the manifestations of thought and action that let so few choose this path for so many. This account is an effort to look squarely in the face of what we as public health workers and our allies are up against.

T.S. Rogers' expression "defensive research" has many more applications today than it had 35 years ago. In fact, much has not changed in society's rules or the patterns of conduct exemplified by individuals, companies, and governments in the asbestos business.

Snapshots of individual and collective human conduct revealed in the history of asbestos offer good material for analysis of what needs to be done differently. An understanding of these discrete events in terms of the relationships of power in society constitutes a framework for seeing what needs to be done. It is hoped that this account will facilitate an understanding of the thoroughly investigated example of asbestos, and that that in turn will contribute toward public health policy measures to assure that, in the future, other epidemics of preventable occupational and environmental disease will be prevented.

Barry Castleman
Baltimore
June 29, 1990

Acknowledgments

The author is grateful for the assistance of a large number of people in the preparation of this book. Historical information and manuscript review were provided by Drs. Wilhelm C. Hueper, Thomas F. Mancuso, Gerrit W.H. Schepers, Irving J. Selikoff, Harriet L. Hardy, Alfred A. Angrist, William E. Smith, Herbert K. Abrams, and Harold L. Stewart. My own contemporaries, Drs. Grace E. Ziem and David Ozonoff, Vicente Navarro, David Egilman and Mr. Stephen P. Teret, were equally helpful in this manner. Attorneys in asbestos litigation who gave generously of their time to assist in the compilation of material and, in a few cases, to review the completeness of corporate knowledge presented include Conard Metcalf, Paul Gillenwater, Russell Budd, Joseph Rice, George Kilbourne, Stanley Levy, Frederick Baron, Ronald Motley, Edward Rubin, Aaron Simon, Karl Asch, David Jacoby, Terry Richardson, David Sheehan, Lawrence Madeksho, Peter Nowinski, Marcia Hughes, and Archibald Wallace, III. Extensive research and clerical work were performed by Robert Mayes, Nancy Tait, Robert Goldberg, Kathy Hunting, Karla Heimann, Dorothea Zitta, Georg Neff, Roger Buker, Peter Moore, Valerie Waudby, Rakesh Madan, Terry Vetters, Scott Hensley, Albert Donnay, Kenneth Silver, Erica Tabachnick, Barbara Castleman, Daniel Berman, Rosemary Twigg, David Gee, Mark Gardner, Deborah Rubin, Ray Sentes, Alan Dalton, Anthony Bale, Paul Edholm, James Fite, Sherwin Zabah, Jean Leger and Joyce Kennedy.

1
The Development of Knowledge About Asbestosis

FROM ANTIQUITY TO REDISCOVERY

The earliest recorded historical recognition of the hazards of asbestos goes back to the time of Christ.[1] In Dr. Thomas Oliver's *Dangerous Trades*, published in 1902, the antiquity of the asbestos health hazard was noted by Adelaide Anderson, Lady Inspector of Factories:[2]

> In the great civilisations of antiquity, whether in the East, West, or in Europe generally, there was sufficient concentration of the forces of labour to produce the intensest forms of the maladies classed by Pliny as 'diseases of slaves'. Some of the most injurious processes known to us now are extremely ancient. To mention but a few: lead and quick-silver mining, the potters' craft, and the textile processes of preparing and weaving asbestos and flax.

Pliny, the ancient Roman historian, referred to the use of transparent bladder skin as a respirator to avoid inhalation of dusts by the slaves.[3] The Romans may well have found that slaves weaving asbestos were becoming disabled to the point that they first could not exert themselves in their work, and then died as their breathing difficulties became severe. The Romans instituted the use of respirators in order to extend the lives of their slaves, much as one might oil a machine to keep it from wearing out too quickly. While the Romans did not have pathologists with microscopes or the science of radiology available to them, they saw gross effects of asbestos inhalation on their workers.

Though pulmonary disease from breathing asbestos dust was discovered by the ancients, nothing more on the subject seems to have been recorded until near the turn of the twentieth century. A fibrous mineral with substantial resistance to heat and chemicals, asbestos found widespread use in insulation, fireproof clothing for high-temperature jobs, and many other industrial applications. The modern asbestos industry, which had started in the 1870s, grew rapidly. And though the devastating pulmonary disease was described at the turn of the century, it would not be until the 1920s that major efforts were mounted to control it.

A Vienna physician wrote in 1897 that emaciation and pulmonary problems in asbestos weavers and their families left no doubt that dust inhalation was the cause. He was concerned about lead and mineral components of the dust, and recommended ventilation and wet processing methods.[4]

In Great Britain, it was the Lady Inspectors of Factories who offered the first words about the hazards of asbestos. Asbestos manufacturing processes were given special attention in 1898 "on account of their easily demonstrated danger to the health of the workers, and because of ascertained cases of injury to bronchial tubes and lungs medically attributed to the employment of the sufferers." The report continued:[5]

> In the case of one particular asbestos works which I visited with Miss Deane, far from any precaution having been taken, the work (sifting, mixing, and carding) appeared to be carried on with the least possible attempt to subdue the dust; hand labour being used where mechanical contrivance was possible to obviate it, and no sort of ventilation being applied. One of the dustiest processes was carried on in a cellar. Recommendations were made for a scheme of applied ventilation to H.M. Inspector in charge of the districts in question, and the carrying out of the necessary works extended into 1899.

In their 1899 report, the Lady Inspectors expressed concern about the manufacture of "non-conducting jacketing for pipes" as a dusty process involving the use of asbestos.[6]

Even in this brutal and primitive era of industrialization, the asbestos industry attracted the prominent attention of the British factory inspectors.

> Of all injurious dusty processes of which I have again in 1906 received complaints none I believe surpass in injuriousness to the workers the sieving, preparing, carding, and spinning processes in asbestos manufacture.

The Lady Inspectors offered an example of a "characteristic complaint" and their findings upon visiting a plant during 1906:[7]

> The breaker, colloquially called the "Devil," produces a great deal of dust; there are two fans in the room, but these are not connected with the machines, so that they merely circulate the dust. Girls from 14 upwards look after the machines. A fortnight after the place is swept down the dust lies half an inch thick on the beams . . .
>
> The complaint gave a mild indication of the thick, fog-like atmosphere of dust that we found. Wherever carding and preparing processes are in progress in such works, unless exhaust ventilation is closely applied with suitable hoods and ducts to the point of generation of the dust, I have found that the atmosphere is of a thick whitey-yellow consistency with larger particles floating about therein.

The inspectors remarked that "at every visit" to asbestos plants, respiratory illnesses and in some cases deaths were reported. Several sample reports of illness were quoted. The writer went on to urge research on workers who had left this industry. Such investigations were "necessary before any true idea can be formed of the effect of this process."

Dr. H. Montague Murray reported on a fatal case of asbestosis to a British parliamentary committee on compensation in 1906.[8] The patient had worked in the "carding room" of an asbestos textile plant, and died at age 33. (Carding is a process of separating textile fibers and laying them in a parallel web, removing impurities in the process.) He told Murray that he was the last survivor of 10 people working in the carding room when he had started 14 years earlier. Murray expressed skepticism on this point ("I have no evidence except his word for that.") and went on to express optimism that efforts to control the dust would prevent the disease. Post-mortem examination showed no evidence of tuberculosis, and Murray attributed the man's death to the asbestos dust damage to the lungs. This is generally regarded as the first "proved" case of pulmonary disease from asbestos in modern times.

There were 16 deaths from pulmonary fibrosis at a French asbestos textile plant, prompting the implementation of local exhaust ventilation and respirators.[9] An Italian doctor reported the deaths of 30 patients employed in asbestos mining and spinning mills, none of whom responded to therapy for tuberculosis.[10]

Meanwhile, the pulmonary disease specialist Collis in England reported five more deaths from lung disease in a plant manufacturing asbestos (insulation) mattresses. His account is among the first to take note of the fundamental fact that "bystanders" in less dusty asbestos jobs were endangered by the dust raised by their co-workers.[11,12] This appeared in an annual report of the Chief Inspector of Factories.

Lady Inspector Whitlock in 1911 visited 24 asbestos factories employing 1074 workers, nearly equally divided by sex.[13]

> Very defective provision for exhaust in the dusty processes in asbestos manufacture was found by Miss Whitlock in most of the factories she visited and in some cases no provision had yet been made... She found a good deal of respiratory trouble in one form or another amongst the workers... In 'mattress' making (for engine covering), a very dusty process... probably the aid of suitable respirators is needed.

Miss Whitlock counselled the plant managers about installation of effectively applied exhaust, noting that some had already taken such measures.

In 1912, Professor J.M. Beattie conducted some experiments on animals and concluded that inhaled asbestos dust caused "a mild degree of fibrosis."[14]

By 1912, there were 3000 to 4000 people employed in the Canadian asbestos mines and mills and one small building products plant. The British Factory Department sent an inquiry about their health. The word came back that in the Bell Asbestos mines and mills all the women "looked strong and healthy, and none of them had any serious objections due to the presence of the dust." Previously, workers had been supplied with respirators, but after the installation of exhaust ventilation they objected to wearing them. This glowing report was marred only by the note that one of the community's oldest doctors believed that asbestos had a weakening effect on some of the workers' lungs.[15]

In 1914, a pathologist in Hamburg called attention to "crystals" in the lung tissue of a deceased 35-year-old asbestos worker.[16] This was one of the first reports of the characteristic appearance of the scarring caused by asbestos in the lungs.

Further inquiry by the British Factory Department in 1917 turned up nothing new regarding asbestos health hazards.[14] That year, in the United States, Pancoast, Miller and Landis reported on the abnormal chest X-rays of 15 asbestos workers, as well as workers in other dusty trades. Asbestos mills were among the dustiest buildings examined by these investigators.[17,18]

In 1918, Hoffman, a statistician with the Prudential Insurance Company, authored a monograph on dusty trades published by the U.S. Bureau of Labor Statistics.[12] He described Murray's case and quoted Collis' entire account from the 1910 British factory report.

But Hoffman went much further, giving a powerful illustration of the insurance industry's ability to identify hazardous trades. He cited Prudential's data showing that 9 of 13 asbestos workers had died before age 45. Hoffman was convinced that the mining and "dressing" of asbestos "unquestionably involve a considerable hazard", despite the fact that "the hygienic aspects of the industry have not been reported upon." In their own way, the insurance companies had *already* seen enough:

> (I)n the practice of American and Canadian life insurance companies asbestos workers are generally declined on account of the assumed health-injurious conditions of the industry.

That 3 of these asbestos workers' deaths were reportedly caused by tuberculosis and 2 were reportedly caused by pneumonia raised concern over the possible role of asbestos trapped in the lungs in causing these deaths. The data pointed to one or more of the following as possible roles for asbestos: 1) asbestos dust in the lungs might reduce a person's resistance to tuberculosis and/or pneumonia infections; 2) asbestos dust in the lungs might reduce a person's resistance to the progress of such infections, once they are contracted; 3) asbestos pneumoconiosis might be a serious disease in itself and be misdiagnosed as tuberculosis and/or pneumonia. Although these are small numbers, it is highly significant that life insurance companies were already refusing to insure asbestos workers, and that Murray had identified a distinct disease as the cause of death in an asbestos worker. Hoffman repeatedly urged research into the health hazards in the growing asbestos industry, decrying the lack of medical literature on the subject.

Case Reports in Medical Journals

Though the English had so far taken the greatest interest in the problem of asbestosis, they had published practically nothing in the medical literature. Starting in 1924, a number of important papers on asbestosis were published in the *British Medical Journal*. Now that asbestosis was discussed in a prominent medical journal, the word spread quickly and was picked up in journals in the United States and other countries. When reports later started to come in from many countries in the

1930s, the authors usually demonstrated an impressive awareness of previous work, which they cited.

The first detailed case report of asbestosis in an individual worker, published in the general medical literature, was by the British pathologist W.E. Cooke in 1924. Dr. Cooke described his patient as having tuberculosis and also "Fibrosis of the Lungs Due to the Inhalation of Asbestos Dust" (the title of the paper).[19] Cooke's report was noted by radiologists Pancoast and Pendergrass in Philadelphia, who also commented on 17 asbestos workers with pneumoconiosis they had examined. "This is another very dusty industry," they wrote.[20]

The subject of Cooke's case report was Nellie Kershaw, who had worked for Turner Brothers Asbestos Company from the age of 13, intermittently after age 26, until she was totally disabled at the age of 31. The Newbold Approved Society approached Turner Brothers in 1922 to pay Ms. Kershaw workers' compensation, on the basis of a doctor's certificate diagnosing her as having "asbestos poisoning."[21] The company replied that "we repudiate the term 'Asbestos poisoning'" and noted that no such condition was listed among the diseases that were compensable under the Workmen's Compensation Act.[22] The company meanwhile wrote to its insurer, "we feel that it will be exceedingly dangerous to admit any liability whatever in such a case and before referring the matter to you, we considered that we ought to do all in our power to repudiate the claim."[23]

Thus unable to obtain sickness compensation from either the National Health Insurance system or her employer, Nellie Kershaw wrote to Turner Brothers, saying "I think it is time there was something from you." She said she was in need of nourishment and had not received a penny during nine weeks off work.[24] The files at Turner & Newall contain no indication that any payment was ever made to Nellie Kershaw or her survivors.

The case was referred to Dr. Cooke two years later, after a coroner's enquiry was reported in the press, raising the possibility that asbestos had contributed to Ms. Kershaw's death at the age of 33. Her treating physician, Walter Joss, wrote that he had seen 10-12 cases a year of lung conditions in patients working with asbestos.[25]

In 1927, Cooke added certain pathologic details about Ms. Kershaw. In this paper, Cooke named the disease "pulmonary asbestosis."[26] The fibrosis contained masses of solid particles presumed to be asbestos fibers. McDonald offered further histologic* findings in an accompanying paper, describing the thickening of the alveolar (lung sac) walls. He also focused attention on the "foreign bodies" throughout the lungs. These characteristic formations were actually coated asbestos fibers and were subsequently referred to as asbestosis bodies or merely asbestos bodies.[27]

Occupational disease expert Thomas Oliver contributed a third article on the clinical picture of two women who were severely disabled by pulmonary asbestosis.[28] He described these cases in a report published in the United States, an abstract of which appeared in the *Journal of the American Medical Association*.[29,30] "*J.A.M.A.*" also carried an account of a presentation on asbestosis by Cooke and Hill at a conference of the Royal Microscopic Society earlier in 1927.[31] In January of 1928 *J.A.M.A.* ran an editorial reviewing Cooke's case and Murray's, commenting that "many other cases seem to have occurred." The editorial acknowledged the existence of "devices for removing the dust" in "modern factories," and concluded:[32]

> Nevertheless, asbestosis, because of its dangers and its unique pathologic features, deserves more attention than it has had.

Another British physician diagnosed asbestosis in a long-term asbestos factory worker in 1928. This was a "pure case," not accompanied by tuberculosis.[33] The British Factory Department investigated this case, the third one of which it had detailed knowledge, and confirmed that a definite pulmonary fibrosis was evident both clinically and radiologically. As a result, a comprehensive survey was started in February, 1928, by Merewether and Price of the Factory Department.[14]

*Histologic refers to the appearance of body tissues under a microscope.

The *British Medical Journal* meanwhile carried a report of several more cases of asbestosis verified by post mortem examination of workers from the mills in a chrysotile asbestos mining district of Rhodesia.[34] The ages of the people were not given, but two were described by the South African pathologist as "adult natives." Child labor was extensively used in the asbestos mining industry of Southern Africa, whose employees did not require as much stamina as workers in the region's rapidly expanding gold mines.

In 1929, the British clinician Haddow reported 4 fatal cases of asbestosis whose average age at death was 41. Two of these were the women Dr. Oliver had examined and reported on. Haddow also had four cases under treatment, women whose average age was 35.[35]

> I know that many workers had drifted away from the asbestos factory because they believed it was unhealthy, whilst many women had ceased work to attend to their homes, and any fibrosis present would readily be overlooked in later years when death overtook them.

Thus, some asbestos workers were apparently able to see (from the impaired condition and deaths of those longest employed at the factories, probably) that grave dangers were attendant upon dusty jobs in asbestos plants. Whether those who knew determined this entirely on their own or with some assistance from the medical profession in unclear.

Haddow reported that the patients he was treating with advanced disease all suffered from shortness of breath upon exertion, had dry cough, rales* at the lung bases in wintertime, and a maximum chest expansion of only one inch. The patients had observed an onset of symptoms after 5 years of work. Chest X-rays showed a characteristic picture of "abnormal radiolucency and marked limitation of diaphragmatic movement." Compensatory emphysema** was observed as the shrinkage of the lungs from fibrosis became severe.

*crackling sounds heard upon chest examination.

**A ballooning out of less affected tissue to compensate for scarring shrinkage in other areas.

A factual analysis of Haddow's paper (including a verbatim listing of his 12 conclusions) and others published in 1927-1929 in Great Britain, including one summarized in *Bulletin of Hygiene*, was compiled by the Sales Promotion Department (Market Analysis Section) of the Johns-Manville Corporation in 1930. The articles were examined at the medical library of the Mt. Sinai Hospital in New York.[36] This clearly demonstrates the accessibility of the British journals in the United States, as well as the fact that asbestosis medical literature was being read by employees of the largest American asbestos company.

There was a considerable amount of research activity on asbestosis in Great Britain in the late 1920s, reflected in a dozen separate medical publications there during 1928-1929.[37] At a British Medical Association meeting on occupational dust diseases, the finding of asbestos bodies at autopsy in the lungs of an asbestos factory neighbor was noted by Haddow. Occupational disease authority Thomas Legge urged that asbestosis be added to the list of compensable occupational diseases.[38] Legge, who had been a participant in the questioning of Montague Murray in 1906, would soon afterward lament:[39]

> Looking back in the light of present knowledge, it is impossible not to feel that opportunities for discovery and prevention were badly missed.

The intensified discussion of asbestosis was not, however, confined to medical circles. By 1929, the district medical officer near the Cape Asbestos factory in East London had diagnosed nine cases of asbestosis. One of several deaths attributed to the disease was the subject of a formal trial with evidence:[40]

> On the instruction of the coroner, an inquest was held with a jury, and the jury brought in the verdict of "asbestos poisoning."

The medical officer's investigations of asbestosis convinced him that the danger extended beyond the factories in which asbestos was used.[40] He observed that "an exposure to asbestos dust over a period of six months (could) produce a definite disability lasting over many years." He expressed the hope that, with the protective measures then being employed, deaths from asbestosis in Barking Town would cease to occur over the succeeding 15 years.

The British Survey of Disease in Asbestos Factories

In 1930, Merewether and Price of the Factory Department completed their investigation of conditions in the asbestos industry, producing an historic report.[41] They chose to study workers actively employed in the asbestos textile industry, because "it was considered advisable to exclude, as far as possible, from the inquiry, all workers exposed to the influence of mixed dusts."[42] The use of 2 to 10 percent of cotton or other vegetable fiber in the carding and spinning textile processes was not seen as an obstacle to the investigation of the fibrotic potential of asbestos dust. Furthermore, asbestos textile mills were centers of relatively large groups of workers. They had employed some individuals for long periods of time, thus giving the researchers an opportunity to observe the effects of varying durations of exposure. Besides, the Factory Department appears to have had no jurisdiction over such people as asbestos insulation workers at construction sites and shipyards.[40] Dr. Merewether described his subject in plain English:[41]

> It is helpful to visualize fibrosis of the lungs as it occurs among asbestos workers as the slow growth of fibrous tissue (scar tissue) between the air cells of the lungs wherever the inhaled dust comes to rest. While new fibrous tissue is being laid down like a spider's web, that deposited earlier gradually contracts. This fibrous tissue is not only useless as a substitute for the air cells, but with continued inhalation of the causative dust, by its invasion of new territory and consolidation of that already occupied, it gradually, and literally strangles the essential tissues of the lungs.

> In common with other essential organs of the body the lungs have a large reserve of tissue for use in emergencies and to permit of a diminution in functional capacity due to advancing age or disease. For this reason, and because fibrosis of the lungs is essentially a local disease, it is only when the fibrosis progresses to the extent of obliterating this reserve, that undue shortness of breath on any extra effort draws the worker's attention to the fact that his health is not what it should be. The other symptoms of the disease such as cough are equally unassuming, and are readily ascribed to some common and trivial cause.
>
> From this point the progress of the disease is more rapid, since it is now encroaching on the remaining sound tissue of the lungs, already only just sufficient to maintain him in his ordinary daily activities. Ultimately, if no acute respiratory infection has precipitated a fatal termination, a stage is reached when the lungs can do little more than maintain life, and the shortness of breath becomes extreme.

Merewether published a lengthy report of his findings in the U.S. the same year as his official government report in England. In both writings he reviewed the history of his government's interest in asbestosis, even offering explanations for the slowness to recognize the problem and take appropriate action.

To the readers of the *Journal of Industrial Hygiene,* he described the early stages of the disease succinctly:[42]

> This disease, insidious in its onset, stealthily advances with but faint warnings of its progress; inexorably it cripples the essential tissues of the lungs, yet for a considerable period causes almost no inconvenience to the worker. As time goes on, however, the lungs find more and more difficulty in re-aerating the blood; and breathing is quickened on slight exertions. Still the worker is able to remain at work, but is aware of his undue shortness of breath on extra effort. Usually, however, he ascribes it to causes other than the dust he is inhaling.

As for the authorities' reasons for so slowly appreciating this threat, Merewether made several points. For one thing, the disease was commonly misdiagnosed even in an advanced stage of development:

> Even in its terminal stages, the disease, deceitful to the last, may masquerade as chronic bronchitis, pulmonary tuberculosis, broncho-pneumonia, or the like.[42]

In addition, the science of radiology had been in its infancy in 1915, but by 1930 had "attained the status of being an indispensable aid to the diagnosis of the dust diseases of the lungs." Further, the asbestos industry had been much smaller at the start of the century, but by the late 1920s had grown substantially. Because of this increase in employment, the Factory Department was more inclined to give priority attention to the health hazards in the asbestos industry.

Merewether and Price examined 374 asbestos factory workers out of an estimated 2,200 who would have met their selection criteria. Those with previous work in other dusty occupations were excluded from the analysis, leaving 363. Fully 95 (26.2%) of those examined clinically definitely had asbestosis, and another 21 had "precursive signs" of the disease (these were given no weight in the analysis). The incidence of disease increased dramatically with the number of years employed in the asbestos industry. (See Table 1.) Excluding those employed under 5 years, the incidence of asbestosis was about 35 percent. Four out of five still working in the industry after 20 years had asbestosis. Cough, cyanosis of the lips (a bluish tinge in the color of the skin due to impaired oxygenation of the blood in circulation), and dyspnea (shortness of breath, especially upon exertion) were each present in 50 to 60 percent of the asbestotics.[42] Well-marked clubbing of the fingertips, another sign of chronic respiratory disease, was seen in a few cases. Rales, or crackling sounds, were also heard upon chest examination of some of the asbestotics.

Chest X-rays of asbestotics had a diffuse, hazy appearance, described as the "ground glass appearance." The most marked

Table 1. Incidence of Fibrosis Relative to Length of Employment[41]

Years Employed	Number Examined	Cases of Asbestosis: Number	Cases of Asbestosis: Group Incidence
0-4	89	0	
5-9	141	36	25.5%
10-14	84	27	32.1%
15-20	28	15	53.6%
20 and over	21	17	80.9%
TOTALS	363	95	26.2%

X-ray changes were in the bases of the lungs, in contrast to silicosis, where changes are mostly in the upper lobes of the lungs. Chest X-ray changes were more subtle than those of silicosis, for a given degree of disability. Asbestosis was usually easily distinguished from tubercular lesions as well on X-ray and by tests for TB bacteria. The asbestosis was a diffuse lung scarring (unlike silicosis which appeared as larger nodules), and the increased density of fibrous tissue caused the characteristic abnormalities seen on the chest X-ray film.

Merewether X-rayed only a minority of the workers examined, and he apparently felt that positive X-ray findings were not a necessary prerequisite to making a diagnosis of asbestosis.[42]

> Clearly, the maturation of asbestos fibrosis is spread over a period of years, and by the time the stage is reached when the features discussed above are, in varying degree, positive, and the radiologic picture is recognizable, the fibrosis is not in its inception, nor even in its earliest stages, but is developed and fairly widespread.

Even taking account of the state of practice in pneumoconiosis radiology in 1930, one important point was established here: that an early stage of asbestosis might not be clearly recognizable from the chest X-rays, and a full clinical examination might pick up cases considered negative or doubtful on X-ray.

Merewether noted that his survey, limited to those at work, would miss some cases of asbestosis among those who had given up work and others temporarily off work for illness and other reasons.

As for the *maturation period* necessary for the development of asbestosis, data from this survey would serve as a guide for the interpretation of subsequent research. No definite cases of fibrosis were found until 5 or more years had elapsed from the start of employment. Afterwards:

> The rate of progress and duration of the disease varies within wide limits. With continued exposure to high concentrations of dust, the fibrosis may be fully developed in from 7 to 9 years, and may cause death after about 13 years exposure, exceptionally in a shorter period. On the other hand, with exposure to less concentrations of dust, the period of maturation of the fibrosis may be extended to 15, 20, or 25 years. There are definite indications, derived from the industrial histories and examination of workers, that a diminution in the concentration of dust in the air breathed, either by change of employment from a highly dusty process to one less dusty, or the effect of methods taken for the suppression of dust, results in a prolongation of this period of maturation of the fibrosis except in the late stages of the disease.

Merewether and Price analyzed the workers' exposure by length of employment and dustiness of the job. They observed that *the degree of fibrosis ultimately produced and the speed with which it developed were directly proportional to the intensity of the exposure sustained.* The public health implications of this were spelled out:

> If this hypothesis is correct, and the evidence points to it, the practical inferences are of very great importance, since it follows that the application of measures resulting in the reduction of the concentration of dust in the air in the neighborhood of dusty asbestos processes will cause, first

> a great increase in the length of time before workers develop a disabling fibrosis, and secondly, the almost total disappearance of the disease, as the measures for the suppression of dust are perfected.

Samples were taken of dust-laden air in the plants, and 51 dust counts were tabulated with a minimal description of each process, whether it was equipped with local exhaust ventilation, and whether there were other processes in the same room.[37] In the vast majority of cases, there were other processes in the room besides the process where sampling was done, greatly confounding attempts to rate the dust risk by process. However, the medical findings did suggest that one group of workers was at lower risk than the rest: "spinners"—those engaged in spinning, twisting, doubling, and plaiting the asbestos threads. This group took longer, on the average, to develop fibrosis, and also appeared to be least exposed to asbestos dust among the work force studied. The dust sample analysis counted dust particles in the air in toto, and did not distinguish fibers from other airborne dust particles. (For further information, see Chapter 4.)

Merewether and Price also made recommendations for the control of dust exposures in asbestos plants. These recommendations covered specifically each major manufacturing industry using asbestos, and in addition included general "house-keeping" practices to be followed by all. In addition, periodic medical examinations of the workers were recommended, to exclude people with lung disease and detect cases of fibrosis and tuberculosis "at the earliest possible moment." The importance of worker education was stressed. Respiratory protection was "only recommended as a second line of defense, and not in substitution for other preventive measures specifically directed to the control of dust as near as possible to its point of origin."

In a magazine article entitled "Workers Who Breathe Death," Merewether's findings were reported. "The only advantage which the less dusty processes have is that it takes longer finally to cripple and disable the worker," the article said.[43]

Government regulation of the industry and compensation for asbestosis were strongly urged.

The Merewether and Price survey was noted in numerous other publications in England and the United States.[44-49] The major medical journals in England promptly carried editorials on it.[50-51]

But the "British monopoly" on asbestosis research was now over, and in 1930 new contributions would emerge from a number of countries. For it turned out that virtually everywhere asbestosis was looked for, it was found.

Other Events of 1930

This year the British activities on asbestosis received considerable attention in the United States medical literature, as the first case reports of asbestosis in the U.S. were published. There was also a conference on pneumoconisis held by the International Labor Office in 1930, at which the subject of asbestosis was repeatedly discussed. Medical reviews of the state of knowledge on asbestosis were published in a number of countries. And the British radiologists observed that cessation of exposure to asbestos would not halt the steady progress of the deadly lung disease, once it was established.

Statistical highlights of Merewether's findings were reported in the *Journal of the American Medical Association* on June 28, 1930, at the time when a bill had just been introduced in Parliament to extend the silicosis provisions of the Workmen's Compensation Act to cover asbestosis as well.[52]

> Supporting the bill, Lord Russell for the government said that many processes in silica working could not show a mortality approaching that for the asbestos industry, in which 14 fatal cases had now been reported and in addition 3 deaths from asbestosis associated with tuberculosis.

Later that year, the *Journal of the American Medical Association* noted Mills' report of an asbestosis case.[53,54] This report, just published in *Minnesota Medicine*, described a severe case of asbestosis in a man who had worked in an asbestos mine in South America long before his death. Mills' alert to doctors in the U.S. was amplified.

> Concerning the relation of physicians of the United States to this industry, Mills pointed out that asbestos is mined and manufactured in many parts of this country, and that pulmonary asbestosis surely will be encountered.

The editorial went on to report that the Workmen's Compensation Act in England had been extended to include asbestosis.

The *Journal of the American Medical Association* was the most widely read medical journal in the United States. By 1920, the *J.A.M.A.* was mailed directly to 48 percent of the physicians in the U.S. and was believed to have reached 80 percent of them.[55] Total circulation of the journal in 1930 was 98,000, including institutions and individual subscribers.[56]

Additional medical case reports and reviews of the literature on asbestosis were published in the U.S. by Lynch and Smith (in *J.A.M.A.*), and Soper, in 1930.[57,58] Dr. Soper began by expressing disappointment with the medical profession's slowness to appreciate the threat of dust hazards in general and asbestos dust in particular. He concluded,

> When there has been exposure to asbestos dust the presence of pulmonary asbestosis should always be suspected.

The International Labor Office held an international conference on silicosis and other dust diseases in Johannesburg, South Africa, in 1930.[59] This was the first of several major conferences held by the I.L.O. bringing together pneumoconiosis experts and knowledge from all over the world. Here, too, it was noted that there was a bill before the British Parliament to provide compensation for workers disabled by asbestosis. Authorities in Great Britain reported that, "Asbestos damaged (the lungs) more rapidly than silica." Incapacitating asbestosis had been observed in South Africa and southern Rhodesia but not in Australia. Engineering dust controls had been installed at an Italian asbestos plant in 1912. An Italian said it was "well known" that blue asbestos (crocidolite from Africa) was more deadly than white (chrysotile, mined in Italy and elsewhere); but no supporting evidence was given.[60] Researchers from the Saranac Laboratory for Research on Tuberculosis (U.S.) contributed a preliminary report on their experiments on guinea pigs inhaling asbestos.

The International Labor Office had stern warnings about asbestos in its encyclopedia, *Occupation and Health,* in 1930:

> All processes from extraction onwards unquestionably involve a considerable hazard, and American and Canadian life insurance companies generally refuse asbestos workers on account of the assumed deleterious conditions in the industry.

The article went on to deplore the lack of more detailed data on the hazard in various branches on the industry, laying stress on the "rapidly increasing development of industries utilizing asbestos."[61] Other treatises on pneumoconiosis and preventive medicine now included sections about asbestosis.[62,63]

In Great Britain, yet another detailed review was based on the experience from treating 37 asbestosis cases.[64] The authors remarked that shortness of breath would eventually lead the worker to "discard the respirator worn hitherto under protest."

Also in the year 1930, additional medical articles on asbestosis were published not only in Great Britain but also in Italy and France.[37,65-67]

Even *The Asbestos Worker,* a monthly journal of the International Association of Heat and Frost Insulators and Asbestos Workers, made reference to asbestosis that year.[68] A medical report from the U.S. Department of Labor's *Monthly Labor Review* was reprinted but without any analysis or interpretation. It is unlikely that the union magazine editor or the insulation workers receiving this report were able to grasp the potential significance for them of this "new form of chronic pulmonary fibrosis," which had so far been reported in asbestos mine and factory workers. Some of the signs and symptoms described ("slight dullness over the base of each lung and deficiency of the respiratory murmur with fine crepitating rales") must also have meant little to the tradesmen who received this report. The subject of asbestosis would not come up again in this union's publications until decades later.

Dr. J.V. Sparks of London journeyed to Los Angeles to present a major paper on asbestosis at the 1930 meeting of the Radiological Society of North America. The paper was published the following year in the Society's journal, *Radiology.*[69] Sparks remarked that, "practically no literature (on asbestosis) has been published in America." Noting that 80 percent of the asbestos used in England came from Canada, he observed that the Americans used the same raw material. And if U.S. industry was built along the same lines as that in England "an effect should be produced on the lungs similar to that produced in England." Sparks and his co-workers at the City of London Chest Hospital had seen 50 cases of asbestosis and had examined 6 records of post mortem findings. These doctors may well have told some of their patients to get out of the asbestos industry, hoping the disease state would stabilize or perhaps even lessen. However, Sparks found any such optimism unjustified:

> It seems reasonable to suppose that after some years of such employment the workers may become affected by the inhalation of asbestos dust and seek other industries. The fact that they cease to be exposed to the dust does not, however, prevent the disease, when once established, from progressing.

Thus, radiologists were able to establish the startling fact that in some cases asbestosis became more serious as time passed, even for workers who had removed themselves from workplaces where they were exposed to asbestos. Not only did these workers fail to recuperate, but their health continued to deteriorate as the asbestos fibers trapped in their lungs produced a steadily increasing fibrosis. The "maturation" period Dr. Merewether had spoken of was still in progress. Sparks,

Wood, and Gloyne at City of London Hospital were seeing time bombs in people's chests that no one could defuse. Sparks said under "Prognosis" that medicine was unable to relieve the patients' chief complaint, dyspnea. He concluded,

> Prophylaxis is all-important and the only hope for the asbestos worker lies in the adoption of proper means of protection against the risk attendant on the inhalation of the fibers.

Dr. Frank Pedley authored two publications on asbestosis in Canadian medical journals in 1930.[70,71] His editorial in the *Canadian Medical Association Journal* was by far the more cautious of the two. In both, Pedley said that mining and milling asbestos might not present the hazard of disease found in factories where asbestos was used. Pedley's editorial acknowledged that,[70]

> The failure to recognize the disease in Canada, however, is no evidence of (its absence), for in other occupations experience has shown that large groups of men may suffer serious occupational effects, which go unrecognized for years.

In his article in *Canadian Public Health Journal,* Pedley began by noting that the Province of Quebec was a leading source of asbestos, and the fibrous mineral had been mined there "for forty years or more." He went on,

> To our knowledge, however, *no case of pneumoconiosis has been reported from asbestos in Canada,* and the general impression among the miners is that the dust is not hazardous. (emphasis added)

He presented figures for overall reported tuberculosis mortality in Thetford Mines compared with the entire Quebec Province. There was no striking excess of deaths in the asbestos mining town.

Pedley then described the asbestos bodies that had been

reported in British literature on asbestosis (variously referred to in the early literature as "asbestosis bodies" and "curious bodies"):

> Unquestionably these 'curious bodies' have stimulated much interest in the disease, asbestosis. Pathologists, whose interest in such a disease might languish, come above at the sight of the 'curious bodies.'

Pedley acknowledged Simson's report of asbestosis in "four Rhodesian miners." Simson's subjects had worked in a mill processing chrysotile asbestos fiber from a nearby mining operation. Chrysotile asbestos, by far the most abundant of the commercial asbestos minerals, is the same type of asbestos that was mined in Canada. Pedley did not attempt to explain how milling chrysotile in Canada presented no asbestosis hazard, while milling this same mineral in Rhodesia and weaving Canadian asbestos in England could both cause asbestosis.[71]

One could imagine reasons for Dr. Pedley's failure to find evidence of pneumoconiosis in the asbestos mining districts—but the truth is that he *did* find numerous asbestosis cases not mentioned in his publications in 1930 or subsequently in the medical literature.

An obscure 1944 report from the Metropolitan Life Insurance Company includes a table of data compiled in 1930 by Pedley and Dr. A. J. Lanza of Metropolitan Life.[72] It shows that, of 195 workers examined in Thetford Mines and Asbestos, Quebec, 42 had asbestosis. Only 76 of these 195 men had been in the industry for more than 10 years. This medical survey was part of an investigation directed by Dr. Lanza at the request of asbestos companies in the United States.[73]

In his 1935 report on factory workers Lanza alluded to the existence of this survey at the asbestos mines, but the latter was never published, nor were its findings acknowledged by Lanza.[74] Pedley did not later correct the false impression left by his 1930 writings in Canadian journals, either.

To sum up developments as of 1930, it may be said that:

1. The signs, symptoms, X-ray appearance, and pathological aspects of asbestosis were rather well understood.
2. The disease was fatal in a number of reported cases.
3. The disease was capable of progressing after exposure to asbestos dust had been discontinued.
4. Even the people still actively employed in asbestos mining, milling, and manufacturing showed a high prevalence of asbestosis; roughly half of those surveyed with 10 or more years in the industry were diagnosed with asbestosis.

As Selikoff and Lee put it, "Asbestosis had now definitely arrived!"[75]

1931-1935: Taking Account of Asbestosis

After 1930, the medical literature continued to grow, with primary case reports and group studies coming out of Europe and the United States. In the meantime, publications increasingly removed from the primary medical journals broadcasted alerts about asbestosis.

In 1931, German writers alone produced nine medical articles on the subject of asbestosis.[37] Two of the more detailed studies, on asbestos factory workers in Dresden and Berlin, found that every worker with more than 10 years of exposure had asbestosis.[76,77]

The German reports were summarized in English in numerous American and English publications.[78-84]

In the United States, Stewart and his co-workers reported two cases of asbestosis seen at autopsy.[85] One of these men had worked nine months in an asbestos plant with no dust controls, and he later developed severe asbestosis that was the main contributing cause of death. The other man worked 9 years in a low-exposure job, wore "silver dust protectors in his nostrils," and still developed a minor grade of asbestosis. As the authors pointed out, the two cases "illustrated nicely the extremes and some of the features of the disease." The authors closed with a plea for adoption of preventive measures.

Chest physicians in South Carolina reported an additional "pure case" of asbestosis in an asbestos textile worker in 1931. The authors surveyed the literature and counted 172 cases of asbestosis in medical journals.[86]

Radiologists Pancoast and Pendergrass reported that they had seen 58 men employed at various occupations in asbestos mining, of whom 15 "showed definite evidence of pneumoconiosis."[87] They did not regard the hazard at the mine as comparable to that in factories, which were dustier.

Gardner and Cummings had exposed guinea pigs to airborne asbestos and produced asbestosis in the animals, which they examined and described pathologically. There was little if any enhancement of the virulence of tuberculous infection by asbestosis.[88]

In 1932, medical examinations were conducted for all 1140 employees of Johns-Manville's factory in Manville, New Jersey. Guidance was obtained from Metropolitan Life doctors Lanza and Fellows in designing the survey. Interpretation of chest X-rays was done by Dr. F. V. Meriwether, chief of the U.S. Bureau of Mines clinic in Picher, Oklahoma; however, Dr. Meriwether was not provided with information on the occupational exposure histories of the workers after their hire by Johns-Manville. The report of this unpublished study shows 327 (29%) of the workers had X-ray evidence of pneumoconiosis, which was called "asbestosis" if the worker had had no prior history of exposure to occupational dust hazards. The company separately tabulated length of service and length of exposure, while noting asbestosis among a number of workers listed as having no exposure. Some of the employees diagnosed by X-ray as having asbestosis, whose "exposure" at Manville was recorded as "none" were two watchmen, a mill wright, packing and shipping department workers, and machinists.[89] Thus Manville plant workers exposed as "bystanders" were identified as asbestosis victims before any such cases were reported in the published medical literature (See chapter 7).

The Children's Bureau of the U.S. Department of Labor convened an expert committee in 1932 to formulate guidelines for the protection of children at work. The committee was unanimous in recommending that minors under 18 be prohibited from working in a number of hazardous occupations. Among those listed were "occupations involving exposure to free silica dust, asbestos dust, or other dusts in injurious quantities."[90] This reference to health hazards in the asbestos industry was reiterated by a labor representative at a 1933 government hearing on the asbestos industry. The hearing was attended by the Presidents of Johns-Manville Corporation and Philip Carey Manufacturing Company, and a representative of Keasbey & Mattison Company.[91]

An I.L.O. bibliography, *Pneumoconiosis,* published in 1932, listed 70 references on asbestos. With the exception of one article on geological occurrence, these were all medical reports about asbestosis.[92] The point of diminishing returns had already been reached, however. The next 70 publications would have little to add to the framework of their predecessors on the subject of asbestosis. The first reports of another scourge, lung cancer with asbestosis, were yet to be written.

London chest physician Philip Ellman published thorough articles on the features of asbestosis in both the U.S. and Great Britain in 1933-1934.[93,94] He described some of his patients, who included: a 22-year-old woman with "early" asbestosis; a 26-year-old woman whose X-ray showed "definite and progressive spread of fibrosis in both lungs in less than 9 months"; and a man with an early stage of asbestosis who had worked for 10 years as a pipe-coverer (insulation worker). Ellman also mentioned that a terrier dog "kept for ratting purposes in an asbestos factory" was "lethalled in its own interest due to the distressing degree of dyspnea the dog suffered." Ellman warned that "Pulmonary asbestosis, once established, is a progressive disease with a bad prognosis." He also said,

> Inhalation of asbestos dust must be expected sooner or later to produce pulmonary fibrosis, depending upon (a) length of exposure and (b) nature and concentration of the dust.

Ellman's clinical description of the asbestotic was vivid, and was one of the earliest comparisons of asbestosis with its better-known cousin, silicosis.

> (A) case of simple silicosis often looks well, declares that he is well, and is even offended when any reflection is cast upon the soundness of his lungs. In contrast to this, a case of asbestosis is cyanotic, emaciated, anxious, and often obviously going downhill. Such, then, is the clinical picture of *sufferers* from asbestosis.
>
> Only by an extension of meaning could the word 'sufferer' be applied to anyone with simple silicosis. (original emphasis)

The publication of Ellman's article in the *British Journal of Radiology* followed another on asbestosis by radiologist W. Burton Wood.[95] Dr. Wood reported that he had had patients with asbestosis that did not worsen after cessation of exposure, as well as others that did.

The British journal *Tubercle* ran separate, comprehensive, three-part articles on asbestosis by Merewether and Gloyne.[14,96] Gloyne described minutely the pathological aspects of asbestosis, and Merewether described almost everything else then known. Merewether began with a description of the asbestos industry's phenomenal growth. Just between 1922 and 1927 Britain's consumption of asbestos had tripled.

Merewether reviewed earlier work, and described the disease as he had in his 1930 Factory Department report. By 1933, he recommended that chest X-rays were "invaluable" in diagnosing asbestosis, "and should never be neglected."

Again and more clearly, the fundamental concepts of the *requisite lung burden* and the *period of maturation of fibrosis* were explained:

> (T)his is important from the practical point of view of prevention, that a certain minimum fibrosis-producing amount, as it were, of asbestos dust must be trapped in the lungs in order to produce a potentially disabling or serious amount of fibrosis, and also that a certain "maturation" period must elapse before that amount of fibrosis is developed.

Pausing to describe two illustrative fatal cases with under 5 years' duration of exposure, he went on to explain the interplay between exposure and the maturation of disease:

> Particulars of cases seem to show that with high concentrations of dust the minimum period of time which must elapse between the commencement of exposure and the production of a serious degree of asbestosis is approximately seven years—which include not only the trapping period of the fibrosis-producing dose of dust, but also the maturation period of the fibrosis, which periods, of course, overlap.
>
> The existence of this, which may be referred to as the fibrosis-producing period, i.e., the period which must elapse from the date of commencing work before a serious degree of asbestosis can be produced, accounts for the fact that it is not until the second five years of employment is reached that appreciable numbers of cases of asbestosis are discovered.
>
> This period of seven years is, of course, the minimum, and few cases mature in this minimum period; in successive years, however, depending on the dustiness of the process in which employed, more cases mature. In the more dusty processes the fibrosis-producing period, as defined above, is commonly eleven years.

The workers themselves were commonly oblivious of the inexorable progress of the disease until it became well advanced, he said.

Dr. Merewether then posed the question "Does Asbestosis Shorten Life?" The answer to this question is "emphatically Yes," he wrote. He presented figures showing that of 42 fatal cases of asbestosis in Great Britain, the average age at death was 41. All but two of these cases were examined post-mortem. The extent of the devastation caused by asbestosis was indicated by a comparison with silicosis:

> The average duration of employment sufficient to cause a fatal degree of asbestosis was only 15.2 years, as compared with 40.1 years for all cases of silicosis.

Merewether concluded that asbestosis was "comparable with the more serious silicosis risks" based on these findings.

In light of the irreversible and progressive nature of asbestosis, he held out little hope for the victims of asbestosis:

> The ultimate prognosis in those with developed asbestosis or in those who have incarcerated in their lungs a fibrosis-producing amount of asbestos dust, even though no appreciable fibrosis or only a slight amount can be detected, is bad. Death from the disease is inevitable sooner or later, if life is not cut short by accident or by some unconnected disease.

He went on to explain that asbestosis needn't even be advanced to cause death. It proved sufficient in some cases simply by destroying the body's *reserve* capacity to deal with other onslaughts in life:[14]

> It is remarkable to what extent the lungs can be affected and yet life in a fair degree of comfort remain. The reserve is, however, so slender that the addition of any burden to the system, in the form of a disturbance of health which would only slightly inconvenience a normal person, may overcome the remaining resistance and precipitate the fatal outcome. It is apparent, therefore, that while the onset of an acute respiratory infection is most ominous, the development of any disease which directly or indirectly throws an added strain on the heart or lungs is of serious import.
>
> For these reasons and from consideration of the features present in recorded fatal cases, *the view is forced upon one that the existence of even a moderate degree of asbestosis is a serious and ever-present potential risk to life.* (emphasis added)

Donnelly, a physician in North Carolina, reported on 15 cases of asbestosis he had seen from the asbestos plants in his area. He emphasized that exposure "for even a comparatively short time is a definite and serious industrial hazard."[97]

> The fact that the condition when once acquired is permanent and more or less rapidly progressive is most important from a public health viewpoint.

Donnelly said it was "the concensus of opinion ... that the protective devices now in use in many plants are most inadequate." He went on to contrast the British asbestos regulations (with their requirements for dust suppression and annual medical examinations of workers) with the lack of such regulations in North Carolina. The same criticism he applied to the matter of workers' compensation for ("almost invariably" total disability from) asbestosis in the two locales. Donnelly also alluded to the damage suits being filed by workers with asbestosis against the factory owners. His presentation was made at the 1933 meeting of the American Public Health Association and was promptly published in the association's journal.[97]

In 1934, Wood and Gloyne published a review of the first 100 cases of asbestosis they had seen.[98] Among the 67 women in their series, "The shortest exposure was six months (2 cases)..." Most of the men and all of the women in this series worked at the same factory. "Among the men the shortest exposure was 11 months..." Thus, these authors reported seeing *at least* 3 cases of asbestosis resulting from less than one year of occupational exposure to asbestos. Presumably, these individuals worked at jobs with heavy exposure to airborne asbestos fibers.

The authors provided brief, individual discussions for only a handful of cases. They noted two that resulted from outdoor exposure to asbestos:

> "...a van boy, aged 18, whose spare time during two and a half years' employment had been spent in mixing powdered asbestos in an open yard..."

> "... a man who had been employed handling asbestos mattresses in the open air at an aerodrome."

Another individual had developed extensive asbestosis from "about 40 years (clerical and administrative work)" at an asbestos factory.

Another man had been exposed to asbestos from thermal insulation materials:

> "...a middle-aged boiler riveter who had served his apprenticeship as a youth in a shop where asbestos was used for lagging pipes..."

It was not stated that this man ever applied insulation to boilers or pipes himself, but if he did it would probably have been only intermittently during his apprenticeship for the boiler riveting trade.[98,99] He did work in close proximity to insulation workers during his apprenticeship and thus was exposed to the dust this work created. He may well have been exposed to dust left in the air around boilers needing repair, from which the old insulation had just been torn off. In any event, it seems clear that if a boiler riveter could get asbestosis from asbestos insulation products, insulation workers must have also been at risk.

This report mentions that two of the asbestosis cases in the series also had carcinoma of the lung. The following year Gloyne issued a separate report on these two cases of lung cancer. (See the Cancer chapter.)

The U.S. asbestos industry produced a study of its workers in 1935, conducted by Lanza and his co-workers at the Metropolitan Life Insurance Company.[67]

> In 1929, the Metropolitan Life Insurance Company was approached by officials representing the asbestos industry in the United States, who were desirous of ascertaining whether asbestos dust was an occupational hazard in their establishments and, if so, what was the nature of this hazard and what should be done to prevent or control it.

The investigation was conducted during the period ending in January 1931, but was not published until four years later.

The scope of the study was described as follows:

> X-ray films were made of 126 persons (108 men, 18 women) working in asbestos plants in the United States. All but five of these were given physical examination. The cases were selected more or less at random from among those having more than 3 years of employment in the industry...

No further clarification was given on the meaning of "selected more or less at random."

Only if there was a consensus of the X-ray readers was a worker classified as having radiologic evidence of asbestosis:

> *The (X-ray) films were read conservatively,* taking into account the physical examination and the age of the individual, *and were classed as positive only when there was no major disagreement* (among the examiners of the X-rays)...(emphasis added)
>
> The films classified as negative for asbestosis were further subdivided into doubtful and negative.

The definite cases of asbestosis were broken down into first stage and second stage, the latter being a more extensive development of the disease.

> Of the total of 126 X-ray examinations, 4 were diagnosed as second degree asbestosis, 63 as first degree, 39 as doubtful, and 20 as negative.

In other words, 53 percent of the workers had asbestosis by a conservative reading of the X-rays, and another 31 percent had some X-ray signs of disease ("doubtful"). Only 16 percent had no signs of asbestosis on X-ray. It should be recalled that these were active workers; those who had left due to illness were not examined.

The majority of persons classified by X-ray as "doubtful" and "negative" complained of cough and/or shortness of breath. Referring to those that were classified as "negative" by X-ray who complained of symptoms, the authors said, "too much emphasis should not be placed on statements of subjective symptoms."

The authors minimized their finding of widespread asbestosis, commenting that, in the cases selected for examination, none had "marked disability." The threat of progressive maturation of fibrosis previously noted by many authorities was not discussed; one of those authorities, Dr. Pancoast at the University of Pennsylvania, had even been consulted by the Metropolitan Life investigators in the interpretation of the X-ray films.

The Met Life study ignored the definitive statistics of the British Factory Department to the contrary and offered no data of its own to support remarks to the effect that, "available information suggests that asbestosis is a milder disease than silicosis." This point was actually a focal concern of the largest U.S. asbestos manufacturer at the time Lanza's work went to press. (See Compensation chapter for details.)

The authors declined to recommend that the industry be regulated, and did not mention that industrial hygiene regulations were in effect in the United Kingdom. These investigators took some air samples and analyzed them for the concentrations of airborne dust. Their data and Merewether's could have provided a preliminary idea of risks at various exposure levels, a beginning toward numerical standards that would protect the workers. However, the Met Life authors declined an effort to relate dust levels to their associated dangers of asbestosis.

They did recommend these things:

1. That the industry seriously face the problem of dust control in asbestos plants.
2. That new employees be examined physically, including X-ray examination of the chest, and rejected for employment if they show tuberculosis or pneumoconiosis.

3. That employees be examined physically, preferably every year, but at least every 2 years, this examination to include an X-ray examination of the chest.
4. That the industry sponsor studies on known cases of asbestosis, as well as studies on effects of asbestosis on the heart and circulation.

CONCLUSION

In summary, asbestosis was by 1935 widely recognized as a mortal threat affecting a large fraction of those who had regularly worked with the material. Severe disease had occurred even among people who had worked for less than one year with asbestos. It was known that the disease process would not become evident for the first few years of exposure no matter how intense the exposure was. Yet slowly but surely, the lung scarring would develop as the mineral fibers accumulated in the lungs and had time to provoke the characteristic response. Moreover, by the time the disease became evident, cessation of exposure could not halt the inexorable progress of the disease caused by the durable fibers already trapped in the lung tissues. To make matters worse still, the compromised lungs of the asbestosis victims rendered them especially vulnerable to respiratory infections. So even a moderate degree of asbestosis was recognized as a threat to life, because of the enhanced risk that an ordinary chest cold could lead to pneumonia and death. In view of this, it is little wonder that Dr. Merewether considered prohibition of the use of asbestos even before the first case reports of lung cancer and asbestosis were published.[14]

REFERENCES

1. Demy, N. Letter to the Editor. *J.A.M.A. 175:* 530 (1961).
2. Anderson, A.M. Historical Sketch of the Development of Legislation for Injurious and Dangerous Industries in England. *Dangerous Trades* (T. Oliver, Ed.) New York: Dutton, 1902, p. 25. Also quoted in

R. W. Goldberg. *Occupational Diseases.* New York: Columbia University Press, 1931, p. 13.

3. Hunter, D. *The Diseases of Occupations* 4th Ed. Boston: Little, Brown & Co., 1969, p. 1009.

4. Netolizky, A. Hygiene der Textilindustrie. *Handbuch der Hygiene.* (Th. Weyl, Ed.) Vol. 8, Industrial Hygiene, Gustav Fischer Publ., Jena, 1102-1103 (1897).

5. *Annual Report of the Chief Inspector of Factories and Workshops for the Year 1898.* London: H.M. Stationery Ofc., 1899, pp. 171-172.

6. *Annual Report of the Chief Inspector of Factories and Workshops for the Year 1899.* London: H.M. Stationery Ofc., 1900, p. 264.

7. *Annual Report of the Chief Inspector of Factories and Workshops for the Year 1906.* London: H.M. Stationery Ofc., 1907, pp. 219-220.

8. Murray, H.M. *Departmental Committee on Compensation for Industrial Diseases Minutes of Evidence. Appendices and Index.* London: Wyman and Sons, 1907, pp. 127-128.

9. Auribault, M. Note sur l'Hygiène et la Sécurité des Ouvriers dans la Filatures et Tissages d'Amiante. *Bull Insp. Trav. Paris: 14:* 120-132 (1906).

10. Scarpa, L. Industria dell'Amianto e Tuberculosi. *Proc. Int. Med. Congr. 18th* 358 (1908).

11. Collis, E.C. Dusty Processes. *Annual Report of the Chief Inspector of Factories and Workshops for the Year 1910.* London: H.M. Stationery Ofc., 1911, p. 188.

12. Hoffman, F.L. *Mortality From Respiratory Diseases in the Dusty Trades (Inorganic Dusts).* Washington, D.C.: U.S. Bur. Labor Statistics Bull. No. 231, 1918, pp. 172-180.

13. *Annual Report of the Chief Inspector of Factories and Workshops for the Year 1911.* London: H.M. Stationery Ofc., 1912, p. 149.

14. Merewether, E.R.A. A Memorandum on Asbestosis. *Tubercle 15:* 69-81, 109-118, 152-159 (1933-1934).

15. Effects of Asbestos Dust on Workers' Health in Asbestos Mines and Factories. *Labour Gazette 12:* 761 (1912). Printed in Ottawa, Canada.

16. Fahr, T. Demonstrationen: Praparate und Microphotogrammes von einen Falle von Pneumokoniose. *Muenchener Med. Woch. 11:* 625 (1914).

17. Pancoast, H.K., T.G. Miller, and H.M. Landis. A Roentgenologic Study of the Effects of Dust Inhalation upon the Lungs. *Trans. Assoc. Amer. Phys.* 32: 97-108 (1917).

18. Pancoast, H.K., T.G. Miller, and H.M. Landis. A Roentgenologic Study of the Effects of Dust Inhalation upon the Lungs. Republished. *Amer. J. Roent. 5:* 129-138 (1918).

19. Cooke, W.E. Fibrosis of the Lungs Due to the Inhalation of Asbestos Dust. *Brit. Med. J. 2:* 147 (1924).

20. Pancoast, H.K. and E.P. Pendergrass. A Review of Our Present Knowledge of Pneumoconiosis, Based Upon Roentgenologic Studies, with Notes on the Pathology of the Condition. *Amer. J. Roent. 14:* 381-423 (1925).

21. Blomley, J. (Newbold Approved Society) letter to Turner Bros. Asbestos Co. (Sept. 1, 1922).

22. Turner Bros. Asbestos Co. letter to Newbold Approved Society (Sept. 15, 1922).

23. Turner Bros. Asbestos Co. letter to London & Lancashire Insurance Co. (Sept. 21, 1922).

24. Kershaw, N. letter to Turner Bros. Asbestos Co. (Sept. 1922). Turner & Newall files.

25. Joss, W.S. note explaining basis for his previous diagnosis of "Asbestos poisoning." Turner & Newall files, No. 052-16-00104.

26. Cooke, W.E. Pulmonary Asbestosis. *Brit. Med. J. 2:* 1024-1025 (1927).

27. McDonald, S. Histology of Pulmonary Asbestosis. *Brit. Med. J. 2:* 1025-1026 (1927).

28. Oliver, T. Clinical Aspects of Pulmonary Asbestosis. *Brit. Med. J. 2:* 1026-1027 (1927).

29. Oliver, T. Pulmonary Asbestosis in Its Clinical Aspects. *J. Indust. Hyg. 9:* 483-485 (1927).

30. Pulmonary Asbestosis. *J.A.M.A. 89:* 2285 (1927).

31. Pneumoconiosis Caused by Asbestos Dust. *J.A.M.A. 89:* 304 (1927).

32. Pulmonary Asbestosis. *J.A.M.A. 90:* 119-120 (1928).

33. Seiler, H.E. A Case of Pneumoconiosis. Result of the Inhalation of Asbestos Dust. *Brit. Med. J. 2:* 982-983 (1928).

34. Simson, F.W. Pulmonary Asbestosis in South Africa. *Brit. Med. J. 1:* 885-886 (1928).

35. Haddow, A.C. Clinical Aspects of Pulmonary Asbestosis. *Brit. Med. J. 2:* 580-581 (1929).

36. *Pulmonary Asbestosis,* Memo Report #22. Market Analysis Section, Sales Promotion Dept., Johns-Manville Corp. (March 21, 1930).

37. Davis, G.G., E.M. Salmonsen, and J.L. Earlywine. *The Pneumokonioses (Silicosis) Bibliography and Laws-Volume 1,* Chicago: Industrial Medicine, Inc., 1934, pp. 153, 166, 182-183, 208-210, 213.

38. Section of Occupational Diseases. *Lancet 2:* 230-231 (1929).

39. Legge, T. Asbestosis. *Industrial Maladies.* London: Oxford University Press, 1934, pp. 190-194.

40. Williams, C.L. *Report of the Medical Officer of Health for the Year 1929.* England: Barking Town Urban District Council, 1930, pp. 62-64.

41. Merewether, E.R.A. and C.W. Price. *Report on Effects of Asbestos Dust on the Lungs and Dust Suppression in the Asbestos Industry.* H.M. Stationery Ofc. (1930).

42. Merewether, E.R.A. The Occurrence of Pulmonary Fibrosis and Other Pulmonary Affections in Asbestos Workers. *J. Indust. Hyg. 12:* 198-222, 239-257 (1930).

43. Workers Who Breathe Death. *John Bull* (June 28, 1930).

44. Notes and Memoranda. *The Engineer 149:* 379 (1930).

45. Pulmonary Asbestosis. *Monthly Labor Rev. 31:* 74-76 (1931).

46. Pulmonary Asbestosis. *Handbook of Labor Statistics 1931 Edition.* Bureau of Labor Statistics Bulletin No. 541, U.S. Dept. of Labor, Washington, 340-342 (1931).

47. Asbestos. *The Engineer 152:* 283 (1931).

48. Mineral Dust in Factories. *Engineering 129:* 577-578 (1930).

49. Industrial Diseases and Poisoning in British Factories, 1930. *Safety Eng. 62:* 353-354 (1931).

50. Pulmonary Asbestosis. *Brit. Med. J. 1:* 789 (1930).

51. Pulmonary Asbestosis. *Lancet 1:* 870-871 (1930).

52. Compensation Act to be Extendeed to Asbestosis. *J.A.M.A. 94:* 2078 (1930).

53. Pulmonary Asbestosis. *J.A.M.A. 95:* 1431 (1930).

54. Mills, R.G. Pulmonary Asbestosis: Report of a Case. *Minnesota Med. 13:* 495-499 (1930).

55. Burrow, J.G. *AMA: Voice of American Medicine.* Baltimore: Johns Hopkins Press, 1963, pp. 52-53.

56. Fishbein, M. *A History of the American Medical Association 1847 to 1947.* Philadelphia: W.B. Saunders Co., 1947, p. 992.

57. Lynch, K.M. and W.A. Smith. Asbestosis Bodies in Sputum and Lung. *J.A.M.A. 95:* 659-661 (1930).

58. Soper, W.B. Pulmonary Asbestosis. A Report of a Case and a Review. *Amer. Rev. Tuberc. 22:* 571-584 (1930).

59. *Silicosis/Records of the International Conference Held at Johannesburg* London: P.S. King & Son, 1930.

60. Lovisetto, D. Pulmonary Asbestosis. *Ibid.* 506-509.

61. Asbestos. *Occupation and Health* Vol. 1, Geneva: International Labour Office, 1930, pp. 189-191.

62. Willis, H.S. Pneumoconiosis and Tuberculosis. *Medicine 9:* 413-506 (1930).

63. Haslam, J.F.C. Pulmonary Asbestosis. *Recent Advances in Preventive Medicine* London: J. & A. Churchill, pp. 258-265 (1930).

64. Wood, W.B. and S.R. Gloyne. Pulmonary Asbestosis. *Lancet 1:* 445-448 (1930).

65. Palmieri, V.M. Pulmonary Asbestosis. *Riforma Med. 46:* 1207 (1930).

66. Dhers, V. Asbestos and Pulmonary Asbestosis. *Med. Travail 2:* 147-172, 187-209 (1930).

67. Dhers' paper summarized in *Abstracts* section, *J. Indust. Hyg. 13:* 49 (1931).

68. The 'Pulmonary Asbestosis' Menace, *The Asbestos Worker* 9(9):9-11 (Sept. 1930).

69. Sparks, J.V. Pulmonary Asbestosis. *Radiology 17:* 1249-1257 (1931).

70. Pedley, F.G. Asbestosis. *Canad. Med. Assoc. J. 22:* 253-254 (1930).

71. Pedley, F.G. Asbestosis. *Canad. Publ. Health J. 21:* 576-577 (1930).

72. Wheatley, G.M. *Tuberculosis and Asbestosis.* 11 pp. (1944). Document No. 2578, Institute of Occupational and Environmental Health, Quebec Asbestos Mining Association, Montreal, Quebec.

73. Lanza, A.J., W.J. McConnell, and J.W. Fehnel. Effects of the Inhalation of Asbestos Dust on the Lungs of Asbestos Workers. *Publ. Health Rep. 50:* 1-12 (1935).

74. Lanza, A.J. and R.J. Vane. Industrial Dusts and the Mortality from Pulmonary Disease. *Amer. Rev. Tuberc. 39:* 419-438 (1939).

75. Selikoff, I.J. and Lee, D.H.K. *Asbestos and Disease* New York: Academic Press, 1978, p. 23.

76. Kruger, E., O. Rostoski, and E. Saupe. Pulmonary Asbestosis. *Arch. Gewerbepath. Gewerbehyg. 2:* 558-590 (1931).

77. Gerbis, H. and Ucko. Asbestosis of the Lung. *Ver. Inn. Med. Berlin* Sitz v. (Dec. 7, 1931).

78. Gerbis, H. and Ucko. Asbestosis of the Lung. *Deut. Med. Woch. 58:* 285 (1932).

79. Gerbis, H. and Ucko. Preceding article, abstract in *Bull. Hyg. 7:* 341-342 (1932).

80. German Work on Pulmonary Asbestosis. *Lancet 2:* 91-93 (1932).

81. Kruger, Rostoski, and Saupe. *Abstracts* section of *J. Indust. Hyg. 14:* 144-145 (1932).

82. Recent Studies of Pulmonary Asbestosis in Germany. *Monthly Labor Rev. 35:* 541-542 (1932).

83. Kruger, Rostoski, and Saupe. Preceding article, abstract in *Bull. Hyg. 6:* 861-862 (1931).

84. Beintker, E. *Arch. Gewerbepath. Gewerbehyg. 2:* 345-358 (1931). in *Abstracts* section of *J. Indust. Hyg. 14:* 120-121 (1932).

85. Stewart, H.L., C.J. Bucher, and E.H. Coleman. Asbestosis. *Arch. Path 12:* 909-916 (1931).

86. Lynch, K.M. and W.A. Smith. Pulmonary Asbestosis II Including the Report of a Pure Case. *Amer. Rev. Tuberc. 23:* 643-660 (1931).

87. Pancoast, H.K. and E.P. Pendergrass. A Review of Pneumoconiosis. *Amer. J. Roent. 26:* 556-614 (1931).

88. Gardner, L.U. and D.E. Cummings. Studies on Experimental Pneumokoniosis. VI Inhalation of Asbestos Dust: Its Effect Upon Primary Tuberculous Infection. *J. Indust. Hyg. 13:* 97-114 (1931).

89. Physical Examinations at Manville Factory (1932). Manville document.

90. Abbott, G. *et al.*, "Report of Advisory Committee on Employment of Minors in Hazardous Occupations," *Monthly Labor Rev. 35:* 1315-1321 (1932).

91. "Hearing on Code of Fair Practices and Competition Presented by Asbestos Industry," National Industrial Recovery Administration, Vol III (Oct. 19, 1933).

92. *Pneumoconiosis.* Études et Documents Série F (Hygiène Industrielle) No. 15. Geneva: International Labor Office, 1932, pp. 34-37.

93. Ellman, P. Pulmonary Asbestosis: Its Clinical, Radiological, and Pathological Features, and Associated Risk of Tuberculous Infection. *J. Indust. Hyg. 15:* 165-183 (1933).

94. Ellman, P. Pneumoconiosis. Part III Pulmonary Asbestosis. *Brit. J. Radiol. 7:* 281-295 (1934).

95. Wood, W.B. Pulmonary Asbestosis. *Brit. J. Radiol. 7:* 277-280 (1934).

96. Gloyne, S.R. The Morbid Anatomy and Histology of Asbestosis. *Tubercle 15:* 445-451, 493-497, 550-558 (1933).

97. Donnelly, J. Pulmonary Asbestosis. *Amer. J. Publ. Health 23:* 1275-1281 (1933).

98. Wood, W.B. and S.R. Gloyne. Pulmonary Asbestosis. A Review of One Hundred Cases. *Lancet 2:* 1383-1385 (1934).

99. Gloyne. Abstract of the preceding article, *Bull. Hyg. 10:* 219-220 (1935). Reprinted in *Pneumoconiosis Abstracts I:* 143 (1953).

2
Cancer

"The sudden change which has taken place in the conditions of life consequent upon the development of modern industry has been associated with a rapid rise in cancer mortality, and this rise is greatest where modern industry is most developed."

Edgar L. Collis and Major Greenwood, *The Health of the Industrial Worker* J. & A. Churchill, London, 160 (1921).

"This is a war just like any other war, and it will be fought with every dirty means."

Wilhelm C. Hueper

INTRODUCTION

The recognition of asbestos as a cancer hazard took place a remarkably short time after the first case reports were published. Clinicians, reading the literature and seeing cases of their own, were able to identify similarities as the evidence mounted, revealing features of the occupational origin of lung cancers in asbestos workers. "Clinical epidemiology" is in fact the way innumerable advances in medicine have emerged over the centuries, and all the early discoveries in the field of industrial carcinogenesis followed this pattern.

Most of the reports published came from England, Germany, and the United States. In the late 1930s these mainly consisted of case reports. In the 1940s, asbestos carcinogenicity was also noted in reviews in the fields of industrial medicine, cancer research, and pneumoconiosis. These articles and editorials appeared in widely read, general medical journals.

As with asbestosis decades earlier, the annual reports of the chief inspector in England became important sources of knowledge on cancer from asbestos. Due to meticulous efforts to compile data on the "complications" of asbestosis at autopsy, the Factory Inspectorate was able to sound early alarms based on impressive statistical evidence. The most notable example was the *Annual Report of the Chief Inspector of Factories for the Year 1947*, whose data and analysis were quickly picked up in medical literature around the world.

Only after the carcinogenicity of asbestos was widely acknowledged was a modern type of epidemiological mortality study published by Doll in England (1955). This confirmed that asbestos workers had suffered a massive increase in mortality from cancer of the lung. Larger studies of this general type would eventually reveal the wide range of target organs for asbestos-induced malignancies.

Discovery of the Cancer Threat with Asbestosis

Some of the earliest reports of cancer in association with asbestosis were made by the British pathologist, Gloyne. He wrote at length on the damage to the pleura and lungs in asbestosis, and reported having seen a case of "squamous carcinoma of the pleura" with asbestosis in 1933.[1] The next year, Wood and Gloyne noted that in 12 autopsied cases of asbestosis, there were two cases of lung cancer in addition to the pleural cancer.[2] In 1935 Gloyne reported in detail on the two cases of lung cancer with asbestosis.[3] He considered the pleural cancer (and an abdominal cancer) unrelated to asbestosis, but suggested the possibility of industrial origin of the lung cancers.

Also in 1935, Lynch and Smith of South Carolina published the first case report of asbestosis and lung cancer in the American literature. The man had worked in an asbestos textile mill for 21 years. Lung cancer was an uncommon disease in 1935, and the occurrence of even one case of asbestosis with lung cancer was noteworthy.[4]

In 1936, Gloyne reported another case of oat cell lung cancer with asbestosis. The man died 21 years after starting work in an asbestos plant.[5]

Egbert and Geiger at Yale published another case report of asbestosis with lung cancer in July, 1936.[6] The patient had worked as a weaver in an asbestos factory for 18 years. He left his job when he developed a disabling pain in his back, and died shortly afterward with lung cancer.

In 1938, Nordmann in Germany published a paper entitled "The Occupational Cancer of Asbestos Workers." He reported 2 new cases of lung cancer with asbestosis, in a 35-year-old woman and a 55-year-old man. They were asbestos textile workers. Nordmann reviewed the cumulative literature and was first to declare that lung cancer was an occupational disease of asbestos workers.[7] He tabulated data from his and all of the earlier reports except Gloyne's 1936 case, which he missed. He cited a number of factors that differentiated these 6 cases from lung cancer then seen in the general population.

Nordmann noted that 3 of the 6 asbestosis/lung cancer victims were young compared to the usual age of people dying with lung cancer (two were 35 and one was 41). In the older ones, entry into the asbestos industry had occurred at an older age. *A consistent finding for all was the length of time elapsed from the start of asbestos work until the time of death: 15 to 21 years.*

In 5 of the 6 cases, the tumors developed in the lower lobes of the lungs, whereas in the general population lung cancer was most common in the upper lobes. By 1938, it was also well recognized that the more extensive fibrosis in asbestosis was found in the lower lobes of the lungs. The occasional finding of multi-focal cancers—the development of more than one primary malignancy in the lungs of one person—also suggested to Nordmann that occupational exposure to a carcinogen was involved.

Finally, Nordmann assembled the scant data on autopsied cases of asbestosis to reveal that an unusually high fraction of these cases had cancer. Referring to Wood and Gloyne's report of 100 cases of asbestosis, he noted that of 12 autopsied cases, 2 (17%) had lung cancer. In Germany, he knew of 12 autopsied asbestotics, and 2 of these also had lung cancer.

One of the cases seen by Nordmann was described in a

companion article by Hornig, who also considered asbestos carcinogenic to the lungs.[8] Both of these German articles were abstracted in *Journal of Industrial Hygiene and Toxicology* in the U.S.[9]

The Senior Medical Inspector of Factories reported that in England, a total of 12 cases of lung cancer had occurred in 103 autopsied cases in which asbestosis was present (11.6%), as of 1938.[10-12] The British radiologist Sparks listed cancer of the lung among the complications seen with asbestosis.[13,14]

Writing for the International Labor Office, Gloyne and Merewether noted the reported association between asbestosis and lung cancer. Acknowledging that asbestos had not been proven to have carcinogenic properties, they advised "there is sufficient evidence to warrant careful observation in the future."[15]

In 1938, Koelsch in Germany reported 3 additional cases of asbestosis with lung cancer, which he had been informed of by Dominici and Baader. Koelsch seems to have been persuaded of the carcinogenicity of asbestos.[16]

Lynch and Smith reported another fatal case of asbestosis with lung cancer in a 50-year-old man.[17] The man had begun work with asbestos 15 years before he died. The authors reviewed other literature on lung cancer with asbestosis, noting that Nordmann considered lung cancer with asbestosis an occupational disease. The authors reported that 2 of the 7 cases of lung cancer they had seen at autopsy over a 12-year period (2,343 autopsies) were in 35 people who exhibited some degree of asbestosis.

By 1939, Baader, a leading industrial medical authority in Berlin, said there was no doubt that lung cancer was an occupational hazard of asbestos workers. Different authors had reported 14 cases of combined asbestosis and lung cancer, he remarked. And despite the lack of recognition under federal compensation law, Baader said the (state) insurance carriers in Germany had nevertheless readily recognized and compensated fatal lung cancer associated with slight asbestosis as an occupational disease.[18] Another reviewer in Germany, Ehrhardt, agreed that the carcinogenicity of asbestos was established.[19]

Two more cases were detailed by Linzbach and Wedler in 1941. This exhaustive account of their own patient, whose cancer developed in a lower lobe of his lung, was combined with notice of another case seen (but not reported in the literature) by Böhme. The authors stressed that, based on English data, asbestotics tended to die before reaching the "cancer age," unlike silicotics. This strengthened the view that asbestosis associated with lung cancer was more than a coincidental finding. These authors, too, said that the frequency of observation of cancer with asbestosis established the occupational derivation of the cancers.[20]

Nordmann and Sorge meanwhile completed an experiment with white mice exposed to chrysotile asbestos in dust chambers. The longest-exposed group of 50 mice was "dusted" for thirteen weeks. The longest survival was barely one third of the normal life span for these mice. Only 10 mice survived 240 days or more, the time when the earliest-appearing lung cancer was found. There were 2 lung carcinomas sustained by the 10 surviving mice, and what were described as precancerous cell changes were commonly found. The authors considered this a complete reproduction of the malignant disease seen in humans.[21]

The same year, two more cases of asbestosis with pulmonary cancer were reported in Quebec, in men who had each worked with asbestos for over twenty years.[22] In both of these cases, the authors described the tumors as "epithelioma pleuro-pulmonaire," though they were believed to have originated in the lungs with metastasis to the pleura.

In 1942, the exhaustive treatise *Occupational Tumors and Allied Diseases* was published in the United States by Dr. Wilhelm C. Hueper.[23] Hueper regarded the evidence on asbestosis and lung cancer as "suggestive" of a carcinogenic risk. He made the same points first stated by Nordmann, and noted that case reports were the first warning of an occupational cancer hazard. He went on to urge extensive clinical, pathological and statistical studies of the cancer risks of asbestos work. Hueper noted that some states in the U.S. with large asbestos plants did not even include asbestosis among compensable occupational diseases. This condition, he said, impeded the application of control measures and the collection of essential information on the hazards of asbestos.

One of Nordmann's co-workers, Welz, reported 2 more cases of lung cancer in individuals who had worked in asbestos factories for 3 and 4 years, respectively. Welz had no doubt as to the causal relationship between asbestosis and lung cancer.[24]

Pathologists Holleb and Angrist in New York reported 2 more cases of asbestosis with lung cancer in 1942.[25] The patients had both been insulation workers for over 20 years. One had experienced increasingly severe disability beginning 15 years before his death, although for the last 10 years of his life he did not work as a pipecoverer. The authors wrote that over a 5-year period, they had seen 59 bronchogenic carcinomas, comprising 2.4% of all routine autopsies. They had seen only 2 cases of pulmonary asbestosis, and in both, there was lung cancer as well. This appears to be the earliest report of asbestosis and lung cancer among insulation workers.

On January 29, 1943 the German (federal) government declared "asbestosis in combination with lung cancer" a compensable occupational disease, acknowledging the lung cancer occurs in clinically slight cases of asbestosis as well as in well-developed asbestosis.[26,27] Thus, the citations of this health hazard in the medical literature since 1938—by Nordmann, Hornig, Koelsch, Welz, Baader, Ehrhardt, Linzbach, and Wedler—resulted in the German government formally recognizing this occupational disease within a period of 5 years. Germany's tradition of industrial disease compensation dated from 1883 and the German Industrial Insurance Act. The United States "system," with private insurers in most states and 50 different state workers' compensation laws, was far behind the standard of compensation for occupational disease that Baader described in practice in Nazi Germany in 1939. In 1942, 24 states in the United States still did not hold employers liable for diseases workers contracted as the result of conditions of their employment.[23]

In 1943, Hueper was no longer doubtful about the occupational origin of lung cancers with asbestosis.[28] The war with Germany precluded his knowing that the German government had formally recognized lung cancer associated with asbestosis as a compensable disease.[29] He wrote:

> Asbestosis cancer of the lung is the most recent newcomer among occupational cancers of this origin. First described in 1935, there are now 18 cases of this industrial cancer on record observed among asbestos workers in England, Germany, and the United States. The latter contributed 5 cases. Inasmuch as the asbestos industry is most extensively developed in this country, asbestosis cancer of the lung has for us a special hygienic and sociologic significance.

Hueper urged that industry take action to control occupational cancer:

> Industry should devote considerably more effort than heretofore in determining the cancerous or noncancerous nature of their numerous products which may be suspected on general grounds in cancerigenic respects... *Industry should make serious attempts to eliminate all potentially cancerigenic agents from further use by the development of suitable substitutes.* (original emphasis)

By 1946, Johns-Manville executive Page Woodard had obtained a copy of this article and sent it out for scientific review.[30]

Dr. H.W. Wedler in Heidelberg filed two reports in 1943 which included pleural tumors with asbestosis along with lung tumors as an occupational disease.[31,32] He reported that in Germany, a total of 29 autopsies had been performed on workers with asbestosis, and there were 4 with lung cancers and 2 with pleural cancers. In a survey of world literature, Wedler found a total of 92 reported autopsies of patients with asbestos disease, in which 14 malignant lung and pleural tumors were found (16%). This exceeded the prevalence of lung cancer he normally found in the general autopsy statistics (2-6%).

Wedler made many of the points raised earlier by Nordmann. He also said he knew of no medical expert in Germany who had taken a stand against compensating workers with asbestosis who developed pulmonary cancer. Even the industry associations conceded this, he reported, as had Welz before him.

Later in 1943, Boemke reported another case of asbestosis with lung cancer. Boemke agreed with other German writers about the occupational origin of the cancer, which arose in the lower lobe of the right lung about 18 years after the patient started work in an asbestos plant.[33]

Summaries of Wedler's shorter paper and the one by Welz were published in 1944 in the British journal, *Bulletin of Hygiene.*[34,35] These abstracts in turn were reprinted in the United States.[36] It is noteworthy that the unfolding literature was continuously surveyed and abstracted in *Bulletin of Hygiene,* and that even at the height of World War II, the British were abstracting the German literature on asbestos diseases.

Homburger at Yale published a report of 3 more cases in 1943.[37] The patients were all in their forties. Homburger's paper contained an excellent tabular presentation of the literature on asbestosis with lung cancer. Homburger reported that from 1918 to 1938 his laboratory had conducted thousands of autopsies and found asbestosis in 8: lung cancer was found in 4 of these, a "remarkably high ... association of the two conditions."

Early Saranac Laboratory Cancer Tests with Asbestos

Homburger's paper heightened the alarm of others, including Leroy Gardner, Director of the Saranac Laboratory for the Study of Tuberculosis. This institution, located in upstate New York, was at that time the most prestigious research center on industrial and infectious pulmonary disease in the United States. Gardner had just written to Dr. Ludwig Hektoen of the National Advisory Cancer Council, requesting funding for an animal inhalation study on the carcinogenicity of asbestos. Dr. Gardner explained that his preliminary animal tests had yielded a positive finding:[38]

> In analyzing the results of a recently completed inhalation experiment on asbestosis, I was startled to discover that a small group of 11 white mice that had been inhaling asbestos dust from 15 to 24 months showed an excessive incidence (81.8%) of pulmonary cancer.

This was contrasted with an 18.8% lung cancer incidence in white mice exposed for 15 or more months to quartz dust. Gardner went on to say that this finding was different from earlier work reported by his staff at Saranac.* Gardner went on to say that he would have attached little significance to his cancer findings in such a small group of animals, were it not for "some 10 reports of pulmonary cancer in cases of human asbestosis." Noting that "Gloyne, Merewether and other English observers contend that asbestos has a specific carcinogenic action," Gardner cited the importance of the issue from the compensation standpoint. Closing his proposal for government funds, Gardner added that the "Asbestos Association" had financed $30,000 worth of other studies over a 7-year period. "I cannot ask them for further contributions," he wrote.

Pressing Hektoen again in September of 1943, Gardner wrote:[39]

> I have always felt that asbestosis probably created no specific predisposition to pulmonary cancer. However, evidence to the contrary continues to accumulate. In the last number of the *American Journal of Pathology,* Homburger reports 3 new cases making a total of 19 in which the two conditions were associated. For this reason, I do not believe that we can afford to neglect the matter much longer.

*This 1938 report was about the failure of pneumoconiosis-producing dusts in general to elicit cancer, and noted briefly that none of 235 guinea pigs exposed to asbestos for unstated periods of time developed pulmonary tumors. It was acknowledged that the experiments were often short-term ones not designed to test for cancer.[40]

Describing it as an unintentional experiment, Gardner meanwhile notified Johns-Manville executive Vandiver Brown about his findings on asbestos carcinogenicity. Here he also reported an 81.8 percent incidence of lung tumors in mice inhaling "long-fibre asbestos" versus 18.8 percent in mice exposed to other dusts for 15 or more months. He also remarked that 3 of 22 mice (13.6%) inhaling "short-fibre asbestos" for no more than twelve months also developed lung tumors; this contrasted with a 1.9% lung tumor incidence in mice exposed to other dusts for 10-12 months. While acknowledging that the results were open to criticism on some grounds, Gardner concluded:

> These observations are suggestive but not conclusive evidence of a cancer stimulating action by asbestos dust... It is hoped that this experiment can be repeated under properly controlled conditions to determine whether asbestos actually favors cancer of the lung.

Dr. Gardner included this information in an annotated outline of a monograph he intended to write on all of his asbestos experiments. This advance summary was provided "for the benefit of the contributors," whose comments and criticisms he welcomed. In his cover letter to Vandiver Brown, Gardner showed an awareness of the importance and sensitivity of the cancer issue:[41]

> The question of cancer susceptibility now seems more significant than I had previously imagined. I believe I can obtain support for repeating it from the cancer research group. As it will take two or three years to complete such a study, I believe it would better be omitted from the present report.

He appears to have conditioned the non-publication of his preliminary findings upon the receipt of a government grant to verify them. The letter continued:

> If it should become possible to make this study, I hope that

> I may count on some of your members to supply me with enough pure, long fibre asbestos for the purpose.

In his annotated outline, Dr. Gardner discussed lung cancer reported in human asbestosis in similar terms to those he used to characterize his unpublished animal experiments:

> The evidence is suggestive but not conclusive that asbestosis may precipitate the development of cancer in susceptible individuals.

In reply, Brown told Gardner he would send photostats of the new report to "the several interested companies."[42] Within two weeks, a copy of Gardner's letter and his monograph outline were mailed from the executive offices of Keasbey & Mattison Company to Turner & Newall in England (the English company had purchased Keasbey & Mattison in 1934). The brief cover letter said in part:[43]

> I have found this outline to be extremely interesting . . . but we feel that reference to the question of cancer susceptibility should be omitted from the report since it is inconclusive.

Turner & Newall's research chief, Dr. Francis, made brief notes on Gardner's report. He acknowledged that Gardner's outline seemed comprehensive, "but the conclusions are not very helpful." With respect to cancer, Francis wrote:[44]

> The reference to the possibility of producing cancer of the lung by inhalation of asbestos fibres is disconcerting but Gardner may be right in this since I understand that there have been one or two cases of deaths due to cancer accelerated by asbestosis, or vice versa.

These comments were transmitted back through industry channels, and Gardner replied to Dr. Francis' remarks in a letter to Vandiver Brown.[45] Gardner reasserted that, "the question of carcinogenic action by asbestos is by no means settled."

He went on to note that, "Gloyne in England is strongly impressed with its probability." Again expressing hope of getting funds for confirmatory animal studies on the issue, Gardner reassured Brown that,

> Until that is done I shall maintain the same attitude and say nothing about our observation (in mice).

Gardner's approach to the federal government for funding cancer experiments was out of character with the laboratory's prior reliance on industry for research support. Gardner's reticence to ask for this support from the asbestos industry may have had its origin in the 1936 agreement he concluded upon accepting industry funds. Specifically, there was this troublesome paragraph:[46]

> The Saranac Laboratory agrees that the results of these studies shall become the property of the contributors and that the manuscripts of any reports shall be submitted for approval of the contributors before publication.

The asbestos industry contact who concluded the arrangements with Dr. Gardner was attorney Vandiver Brown of Johns-Manville Corporation. Brown was quick to note that the Saranac Lab annual report for 1938 and an excerpt from the Air Hygiene Foundation *Digest* contained references to Gardner's asbestos research work. In both cases, Brown wrote to Sumner Simpson, President of Raybestos-Manhattan, expressing umbrage at Gardner's non-observance of his contractual obligations.[47,48] Simpson agreed that Gardner was "not living up to his agreement," and mused:[49]

> The reports may be so favorable to us that they would cause us no trouble, but they might be just the opposite, which could be very embarrassing.

It is not hard to imagine what the asbestos companies would have said about publishing animal studies showing that asbestos caused cancer.

The apprehensions of his benefactors, whose research funding was re-approved on an annual basis, was definitely made known to Dr. Gardner. Dr. Harriet Hardy visited Gardner shortly before his death in 1946, and recalled that he was "very much distressed because he said Johns-Manville wouldn't allow him to publish his findings."[50]

Dr. Gardner's request to the National Advisory Cancer Council was considered at that group's January, 1944 meeting.[51] Objections were raised that: 1) the large experiment contemplated by Gardner at a cost of $10,000 was excessive; and 2) the Saranac Lab was inexperienced in cancer research, in which the strain of animals tested could have widely varying spontaneous background levels of lung tumors. The discussion was concluded by the consideration that it was "evident on the surface" that asbestos workers should be protected from dust, on general principles. As Dr. J.J. Murphy put it,

> You know you can produce a fibrosis, and the possibility of occasional cancer must also come into the picture. But I don't believe that this information would be of any tremendous value.

Gardner's application for funding was rejected.

In the aftermath of this disappointment, Gardner never realized that his presumed ally on the committee (Dr. Rhoads of Memorial Hospital) had not urged funding of Gardner's project.[30,51]

No evidence has come to light that Gardner actually asked the asbestos companies to fund animal studies on asbestos carcinogenicity. However, in a "Dear Page" letter (1946) to Johns-Manville executive Page Woodard, ("Roy") Gardner expressed the hope that he would some day be given the chance to review "all (chest X-ray) films" of actively employed Johns-Manville workers.[30]

> If a large enough number of such films were reviewed by one central agency, I am quite sure that we would have evidence to controvert the implications of the case reports now in the medical literature.

Whether Gardner really believed that surveys of employed workers could provide legitimate answers to the lung cancer question or was orienting his "pitch" to obtain a large work contract is a matter for speculation.

There were, however, certain aspects of Leroy Gardner's research that the industry was anxious to see in print. Thomas Gatke, President of one of the sponsoring companies, felt that Gardner had shown by 1946 that only particles larger than 5 microns in size were injurious. Such large fibers, Gatke said, could be arrested by the use of approved respirators.[52]

> With these two facts established, and *without injections of possibilities of cancer,* etc., etc., we would have something definite and worthwhile to combat the claims of these country doctors who set themselves up as experts but have actually had no experience beyond what they read in books, and whose statements have been accepted by the courts as more or less authentic because we have had no expert testimony based on such experience as Dr. Gardner's. (emphasis added)

When Gardner died unexpectedly in October of 1946, the Saranac Laboratory turned to Dr. Anthony Lanza at Metropolitan Life. Lanza was made a member of the Board of Trustees of the Trudeau Foundation, parent organization of the Saranac Laboratory. Lanza decided to send Gardner's papers to Dr. Kenneth M. Lynch. Lynch, a pathologist who had published several papers on asbestosis and cancer, had become Dean of the Medical College of the State of South Carolina. He had also been known to the President of Raybestos-Manhattan as "the doctor in charge of our spinning plant in North Charleston."[53] Lanza explained that Gardner had been "doing some work for Johns-Manville and had promised them a report." The Saranac Laboratory was willing to "pay an adequate fee" to produce that report.[54]

At a meeting with Johns-Manville executives in January, 1947, Lanza reported that Dr. Gardner's notes had been sent to Dr. Lynch to determine whether they could be put into publishable form. A.R. Fisher (then a Vice President of Johns-Manville) said a report could be of help in Canada "to offset the effects of a lot of propagandizing that has been done in relation to the harmful effects of asbestos dust." Vandiver Brown emphasized that the contract with Saranac barred any publication "without our consent." He was concerned that Lynch might want to include "objectionable material from our point of view, as, for example, any relation between asbestos dust and cancer."[55]

Two months later, Saranac Field Director Manfred Bowditch summarized Gardner's findings in a one-page letter to Brown. The 81.8% incidence of lung cancer among mice inhaling long-fiber asbestos was given as one of Gardner's main findings.[56] Brown replied that he was very much concerned by that, and did not recall such an abnormal incidence of lung cancer.[57] Bowditch answered that the cancer data was in the "Outline of Proposed Monograph on Asbestosis" acknowledged by Brown on March 1, 1943.[42]

Hearing nothing encouraging from Dr. Lynch, Bowditch at Saranac invited him to present a paper at its sixth symposium, scheduled for late September of 1947. But there were conditions:[58]

> The asbestos interests quite rightly feel that this should only be done if your work has been completed early enough to permit adequate consideration of your report well in advance of the proposed delivery.

Lynch wrote that he'd rather put that off for awhile.

Lynch finally wrote that it would be best to let Gardner's work speak for itself rather than impose a viewpoint that would not accurately represent him.[59] His note was vague about the specifics.

Lanza replied that he agreed with Lynch about publishing Gardner's work and said he was going to Saranac to confer with Dr. Arthur Vorwald, who had just been named Gardner's successor. The insurance industry doctor also explained to Lynch that:[60]

> (T)here has been quite a stirring up of activity on the part of State Industrial Commissions in the United States and Canada, with the result that there has been threatened legislative actions or procedures based upon assumptions as to the effects of asbestos which may or may not be correct.
>
> All concerned are looking to Saranac for a reply to their questions and it would be an immense help to both industry and constituted authorities if they could believe that some of the fruits of Dr. Gardner's activities will soon be available.

Two weeks later, Lanza wrote that he and Vorwald agreed that it would be desirable to present as much of Gardner's material "as workable" within a short time.[61] Would Dr. Lynch send excerpts for their consideration?

Lynch had received an unfinished report on experimental studies of asbestosis and a copy of Gardner's "Outline of Proposed Monograph on Asbestosis," which had been sent to Vandiver Brown in 1943. Dr. Lynch now advised Lanza that these two works should be joined together and published in the *Journal of Industrial Hygiene and Toxicology,* where Gardner's earliest studies on asbestosis were published in 1931. Lynch was especially impressed with the latter part of the Outline (which included a discussion of Gardner's unpublished, "unintentional" cancer studies).[62]

Dr. Vorwald had just returned to Saranac after five years with the Navy. Despite his long absence and his acknowledgement that Gardner's manuscript was a significant contribution, he wrote,[63]

> Its publication alarms me, however, lest other evidence accumulated in the past several months might have caused Dr. Gardner to revise some of the statements which he recorded at that time. In his interests and also because of *the Laboratory, which must continue* as a lasting memory in his honor, I know you will agree with my alarm. I am sure that Dr. Lanza would concur. (emphasis added)

Lanza wrote that he didn't understand what Vorwald meant but invited Lynch to be his and Vorwald's guest at Saranac two weeks later (mid-August).[64] Lynch declined, leaving the entire matter for the other two to resolve.

Vorwald convinced Lanza he could expect to have a report of the Saranac asbestos research completed by November.[65] A.R. Fisher meanwhile expressed concern over the activities of doctors in Quebec and suggested that any draft report from Saranac be shown to the members of the Quebec Asbestos Producers Association.[66,67]

Vorwald had still not produced his report on the asbestos studies by the following March, prompting Johns-Manville executive J.P. Woodard to write to Lanza for help in coaxing Vorwald. "I am quite disturbed over the possibility that we may get hit with some bad situations before we have the information that we hope these studies will disclose," he wrote, referring to "considerable agitation, both in Canada and on the West Coast."[68] Woodard also wrote an anxious letter directly to Vorwald.[69]

By June, Vorwald had overrun a deadline he had set for himself and was unwilling to set another. Woodard wrote about a "real ferment" in Quebec over articles in magazines and newspapers on industrial diseases, and expressions of concern by the unions.[70] He continued writing about "agitation" in Canada and pressed Vorwald again in July to offer a deadline.[71] Vandiver Brown meanwhile asked the New Jersey Department of Labor to delay setting its "Asbestos Code" until the Saranac report was available.[72]

The Saranac Laboratory finally produced a report of its research on experimental animals dated September 30, 1948, and sent 15 copies to Johns-Manville.[73,74] Vandiver Brown first informed Ernest Muehleck at Keasbey & Mattison and J.F.D. Rohrbach at Raybestos-Manhattan. He urged elimination of references to tumors and pneumonia. He also recommended that the report be limited to animal studies, for which "our right to criticize and suggest changes before publication, or even to forbid publication, is unquestionable." Brown wrote that time was of the essence in getting out a report "as a counter agent to opinions being expressed and conclusions arrived at by Quebec physicians and officials upon the basis of surmise, social ideology, and inadequate information."[75]

A few days later, Brown invited executives from the following companies to meet at the Johns-Manville Boardroom to discuss the Saranac report on November 11, 1948:

American BrakeBlok Div. of American Brake Shoe & Foundry

Gatke Corporation

Keasbey & Mattison Company

Raybestos-Manhattan, Inc.

Russell Manufacturing Company

Thermoid Company (Southern Asbestos)

Union Asbestos and Rubber Company

United States Gypsum Company

To each, he sent a copy of the report from Saranac, asking that it be treated with the utmost confidence. Brown asked that each addressee return his copy of the draft report by the time of the meeting, concluding: "It is obviously undesirable that the report in its present form receive any distribution or publicity outside a limited number of people in our respective organizations."[76]

American Brake Shoe Medical Director Lloyd Hamlin saw nothing in the draft report that he thought warranted concern from a legal viewpoint: "Similar reports are frequent in the literature not only from this country but also from abroad."[77] That company's Executive Vice-President, W.T. Kelly, sent Hamlin's comments and asked Brown to act on his company's behalf at the meeting.[78] U.S. Gypsum also wrote that it would not be sending a representative but asked Brown to represent its interests.[79] The other firms, except for Russell Manufacturing, each arranged to send an executive to the meeting.[80-84]

The day after the meeting was held, Vandiver Brown reported to W.T. Kelly and sent a copy to U.S. Gypsum's J.W.

Butler.[85,86] "It was the unanimous opinion," he wrote, "that the reference to cancer and tumors should be deleted and this is a point we will insist upon for the following reasons..." The first reason given was that the experiments were not "directed" toward determining the incidence of cancer from asbestos exposure. The other "reasons" were remarks excerpted from Gardner's letters and Outline, in some of which Gardner had assured Brown he did not intend to publish his "unintentional" cancer studies.

The only other scientific issue addressed in Brown's letter was pneumonia in the test animals. "(W)e will not request that this be deleted but merely that is be modified somewhat with the view of placing more emphasis on the factors which made it doubtful whether the disease developed as a result of dust exposure."[85]

Vandiver Brown also informed Kelly that all copies of the "tentative and confidential report" had been retrieved except the one held by Dr. Hamlin. He asked for its return: "Everyone felt it would be most unwise to have any copies of the draft report outstanding if the final report is to be different in any substantial respect. The feeling of the representatives of the various companies was very emphatic on this point."[85] Kelly replied that he would ask Hamlin to return the draft.[87]

Page Woodard's minutes of the November 11, 1948 meeting were circulated to the participating corporate representatives later that month. Cover letters informed the recipients that Dr. Lanza had agreed to deal directly with Saranac on the companies' behalf in "putting (the report) in the shape that we agreed upon."[88,89]

Dr. Lanza was assured by Vorwald that the companies need not be alarmed, for it was Saranac's policy to submit articles on asbestos research for review by the sponsors before publication.[90] Lanza had just moved to New York University to establish an "Institute of Industrial Medicine." He advised Vorwald of the changes that were requested by the underwriting companies. "It was the feeling of this group that all references to cancer or tumors should be omitted," he began, citing relevant parts of the draft. "This request would likewise call for the elimination of any tables relating to this subject matter."[91]

Professor Lanza continued: "The group felt there might be included under 'Conclusions' a reference to the non-progressive character of the fibrosis produced by asbestosis." Other revisions more along the lines of editorial changes were also prescribed. "It was decided," Lanza wrote, that after the revisions were made, the paper should be published "as promptly as possible." Any report on human asbestosis should be published separately, he concluded.[91]

On March 3, 1949, Vandiver Brown announced to the other firms that a report had been received from Saranac adopting "the substance of all the suggestions that were made by representatives of the underwriting group." A copy was also enclosed with each letter. Brown hoped that the findings would now be promptly published in the *Journal of Industrial Hygiene*," with an appropriate introduction by Dr. A.J. Lanza."[92] Copies of the report were also sent to Ivan Sabourin, counsel to the Quebec Asbestos Mining Association, and to the New Jersey Department of Labor.[93]

In Quebec, the fears of Johns-Manville executives had by this time been borne out with the publication of Le Doux's incendiary exposé on asbestosis and continuing newspaper reports along those lines. Johns-Manville operations had been the first ones closed in February, 1949, in the beginning of an historic strike at the asbestos mines (described in next chapter).

The delays in publication continued, prompting complaints from Thomas Gatke (and later others), who wanted the Saranac study to combat workers' compensation claims.[94,95] Vorwald finally submitted his paper for publication in September of 1950. It appeared in print early in 1951, in the successor publication to *Journal of Industrial Hygiene*, the *A.M.A. Archives of Industrial Hygiene and Occupational Medicine*.[96] The Industrial Medical Association gave Vorwald its annual Merit in Authorship Award for this paper.[97]

In mailing reprints to the other sponsoring firms, Vandiver Brown wrote of the 15-year effort at Saranac, "I believe we are entitled to conclude that the project was worthwhile."[98]

Vorwald's original report of September 30, 1948 was located in 1979 among his unpublished papers, at the Armed Forces Institute of Pathology. The surviving copy is marked, "Revised," and bears notations throughout in Vorwald's handwriting with changes whereby it was revised as of January 31, 1949.[74]

Additional Reports and Reviews Published in the 1940s

In the 1940s, an increasing number of medical reviewers around the world commented on the carcinogenicity of asbestos. These papers came from Canada, Norway, Italy, and France at first.[99-101,313]

Occupational causes of cancer of the bladder had been identified in the early decades of this century, in dye manufacturing. So it is perhaps not surprising that by 1943 the carcinogenicity of asbestos was noted in a review in the *Journal of Urology*.[102]

The following year, New York State health official Morton Levin published a paper on cancer epidemiology that he had presented to the Health Officers Section of the American Public Health Association. He named a variety of exogenous agents including asbestos, which he said was "possibly" carcinogenic.[103] Massachusetts health officials Tabershaw and Bowditch wrote that the finding of an increased incidence of lung cancer in persons with asbestosis "seems too significant to be overlooked."[104] The word was now going out to a broad audience.

The *Journal of the American Medical Association (J.A.M.A.)* published an editorial entitled "Environmental Cancer" on November 25, 1944.[105] The editorial warned that the most numerous and important environmental cancers were occupational. One of the agents "known or suspected to cause occupational cancer" was asbestos. The article stated that 5,000 to 9,000 cases of occupational cancer had been recorded, and that there was clearly under-reporting of cancers attributable to occupation. Organized investigation of occupational cancer was urged, for the purposes of early detection, improved prognosis, and cancer prevention through the elimination of carcinogenic agents.

The author of this editorial, not identified in the journal, was Wilhelm Hueper.[29] In 1946, Hueper published an article on occupational cancer in *J.A.M.A.* and another one in *Occupational Medicine,* both of which identified asbestos and other industrial materials as causes of cancer.[106,107] Hueper made a number of specific recommendations for effective control of the nation's industrial cancer hazards, and concluded that the great majority of industrial cancers could be eliminated. He ended with an impassioned plea for action:

> The continued occurrence of occupational cancers, on the other hand, represents a challenge not only to the intelligence but also to the social conscience of human society, because industrial cancers may be compared to a biologic time bomb having a delayed time fuse which may be placed in the body of the victim without his knowledge and realization and which may display its deadly effect many years later when the conditions connected with its introduction are often forgotten.[107]

The carcinogenic potential of asbestos was mentioned again in the French literature in 1946, in reports on asbestosis.[108,109] Rousseau of Quebec also described one of his cases of asbestosis with lung and pleural cancer (previously published in 1941), in a paper on asbestosis published in France.[110] Rousseau urged that a study committee independent of politics and the asbestos companies be empowered to investigate conditions in the industry.

In Great Britain, Kennaway and Kennaway published an analysis of death certificate data on lung cancer and occupation. Among persons in whose death asbestosis played a role, these authors found 8 cases of lung cancer. They believed the frequency of lung cancers was disproportionately high for the number of workers exposed to asbestos.[12] Perry, also from Great Britain, agreed that asbestos was a carcinogen.[111]

Physicians at the Massachusetts General Hospital added a

report of pleural mesothelioma in a man aged 37 whose work was cutting asbestos insulating boards. The only treating doctor to comment on the matter thought the man's asbestosis was not a factor in the development of pleural cancer. These physicians commented on the extreme rarity of pleural mesothelioma, a tumor whose very infrequent occurrences had been passed off by some writers as metastases from other primary cancer sites in the body. In this case, "every organ" was searched for a primary cancer focus elsewhere, but none was detected at autopsy.[112]

Boemke published another paper in 1947 on the pathology of dust diseases, recalling his own case and reports by others associating lung cancer with asbestosis. Boemke said there was no doubt that asbestos was responsible for the development of the lung tumors.[113]

The following year the British pathologist Cureton reported lung cancer with asbestosis in a woman who died at 37. This woman had worked for 7 years in "a factory making asbestos pipecovers," starting at the age of 15. The woman's aunt had worked in the same factory and died at age 40 from asbestosis. The author considered his patient unusually young compared to others who died of squamous cell carcinoma of the lung.[114]

Lung cancer in combination with asbestosis became a compensable occupational disease in Czechoslovakia in 1948.[115] Germany, which had implemented a similar compensation provision during World War II, continued that after the War.[116,117]

In Italy, Saita reviewed the literature on "Occupational Tumors of the Lung" (title) in 1948. The English summary at the end of this report was reproduced in *Bulletin of Hygiene,* and said in part:[118,119]

> The conclusion is that only asbestos dust and coal tar derivatives possess an undoubted carcinogenic power on the lungs...

Lynch in South Carolina updated his group's findings in 1948.[120] The cumulative incidence of lung cancer with asbestosis was 3 out of 40, or 7.5%. This was contrasted with the 1% incidence of lung cancer seen in the authors' previous ten years of general autopsy experience. They had also diagnosed lung cancer in an asbestos worker still living. In his discussion of Dr. Lynch's presentation, Dr. Leopold Brahdy said it was his "tentative conclusion" that lung cancer was an occupational disease of asbestos workers.[121]

The Factory Inspectorate Report on Asbestosis and Cancer

The Chief Inspector of Factories produced cumulative statistics and analysis for all known cases of asbestosis in the United Kingdom from 1924 to 1946 in his annual report for the year 1947.[122] In a total of 235 deaths either caused by asbestosis or in which asbestosis had been found at autopsy, cancer of the lungs or pleura was present in 31 (13.2%). This was contrasted with the incidence of such cancers in silicotics (1.32%), which was similar to that of the general population. In other words, the expected number of lung cancers then in a series of 235 autopsies would have been 2 or 3 and instead, there were 31. The chance that as many as 31 lung cancer cases in 235 would occur if their real likelihood was only the same as that of the general population (1%) is remote—less than 1 in a million. This report was often cited in later papers. The large number of asbestosis cases with lung cancer pointed unmistakably to an occupational origin of these cancers.

A 1949 editorial in the *Journal of the American Medical Association* ("Asbestosis and Cancer of the Lung") discussed the cancer statistics published by the Chief Inspector of Factories. The editorial cited epidemiological and experimental evidence suggesting that asbestos workers were at an increased risk of lung cancer. It characterized this cancer risk as "probable," and stated that workers in asbestos-consuming industries should be considered at risk along with manufacturing plant workers.[123] This unsigned *J.A.M.A.* editorial was also written at the request of the editor by Wilhelm Hueper.[29] Members of the Industrial Hygiene Foundation, a group of more than 300 industrial and insurance companies, received a summary of this editorial in the *Industrial Hygiene Digest.*[124] Dr. L.W. Smith echoed these concerns, writing later that year, and further publicizing the British data.[125]

The Scientific American Article

The same month the Chief Inspector of Factories published his annual report for the year 1947, an article called "Cancer and Environment" was published in *Scientific American.*[126] This report by Groff Conklin listed asbestos in a table of "carcinogens known to be present in human environment," and in another graphic display showed that the target organ for asbestos cancer was the lung. Excerpts from Conklin's article were read at the April 7, 1949 general meeting of the Asbestos Textile Institute (ATI). One of those present, George Marshall, wrote for "clarification" to Dr. A.J. Lanza at the Metropolitan Life Insurance Company. Lanza's associate, Dr. W.J. McConnell, replied that, "During the last few years, quite a number of articles claim that carcinoma of the lungs was found due to asbestos." McConnell said he had seen no evidence in his own work to support the asbestos-cancer relationship and closed: "However, time will prove whether they are right or wrong."[127]

Dr. Wyers' Report from Cape Asbestos

Wyers' report on 115 fatal cases involving asbestosis in England offered statistics on the incidence of accompanying lung and pleural cancer.[128] There were 17 such cancers in all, and they were referred to as one entity: "The proportion of pulmonary cancers in the series was therefore 14.8%." Seven others died with cancer of other organs. The author's discussion concerned how asbestos caused cancer, not whether it did.

It was striking that the pulmonary cancer cases had the longest exposure to asbestos and died on the average at an older age than any other subgroup in the series. The average age at death for the Wyers' 115 cases was 40.8 years and the average duration of asbestos exposure was 10.4. For those with pulmonary cancer, the average age at death was 52 years, and the average duration of exposure was 17.3 years. This finding was quite consistent with earlier remarks by Linzbach and

Wedler that the cancer rate of asbestotics was misleadingly low because so many died before the cancer age.

Wyers was the medical officer of the Cape Asbestos Company. Cape's utter lack of industrial hygiene in its South African mining activities at that time have been described by Schepers, who saw "radiologic asbestosis with cor pulmonale" in Black children less than 12 years old.[129]

Dr. Schepers' Visit to America

Dr. Gerrit Schepers was a specialist in occupational lung diseases in South Africa, and in 1949 he came to the United States. He was formally associated with Dr. Anthony J. Lanza, at the Institute of Industrial Medicine at New York University. With the help of Lanza, Schepers gained access to the Saranac Laboratory, the Johns-Manville mining operation in Quebec, and Johns-Manville plants in Lompoc, California, and Waukegan, Illinois.[130]

In his three weeks at Saranac, he examined the "large accumulation of lung tissues from deceased employees" which had been arriving at the laboratory since 1942. Schepers noted a group of 11 cases of pulmonary cancer including 2 pleural mesothelioma cases from the Canadian asbestos mines and mills.

After leaving Saranac, Dr. Schepers visited the Canadian mines and became acquainted with Dr. Kenneth W. Smith of Johns-Manville. The company's large mine was immediately upwind of the town of Asbestos, Quebec, where Smith worked. One of Schepers' main interests was the question of compensability of lung cancer as an occupational disease in asbestos workers. He was surprised to find that Dr. Smith seemed unaware of the cancer material at the Saranac Lab. It had been taken there by automobile by the attorney for the Quebec Asbestos Mining Association (Q.A.M.A.), Ivan Sabourin. Reports of the lab findings had in turn been sent back to Mr. Sabourin, and Dr. Smith apparently had not been told about them before meeting with Dr. Schepers.

Schepers also met Dr. Paul Cartier, who ran a clinic in Thetford Mines, an asbestos mining town nearby in Quebec.

One of Cartier's recent patients had been the Treasurer of Asbestos Corporation, Ltd. This man had died from pleural mesothelioma after 29 years of office work at the company.[131]

To Dr. Schepers' surprise, he was told by Dr. Lanza that he would have to write a thesis to complete his work at New York University. He had already been required by the South African government to write a technical appraisal, incorporating notes and observations from his trip to America. He submitted this to Dr. Lanza.

Dr. Schepers' sworn testimony on what happened next speaks for itself:[130]

MR. KAZAN: Q. Let me ask you this, Doctor. After you turned the report in to Dr. Lanza, did you receive any communication from the Johns-Manville Corporation or any of its officers?
A. I ended up in the office of the chief counsel of the Johns-Manville Corporation in New York City.
Q. What was that gentleman's name?
A. Mr. Vandiver Brown.
Q. Did anyone accompany you to his office?
A. Dr. Lanza.
Q. Whose idea was this visit?
A. Mr. Vandiver Brown's idea.
Q. And do you recall your conversation with Mr. Brown on that date?
A. He had a copy of my thesis on his desk.
Q. Do you know where he got that copy?
A. Well, the only source could have been Dr. Lanza.
Q. Was the only copy that you distributed to anyone the copy you gave Dr. Lanza?
A. Yes, sir.
Q. And was that the copy that was on Mr. Brown's desk?
A. Yes, sir.
Q. All right. And what, if anything, did Mr. Brown tell you with respect to that report?
A. He asked me to suppress it and not publish the information in it.

Q. Did he explain to you why?
A. He said it would be harmful to the economic interests of his company.
Q. Can you be more specific with respect to what portions of the report he found objectionable?
A. He did not wish to have the fact revealed that cancer had been reported in the Canadian asbestos miners and millers.
MR. LUNDQUIST: Could we have that date of that conversation, Doctor?
THE WITNESS: That was in August of 1950.
MR. LUNDQUIST: August of 1950?
THE WITNESS: Yes, sir.
MR. LUNDQUIST: Thank you.
MR. KAZAN: Q. What did Mr. Brown tell you with respect to that report?
A. Well, I can—I think I would be told that I am telling hearsay if I told you what he said, but I can tell you what I said.
Q. That's the Judge's job to tell you if you can't answer. So, would you tell us please as best as you can recall what Mr. Brown told you that he found objectionable or inappropriate with respect to your publishing this information?
A. Well, the one was the cancer issue which he did not want to have revealed. The other was the fact that I had mentioned the extreme severity of the asbestotic disease which I had seen in the cases from Saranac, and also the extreme dustiness of the working environment of the men at the Waukegan Plant and at the Lompoc Plant.
Q. Did Mr. Brown in any way tell you that this was confidential or privileged information?
A. He suggested that I had been their guest, their privileged guest, and therefore should respect the confidence of the company and not mention what I had seen.
Q. And what, Doctor, was your response?
A. I told him that I would release the information to the South African Government, because that was my duty.
Q. Did you in fact do so?
A. Yes.

Q. Do you know what happened to your report once it was delivered by you to the South African officials?
MR. LUNDQUIST: I am going to object if he's going to give us any hearsay in response to this unless he knows of his own knowledge, your Honor.
THE COURT: Well, I think that's what it calls for. Do you know of your own knowledge what occurred?
THE WITNESS: Yes. My—there had been communication between our—
MR. LUNDQUIST: Excuse me, Doctor. Was this told to you or did you observe it and determine it by yourself?
THE WITNESS: I was told by the Director of the Pneumoconiosis Bureau.
MR. LUNDQUIST: Okay. That's as far as it goes. It's hearsay, and I object to it.
THE COURT: It sounds like it.
MR. KAZAN: Q. Doctor, did your report ever see the light of day once it got into the South African government?
A. No, it was suppressed.

The Saranac Lab's Cancer Studies for the Quebec Asbestos Mining Association

In the meantime Merewether presented the British asbestosis-cancer statistics to the Canadian Medical Association, and his paper was published in the Association's journal in February, 1950. Merewether expressed disappointment that death from wholly preventable pneumoconioses remained a problem. This occurred because these deaths did not make headlines like those caused by accidents or dramatic epidemics, he said. He also wrote:[132]

> It can be said with certainty, however, that a few months exposure to silica or asbestos in gross... concentrations will eventually cause death.

This was immediately picked up by Dr. Kenneth Smith, who wrote to Dr. Vorwald at Saranac about the article.[133]

Vorwald spoke with Merewether at the I.L.O. pneumoconiosis conference in Australia the next month. Upon his return he wrote to Dr. Smith. Speaking of Merewether's recent publication, Vorwald said,[134]

> It certainly is a dilly, and, as you do, I take strong exception to some of his statements. Why or how he comes to many of his conclusions is beyond me. Even at that, however, I continue to like him.

Getting down to business, he continued,

> Paul (Cartier) tells me of another storm which is brewing in Quebec, this time concerning a case of asbestosis with cancer. I am most anxious to get on with the survey of all available data before the storm really breaks. As you know, fishing is always best just before rather than immediately after the storm.

Dr. Merewether was no doubt aware of the difficulties his publications presented to the asbestos industry. His courage in placing his new cancer statistics in the Canadian medical literature can be appreciated in light of the remarks of a "colleague" at the time of his death:[135]

> Merewether lived at a time when the publication of original papers by serving Civil Servants was, at the very least, not actively encouraged...

After Dr. Gardner's death in 1946, his successor Dr. Arthur Vorwald expressed an interest in cancer immediately upon taking the reins as the Laboratory's director. In late 1950, Vorwald sent a proposal around to a number of asbestos mining companies in Quebec. On November 7, 1950, he met with industry representatives (J.P. Woodard of Johns-Manville and attorney Ivan Sabourin of the Quebec Asbestos Mining Association) and their consultant, Dr. A.J. Lanza. In proposing to do animal inhalation tests, Vorwald explained:[136]

Dr. E.R.A. Merewether, H.M. Senior Medical Inspector of Factories, U.K. Ministry of Labour and National Service. (*Courtesy of the U.K. Health and Safety Executive.*)

> We hope to show or prove that cancer incidence is not increased among these animals even if dusted.

It was agreed that the report would "be available only to the underwriting companies and not made generally available until it has been reviewed with and by the companies." Thus, with approval of the companies in Q.A.M.A. and top management at Johns-Manville, the arrangements were concluded.

The only trace of these studies that remains is an interim report in May, 1952, by which time mice had been exposed to airborne asbestos dust for 14 months.[137] Vorwald found "a trend toward a greater incidence of tumors in the exposed animals than in the control animals." Though the excess was not yet statistically significant, Vorwald anticipated that a continuing incidence of tumors such as he had been seeing would tip the scales in favor of asbestos carcinogenicity.

> The final phases of this experiment will be of great importance since at the most recent period when animals were killed for study, the incidence of tumors had increased and the increase seems to be more pronounced among the animals exposed to asbestos dust than among the non-exposed control animals.

This research was never published, and no final report of the study has come to light. QAMA apparently deferred sponsoring epidemiological studies until 1956.

More Reports and Reviews Linking Asbestos and Cancer

Merewether's statistics associating asbestosis with cancer of the lung and pleura were cited by Doig (also with the Factory Department), who wrote: "evidence is accumulating that cancer of the lung is unduly frequent in asbestos workers."[138] Similar comments and reviews were published by Fischer, Frost, Eickhoff, Middleton, G.C. Smith, Silson, and Gloyne in the years 1949-1951.[139-145]

Hueper, who had become Chief of the Environmental Cancer Section of the U.S. National Cancer Institute, noted in 1951 that most of those who had written on the subject had concluded that there was a causal relationship between asbestosis and lung cancer.[146]

Owen in England reported another case of asbestosis with lung cancer in 1951. The victim died at age 39, and his only exposure to asbestos had been a 12-month job in a London asbestos factory 20 years before.[147]

Another fatal case of asbestosis with lung cancer was reported in New York that year in a 40-year-old man. He had worked as a pipecoverer starting in 1940 and had been a plumber before that. The authors (one of whom had reported 2 earlier deaths from these causes in insulators) introduced their report with a review of earlier literature. They concluded:[148]

> (The association of carcinoma in cases of asbestosis) emphasizes the hazards of industrial exposure, the compensability of the cancerous process as well as asbestosis and the need of careful preventive measures.

A tabular presentation of the literature on cases of lung cancer with asbestosis was published in 1952 by Behrens. He reviewed the cumulative world literature and his own experience for the frequency of lung cancer with asbestosis and compared that with the reported rate of lung cancer with silicosis. He counted a total of 509 autopsied cases of asbestosis in which 44 (14.2%) had lung cancer. For silicosis, there were only 35 cases with lung cancer out of 2,475 autopsy reports (1.4%).[149]

Hardy of the Massachusetts Institute of Technology referred to prior case reports of asbestosis with lung cancer in an insulation worker and in a man who "worked for seven years sorting and carding asbestos fibers intended for insulation manufacturing." She concluded,

> These cases have particular significance since there are nearly 10,000 workers exposed to varying amounts of asbestos in American industry, many of them in some operations not properly safeguarded against a potential carcinogen.

Hardy used the term "potential carcinogen" though she seemed convinced by Merewether's 1947 statistics.[150] The use of such an expression does raise the point that, whether one was inclined to accept the carcinogenicity of asbestos as proven or await further data before drawing a conclusion, one had to acknowledge the immediate responsibility for taking preventive measures.

Werber added another report of asbestosis and lung cancer, which the author believed was the first case in the literature to be operated upon with success. The cancer was presumed to be occupationally caused.[151] Others to comment positively on the relation between asbestosis and lung cancer were Mayers, Sroka, and Grosse.[152-155]

Dr. W.E. Smith, at New York University, still felt that there had been inconclusively few reports of lung cancer with asbestosis in Germany, the United States, and Canada. However, he seemed persuaded that a cancer hazard with asbestosis had been demonstrated in England, where dust control regulations had been in force since 1933. Smith had recently been informed by Dr. Merewether that although lung cancer had been found predominantly among people who started work in the asbestos industry before the industrial hygiene rules took effect, some cases had also been diagnosed in individuals first exposed afterwards. While the latter could have been unrelated to occupation in the regulated era, Smith acknowledged that people starting their employment in the 1930s "are only now reaching the mean age at which tumors might be expected to appear."[156,157]

In the published discussion of one of Smith's papers, Dr. A.J. Lanza offered this incredible critique of Merewether's data:[158]

> I think it is important to distinguish between cases of clinically recognizable and fatal lung cancer, on one hand, and cases in which the diagnosis of lung cancer has been made as more or less of an incidental finding at autopsy, on the other. The English claim for an association between lung cancer and asbestosis has been based, it seems to me, on data obtained from lungs that a pathologist has searched with a microscope. I wonder how many cases of lung cancer would be found if lungs from any sort of population were subjected to the same minute scrutiny?

Smith responded that the British Pneumoconiosis Board handled silicosis cases the same way as asbestosis cases, and so the silicotics could serve as a control group. In fact, the silicotics had an almost identical incidence of lung cancer as the general population, one tenth the incidence of lung cancer in asbestotics. In addition, many of the pathologists reporting excess lung cancer in asbestotics had done thousands of autopsies of the general population, and cited them as a comparison or "control" group. Further, no autopsy series of asbestotics was reported as having a "normal" rate of lung cancer.

Another person who commented after Dr. William Smith's report on European research on occupational cancer was Dr. Paul Cartier, of the Thetford Industrial Clinic in Quebec.[158] Cartier reported that his clinic had detected "eight cases of primary cancer of the lung" among an asbestos mine and mill working population of 4000. Other cases were suspected, but only those cases confirmed by an autopsy (or biopsy) were included. Of the eight cases described, two were called "pleural mesothelioma." The degree of concomitant asbestosis of the lungs was given as "none" or "minimal" for six of the seven for whom this data was provided. Cartier expressed the opinion that more study would be required, and looked askance at the "variety" of malignancies found.

Smith, however, had no trouble believing that asbestos, like polycyclic hydrocarbons and other carcinogens, could attack multiple target organs. The mention of pleural mesothelioma reminded Smith of material he had discussed with other pathologists in England:[158]

> I am interested in your observation of two cases of pleural mesothelioma. This is a rather rare tumor. In examining pathological material sent us from England by Dr. Hinson, we found among six cancerous asbestotic lungs two presenting alveolar cell carcinoma. These tumors are often diagnosed as "pleural mesothelioma." I should very much like to exchange slides with you.*

Smith's main interest was animal testing of dangerous industrial materials. He felt that published experimental studies on asbestos' carcinogenicity were insufficient, and was anxious to conduct such studies himself. He was then unaware of the positive carcinogenicity studies of Gardner, suppressed by Vorwald at the direction of asbestos companies and Dr. Lanza. After examining this material for the first time in 1989, Dr. Smith said, "It would have been of interest and importance to people studying the problem at that time."[160]

The Seventh Saranac Symposium

In September of 1952, the Saranac Laboratory held another one of its scientific conferences. However, unlike the others, the Seventh Saranac Symposium was never published. Only fragmentary information survives, and has come to light in recent years. Attendees included Drs. W.C. Hueper, A.J. Vorwald, E.R.A. Merewether, K.W. Smith (Johns-Manville), J.F. Knox

*These tumors of the pleura were also called "endotheliomas" in reports of this era.[159]

(Turner Brothers Asbestos), A.J. Lanza, K.M. Lynch, O.A. Sander, R.T. Johnstone, and medical directors from a number of industrial corporations. Hugh Jackson (Johns-Manville) and Edward Ames (Owens-Corning Fiberglas) were also on the guest roster preserved by Dr. Vorwald.[161]

Dr. Merewether provided up-to-date statistics from his country at the session on "Pneumoconiosis and Pulmonary Cancer." Dr. Cartier presented an evaluation of pulmonary cancers found at autopsy in Quebec asbestos mine and mill workers. Vorwald's incomplete records of the Symposium contain no indication that he presented his preliminary animal data from the Q.A.M.A. study.[161]

Merewether reported that a total of 306 deaths involving asbestosis were known to British authorities. Excluding 10 "where there is also cancer of other sites other than the lungs," he found that 48 (16.2%) of the remaining 296 deaths were associated with cancer of the lung. This was an increase from 13.2 percent disclosed as of 1949:

> (T)he cumulative percentage of deaths with complicating cancer of the lungs is rising rather than falling.

Merewether believed that very few deaths involving asbestosis escaped notice of the authorities in his country.

He further remarked that cases of massive fibrosis within 5 to 7 years from commencement of work were no longer seen, and as people lived longer in the industry more lived long enough to get cancer:

> The duration of exposure which results in death from asbestosis is lengthened, the age of death is increasing and the fibrosis found at autopsy is less. This means that cases of asbestosis are limited to the cancer-occurring age period, and if—and I say if there is a relationship between asbestosis and cancer of the lung... then we would expect an increased incidence of cancer of the lung over that found in the general population...

Lanza suggested that the British must have had more problems because they used different varieties of asbestos than Canadian chrysotile. When asked to reply, Merewether shot back:

> (I) think Dr. Lanza is misinformed about the proportions of asbestos used and where they are used in England. The original cases of asbestosis, 50 years ago, were all Canadian asbestos.

Later on England also used amosite and crocidolite from South Africa, Merewether said. He called on Dr. Knox of Turner Brothers Asbestos Company to describe the kind of asbestos used at his firm's large plant and comment on whether there had been cases of cancer there.

Most unfortunately, the transcript remaining is very incomplete and a large number of pages are missing—including any reply Dr. Knox may have offered. But Merewether's skepticism about the relative innocuousness of the most abundant variety of asbestos (chrysotile) was apparent.

Dr. Cartier's presentation began with the acknowledgment that 58 cases of pulmonary cancer and asbestosis had been reported in medical literature as of 1950. Considering the size of the industry, Cartier did not think that figure was significant. While granting that there seemed to be a cancer problem in the British asbestos industry, he questioned a lack of confirmatory reports from the South African mines, the mines of Quebec, and the asbestos textile industry of the U.S.[161]

Cartier's own investigation included an evaluation of 53 chrysotile asbestos mine and mill workers with 17 to 40 years in the industry who had died and been autopsied. He used the tabulation shown on the next page to display his findings. From the data in Table 1, one would think there was a high risk of lung cancer in the chrysotile asbestos mining industry, a risk that extended to the employees with light- and moderate-exposure jobs. But Cartier concluded instead:[161]

Table 1. Comparative Incidence of Pulmonary Cancer in Two Groups of Autopsied Asbestos Miners

	Employees With Asbestosis	Employees Without Asbestosis	Total
Number Autopsied	34	19	53
Number of Pulmonary Cancer	4	6	10
Percent in each Group	11.7	31.5	

> (T)his table does not reveal a statistical evidence of a causal relationship between asbestos*is* and pulmonary cancer. (emphasis added)

This epidemiological nonsense was not to be held up to the light of day by publication in the scientific literature.

A year later, Cartier presented slightly updated figures at a conference moderated by Dr. Lanza. By this time, 40 asbestotic mine and mill workers under his observation had died and been examined post mortem. Six (15%) had died from bronchogenic carcinoma. Cartier admitted that this was a matter of "special interest" but declined an effort to fully discuss the cancer relationship:

> I just want to say that there are seven other patients with bronchogenic carcinoma among the employees who did not have asbestosis.

The reader will note that Cartier has so far reconstructed his Saranac presentation as shown above in Table 2.

In the space of these two reports the number of pulmonary cancers had gone up 30 percent (to 13). But Cartier concluded once again that *asbestosis* did not cause cancer:

> Therefore, the part played by the asbestotic fibrosis (in the lung cancer/asbestosis cases) remains questionable.

Once again, Dr. Cartier did not say that asbestos did not cause cancer. The incidence of pulmonary cancer among the non-

Table 2. Comparative Incidence of Pulmonary Cancer in Two Groups of Autopsied Asbestos Workers

	Employees With Asbestosis	Employees Without Asbestosis	Total
Number Autopsied	40 (34)	? (19)	? (53)
Number of Pulmonary Cancer	6 (4)	7 (6)	13 (10)
Percent in each Group	15 (11.7)	? (31.5)	

Note: Numbers from Table 1 in parentheses for comparison.

asbestotic miners was undoubledly still even higher than among the asbestotics (whose rate was 15 percent—very similar to the figures tallied by Merewether and Behrens). But this article, which *was* published, withheld that figure from the scientific community.[162]

The Louvain Symposium

At this time, a worldwide trend of increasing lung cancer rates was clearly evident. Dr. W.E. Smith was present at an international meeting of experts on the pathogenesis of lung cancer, convened in Belgium in 1952 under the chairmanship of Dr. Harold L. Stewart of the National Cancer Institute (U.S.). Their report, authored by scientists from seven countries, was published the following year. The carcinogenicity of asbestos and other materials was unequivocally acknowledged by this panel.[163-166]

The journal in which the Symposium's conclusions and recommendations were published editorialized,[167]

> It seems to be beyond discussion that cancer of the lung is sometimes caused by occupational exposure to asbestos and chromates, and occurs with higher frequency among gas-workers and miners in certain mines.

Other Reports in the Early 1950s

In Hamburg, a city with asbestos manufacturing and large shipyards, König found 5 more cases of lung cancer among 16 asbestosis patients seen at autopsy.[168]

Dr. Wilhelm C. Hueper, Chief of the Environmental Cancer Section, U.S. National Cancer Institute, 1948. (*Courtesy of Dr. Thomas F. Mancuso.*)

In 1953, the German pathologist, Weiss, reported a case of cancer of the pleura in an insulation worker with asbestosis. Referring to Wedler's findings (of pleural cancer with asbestosis) and his own, Weiss concluded that pleural cancer (i.e., mesothelioma) was an occupational hazard of asbestos workers.[169,170]

Boemke added another report of two cases, people who had worked in asbestos factories. Both had asbestosis and died

Dr. W.C. Hueper and Dr. H.L. Stewart at the National Cancer Institute, 1977. (*Courtesy of Dr. Stewart.*)

from tumors originating in lower lobes of their lungs. Boemke again asserted that the relationship between asbestosis and lung cancer was indisputable.[171] This paper, and his 1947 report in the same journal (also linking asbestos with cancer), were summarized in *Chemical Abstracts*.[172,173]

In the U.S. Isselbacher and co-workers reported additional cases of lung cancer with asbestosis in an insulation handler and an asbestos mill worker, both smokers. The authors considered the association between asbestosis and lung cancer to be "more than coincidence," based on their review of the literature.[174] An average of 5 analyses recorded in the literature gave a 13.8% incidence of lung cancer with asbestosis at autopsy, contrasted with 0.8 to 2.4% in routine autopsies of the general population. Moreover, cancer of the lung with asbestosis had occurred in a far higher proportion of females than did lung cancer in the general population, again pointing to an occupational origin. These investigators also noted that in about four-fifths of the cases in the literature, the tumor originated in the lower lobes of the lungs, in contrast with lung cancer in the general population where cancers more often arose in the upper lobes.

Sometime between 1952 and 1954, Dr. Herbert K. Abrams wrote an article, "Cancer in Industry," which was distributed by the American Cancer Society. It listed asbestos as an occupational cause of lung cancer. Industrial hygiene safeguards and "education of the worker" were recommended.[175] Under "Cancer," the *Encyclopedia Britannica* observed that respiratory cancers "occur in workers who are exposed to the inhalation of ... asbestos dust."[176]

California health officials studied the relation of occupation and smoking habits to lung cancer rates.[177,178] Histories of occupation and smoking were taken for 518 lung cancer patients and 518 matched control hospital patients. There were 10 lung cancer patients with 5 or more years' work with asbestos exposure, and only 1 control patient in such occupations (steamfitters, boilermakers, and asbestos workers). Controlled for the effects of cigarette smoking, this finding was "on the borderline of statistical significance at the 95% level."

Also in 1954, Eckardt (Esso) and Drinker (Harvard) authored an editorial describing asbestos as among the "most suspect human pulmonary carcinogens."[179]

Leicher in West Germany meanwhile published a disturbing report of a case of peritoneal mesothelioma with asbestosis in an asbestos factory worker. The man died 33 years after starting to work with asbestos. Asbestos was identified in the tumor. Leicher considered the cancer to be of occupational origin, noting that such tumors were very rare in the general population.[180-181]

1955: Doll's Study and Other Events

In 1955, major studies were published on cancer in the asbestos textile industry.

Bonser and co-workers, reporting on post-mortem examination of 72 factory workers with asbestosis, found 2 pleural and 4 peritoneal cancers. Lung cancer was present in another 12 cases, accounting for one sixth of all deaths (16.7%). The authors called attention to the "very high number" of primary peritoneal cancers in such a small group of subjects. They were hopeful that the 1933 industrial hygiene rules would reduce or even lead to the disappearance of the cancer risk of asbestos factory workers. Although this study concerned workers in England, it was published in the United States.[182]

Doll, referring to Hueper's unpublished presentation at the Seventh Saranac Symposium, alluded to the fact that a majority of writers considered the causal relationship between asbestosis and lung cancer either proved or highly probable.[164] Doll was in that majority.[183] He noted that, on the other hand, a minority consisting of Cartier, Warren, Lanza, and Vorwald remained skeptical; and this, he said, had prompted him to do an epidemiological study.

Doll found that of 105 asbestos textile workers examined at autopsy from 1935-1953, 18 had lung cancer. Fifteen of them also had asbestosis, and their average period between the start of asbestos work and death was 28.4 years. Follow-up studies of 113 men with at least twenty years' exposure showed that 39 deaths had occurred, whereas only 15.4 would have been expected based on general mortality rates. The excess was entirely due to pulmonary cancer (11 against 0.8 expected) and other respiratory and cardiovascular disease (22 against 7.6 expected). One death from "endothelioma of the pleura" was counted as a lung cancer. Doll wrote that with the regulation of conditions in the industry in the early 1930s, the cancer risk had declined.[164] However, in 1955, he had no way of knowing how much the cancer risk would come down with reduced exposure—or how much it would rise with the decline of asbestosis as a competing cause of death in these workers.

Doll did *not* speculate on whether the asbestos workers' smoking habits played a role in producing the tenfold excess rate of lung cancer. Though himself a contributor of studies linking cigarettes to lung cancer, Doll apparently saw no likelihood that the asbestos workers could have smoked that much more than other men their age in the general population. Lacking smoking histories for the deceased workers, he could not study the separate and combined impacts of occupation and smoking on the lung cancer rates of the asbestos workers.

Dr. John Knox, medical officer for Turner & Newall, was really the architect and principal author of the study published by Doll. The original version of this study was completed by mid-1954. "On completion, we sought permission to publish, and this, to my great surprise, was refused by the Company," a mortified Dr. Knox wrote in a personal letter to Dr. William E. Smith.[184] "The headline news about lung cancer has scared people over here and it was thought we might attract undesirable publicity," Knox explained. Doll wrote to Knox, "I was shocked to hear of the decision of your Board not to approve publication of our proposed paper." Insisting that "any positive findings with regard to the cause of cancer must be made available to all research workers," Doll said he would not have participated, had he imagined that there would be restraints on publication.[185] When Doll then moved to publish the report by himself, Turner & Newall threatened to take legal action against Doll, who worked at the government's Medical Research Council. The Council's attorney rebuffed the company, and Doll published the results of the study. But the paper Doll published was different from the original in one important way: there was an almost desparate effort throughout to reassure readers that the occupational cancer hazard in Britain's asbestos industry was a thing of the past.[164,184] Gone was the last sentence of the original manuscript by Knox and Doll, which read:

> Insufficient data are available to determine whether the risk has yet been eliminated by the improved conditions which now exist.

Dr. William Smith, still eager to do animal tests with asbestos, brought Knox's letter to Dr. Lanza's attention. Dr. Smith remembered Lanza's reaction more than 20 years later:[186]

> I recall Dr. Lanza responding to this by becoming very irate and repeating his assertion that all this business about chemicals causing cancer was going to blow over, and the cancer investigators were a lot of troublemakers, and it was my impression that this was the immediate cause for his advising me that my employment at (New York University) would not continue.

Smith made similar comments in an interview with a writer from *Cavalier* magazine published in 1962, even naming Lanza (who was still living). He went on to describe his misfortune as part of a larger and more serious problem:

> I consider myself expendable... But I see one cancer scientist after another pushed out of his work and perhaps out of his career... What happened to me I've seen experienced by other investigators who became too inquisitive about carcinogens in a company's product or manufacturing processes. Government, university, and industrial research in this field has been obstructed, while apologists for carcinogens are in great demand at $50,000 a year. You have to play ball with some large corporations if you want to hold your job—at the expense of employees and the public.[186]

The *Lancet's* editors also reacted strongly to Doll's report. "Doll now confirms suggestive evidence that lung cancer is an occupational hazard of asbestos workers."[187] Dr. Knox, in his response to the *Lancet* editorial, did not dispute this conclusion.[188]

In its editorial on Doll's paper, the *British Medical Journal* echoed Doll's conclusion that the excess risk of contracting lung cancer "had become progressively less as the duration of employment under the old dusty conditions decreased."[189] But only one of the 15 deaths from lung or pleural cancer and asbestosis had taken place less than 23 years from the onset of asbestos exposure. The follow-up period in Doll's study after the implementation of dust control regulations in Great Britain was barely 21 years. Given the long latency of lung cancer from asbestos, it was premature to claim that the 1933 dust controls had brought the lung cancer problem under control.[164]

On the contrary, the Factory Inspectorate's update of the picture nationwide in Britain showed that lung cancer accompanying asbestosis was increasing steadily, from an already staggering rate.[190] The figures reported in the annual report of 1947, those in the 1954 report, and the breakdown of the more recent cases are shown in Table 3. Presumably, the compiler of the data, Dr. Merewether, was still counting cancers of the pleura under the category "cancers of the lung." This would have rendered the figures for the time intervals properly comparable in the 1954 report.

Asbestosis victims were living longer, the result of dust controls and regulations prohibiting the employment of children under 18 in asbestos factories. The average age at death

Table 3. Proportion of Lung Cancer Deaths with Asbestosis

	1924-1946	1924-1954	1947-1954
deaths caused by asbestosis or in which asbestosis had been proved at autopsy	235	344	109
number of these in which lung cancer was also present	31 (13.2%)	55 (16.0%)	24 (22.0%)

Table 4. Average Age at Death

	Asbestosis	Asbestosis with Tuberculosis	Asbestosis with Cancer of the Lung
as reported in December, 1933	40.8	41.6	—
cumulatively through 1946	47.5	39.0	52.1
cumulatively for all cases, 1924 through 1954	49.1	40.5	52.7

for asbestotics had been barely over 40 in Merewether's 1933 article.[191] (See Table 4)

A little arithmetic shows that people dying with asbestosis in Great Britain in the years 1947-1954 reached an average age of 55. [This calculation excludes asbestotics who also had tuberculosis or lung cancer.] Those dying in these years with both asbestosis and pulmonary cancer reached an age of 53.6, on the average. And the steady rise in lung cancer confirmed the fact that more and more people with asbestosis were living long enough to get cancer.

NEGATIVE OPINIONS ON ASBESTOS AS A CAUSE OF CANCER

Let us interrupt the chronology of events to recall Doll's reference to the minority who remained skeptical about the carcinogenicity of asbestos. Those named were: Warren, 1948; Cartier, 1952; and "according to Hueper, Lanza and Vorwald."

Dr. Shields Warren had written a brief editorial on occupational cancers, with only this perplexing reference to asbestosis:[192]

> It is well to remember that the mere occurrence of a tumor in conjunction with a recognized occupational disease may be fortuitous, as in the case of a cancer of the bronchus in a person already suffering from asbestosis.

It appears that Warren's main interest at this time was radiation, not asbestos and chemical carcinogens. Here, his obstructionist role was singled out in an anecdote told to the AFL-CIO Executive Council by Dr. Wilhelm Hueper. Dr. Hueper had proposed a U.S. government investigation of the lung cancer risks of Colorado uranium miners, mindful of the already well-documented radiation cancer hazard of miners in the Erz mountains of Central Europe. Hueper told this story:[193]

> When this investigation was first proposed by me in 1948, after I had just joined the National Cancer Institute, the application for a grant for conducting this investigation to be made to the Colorado State Health Department was placed before the National Advisory Cancer Council. It was adopted upon my advice, over the protest of one of its members, Dr. Shields Warren, who at that time was Director of the Division of Biology and Medicine of the Atomic Energy Commission. *Dr. Warren rather foolishly claimed that uranium ore miners in Colorado sustained a greater exposure to ionizing radiation from cosmic rays than from exposure to radioactive dust and gases in the mines.* Defeated in the National Advisory Cancer Council to block this study, he tried then equally unsuccessfully to prevent the approval of this application by the Surgeon General through a letter of protest addressed to (the Surgeon General). (emphasis added)

Senate investigators have found that, although the cancer risks were recognized by Warren's group at the A.E.C. by 1948, weapons plant workers were, as a matter of policy, not warned that they were at high risk of getting lung cancer.[194]

Even without knowing that Dr. Warren said that cosmic ray exposure to Colorado residents was a comparable cancer threat to radiation in the uranium mines, one could hardly attach much significance to his contemporary remark about asbestos lacking any scientific support.

Hueper's reference to Vorwald's and Lanza's skepticism on the relationship between asbestos and lung cancer (cited by Doll) probably came from the First National Cancer Conference. The Proceedings of this 1949 meeting mentioned that 14 cases of carcinoma of the lung had been observed in association with 92 cases of asbestosis confirmed through autopsy. The record of this panel discussion, moderated by Dr. Hueper, continued:[195]

> The clinical experience of Lanza and the experimental work of Vorwald have not revealed any carcinogenic properties which can be attributed to asbestos.

This conference predated the decision of Q.A.M.A. to fund confidential animal studies on asbestos and cancer under Vorwald's direction and with Lanza's encouragement. The experimental work of Vorwald's former chief, Gardner, was apparently not discussed.

Like his predecessor Gardner, Vorwald provided medical reports to asbestos firms and others in workers' compensation cases. His confidential pathology reports would presumably contain candid expressions of Vorwald's viewpoints. In one such report (March 6, 1954) on a Quebec miner, he wrote that the underlying asbestosis was a "factor which operated to produce the cancer present in his lung."[196]

Cartier's research on asbestos and cancer has already been discussed. Of the four detractors named by Doll in 1955, only Warren appears to have been independent of research and consulting relationships with the asbestos industry.

It is important to note that in the normal course of development of scientific knowledge, absolute unanimity of opinion is extraordinarily rare. Even widely accepted ideas in science are regularly questioned by investigators who either require a high degree of proof to be convinced or have alternative theories of their own consistent with the available evidence. In science, skepticism is a tradition.

However, the exercise of judgment in the absence of irrefutable proof is also a tradition. Particularly in matters relating to public health, withholding judgment and action until faced with absolute certainty can be disastrous. (One does not wait for a cholera epidemic to spread to regions where the most reliable diagnosticians practice medicine before deciding to take action, for example.) The weight of independent scientific opinion in 1955 favoring the idea that asbestos caused cancer can be better appreciated in this context.

Other Developments in 1955

In an article on medical aspects of cigarette smoking, the monthly magazine *Consumer Reports* included a display of "Possible Industrial Causes of Lung Cancer." Included were "asbestos from asbestos mining, processing, and weaving" and 6 other substances.[197]

The minutes of the Asbestos Textile Institute the next month reflect concern about burgeoning publicity:[198]

> There is increasing publicity both in the professional and popular literature concerning the relationship of asbestosis to cancer ... For example, in the Consumers Reports, a popular publication of national distribution, one of the member companies reported that they currently have a workmen's compensation case claiming that pulmonary cancer was caused by exposure to asbestosis. (sic)

A conference on occupational chest disease was held at Saranac Laboratory, papers from which were published in the (A.M.A.) *Archives of Industrial Health* later that year. One of these was by Dr. A.I.G. McLaughlin, of the British Factory Inspectorate. Referring to cancer, he said:[199]

> The connection between asbestosis and cancer of the lung is becoming clearer, and in one series of 100 autopsies on asbestosis cases there were 25 cases of cancer of the lung.

Lynch and Pratt-Thomas reported details of two more cases of lung cancer with asbestosis in South Carolina. They had seen 4 cases of lung cancer in 49 autopsies of people with asbestosis (8.3 percent). This was more than 5 times the lung cancer rate seen in their hospital service during that time (1.5 percent). They concluded:[200]

> Statistical inference from this and other series does not allay the suspicion that there may be an association between the two conditions.

Responding to a question on the compensation status of lung cancer with asbestosis, Dr. Pratt-Thomas said that in some cases the compensation boards were issuing awards in favor of the claimants.

Hueper authored a Public Health Service Monograph on environmental causes of lung cancer in 1955. By this time, there were 99 published cases of asbestosis and cancer of the lung, including some duplication of cases among British authors.[201] Hueper was also struck by the large proportion of women with asbestosis and lung cancer. For lung cancer in the general population was primarily a disease of men, but among men and women with asbestosis any difference of risk between the sexes appeared to be much less.

Hueper referred to Merewether's figure of 44.2 as the average age at death for asbestosis (this included cases of asbestosis with tuberculosis) versus 52.1 years for asbestosis and lung cancer. He went on to declare that many asbestotics had died before they had time to develop cancer. So Hueper reiterated that the reported association of lung cancer with asbestosis was conservatively biased because the cancer risk from asbestos had been partially eclipsed by the competing mortal risk from asbestosis.

In September of 1955, the National Cancer Institute convened a "Conference on Environmental Carcinogens." Expert panels reviewed the evidence on a number of substances including asbestos. The asbestos panel consisted of Dr. William E. Smith as discussion leader, Dr. Kenneth W. Smith (medical director Johns-Manville), and Dr. Arthur J. Vorwald (fired by the Saranac Laboratory in 1953, he had gone to Wayne University in Detroit).

The summary sheet on asbestos produced at this meeting said this about the epidemiological evidence on lung cancer:

> English reports are very suggestive—13% of asbestosis deaths had carcinoma compared to 1.3% of silicotics.

> Canadian workers—6 cases of lung cancer in 52 autopsies (11%). All of the participants were impressed but on the whole felt that more studies in greater detail were needed.

The experimental evidence was rated inadequate, and Vorwald's experiments for Q.A.M.A. do not appear to have been discussed. The score sheet read "O" (no evidence available) on experimental evidence in both rats and mice. The panel concluded, under "general aspects":[202]

a. Worker studies have been very suggestive but no great reliance can be placed on the data assembled to date. Additional studies are needed.
b. The laboratory investigations reported do not confirm the human experience although only scanty observations are available.
c. *Widespread hazard if a causal relationship is established due to many uses of this material under various conditions.* (emphasis added)

None of these details were published, in Vorwald's review of the session, except the marks on the score sheets for each substance considered. Under epidemiologic evidence of lung cancer from asbestos was a question mark (?).[203]

Just before the conference at the National Cancer Institute the Asbestos Textile Institute's Air Hygiene Committee met, with guests Paul Cartier and Ivan Sabourin from Q.A.M.A. Dr. Cartier said additional research was needed. Attorney Sabourin was apparently less skeptical:[204]

> Mr. Sabourin stated that the present major health problems of the industry pertained to the relationship of heart difficulties and cancer to asbestos exposure.

In Dresden, Bohlig and Jacob concluded that the occurrence of cancer among asbestos workers (with and without asbestosis) was not as frequent as many people believed. Still, they were convinced of an occupational origin by the predisposition of lung cancer in asbestos workers for the lower lobes of the lungs; the relatively high mortality from this cause among women in the asbestos industry; and the high number of serosal tumors (mesotheliomas) of the pleura and peritoneum in the reported literature.[205] Güttner meanwhile reported cases of asbestosis in conjunction with lung cancer in two Dresden workers.[206]

In Italy, a case of asbestosis with lung cancer was reported separately by Portigliatti-Barbos and Rombola. The woman was 49 when she died. Because of what one author attributed to "bureaucratic delays" the autopsy did not take place until 94 days after death. Despite "uncommon individual luck," as it was expressed by the dissector, it was possible to diagnose both the asbestotic process and the lung cancer, which had been diagnosed during the patient's life.

Rombola, citing W.E. Smith and Lanza, questioned the lack of published experimental confirmation of asbestos carcinogenicity; but he tended to accept that the British and German authors had identified an industrial cancer hazard. Rombola tried to reconcile the lower reported cancer incidence in the U.S., Canada, and Italy with the higher incidence in England and Germany. He proposed that the white (chrysotile) asbestos mined in Canada and Italy might be carcinogenically different from the African blue (crocidolite) asbestos.[207]

Portigliatti-Barbos thoroughly reviewed the literature and flatly concluded that there was no doubt of a relationship between asbestosis and pulmonary cancer.[208]

Hueper authored an editorial on asbestosis in the *American Journal of Clinical Pathology*.[209] He noted that lung cancer with asbestosis had been compensated as an occupational disease in Germany and Canada. Hueper also reported that O'Donnell in Pennsylvania had found 10 lung cancer cases in asbestotics, bringing the world total to 127 reported cases of asbestos-associated cancer of the lung. Hueper also warned that asbestos air pollution might be responsible for neighborhood cases of asbestosis and cancer of the lung. Hueper's editorials, books, and review articles on asbestos (and generally, environmental cancer) alone would have kept anyone who read them well-informed about the advances in the field.

Industry Reaction

Hueper's publications and other activities were a subject of intense interest at meetings of the Asbestos Textile Institute.

The A.T.I. Board of Governors met on March 7, 1956 to receive the report of the Air Hygiene Committee. Referring to concerns about court actions, the minutes went on to say:[210]

> Dr. (K.W.) Smith (Johns-Manville) strongly recommended that (A.T.I.) initiate a program of investigation and publicity to counteract the unfavorable publicity presently directed to the asbestos industries as a result of the work of Dr. Hueper.

The position of the industry at this point, scientifically speaking, is indicated by a sentence in the A.T.I. Air Hygiene Committee report:[211]

> Dr. Smith indicates that he has no evidence that there is *not* a relationship between asbestosis and cancer. (original emphasis)

Smith urged that studies be conducted which might provide a basis for countering the "derogatory literature now being circulated throughout the United States and Canada."[211] In fact, the Saranac Laboratory and the Industrial Hygiene Foundation were proposing just such studies to the industry at the time.

Dr. Vorwald's successor at Saranac Laboratory was Dr. Gerrit Schepers. Dr. Schepers had no idea that both Gardner and Vorwald had conducted experimental cancer assays under sponsorship of some of the same companies he was addressing. On October 6, 1954, Schepers appeared before members of the A.T.I. and presented a detailed review of the published literature on asbestosis and cancer from asbestos. He told the industry representatives that they stood accused of using a product that caused cancer as well as asbestosis, and said the only way to answer this challenge would be with research.[212] In attendance were doctors representing Johns-Manville, American Asbestos, Keasbey & Mattison, Raybestos-Manhattan, Southern Asbestos, and Asten-Hill.[213]

Schepers offered to do pathological analyses of tissue specimens from deceased industry employees. The A.T.I. Air Hygiene Committee tentatively agreed to conduct such studies:[214]

> After a series of case studies, Dr. Schepers will summarize and report to the Institute membership his findings and observations.

The A.T.I. hygiene committee minutes further explained the low cost and potential economic importance of the research:[172]

> The cost for each member is nominal and immediate value is obtained through the case reports which provide a basis for equitable settlement of Workmen's Compensation claims.

Despite this, and the pressure the industry faced at the time, the A.T.I. General Meeting was cool to the idea of Schepers' studies. In a meeting on June 9, 1955, attended by representatives of 13 companies, the minutes record this reaction:[215]

> The (autopsy) program listed was considered ill-advised at this time due to its implication that a relationship existed between asbestosis and carcinogenic development, a condition which, to date, has not been established although it has been given rather widespread publicity in the press.

Early in 1956, representatives of Owens-Corning Fiberglas (OCF) Corporation asked Dr. Schepers for a "letter incorporating favorable statements" about Saranac's studies on OCF fibrous glass.[216] In his letter, Schepers recommended tests to determine whether fibrous glass was carcinogenic.[217] Comparing it to asbestos, Schepers said, "I suppose you already know that asbestos is fairly well incriminated as a carcinogen." Chagrined OCF attorney John Black remarked that Schepers' letter was "certainly nothing that we could show to consumers or a union."[216] OCF sold asbestos and fibrous glass products at that time.

Soon afterward, the Saranac Laboratory was closed.

In 1956, the A.T.I. Air Hygiene Committee took up a proposal for an "Epidemiological Study of Lung Cancer in Asbestos Workers for the Asbestos Textile Institute." This one came from the Industrial Hygiene Foundation, and the idea was supported by Dr. Kenneth W. Smith. I.H.F. had submitted a similar proposal to Q.A.M.A., and work on that was just starting.[218]

The A.T.I. decided on March 7, 1957 by a 6 to 2 vote to reject the I.H.F. proposal. The reasons given were:[219]

1. It was decided that as the Q.A.M.A. has a similar program, we should not enter into a program of our own as the results of the Q.A.M.A. investigation will be made available to us upon the conclusion of that investigation.
2. *There is a feeling among certain members that such an investigation would stir up a hornet's nest and put the whole industry under suspicion.*
3. We do not believe there is enough evidence of cancer or asbestosis in this industry to warrant a survey. (emphasis added)

A companion proposal from I.H.F. for an $8000 "environmental dust survey" was also rejected unanimously as needlessly expensive "after much discussion" by the Committee:[219]

> It was our opinion that we can locate our own trouble spots involving high dust counts and correct them, and perhaps later on we could use the facilities of Travelers Life Insurance Company laboratories to make a comparison of dust counts for little or no expense similar to the survey made by the committee three years ago.*

The A.T.I. also received a proposal by Dr. Kenneth M. Lynch, still President of the Medical College of South Carolina. Lynch wanted industry support for his experiments on laboratory animals exposed to asbestos dust. Lynch had been doing work for a member of the A.T.I. "in an effort to clarify the relation of asbestosis and cancer of the lung." The committee decided to thank Dr. Lynch "for his interest in Industry and its problems" but rejected his proposal.[218]

*At this time nothing more about the earlier collaboration with Travelers has yet come to light.

Dr. Lynch subsequently published his findings, suggesting tumorigenicity of asbestos inhaled by mice. However, he felt another animal species should be used, and described his own feelings as equivocal. By this time ten years had passed since Lynch had obtained a copy of Dr. Gardner's 1943 "Outline" detailing positive cancer studies. The Saranac lab was gone, and still Lynch did not publish Gardner's startling findings (the 81.8% rate of lung cancer in mice inhaling "long-fiber asbestos" for 15 or more months); instead, he disclosed only the 13.6% rate of tumors in mice inhaling "short-fiber asbestos" for no more than 12 months and then misrepresented Gardner as having said the results were "merely suggestive."[220]

The Industrial Hygiene Foundation Cancer Study

Dr. Hueper carried the battle against occupational cancer into Canada in 1954. In presentations at the First Canadian Cancer Research Conference (Honey Harbor, Ontario) and the Annual Convention of the International Association of Industrial Accident Boards and Commissions (Quebec), he included asbestos among the industrial causes of cancer described.[221,222] An asbestos industry observer of the Quebec presentation remarked:

> Dr. Hueper referred frequently to asbestos, and almost all of the slides used to demonstrate pulmonary cancer were of cases involving both asbestosis and cancer.[223]

The statistician of the National Cancer Institute of Canada was concerned about cancer in the asbestos mining district. However, his plan to do an epidemiologic survey was dropped when Q.A.M.A. agreed to finance a study of is own.[224] This work was undertaken by I.H.F. in 1956, and a report of the findings was completed in 1957.[225]

The work force in the I.H.F. study consisted of every asbestos miner employed in 1950 with 5 or more years of exposure. This cohort of nearly 6000 was followed for six years and an effort made to identify all deaths from primary cancer of the lung. In all, Braun and Traun identified nine cases of proven primary lung cancer and three "suspected" ones. All twelve were cigarette smokers.[226]

Using the mortality experience of Quebec Province as a control, the authors calculated that about 8 lung cancer deaths would have been expected. Even counting both proven and suspected cases together, the excess of deaths in the cohort did not quite reach the point of statistical significance at the 95% confidence level.

On the other hand, no such comparison was provided in the published report between the lung cancer mortality of the miners and that which would have been expected in the rural areas where they lived. One Table (No. 22) showed that the death rate from lung cancer was 9.4 and 9.8 per 100,000 man-years in rural districts and 22.6 for the entire Province. The main reason for the difference was the presence of the cities of Montreal (32.3) and Quebec (no figure given) in the Province. Had the control group chosen for comparison been rural, the finding of just the 9 cases of (proven) lung cancer would have been more than 2 ½ times the expected number, and it would also have been statistically significant.

I.H.F.'s original report to Q.A.M.A. included a section called "Asbestosis and Lung Cancer." Here, it was noted that four of the nine "proved" lung cancer decedents had also been diagnosed as having asbestosis. These diagnoses were based on autopsy findings and chest X-rays of the workers. The total number of employees dying with asbestosis in this period was 32, and so the incidence of accompanying lung cancer was 4 out of 32 (12.5%). The significance of such a disproportionately high fraction of lung cancer among those dying with asbestosis was acknowledged by Dr. Braun in his report to Q.A.M.A.

Braun offered the explanation that asbestosis was being grossly under-diagnosed at the asbestos mines, thus causing the alarmingly high proportion of deaths from lung cancer among asbestotics. However, this would have reflected badly on the Canadian asbestos industry, which had been operating a chest clinic at Thetford Mines and sending tissue specimens to the Saranac Laboratory since the early 1940s. Braun acknowledged that the 12.5% incidence of lung cancer among asbestotics at autopsy was a figure consistent with although "slightly lower than those quoted by authors who confined themselves to this type of comparison."[181]

In the Conclusions, he said:

> (T)he results suggest that a miner who develops the disease asbestosis does have a greater likelihood of developing cancer of the lung.

This information on lung cancer among miners dying with asbestosis was deleted in the published report, and the nettlesome problem of explaining its meaning was thus disposed of.[226]

A "condensed" version was sent from Q.A.M.A. for review by Kenneth Smith and Hugh Jackson at Johns-Manville headquarters in New York. In a letter to Q.A.M.A. lawyer Ivan Sabourin, Dr. Smith wrote:[227]

> We have noted the deletion of all references to the association of asbestosis and lung cancer in this condensation. While we believe that this information is of great scientific value, we can understand the desire of Q.A.M.A. to emphasize the exposure of the asbestos miner and not the cases of asbestosis...
>
> It must be recognized, however, that this report will be subjected to criticism when published because all other authors today correlate lung cancer and cases of asbestosis.

Dr. Hueper was acknowledged by Braun and Traun as the most prolific writer on the subject of asbestos and cancer.[226] However, Hueper denounced their report as,

> statistical acrobatics which tend to obscure incriminating evidence on hand by use of a highly biased population group as a 'normal' standard.

He explained,

> It is a well-known fact that urban populations in all industrialized countries have a decidedly higher lung

> cancer death rate than that in rural regions. Since the asbestos mines are situated in rural areas in Quebec and are not located within the fume zones of Quebec and Montreal, where a high lung cancer rate prevails (Montreal rate 32.3), the lung cancer death rate of the asbestos miners, which stands at 33.8 per 100,000, has to be compared with the rates present in rural counties of the Province of Quebec. According to the data provided on this point by Braun and Traun, their conclusion is patently incorrect and grossly misleading and results in obscuring the existence of a markedly elevated lung cancer rate for members of this working group.[228]

A few years later, Dr. Thomas Mancuso published a detailed critique of his own. He stressed: the large "dilution factor" of (66%) workers aged 44 or less; the short period of follow-up compared to the latent period for cancer from asbestos; and limitations imposed by the selection and manner in which the controls were used. Mancuso also pointed out that the senior members of the cohort were a "survivor group," which excluded their contemporaries who had already died.[229]

Braun and Truan's report suffered none of these criticisms the week of its publication, however. That coincided with a medical symposium and public relations event orchestrated at the Queen Elizabeth Hotel in Montreal by the Quebec Asbestos Mining Association: "a complete success," reported Q.A.M.A. lawyer Sabourin to member companies.[230]

Remaining Doubters

There remained a few who still questioned whether asbestos had been proven carcinogenic. Hammond considered the data on asbestos workers suggestive, but not definitive, in 1956.[231] Stokinger referred to the reports of Doll and Cartier, but considered the numbers too small to establish a causal relationship. He cited a presentation by Lanza to the effect that the high rate of lung cancer in asbestos workers in England was not paralleled in the U.S. and Canada.[232] Hinshaw and Garland said in 1956 that the hypothesis that asbestosis predisposed to lung cancer had not been fully confirmed.[233] More recently, Dr. Hinshaw has testified as an expert on the history of asbestos disease. In the 1980 edition of his book, Dr. Hinshaw used a graph from Becklake showing that asbestos' carcinogenicity was "established" in the mid-fifties and that a "probable" association of asbestos exposure with lung cancer dated from the early 1940s.[234]

Bohlig and Jacob at first were equivocal about their own data, but were unwilling to take issue with the existing body of literature linking asbestosis and cancer. They found the lung cancer death rate among German asbestos workers unremarkable, but among the asbestotics who died up to the year 1956, there were 5 with lung cancer out of a total of 34.[235,236]

In answer to an inquiry in *J.A.M.A.*, as late as 1961, Dr. Rutherford Johnstone asserted,[237]

> In the American literature there is no evidence that there is a relationship between asbestosis and lung cancer.

When challenged by Dr. George Trimble citing case reports from the U.S. and the opinions of American authors, Johnstone explained:[238]

> (T)here is no epidemiological evidence of such among American workers.

He again emphasized the separateness of the "English experience with asbestos" and referred readers to two references of questionable relevance.

In 1963, Lanza's book, *The Pneumoconioses*, still held out doubts on the asbestosis-cancer link. The chapter on asbestosis was by Dr. Kenneth W. Smith.[239] Only a small excerpt will be included here, for its interest in light of the I.H.F. correspondence of 1957:

> Some observers in the past few years have associated various conditions such as lung cancer ... with the as-

> bestos worker. No attempt was made to associate the disease with the clinical, radiological, and pathological entity, known as asbestosis.

Smith asserted that in his 18 years' experience with workers exposed "only to chrysotile fiber, there were no more cases of pulmonary malignancy than among the general population."

Looking back with assistance from the Asbestos Information Association (the industry trade group in Washington), Dr. Philip Enterline found second-hand reference to one other scientist who reportedly questioned the carcinogenicity of asbestos—Dr. Leroy Gardner.[240] However Dr. Gardner died in 1946, and from the unpublished material already cited, appears to have been changing his mind on that issue in 1943.[39,41]

National Differences in Asbestos Carcinogenicity

Writers such as Levin, Johnstone, and others were willing to conclude that a cancer hazard had existed in the British asbestos plants, and accept the consensus view in Germany that asbestos was carcinogenic there.[207,237,241] But there was an implication, if not an explicit statement, that "foreign" industries and workers were different. Let us trace these national interpretations back in time, specifically with respect to cancer in industry.

Hueper reported that an early proponent of the differing national susceptibility hypothesis was insurance statistician Frederick Hoffman:

> F. Hoffman complacently noted about this matter in 1928 that the scarcity of recorded industrial cancers in the United States was attributable to the fact that the workers in America are unusually intelligent and susceptible to educational influence, desire to know the truth and facts of a given situation and frequently govern their conduct accordingly...
>
> As industrial cancers are not notifiable diseases in most of the states and as American industries have shown so far

> great reluctance in placing their cases of occupational cancer on record, there exist in this country only incomplete data as to the actual number and variety of these disease conditions, their causes and the agents and operations responsible for their development. This evident lack of proper appreciation of the importance of industrial cancer in the United States stands in sharp contrast to the unrestricted and wide publicity which these tumors have received for many years in other industrialized countries, such as England, Germany, and Switzerland, in which industrial cancers are compensable and notifiable industrial diseases and from which for this reason relatively reliable and complete official information concerning them is available.[107]

Following extensive reports on asbestos and cancer, one would think the burden of proof was on the asbestos industries worldwide to show that they did *not* have a cancer problem—rather than quibble about trivial differences, real and imagined, between the industrial hazards of asbestos in each and every country.

Hueper came back to this theme in 1959, in an unpublished presentation to the Executive Council of the AFL-CIO:[193]

> It is idle to speculate about the relative intelligence and self-reliance of industrial workers of different countries and their alleged influence upon the frequency and prevention of industrial cancers. Then, too, it is more than doubtful whether American workers actually have a better opportunity to acquire information than their colleagues in other countries. American workers seemed to be as severely affected as those employed in the same industries and specific operations in other countries ... My own observations on the allegedly more extensive use of mechanical handling systems in American plants having industrial cancer hazards do not support such a claim, considering the conditions encountered in the aromatic amine and dye industry, in the chromate manufacturing

> industry, in the asbestos industry, in the coke oven and coal tar fractionation industry, in tarred paper pipes manufacturing industry, asphalt industry, as well as in the petroleum industry, uranium plants and asphalt shingle industry.

Accusing the asbestos industry in Quebec of not publishing information about cancer at the chrysotile mines, Hueper even slipped in a remark about (less successful?) efforts in Europe to suppress publication:

> One may further wish to obtain a satisfactory explanation of a request made to a foreign investigator of lung cancer among European asbestos workers to suppress for so-called "patriotic" reasons the publication of his paper incriminating the asbestos industry.

*More Reports of Lung Cancer, Mesothelioma, and Other Cancers from Asbestos**

Large numbers of cancer cases among asbestotics were reported in the years 1957-1963. From the U.S. came a report by O'Donnell and Mann, who had seen 27 cases of asbestosis at autopsy or in surgery. Lung cancer was found in 13 of these asbestos textile workers, and in all of them the primary site of tumor growth was in the lower lobes of the lungs.[242] The workers had been employed at the Raybestos-Manhattan plant in Manheim, Pennsylvania.

German writer Böhme used government records to add to his own material, comprising 125 patients compensated for disability from asbestosis. Of this number, 31 had died, including 14 (45%) with lung cancer. The author counted here one case of "endothelioma of the pleura" accompanying slight asbestosis. Though moderate or severe asbestosis was present in most of his lung cancer cases, Böhme speculated that lung

*Numerous review articles and case reports assigning asbestos a carcinogenic rule, published after 1955, are not included in this chapter. Some of these articles are cited elsewhere (e.g., Chapter 5).

cancer from asbestos might also arise in the absence of asbestosis.[243]

König in Hamburg, who had published a brief report on 16 autopsied cases of asbestosis earlier, brought his findings up to date in 1960. Out of 36 cases of asbestosis, there were 7 with lung cancer as well, and another 4 with primary pleural tumors. The pleural tumors were attributed to the asbestos exposure, based partly on the early observations of Wedler. There were also 3 patients in this group who died from primary cancers of the peritoneum, and 6 from cancers of the stomach, esophagus, and colon. An analysis showed that the cancer hazard did not appear to be related to the degree of asbestosis in these patients.[244]

Böhme and König both took issue with Bohlig and Jacob for relating cancer incidence to a population of living asbestos workers.

Keal reported on another 42 cases of asbestosis seen at London Hospital. There were 14 people with lung cancer in this group, including 4 women who were all non-smokers. Keal was especially interested in the large number of peritoneal cancers, 1 in a man and 8 in women. He suspected ovarian cancer, as this was far more common than peritoneal cancer and could conceivably have metastasized to the peritoneum in some of these cases.[245]

The average time from onset of exposure to development of cancer was 25 years for lung cancer with asbestosis, and 30 years for peritoneal cancer. Keal recalled Hueper's earlier conclusion that many asbestosis patients died from asbestosis before their lung cancers had had time to develop. Keal also noted that two of his cancer patients had been removed from asbestos exposure for many years and had had no symptoms or radiological changes attributable to asbestosis. The occupations of the patients were tabulated and covered a wide range of exposure in asbestos product manufacture and use.[245]

Dunn and co-workers prospectively followed a group of nearly 8000 "asbestos workers" in California for the years 1954-1958. After corrections for cigarette smoking, the number of lung cancer deaths was excessive (22 vs. 15.6 expected) but not so excessive as to be statistically significant. The authors considered their findings on asbestos workers and others in the study preliminary and requiring "at least five years" of additional follow-up time.[246]

Another large number of asbestosis cases with accompanying lung cancer was reported by doctors in Seattle, Washington. Many of these patients were construction workers in insulating and other trades.[247]

By 1955, mesothelioma of the pleura had been reported in asbestos workers by a number of authors (Gloyne, 1933; Wedler, 1943; Mallory *et al.*, 1947; the Factory Inspectorate and Wyers of Cape Asbestos in 1949; Cartier, 1952; Weiss, 1953; Doll, 1955 at a Turner Brothers Asbestos plant; Bonser and coworkers, 1955). There were additional cases reported over the next few years in Italy, the U.S., Canada, Britain, and the Netherlands, in addition to the German studies just mentioned.[226,243,244,248-250,312]

But a report of 33 cases of these extremely rare pleural cancers in South Africa quickly focused worldwide attention on mesothelioma as an asbestos cancer. In 32 of these cases, an occupational or environmental history of exposure to asbestos was obtained. In the latter, the exposures clustered around the crocidolite mines of the North West Cape Province.[251]

Hueper had injected rats intrapleurally with asbestos in an experiment published a few years earlier. But only 10 animals lived more than one year, and none of them developed tumors.[252] Wagner duplicated this study using a larger number of animals and in 1962 reported finding a few tumors in rats which had received chrysotile and crocidolite asbestos injections. This confirmed the capacity of these types of asbestos to cause mesothelioma.[253]

Meanwhile, additional human findings poured forth. Many of the mesothelioma victims reported on at this time were construction and shipyard workers.[254-258] McCaughey reported 15 cases in Belfast, mostly shipyard workers. Lung sections from 12 showed asbestos bodies but these were numerous in only one case. As Smither, Gilson, and Wagner said in calling for reports on mesothelioma,[259]

> There appears to be no correlation between the severity of any pulmonary asbestosis and the occurrence of these tumors.

By this time, mesotheliomas of the peritoneum were likewise suspect. [The serosal membranes enclosing the lungs, abdomen, and heart are called the pleura, peritoneum, and pericardium, respectively. The cells making up these membrane linings are called mesothelial cells.] After Leicher's report in 1954, these tumors were noted in asbestosis patients by Bonser and her co-workers (1955), Böhme (1959), König (1960), and Keal (1960), as already mentioned. Wagner and co-workers (1960) had also seen one person with peritoneal mesothelioma. Additional reports of peritoneal mesothelioma with asbestosis were published in 1958-1961 in England and the Netherlands.[250,260,261] Schmähl had already demonstrated that asbestos injected intraperitoneally readily produced tumors in rats surviving longer than 15 months.[262]

In an epidemiological study of workers employed as of 1938 in an asbestos products plant followed through 1960, Mancuso and Coutler found an excess of deaths from lung cancer (19 vs. 5.6 expected). Upon review of histological slides available for some of the deaths in this cohort, 5 cancers of the peritoneum were identified. This was extraordinarily high in a population in which only 186 deaths had been traced.[263]

Campbell had found 4 pleural mesotheliomas in 3,533 consecutive autopsies.[264] As late as 1960, Willis questioned whether true, primary, mesothelial tumors occurred at all.[265] Others had, meanwhile, published reports of these rare tumors without making any connection as to their etiology.[266-269]

By 1964, there was little reason to doubt that asbestos was a cause of mesothelioma. As additional cases were reported in Great Britain, an epidemiological study was published in the United States that would ultimately compel unanimity of opinion.[270-272]

This study, published in the *Journal of the American Medical Association*, showed the mortality experience of asbestos insulation workers. Followed up more than 20 years from the onset of exposure, these men sustained grossly excessive mortality from lung cancer, mesothelioma, and gastrointestinal cancer, in addition to asbestosis.[272] This work has been continually updated, and by 1979 excess risks from cancers of the kidney, larynx, pharynx and buccal cavity were also evident in insulation workers.[273]

After the publication of their first epidemiological paper on insulators, Drs. Selikoff and Churg organized an international conference under the auspices of the New York Academy of Sciences, entitled "Biological Effects of Asbestos." Over 700 pages of scientific presentations were made at that conference, published in Volume 132 of the *Annals of the New York Academy of Sciences* in 1965.

Appendix 1 of these proceedings is the Report and Recommendations of the Working Group on Asbestos and Cancer, organized by Drs. Mancuso and Wagner and convened under the auspices of the International Union against Cancer. The delegates included a virtual Who's Who in the science of asbestos health effects. Also on the panel were Dr. J.F. Knox of Turner Brothers Asbestos Company, and Dr. W.J. Smither of Cape Asbestos Company. Dr. Kenneth W. Smith of Johns-Manville was invited but declined to attend.

The Working Group had this to say about the association of asbestos dust and cancer, at its meeting in October, 1964:[274]

> There is evidence of an association between exposure to asbestos and malignant neoplasia. This has been established mainly on information from Germany, Italy, South Africa, the United Kingdom, and the United States of America.
>
> The types of tumors which have been shown to be associated with exposure to asbestos dust are:
>
> 1. carcinoma of the lung
> 2. diffuse mesothelioma of the pleura and peritoneum
>
> There is some suggestion of an association also with gastrointestinal carcinoma, and possible ovarian tumors.

Table 5. Publications on Mesothelioma and Asbestosis 1933-1960

Author(s), Year	Cases Reported	Ref. No.	Comment
Gloyne (1933)	1	1	"no evidence at the moment" that pleural cancer was related to asbestosis
Wood and Gloyne (1934)	1	2	same as above
Wedler (1943)	2	31	asbestos considered the cause of pleural mesothelioma
Wedler (1943)	2	31,34,36	same as above; abstracted in U.K. and U.S.
Mallory, Castleman, and Parris (1947)	1	112	pleural mesothelioma not attributed to the man's asbestos exposure
Annual Report of the Chief Inspector of Factories for the Year 1947 (1949)	?	122	cancers of the lung and pleura counted together in demonstrating excess incidence among asbestotics
Wyers (1949)	1	128	"endothelioma of the pleura" counted among pulmonary tumors in asbestos workers
Doig (1949)	—	129	review article mentions cancers of lung and pleura in asbestos workers
Cartier (1952)	2	158	degree of asbestosis in miners dying with pleural mesothelioma assessed as "minimal" and "none"
Smith (1952)	2	158	pathological material from asbestosis victims in England

Table 5. (cont'd.)

Author(s), Year	Cases Reported	Ref. No.	Comment
Weiss (1953)	1	169	asbestos considered the cause of pleural tumor in insulation worker
Kraussler and Seyss (1954)	—	170	cited Weiss' case
Leicher (1954)	1	180, 181	asbestos considered the cause of peritoneal tumor in asbestos factory worker: report abstracted in *Bulletin of Hygiene*
Bonser, Faulds, and Stewart (1955)	6	182	2 pleural and 4 peritoneal cancers among 72 asbestosis victims seen at autopsy
Doll (1955)	1	164	"endothelioma of the pleura" counted among pulmonary cancer cases
Jacob and Bohlig (1955)	—	205	considered reports of mesothelioma evidence of asbestos' carcinogenicity
Francia and Monarca (1956)	1	248	pleural mesothelioma and asbestosis in a man who worked 17 years in an asbestos factory
Williams (1957)	2	312	endothelioma of the pleura in asbestos workers
Van der Schoot (1958)	3	250	pleural cancer in insulation workers
Schornagel (1958)	1	250	peritoneal mesothelioma in an insulation worker
Braun and Truan (1958)	1 or more	226	mesothelioma a cause of death among miners dying after the follow-up period of the epidemiological study

(*continued*)

Table 5. (cont'd.)

Author(s), Year	Cases Reported	Ref. No.	Comment
Böhme (1959)	1	243	"endothelioma of the pleura" with slight asbestosis
König (1960)	7	244	4 pleural and 3 peritoneal cancer deaths among asbestos workers; asbestos considered the cause of pleural mesothelioma
Keal (1960)	9	245	peritoneal tumors with varying degrees of asbestosis
Eisenstadt and Wilson (1960)	2	249	pleural mesothelioma in oil refinery foremen, one with asbestosis
Wagner, Sleggs, and Marchand (1960)	33	251*	pleural mesothelioma associated with occupational and environmental exposure to asbestos in 32 cases
Schepers (1960)	—	287	reference to mesothelioma as an asbestos disease in text on occupational lung diseases
Gough and Heppleston (1960)	—	288	reference to pleural tumors as a consequence of asbestosis in proceedings of 1957-1958 symposium on occupational lung diseases
Hugh-Jones (1960)	—	289	pleural nesothelioma taken to indicate that a patient has worked in asbestos dust

*The first of these cases reported by Wagner in *Proceedings of the Pneumoconiosis Conference held at the University of Witwatersrand, Johannesburg 9th - 24th February, 1959* (A.J. Orenstein, Ed.), Little, Brown and Co. Boston (1960)

Other Sources of Information on Asbestos and Cancer

While the primary literature on asbestos carcinogenicity expanded, secondary and tertiary references also emerged. For example, a number of specialized texts in industrial medicine and hygiene included positive commentary and republished data on the asbestos-cancer link. Some of these were:

Author (Year)	Ref. No.
Hueper (1942)	23
Hamilton and Hardy (1949)	275
Drinker & Hatch (1954)	276
Davies (1954)	277
Hunter (1955)	278
McGee (1956)	279
Merewether (1956)	280
Lloyd-Davies (1957)	281
Fairhall (1957)	282
Holt (1957)	283
Dubois and Geiling (1959)	284
Eckardt (1959)	285
Ahlmark, Bruce, and Nyström (1960)	286
Schepers (1960)	287
Gough and Heppleston (1960)	288

A minority of texts in this field in the Fifties mentioned the asbestos-cancer issue and offered more guarded opinions on it.[233,289,290] In general, the more detailed the review of the literature, the more likely it was to be positive about the association.

The carcinogenic properties of asbestos were also noted in more general and basic texts on such subjects as cancer, chest disease, pathology, and internal medicine. Examples include:

Author (Year)	Reference No.
Bauer (1949)	116
Boyd (1950)	291
Harrison (1950)	292
Cappell (1951)	293

Author (Year)	Ref. No.
Ellman (1952)	294
Hadfield (1953)	295
Herbut (1955)	296
Weller (1955)	297
Richardson (1956)	298
Hunter (1956)	299
Bignall (1958)	300
Cecil and Loeb (1959)	301

Closer to developments in occupational medicine were specialized journals publishing abstracts, or short summaries, of primary medical reports. Articles on asbestosis and cancer published all over the world were abstracted in English soon after they appeared, in *Journal of Industrial Hygiene and Toxicology* (U.S.), *Bulletin of Hygiene* (U.K.), and *Industrial Hygiene Digest* (U.S.). (See also "Abstracts," in Chapter 10.) Enterline's recent reviews of the literature on asbestos and cancer apparently overlooked the existence of these excellent abstracting publications in the field of industrial medicine. In explaining what he called the international lag, Enterline seized upon Hueper's German origins as an explanation for his early agreement with "the position of the Germans" on asbestosis and lung cancer ("German literature was probably easily known to him since he was German born and educated."). This simplistic explanation not only overlooks the existence of English-language abstracts and references to the German literature (which Hueper used and to which he contributed), but also overstates the importance of American scientists being raised in Germany as a prerequisite to understanding German scientific writings in their own fields of research.[240,290] As to the recognition that mesothelioma was caused by asbestos exposure, Enterline considered the issue "fairly well resolved "by 1953.[290])

By 1957, the carcinogenicity of asbestos was sufficiently well known to receive note in a second common encyclopedia, the *Encyclopedia Americana.*[302]

Some Historical Comments of Asbestos Industry Medical Experts on Asbestos Carcinogenicity

The apparent acceptance of asbestos' carcinogenicity by Dr. Wyers of Cape Asbestos and Dr. Knox of Turner Brothers Asbestos in England has already been discussed.[128,188] However, others who later became asbestos industry medical directors have also contributed opinions on the historical recognition of asbestos as a cancer hazard and related issues.

Dr. Hilton C. Lewinsohn succeeded Dr. Knox as medical officer for Turner Brothers Asbestos in the late 1960s. He later took similar posts with Raybestos-Manhattan (now called Raymark) and then Union Carbide in the United States. In 1974, Dr. Lewinsohn credited Merewether with having "first demonstrated a clear-cut association between asbestosis and lung carcinoma" in 1949.[303]

Dr. Paul Kotin was hired by Johns-Manville as Senior Vice President for Health, Safety, and Environment in 1974. Previous to that he had done experimental work in environmental cancer pathology since meeting Dr. Wilhelm Hueper in the early 1950s. Kotin's reviews named asbestos as a carcinogen starting in 1956.[304,305] At that time, he said there was "no convincing evidence" that tobacco smoking caused lung cancer.[304]

Kotin was also a staunch advocate of the no-threshold theory of carcinogenesis prior to his employment as a corporate executive.[306-308] This was exemplified in his response in a withering exchange with the Chairman of the Joint Committee on Atomic Energy (U.S. Congress) in 1969:[307]

> As experimental models have developed their sensitivity has increased and essentially one could have predicted this on the basis of what we know about the fundamental aspects of carcinogenesis—and here is dogma about which there is considerable controversy—but a very respectable body of opinion maintains that there is no threshold for the action of a carcinogen, and that therefore limitations in data are the results of our inadequate models rather than

> the presence of a threshold. For what it is worth, I belong to that group that maintains there is at present no evidence for a threshold, but I would say biological data make such a position a reliably speculative one.

The next year, Kotin co-authored a report to the Surgeon General eloquently stating the basis for the no-threshold concept.[308]

By late 1973, there was a shift in his emphasis though not a direct reversal on the threshold issue:[309]

> (C)ancer induction most frequently requires prolonged periods of exposure to carcinogenic agents... this interval is best measured in years and decades...

At the Asbestos Information Association's 1974 Government-Industry Conference, Kotin crossed the line and defended the threshold concept as it related to asbestos:[310]

> (A) threshold or safe level of exposure probably exists. Stated differently, and as indeed extensive biological data can support, exposure at certain levels does not increase the risk to related diseases.

In 1978 Kotin was asked by a television interviewer, "Didn't you once say there was no such thing as a safe level of exposure for any carcinogen?" He replied, "I sure did, and I said it as part of the Surgeon General's committee in 1970 ... I guess I'll tell you I'm smarter now."[311]

CONCLUSION

The carcinogenicity of asbestos was recognized by Nordmann, Hornig, and Koelsch in Germany in 1938. Others in Germany added material of their own, and the unanimity of opinion of the experts in that country is reflected by the compensability of lung cancer with asbestosis nationwide in Germany in 1943.

British and American authors contributed additional case reports and analyses, and were expressing positive views on the association of asbestosis and lung cancer in the 1940s. Many authors were especially impressed by: 1) the unusually large proportion of lung cancers among asbestos workers originating in the *lower* lobes of the lungs, 2) the consistently long time elapsed from the onset of exposure until the development of cancer; and 3) the very high percentage of cases of lung cancer among workers with asbestosis seen at autopsy. Indeed, these autopsy studies comprised the earliest epidemiologic support for the relation between asbestos and cancer.

Along this last line, the publication of British cancer statistics in the *Annual Report of the Chief Inspector of Factories for the Year 1947* stands as a milestone. There was no reason to question that a cancer hazard among asbestosis victims had been identified, and the utter lack of such a finding among silicosis victims in Britain served as an excellent control. The proportion of lung cancer deaths among silicotics was roughly the same as that in the general population.

For those who doubted that asbestos was carcinogenic after 1950, Doll's report in 1955 should have been persuasive. But as Hueper reported in the early 1950s, the majority was already convinced before that time.

The unpublished records cited in this accounting show U.S. asbestos industry officials to have been concerned about cancer and aware of medical reports by 1943. Some of the more startling data were actually published by the medical officer of Cape Asbestos, Hubert Wyers, in 1949. Dr. Hueper was meanwhile being quoted in popular writings, and this along with his scientific reports were matters of great concern to members of the U.S. asbestos industry by the mid-1950s.

In the meantime, scattered reports of mesothelioma appeared in the literature on industrial medicine and hygiene. The German authors, once again, showed a readiness to accept these as asbestos cancers that would be amply vindicated in the 1960s.

It remained for epidemiologists not to document the cancer risk but quantify its extent in the asbestos industry, to identify the numerous types of cancer caused by asbestos, and further track the danger across property lines into the community (using rare mesothelioma as a marker).

Neighborhood and household-contact asbestos disease are discussed in Chapter 7. Other aspects of asbestos carcinogenicity are discussed in Chapters 3 and 4.

REFERENCES

1. Gloyne, S.R., "The Morbid Anatomy and Histology of Asbestosis," *Tubercle 14:* 550-558 (1933).
2. Wood, W.B. and Gloyne, S.R., "Pulmonary Asbestosis: A Review of One Hundred Cases," *Lancet 2:* 1383-1385 (1934).
3. Gloyne, S.R., "Two Cases of Squamous Carcinoma of the Lung Occurring in Asbestosis," *Tubercle 17:* 4-10 (1935).
4. Lynch, K.M. and Smith, W.A., "Pulmonary Asbestosis III: Carcinoma of the Lung in Asbesto-Silicosis," *Amer. J. Cancer 24:* 56-64 (1935).
5. Gloyne, S.R., "A Case of Oat Cell Carcinoma of the Lung Occurring in Asbestosis," *Tubercle 18:* 100-101 (1936).
6. Egbert, D.S. and Geiger, A.J., "Pulmonary Asbestosis and Carcinoma," *Amer. Rev. Tuberc. 34:* 143-150 (1936).
7. Nordmann, M., "Der Berufkrebs der Asbestarbeiter," *Z. Krebsforsch. 47:* 288-302 (1938).
8. Hornig, F., "Clinical Considerations on the Question of Industrial Cancer of Asbestos Workers," *Z. Krebsforsch. 47:* 281-287 (1938).
9. Abstracts of the two preceding papers (by L. Teleky). *Abstracts of the Literature of Industrial Hygiene,* suppl. to *J. Indust. Hyg. Tox. 20:* 184 (1938).
10. *Annual Report of the Chief Inspector of Factories for the Year 1938.* London: H.M. Stationery Ofc., 1939, p. 81.
11. Home Office. *Annual Report of the Chief Inspector of Factories for the Year 1938.* Abstract in *Bull. Hyg. 15:* 69-70 (1940).
12. Kennaway, E.L., and N.M. Kennaway, "A Further Study of the Incidence of Cancer of the Lung and Larynx," *Brit. J. Cancer 1:* 260-298 (1947).
13. Sparks, J.V., "Asbestosis," *Brit. J. Radiol. 2:* 371-377 (1938).
14. Abstract of preceding paper, *Abstract of the Literature of Industrial Hygiene,* suppl. to *J. Indust. Hyg. Tox. 21:* 54 (1939).
15. Gloyne, S.R., and E.R.A. Merewether, "Asbestos," *Supplement*

to Occupation and Health: Encyclopedia of Hygiene, Pathology, and Social Welfare, Geneva: International Labor Office, 1938.

16. Koelsch, F. "Lungenkrebs und Beruf," *Acta Unio Int. contra Cancrum 3:* 243-251 (1938).

17. Lynch, K.M. and Smith, W.A., "Pulmonary Asbestosis V. A Report of Bronchial Carcinoma and Epithelial Metaplasia," *Amer. J. Cancer 36:* 567-574 (1939).

18. Baader, E.W., "Asbestose," *Deut. Med. Woch. 65:* 407-408 (1939).

19. Ehrhardt, "Today's Position in the Fight against Abestosis," *Arbeitsschutz* (No. 7) 191-193 (1940).

20. Linzbach, A.J. and H.W. Wedler, "Beitrag zum Berufskrebs der Asbestarbeiter," *Virchows Arch. Path. Anat. 307:* 387-409 (1941).

21. Nordmann, M. and A. Sorge, "Lung Cancer from Asbestos Dust in Animal Experiments," *Z. Krebsforsch. 51:* 168-182 (1941).

22. Desmeules, R. *et al.*, "Amiantose et Cancers Pulmonaires," *Laval Med. 6:* 97-108 (1941).

23. Hueper, W.C., *Occupational Tumors and Allied Diseases*, Springfield, Ill.: Charles C. Thomas, 1942, pp. 399-405.

24. Welz, A., "Further Observations of Occupational Cancer Among Asbestos Workers," *Arch. Gewerbepath. Gewerbehyg. 11:* 536-550 (1942).

25. Holleb, H.B. and A. Angrist, "Bronchiogenic Carcinoma in Association with Pulmonary Asbestosis," *Amer. J. Path. 18:* 123-131 (1942).

26. Fourth Schedule of Extension of Compensation for Industrial Accidents and Diseases. *Reichsgesetzblatt*, Part 1, No. 14 (Jan. 29, 1943).

27. Bauer, M., *Arbeit und Gesundheit/Die Entschadigungspflichtigen Berufskrankheiten*, Stuttgart: Georg Thieme, 1953, pp. 107, 157-158.

28. Hueper, W.C., "Cancer in Its Relation to Occupation and Environment," *Bull. Amer. Soc. Contr. Cancer 25:* 63-69 (1943).

29. Hueper, W.C., Personal communication to the author (1977).

30. Gardner, L.U. (Saranac Laboratory) letter to J.P. Woodard (Johns-Manville) May 8, 1946.

31. Wedler, H.W., "Lung Cancer in Asbestosis Patients," *Deut. Arch. Klin. Med. 191:* 189-209 (1943).

32. Wedler, H.W., "Asbestose und Lungenkrebs," *Deut. Med. Woch. 69:* 575-576 (1943).

33. Boemke, F., "Asbestosis and Lung Carcinoma," *Frankf. Ztschr. Path. 57:* 569-577 (1943).

34. Wedler, H.W., "Asbestose und Lungenkrebs," *Bull. Hyg. 19: 362 (1944).*

35. Welz, A., "Further Observations on Occupational Carcinoma in Asbestos Workers," *Bull. Hyg. 18:* 651 (1943).

36. Welz and Wedler abstracts from *Bull. Hyg.* reprinted in *Abstracts of the Literature of Industrial Hygiene,* supplement to *J. Indust. Hyg. Tox. 26:* 8, 183 (1944).

37. Homburger, F., "The Co-incidence of Primary Carcinoma of the Lungs and Pulmonary Asbestosis." *Amer. J. Path. 19:* 797-807 (1943).

38. Gardner, L.U. (Saranac Laboratory) letter to L. Hektoen (Committee on Cancer Research of the National Cancer Institute), March 15, 1943.

39. Gardner, L.U. letter to L. Hektoen (Sept. 29, 1943).

40. Vorwald, A.J. and J.W. Karr, "Pneumoconiosis and Pulmonary Carcinoma," *Arch. Path 14:* 49-57 (1938).

41. Gardner, L.U. letter to V. Brown (Johns-Manville Corp.) and attached Outline of Proposed Monograph on Asbestos (Feb. 24, 1943).

42. Bowditch, M. (Saranac Laboratory) letter to V. Brown (Mar. 24, 1947). Refers to a Mar. 1, 1943 letter from Brown to L.U. Gardner. Manville files.

43. Muehleck, E. (Keasbey and Mattison Co.) letter to W.W.F. Shepherd (Turner and Newall, Ltd.), March 8, 1943. (Produced in discovery by T & N)

44. Dr. Francis (Turner & Newall) notes on outline of the proposed monograph by Dr. Gardner (May, 1943). Turner & Newall document.

45. Gardner, L.U. letter to V. Brown (June 9, 1943). Turner & Newall document.

46. Gardner. L.U. letter to V. Brown (Nov. 23, 1936).

47. Brown, V. letter to S. Simpson (President of Raybestos-Manhattan), May 3, 1939.

48. Brown, V. letter to S. Simpson (May 10, 1940).

49. Simpson, S. letter to V. Brown (May 4, 1939).

50. Richards, B., "New Data on Asbestos Indicate Cover-Up of Effects on Workers," *Washington Post* (Nov. 12, 1978). Confirmed by Dr. Hardy (1982).

51. Proceedings, Twenty-Fourth Meeting National Advisory Cancer Council/National Cancer Institute. NCI Files No. 16-5-2. National Institute of Health, pp. 21-26 (Jan. 8, 1944).

52. Gatke, T. (President, Gatke Corp.) letter to J.F.D. Rohrbach (Executive Vice President, Raybestos-Manhattan), August 12, 1946.

53. Simpson, S. (President, Raybestos-Manhattan), letter to L.U. Gardner (May 17, 1938).

54. Lanza, A.J. (Metropolitan Life Insurance Co.), letter to K.M. Lynch (Med. Coll. State of S.C.), Dec. 26, 1946.

55. Hamilton, J.R., "Minutes of Meeting Held January 21, 1947 at General Headquarters to Receive and Discuss Report of Dr. A.J. Lanza re the Status of Diatomaceous Earth Dust Experiments, as Determined on His Recent Trip to the Saranac Laboratory." 6 pp.

56. Bowditch, M.F., letter to V. Brown (Mar. 18, 1947).

57. Brown, V., letter to M. Bowditch (Mar. 21, 1947).

58. Bowditch, M. (Saranac Laboratory), letter to K.M. Lynch (Apr. 22, 1947).

59. Lynch, K.M., letter to A.J. Lanza (June 30, 1947).

60. Lanza, A.J., letter to K.M. Lynch (July 2, 1947).

61. Lanza, A.J., letter to K.M. Lynch (July 14, 1947).

62. Lynch, K.M., letter to A.J. Lanza (July 23, 1947).

63. Vorwald, A.J. (Saranac Laboratory), letter to K.M. Lynch (Aug. 1, 1947).

64. Lanza, A.J., letter to K.M. Lynch (Aug. 4, 1947).

65. Woodard, J.P., memorandum to A.R. Fisher *et al.* (Aug. 19, 1947).

66. Fisher, A.R., memorandum to J.P. Woodard (July 22, 1947).

67. Fisher, A.R., memorandum to J.P. Woodard (Oct. 29, 1947).

68. Woodard, J.P., letter to A.J. Lanza (Metropolitan Life Insuance Co.), Mar. 15, 1948.

69. Woodard, J.P., letter to A.J. Vorwald (Mar. 15, 1948).

70. Woodard, J.P., letter to A.J. Vorwald (June 1, 1948).

71. Woodard, J.P., letter to A.J. Vorwald (July 21, 1948).

72. Brown, V., letter to C. George Krueger (New Jersey Dept. of Labor), Aug. 16, 1948.

73. Durkan, T.M. (Saranac Laboratory), letter to J.P. Woodard (Oct. 12, 1948).

74. Vorwald, A.J., *Asbestosis*, report to the Johns-Manville Corporation (Sept. 30, 1948). Vorwald archives, Armed Forces Institute of Pathology, Washington, D.C.

75. Brown, V., memorandum to E. Muehleck (Keasbey & Mattison Co.) and J.F.D. Rohrbach (Raybestos-Manhattan), Oct. 22, 1948.

76. Brown, V., letter to other sponsoring companies (Amer. Brake Shoe, Gatke Corp., Keasbey & Mattison, Raybestos-Manhattan, Russel Mfg., Thermoid, Union Asbestos & Rubber, U.S. Gypsum), Oct. 27, 1948.

77. Hamlin, L.E. (American Brake Shoe), memorandum (Nov. 3, 1948).

78. Kelley, W.T. (Amer. Brake Shoe), letter to V. Brown (Nov. 8, 1948).

79. Butler, J.W. (U.S. Gypsum), telegram to V. Brown (Nov. 10, 1948).

80. Silverman, L. (Union Asbestos & Rubber Co.), letter to V. Brown (Nov. 8, 1948).

81. Russell, T.M. (Russell Mfg. Co.), letter to V. Brown (Nov. 8, 1948).

82. Gatke, T. (Gatke Corp.), letter to V. Brown (Nov. 8, 1948).

83. Pardoe, W.T. (Thermoid Co.), letter to V. Brown (Nov. 9, 1948).

84. Rohrbach, J.F.D. (Raybestos-Manhattan), letter to V. Brown (Oct. 28, 1948).

85. Brown, V., letter to W.T. Kelly (Nov. 12, 1948).

86. Brown, V., letter to J.W. Butler (Nov. 12, 1948).

87. Kelly, W.T., letter to V. Brown (Nov. 16, 1948).

88. Woodard, J.P., memorandum to V. Brown and A.R. Fisher (Nov. 30, 1948).

89. Woodard, J.P., letter to T. Gatke (Nov. 30, 1948).

90. Vorwald, A.J., letter to A.J. Lanza (Dec. 6, 1948).

91. Lanza, A.J., letter to A.J. Vorwald (Dec. 14, 1948).

92. Brown, V., letter to other sponsors (Mar. 3, 1949).

93. Brown, V., letter to I. Sabourin (Quebec Asbestos Mining Association), Mar. 8, 1949.

94. Gatke, T., letter to V. Brown (June 14, 1949).

95. Gatke, T., letter to V. Brown (June 29, 1949).

96. Vorwald, A.J., T.M. Durkan, and P.C. Pratt, "Experimental Studies of Asbestosis," *Arch. Indust. Hyg. Occup. Med. 3:* 1-43 (1951).

97. Selleck, H.B., and A.H. Whittaker, *Occupational Health in America*, Detroit: Wayne State Univ. Press, 1962, p. 458.

98. Brown, V., letter to other sponsoring companies (Mar. 21, 1951).

99. Macklin, M.T. and C.C. Macklin, "Does Chronic Irritation Cause Primary Carcinoma of the Human Lung?" *Arch. Path. 30:* 924-955 (1940).

100. Wolff, A., "Asbestosis Pulmonum," *Nordisk Hyg. Tidskr. 21:* 1-40 (1940).

101. Lecoeur, J., "L'Étude des Cancers Professionelles," *Presse Medicale 50:* 415-418 (1942).

102. Davis, E., "Chemical Carcinogenesis, Drugs, Dyes, Remedies, and Cosmetics with Particular Reference to Bladder Tumors," *J. Urol. 49:* 14-27 (1943).

103. Levin, M.L. "The Epidemiology of Cancer," *Amer. J. Publ. Health 34:* 611-620 (1944).

104. Tabershaw, I.R. and M. Bowditch, "Industrial Hygiene in 1944," *New Engl. J. Med. 231:* 706-710 (1944).

105. "Environmental Cancer," *J.A.M.A. 126:* 836 (1944).

106. Hueper, W.C., "Industrial Management and Occupational Cancer," *J.A.M.A. 131:* 738-741 (1946).

107. Hueper, W.C., "Significance of Industrial Cancer in the Problem of Cancer," *Occup. Med. 2:* 190-200 (1946).

108. Policard's discussion in Luton, Chamepeix and Faure, "A Case of Pulmonary Asbestosis," *Arch. Maladies Profess. 7:* 299-302 (1946).

109. Luton, P. and J. Champeix, "Study of Asbestosis," *Arch. Malad. Profess. 7:* 365-378 (1946).

110. Rousseau, L., "Some Considerations on Asbestosis." *Sem. Hôp. Paris 23:* 1811-1814 (1947).

111. Perry, K.M., "Diseases of the Lung Resulting from Occupational Dust Other than Silica," *Thorax 2:* 91-120 (1947).

112. Mallory, T.B., B. Castleman, and E.E. Parris, "Case Records of the Massachusetts General Hospital," *New Engl. J. Med. 236:* 407-412 (1947).

113. Boemke, F., "The Pathology of Dust-Induced Diseases," *Medizin. Monatsschr. 1:* 2-6 (1947).

114. Cureton, R.J.R., "Squamous Cell Carcinoma Occurring in Asbestosis of the Lung," *Brit. J. Cancer 2:* 249-253 (1948).

115. *Third International Conference of Experts on Pneumoconiosis, Feb.-March, 1950, Record of Proceedings.* Geneva: International Labour Office, 1953, p. 235.

116. Bauer, K.H., *Das Krebsproblem,* Berlin: Springer-Verlag, 1949, pp. 238-239.

117. Tabershaw, I.R., "Report on Industrial Hygiene in the Western Zone of Germany," *Arch. Indust. Hyg. 3:* 298-315 (1951).

118. Saita, G., "Occupational Tumors of the Lung," *Med. Lavoro 39:* 105-116 (1948). (English summary at end)

119. Saita, G., "Occupational Tumors of the Lung." Abstract in *Bull. Hyg. 23:* 865 (1948). Reprinted in *Pneumoconiosis Abstr. II:* 67 (1954).

120. Lynch, K.M. and W.M. Cannon, "Asbestosis: VI. Analysis of 40 Necropsied Cases," *Dis. Chest 14:* 874-885 (1948).

121. Brahdy, L., "Discussion," *Dis. Chest. 14:* 885-888 (1948).

122. *Annual Report of The Chief Inspector of Factories for the Year 1947* London: H.M. Stationery Ofc., 1949, pp. 79-81.

123. "Asbestosis and Cancer of the Lung," *J.A.M.A. 140:* 1219-1220 (1949).

124. "Asbestosis and Cancer of the Lung," *Indust Hyg. Digest 13:* abstract 867 (Aug. 1949).

125. Smith, L.W., "Pneumoconiosis and Lung Cancer," *Compensation Med. 2:* 3-10 (1949).

126. Conklin, G., "Cancer and Environment," *Scient. Amer. 180:* 11-15 (1949).

127. Asbestos Textile Institute, Minutes of General Meeting April 7, 1949. And also, letter from W.J. McConnell (Metropolitan Life) to George W. Marshall (Raybestos-Manhattan), May 26, 1949 (attached to ATI minutes of June 13, 1949).

128. Wyers, H., "Asbestosis," *Postgrad. Med. J. 25:* 631-638 (1949).

129. Schepers, G.W.H., "Discussion," *Ann. N.Y. Acad. Sci. 132:* 246-247 (1965).

130. Schepers, G. Testimony in *Bob Alan Speake v. Johns-Manville Corp. et al.* Superior Court of the State of California, Vol. II, 86-105 (Dec. 14, 1981).

131. Case IM 573, Arthur J. Vorwald's Private Patient Files, Armed Forces Institute of Pathology, Walter Reed Hospital, Washington, D.C.

132. Merewether, E.R.A., "The Pneumokonioses: Developments, Doubts, Difficulties," *Canad. Med. Assoc. J. 62:* 169-173 (1950).

133. Smith, K.W. (Johns-Manville) letter to A.J. Vorwald (Feb. 8, 1950). Vorwald archives.

134. Vorwald, A.J. (Saranac) letter to K.W. Smith (Apr. 18, 1950).

135. Edward Rowland Alworth Merewether C.B., C.B.E., M.D., F.R.C.P., D.I.H., F.R.S.E. *Lancet 1:* 477-478 (1970).

136. Minutes of Discussions Held at Saranac Lake on Nov. 7, 1950 (Confidential), by J.P.W. (Woodard), Nov. 14, 1950. Vorwald Archives, Armed Forces Institute of Pathology, Walter Reed Hospital.

137. Vorwald, A.J. *First Interim Report/Asbestosis and Pulmonary Cancer* (to QAMA) Saranac Laboratory, Saranac Lake, N.Y. (May 7, 1952). Vorwald Archives, Washington, D.C.

138. Doig, E.T., "Other Lung Diseases Due to Dust," *Postgrad. Med. J. 25:* 639-649 (1949).

139. Fischer, W., "Lung Cancer," *Zentralbl. Allgemeine Pathologie Pathol. Anat. 85:* 193-212 (1949).

140. Eickhoff, in *Die Staublungenerkrankungen* (K. Jötten and H. Gartner, editors) Darmstadt: D. Steinkopff, 1950, pp. 125-126.

141. Frost, J., "Three Cases of Asbestosis," *Ugeskr. Laeger 112:* 1284-1289 (1950).
142. Middleton, E.L., "Silicosis and Other Pneumoconioses," *Brit. Med. Bull. 7:* 47-51 (1950).
143. Smith, G.C., "Occupational Factors in Pulmonary Dust Disease," *Med. J. Australia 2:* 777-782 (1950).
144. Silson, J.E., "Dust Inhalation in Relation to Pulmonary Disease," *Dis. Chest 18:* 562-573 (1950).
145. Gloyne, S.R., "Pneumoconiosis," *Lancet 1:* 810-814 (1951).
146. Hueper, W.C., "Environmental Lung Cancer," *Indust. Med. Surg. 20:* 49-62 (1951).
147. Owen, T.K., "Carcinoma and Asbestosis of the Lung: Report of a Case," *Brit. J. Cancer 5:* 382-383 (1951).
148. Stoll, R., R. Bass, and A.A. Angrist, "Asbestosis Associated With Bronchogenic Carcinoma," *Arch. Intern. Med. 88:* 831-834 (1951).
149. Behrens, W. Über Klinik und Pathologie der Asbestosis," Z. *Unfallmed. Berufskrankh. 45: 129-140, 179-188 (1952).*
150. Hardy, H.L., "Occupational Medicine," *New Engl. J. Med. 247:* 473-483 (1952).
151. Werber, M., "Lungen-Asbestose und Karzinom," *Zentralbl. Arbeitsmed. Arbeitsschutz 2:* 179-180 (1952).
152. Mayers, M.R., "Occupational Disease Diagnosis," *N.Y. State J. Med. 52:* 2381-2385 (1952).
153. Mayers, M.R., "Industrial Cancer of the Lungs," *Compensation Med. 4:* 11-18 (1952).
154. Sroka, K.H., "Occupational Disease Caused by Asbestos," *Krebsarzt 7:* 167-171 (1952).
155. Grosse, E., "About Occupational Cancer," *Z. Krebsforsch. 59:* 180-190 (1953).
156. Smith, W.E., "Survey of Some Current British and European Studies of Occupational Tumor Problems," *Arch. Indust. Hyg. Occup. Med. 5:* 242-262 (1952).
157. Smith, W.E., "An Evaluation of Claims for Occupational Factors in Cancer of the Lungs," *Acta Unio Internat. contra Cancrum 8:* 476-483 (1952).
158. "Abstract of Discussion." *Arch. Indust. Hyg. Occup. Med. 5:* 262-263 (1952).
159. Hochberg, L.A., "Endothelioma (Mesothelioma) of Pleura," *Amer. Rev. Tuberc. 63:* 150-175 (1951).
160. Smith, W.E., Personal communication to the author (1990).

161. Archives of Dr. Arthur J. Vorwald. Armed Forces Institute of Pathology, Walter Reed Hospital, Washington, D.C.

162. Cartier, P., "Some Clinical Observations of Asbestosis in Mine and Mill Workers," *Arch Indust. Health 11:* 204-207 (1955).

163. Stewart, H. *et al.* "Symposium on the Endemiology of Cancer of the Lung," *Acta Unio Internat. contra Cancrum 9:* 440-446 (1953).

164. Doll, R., "Mortality from Lung Cancer in Asbestos Workers," *Brit. J. Indust. Med. 12:* 81-86 (1955).

165. Doll, R., "Etiology of Lung Cancer," *Adv. Cancer Research 3:* 1-47 (1955).

166. Goldblatt, M.W., "Occupational Carcinogenesis," *Brit. Med. Bull. 14:* 136-141 (1958).

167. "The Endemiology of Cancer of the Lung," *Acta Unio Internat. contra Cancrum 9:* 437-439 (1953).

168. König, J., "Concerning the Histogenesis of Pulmonary Asbestosis," *Zentralbl. Allgem. Pathologie Pathol. Anat. 88:* 220 (1952).

169. Weiss, A., "Cancer of the Pleura with Lung Asbestosis in Vivo Morphologically Ascertained," *Medizinische 3:* 93-94 (1953).

170. Kraussler, J. and R. Seyss, "Zur Frühdiagnose mittels Vergrösserungsaufnahmen," *Z. Unfallmed. Berufskrankh. 47:* 59-64 (1954).

171. Boemke, F., "Lung Carcinoma in Asbestos Pneumoconiosis," *Med. Monatsschr. 7:* 77-81 (1953).

172. "The Pathology of Diseases Due to the Inhalation of Dust," *Chem. Abstr. 42:* c. 9002-9003 (1948).

173. "Lung Carcinoma Caused by Asbestos Inhalation," *Chem. Abstr. 47:* c. 4471 (1953).

174. Isselbacher, K.J., H. Klaus, and H.L. Hardy, "Asbestosis and Bronchogenic Carcinoma," *Amer. J. Med. 15:* 721-732 (1953).

175. Abrams, H.K., deposition in *Alcorn v. Manville et al.* Case No. 82-CV-0527, Dist. Court, Boulder Co., CO (Apr. 22, 1986). Exhibit: "Cancer in Industry," Amer. Cancer Soc., N.Y.

176. "Cancer," *Encyclopedia Britannica*, Vol. 4, p. 731 (1952).

177. Breslow, L. *et al.*, "Occupations and Cigarette Smoking as Factors in Lung Cancer," *Amer. J. Pub. Health 44:* 171-181 (1954).

178. Breslow, L., "Industrial Aspects of Bronchiogenic Neoplasms," *Dis. Chest 28:* 421-430 (1955).

179. Eckardt, R.E. and P. Drinker, "Experimental Lung Cancer," *Arch. Indust. Hyg. Occup. Med. 9:* 449-450 (1954).

180. Leicher, F., "Primary Epithelial Tumor of the Peritoneum in Asbestosis," *Arch. Gewerbepath. Gewerbelhyg. 13:* 382-391 (1954).

181. Leicher, F., Abstract of preceding article. *Bull. Hyg. 30:* 324 (1955). Reprinted in *Pneumoconiosis Abstracts Vol. 3* Pitman Medical Publ. Co. London, 179 (1959).

182. Bonser, G.M., J.S. Faulds, and M.J. Stewart, "Occupational Cancer of the Urinary Bladder in Dyestuffs Operatives and of the Lung in Asbestos Textile Workers and Iron-Ore Miners," *Amer. J. Clin. Path. 25:* 126-134 (1955).

183. Doll, R., "Bronchial Carcinoma: Incidence & Aetiology," *Brit. Med. J. 2:* 521-527 (1953).

184. Knox, J.F., letter to W.E. Smith (June 6, 1954), and attached report by J.F. Knox and R. Doll, "Mortality from Lung Cancer among Asbestos Workers." Also, Gee, D. (General, Municipal, Boilermakers & Allied Trades Union, U.K.), personal communication.

185. Doll, R. (Medical Research Council), letter to J.F. Knox (June 8, 1954).

186. Deposition of William E. Smith. *Helen May Jackson v. Johns-Manville et al.* Western Distr. U.S. Distr. Court Michigan 77-410CA (Nov. 28, 1978). Including exhibit, T. Irwin, "On the Job Cancer—the Killer They Won't Track Down," *Cavalier* (Jan. 1962); which starts with Drew Pearson's report, "Cancer Probers Stilled," (Nov. 19, 1959).

187. "Lung Cancer in Asbestosis," *Lancet 1:* 1163 (1955).

188. Knox, J.F., "Lung Cancer in Asbestosis," *Lancet 1:* 1275-1276 (1955).

189. "Cancer of the Lung in Industry." *Brit. Med. J. 2:* 780-781 (1955).

190. *Annual Report of the Chief Inspector of Factories for the Year 1954* London: H.M. Stationery Ofc., 1955, pp. 190-193.

191. Merewether, E.R.A., "A Memorandum on Asbestosis," *Tubercle 15:* 109-118 (1933).

192. Warren, S., "Pathologic Aspects of Occupational Tumors," *Occup. Med. 5:* 249-251 (1948).

193. Hueper, W.C., "Organized Labor and Occupational Cancer Hazards," Presented to the Executive Council of the AFL-CIO, Summer of 1959. Unpublished papers of Dr. Wilhelm C. Hueper, National Library of Medicine, Bethesda, Maryland.

194. *Early Health Problems of the U.S. Nuclear Weapons Industry and Their Implications for Today*, Rept. of Majority Staff of U.S. Senate Comm. on Gov't. Affairs, Washington (1989).

195. "Pulmonary Cancer," *Proceedings of the First National Cancer Conference*, New York: American Cancer Society, 1949, p. 249.

196. Vorwald archives patient file P-53-590, Armed Forces Institute of Pathology, Walter Reed Hospital, Washington, D.C.

197. Medical Aspects of Cigarette Smoking. *Consumer Reports 20:* 67-73 (1955).

198. Minutes of the Air Hygiene Committee Meeting. Asbestos Textile Institute (March, 1955).

199. McLaughlin, A.I.G., "The Dust Diseases in Great Britain," *Arch. Indust. Health 12: 83-98 (1955).*

200. Lynch, K.M. and H.R. Pratt-Thomas, "Carcinoma of the Lung in Asbestosis," *South. Med. J. 48:* 565-569 (1955).

201. Hueper, W.C. *A Quest Into the Environmental Causes of Cancer of the Lung.* Washington: Public Health Service Publication No. 452, 1955, pp. 35-38.

202. Conference on Environmental Carcinogens (1955) in, Unpublished Papers of Wilhelm C. Hueper, National Library of Medicine, Bethesda, Maryland.

203. Vorwald, A.J., "Environmental Aspects in the Etiology of Lung Cancer," *Proceedings of the Third National Cancer Conference* Philadelphia: J.P. Lippincott Co., 1957, pp. 462-468.

204. Minutes, Air Hygiene Committee, Asbestos Textile Institute (Sept. 7, 1955).

205. Jacob, G. and H. Bohlig, "The Roentgenologic Complications of Pulmonary Asbestosis," *Fortschr. Rontgenstrahlen Roentgenpraxis 83:* 515-525 (1955).

206. Güttner, H.G., "Lung Cancer and Asbestosis, *Z. Ärztl. Fortbild. 49:* 388-392 (1955).

207. Rombola, G., "Asbestosis and Lung Cancer in the Case of an Asbestos Spinner," *Med. Lavoro 46:* 242-250 (1955).

208. Portigliatti-Barbos, M., "Considerations on the Association Between Asbestosis and Pulmonary Carcinoma," *G. Accad. Med. Torino No. 1-6:* 91-107 (1955).

209. Hueper, W.C., "Silicosis, Asbestosis, and Cancer of the Lung," *Amer. J. Clin. Path. 25:* 1388-1390 (1955).

210. Minutes of Meeting of the Board of Governors, Asbestos Textile Institute (March 7, 1956).

211. Minutes of Air Hygiene Committee, A.T.I. (March 7, 1956).

212. Schepers, G.W. Personal communication to the author.

213. Asbestos Textile Institute Air Hygiene Committee. Report of Meeting Dated 10/6/54.

214. Minutes of the Air Hygiene Committee, A.T.I. (June, 1955).

215. Minutes, General Meeting, A.T.I. (June 9, 1955).

216. Black, J.D. (Owens-Corning Fiberglas), intra-company corr. to Dr. C. Bishop (Feb. 8, 1956). OCF document marked, WHY FILE THIS?

217. Schepers, G.W.H. (Saranac Laboratory), letter to M.D. Burch (Owens-Corning Fiberglas), Feb. 6, 1956.

218. Minutes, Air Hygiene Committee, A.T.I. (June 4, 1956).

219. Minutes, Air Hygiene and Manufacturing Committee, A.T.I. (March 7, 1957).

220. Lynch, K.M. *et al.*, "Pulmonary Tumors in Mice Exposed to Asbestos Dust," *Arch. Indust. Health 15:* 207-214 (1957).

221. Hueper, W.C., "Environmental Lung Cancer," *Canadian Cancer Conference Vol. 1,* R.W. Begg, ed. New York: Academic Press, 1955, pp. 186-236.

222. Hueper, W.C., "Occupational Cancer Hazards," *Workmen's Compensation Problems 1954* (Washington: U.S. Bur. Labor Standards Bull. 180, 1955), pp. 126-144.

223. Jackson, H.M., Minutes of the Air Hygiene Committee, A.T.I. (Dec. 1, 1954).

224. Hueper, W.C., "Occupational and Nonoccupational Exposures to Asbestos," *Ann. N.Y. Acad. Sci. 132:* 184-195 (1965).

225. Braun, D.C., *An Epidemiological Study of Lung Cancer in Asbestos Miners,* prepared for Quebec Asbestos Mining Association, September 1957, pp. 47-55, 75-76.

226. Braun, D., and T. Traun, "An Epidemiological Study of Lung Cancer in Asbestos Miners," *Arch. Indust. Health 17:* 634-652 (1958).

227. Smith, K.W., letter to I. Sabourin (Dec. 30, 1957). Files of Industrial Health Foundation, Pittsburgh.

228. Hueper, W.C., "Environmental and Occupational Cancer Hazards," *Clin. Pharm. Therap. 3:* 776-813 (1962).

229. Mancuso, T., "Discussion," *Ann. N.Y. Acad. Sci 132:* 589-594 (1965).

230. Sabourin, I. "Re: Symposium June 16, 17, 18, 1958/Queen Elizabeth Hotel, Montreal," memo to members of Q.A.M.A. (June 22, 1958).

231. Hammond, E.C., "Etiology of Bronchogenic Carcinoma," *Bull. Cancer Prog. 6:* 156-168 (1956).

232. Stokinger, H.E., "In the Field of Toxicology," *Amer. Indust. Hyg. Assoc. Quart. 17:* 340-344 (1956). Also, Stokinger, H.E., "Toxicologic Aspects of Occupational Hazards," *Ann. Rev. Med. 7:* 177-194 (1956).

233. Hinshaw, H.C. and L.H. Garland, *Diseases of the Chest*, Philadelphia: W.B. Saunders Co., 1956, pp. 666-667.

234. Hinshaw, H.C., and J.F. Murray, *Diseases of the Chest*, 4th ed. Philadelphia: W.B. Saunders Co., Philadelphia, 1980, p. 723.

235. Bohlig, H. and G. Jacob, "Incidence of Lung Cancer Among German Asbestos Workers," *Deut. Gesundheitsw. 13:* 1101-1103 (1958).

236. Bohlig, H., G. Jacob, and B. Kallabis, "Morbidity and Pathology of Lung Cancer Due to Asbestos," *Z. Unfallmed. Berufskr. 52:* 64-78 (1959).

237. Silicosis and Cancer, *J.A.M.A. 176:* 81 (1961).

238. Silicosis and Cancer, *J.A.M.A. 178:* 352-353 (1961).

239. Lanza, A.J., *The Pneumoconioses*. New York: Grune and Stratton, 1963, p. 24.

240. Enterline, P.E., "Asbestos and Cancer: The International Lag." *Amer. Rev. Resp. Dis. 118:* 975-978 (1978).

241. Levin, M.L., "Etiology of Lung Cancer: Present Status," *N.Y. State J. Med. 54:* 769-777 (1954).

242. O'Donnell, W.M. and R.H. Mann, "Asbestos: An Extrinsic Factor in the Pathogenesis of Bronchogenic Carcinoma," *Amer. J. Path. 33:* 610 (1957).

243. Böhme, A., "Asbestosis and Lung Carcinoma," *Arch. Gewerbepath. Gewerbehyg. 17:* 384-395 and 457-461 (1959).

244. Koñig, J., "Asbestosis," *Arch. Gewerbepath. Gewerbehyg. 18:* 159-204 (1960).

245. Keal, E.E., "Asbestosis and Abdominal Neoplasms," *Lancet 2:* 1211-1216 (1960).

246. Dunn, J.E., G. Linden, and L. Breslow, "Lung Cancer Mortality Experience of Men in Certain Occupations in California," *Amer. J. Publ. Health 50:* 1475-1487 (1960).

247. Cordova, J.F., H. Tesluk, and K.P. Knudtson, "Asbestosis and Carcinoma of the Lung," *Cancer 15:* 1181-1187 (1962).

248. Francia, A. and G. Monarca, "Asbestosis and Pulmonary Carcinoma," *Minerva Med. 47:* 1950-1959 (1956).

249. Eisenstadt, H.B. and F.W. Wilson, "Primary Malignant Mesothelioma of the Pleura," *Journal-Lancet 80:* 511-514 (1960).

250. Van der Schoot, H.C.M., "Asbestosis and Pleural Tumors," *Ned. T. Geneesk. 102:* 1125-1126 (1958) with discussion by Schornagel.

251. Wagner, J.C., C.A. Sleggs, and P. Marchand, "Diffuse Pleural Mesothelioma and Asbestos Exposure in the North Western Cape Province," *Brit. J. Indust. Med. 17:* 260-271 (1960).

252. Hueper, W.C., "Experimental Studies in Metal Cancerigenesis, XI, Tissue Reactions in Rats and Rabbits after Parenteral Introduction of Suspensions of Arsenic, Beryllium, or Asbestos in Lanolin," *J. Nat. Cancer Inst. 15:* 113-124 (1954).

253. Wagner, J.C., "Experimental Production of Mesothelial Tumors of the Pleura by Implantation of Dusts in Laboratory Animals," *Nature 196:* 180-181 (1962).

254. Sleggs, C.A., P. Marchand, and J.C. Wagner, "Diffuse Pleural Mesotheliomas in South Africa," *S. Afr. Med. J. 35:* 28-34 (1961).

255. McNulty, J.C., "Malignant Pleural Mesothelioma in an Asbestos Worker," *Med. J. Australia 2:* 953-954 (1962).

256. McCaughey, W.T.E., O.L. Wade, and P.C. Elmes, "Exposure to Asbestos Dust and Diffuse Pleural Mesothelioma," *Brit. J. Med. 2:* 1397 (1962).

257. Eisenstadt. H.B., "Pleural Asbestosis," *Amer. Practitioner 13:* 573-578 (1962).

258. Castleman, B. and B.U. Kibbee, "Case Records of the Massachusetts General Hospital," *New Engl. J. Med. 269:* 747-754 (1963).

259. Smither, W.J., J.C. Gilson, and J.C. Wagner, "Mesotheliomas and Asbestos Dust," *Brit. Med. J. 2:* 1194-1195 (1962).

260. Heard, B.E. and Williams, R., "The Pathology of Asbestosis with Reference to Lung Function,' *Thorax 16:* 264-281 (1962).

261. Frenkel, M. and H. de Jager, "Peritoneal Mesothelioma associated with Pulmonary Asbestosis," *Jaarboek van Kankeronderzoek en Kankerbestrijding in Nederland 11:* 99-106 (1961).

262. Schmähl, D., "Carcinogenic Effect of Asbestos in Implantation in Rats," *Z. Krebsforsch. 62:* 561-567 (1958).

263. Mancuso, T.F. and E.J. Coulter, "Methodology in Industrial Health Studies," *Arch. Environ. Health 6:* 210-226 (1963).

264. Campbell, W.M., "Pleural Mesothelioma," *Amer. J. Path. 26:* 473-487 (1950).

265. Willis, R.A., *The Pathology of Tumors:* 3rd ed., Washington: Butterworth, 1960, p. 181.

266. Klemperer, P. and C. Rabin, "Primary Neoplasms of the Pleura," *Arch. Path. 11:* 385-412 (1931).

267. Stout, A.P. and M.R. Murray, "Localized Pleural Mesothelioma," *Arch. Path. 34:* 951-964 (1942).

268. Godwin, M.C., "Diffuse Mesothelioma," *Cancer 10:* 298-319 (1957).

269. McCaughey, W.T.E., "Primary Tumours of the Pleura," *J. Path. Bact. 76:* 517-529 (1958).

270. Lawson, J.P., "Exposure to Asbestos Dust," *Brit. Med. J. 1:* 467 (1963).

271. Enticknap, J.B. and W.J. Smither, "Peritoneal Tumours in Asbestosis," *Brit. J. Indust. Med. 21:* 20-31 (1964).

272. Selikoff, I.J., E.C. Hammond, and J. Churg, "Asbestos Exposure and Neoplasia," *J.A.M.A. 188:* 22-26 (1964).

273. Selikoff, I.J., E.C. Hammond, and H. Seidman, "Mortality Experience of Insulation Workers in the United States and Canada, 1943-1976," *Ann. N.Y. Acad. Sci. 330:* 91-116 (1979).

274. "Report and Recommendations of the Working Group on Asbestos and Cancer." *Ann. N.Y. Acad. Sci. 132:* 706-721 (1965).

275. Hamilton, A. and H.L. Hardy, *Industrial Toxicology* 2nd ed., New York: Paul B. Hoeber, 1949, pp. 447-448.

276. Drinker, P. and T. Hatch, *Industrial Dust,* 2nd ed. New York: McGraw-Hill, 1954, pp. 46-47.

277. Davies, C.N., *Dust is Dangerous,* London: Faber & Faber, Ltd., 1954, p. 17.

278. Hunter, D., *The Diseases of Occupations,* Boston: Little, Brown & Co., 1955, p. 881.

279. McGee, L., *Industrial Medicine,* 3rd ed. Philadelphia: University of Pennsylvania Press, 1956, p. 91.

280. Merewether, E.R.A., *Industrial Medicine and Hygiene, Vol III,* London: Butterworth & Co., 1956, pp. 115, 215-218.

281. Lloyd-Davies, T.A., *The Practice of Industrial Medicine,* 2nd Ed. London: J. & A. Churchill, 1957, p. 160.

282. Fairhall, L.T., *Industrial Toxicology,* 2nd ed. Baltimore: Williams & Wilkins Co., 1957, p. 21.

283. Holt, P.F., *Pneumoconiosis,* London: E. Arnold, 1957, pp. 142-159.

284. Dubois, K.P. and E.M.K. Geiling, *Textbook of Toxicology,* New York: Oxford University Press, 1959, p. 110.

285. Eckardt, R.E., *Industrial Carcinogens,* New York: Grune & Stratton, 1959, pp. 4, 99-101.

286. Ahlmark, A., T. Bruce, and A. Nyström, *Silicosis and Other Pneumoconioses in Sweden,* Stockholm: Svenska Bokförlaget, 1960, pp. 353-357.

287. Schepers, G.W.H., "Occupational Chest Diseases," *Modern Occupational Medicine,* 2nd ed. A.J. Fleming, C.A. D'Alonzo, and J.A. Zapp, eds. Philadelphia: Lea & Febiger, 1960, pp. 463-470.

288. Gough, J. and A.G. Heppleston, "The Pathology of the Pneumoconioses," *Industrial Pulmonary Diseases,* E.J. King and C.M.

Fletcher (eds.) Boston: Little, Brown & Co., 1960, pp. 23-36.

289. Hugh-Jones, P., "Complications of Asbestosis," *Br. Med. J.I.:* 1345-1353 (1960).

289. Von Oettingen, W.F., *Poisoning/A Guide to Clinical Diagnosis and Treatment,* Philadelphia: W.B. Saunders Co., 1958, pp. 247-248.

290. Enterline, P.E., N. Sussman, and G.M. March, *Asbestos and Cancer/The First Thirty Years,* copyright by P. Enterline, Pittsburgh (1978).

291. Boyd, W., *The Pathology of Internal Diseases,* Philadelphia: Lea and Febiger, 1950, pp. 173-174.

292. Harrison, T.R., *Principles of Internal Medicine,* Philadelphia: Blackiston Co., 1950, p. 771.

293. Cappel, D.F., *Muir's Textbook of Pathology,* Baltimore: Williams and Wilkins Co., 1951, pp. 427-428.

294. Ellman, P., *Essentials in Diseases of the Chest for Students and Practitioners,* London: Oxford University Press, 1952, p. 266.

295. Hadfield, G., *Recent Advances in Pathology,* New York: Blackiston Co., 1953, pp. 222-223.

296. Herbut, P.A., *Pathology,* Philadelphia: Lea & Febiger, 1955, p. 150.

297. Weller, C.V., *Causal Factors in Cancer of the Lung,* Springfield, Ill.: Charles C. Thomas, 1955, pp. 53-56.

298. Richardson, J.S., *The Practice of Medicine,* London: J & A Churchill Ltd., 1956, p. 162.

299. Hunter, D., *Price's Textbook of the Practice of Medicine,* London: Oxford University Press, 1956, pp. 1012-1013.

300. Bignall, J.R., (Ed.), *Carcinoma of the Lung,* Vol 1 Edinburgh: E & S Livingstone Ltd., 1958, p. 50.

301. Cecil, R.L., and R.F. Loeb, *A Textbook of Medicine,* 10th ed. Philadelphia: W.B. Saunders Co., 1959, p. 993.

302. "Industrial Hygiene," *Encyclopedia Americana 15:* 88 (1957).

303. Lewinsohn, H.C., "Health Hazards of Asbestos: A Review of Recent Trends," *J. Soc. Occup. Med. 24:* 2-10 (1974).

304. Kotin, P., "The Role of Atmospheric Pollution in the Pathogenesis of Pulmonary Cancer," *Cancer Res. 16:* 375-393 (1956).

305. Falk, H.L. and P. Kotin, "Chemical and Biological Consideration of Atmospheric Carcinogenic Agents," *J. Air Pollut. Contr. Assoc. 7:* 12-14 (1957).

306. Kotin, P., "Experimentally Weak Carcinogens," *Cancer Res. 18:* 1-3 (1958).

307. Kotin, P. *Radiation Standards for Uranium Mining.* Hearings before the Joint Committee on Atomic Energy, U.S. Congress, March 17-18, 1969, pp. 58-62.

308. Saffiotti, U. *et al., Ad Hoc Committee on the Evaluation of Low Levels of Environmental Chemical Carcinogens.* Report to the Surgeon General, U.S. Public Health Service, 20 pp. (April 22, 1970).

309. Kotin, P., "Mutagenic and Carcinogenic Problems Associated with Air Pollutants," *Proceedings of the Conference on Health Effects of Air Pollutants* (National Academy of Sciences), Oct. 3-5, 1973. U.S. Senate Committee on Public Works, Ser. No. 93-15, pp. 603-617 (1973).

310. Kotin, P. Remarks at *Asbestos Information Association Government—Industry Conference.* September, 1974, pp. 34-47 in conference proceedings printed by A.I.A., Washington.

311. *ABC News Closeup—Asbestos: The Way to Dusty Death.* Broadcast July 14, 1978. Quotes in ABC's press release on the program (June 29, 1978).

312. Williams, W.J. "Alveolar Metaplasia: Its Relationship to Pulmonary Fibrosis in Industry and the Development of Lung Cancer," *Br. J. Cancer 11:* 30-42 (1957).

313. Mottura, G. and E. Fagiano, "Pathological Anatomy and Pathogenesis of Asbestosis," *Rass. Med. Ind. II:* 233-284 (1940). In *Chem. Abstr. 36:* 3581 (1942).

3
Compensation: The Final Check-Up

"I can think of no better way of illustrating management's view of compensation for industrial accidents and occupational diseases than to tell you what great concern was felt by my own company—Johns-Manville Corporation—when, after having decided to erect a new insulating board plant in southwest Mississippi, we learned that this was the one state in the Union which had no workmen's compensation law. Of course, we went ahead with our plans but we are hoping that early corrective measures will be taken by the state legislature. . . . It remains our firm conviction that the worst Workmen's Compensation Commission is preferable to the best jury when the issue of compensation for an industrial injury is drawn between a laborer and his corporate employer."

Vandiver Brown, 1947, at Sixth Saranac Symposium (*Pneumoconiosis,* Paul Hoeber, pp. 567-568, 1950)

EARLY HISTORY OF WORKERS' COMPENSATION

Switzerland was the first country to provide for disablement from occupational injuries and diseases. In 1877, 45 substances used in industry were listed as specified causes of occupational disease. Germany followed this example a few years later, and Austria established workers' compensation for occupational diseases in 1897.[1]

The German Industrial Insurance Act, enacted in 1883, was

one of the first national schemes for providing compensation to injured workers. It seems remarkable that Bismarck, who was supported by industrialists and landowners, would have enacted state insurance for sickness, accidents, and old age in the 1880s. However, the purpose of these measures of state socialism was to woo German workers from the Social Democratic Party and de-fuse revolutionary tendencies among them. Bismarck was opposed to regulation of working hours or working conditions; i.e., the system mainly responsible for producing occupational injuries and diseases in the first place.

In England, the industrial age caused widespread misery in the first half of the 19th century. Describing the number of people in Manchester maimed by machinery, Engels said in 1845: "it is like living in the midst of an army just returned from a campaign."[2] The average age at death for working class English people in the mid-19th century was less than half of that for upper middle class people. During this brutal period of industrialization, the working people in Manchester and Liverpool died in their teenage years, on the average.[3] Labor protection laws of that era were mainly directed toward curbing the most extreme exploitation of children in industry.

Britain's Workmen's Compensation Act of 1897 was introduced by a conservative government. It set up a system to compensate workers disabled by injuries (but not diseases) on the job regardless of fault. Interestingly, the unions preferred to be able to go to trial before a judge and sue for negligence rather than have this no-fault legislation.[4] It is unclear how much management support for this legislation arose respectively from: 1) concern over losing such suits before judges from the same social strata as the factory owners; and 2) concern over the expense of high-priced legal representation even in the successful defense of claims.

The initial failure of the English Workmen's Compensation Act to cover any occupational diseases was denounced by Dr. Thomas Oliver in his 1902 text, *Dangerous Trades*. Oliver rejected the idea that "hazard pay" somehow offset this injustice:

> No high wages paid to men to undertake work in a

> dangerous trade, even if it were always the case that such were paid, can adequately compensate the affected workman for the loss of health occasioned by following a dangerous occupation. Many dangerous trades are far from being highly paid. The class of workmen who are affected by these industries are usually very poor, their occupation is often interrupted, and they are not organized into unions, so that they neither contribute to the funds of, nor do they receive benefits from, a Friendly Society.[5]

When Britain cautiously allowed compensation for occupational diseases, it was limited to specific diseases and industries where the risk of each arose. The schedule of hazardous materials covered in the original Act of 1906 included phosphorous, arsenic, mercury, and lead. By 1918 various effects of carbon disulfide, nickel carbonyl, tetrachloroethane, and chromium compounds were added.[6] Silicosis, well known in 19th century England, was not included until 1918; asbestosis was added in 1931.

In the United States, as in Europe, the establishment of workers' compensation systems appears to have been an effort to forestall potentially more onerous consequences to industry. Workers' personal injury suits in the U.S. were decided by juries of ordinary citizens, not patrician judges. The occupational safety and health issue was a growing threat wielded by the many injured plaintiffs and their lawyers, trade unionists, and social reformers.[7]

Industrial accidents took a staggering toll in the U.S. in the first years of this century. The death count was placed at over 15,000 per year.[8] In the meantime, jury trials occasionally yielded large awards and substantial publicity. Some reformers targeted the employers' legal defenses under the laws, weakening them and paving the way for more and larger jury verdicts.

The common law defenses of the employers amounted to:

1) the worker had been careless (contributory negligence)

2) the worker had assumed the risk in taking the job
3) a fellow employee and not management was at fault.

Occupational diseases were almost completely overlooked at this time (by the workers if not management), but an additional defense of employers here would be the claim that the health hazard was not a recognized and hence foreseeable one. Employers, although generally able to win these cases, were still facing increasingly large legal expenses.

In a report of an investigation supported by the Russell Sage Foundation, Eastman criticized the common law system's inadequacies and urged the creation of a system of workers' compensation in 1910.[9] This would replace the common law suits with a "no-fault," limited liability system administered by state industrial accident commissions. The unions were all in favor of just compensation for work-related disability and death. It was assumed that appropriate enactment of provisions for obtaining such compensation would both benefit the disabled and induce management to better protect those actively employed. But workers' compensation laws were also seen as a potential threat on both fronts, should their actual effect be to only minimize employers' liability. The powerful railroad workers' union opposed workers' compensation, and union reluctance to go along with the new scheme was largely eliminated by excluding railroad workers from inclusion under state workers' compensation laws.

The corporations were thus able to avoid jury trials and have compensation claims quietly decided by administrative agencies. Through the political appointment process (including "promotions" and transfers), and various time-honored forms of friendly persuasion (e.g., lucrative offers of jobs in the private sector), they could reduce the risk that commissioners would act with great zeal in granting disability compensation. Through the legislatures, the employers were able to set low limits for both medical and disability payments which they could be ordered to pay. They could also legislatively impose procedural obstacles and stall the processing of claims, through inadequate appropriations and salary levels for commissioners and staff, etc. Between 1911 and 1920, all but six states established workers' compensation laws.[10]

One aspect in the workers' compensation law of great interest to employers was the limitation of attorneys' fees. The purveyors of these limitations claimed that they wanted to keep ambulance-chasing lawyers from starting a medico-legal racket or holding up their worker clients for extravagant legal fees. But whatever the justification offered may have been, the result was that workers' compensation law was rendered about as non-lucrative as criminal law. The field was thus sufficiently uninviting to be generally overlooked by the mainstream legal profession. What few "labor lawyers" had occasion to take on workers' compensation cases were no match for the skilled and well-paid opposition, which came to include "industrial physicians" hired or consulted to work with attorneys in the defense of compensation claims.

By 1920 the unfairness of the compensation apparatus was so evident to the authorities in Pennsylvania that they asked the legislature for $12,000 as an appropriation for attorneys' fees to help claimants.[11] Meanwhile, the overall cost of workers' compensation insurance and claims was costing employers a very affordable 1 percent of payroll.[10]

Thus, the origins of workers' compensation in the United States, England and Germany were similar. In all three countries, the legislation was introduced by business interests or conservative governments to defuse labor unrest and control the long-term costs of occupational injuries.

Occupational diseases had been completely overlooked in most of the American workers' compensation laws. But during the second decade of this century, Dr. Alice Hamilton investigated a number of industries in which severe health hazards existed. Her reports and those of her co-workers were published by the U.S. Bureau of Labor Statistics, dealing with lead poisoning, the rubber industry, the printing trades, dyes, carbon monoxide, and silicosis. By the Twenties, the compensation boards were starting to see some disease claims, and they applied their laws to these claims in interesting ways.

The early application of workers' compensation law to occupational diseases was memorably recorded by the chairman of the Pennsylvania Workmen's Compensation Commission in 1921:[11]

> Up in Massachusetts they boast they have an act which covers industrial diseases. It was an accident that they have such a law, as they never intended to write such a law. In the phrase "personal injury by accident" they left out the words "by accident." They intended to put in the usual words but they left out the words "by accident", and the supreme court says, "Why, you have occupational diseases covered." California has such a law by design, but every time I hear a Massachusetts representative boasting of her occupational disease compensation law I feel like reminding him that she only has it by accident.

In 1920 the compensation systems in only seven states made provision for occupational diseases. The exclusion of occupational diseases from coverage under most of the state workers' compensation systems continued through the 1920s, resulting from:

1) limiting the scope of the law to injuries "by accident"
2) adverse rulings of the courts and commissions
3) express provisions in the compensation acts themselves

But this also meant that, since workers' compensation didn't apply, it also wasn't a bar to the bringing of civil suits against employers in occupational disease cases.

It would not be until the 1930s with severe unemployment in the Great Depression, that workers with occupational lung diseases would seek compensation *en masse* through the industrial accident boards and civil courts. By 1934, suits demanding $300 million had been filed by workers seeking compensation for pneumoconioses.[12]

The expense of occupational disease compensation to industry had risen suddenly from insignificance to a major expense by 1935. The industries and their insurers at that time were terrified that all-inclusive occupational disease laws left open the possibility that courts and industrial commissions would hold industries and their insurance carriers liable for all forms of ill health in any way contributed to by work. It was by then well known that silicotics commonly developed tuberculosis, and asbestotics were prone to develop pneumonia. Would deaths from these common causes be charged to employers in thousands of cases where the individuals had worked in dusty trades?

Little historic material has been written about how the employers and insurers kept workers' compensation for occupational disease from becoming the tremendous ongoing expense it threatened to be in 1935. However, one aspect of the compensation laws that played a major role were the statutes of limitations they all had. Typically, a claim had to be filed within one or two years of leaving employment—the dust diseases and occupational cancer were known to have long latent periods, and employers could simply fire employees before they had time to develop disease. Alternatively, if the employee had ever been told he had a dust disease, he might find his claim "statute-barred" a few years later when he found it necessary to file a claim for disability.

Some U.S. laws enacted in the mid-1930s (New York, Michigan, Pennsylvania, Ohio) adopted the so-called "principle of limited and graduated liability." This excluded from coverage persons no longer employed in the industry at the time the law took effect. Graduated liability provisions set compensation limits for other workers based on the amount of time they had been employed in the hazardous work after the law took effect, before they became disabled. In this way, the affected industries were able to avoid facing a tidal wave of liability for disability claims following the inclusion of occupational diseases in the state workers' compensation laws. The insurers had balked at paying off claims for past years' coverage, during which time only occupational injuries had been covered by law. The industrial companies, on the other hand, had had to press for a phase-in of occupational disease coverage under workers' compensation, in order to be able to continue to purchase insurance at affordable rates for their accrued liabilities.[13] And so, by phasing in the laws' impact, both the employers and insurers were able to largely escape liability to the disabled workers and their families. As in the case of England's compensation law for silicosis and asbestosis, such a law *invited* employers to discharge workers who were disabled before the date it took effect.[14]

Another aspect of laws serving to limit liability were provisions for only *partial medical coverage.* A worker who won a compensation award in Georgia as late as 1974 could get only $5000 in medical coverage from the employer—West Virginia and Wyoming were even worse. In South Carolina, coverage was limited to 10 weeks, in Missouri 180 days.[15]

A device started in Maryland around 1939 and adopted in some other states was the incorporation of a "medical board" into the workers' compensation commission. The imposition of a medical board meant an additional lengthy period of delay in processing of occupational disease claims by the commission, a condition which heavily favored the employer. The pro-employer bias of these medical boards is indicated by the fact that 2 of the 3 members of the Maryland medical board resigned in disgrace in 1981, following disclosures of conflicts of interest over their more lucrative roles as company doctors. In 1983, the Maryland Medical Board for Occupational Diseases was abolished by the legislature at the insistence of labor unions.

Some state laws required a minimum 5 or more years' duration of employment in a pneumoconiosis-producing industry. Scientifically, this was unjustified, since it had long been known that silicosis and asbestosis could be produced by shorter periods of work in dust.

Additional legal obstacles were imposed because of the numerous jurisdictions involved. Many workers traveled a great deal in their trades to find work. They would later be confronted by workers' compensation laws saying they had to have worked for some minimum number of consecutive months at a time in the state within the past ___ years to qualify. If they worked on ships, there might be additional confusion over whether they should bring a compensation claim or a suit in admiralty court.

An important structural feature of the workers' compensation systems in the U.S. is that, in most states, insurance coverage has been provided by private insurers. The private insurers, unlike state insurance carriers, had a common interest with their industrial insureds to litigate even meritorious claims. This exhausted the resources of claimants and set them up for either dismissal or a negotiated settlement for a pittance. Equally important, it set an example for co-workers and attorneys who might have been thinking of filing additional claims. Thereby, insurance premiums could be held competitively low without necessarily controlling the known hazards in the workplace.

The situation could be very different with a state insurance carrier that didn't have to concern itself with competition for the lowest insurance rates on the one hand and the desire to maximize profits on the other. The American pioneer in occupational medicine, Dr. Alice Hamilton, was impressed with this fact as a guest of her counterparts in Russia in 1924.[16] In Germany, where there had been state insurance carriers since the time of Bismarck, people with asbestosis were compensated for subsequent development of lung cancer as early as 1939.[17]

The very opposite role played by private insurers in the U.S. was personified by Dr. A.J. Lanza. Lanza had been with the U.S. Public Health Service, and was hired by Metropolitan Life Insurance Company in the Twenties. An expert on dust diseases, he was selected by the U.S. asbestos industry to conduct a health survey of factories and mines. The factory survey was published in 1935, four years after it was finished, and contained numerous understatements regarding the severity of the asbestosis problem (the study of the miners was never published). Key phrases were changed, deleted, and inserted in the galley proof stage by Lanza at the request of asbestos industry lawyers. Lanza was a frequent consultant to the asbestos companies on workers' compensation claims and on confidential animal studies on asbestos' carcinogenicity that were never published.

The dominant political lobbying role of private insurers in minimizing compensation paid to workers with occupational diseases persists to this day. Archaic provisions in the state compensation laws, where blatant social injustices still masquerade as administrative conveniences, testify to the power exercised by industries and insurers in the state legislatures. Until mid-1984, occupational cancer was not compensable under New York State workers' compensation law unless the disease was contracted and the claim filed within one year of leaving the employment that caused the cancer.[18] New York was also one of the few states where the victim of a dangerous product must bring a civil suit within 3 years of the last exposure, rather than within a comparable period after the manifestation of illness, as in most other states. This insidious law barred several thousand New York asbestos victims from filing personal injury suits, because the statute of limitations had lapsed before they developed asbestosis and cancer.[19] Finally, in 1986, New York enacted a "revival statute," allowing victims of asbestos (and a few other occupational and environmental hazards) one year to file suits previously barred by the statute of limitations.

The industrial firms and their insurers were acutely aware of the pivotal role of physicians in determining what is job-related, what is disease, what is disability (and if so how much). Accordingly, the few doctors who tried to conduct legitimate scientific inquiries faced relentless persecution. Such people soon found their careers threatened or destroyed and their motives impugned by powerful business interests.[20-24]

It was commonly recognized in the field of occupational health in the period before 1970 that considerable information on health hazards was withheld from publication.[25, 26] The Industrial Hygiene Foundation did thousands of plant industrial hygiene surveys for member companies starting in 1937, and kept all the findings confidential. When approached by plaintiffs' attorneys in asbestos litigation in 1979 to produce such records, they were all destroyed under a new "policy."

The Saranac Laboratory ran a similar business doing animal tests on hazardous dusts. Contracts for doing such testing contained explicit provisions or at least understandings whereby industrial sponsors could control any publication of the findings. Hueper claimed that after he left DuPont's Haskell Laboratories in 1938, toxicological research that was bad for business was treated as a trade secret and withheld from publication.[22]

Before 1970, the dearth of qualified, independent professionals and published scientific literature contributed to the state of ignorance of the trade unions. The unions, thus less aware of the magnitude and insidious nature of the occupational disease problem, were more likely to miss subtle subversion of the compensation structure.

Businesses with health hazards from the classical dusts have long conducted programs of medical examination, including chest X-rays. The main purposes were:

1) to reduce the cost of workers' compensation
2) to reduce the cost of hospital and surgical insurance
3) to reduce absenteeism
4) to reduce labor turnover and increase efficiency

But some firms who regularly examined employees were reluctant to inform workers who were developing pneumoconioses. It was not until the 1970s that this was exposed (in legal discovery against Johns-Manville in California, in OSHA hearings over a citation against Bethlehem Steel in Baltimore, and in an OSHA inspection of medical records at a DuPont plant in New Jersey), with the result that obscure provisions of workers' compensation laws have finally been used to bring suit directly against employers. These provisions, not present in every state law, say that the employer can be sued for *intentionally* harming the worker. In states whose workers' compensation laws have no intentional tort provisions, cases have been brought on the contention that limited liability under workers' compensation law doesn't apply to these particular cases. In the present civil suits proceeding in New

Jersey, Maryland, California, Ohio, West Virginia, and elsewhere, the workers and their families are demanding full compensation for lost earnings and medical costs, additional damages for pain and suffering, and punitive damages. Courts in New Jersey have allowed such claims to be pursued against DuPont by its chemical plant construction trades employees.

The industries with dust and chemical hazards have long been aware of the potentially ruinous cost of compensating employees disabled by occupational diseases. By the force of sheer economic power, applied through the courts, the legislatures, administrative agencies, the professions, and the universities, business interests were able to downplay the importance of occupational diseases and avoid compensating most of the affected workers. The result has been the physical and economic devastation of millions of American workers and their families, the wanton pollution of our environment with the same poisons that ruined the health of many workers, and the legacy of a social structure that still treats disabled workers like mendicants and gives the responsible parties every benefit of the doubt.

The asbestos industry's response to the problem of occupational disease compensation is thus an example of an even more widespread pattern, vividly seen through the documentation and testimony unearthed through legal discovery.

COMPENSATION FOR ASBESTOS DISEASE

The history of asbestos disease compensation is important for a number of reasons. Doctors can publish articles in medical journals and offer whatever conclusions they have, but what is written does not suddenly become common knowledge. It takes some time to percolate past the comparatively small groups of specialists in pathology, radiology, and clinical medicine, to reach the general practice doctors who see people from the local asbestos factory. It may take longer for these physicians to broach the subject of occupational disability and death compensation to their patients and their families. Since compensation is usually sought through a complicated, formal process, the service of an attorney is also required. The prosecution of a successful compensation claim may be an arduous process—even in cases where the opposition is limited to scientifically legitimate issues, and no deliberate hardships are inflicted upon the claimant, the case must still be proved scientifically.

What this amounts to is that an award of compensation (for disability or death) constitutes society's formal recognition of cause and effect for occupational diseases. Compensation comes only *after* an adequate body of scientific knowledge accumulates, with rare exceptions. Thus, precedents in the compensation field are tremendously important in that they serve notice on industry (and, where the industry is insured by private carriers, on the insurance industry as well). To the extent that defendants in compensation suits use the procedural means available to exhaust the resources of claimants, they can hardly turn around and then profess ignorance of the results after the compensation is ordered to be paid.

England was the first nation to formally recognize asbestosis as a compensable occupational disease. In the United States, the situation varied from state to state. Some states had laws allowing compensation for any disease attributable to occupation; others, like the English, had schedules of compensable diseases and statutory requirements further limiting eligibility for compensation.

Asbestos manufacturers in the U.S. were generally aware of asbestosis in the 1930s. It was a severe problem, commonly affecting half of the long-term factory employees. The companies saw that the cost of compensating disabled employees could be devastating, and the issue of compensation was thus a concern of top management in the Thirties.

Industry fears about the spread of information on asbestos diseases can be best understood from this standpoint. Failure to stress the gravity of the hazard in employee training, and failure to notify employees that their chest X-rays were starting to show fibrosis may be traced to concerns about compensation. Industry apprehension over publications of all kinds describing asbestos disease can be similarly explained. Newspaper stories incited suits by workers awakened to the cause of their lung problems, while articles in professional journals provided support for the compensation actions. The industry's own contributions to the medical literature and the suppression of some industry-sponsored research appear to have been significantly motivated by compensation considerations.

The industry attempted to hold down compensation costs in different ways over the years. In the 1930s, the companies could still claim that asbestosis had "just been discovered" and so absolve themselves from liability in negligence suits. By the 1940s, time had so eroded the "ignorance defense" in negligence cases that members of the industry came to prefer workers' compensation boards to civil courts. Liability in a workers' compensation case was, after all, limited by statute to significantly less than the full compensation obtainable in a common law trial before a jury.

Workers' compensation was becoming more than just an insurance problem for asbestos manufacturers by the 1950s. By then, a medical consensus had formed that asbestos caused lung cancer, which had risen to become the most common form of cancer in U.S. males. Moreover, major asbestos manufacturers learned first-hand about the afflictions of asbestosis and lung cancer in users of their insulation products, whom they had employed in their contracting divisions. The compensation claims filed by these workers in the 1950s presaged the deluge of product liability suits that would come in the 1970s, 1980s, and 1990s.

In the absence of direct preventive measures, society's provisions for the compensation of occupational disease bore the brunt of the burden of prevention. In the United States, this situation prevailed at least until the passage of the Occupational Safety and Health Act of 1970. Compensation is thus a major theme of the history of the asbestos problem of today.

Asbestos Compensation in the Early Years: Damage Suits

The year W.E. Cooke named the disease asbestosis, 1927, a foreman in the weaving department of a U.S. asbestos factory filed a claim for workers' compensation. The Massachusetts

Industrial Accident Board awarded the man compensation for disability from occupational lung disease.[27] Three years later, another claimant with asbestosis in Connecticut was awarded compensation.[28]

In many states, the workers' compensation laws either did not cover occupational diseases or applied only to designated industrial diseases, and workers seeking compensation for "unlisted" ailments had to sue their employers in civil court. Dr. Anthony J. Lanza, Assistant Medical Director of the Metropolitan Life Insurance Company, remarked that "the damage suit situation" prompted employers to deal with asbestosis:[29]

> Silicosis and asbestosis burst upon the amazed consciousness of American industry during the period 1929-1930... Arising out of the period of economic depression, the situation with respect to silicosis and asbestosis became manifest as a medico-legal phenomenon of a scope and intensity that was at once preposterous and almost unbelievable. Damage suits, under the common law, were instituted against employers by employees, alleging pulmonary dust diseases, in industrial centers all over the United States, to an amount in excess of 100 million dollars.

Beginning in 1929, attorney Samuel Greenstone brought suits against the Johns-Manville Corporation on behalf of 11 employees and former employees alleging disability from lung damage.[30] The negligence suits typically demanded $50,000 for total disability and specifically charged that the Manville, N.J. plant management had failed to provide:

1. a safe place to work
2. masks and other safety appliances, and
3. a proper ventilating system at the plant.

At least 3 of these complaints were served on A.R. Fisher, who rose to be the President of Johns-Manville in the early 1950s.

Perhaps due to questionable practices Mr. Greenstone used in soliciting these cases, Johns-Manville lawyers were able to negotiate a settlement of $30,000 for all the cases and obtain Greenstone's written assurance that he "would not directly or indirectly participate in the bringing of new actions against the Corporation." Settlement by the company President was thus authorized at a meeting of the J-M Board of Directors on April 24, 1933.[31]

Later that year, A.R. Fisher, manager of the Manville plant, received a confidential note from corporate Vice President S.A. Williams, referring to advice received by a plant doctor at another location (Waukegan, Illinois). Dr. A.J. Lanza's "verbatim" responses to questions were enclosed. Asked whether employees should "definitely be made aware that asbestos is hazardous to their health" by means of posters, Lanza had reportedly said he doubted the hazard justified that: "This is especially true in view of the extraordinary legal situation."[32]

In 1935, Johns-Manville was hit with another volley of lawsuits (about 20) from former employees at its Waukegan, Illinois plant. These workers alleged injury due to asbestos and other dusts in the workplace. The courts first rejected Johns-Manville's assertion that occupational disease was covered exclusively under the state workers' compensation law; but later, they threw out the suits against Johns-Manville, ruling that the workers had no right to either bring such suits under common law or file workers' compensation claims. The Illinois legislature promptly expanded the compensation law to include occupational disease, and the state distributed thousands of pamphlets to publicize the changes. A railroad industry doctor, acknowledging problems of exposure to asbestos and other dusts in railroads, worried that publicity about the Illinois law would create a "fear complex" along with unjustified compensation suits or claims.[33-36]

Workers' Compensation Law in Great Britain

In 1931, Great Britain had formally included asbestosis under the Workmen's Compensation Act. There were restrictions of coverage, however:[14]

> (A) successful claim can only be made if the sufferer has worked in an industry or process included in a compensation scheme; the mere fact that a claimant is suffering from (asbestosis) does not entitle him to compensation from his employer. His condition must be due to employment in one or more of the specified processes.

A medical board was set up to screen compensation applications. One drawback of the compensation scheme was that it did not explicitly include any users of asbestos products, such as insulation workers. "Breaking, ... mixing ... of asbestos or any admixture of asbestos" could conceivably have applied to insulators, but in England insulators apparently did not obtain compensation for asbestosis until the late 1940s or the early 1950s.[37,38]

A grievous defect of British asbestosis compensation was the provision that workers who had left the industry three or more years before filing a claim were ineligible. Even before the compensation scheme for asbestosis was finalized, there was controversy over the eligibility of women, many of whom had left their jobs in asbestos factories years before becoming crippled with asbestosis.[39,40]

In the case of an English woman who died in 1931 from asbestosis and tuberculosis eight years after leaving her factory job, the Home Secretary was pointedly asked to do something about the arbitrary statute of limitations. The response was that even aside from the time limit, compensation in that case was barred by the fact that the woman was not employed in the industry as of May 1, 1931.[41] In other words, the compensation law excluded everyone in the country with asbestosis who had already been disabled, retired, or fired by the time the compensation scheme took effect.

As of 1950, these defects in the law apparently remained. That year, Livingstone and Street reported on a man with asbestosis who had worked from 1924 to 1929 as an "asbestos crusher."[42]

> The case was referred to the Pneumoconiosis Medical Panel as a matter of interest, but as the man had not

worked in the asbestos industry for 20 years he was adjudged ineligible to recover compensation under any existing scheme.

Industry "Editing" of Medical Publications: Lanza's Surveys

When the compensation issue first arose, the American asbestos industry commissioned studies of the workers' health. The work was directed by Dr. Anthony J. Lanza of the Metropolitan Life Insurance Company. Although the examinations of the workers and dust counts were completed by January, 1931, publication of a report was delayed until 1935.[43]

Lanza and his co-workers examined 126 asbestos factory workers "selected more or less at random from among those having more than 3 years of employment in the industry." By a conservative reading of their X-rays, 53 percent of the workers were judged to have asbestosis; and most of those classed as having "doubtful" or "negative" X-rays complained of cough and shortness of breath. With Pedley in Canada, Lanza conducted a medical survey of 195 asbestos miners in Thetford Mines and Asbestos, Quebec, and found 42 cases of asbestosis (only 76 of the miners had had more than 10 years' exposure).[44]

The larger survey finding asbestosis in the miners in Canada was *never* published in the medical journals. Yet, years later, Lanza called it one of "the confusing aspects of this disease," that: "The cases described have originated in textile and other asbestos fabricating plants and not in connection with the mining of asbestos."[45]

Correspondence remaining from 1934 suggests that the compensation issue may have been crucial in the decision to finally publish Dr. Lanza's research on asbestos factory workers. By 1935, compensation had become a pressing concern of industry executives. Lanza sent a galley proof of his article to Johns-Manville lawyer Vandiver Brown, who passed it along to Newark attorney George Hobart (who had earlier negotiated the settlement of asbestosis lawsuits brought by Samuel Greenstone). Hobart explained that the New Jersey Legislative Commission was considering the addition of silicosis to the list of occupational diseases under the New Jersey compensation law. Hobart worried that asbestosis might also be recognized as a compensable disease:[46]

> (W)e have consistently urged that there is a substantial difference between silicosis and asbestosis . . . and . . . we have urged that asbestosis should not at the present time be included in the list of compensation diseases, for the reason that it is only within a comparatively recent time that asbestosis has been recognized by the medical scientific professions as a disease—in fact one of our principal defenses in actions against the company on the common law theory of negligence has been that the scientific and medical knowledge have been insufficient until a very recent period to place upon the owners of plants or factories the burden or duty of taking special precautions against the possible onset of the disease to their employees.

Brown and Hobart were well aware of the fact that if asbestosis became a compensable disease under the workers' compensation code, workers would not have to prove that the employer was at fault as required in negligence suits.

Before even receiving Hobart's reply, Vandiver Brown focused on a sentence Dr. Lanza had deleted from his initial report, to the effect that, "Clinically, it (asbestosis) is of a type (of disease) milder than silicosis."[47,48] Brown had suggested to Lanza, and Hobart agreed, that the sentence must be reinserted but could be reworded to "Clinically, *from this study* it appeared to be of a type milder than silicosis" (emphasis added).[46] The exact wording didn't matter, Hobart said, but that sentence must be included in some form:

> Here again I have in mind the probability that the New Jersey Commission will introduce a bill in the Legislature which opens in January of 1935; and if it is the policy of Johns-Manville to oppose any bill that attempted to in-

> clude asbestosis, as compensable, it would be very helpful to have an official report to show that there is a substantial difference between asbestosis and silicosis; and by the same token it would be troublesome if an official report should appear from which the conclusion might be drawn that there is very little if any difference between the two diseases.[46]

Vandiver Brown sent a copy of Hobart's 3-page letter to Dr. Lanza, asking that the contents be given "your most serious consideration."[49] Two weeks later, on January 4, 1935, Lanza's paper appeared in *Public Health Reports* with the sentence from Hobart's letter in conclusion number one, word for word.[43] Other changes requested by the lawyers were also made by Lanza.

It certainly appears plausible, from this record, that Lanza was asked to get his work into print so that the asbestos companies would have a tool to lobby against compensating asbestosis in New Jersey (and perhaps elsewhere). However, in the years since Lanza had originally written his findings, Merewether in England had published statistics (1933) showing that asbestotics were dying far younger than silicotics and after careers less than half as long (silicotics died on the average 40 years after starting work, compared to a figure of only 15 years for asbestotics).[50] Lanza was almost certainly aware of Merewether's work at this time, as he was a leading authority on asbestosis and referred to this article of Merewether's in his lengthy text, published in 1938.[29] These statistics were also published in the Annual Report of the Chief Inspector of Factories for the Years 1931-1933, and reprinted in the U.S. in *Monthly Labor Review*.[51-53] Ellman also described asbestosis as a cause of more pronounced suffering than silicosis in papers published in the U.S. in 1933 and in the U.K. in 1934.[54,55] Attorney Brown immediately noticed that the crucial sentence was deleted and quite possibly perceived that the publication of Lanza's report could backfire and hasten legislative recognition of asbestosis. By this time, the report had already been submitted for publication and was in the galley proof stage, and could hardly be withdrawn. So, as Brown realized and Hobart stressed, the report would have to be edited—and it was.

In the state of New Jersey, where Johns-Manville had its largest manufacturing plant, asbestosis and silicosis were not listed as compensable diseases until 1945.[56] By this time, Vandiver Brown had changed his mind on the comparative costs of civil suits and workers' compensation for asbestosis (see opening quote of this chapter).

The Asbestos Magazine Letters

The English radiologist W. Burton Wood published an article on the chest X-rays of asbestos workers in the May, 1929 issue of *Tubercle*.[57] An abstract of this paper appeared in *Bulletin of Hygiene*, also printed in England.[58] This in turn was summarized and discussed in *Monthly Labor Review*, a publication of the U.S. Bureau of Labor Statistics.[59] Finally, this last item was picked up by the trade magazine of the asbestos industry in the United States, *Asbestos*.[60] The magazine not only informed its readers that much had been written in England about asbestosis, but went on to say, "The Bureau urges the establishment of efficient exhaust systems and the introduction of other safety methods."

This article appeared among advertisements of asbestos companies from all over the world, including Ehret Magnesia Manufacturing Company, Philip Carey Manufacturing Company, Johns-Manville, Keasbey & Mattison Company, Asbestos Corporation Limited, Ruberoid Company, and Cape Asbestos.[60] That very month, the Merewether and Price report was laid before Parliament by the Chief Inspector of Factories. Merewether's monumental contribution to the literature on asbestosis was not, however, cited in *Asbestos*. In fact, the subject of asbestosis received no attention at all in the trade magazine for many years after March, 1930.

By 1935, the editor of *Asbestos* had asked Raybestos-Manhattan President Sumner Simpson "on several occasions" about the possibility of publishing something on asbestosis. The apprehension of the companies over articles on asbestosis appearing among their advertisements in *Asbestos* was understandable. Copies of such publications introduced by plaintiffs in negligence suits would have shattered the "ignorance" defense described by Hobart in his letter to Vandiver Brown.[46] To compound this danger, the trade magazine was avidly read by sales and marketing personnel in the asbestos industry. The raised awareness of such people about asbestosis, which demonstrably occurred with the publication of the March, 1930 article, was bound to be counter-productive from a purely business standpoint.[61] The editor of *Asbestos* wrote:

> Always you have requested that for certain obvious reasons we publish nothing, and naturally your wishes have been respected.[62]

Sumner Simpson passed the renewed request along to Vandiver Brown. He acknowledged that the magazine had been "very decent about not reprinting the English articles" on asbestosis.[63] Brown replied on October 3, 1935:[64]

> I quite agree with you that our interests are best served by having asbestosis receive the minimum of publicity.

In 1939, the editor of *Asbestos* wrote to Sumner Simpson, again expressing eagerness to run an article on asbestosis. But still, nothing more had been said about the mortal hazard of the asbestos industry:[65]

> Of course we understand that all this information on asbestosis is to be kept confidential and that nothing should be published about asbestosis in *Asbestos* at present.

As late as November 3, 1941, a letter from Brown to Simpson shows why the magazine was still mute on the subject. In this letter, Vandiver Brown related a conversation he'd had with A.S. Rossiter, editor of *Asbestos,* about publishing a review of a book on pneumoconiosis.[66]

> (I) told her in substance that... I felt there was considerable likelihood that a number of her subscribers would dislike an article on this subject in the trade magazine of the Asbestos Industry. I had in mind the ostrich-like attitude which has been evidenced from time to time by some members of the Industry. While I did not over-emphasize this point with Miss Rossiter, but merely suggested she give it consideration, I am inclined to believe she will omit any review of the book in question.

Nothing more about the health hazards of asbestos appeared in the trade magazine until 1969.

> [The 1935 *Asbestos* magazine letters are reproduced in full in Appendix 1.]

RISING TIDE OF COMPENSATION IN THE 1930s

Insurance carriers' concern about asbestos was evident by 1932.[67] Asbestos manufacturing was listed along with industries with silicosis, lead, and serious chemical hazards as receiving special attention "for some time" in insurance underwriting. But the closing paragraph of a 1932 occupational disease report in *The National Underwriter* was reserved for asbestos:

> Any processes involving asbestos are considered especially hazardous, for the asbestos fibers appear to be difficult to expel from the lungs.

The Supreme Court of North Carolina (*McNeely v. Carolina Asbestos Co.*, May 23, 1934) determined that the occupational disease, asbestosis, contracted unexpectedly and gradually over a long time, if due to the employer's failure to provide means of prevention, was an injury "by accident" and was compensable under the state Workmen's Compensation Act.[68] There had been many civil suits filed against employers by workers with asbestosis in North Carolina, according to Dr. J. Donnelly.[69]

Insurance executive F.R. Jones wrote that the *McNeely* case and others like it injected elements of uncertainty that rendered the hazards of asbestosis and silicosis "often uninsurable at practicable rates." Jones went on to discuss the workers' compensation insurance rates in New York, following that state's recognition of asbestosis and other diseases under the Workers' Compensation law in 1935. He wrote that even though the rates were high, "their adequacy . . . is generally doubted." Jones said the State Fund charged even higher rates to companies rejected by the private insurance carriers. This, in turn, was driving operations with dust hazards out of New York, and at the same time fueling (successful) efforts to weaken the New York compensation law.[68]

Jones was the General Manager of the Association of Casualty and Surety Executives, and in 1935-1936 he issued urgent warnings to the effect that dust diseases were a mortal menace to industry. He called for the development of minimum engineering standards, "to impress backward industrialists, to guide and support insurers in granting or refusing coverage, and to furnish a scientific basis for regulations kept open to continual revision . . ."[70,71] In this way, Jones hoped occupational diseases could be reduced to exceptional misfortunes instead of routine ones.[72]

He was much alarmed about the perils to business posed by occupational disease compensation, which had risen from insignificance to a major expense, along with taxes and unemployment insurance, in three years' time. All-inclusive occupational disease laws, Jones said, "should be avoided like sin" because they would leave open the possibility that courts and industrial commissions would then hold industries and their insurance carriers liable for all forms of ill health in any way contributed to by work.[72,73]

To confront the dust disease threat, a meeting of about 250 people representing over 50 industries with industrial disease problems was held on January 15, 1935. According to Vandiver Brown's memorandum of the meeting, speakers included attorney A.C. Hirth of Owens-Illinois, Dr. A.J. Lanza of Metropolitan Life, Dr. R.R. Sayers from the U.S. Public Health Service, Dr. Philip Drinker of Harvard, and insurance lobbyist F.R. Jones.[74]

Reviewing the discussions, Brown wrote,

> Only two forms of dust, namely, free silica and asbestos, are definitely known to produce disabling fibrosis of the lung.

Turning to problems common to all, the meeting then focused on what Brown called "the menace of ambulance chasing lawyers in combination with unscrupulous doctors." This menace to employers was seen to be greatest where juries decided the facts in each case. Brown then quoted a speaker who urged that "the strongest bulwark against future disaster for industry is the enactment of properly drawn (workers' compensation laws)." Such legislation would:

1. "eliminate the jury" and replace it by an appointed medical board within the workers' compensation system;
2. "eliminate the shyster lawyer and the quack doctor" by strictly limiting their fees under the law; and
3. "permit the correcting of initial mistakes in the making of awards" by establishing hearing procedures where new evidence could be offered to contest awards of compensation

One outcome of these compensation-related industry concerns was the formation of the Air Hygiene Foundation in 1936 (renamed Industrial Hygiene Foundation in 1941). Established under the auspices of the Mellon Institute, this organization provided a means for doing confidential studies and compiling medical, legal, and industrial hygiene knowledge for the member companies.

At this time, one consulting physician to the insurance industry observed, "The asbestos industry has been a bad risk for the carriers, and those taking them have been losing money for years, due to asbestosis and silicosis."[75]

Raybestos-Manhattan was one company beset with compensation claims over asbestosis. The Public Health Service requested permission to examine the employees at R-M's North Charleston, S.C. plant, in 1936. R-M President Sumner Simpson advised his plant manager:[76]

> For our own information, I should like to have an X-ray of all the employees, and if we could get this information from the United States Department of Health without it being placed in the hands of every "Tom, Dick, and Harry" in the country, I would be willing to let them make the X-rays, as it would be one way of getting them without arousing very much suspicion on the part of the employees. It would, no doubt, be interpreted as having some connection with the Social Security Act, but I certainly do not want to bring a lot of suits down on us just about the time we are getting through with the old ones.

Simpson and his plant manager then consulted with Dr. A.J. Lanza, who reassured them that Public Health Service reports were anonymous and individual records of the Service were held confidential. Lanza was especially complimentary about one of the government investigators:[77]

> Dr. Sayers has had wide industrial experience and enjoys the highest favor and confidence of industrialists and employers all over the United States.

Simpson then wrote to the plant manager again.[78]

> (Y)ou may advise the Public Health Service that they may take the (chest X-ray) pictures, with the understanding that they are not available for any purpose whatever except public health information, and you want to stress the fact that we do not want them given to shyster lawyers and doctors so as to be the subject of suits, for, as you know, we have had enough adjustments for any one company.

With compensation costs very much in mind, Sumner Simpson and Vandiver Brown of Johns-Manville decided to sponsor confidential animal experiments at the Saranac Laboratory for Research on Tuberculosis, in upstate New York. Simpson solicited contributions from top executives of four other asbestos companies[79] in 1936, noting,

> (W)e should have all the information we can possibly get to submit to the Compensation Commissioners of the various states when the question of asbestosis comes up.

Another person involved in the spate of workers' compensation claims was Dr. John B. Hawes, Jr. of Boston.[80]

> ...dust is the source of one of the most vicious rackets inflicted in this country...The basis of this racket is founded on (1) ignorance on the part of the workingman, (2) ignorance on the part of doctors as to what dusts are dangerous and (3) unscrupulous and mercenary lawyers.

He went on to decry the alliance of clever, crooked lawyers with ignorant and even unscrupulous doctors who were bringing unjustified claims against a woolen mill, a charity employing a cotton cloth cutter, a steel wire drawing operation, and the cement industry. Hawes went on to then talk about silicosis and describe the clinical signs of asbestosis.

> I have seen nearly 75 men and women that have been exposed to asbestos dust and have found that the one striking sign in those in whom I have made a positive diagnosis has been a greatly diminished chest expansion, rarely over *one inch.* (original emphasis)

He concluded that asbestosis claims were no medicolegal racket:

> There is not the slightest doubt, however, in my mind at least, that asbestos dust is the most dangerous of all dusts.

> Asbestosis is able to produce permanent and total disability in a remarkably short length of time, even after only 2 or 3 years' exposure and occasionally less, as compared with the much slower and more gradual action of pure silicon and the great majority of silicates.

Dr. Hawes' patients had worked at the Multibestos plant of the Dewey & Almy Chemical Company (which in turn became part of W.R. Grace & Company).[81] The company president, Bradley Dewey, was also convinced that asbestosis was "a very serious and sometimes fatal disease." Dewey suspected that his shift to Rhodesian and Russian chrysotile from Canadian chrysotile asbestos had something to do with this epidemic of disease; but Drs. Lanza and Gardner disagreed.[82-84] Lanza observed:

> Mr. Dewey points out that Multibestos ran for years without much trouble. Of course, the reason was that nobody knew anything about asbestosis. I am not quite sure what he means when he says "trouble" but I suspect he means "lawyer trouble" which, of course, has nothing to do with the issue. The same comment holds good for the plants of his competitors. They did not have any trouble either—until the shysters got busy.[84]

Radiologists Arial George and Ralph Leonard had been increasingly disturbed by Dr. Hawes' testimony in asbestosis compensation cases. They had examined asbestos factory workers in the U.S. one year before the industry approached Dr. Lanza at Metropolitan Life to do his survey.[85] Their account shows first of all the importance of compensation in forcing the conversion from dry to wet processes:

> In 1928, we began the intensive study of those exposed to the asbestos hazard in one of the large industrial plants in Massachusetts, where brake lining was manufactured ...Dry weaving was first used and then changed to wet weaving. This change was brought about by the fact that

> in 1928 and 1929 there were numerous cases which showed symptoms, referable to the lungs, characterized by increased difficulty in breathing on exertion, cough, sleeplessness, and loss of weight...in 12 cases X-ray examination revealed changes in the lungs, upon which we based our diagnosis of asbestosis.

The insurance carrier then paid to settle these 12 disability claims. By 1933, the workers' compensation insurance premiums "had pyramided to 15 percent of the payroll, and the carriers were rather indifferent to the taking on of this risk." A large insurance firm then insisted on having clinical and X-ray examinations done of all 800 employees in the plant *before* agreeing to provide coverage. The examinations were performed by Drs. George and Leonard, who found three cases that were "definitely advanced." These workers "would not, on account of the high wages they were earning, change their occupations." When the plant closed in 1936, one of these men filed a compensation claim, and the other two "disappeared into other industries."

After the plant closed, 90 workers filed claims. Once again, they were X-rayed and physically examined by George and Leonard, who now found that 12 more had asbestosis, and three others were "questionable" cases. The insurer then put the 12 either on compensation payments or agreed to "lump-sum settlement in excess of $50,000." Of the remaining 78, 30 cases came to trial, furnished with a lawyer from the Legal Aid Society and Dr. Hawes as the medical expert. Hawes had made a positive diagnosis on these 30 cases after clinical and X-ray examination. The State "Panel Doctors" then decided 10 of these cases, ruling with Dr. Hawes and against Drs. George and Leonard. The complaint by the latter two was that despite marginal X-ray findings, these cases were decided, "giving the benefit of the doubt to the workmen." They then proceeded to decry Hawes for excessive reliance on history of exposure and his assumption that asbestosis was a progressive disease.

George and Leonard then returned to the 12 individuals who had been compensated for disability and discharged back in 1928-29.[85]

> At one of the hearings they were recalled by the insurance company to illustrate that these 12 who had been found positive by both clinical and X-ray examination *were, by their own testimony, free of all symptoms, and except for several women in the group, were doing laborious work in their new occupations.* (emphasis added)

George and Leonard went on to conclude that asbestosis was thus not a progressive disease, apparently based on the accounts of the patients as elicited at a hearing by the insurance company lawyer. No confirmatory X-ray or clinical examinations were mentioned, and perhaps for this reason this report of mass recovery from asbestosis is unique in the literature.

In marked contrast, the *Employers' Group Engineering Manual* advised insurance industry representatives that,[86]

> A potential asbestosis hazard is to be looked for wherever asbestos dust is created... In the opinion of certain authorities it is established that asbestos may cause disability and death, and that any well-defined case of asbestosis is very likely to progress to a fatal conclusion.

Three Stories of Compensation

What follow are examples from the 1940s about asbestos disease compensation and the ways it informed and influenced business conduct. The first anecdote describes what happened when officials from a smaller asbestos company asked Johns-Manville executives how they managed the problem of asbestosis. The second discusses the plan of a fiber-glass insulation manufacturer to capitalize on the health issue in competing with asbestos. The last story shows how industry officials confirmed that asbestos had killed some of their employees, and then sometimes paid cash settlements to the workers' widows.

A Lobster Lunch with Vandiver Brown

The United Asbestos and Rubber Company manufactured amosite asbestos insulation in Paterson, New Jersey.[87]

Former Chairman of the Paterson Industrial Commission, Charles H. Roemer, who was unaccustomed to the rich fare he enjoyed as a guest at Johns-Manville, recalled the following story in a sworn affidavit filed in 1982. The document's text is reprinted in its entirety.[88] It offers a unique glimpse of the corporate policy of Johns-Manville on asbestos and health in the early 1940s.

1. I am an attorney who was admitted to practice in the State of New Jersey in 1920 and presently maintain an office at 99 Broadway, Elmwood Park, Bergen County, New Jersey.
2. I was born February 5, 1899 and am presently under the care of Dr. David Roth.
3. Sometime in 1942-43, I was advised by my cousin, Dr. Jacob Roemer, that in the course of reviewing chest X-rays of employees at the Union Asbestos and Rubber Company's Paterson plant he had observed a significant number with lung changes which he believed were due to exposure to asbestos. Dr. Roemer suggested that the men be advised of his findings and that they secure outdoor employment which did not involve exposure to asbestos dust. Dr. Roemer said unless this was done immediately the men would suffer from painful asbestos diseases.
4. Immediately I reported what Dr. Roemer said to Robert Cryor, the Union Asbestos and Rubber Company Plant Manager, and Edward Shuman, the Assistant Plant Manager.
5. I was then informed that in accordance with the labor union contract, the 5 or 6 employees in question could not be discharged without the consent of the union. The union refused to consent to their dismissal.
6. I then suggested that since Johns-Manville was the largest asbestos company in the country, we should set up an appointment to see how they were handling the asbestos health problem.
7. Mr. Cryor and Mr. Shuman set up an appointment with Johns-Manville. Shortly thereafter, Mr. Cryor, Mr. Shuman and I met with Vandiver Brown, General Attorney for Johns-Manville and the President of the corporation, at Johns-Manville corporate headquarters in New York City.

8. We advised the Johns-Manville officials of Dr. Roemer's findings and asked them if Johns-Manville's physical examination program had turned up similar findings and, if so, what Johns-Manville was doing about it.

9. In response, Vandiver Brown stated that Johns-Manville's physical examination program had, indeed, also produced findings of X-ray evidence of asbestos disease among workers exposed to asbestos and that it was Johns-Manville's policy not to do anything nor to tell the employees of the X-ray findings. Vandiver Brown went on to say that it was foolish for us to be concerned and that if Johns-Manville's workers were told, they would stop working and file claims against Johns-Manville, and that it was Johns-Manville's policy to let them work until they quit work because of asbestosis or died as a result of asbestos-related diseases.

10. Thereafter, we contacted Dr. Lanza at Saranac Lake, who was in charge of an asbestos exposure study and we were unable to gather any further advice or information from him.

Owens-Corning "Fiber-glass Itch Documents"

In the early 1940s, Owens-Corning Fiberglas (OCF) Corporation was facing marketing difficulties and objections by the Asbestos Workers (insulators) union. Some of the union members were having skin reactions from handling fiber-glass insulation, and there was talk of charging premium rates for using the material. Several steps were taken to overcome "market resistance" to fiber-glass, capitalizing on the greater health hazard of asbestos products.

The company prepared a brochure in 1941 or 1942, featuring a letter from the Aetna Life Insurance Company to OCF Public Relations Manager Edward C. Ames. The letter cited a 35 percent reduction in sickness and hospitalization insurance for OCF's employees. It noted further that OCF was covered by insurance for "Products Liability at an extremely low rate." The lack of any claims on this front was offered as an indication "that there is no hazard in the use of fiberglass or any of its products." On the subject of workers' compensation rates, the Aetna letter said, "(W)e feel the hazard (from fiber-glass) is much less than in the manufacture of Rockwool, Slagwool, Asbestos, or any of the so-called 85% magnesia products." It is not clear how widely this brochure, which seems to have been intended for employers, was distributed.[89,90]

To counter union resistance, a plan of action was drafted by Public Relations Manager Ed Ames. It began,

> Gather as a weapon-in-reserve an impressive file of photostats of medical literature on asbestosis. Available are two bibliographies covering medical literature to 1938, citing references to scores of publications in which the lung and skin hazards of asbestos are discussed. This file would cover five or six hundred pages...[91]

This weapon in reserve would be used, if necessary, to "conceivably bring about the overthrow of the present Union leadership" if the union officials maintained their position against fiber-glass. The plan was also summarized in a memorandum to Harold Boeschenstein, who was the President of Owens-Corning from its founding in 1938 until sometime in the 1960's.[91] He was also a director on the Board of Owens-Illinois, which owned half of Owens-Corning in 1942. The weapon-in-reserve never was deployed, and the union's false sense of security about asbestos remained undisturbed. In 1944, Ed Ames confirmed that a Toledo physician was caring for a man who had left the insulation trade due to asbestosis.[92] More than ten years later, when the union was again threatening to charge a premium for work with fiber-glass, Owens-Corning was dealing extensively in both fiber-glass ("Fiberglas") and asbestos ("Kaylo") insulations. The subject of asbestosis came up often in Owens-Corning documents from the 1956-1957 period.

Saranac Compensation Reviews for Manufacturers

Rose Bertogliat, widow of a Johns-Manville foreman at the Waukegan, Illinois plant, approached the company in 1947 seeking compensation payments for the death of her husband.

Sections from Dominic Bertogliat's lungs were sent by the company to Dr. Vorwald at the Saranac Laboratory, who concluded that Mr. Bertogliat must have suffered "considerable respiratory difficulty" with his asbestotic lungs. J-M headquarters safety engineer Hugh Jackson, who had worked with Mr. Bertogliat at Waukegan, wrote back that, "appropriate steps have been taken... toward the settlement of this case." But Jackson was "particularly concerned that the type of exposure to which Mr. Bertogliat was subjected should produce the evident results." He continued,

> To our way of thinking, although he had worked in the general area for a number of years, the degree of exposure was relatively slight. That is, he was subjected not to a concentrated exposure of any particular part of the process but rather only to that of the general atmosphere. Since there are numerous others who also have this type of exposure, I would appreciate your opinion as to whether Mr. Bertogliat might have had some individual susceptibility to the asbestos irritation and/or whether we should anticipate others with similar exposures to be similarly affected. (Aug. 13, 1948).

Dr. Vorwald replied on August 19, 1948, that "I can see no other alternative than to anticipate others with similar exposures to be similarly affected."[93]

The implications of Mr. Bertogliat's experience would appear grave for others at the J-M Waukegan plant; and for workers elsewhere exposed to asbestos manufacturing and fabrication dust as "bystanders."

Saranac provided similar services directly and indirectly to other U.S. asbestos manufacturers. In 1944, the Saranac lab pathologically verified asbestosis in the lung tissues of an Ohio man who had died at age 42. The man had worked at Philip Carey Manufacturing Company for 25 years making "air cell" pipe insulation. The only parts of the process in which the asbestos was not wetted were "cutting and squaring ends of finished material," and some exhaust ventilation was reportedly provided. Dr. Robert J. Ritterhoff, who performed the autopsy before sending lung sections to Saranac, discussed the findings with an official of the Carey company. It was the doctor's understanding that the company then arranged to pay the widow a cash settlement, and no workers' compensation claim was filed.[94,95]

In 1949, Dr. Vorwald analyzed lung tissues from a deceased employee of the Paterson, New Jersey, plant of Union Asbestos and Rubber Company. He concluded that the man had died from lung cancer and had suffered from moderately advanced asbestosis. Vorwald sent his report to a company Vice President, Robert E. Cryor, who had been plant manager at Paterson. Vorwald wrote that it was his "current opinion" that there was no causal relationship between asbestos and lung cancer.[96]

Published Literature on Compensability of Asbestosis Disability in Asbestos Product Users

Some medical papers on asbestos disease mentioned the issue of workers' compensation. These, together with relevant legal literature, provide a partial record of asbestos disease compensation received by asbestos product users in various countries. Disability compensation was paid to handlers of asbestos insulation products in several countries in the Thirties. By the 1950s, such claims became much more numerous.

Perhaps the first report of disability compensation to an asbestos product user was made public by a physician with the U.S. government. Dr. Albert Russell, of the Public Health Service, reported in 1932 that a maintenance worker in a government hospital was compensated for asbestosis, which he developed as a consequence of handling pipe insulation.[62] Russell's presentation was attended by an audience composed primarily of doctors, lawyers, and insurance company officials. (Insurers represented included Liberty Mutual and Employers Mutual.) With Russell's report and others that soon followed, the mortal risk of asbestosis to insulation workers—or asbestos workers, as they were commonly called in the U.S.—was demonstrated. This knowledge substantially expanded the size of the working population demonstrably endangered by asbestos.

Asbestosis became a compensable disease in Germany in 1936, and the following year a shipyard insulation worker was compensated for disability. This individual when examined at autopsy was determined to have died from asbestosis.[98] Finland began to award workers' compensation for asbestosis to insulation installers in 1938.[99]

The total number of asbestosis case reports in the world literature among *asbestos product users* was small in 1938. But the disease had been well characterized by this time, and its manifestation in asbestos insulation workers was accepted by compensation authorities in at least 3 countries. In Great Britain, asbestosis was reported in an insulation worker and a boiler riveter, but if compensation for disability was awarded it was not noted in the medical literature.[54,55,100]

In 1943, asbestosis became a compensable occupational disease in Italy, with employers' insurance required for asbestos mining and manufacturing, and fabrication of asbestos cement. Compensation claims could be filed up to 10 years after cessation of asbestos work.[101] It was later explained that, "Special emergency legislation to provide compensation for silicosis and asbestosis was enacted in 1943 when thousands of claims were being brought before the courts of civil law."[102]

Canepa, reporting a high prevalence of asbestosis among shipyard insulators in Genoa, noted that the Italian compensation law was written too narrowly to apply to all those at risk of asbestosis (particularly insulators who had not worked with asbestos cement). He urged changes in the language of the statute, and also pleaded for an automatic removal of least-affected (but not yet disabled) workers with provision of a 6-month "transition income." Canepa argued that it should not be necessary to await the development of disability before triggering the protection of the insurance law.[103]

Following the Second World War a new system of compensation was established in Great Britain under the National Insurance (Social Security) scheme. Workers' compensation claims in the United Kingdom are not accessible for complete

Table 1. Compensation for Disability from Asbestosis

Country	Year	Inclusiveness of Coverage Reported	Ref.
U.K.	1931	not explicitly extending to product users	14
	1949-50	handlers of thermal and electrical asbestos insulation	37,38,104
U.S.	1927	plant foreman	27
(Mass.)			
	1932	maintenance worker handling insulation	97
GERMANY	1936	not limited;	98
	1937	shipyard insulator	
FINLAND	1938	insulator	99
ITALY	1943	plant workers and asbestos cement fabrication workers	101
NETHERLANDS	1945	notlimited	198
CZECHOSLOVAKIA	1948	not limited	101
DENMARK	1950	not apparently limited	105
SWITZERLAND	1952	not apparently limited	106
SWEDEN	(1956-1960)	insulators	107

review. However, some cases were appealed and thus appear in the legal literature. Two such cases involve the question of whether workers exposed to the asbestos dust from handling electrical and thermal insulation qualified under the statutes applying to asbestosis.[38,104]

The first of these appeals was heard in 1949, and involved a workman who had removed the asbestos coverings on copper wire in a scrap metal reclaiming operation. Even granting that less than half of the cables he handled were insulated with asbestos, the Commissioner entitled the man's claim to be awarded with the presumption that his disease was due to the nature of his employment. The Commissioner stated that the language of the law did not justify a restriction on the "meaning or scope of the phrase" in the law, "working or handling asbestos."[104]

In 1950, another workers' compensation claim was appealed to the Commissioner under the industrial injuries statutes of the United Kingdom. The man had made a claim for pneumoconiosis from dismantling brickwork in boilers and insulating steam pipes. The Commissioner found that the latter occupation entitled the claimant to file for disability under the provision of the law applying to "occupation involving the working or handling of asbestos."[38]

In the years 1955-1963, there were 72 new cases of asbestosis diagnosed in Great Britain among insulation workers. All but 3 had filed claims for disability. Thirteen more cases were diagnosed among asbestos sprayers, all of whom had filed for workers' compensation. These 85 cases constituted over one third of all those diagnosed in the years 1955-1963 in Great Britain.[37]

Cancer

It has already been noted that cancer in combination with asbestosis was recognized as a compensable occupational disease in Germany as early as 1939, and codified there nationwide in 1943. Czechoslovakia followed with a similar provision in its compensation law in 1948.[17,101,108-110] (Details in Chapter 2.)

Meanwhile, Hueper in the United States called attention to

the mounting evidence of asbestos' carcinogenicity and decried the non-compensable status of occupational diseases in states where there were large asbestos plants:

> Such a condition militates against an effective hygienic control of an important industrial hazard, and impedes the collection of pertinent and essential information in regard to the incidence, nature, and potentialities of an occupational disease growing steadily in general significance."[111]

In 1943 Hueper positively identified asbestos as a cause of lung cancer. Here, he pointed to the spectre of liability as the motive for the underreporting of occupational cancers in the United States:

> Industrial concerns are in general not particularly anxious to have the occurrence of occupational cancers among their employees or of environmental cancers among the consumers of their products made a matter of public records. Such publicity might reflect unfavorably upon their business activities, and oblige them to undertake extensive and expensive technical and sanitary measures in their production methods and in the types of products manufactured. There is, moreover, the distinct possibility of becoming involved in compensation suits with extravagant financial claims by the injured parties. It is, therefore, not an uncommon practice that some pressure is exerted by the parties financially interested in such matters to keep information on the occurrence of industrial cancer well under cover. It is for these reasons that the statistical data being presented here concerning the incidence of occupational cancers as caused by the different industrial agents represent only those made public.[112]

By the end of 1945, only 32 states had workers' compensation laws providing coverage for occupational diseases.[113]

Dr. Leopold Brahdy, a New York state workers' compensation official, wrote in 1948 that "the evidence warrants the *tentative* conclusion that asbestos workers do have a higher risk of lung cancer."[114]

In 1950, Johns-Manville plant worker Vernon Hall died with advanced asbestosis and lung cancer. Memoranda from the files of the Saranac Laboratory show that safety specialist Hugh Jackson at J-M headquarters was apprised of the possibility that a compensation claim might be brought against the company.[115] That year, a supervisor at Raybestos-Manhattan's Manheim, Pennsylvania plant was paid $4,500 compensation for "asbestosis-carcinoma."[116]

Anton Szczesniak, a longtime employee of Union Asbestos and Rubber Company (Unarco), died in 1951 from cancer of the intestinal tract. Company records note that "He had been at the head of the list of potential liability cases of those suffering from asbestosis." As a result, the company paid the man's widow $2,000 to release any claims she might have against Unarco, in 1952.[117]

In Massachusetts a 41-year-old man died with severe asbestosis, cor pulmonale, adenocarcinoma of the lower lobe of his left lung, and metastases. He had worked for 12 years in a "very poorly run" asbestos mill, and he had stopped working there two years before admission to the hospital. He was barred from making a workers' compensation claim because the legal time interval had passed between the time he left work and the time he complained of symptoms.[118]

In contrast, West German compensation law was flexible enough in 1953 for an insulation worker with pleural cancer (mesothelioma) to receive workers' compensation while still living.[119]

Wilhelm Hueper, Chief of the Environmental Cancer Section at the National Cancer Institute, made a presentation at the 1954 meeting of the International Association of Industrial Accident Boards and Commissions. The meeting was held in Quebec, about an hour's drive from the asbestos mines. Hueper began with a table showing the number of published cancer cases for each of about 15 industrial materials, including asbestos. He urged numerous measures to prevent and control exposure to carcinogens; identify cases of occupational cancer through mandatory reporting to health officials; and fairly compensate stricken workers through equitable laws. Statutes of limitations barring claims by those whose disease was still latent until after the statute was tolled—commonly found in state laws in the U.S.—were to Hueper the "main defect" in workers' compensation laws in their application to job-related cancer.[120]

Hueper wrote in 1955 that a Canadian asbestos worker had been compensated for lung cancer.[121] He urged that:

> The available scientific evidence is adequate for recognizing asbestosis cancer of the lung for medicolegal reasons as an occupational disease.

Hueper's activities and publications immediately attracted the interest of members of the Asbestos Textile Institute, who were concerned about the implications of a 1956 workers' compensation case in Pennsylvania.[122] Dr. Hueper had testified in this Pennsylvania compensation claim, involving a worker with asbestosis and lung cancer. Commenting on the fact that compensation was awarded, an insurance official noted,

> It is particularly alarming as Penna. law is not as liberal as most state laws in allowing awards for (complications attributed to occupational diseases).

The same memorandum goes on to paraphrase one of Hueper's publications as saying that "anyone living near an asbestos plant can get lung cancer." It continues,

Table 2. Compensation for Cancer Accompanying Asbestosis

Country	Year	Types of Cancer	Ref.
Germany	1939	lung	17
(nationwide)	1943	lung	108
West Germany	1953	pleura	119
Czechoslovakia	1948	lung	101
U.S. (Pa.)	1950	lung	116
(Mass.)	1953	lung	124
Canada	1955	lung	121
England	prior to 1960	lung	125
South Africa	prior to 1960	lung	126

> Hueper has been quite reliable in proving the cancer causing properties of quite a number of commodities but very reliable medical opponents say he goes off the deep end and accuses other materials of having cancer causing properties without sufficient factual basis for his statement. Dr. Kenneth Smith of Johns-Manville accuses him of the latter in the case of asbestos.

The high death rate from lung cancer in the general population was viewed with awesome liability implications by the asbestos textile companies and their insurance carriers, in the event that asbestos work might be widely held responsible for causing this disease:[122]

> Out of every one hundred people employed in asbestos industries (or any other industry for that matter) three will die of lung cancer. With a "mad dog" like Dr. Hueper loose on the subject of asbestos, future claim results can be alarming.[126]

Workers' Compensation Claims by Insulators against Contracting Divisions of Asbestos Product Manufacturers

Major manufacturers of asbestos-containing insulation were also in the construction contracting business. Johns-Manville, Armstrong Cork, Philip Carey, Owens-Corning, Fibreboard, and Mundet Cork had contracting divisions that bid on construction and shipyard jobs, and then hired insulation workers as needed to install their products. When these workers became disabled from asbestosis and filed for workers' compensation, the contracting arms of the asbestos insulation manufacturing companies were named as defendants. Most of these claims involved numerous defendants.

The claims appear to have been bitterly contested, with payments delayed through every legal means, and the defendants aware that claimants had asbestosis from handling their insulation products. The filing of such claims constituted notice to the manufacturers that their products were dangerous; and the importance of this fact is not diminished by the fact that some of the individual claims were dismissed.

Through legal discovery and direct approaches to workers' compensation boards in a number of states, an effort was made to look up the records of the old "contract unit" claims, starting in 1978. The findings cannot be presumed complete by *any* means. Only one company (Armstrong Cork) produced a list of its compensation claims in response to discovery motions. There were frequently other defendants involved. Major limitations were posed by the availability and accessibility of state records. Many states (e.g., Texas) did not retain records going back to the 1950s. Others (e.g., New York, Massachusetts) were extremely guarded about allowing access to the old records of compensation proceedings; the records were held to be confidential, accessible only to the parties involved or their designated representatives.

Where no leads were available, the volume of claims rendered a full records search impossible. Usually, injury and illness records were not separated; and there was no "employer index" or register book to screen out extraneous material from upwards of 100,000 claims per year in the more populous states.

The earliest located compensation claim by an insulation worker in general industry was that of Henry Moore in California. He worked for Johns-Manville distributor Western Asbestos and was compensated for asbestosis in 1940.[123]

The earliest of the Armstrong Cork Company's asbestosis claims so far located was filed by Richard Rothwell in Massachusetts in 1952. Mr. Rothwell was an insulation worker who had asbestosis and died from lung cancer. Armstrong Cork managed to escape liability, arguing that Mr. Rothwell's tumor had probably existed at the time he began work for Armstrong. Compensation was awarded in December, 1953, with lung cancer accepted as a result of Rothwell's occupation.[124]

In 1953, former insulator Floyd Hyatt was told by his doctor that he had asbestosis. He filed a compensation claim against Armstrong Cork in Florida. Armstrong's insurer (successfully) appealed the case to the Florida Supreme Court to avoid paying any more than $5,000, the limit provided under the law at the time of Mr. Hyatt's last exposure (1945). The employer had previously contended that Hyatt's claim was barred by the statute of limitations, but the Workmen's Compensation Commission ruled that the clock did not start running until Hyatt discovered that he had an occupational disease. The record is clear that Hyatt was totally disabled by asbestosis in 1953. The Supreme Court of Florida adjudicated his case in 1960.[127]

In Connecticut, insulator Edward Campbell filed for compensation for asbestosis against companies including Johns-Manville, Armstrong, and R.A. Keasby. In this case, a $6,000 compromise settlement was submitted by the parties involved and approved by the Workmen's Compensation Commission in December, 1955.[128]

California led the other states in the number of contract unit compensation claims filed against Armstrong Cork. State records facilitated searching back to 1954 (25-year retention), using the intake register as an employer index, along with Armstrong's list of claims. There may have been earlier claims whose records were lost.

Two of the most extensive claims proceedings were those initiated by James Whitcomb Riley and Ervey O. McCarrell, both of Los Angeles.[129,130] Riley initially filed against Johns-Manville, Armstrong Cork, Fibreboard, and some local contracting firms, in 1957. Within months, Owens-Corning Fiberglas was added as a defendant. The state Industrial Accident Commission agreed that he was totally disabled by pneumoconiosis and tuberculosis as of 1957, and compensation payments were ordered. Whereupon, defendants involved moved to join all employers in Mr. Riley's 37-year career as an insulator. This brought in Philip Carey in late 1960. Mr. Riley died in January, 1961, and his widow Grace filed for death benefits. Later that year, the Industrial Accident Commission even had to penalize defendants (ultimately numbering more than 50 contracting firms and insurance companies) for "Willful Failure to Pay Compensation, and Death Benefits."

Mr. McCarrell also initiated lengthy compensation proceedings against Armstrong Cork in 1956. An insurance adjuster for Travelers wrote on June 20, 1958, that reserves in McCarrell's case amounted to over $19,000 for disability and medical expenses:

> This case is becoming very complicated and costly, due to the advance (sic) state of asbestosis... We are endeavoring to join numerous other defendant employers...

Within a short time, Johns-Manville, Fibreboard, and Owens-Corning were brought in as additional defendants, along with numerous local contractors. On January 14, 1960, a Compromise and Release Agreement was approved by the Industrial Accident Commission, wherein Mr. McCarrell received a payment of $13,500.

Armstrong claims adjuster R.C. Schiedt, Jr. was clearly concerned by the volume of claims. In McCarrell's case, he wrote,

> These asbestos claims are on the increase and we are wondering if the manufacturers of this high temp insulation which we use could be of some assistance in the defense of these claims. (March 1, 1957)

The year before, Armstrong had begun manufacturing an asbestos-containing insulation product.

John Swartout's claim was filed in San Francisco at the end of 1955 against J-M distributor Western Asbestos Company.[131] Upon the award of compensation in 1958, Western sought to join Johns-Manville and Armstrong (by whom Swartout was employed until his discovery that he had asbestosis and was forced to give up working). The lawyer for their insurer responded that these firms' employment of Mr. Swartout "was either outside the State of California, under contracts of hire not made in California, or involved the use of insulation materials other than asbestos." It was not denied that the man was totally disabled from asbestosis and died from its complications (cor pulmonale) as a result of his occupation, which was insulation work.

Further information on the contract unit workers' compensation claims is contained in Tables 3 and 4.

Table 3. Armstrong Cork Company Workers' Compensation Claims Asbestosis in Insulation Workers

Claimant	Date of Notice	Where Filed	Other Asbestos Manufacturer Defendants	Outcome	Comment
Rothwell, Richard	4-26-52	Mass. Industrial Accident Board	—	Compensation awarded for asbestosis/lung cancer (1953)	Armstrong dismissed-tumor existed when Rothwell was hired by Armstrong in March of 1952
Kish, Harry	1-16-53	California Industrial Accident Commission (S.F.)	Plant Rubber and Asbestos Works (Fibreboard) and Johns-Manville	compromise settlement of $2750/asbestosis death (1955)	—
Munger, Lewis	8-7-53	Michigan Workmen's Compensation Dept.	Johns-Manville joined in case 10-23-59	total disability and death benefits including funeral/ asbestosis	—
Hyatt, Floyd	9-10-53	Florida Industrial Commission Workers' Compensation Division	—	compensation awarded/disabling asbestosis	appealed to Florida Supreme Court by Armstrong

Cuthbertson, Jack	11-15-54	California Industrial Accident Commission (S.F.)	Plant Rubber and Asbestos Works (Fibreboard) and Mundet Cork dismissed as defendants	awarded medical costs/asbestosis (1956)	—
Campbell, Edward	12-16-54	Workmen's Compensation Commission of Connecticut (Hartford)	Johns-Manville, Mundet Cork	compromise settlement $6000/ asbestosis (12-20-55)	—
Swartout, John	12-28-55	California I.A.C. (S.F.)	Johns-Manville, Mundet Cork, Philip Carey	1958 award of compensation for asbestosis, terminating in fatal cor pulmonale	4-11-60 note from lawyer for J-M and Armstrong claimed he had not been employed doing *asbestos* insulation in the state of California by either firm.
McCarrell, Ervey	12-10-56	California I.A.C. (L.A.)	Johns-Manville, Owens-Corning, and Fibreboard joined as defendants (4-23-59)	Compromise settlement $13,500 (1-14-60) asbestosis	—

Claimant	Date of Notice	Where Filed	Other Asbestos Manufacturer Defendants	Outcome	Comment
Hartwig, Henry	2-19-57	Wisconsin Industrial Commission	—	$15,540 compromise "award", permanent total disability/asbestosis	Armstrong had employed Hartwig but avoided liability
Coll, Vincent	1-15-57	New York Workmen's Compensation Board	—	award for permanent total disability $684 (July 30, 1957) asbestosis	Coll died from cancer the day after being awarded compensation
Riley, James	7-15-57	California I.A.C. (L.A.)	Johns-Manville, Fibreboard, Owens-Corning (1958); Philip Carey was joined in case in 1960	award for permanent total disability (11-27-59), pneumoconiosis and tuberculosis. Death benefits awarded (8-3-61) lung cancer	Riley was an insulator for 37 years. There were 32 employer defendants.
Haake, Harry	7-25-57	Workmen's Compensation Commission of	Johns-Manville	Compromise settlement $3363.60 (9-17-59) asbestosis	An insulator for 37 years. J-M employment out of state;

		Connecticut (Hartford)		death case	J-M dismissed as defendant.
Strickland, Fred	10-31-57	California I.A.C. (S.F.)	Owens-Corning	Settlement $650 (asbestosis aggravating pre-existing tuberculosis)	Treating physician Dr. Hinshaw
Shepard, James	2-3-58	Massachusetts I.A.B.	—	settlement $5,891.29 (asbestosis death claim) 1960	Armstrong concerned over failure to use preemployment examinations to screen new hires
Spencer, Thomas	5-21-58	Pennsylvania Bureau of Workmen's Compensation	—	settled	Armstrong indicates no payment in this case
Zini, Robert	6-19-58	California I.A.C. (S.F.)	—	disallowed (asbestosis/lung cancer)	

Claimant	Date of Notice	Where Filed	Other Asbestos Manufacturer Defendants	Outcome	Comment
Reed, Clarence	12-29-58	Texas Industrial Accident Board (Austin)	(not known)	settled $500 (1960) asbestosis	employed only one month by Armstrong, other employment not indicated
Thorsted, Roy	4-27-59	California I.A.C. (Oakland)	—	disallowed 12-30-59 (asbestosis)	3-17-60 Schiedt letter to Edgar "As you know, these pneumoconiosis and asbestosis claims are on the increase in many sections of the country."
Bond, Thomas	7-7-59	State of Washington Department of Labor and Industries	—	Status unknown	—

Cuthbertson, Robert	7-22-59	California I.A.C. (S.F.)	—	denied (12-15-59)	letter from Schiedt to Hanna and Brophy 7-29-59 "We know your attorneys both in your San Francisco and Oakland offices have had considerable experience handling asbestos claims."
Viall, Lloyd	8-10-59	Nevada Industrial Commission	—	"status unknown"	7-5-59 Schiedt letter to Taylor: "If the number of lung claims keep on increasing as they have in the past several weeks, most of your time will be spent on asbestosis and pneumoconiosis claims."

Claimant	Date of Notice	Where Filed	Other Asbestos Manufacturer Defendants	Outcome	Comment
Curtis, Harvey	7-16-59 (Owens-Corning)	Michigan Workmen's Compensation Dept.	Johns-Manville, Armstrong	settled for $5250 (asbestosis 50% responsible for disability) 11-2-61	Hearing notice sent to Armstrong and J-M 1-19-61. Armstrong first informed of claim in 7-29-60 letter
Kendrick, Lloyd	11-16-59	State of Wash. Department of Labor and Industries	—	settled (pneumoconiosis)	Board of Industrial Insurance Appeals said his disease was compensable
Streithorst, L.	3-3-60	California I.A.C. (S.F.)	Fibreboard	"dismissed" (asbestosis)	death attributed to stomach cancer
Dean, William (widow: Mary)	9-19-60	New York Workmen's Compensation Board	Mundet Cork	settled (asbestosis)	2-10-61 letter Schiedt to Hoff: "Our file indicates William Dean's death, December 6, 1959, was caused by asbestosis."
Harding, Clifford	1-12-61	California I.A.C. (S.F.)	Owens-Corning	settled for $3300 in addition to sums	—

				paid previously (asbestosis)	
Gronenthal, John	8-16-61	State of Washington Board of Industrial Insurance Appeals	Owens-Corning	"status unknown" asbestosis/lung cancer	appellate order attributed asbestosis, lung cancer, and death from cor pulmonale to insulation dust exposure (11-30-62)
Gilivich, Steve	11-29-61 (Mundet Cork, Fibreboard)	California I.A.C. (Oakland)	Philip Carey, Owens Corning (and Armstrong) joined as defendants 8-29-62	settled $7968 (asbestosis) 12-22-64	—
Wyss, John	1-10-62	California I.A.C. (Oakland)	Owens-Corning, Mundet Cork, Fibreboard	$6500 settlement (asbestosis) 1966	—
Miller, Arthur	2-21-62	California I.A.C. (L.A.)	Fibreboard, Mundet Cork	"dismissed" (asbestosis)	—
Greischar, Paul	4-24-62	California I.A.C. (Oakland)	Fibreboard, Owens-Corning joined as defendants (8-23-63)	settled $8735 in addition to sums paid previously (asbestosis) 4-5-66	—

Claimant	Date of Notice	Where Filed	Other Asbestos Manufacturer Defendants	Outcome	Comment
Staples, John	5-17-62	California I.A.C. (Long Beach)	Owens-Corning, Mundet Cork	settlement $9250 (asbestosis) 2-1-63	partial disability at age 37
Onofrio, Anthony	6-25-62	Connecticut Workers' Compensation Commission (New Haven)	Philip Carey, Johns-Manville	settlement or comp. awarded	
Brodale, Frederick (widow, Irene)	7-13-62	California I.A.C. (Oakland)	—	settled $1500 (lung cancer)	Cremation prevented pathological verification
Kingston, George	10-16-62	Minnesota Industrial Commission	—	settled $13,500 (asbestosis) 3-27-63	—
Brokenshire, Leonard	3-15-63	California I.A.C. (Los Angeles)	Owens-Corning, Mundet Cork	award for $13,000 (asbestosis) 11-6-63	

Novak, Edward	3-27-63	California I.A.C. (L.A.)	Fibreboard (11-15-65)	settled $5500 (asbestosis) 8-18-66	—
Faulkner, John	4-9-63	California I.A.C. (Long Beach)	Fibreboard	settled	—
Goans, Robert	8-8-63	California I.A.C. (Oakland)	Fibreboard, Mundet Cork, Johns-Manville, Owens-Corning	settled $6750 (asbestosis) 8-3-64	—
Wines, Bernard	1963	Michigan Workmen's Compensation Department	—	—	—

Table 4. States' Workers' Compensation Records (1978 Survey)

State	Claim File Retention	Employer Index	Public Access	Remarks
California	up to 25 yrs.	+	+	Register used as employer index
Massachusetts	early 1940s—	+	–	File given only to parties in the claim
Pennsylvania	1960—	–	?	
Indiana	up to 10 yrs	–	?	
Connecticut	at least as far back as 1954	–	+	3 claims districts in state
Texas	1960—	–	+	
New Jersey		–	–	file given only to parties in the claim
Washington	at least back to 1960	–	+	some files were available, others could not be located
Ohio	up to 10 years after file closed	+	–	Occup. disease claims listed separately from "injuries," files at three locations, suponea required to obtain file access

Table 4. States' Workers' Compensation Records (1978 Survey) (cont'd)

State	Claim File Retention	Employer Index	Public Access	Remarks
Illinois	1913—	+	+	Only fragmentary records retained
Wisconsin	up to 10 yrs after file closed	–	–	
Michigan	at least back to 1954	–	+	2 or 3 files requested were unavailable; but a bigger one was retrieved
Maryland	at least 20 years	–	+	
New York	1959—for all claims in the state; back much farther for NYC area cases	+ (1941—)	– (?)	a specific file was retrieved; general search discouraged

Lawsuits by Product Users Against Asbestos Manufacturers

Damage suits against asbestos manufacturers which went to trial in the early 1970s are well known in legal circles. What is much less well known is that similar tort claims had been filed years earlier and settled quietly or dismissed. Four civil suits against asbestos product manufacturers have come to light, in which liability for the effects of asbestos product use was an issue prior to 1962. These civil suits constituted notice to manufacturers that asbestos and asbestos products were a health hazard to workers using them.

Aycock Corporation was a construction contracting firm based in Texas that that was purchased by Johns-Manville. The Johns-Manville Board of Directors minutes of June 26, 1933 described the Aycock firm as a "wholly owned subsidiary." Later in 1933, Aycock Corporation was sued by Bernard Dugan, who had worked for Aycock "for a long time" as a laborer mixing asbestos in repair and construction work.[132] Attesting that his lungs were so damaged that he was permanently and totally disabled, and stating that his impairment was not covered by the workers' compensation law, Dugan sued Aycock for negligence. He specifically claimed that Aycock Corporation knew, or by the exercise of ordinary care would have known that, "asbestos fumes and particles were likely to be breathed into (Dugan's) lungs and to injure him... yet failed to warn plaintiff of the dangers... carelessly and negligently failed to furnish any instrument, or device for the mixing of said ingredients with safety to plaintiff and other employees, or any mask, or device or other protection to be used over his nostrils and mouth..."[132] It appears that Mr. Dugan died in 1934, and the lawsuit was dismissed.[133]

There were also two damage suits filed by insulation workers in 1957 and 1961 against Johns-Manville.

The first of these cases was brought by Frederick LeGrande, who had been an insulation worker for about 30 years.[134,135] A complaint was filed in U.S. District Court in New Jersey, stating that LeGrande had not been warned of the danger of breathing dust from the asbestos products he handled. Mr. LeGrande asked for a jury trial and $500,000 in damages. At this time, Mr. LeGrande asserted that he was disabled by asbestosis and had ceased work involving the handling of insulation. He had worked for J-M distributor H.W. Porter a Co.

When Johns-Manville failed to respond to LeGrande's lawyer's interrogatories, a Court Order was obtained directing the company to do so. The Answers to Interrogatories in this early damage suit, made under oath, set the tone for future proceedings (and contained factual errors).

> This deponent has no knowledge of any case of asbestosis ever being contracted by an applicator. Asbestosis was first contracted by an employee of this defendant at one of its plants in 1946...

> Since *this defendant never received notice of any claim of asbestosis resulting to any persons other than our employees who were engaged in the manufacture of the products,* we had no reason to issue any warnings, instructions, or preventions to any other persons. (emphasis added)

As the jury was about to be selected for trial, Johns-Manville offered $35,000 to settle the case out of court, and this was accepted in March of 1959.

Fred C. Wenham was an insulation worker who developed asbestosis and lung cancer. A workers' compensation claim was filed against Mr. Wenham's employer, and a wrongful death case was filed against Johns-Manville in U.S. District Court in New Jersey.[136,137] This case was also settled out of court, for about $10,000, and most of that was remitted back to the workers' compensation carrier that had insured Mr. Wenham's employer.

Eagle-Picher Company was sued in 1960 by Gladys Faciane, widow of insulator Clarence A. Faciane. Mr. Faciane had died from lung cancer. An amended petition filed with the court in Louisiana on March 15, 1961 named as additional defendants Armstrong Contracting and Supply, Johns-Manville, Owens-Corning Fiberglas, Ruberoid, U.S. Rubber, Philip Carey, Mundet Cork, Nicolet Industries, Keasbey & Mattison, Baldwin-Ehret-Hill, Pittsburgh-Corning, and tobacco manufacturers R.J. Reynolds and P.F. Lorillard.[138] The product liability case was dismissed because the widow could not prove whose products her husband had used.

Corporate Compensation Meetings at Manville

The compensation claim files and court documents are valuable, but offer little direct insight into the company's internal reaction to the compensation toll among both its employees and its customers.

By the late 1950s, there were regular meetings of the compensation committee at Johns-Manville's main (Manville, New Jersey) plant. At these meetings were Medical Director Ken

Smith, plant engineer Cliff Sheckler, nurse Hahn, and a couple of others. Some excerpts of their notes:[139]

Sigmund Skirzenski, age 52, advanced pneumoconiosis
Sheckler: Should we change him?
Smith: Won't make any difference. Do not transfer, retire if necessary.

Alphonso Desantis, age 50
Hahn: Should these men be advised?
Sheckler: We can put transite pipe out of business from this list alone.

John Hudak, 58, moderately advanced pneumoconiosis
Smith: Has he been counselled?
No.
Smith: I see no reason to bring in a man like this it is dangerous.

Anna Blanik, 49, moderately advanced asbestosis
DuBow: She is very nervous. If she is called in, she will get hysterical and I am sure you will have a claim on your hands.
Hahn: If she is transferred to another job, wouldn't that also precipitate something?
DuBow: Mrs. Blanik is working with no complaints. It is one year since she was (health counselled).
Smith: As a doctor, you can't leave her where she is today.
DuBow: Taking her off the job will not change things. The damage has been done.

Stella Krzesewski, 41, moderate to advanced asbestosis
Sheckler: No health counselling.

Patsy Infante, 53, 33 years in asbestos
Getter: Records indicate asbestosis in 2/51. Man was advised about dust in his lung in 1/55.(Sic)

Dishonesty toward employees was self-perpetuating. Management's dilemma was clearly expressed in a 1963 internal memo describing similar activities at another J-M plant:[140]

(1) From a moral standpoint, employees identified as having pneumoconiosis should be told of their condition promptly.

(2) From an ethical standpoint, Doctors should tell these people of their condition promptly.

(3) From a practical standpoint, if we tell 25 persons they are pneumoconiotic within the next 2 to 6 weeks, there may be an undesirable panic or near-panic.

Workers at Manville describe factory conditions in the 1950s as extremely dusty. Dust counts recorded by the company in 1954 frequently exceeded 5 million particles per cubic foot of air, and ranged as high as several hundred MPPCF.*[141] The air pollution from the factory covered the town with asbestos dust. The Manville victims group successfully campaigned in 1980 to improve workers' compensation payments for people in New Jersey whose occupational diseases developed years after they had left their jobs.[142]

The Law Journals and Informal Consultation with Insurance Officials on Compensation Matters

Manufacturers of asbestos products may also have been aware of compensation proceedings that did not concern them directly. William Muldoon was a pipe coverer for 25 years, and was compensated for total disability from asbestosis combined with tuberculosis.[143,144] Another worker had tuberculosis as well as asbestosis after working as an asbestos sprayer's helper in closed quarters of the ship.[145] Cases like these, appealed for various reasons, became publicly known through the law journals and "downstream" literature.

In addition, the knowledge obtained by insurance companies sometimes made its way back to the asbestos manufacturers. Dr. A.J. Lanza, as a recognized expert on pneumoconiosis with Metropolitan Life Insurance Company, served as a conduit for all types of information on asbestosis, and was consulted by government health officials as well as industry. Massachusetts health officials contacted Lanza about a doctor's report of asbestosis in a shipyard worker in 1942. This was at the Quincy yard, operated by Bethlehem Steel Company and

*A crude guideline or tentative threshold limit value had been suggested by the U.S. Public Health Service in 1938. This value was 5 MPPCF. For further details, see chapter on Thresholds and Standards.

visited by Dr. E.R.A. Merewether during the war. (See Chapter 5, Table 8)[146]

At the end of 1942, Sumner Simpson wrote to Dr. Lanza about a former long-term Raybestos-Manhattan employee who had taken a job at a nearby Navy yard in Charleston, South Carolina. Here, the man had been diagnosed as having asbestosis by Dr. W.A. Smith (co-author with Dr. Kenneth Lynch of four medical articles on asbestosis and cancer). Simpson wrote,

> Dr. W.A. Smith, whom I consider to be a crank on the subject of Asbestosis, for as soon as he finds out that anyone has worked for the Asbestos Company, he puts him down as suffering from a case of Asbestosis, has not only told us that this party has Asbestosis, from which he will die, but he told the party himself that he was suffering from Asbestosis." (sic)

This letter to Lanza was sent via William McConnell at Metropolitan Life, to whom Simpson expressed thanks for having "made a great many personal sacrifices to be present to testify and assist us" in dealing with compensation claims brought by employees.[147,148]

But even a lowly claims examiner could pass the word along on a compensation problem. W.E. Shoemaker, of American Mutual Life Insurance Company, was investigating a claim by Samuel P. Knopp, a former insulator in Baltimore.[149] Mr. Knopp had been an insulation worker and a 2-pack-a-day smoker for at least 19 years, and died with lung cancer and pneumoconiosis. The case was referred to the Chief Medical Examiner, Dr. Russell S. Fisher, who advised the defense attorney that the plaintiff had a strong case (citing papers by Doll and Hueper). After consulting with his superiors, Shoemaker phoned Dr. Kenneth W. Smith, Medical Director of Johns-Manville, who advised him to examine lung sections for "other toxic materials" and emphasize the smoking history. Though Smith declined to testify, he did refer Shoemaker to Dr. A.J. Lanza for expert medical testimony.

> Dr. Smith advised that Dr. Lanza has just completed a study in an asbestos brake lining plant in Manheim, PA. in order to determine the incidence of cancer among asbestos exposed workers. I believe you can rest assured that Dr. Lanza must not have found much cancer in this plant or Doctor Smith would not be recommending him.
>
> [No such study was reported by Dr. Lanza, nor has any other trace of it been found.]

Shoemaker continued,

> (Dr. Smith) said that where a claim for lung cancer among (J-M employees) did arise, they have only paid for it on the basis of the employee showing evidence of advanced stages of asbestosis—mainly because of what they feel to be their moral responsibility although, of course with the selfish reason of making a quiet settlement rather than having the case recorded in the law journals.

Memoranda and reports by Shoemaker and his co-workers at American Mutual mostly pertain to the compensation coverage provided to Keasbey & Mattison Company. Dust surveys by American Mutual in 1956 and 1958 yielded measurements as high as 90 and 63 MPPCF, respectively, and the insurance people spoke with growing exasperation about the management's unwillingness to clean up its Meredith, N.H. plant.[150,151] Ten asbestosis compensation claims in Pennsylvania over a two-year period cost this manufacturer $33,000 in extra insurance premiums.[152]

Asbestosis Compensation in U.S. Navy Shipyards

The U.S. Navy Yard in Charleston, South Carolina (where Dr. W.A. Smith worked), began annual screening of "all workers employed in handling asbestos" in 1939, as Sumner Simpson discovered within a short time. The Yard Dispensary conducted physical examinations and took chest X-rays of these workers.[153,154] Industrial hygiene practices at Naval shipbuilding yards varied widely in the mid-1940s, as Fleischer and his co-workers demonstrated.[155] The use of respiratory protection was advised in some shipyards during World War II but not insisted upon.[156] This was the case despite the Navy's publication of "Minimal Requirements for Safety and Industrial Health in Contract Shipyards," in 1943. The "requirements" included the segregation of dusty work, use of exhaust ventilation and respirators, and periodic medical examinations of workers handling asbestos insulation materials.[157]

Although Fleischer and co-workers reported several cases of asbestosis in U.S. Navy yards, they said nothing about compensation for disability. The Long Beach (California) Naval Shipyard was apparently among the first to confront the question of compensation.

By 1958, at least one former employee there was receiving compensation for asbestosis, which probably was started in 1956.[158,159] Surveys conducted in 1958 through 1961 identified additional cases of asbestosis including two on compensation as of June, 1961.[159] Marr reported in 1964 that five Long Beach Naval Shipyard insulators were retired on disability compensation for asbestosis, and another had received such payments until he died of asbestosis in 1962.[160]

The Mancuso Documents

The Navy's response to compensation matters could be said to have been as disorganized as its approach to prevention of asbestosis in the first place. This cannot be said of many asbestos companies, who managed compensation affairs at high levels. An example of this is provided by records of the Philip Carey Manufacturing Company in the early 1960s.

The Indiana State Board of Health informed Carey executive Louis Pechstein early in 1961 that asbestos in "Carey-temp" insulation was "toxic." Carey's own contract insulators had complained to the health authorities.[161] In addition to the contract unit compensation claims already noted in Table 3, Carey was directed to pay William E. Latto compensation for permanent and total disability in 1962. Mr. Latto had been an insulation worker for 35 years, and filed his claim in Ohio in 1961.[162]

In 1962, at the recommendation of consulting actuaries, Carey hired Dr. Thomas Mancuso as Consulting Medical Director for "long range development of a plan for company-wide observations relative to sickness and mortality, data of other plants at different geographical locations, and evaluation of medical services in relation to employee exposure, and the resolution of potential or actual industrial health problems."[163] It was hoped that:

> From the claims standpoint, Dr. Mancuso, as a nationally accredited expert, can help us differentiate an expensive asbestosis or silicosis case from non-occupational illness such as cancer and bronchitis, and make the defense stand up.[164]

The author of this prediction was Louis A. Pechstein, Assistant Secretary of the company.

Dr. Mancuso conducted a survey of conditions at the Ohio plant and recommended extensive industrial hygiene changes, not only inside the plant but in terms of consumer warnings and air pollution control. These recommendations were couched in terms of promoting public and consumer protection while avoiding lawsuits and compensation claims.[165]

In August of 1963 Dr. Mancuso transmitted to the company a series of scientific reports on the effects of asbestos, of asbestosis, lung cancer and mesothelioma that occurred among insulators, neighbors, and workers in manufacturing processes. These reports included the findings of Dr. Irving Selikoff (8 months prior to their publication), on the very high death rate from cancer and asbestosis among insulation workers.[165] Mancuso reported not only to lesser officials, but also to John W. Humphrey, President of the company.[166,167]

He warned of the fallacy of any asbestos manufacturing company relying upon the Braun-Truan (Industrial Hygiene Foundation) report to deny lung cancer compensation claims or liability; because, in Mancuso's analysis, the study was scientifically flawed.[167]

Dr. Mancuso submitted a confidential report to top management on Sept. 23, 1963. The report contained specific recommendations that applied to each of the company's operations, including the Canadian asbestos mines and processing plants, for the prevention and control of occupational diseases, for the control of air pollution and for the provision of technical advisory services to product users. Mancuso advised the officials of the company to discontinue their national practice of putting sub-contractor insulators on their payroll because of the occupational disease liability.[168] Referring to the overall industry response to the cancer threat, he said:

> Internally, within the company, the question has been raised as to why medical problems, particularly relating to cancer and asbestos, were not recognized before. Actually, they were recognized, but the asbestos industry chose to ignore and deny their existence...
>
> It is also possible that there was no desire by these companies to recognize the problem because of the workmen's compensation implications.

Mancuso's analysis of the asbestos industry's conduct was similar to a more general analysis published by a British factory inspector. This man, Bryan Harvey, had studied at the Harvard School of Public Health and learned about the American system from people including Philip Drinker. Harvey said:[169]

> While compensation insurance, the backbone of the American system, has done so much to stimulate the control of known occupational hazards, it may not to the same extent encourage either the medical profession or the industrial hygienists to discover new industrial diseases and hazards. British industry as a whole has come to accept perhaps more readily the implications of research into industrial disease and does not now to any marked degree contest their results. American industry in insisting on scientific proof of toxic dangers and their presence in the atmosphere seems to delay to some extent the application of measures of control, and this may account for some occupational diseases being undiagnosed in the United

> States while in this country they are accepted without controversy.

Carey continued to manufacture asbestos insulation, without affixing warning labels, for the rest of the 1960s.

Compensation at the Asbestos Mines in Canada

The compensation story would not be complete without a discussion of the situation in Quebec, where the Provincial economy was heavily dependent on asbestos mining. The mines were the largest in the world, and owned for the most part by companies in the United States and England. Asbestos mining companies began to send pathological material and chest X-rays for review by the Saranac Laboratory in 1942. Dr. Gardner and his successor Dr. Vorwald examined the tissue specimens sent by Ivan Sabourin, the lawyer for the industry association, and wrote medical reports of their findings. In the late 1940s Johns-Manville officials Hugh Jackson and Dr. Kenneth Smith also started sending material in to Saranac, from deceased employees at the mines and manufacturing plants. Many of the reports from Saranac were used in the defense of compensation claims.

At the outset in developing a relationship with Dr. Gardner, Sabourin took the liberty of rewriting the doctor's "opinion" in an asbestosis case and sending back his revised version for Gardner's signature. Explaining some of the changes, the lawyer wrote (May 6, 1942):

> I have also deleted from your opinion, as worded for the benefit of my clients, portions which I submit to you respectfully do not seem to alter the meaning of the opinion as a whole, that is of the conclusions, yet are very informative but need not be tabled at this stage unless in rebuttal.

Sabourin explained,

> For instance, I have deleted the report of chemical analysis as I should prefer not to give these data until it has become opportune.

The file of this case contains no indication that Dr. Gardner objected to the attorney's assistance in writing medico-legal opinions.[170]

Sabourin and Dr. Cartier at the Thetford Industrial Clinic then proceeded to send another 36 cases to Saranac for review between 1942 and the departure of Dr. Vorwald in 1953. More than half of these cases were identifiably the subjects of workers' compensation claims. The largest single source of material was Asbestos Corporation Limited (17 cases by 1953), followed by Bell Asbestos Mines (11 cases), Johns-Manville (5 mine workers), and Johnson's Company (6 cases). At least 7 of the asbestos miners were diagnosed as having died with lung cancer in combination with varying degrees of asbestosis.[171]

The claim of Alphonse Labbé appears to have been the first case fought in Canada over the compensability of lung cancer in an asbestos miner. More than three days of testimony were heard, with Dr. Lanza active in the defense of Bell Asbestos Mines (subsidiary of Turner & Newall, U.K.).[172] Q.A.M.A. lawyer credited Lanza with "debunking certain alleged figures, relating to cancer incidence in asbestos workers in the British Isles."

In 1949, an historic strike occurred, largely due to widespread anger over the unhealthy conditions in the mines and mills. Documentation from this era also tells us something about the state of occupational disease compensation available to the asbestos miners. Familiar patterns of information concealment are seen here, too.

Starting on January 12, 1949, *Le Devoir,* a Montreal newspaper, began to carry tragic and vivid reports by Burton Le Doux.[173] Le Doux's report, *Asbestosis,* was also printed in English.[174] For the next month almost daily news reports in *Le Devoir* discussed asbestosis in the miners. Le Doux described cases of individuals crippled by asbestosis contracted from working in mines of Quebec Asbestos Corporation, owned by Philip Carey Manufacturing Company of the U.S.A. He charged both the company and the Provincial government with "criminal negligence," describing the unhealthy conditions in the asbestos mining region as a "charnel house." As of 1948, Le

Doux wrote, no one from Carey's East Broughton mines had ever brought suit against the company for compensation, much less received an award. He assailed the local doctors, one of whom reportedly said,

> If we told the workmen of East Broughton that they were affected by asbestosis, it would cost the Company too much money.

The lack of compensation claims was thus ascribed to the workers' ignorance, corrupt government officials and doctors, and the forbidding complexities of the legal system.[174]

Le Doux's articles aroused a great deal of feeling, and may have played a critical role in what followed. Contract negotiations had begun in December, 1948, and on February 14, 1949 the union decided not to submit the issue to arbitration. The strike started at Johns-Manville's mine in Asbestos, Quebec and immediately spread to Thetford Mines, crippling the asbestos industry for the next five months. During this time, press accounts in *Le Devoir* and other newspapers continued to emphasize the industrial hygiene demands of the strikers. Practically the only mines that kept running during the strike were relatively small, marginal operations of Philip Carey in East Broughton, where Le Doux had done his initial investigations.

Pierre Elliott Trudeau's account, *The Asbestos Strike,* noted that[173]

> Among the events which most concerned the miners, we should mention their long struggle to get asbestosis recognized as an industrial disease. In 1949, this struggle had won them only a partial victory, because monetary compensation was still granted only to those whose health had been impaired by asbestos dust for a period of *5 years* or more. (emphasis added)

Although the unions did induce some outlays for dust control by the mining companies ($5,500,000 set aside for this purpose by Johns-Manville), the compensation law appears not to have been changed by the strike.

Just as the strike was about to begin, Johns-Manville completed a medical survey of 708 workers at its mine in Asbestos, Quebec.[175] Dr. Kenneth W. Smith reported to J-M top management that 59 of these men were "probable compensation claims." He went on,

> Elimination of the dust in their working areas, or transferring them to non-dusty jobs will help the men, but will not prevent claims for compensation being submitted.

Smith said that, although some of the miners had asbestosis, none were yet disabled, and so none had been told they had asbestosis. Smith even recommended (with no apparent success) that when a man did become disabled, the company should itself submit the compensation claim and pay the man for his disability.

Dr. Arthur Vorwald of the Saranac Laboratory was presented as a medical expert to a Quebec arbitration tribunal during the 1949 strike. He told the panel,[176]

> I would like to compare lungs with our two arms, two legs, and our two eyes. When one goes bad we can use the other one, and we have two lungs in case of disease.

In Thetford Mines, one clinic has serviced several asbestos companies (Bell Asbestos Mines, Lake Asbestos, Carey's Canadian mines, and Asbestos Corp. Ltd.) since around 1940. In 1975, the Thetford Mines clinic was exposed in the *Montreal Star* as telling miners they were in good health, while some had such severe asbestosis that it killed them within the next two years.[177] Despite Dr. Cartier's protestations of good intent, it is apparent that his practices as director of the Thetford Clinic since 1940 lessened the companies' workers' compensation outlays.[177]

Obstacles to Workers' Compensation

In the 1940s, one would perhaps not have expected to find many workers compensated for disability from occupational cancer. The New York State Workmen's Compensation Board reported that in 1948, there were 4 compensated cancer claims in New York (out of over 100,000 workers' compensations cases "closed" in that year). In 1947, there were none.[178]

The epidemiological studies on insulators by Dr. Irving Selikoff and his co-workers, reported in the literature in 1964-1965, are credited even by the asbestos industry with establishing unequivocally the existence of a cancer hazard from occupational exposure to asbestos.[179,180] Yet even after the big asbestos conference held by the New York Academy of Sciences in 1964, the New York Workmen's Compensation Board was not deluged with claims. (See Tables 5-6.)

Table 5 shows that in New York, a state with nearly one tenth of the U.S. population and where there are some of the best hospitals in the country, only about 5 people a year have been

Table 5. Occupational Diseases: Cancer
Number of Cases and Amount of Compensation[1]

Compensated Cases Closed, New York State, 1966 – 1981

Year of closing	Number of cases	Amount of compensation
1966	6	$ 64,631
1967	3	8,773
1968	6	30,386
1969	4	23,334
1970	7	28,207
1971	9	111,301
1972	6	44,409
1973	4	48,041
1974	6	47,343
1975	1	850
1976	2	65,954
1977	5	67,649
1978	3	66,021
1979	5	64,209
1980	7	171,913
1981	10	681,870

[1]Includes the estimated value of future payments for death, permanent total, and non-schedule permanent partial disability cases. Does not include the cost of medical and hospital care.

compensated for occupational cancer.[181] In some states, there has probably not yet been a single compensated occupational cancer case (as of 1978, two states had not yet even awarded anyone compensation for asbestosis).[182] Nationwide, the figure would appear to be on the order of no more than several hundred compensated cases of occupational cancer from all causes per year under workers' compensation. This can be contrasted with National Institute for Occupational Safety and Health (U.S.) estimates of 100,000 deaths from occupational disease per year, the U.S. Department of Health, Education, and Welfare's long-term projections of over 50,000 cancer cases per year from asbestos alone, an estimate by Dr. Nicholson and

Table 6. Asbestosis and other Dust Diseases[1]
Number of Cases and Amount of Compensation
Compensation Cases Closed, New York State, 1966 - 1981

Year of closing	Number of cases	Amount of compensation awarded[2]
1966	15	$ 317,939
1967	4	147,619
1968	21	421,707
1969	10	257,240
1970	19	336,038
1971	19	433,099
1972	17	493,433
1973	20	433,624
1974	19	510,343
1975	28	1,026,901
1976	19	812,871
1977	29	1,545,577
1978	37	1,205,001
1979	43	1,780,682
1980	43	2,755,600
1981	27	1,880,660

[1]Does not include silicosis, but includes other dust diseases. Roughly two thirds of these claims are asbestosis cases (29 in 1980 and 16 in 1981).

[2]Includes estimated present value of future payments for death, permanent total, and non-schedule permanent partial disability cases. Does not include the cost of medical and hospital care.

his co-workers of 9500 asbestos-related cancer deaths per year currently and Doll and Peto's figure of 8,000 to 12,000 occupational cancer deaths per year in the U.S. (4,000 to 8,000 from asbestos).[183-186] Admittedly, there are no good figures on the incidence rate of occupational cancer, but it appears that far less than one percent receive compensation. A report to Congress in 1980 concluded that 5 percent of those *severely disabled from an occupational disease* received workers' compensation.[187] The plight of the insulation workers illustrates in part why this is so.

A claim must be made in the state where disability-producing work took place. In the Asbestos Workers' Union, men travelled all over the country doing contract work on the construction and maintenance of industrial plants, power plants, and ships. Disease developed long after exposure, and it was not uncommon for a man to find out he had asbestosis or cancer after he had moved far from the scene of the crime, so to speak. Then, to receive compensation, the worker was required to get on a plane back to New Jersey or Texas, hire a lawyer to take on the case, fly in his doctor to testify, produce the old employment records, name as defendants all the firms that employed him using asbestos (and maybe the products used as well), be prepared to prove that his disease could not have occurred from other employment or personal habits (e.g., smoking), and of course, show that his work within that state was sufficient to produce the disease. There would follow the usual sparring by insurance carriers' lawyers, who might argue that on-ship insulation work was not in the legal jurisdiction of the state compensation law, that the statute of limitations had run out before the claim was filed, and so on. This would be followed by company-paid physicians' testimony that the disease was of questionable occupational origin, and in their expert opinion the X-rays were not indicative of any more than 22 percent disability. Disability from pneumoconiosis might not be compensable unless it was total, and even total disability might not be compensable if the worker managed to find a desk job and still earn a living despite severe damage to his lungs. After several years of re-scheduling hearings to meet the convenience of all the judges, lawyers and doctors involved, the man might live to be offered a compromise-and-release agreement by the defendant companies or even a compensation award by the state compensation board. While all the litigation went on, the man had to somehow come up with the means to pay his medical bills and support his family. Should he resort in his desperation to taking a job, he could expect to have the defendants' lawyers introduce this as evidence that he was not really disabled at all. If a disability or death award was finally granted, the worker or his widow would, of course, have to pay the attorney's fee out of it.

Medical coverage was limited in many states to a set length of time or total financial outlay by the employer. Past limits on medical coverage included dollar amounts (e.g., $10,500 in Kansas, $3,000 in West Virginia, $880 in Wyoming) and short time limitations as recently as 1974.[15] So there was even less of an incentive to file for compensation for occupational disease in earlier times where less liberal "benefits" were provided by the laws. In some cases, workers had to know enough to choose among states where they had worked, to avoid restrictive statutes of limitations and ceilings on medical coverage.[182] Unlike most of the obvious defects of workers' compensation laws, limits on medical coverage appear to have been eliminated in all 50 states.[188]

Workers' compensation awards for occupational diseases can be pitifully small in cases where exposure occurred long ago and the claim is not barred by the statute of limitations. Asch gives an example of a man who only worked with asbestos in the 1920s and died from mesothelioma in 1975. The compensation judge awarded death benefits to the man's widow of $15 a week based on the man's salary of $17.50 a week at the time he was working for Johns-Manville.[189]

It is not surprising, given the adverse legislation and administration of workers' compensation laws in the United States, that the workers began to bring civil suits against the manufacturers of asbestos products and the suppliers of the asbestos fiber they had handled.

Chapter Eleven

Manville Corporation, as it is now called, faced 16,500 unresolved lawsuits for asbestos disease in August of 1982. Manville had won 41 out of 96 cases taken to trial and settled 3,344 cases out of court. In 1982, additional cases were being filed at the rate of *500 per month*. Jury awards for punitive and compensatory damages, sometimes in excess of $1 million, had become increasingly frequent. In 1981, five juries returned verdicts for punitive damages against the company. During the first half of 1982, Manville was found liable for punitive damages in five more suits averaging $616,000 per case.* The legal defense fees were placed at "close to $2 million a month," by mid-1982. Auditors of Manville's annual report to stockholders had by 1980 concluded that the ultimate costs of the litigation "cannot be reasonably determined."[190-193]

On August 26, 1982, Manville Corporation filed for reorganization under the protection of the federal bankruptcy laws. Board Chairman John A. McKinney asserted that "our businesses are in good shape despite this recession," but added, "we are completely overwhelmed by the cost of the asbestos health lawsuits filed against us."[192] The first asbestos manufacturer to file for reorganization under Chapter 11 of the bankruptcy code was UNR Industries (formerly Unarco), several months before Manville. Amatex became the third asbestos defendant to file under Chapter 11 later in 1982.

Epidemiology consultants had advised Manville management that 52,000 such suits in all might eventually be filed. With Manville's average cost of settling claims up to $40,000 each in 1982, other consultants projected a $2 billion estimate for the ultimate cost to the company.[193]

One reason the company went to the bankruptcy court, thereby halting the progress of all damage suits against it, was

*Punitive damages are assessed in addition to damages to compensate for the injury and loss (compensatory damages) when the conduct of the defendant is a gross deviation from societal standards. The purpose is to punish the defendant for past misconduct and to set an example for others to deter them from engaging in similar activities.

because its insurance carriers were refusing to pay hundreds of millions of dollars in product liability insurance coverage, purchased by Manville from 1947-1976.[192,194] The insurers claimed that Manville had hidden information on asbestos hazards from them. Manville then sued 27 insurance companies in 1980, and not until 1985 did the complex trial of this case begin (as settlements were announced with some of the insurers and plaintiffs' attorneys criticized the terms of the first proposed settlements before Judge Lifland). Strained by the litigation of cases that Manville insisted were covered by insurance, along with punitive damage awards (which are not covered by insurance), the corporate management decided to submit to court-supervised direction of its affairs in 1982.

Another reason why Manville took this drastic step was to get the attention of the U.S. Congress, which has been considering various proposals for an "asbestos compensation act" since 1977. All but one of these bills would have completely stopped the filing of new lawsuits. The early proposals called for an industry/government fund and a federally administered procedure for adjudicating claims. Disability compensation would have been limited to about $13,000 a year. The 1985 version, the "Asbestos Workers' Recovery Act," was soundly criticized and denounced as another industry bail-out bill by asbestos victims' groups. Representative Pat Williams finally introduced a bill that had the full support of organized labor; but his Federal Occupational Disease Compensation Act did not impede the filing of civil suits under existing law. It will therefore faced united opposition from industrial and insurance interests.

As the asbestos litigation expanded, Congress has shown little interest in legislating an end to it and creating an expensive, federally-managed system for handling thousands of claims per year. Not a single member of Congress has risen to defend the innocence of the asbestos industry. More recent bills to create a compensation fund financed solely by industry have been coolly greeted by the industry.

Not the least of Manville's reasons for filing under Chapter 11 was the hope that the bankruptcy court would favorably resolve the issue of future claims. Normally, a company emerging from reorganization in bankruptcy court has arranged to settle all debts from its past activities. But some bankruptcy courts have been loath to concoct any scheme to prospectively pay people who haven't yet developed asbestos disease claims but will in the future. These courts were at a loss to find anyone who could really be said to represent future plaintiffs and negotiate on their behalf.

Meanwhile, Manville's legal costs continued to be close to near $2 million a month, and the lawsuits continued to be filed. Over the six years of the Manville Chapter 11 "reorganization," more than $106 million was billed for fees and expenses by law firms, accountants, and investment bankers. The company initially offered $400 million to settle 20,000 outstanding cases (an average of $20,000 each), to cover its share of the liability in these cases. Included in the total were several thousand cases filed against Manville after the company sought the refuge of the bankruptcy court. Plaintiffs' attorneys demanded at least $32,500 per case, the figure Manville had given for its payments in 1982, net of legal defense costs.

Finally, a bankruptcy reorganization plan was finalized in 1988, creating a "trust" with Manville's insurance coverage and other payments to be made over a 25-year period. By 1990, the funding initially provided was nearly exhausted from the initial settlements of older cases (See final chapter for further discussion of Manville trust.)

In enacting the Bankruptcy Amendment and Federal Judgeship Act of 1984, Congress made the Chapter 11 escape route considerably less appealing to asbestos litigation defendants. This legislation protects the right of trial by jury in federal courts for plaintiffs with personal injury and wrongful death cases, even against companies in Chapter 11.

CONCLUSION

We can conclude from all this that most workers with asbestosis and cancer from asbestos didn't file workers' compensation claims or damage suits. However, the industry and its insurers were very much aware of those who did, and the defense of compensation claims and suits was a concern to top management at least as early as the 1930s.

Only fragmentary records have been discovered regarding compensation, compared to what must once have existed. State agencies have long since destroyed their records of the early claims (pre-1950) in most cases, and in some states where the records have been preserved they are guarded against public access. Despite the openness of the original proceedings, records of them are thus excluded from our consideration. For the most part, the defendants and their insurance carriers have been at a loss to produce their own records regarding asbestos disease compensation.

What may have begun as a shortsighted reaction became the *modus operandi* of the industry's top managers: let the lawyers handle it, buy insurance and hire medical experts as necessary, and minimize the cost of the claims by every legal and political means. Dust control as a means of claims cost control was economically unattractive because of its high initial and operating cost and its rather delayed reduction in disease incidence and severity. It was cheaper to rig the compensation laws with short statutes of limitations and miserly limits of medical liability.

Asbestos victims have consequently found product liability suits attractive, despite the long wait before trial, the expense, and even the subrogation rights of their employers' insurers who have paid some of them workers' compensation. It remains to be seen if the defendant companies will be able to stem this tidal wave of liability through the legislative process.

Bills to do away with the concept of strict liability, limit pain and suffering awards, lower plaintiffs' attorneys fees, make losing plaintiffs pay defendants' legal fees, increase the burden of proof for punitive damages, and in other ways discourage personal injury suits have been urged upon the Congress with increasing fervor, though not yet with success. Business alliances involving hundreds of manufacturers, insurers, and trade associations, have come ever closer to succeeding in getting such bills enacted by Congress, with support from the Reagan administration.[195]

In the state legislatures, the asbestos litigation defendants and others with similar problems have been more successful.[196] Changes introduced into state tort laws have followed these lines:

- imposition of ceiling amounts that plaintiffs can be awarded for non-economic loss, as for pain and suffering
- elimination of "joint and several liability," whereby damages for an extinct or bankrupt defendant would have been assessed to viable co-defendants rather than deducted at the expense of the injured party
- erection of statute of limitations so that no damage suit can be filed more than (10 or so) years after the sale of the product
- introduction of additional defenses to damage suits (e.g., absence of a government standard connotes acceptability—a state-of-the-art defense)

Compensation was seen as the Achilles Heel of the asbestos industry long ago. Dr. Donnelly's bitter words in 1936 have proved prophetic:[192]

> An industrial worker is entitled to every protection that may safeguard his health, so that he may earn a livelihood for himself and family for at least a reasonable period of years in the work in which he is most skilled. If he is prevented from continuing in such work because of impairment or health through no fault of his own, he is entitled to some remuneration for his loss of earning power. That protection of asbestos workers has been woefully lacking in the past has been definitely shown. It is imperative that such protection, as nearly complete as possible, be provided by mill owners. *Efficient protective devices will be far less expensive in the final check up than the aggregate of numerous claims for compensation and frequent damage suits.* That complete protection can be afforded by

> the devices in use at the present time seems to be somewhat doubtful, but workers are entitled to the highest type of protection which the engineers familiar with the hazard can provide. (emphasis added)

What Donnelly might not have imagined, with asbestosis and asbestos cancer taking an increasing toll of death and disease over the next 40 years, was that compensation costs could be held in check for as long as they were. And because of the long latency of asbestos diseases, the businessmen running many asbestos companies apparently chose to put off the day of reckoning for as long as they could. Sumner Simpson handed it down to his son William Simpson. Dr. Lanza retired as a Professor of Industrial Medicine at New York University, and today research laboratories at the school's Tuxedo Park, N.Y. campus are named in his honor. [Further discussion of asbestos compensation and efforts to get N.Y.U. to rename the Lanza laboratories is included in the last chapter]

REFERENCES

1. Barth, P.S. and H.A. Hunt, *Workers' Compensation and Work Related Illnesses and Diseases,* Cambridge: MIT Press, 1982, pp.2-8.

2. Engels, F. *The Condition of the Working Class in England in 1844,* (published 1845), Woodstock, New York: Beckman Publ. edition, 1973.

3. Doyal, L., *The Political Economy of Health,* Boston: South End Press, 1981, pp. 50-51.

4. Clutterbuck, R.C., "The State of Industrial Ill-Health in the United Kingdom," *Internat. J. Health Serv. 10:* 149-160 (1980).

5. Oliver, T., *Dangerous Trades,* London: John Murray, 1902, p. 13.

6. *Standardization of Industrial Accident Statistics,* U.S. Bureau of Labor Statistics Bull. 276, 1920, pp. 98-99.

7. Bale, A., "Assuming the Risks: Occupational Disease in the Years Betore Workers' Compensation," Am. J. Indust. Med. 13: 499-514 (1988).

8. Hoffman, F.L., *Industrial Accidents,* U.S. Bur. Labor Bull. No. 408 (1908).

9. Eastman, C., *Work-Accidents and the Laws,* New York: Russell Sage Foundation, 1910.

10. Berman, D., *Death on the Job,* New York: Monthly Review Press, 1978, pp. 20-21.

11. Mackey, H. *Seventh Annual Meeting Internat. Assoc. Indust. Accident Boards and Commissions,* U.S. Bur. Labor Statistics Bull. No. 281, 1921, p. 429.

12. Trasko, V.M., "Socioeconomic Aspects of the Pneumoconioses," *Arch. Environ. Health 9:* 521-528 (1964).

13. Sayer, H., "The Trend in Occupational Disease Legislation," *Trans. 27th Nat. Safety Congress,* Chicago: Nat. Safety Council, 1938, pp. 211-219.

14. Sutherland, C.L., "Workmen's Compensation in Pulmonary Disease," *J. State Med. 40:* 709-715 (1932).

15. Workmen's Compensation and Unemployment Insurance under State Laws, January 1, 1974. AFL-CIO, Washington, D.C.

16. Hamilton, A., *Exploring the Dangerous Trades,* Boston: Little, Brown & Co., 1943.

17. Baader, E.W., "Asbestose," *Deut. Med. Woch. 65:* 408-409 (1939).

18. Steingut, R., and I.J. Selikoff, "Perspectives on Disability Compensation for Occupational Diseases," International Conference on Disability Compensation for Occupational Diseases, New York, June, 1984.

19. Brodeur, P., and M.P. Thornton, "No Way to Treat New York's Asbestos Victims," *New York Times,* Nov. 30, 1985.

20. Felton, J., "Occupational Medicine in the United States," *Clinical Medicine for the Occupational Physician* (M. Alderman and M.J. Hanley, eds.), New York: Marcel Dekker, 1982, pp. 1-23. And personal communication to the author.

21. Hardy, H.L. *Challenging Man-Made Disease,* New York: Praeger, 1983. And personal communication to the author.

22. Hueper, W.C. *Adventures of a Physician in Occupational Cancer: A Medical Cassandra's Tale* (unpublished), National Library of Medicine, Bethesda, MD, 1976, pp. 218-236. And personal communication to the author.

23. Irwin, T. "On the Job Cancer—The Killer They Won't Track Down," *Cavalier* (Jan. 1962).

24. Sicherman, B. *Alice Hamilton: A Life in Letters,* Cambridge: Harvard University Press, 1984.

25. Golz, H.H., *et al.,* "Report of an Investigation of Threshold Limit Values and Their Usage," *J. Occup. Med. 8:* 280-283 (1966).

26. Stokinger, H.E., "Current Problems of Setting Occupational Exposure Standards," *Arch. Environ. Health 19:* 277-281 (1969).

27. Lanza, A.J., "Asbestosis," *J.A.M.A. 106:*368-369 (1936).

28. "Workmen's Compensation for Silicosis," *Safety Eng. 57:* 71-74 (1934).

29. Lanza, A.J. (ed.), *Silicosis and Asbestosis,* London and New York, Oxford Univ. Press, 1938, pp. 64, 405-406.

30. *Anna Pirskowski vs. Johns-Manville Corp.* U.S. Distr. Court, New Jersey. Filed May 28, 1929 and dismissed June 13, 1934. Similar cases filed by other Johns-Manville workers: F. Bartus, C. Perone, J. Perrone, J. Zackwiejz, H. Zackwiejz, P. Lasin, R. Marshall, A. Strelec, S. Rinaldo, A. Graziosi, V. DeMuro, J. Stepka, V. Stepka, M. Stepka, and M. Grabow (all represented by attorney S. Greenstone).

31. Minutes of Meeting of the Board of Directors of Johns-Manville Corporation, New York, April 24, 1933.

32. Williams, S.A., letter to A.R. Fisher (Aug. 29, 1933); and attachment, "Questions Asked Dr. A.J. Lanza and His Answers Verbatim."

33. *Norwood, W. v. Johns-Manville, Inc.* filed March 23, 1935 in Lake County, Illinois Circuit Court. Similar suits were filed by C. Jacobs, W. Canedy, D. Irons, F. Pool, F. Bankhead, W. Cunningham, L. Nixon, A. Peele, S. Clark, F. Dixon, J. Benett, E. Norwood, J. Simmons, C. Gaines, J.H. Nye, S. Ruthkowski, J. Tillis, C. Barney, A. Belcher, R. Worthington, E. Hacker (attorneys for these people were L.M. Tarpey, D.H. Berg, and L.T. Bailey). Each of these suits was removed to the jurisdiction of the federal court.

34. Norris, L.V., "Occupational Disease Claims," *Insur. Index 14-15:*75 (1935). Abstract in Davis, G.G. *et al., The Pneumokonioses Book III* Chicago: Medical Press, 1937, pp. 547-548.

35. Moss, D.B., "Occupational Diseases—The Illinois Law," *Proceedings of the Seventeenth Annual Meeting of the Medical and Surgical Section,* Association of American Railroads, Atlantic City, N.J. 17-22 (1937).

36. *Vogel v. Johns-Manville Products Corp.* N.E. 2d 716 (1936).

37. McVittie, J.C., "Asbestosis in Great Britain," *Ann. N.Y. Acad. Sci. 132:*129-138 (1965).

38. Industrial Disablement Benefit C.W.I. 53 /50 (K.I.) *Reported Decisions of the Commissioner under the National Insurance (Industrial Injuries) Acts.* Vol. 1. 1948-1952. London: H.M. Stationery Ofc. 1955.

39. "Asbestosis Among Women," *Brit. Med. J. 1:*278 (1929).

40. "Asbestosis and Silicosis," *Brit. Med. J. 1:*379 (1929).

41. "Woman's Death from Asbestosis," *Lancet 2:*775 (1931).

42. Livingstone, R. and Street, E.W., "A Case of Pulmonary Asbestosis," *Brit. Med. J. 1:*939 (1950).

43. Lanza, A.J., McConnell, W.J., and J.W. Fehnel, "Effects of the Inhalation of Asbestos Dust on the Lungs of Asbestos Workers," *Publ. Health Rep. 50:*1-12 (1935).

44. Wheatley, G.W. *Tuberculosis and Asbestosis,* Metropolitan Life Insurance Co. (1944). This report includes data on asbestosis in asbestos miners from the 1930 study of F. Pedley and A. J. Lanza. Ref. 43 also alludes to the miners survey.

45. Lanza, A.J. and R.J. Vane, "Industrial Dusts and the Mortality from Pulmonary Disease," *Am. Rev. Tuberc. 39:*419 (1939).

46. Hobart, G., letter to V. Brown, December 15, 1934.

47. Lanza, A.J. *et al.,* "Effects of The Inhalation of Asbestos Dust upon the Lungs of Asbestos Workers," Metropolitan Life Insurance Company, New York, 1930.

48. Brown, V., letter to A.J. Lanza, December 10, 1934.

49. Brown, V., letter to A.J. Lanza, December 21, 1934.

50. Merewether, E.R.A., "A Memorandum on Asbestosis," *Tubercle 15:* 69-81, 109-118, and 152-159 (1933-1934).

51. "Industrial Diseases and Poisoning in British Factories, 1931," *Monthly Labor Rev. 35:*834-836 (1932).

52. "Industrial Diseases and Poisoning in British Factories, 1932," *Monthly Labor Rev. 37:*864-866 (1933).

53. "Industrial Diseases and Poisoning in British Factories, 1933," *Monthly Labor Rev. 39:*1398-1400 (1934).

54. Ellman, P., "Pulmonary Asbestosis: Its Clinical, Radiological, and Pathological Features, and Associated Risk of Tuberculous Infection," *J. Indust. Hyg. 15:*165-183 (1933).

55. Ellman, P., "Pneumoconiosis. Part III Pulmonary Asbestosis," *Brit. J. Radiol. 7:*281-295 (1934).

56. Napier, A.J., Chief Judge of Compensation, State of New Jersey, Personal communication (Aug. 29, 1978).

57. Wood, W.B., "Pulmonary Asbestosis," *Tubercle 10:*353-363 (1929).

58. Wood, W.B., "Pulmonary Asbestosis," *Bull. Hyg. 4:*978 (1929).

59. "Pulmonary Disease Caused by Asbestos Dust," *Monthly Labor Review 30:*82 (1930).

60. "Pulmonary Asbestosis," *Asbestos 11:*20 (March, 1930).

61. "Pulmonary Asbestosis," Memo Report #22, Market Analysis Section, Sales Promotion Dept., Johns-Manville Corp., New York (March 21, 1930).

62. Rossiter, A.S. (*Asbestos* magazine), letter to S. Simpson (Raybestos-Manhattan), September 25, 1935.

63. Simpson, S. (Raybestos-Manhattan), letter to V. Brown (Johns-Manville), Oct. 1, 1935.
64. Brown, V., letter to S. Simpson, Oct. 3, 1935.
65. Rossiter, A.S., letter to S. Simpson, March 23, 1939.
66. Brown, V., letter to S. Simpson, Nov. 3, 1941.
67. "Occupational Diseases are Not Generally Understood," *Nat. Underwriter 36*:28 (Dec. 15, 1932).
68. Jones, F.R., "Occupational Disease Compensation," *Industr. Med. 5*:179-183 (1936).
69. Donnelly, J., "Pulmonary Asbestosis," *Am. J. Publ. Health 24*:1275-1281 (1934).
70. Jones, F.R., "Occupational Diseases," *Mech. Eng. 57*:90-91 (1935).
71. Jones, F.R., articles abstracted in *The Pneumoconioses (Silicosis) Literature and Laws Book III* by G.G. Davis, E.M. Salmonsen, and J.L. Earlywine (Chicago: Chicago Medical Press, 1937), pp. 385-391.
72. Jones, F.R., "Problems in Compensation for Occupational Diseases," *Indust. Med. 4*:222-224 (1935).
73. "Jones Gives Answers to Disease Problems," *Insur. Field 64*:10 (1935).
74. Brown, V., letter to M.F. Judd (Raybestos-Manhattan), Jan. 22, 1935, and attached "Memorandum Re: Mellon Institute of Industrial Research Symposium on Dust Problems—Pittsburgh, Jan. 15, 1935."
75. George, A., *Discussion of Industrial Accidents and Diseases*, 1935 Convention of the International Association of Industrial Accident Boards and Commissions, Asheville, N.C. United States Division of Labor Standards Bull. No. 4, Washington, pp. 80-82 (1936).
76. Simpson, S., letter to E.H. Jeffords, Oct. 31, 1936.
77. Lanza, A.J., letter to J. Mitchell (attorney in Charleston, S.C.), Oct. 30, 1936.
78. Simpson, S., letter to E.H. Jeffords, Nov. 5, 1936.
79. Simpson, S., letters to V. Brown (Johns-Manville), F.H. Schluter (Thermoid Rubber Co.), A.S. Blagden (Keasbey and Mattison Co.), H.D. LaMont (Asbestos Manufacturing Co.) and G.M. Williams (Russell Manufacturing Co.), Nov. 10, 1936.
80. Hawes, J.B., "Dangerous Dusts," *New Engl. J. Med. 216*:162-165 (1937).
81. Bowditch, M. (Massachusetts Div. Occup. Hyg.), letter to A.J. Lanza (Metropolitan Life), Dec. 10, 1937.
82. Dewey, B. (Dewey & Almy Chemical Co.), letter to M. Bowditch (Feb. 23, 1938).
83. Gardner, L.U. (Saranac Laboratory), letter to M. Bowditch (Mar. 22, 1938).

84. Lanza, A.J., letter to M. Bowditch (Mar. 8, 1938).
85. George, A.W. and R.D. Leonard, "An X-Ray Study of Workmen in the Asbestos Industry Covering a Period of Ten Years," *Radiology 33*:196-202 (1939).
86. "Asbestosis," *The Employers' Group Engineering Manual,* (June 1, 1937), pp. 1-2. Produced in *Commercial Union v. Pittsburgh Corning,* E. Dist. PA. CA-81-2129.
87. Selikoff, I.J., E.C. Hammond, and J. Churg, "Carcinogenicity of Amosite Asbestos," *Arch. Environ. Health 25*:183-186 (1972).
88. Affidavit of Charles J. Roemer. U.S. Bankruptcy Court, Southern District of New York. *In re Johns-Manville Corporation et al.,* Debtors (Sept. 29, 1982).
89. Complete brochure ("Aetna says Fiberglas Workers Enjoy . . .") in files of Industrial Health Foundation, Pittsburgh, PA.
90. Hill, J. (General Agent, Aetna Life Insurance Co.), letter to Edward Ames (Owens-Corning Fiberglas), June 11, 1941.
91. Ames, E.C., "Asbestos Workers Union," memorandum to E.J. Marshall (OCF); and untitled memorandum to H. Boeschenstein (OCF), both Jan. 7, 1942.
92. Ames, E.C., letter to Dr. A.E. Canfield (Nov. 22, 1944); and letters from Canfield to Ames (Nov. 21, 1944 and one undated).
93. Dominic Bertogliat file (P. 48-415), Vorwald archives, Armed Forces Institute of Pathology, Walter Reed Hospital, Washington, D.C.
94. Vorwald archives patient file P-44-326, Armed Forces Institute of Pathology.
95. Deposition of Dr. Robert J. Ritterhoff, Cincinnati, Jan. 30, 1986 *State of Maryland v. Keene Corp. et al.* Civ. No. 1108600, Circuit Court, Anne Arundel County, MD.
96. Vorwald archives patient file P-48-430, Armed Forces Institute of Pathology.
97. Russell, A.E., *Effects of Dust Upon the Respiratory System* (Proceedings of a conference held by the Industrial Commission of Wisconsin, November, 1932), Democrat Press, p. 180.
98. Kuhn, A., "Illness Among Dock Workers at Wilhelmshaven with Special Reference to Industrial Accidents and Disease." *Arch. Gewerbepath. Gewerbehyg. 10*:133-150 (1940).
99. Ahlman, K. and Siltanen, E., "Exposure of Insulation Workers to Asbestos Dust," *Work-Environment-Health 8*:1-5 (1971).
100. Wood, W.B. and Gloyne, S.R., "Pulmonary Asbestosis/A Review of One Hundred Cases," *Lancet 2*:1383-1385 (1934).

101. *Third International Conference of Experts on Pneumoconiosis, Sydney, February-March, 1950, Record of Proceedings.* (Geneva: International Labour Office: 1953) pp. 235-247.

102. Vigliani, E.C., "The Proposed New Insurance Schedule of Occupational Diseases, Suggested Modifications Made in the Light of Experience at the Milan Clinica del Lavoro," *Med. Lavoro 43:*343-355 (1952). Abstract in *Bull. Hyg. 28:*431 (1953).

103. Canepa, G., "Asbestosis in Port Workers," *Zacchia 12:*188-205 (1949). [English summary at end.]

104. Industrial Disablement Benefit C.S.I. 68/49 (K.1.) *Reported Decisions of the Commissioner under the National Insurance (Industrial Injuries) Acts.* Vol. 1. 1948-1952. London: H.M. Stationery Ofc., 1955.

105. Frost, J., "Three Cases of Asbestosis," *Ugeskrift for Laeger 112:*1284-1289 (1950).

106. Stökly, A., "New Schedules of Compensable Industrial Diseases," *Z. Unfallmed. Berufskrankh. 46:*106-110 (1953). Abstract in *Bull. Hyg. 29:*376 (1954).

107. Ahlmark, A., Bruce, T., and A. Nyström, *Silicosis and Other Pneumoconioses in Sweden,* Stockholm: Svenska Bokförlaget, and London: W. Heinemann, Ltd, 1960, pp. 353-357.

108. "Fourth Schedule of Extension of Compensation for Industrial Accidents and Diseases," *Reichsgesetzblatt* Part 1, No. 14 (Jan. 29, 1943).

109. Tabershaw, I., "Report on Industrial Hygiene in the Western Zone of Germany," *Arch. Indust. Hyg. 3:*298-315 (1951).

110. Bauer, K., *Das Krebsproblem,* Berlin: Springer-Verlag, 1949, pp. 238-239.

111. Hueper, W.C., "Cancers of the Respiratory System," *Occupational Tumors and Allied Diseases,* Springfield, Ill: Charles C. Thomas, 1942, p. 405.

112. Hueper, W.C., "Cancer in Its Relation to Occupation and Environment," *Bull. Amer. Soc. Control Cancer 25:*63-69 (1943).

113. Hueper, W.C., "The Significance of Industrial Cancer in the Cancer Problem," *Cancer Res. 7:*47-48 (1947).

114. Brahdy, L., "Discussion," *Dis. Chest 14:*885-888 (1948).

115. Jackson, H., "Industrial Disease Claims/Vernon Hall, Deceased April 28, 1950," Memorandum for Waukegan plant, June 14, 1950. And Vorwald's report in Vorwald archives patient file P-50-495, Armed Forces Institute of Pathology.

116. Answers to Interrogatories, Raybestos-Manhattan Inc.

117. Minutes of Meeting Administrative Committee-Fibrous Products Division, July 9, 1951. And Balch, J.H. (Unarco Vice President), letter to W.S. Haines (Safety and Claims Service, Inc.), April 4, 1952.

118. Castleman, B., and V.W. Towne, "Case Records of the Massachusetts General Hospital," *New Engl. J. Med. 246*:867-872 (1952).

119. Weiss, A., "Pleural Cancer with Asbestosis of the Lungs, Observed Morphologically in Vivo," *Medizinische 3*:93-94 (1953).

120. Hueper, W.C., "Occupational Cancer Hazards," *Workmen's Compensation Problems 1954*. U.S. Bur. Labor Stds. Bull. 180 (1955), pp. 126-144.

121. Hueper, W.C., "Editorials/Silicosis, Asbestosis, and Cancer of the Lung," *Amer. J. Clin. Path. 25*:1388-1390 (1955).

122. Minutes of the Air Hygiene Committee, Asbestos Textile Institute (March 7, 1956).

123. Moore, H.C. Claim No. 68064, Findings and Award, Industrial Accident Commission, San Francisco (Sept. 25, 1940).

124. Rothwell, R.J. Claim No. B7131799 Industrial Accident Board, Boston, Mass. Records at the Board and others procured on discovery from Armstrong Cork.

125. Schepers, G.W.H., "Occupational Chest Diseases," *Modern Occupational Medicine*, 2nd ed., A.J. Fleming, C.A. D'Alonzo, and J.A. Zapp, eds. (Philadelphia: Lea & Febiger, 1960), pp. 463-470.

126. Shoemaker, W.E. Memorandum to N. Kley (American Mutual Liability Insurance Co.). "Asbestos Textile Institute—3/7/56 Air Hygiene Committee Meeting." March 13, 1956.

127. *Hyatt v. Armstrong Cork*. Florida Supreme Court No. 30,185, April 13, 1960. Digested in *Workmen's Compensation Law Reports*, May 24, 1960.

128. *Campbell, E. v. Johns-Manville et al.*, records at Workmen's Compensation Commission of Connecticut, Hartford, Connecticut, 1955. And records provided in discovery by Armstrong Cork.

129. *Riley, J.W. v. Johns-Manville Products, et al.*, Case No 57LA 182-835, Industrial Accident Commission of the State of California, Los Angeles. And records provided in discovery by Armstrong Cork.

130. *McCarrell, E.O. v. Armstrong Cork Co. et al.*, Case No. 56LA 176-684. Industrial Accident Commission of the State of California, Los Angeles. And records provided in discovery by Armstrong Cork.

131. *Swartout, J.E. v. Western Asbestos Company et al.*, Claim No. SF169-171, Industrial Accident Commission of the State of California, San Francisco. Also records provided in discovery by Armstrong Cork.

132. *Dugan v. A.V. Aycock Company, Aycock Corporation, and R.V. Aycock*, Circuit Court of Jackson County, Missouri, at Kansas City (November term, 1933).

133. Gillenwater, P.T. (Knoxville, Tennessee) Personal communication to the author (1982).

134. *LeGrande, F. v. Johns-Manville Products Corp.*, Civil No. 741-57, U.S. District Court for the District of New Jersey.

135. Deposition of William L. Brach, attorney for F. LeGrande, *LeGrande, F. v. Johns-Manville Products Corp.*, taken by P.T. Gillenwater of Knoxville, TN in Springfield, N.J. December 22, 1980.

136. *Wenham, F.C. v. Johns-Manville Products Corp.*, Civil No. 125-61 U.S. District Court, District of New Jersey.

137. Deposition of Franklin Swersky, attorney for F.C. and B.V. Wenham, *Wenham, F.C. v. Johns-Manville Products Corp.*, Taken by P.T. Gillenwater of Knoxville, TN in East Orange, N.J. on December 22, 1980.

138. *Gladys Faciane v. The Travelers Insurance Company, Eagle Picher Company, et al.*, No. 77,004, Div. C, 19th Judicial District Court, Parish of East Baton Rouge, Louisiana.

139. Minutes of the Johns-Manville Compensation Committee Meetings, Manville, N.J., 1957-1958. Authenticated in depositions of C. Sheckler, a member of the Committee.

140. Smith, R.C., "Pneumoconiosis Cases," Confidential (Jan. 12, 1963). Manville document.

141. Notebooks recording dust counts in the Manville plant of Johns-Manville, 1952-1954, in the possession of Karl Asch, Elizabeth, N.J.

142. Kowalski, Ted, Personal communication to the author (1982).

143. *Muldoon, W. v. C.S. Woods Co. and Liberty Mutual Insurance Co.*, 186 New York Supp. 107-909 (Supreme Court, Appellate Div. June 9, 1959).

144. *Muldoon, W. v. Charles S. Woods Co.* New York Supreme Court Appellate Div. No. 1397, June 9, 1959. *Workmen's Compensation Law Reports* pp. 3048-3049, Commerce Clearing House, Inc. 1959.

145. *Lacomastic Corp. vs. Parker,* U.S. District Court, Maryland. Admiralty No. 2617, Feb. 9, 1944. *Workmen's Compensation Law Reporting Service,* Commerce Clearing House, Inc. March 21, 1944, p. 1068.

146. Bowditch, M. (Mass. Div. Occupational Hygiene), letters to A.J. Lanza (Metropolitan Life Insurance Co.), Feb. 13, and 17, 1942. Obtained from the Massachusetts Department of Occupational Hygiene, Boston.

147. Simpson, S., letter to A.J. Lanza (in military service on leave from Metropolitan Life), Dec. 29, 1942.

148. Simpson, S., letter to W.J. McConnell (Metropolitan Life), Dec. 29, 1942.

149. Shoemaker, W.E., Memorandum on *S.P. Knopp v. Leroy Insulating Co.* to Blaine, March 20, 1962 (American Mutual Liability Insurance Co.) Also letter of Dr. R.S. Fisher (Chief Medical Examiner, State of Maryland) to A.M. Porth, Feb. 3, 1962.

150. Shoemaker, W.E., Memorandum on Keasbey and Mattison Co. September 26, 1961, and other documents provided by American Mutual Liability Insurance Co. in discovery.

151. Skinner, J.B. *Report of Occupational Disease Study Keasbey and Mattison Co. Meredith, N.H.* American Mutual Liability Insurance Co., December, 1956.

152. Childs, H.B., "Workmen's Compensation Insurance," Memorandum to R.R. Porter (Keasbey & Mattison Co.) April 18, 1960.

153. Alden, H.S. and W.M. Howell, "The Asbestos Corn," *Arch. Dermat. Syphil. 49:*312-314 (1944).

154. "Hazard of Asbestosis," *Annual Report of the Surgeon General, U.S. Navy* (for 1939), Washington, pp. 24-25 (1941).

155. Fleischer, W.E. *et al.*, "A Health Survey of Pipe Covering Operations in Constructing Naval Vessels," *J. Indust. Hyg. Tox. 28:*9-16 (1946).

156. Stoll, R., Bass, R. and A.A. Angrist, "Asbestos Associated with Bronchogenic Carcinoma," *Arch. Internal. Med. 88:*831-834 (1951).

157. "Minimum Requirements for Safety and Industrial Health in Contract Shipyards," *Indust. Med. Surg. 12:*259-263 (1943).

158. *Occupational Health Hazards.* Release No. 29. U.S. Navy, p. 32 (1961).

159. Hetzel, V.L. *Long Beach Naval Shipyard Study of Asbestos Workers in Relation to Asbestosis* (3-16 June, 1961).

160. Marr, W.T., "Asbestos Exposure During Naval Vessel Overhaul," *Amer. Indust. Hyg. Assoc. J. 25:*264-268 (1964).

161. Edwards, A. (Indiana State Board of Health), letter to L. Pechstein (Philip Carey Manufacturing Co.), Feb. 17, 1961. And Pechstein's Note to File (Feb. 21, 1961).

162. Latto, W.E. State of Ohio Bureau of Workmen's Compensation Claim No. OD 117279. And records of John T. Cantlon, consulting actuaries.

163. Cantlon, J.T., letter and attachment to L.A. Pechstein (Sept. 27, 1962).

164. Pechstein, L.A. (Philip Carey Manufacturing Co.) "Occupational Health of Employees," September 14, 1962 memorandum.

165. Mancuso, T.F., letter to L.J. Knippa (plant manager, Philip Carey Manufacturing Co., Cincinnati, Ohio), May 23, 1963.

166. Mancuso, T.F., letter to L.J. Knippa, August 15, 1963.

167. Deposition of Dr. Thomas F. Mancuso taken by Thomas Henderson of Pittsburgh, PA, on October 17-18, 1979.

168. Mancuso, T.F., "The Philip Carey Manufacturing Company Occupational Health Program," September 23, 1963 (11 pages).

169. Harvey, B. "Some Personal Observations on Industrial Health in the United States of America," *Br. J.Ind. Med. 11:* 222-226 (1954).

170. Vorwald archives patient file P-42-271, Armed Forces Institute of Pathology.

171. Vorwald archives patient files, Armed Forces Institute of Pathology.

172. Vorwald archives patient file P-50-500, esp. letter from I. Sabourin to A.J. Vorwald (July 6, 1951) and letter from P. Cartier (Thetford Industrial Clinic) to A.J. Vorwald (Feb. 21, 1952). Armed Forces Institute of Pathology.

173. Trudeau, P.E. (ed.) *The Asbestos Strike* (Toronto, J. Lorimer and Co., 1974), pp. 183-188, 199, 203, 239-247. (Originally published in French in 1956 as *La Grève de l'Amiante).*

174. LeDoux, B., *Asbestosis,* January, 1949, 55 pp.

175. Smith, K.W., "Industrial Hygiene Survey of Men in Dusty Areas," submitted to V. Brown and J.P. Woodard by A.R. Fisher by Confidential memorandum dated February 3, 1949.

176. Tataryn, L. *Dying for a Living,* Toronto: Deneau and Greenberg, 1979, p. 28.

177. Freed, J., "Asbestos Clinic Let Sick Men Work," and C. Arpin, "Chief Doctor Says He Tried 'To Be Human,'" *The Montreal Star,* March 20, 1975.

178. Allen, E.S., "Abstract of Discussion," *Arch. Indust. Hyg. Occup. Med. 5:*276 (1952).

179. Selikoff, I.J., Hammond, E.C. and Churg, J., "Asbestosis and Neoplasia," *J.A.M.A. 188:*22-26 (1964).

180. "Report and Recommendations of the Working Group on Asbestos and Cancer," *Ann. N.Y. Acad. Sci. 132:*706-721 (1965).

181. *Occupational Diseases.* Records of the New York State Workers' Compensation Board, Office of Research and Statistics, 1983.

182. Steinfurth, R.J., "Care of the Injured Worker: A Labor Perspective," *Ann. N.Y. Acad. Sci. 330:*521-523 (1979).

183. Ashford, N.A., *Crisis in the Workplace: Occupational Disease and Injury* (Cambridge: MIT Press, 1976).

184. Bridbord, K. *et al., Estimates of the Fraction of Cancer in the United States Related to Occupational Factors.* U.S. Department of Health, Education, and Welfare. Washington, D.C., September 15, 1978.

185. Nicholson, W.J., Perkel, G. and I.J. Selikoff, "Occupational Exposure to Asbestos: Population at Risk and Projected Mortality—1980-2030," *Amer. J. Indust. Med. 3:*259-311 (1982).

186. Doll, R., and R. Peto, "The Causes of Cancer," *JNCI 66:*1197-1312 (1981).

187. Marshall, R. *An Interim Report to Congress on Occupational Diseases* U.S. Dept. of Labor, Washington, D.C. 1980.

188. Workers' Compensation and Unemployment Insurance under State Laws, January 1, 1982. AFL-CIO, Washington, D.C.

189. Asch, K., "Asbestos Law: Victims' Rights and Industry's Reaction," *Ann. N.Y. Acad. Sci. 330:*255-272 (1979).

190. Maxwell, N., "Manville Tries to Fight Wave of Problems, Including Costly Rise in Asbestos Lawsuits," *Wall Street J.* (June 9, 1982).

191. Manville Corp. Form 10-K (report filed with the U.S. Securities and Exchange Commission) for the year 1981, pp. 24-29 (1982).

192. "Manville's Big Concern as It Files in Chapter 11 is Litigation, Not Debt," *Wall Street J.* (Aug. 27, 1982).

193. *Asbestos: The Way to Dusty Death.* ABC News, New York (Dec. 27, 1982).

194. Solomon, S., "The Asbestos Fallout at Johns-Manville," *Fortune:*196-206 (May, 1979).

195. Brodeur, P., *Outrageous Misconduct: The Asbestos Industry on Trial,* New York: Pantheon Books, 1985, pp. 350-354.

196. Castleman, B.I., *Corporate Criminal Liability,* Hearings before the Subcommittee on Crime of the Committee on the Judiciary, U.S. House of Representatives, on H.R. 4973. Serial No. 71, U.S. Gov't Printing Ofc. (1981), pp. 36-77.

197. Donnelly, J., "Pulmonary Asbestosis: Incidence and Prognosis," *J. Indust. Hyg. 18:*222-228 (1936).

198. Swuste, P.H.J.J., Burdorf, A., and J.A.M. Klaver, *Asbest/het inzicht in de schadelijke gevolgen in de periode 1930-1969 in Nederland.* Delft: Delft Univ. Press, 1988, pp. 44-45. And personal communication to the author from Paul Swuste (1990).

4

Thresholds and Standards

"(W)here (asbestos particles) are allowed to rise and remain suspended in the air of a room, in any quantity, the effects have been found to be injurious, as might have been expected."

The Lady Inspectors of Factories, *Annual Report of the Chief Inspector of Factories and Workshops for the Year 1898*, p. 172 (1899).

"Although (The 1931 British Asbestos Industry Regulations) required that no asbestos dust should enter the workroom, they were so riddled with loopholes... that the requirement was from the outset no more than a pious aspiration."

Asbestos in the air (Editorial). *Lancet 1:* 944-945 (1976).

"If you poison your boss a little bit each day it's called murder; if your boss poisons you a little each day it's called a Threshold Limit Value."

—James P. Keogh, M.D.

SOCIAL ORIGINS AND NATURE OF DIRECT MEASURES TO PREVENT OCCUPATIONAL DISEASE IN THE UNITED STATES

The industrial age was rife with physical hazards, as expanding urban industries absorbed workers arriving from the countryside. Moving machinery, high pressures and temperatures, and other high energy hazards to the human body were ubiquitous. Along with these came acute health hazards such as carbon monoxide asphyxiation, sort of a cross between a safety hazard and a health hazard. And there were also well-documented health risks, such as silicosis, and mercury and lead poisoning, from substances whose main route of entry to the body was by inhalation.

It followed that limits on the concentrations of the acutely hazardous substances in the workplace air could, if followed, prevent the most harmful effects on the workers. Management had economic incentives for determining some of these limits and observing them, for otherwise workers could be overcome by carbon monoxide or solvent fumes, with disastrous effects on the expensive machinery and interruptions in production. Even such effects as eye and respiratory tract irritation could be a cause of lowered productivity, if uncontrolled.

With more chronic health hazards there was decidedly less of an economic interest in limiting exposure. These insidious causes of ill health in the workers posed no threat to the rhythms of industrial processes. Asbestos, which causes no acute toxic response and does not manifest its chronic effects for at least 5 years—effects which were easily confused with common non-occupational lung diseases 60 and more years ago—is a good example of a severe but non-acute occupational health hazard.

And so the first attempts to develop guidelines for ceiling exposures to toxic air contaminants in the workplace centered on irritating gases: sulfur dioxide, halogens, ammonia, acid fumes. K.B. Lehmann's method was to order his laboratory servant to spend one hour in the housekeeper's laundry room, where a calculated amount of volatile test fluid was poured out and vaporized. The servant was periodically observed, and in this way a concentration was determined to be "just tolerable for short-term exposure."[1] Lehmann also conducted experiments on various animal species. Lehmann's work over a century ago was the first use of quantitative evaluations based on chemical analysis for the development of quidelines for workplace exposure.[2] Animal experiments were also used in the nineteenth century for recommending workplace air limits for the deadly, colorless, odorless gas, carbon monoxide.[3]

Short lists of harmful concentrations of contaminants in air appeared in 1912 and 1921; and in 1927, the American Chemical Society published for 25 "noxious gases" limits for acute toxic effects and "maximum concentrations allowable for prolonged exposure."[4] In 1940, authorities in Massachusetts published "suggested" maximum concentrations for 41 toxic substances used in industry.[5]

Official occupational health guidelines and regulations in Britain and Germany followed another approach. These rules were developed in terms of general engineering controls, plant design features, and specific work practices to follow in controlling the hazards. Monitoring the worker's health was required, but monitoring the workplace air was not. The idea of a measured ceiling concentration for worker exposure was not adopted in Europe. That was an American approach: set some limit, and leave it to management to use its "ingenuity" to comply by whatever means it chose. Modern workplace standards use a combination of these requirements, both ceiling limits and work practice/engineering controls. Of course the results were similar when the guidelines—of whichever kind—were not followed, as was very often the case.

In the United States, a number of health hazard evaluations were performed starting in the second decade of this century by the U.S. Public Health Service. It is important to consider how these studies were arranged, conducted, and reported in order to understand their role in the setting first of U.S. guidelines, and later standards for substances including asbestos.

Both labor and health agencies within the U.S. government supported and published research on health hazards in industry (many of which had already been described in Europe). These reports included basic observations of health hazards by Dr. Alice Hamilton and others (published by the Bureau of Labor Statistics), and more comprehensive investigations by the U.S. Public Health Service. The Social Security Act of 1935 made federal funds available for state and local industrial hygiene programs, and by 1939 thirty such units were operating. With the added impetus of the war effort to "conserve manpower," these industrial hygiene units numbered 47 by 1945.[6] Unions and their political allies got occupational safety and health on the Chief Executive's agenda following World War II, with annual President's Conferences on Occupational Safety. Between 1947-1950 federal grants-in-aid were allocated for industrial hygiene units, as Public Health Service personnel on loan were withdrawn from states and replacements were trained.[6] In this period, only Delaware and Nevada still did not have any programs.

The Public Health Service ceased publishing health hazard evaluations in industry in the late 1940s. Following the Donora, Pennsylvania disaster in 1949, the agency directed some of its resources formerly committed to occupational health to the new field of air pollution and health. Health departments in Pennsylvania (1949), Maryland (1951), and other states kept industrial hygiene divisions at least in name by adding air pollution responsibilities while resources for occupational health were cut back.[6]

Beyond these facts lies a more sordid story. Dr. Wilhelm Hueper, who was Chief of the National Cancer Institute's Environment Cancer Section from its genesis in 1948 until 1964, ascribed the reticence of the Public Health Service in occupational and environmental cancer prevention to "political pragmatism providing a convenient cover for personal greed and corruption."[7] Looking back on nearly 3 decades of government performance in 1976, Hueper described the problem as a structural one in American society: "the same old game is still played by new men with the old cards."[8] Hueper supported his assertions with numerous examples drawn from his personal experience with federal and state health officialdom. His examples included cover-ups of: scrotal cancers among oil refinery workers, by the Ohio State Health Department; tumors in animals fed waxes used in milk cartons, by the National Cancer Institute; and occupational lung cancer in Colorado uranium miners, by the National Cancer Institute.

It must be borne in mind that U.S. government inspectors did not have the right of entry into general industrial workplaces until the 1970s (with passage of the Occupational Safety and Health Act of 1970). In prior decades, the Public Health Service depended on what Hueper called "harmonious relations with industry" to even conduct its industrial hygiene studies. Not surprisingly, the Service's published findings and recommendations were minimally offensive and burdensome to industry. Government and industry participants were well aware that, eventually, enforceable state regulations might follow along the lines of the P.H.S. recommendations. Had the government hygienists published stronger reports, they risked not only widespread industry non-cooperation but also lobbying by industrial parties to cripple or kill their small program through the annual Congressional appropriations process. Political operatives at the highest levels of the Public Health Service were also mindful of the problems their published findings could cause for employment and later the War effort in the years 1930-1945. (These were the most productive years of the Service in industrial hygiene.)

By 1951, with its appropriations budget soaring, the Public Health Service's National Cancer Institute acceded to industry demands and restricted research on occupational cancer. Dr. Hueper was forbidden to contact industry and state health departments by the Surgeon General. Later in the 1950s, his bosses in the Public Health Service prevented Dr. Hueper from appearing and presenting findings at scientific meetings. His review articles were withheld from publication for extended "peer review," including surreptitious reviews by DuPont medical men.[8,9]

The power of business interests was at least equally dominant at the state and local level. By 1950, Delaware, self-proclaimed "Chemical Capital of the World," was one of the only two states in the country that had not set up an industrial hygiene program. No doubt a large part of the reason for this is the success of the state's leading employer, DuPont, in projecting the image of a "benevolent employer" while maintaining a stranglehold on the economic and political life of Delaware. By the use of skillful propaganda, token changes, and the promotion to management or dismissal of worker leaders, etc., DuPont has been eminently successful in thwarting union drives to this day. Through its dominance in every aspect of community life (control of the United Fund; ownership of the newspapers and magazines; control of the banks; board of directors membership and charitable donations to public and private schools, hospitals, museums, churches and community groups; control of the Delaware Bar Association; ownership and control of development interests, etc.)—DuPont and other firms faced essentially no organized opposition for generations in what Ralph Nader's researchers have called *The Company State.*[10,11]

Industrial hygiene programs of most other states prior to 1970 could hardly be characterized as regulatory, however. Typically, these operations were small and had no enforcement powers. Widespread, uncontrolled exposure to industrial health hazards consequently went mostly uninspected by government officials. The government personnel were often not well trained in occupational safety and health. Few states or local agencies employed an occupational health physician. Few agencies had the necessary sampling gear and laboratory facilities to do proper inspections of the workplace. Government salaries were low, and the more qualified industrial hygienists were commonly attracted by offers of better pay in industry. The federal government's withdrawal from the field in the 1950s was thus accompanied by rapid attrition at the state and local levels.

At least some union leaders were aware of the workers' tragic situation in those years and pleaded for both more humane conduct by industry and federal legislation.[12] The ignorance of the unions about the magnitude of the occupational disease problem had a lot to do with their limited efforts to bring about reforms. Underlying causes of labor ignorance on this issue included: 1) the abject lack of study of these problems by industry and government; 2) the suppression and misleading reporting of some research that was done by industry and its contractors; and 3) the dearth of labor-oriented professionals in the field of industrial hygiene and medicine. The response of the unions would probably have been much greater even if only the third cause of their ignorance had not existed. There was, after all, an abundant global body of literature in print on occupational health hazards and means for controlling them. Health professionals allied with unions could have had an enormous impact.

But before 1970, most employment available in occupational health was in industry. University faculty depended on industry good-will for research funding, consulting, and field experience and jobs for their students. The few government jobs were poorly paid, irregularly funded, and hardly equipped with the necessary resources either legally or technically. There were no full-time jobs in occupational health in the unions.

The industrial physicians were organized into a professional association in the U.S. starting in 1916 (American Association of Industrial Physicians and Surgeons, now called American Occupational Medical Association). The demand for industrial physicians grew rapidly, as employers sought to "combat Bolshevism from within" by placating labor in the years immediately following the Russian revolution and the World War's devastation of European industries. The industrial physicians' group met regularly and issued its own journals starting in 1932. *Industrial Medicine,* the first of these journals, contained not one strong editorial (over 20 years publication) decrying the uncontrolled threats of occupational disease so widespread in industry. Papers describing newly discovered health hazards in industry were extremely rare. In contrast, there appeared an abundance of papers on malingering, absenteeism, and emotional factors in employee health.

Dr. Carey McCord, a frequent contributor and in later years the editor of *Industrial Medicine,* spoke at the annual congress of the National Safety Council in 1933. He warned that "plaintiff prone juries" constituted good cause for chest X-ray screening of new hires. He advised employers against apprising "any undisabled workman of his condition," and went on to assert that, "about four out of five litigants alleging dusty lung diseases are in fact free of such diseases." No evidence was offered to support this contention. Dr. McCord proceeded to then prescribe 11 medico-legal defenses to occupational disease claims, "claims richly deserving defeat."[13]

The industrial physicians' group was as much a social club as a professional organization, with great attention paid to such details as new member admissions, raising the status of members, and giving out awards at annual meetings.[14] Only in 1976 did the American Occupational Medical Association, then 4,000 strong, adopt a code of ethics and establish an ethics committee. The Chairman of the ethics committee in 1984 did not know of a single example of censure of a member by the committee, however.[15]

The American Medical Association established a Council on Industrial Health in 1938. Though speakers such as unionists and industrialists were invited to the annual Congresses held by the Council, the key players were industrial physicians and their consultants in the insurance industry, private practice, and academia. The *Journal of the American Medical Association (J.A.M.A.)* published short summaries of these meetings typified by the following excerpts from the report of 1953: "For every case of occupational disease, (Dr. R. Johnstone) said, there are a thousand cases of fear, frustration, and futility arising from a failure in human relations." At the same meeting, the President-Elect of the A.M.A. chimed in with praise of "unlimited medical advances that are possible under the system of free enterprise."[16] These meetings were not scientific discussions about occupational health, and the A.M.A. Council on Industrial Health was eventually eliminated as a result of budgetary constraints.[17]

The industrial medicine and hygiene establishment opposed mandatory industrial hygiene standards. Industry lawyer Theodore Walters of Baltimore said administration of workplace limits "in a police sense" would be a "tool in the hands of labor unions," at the 1954 annual meeting of the Industrial Hygiene Foundation. Harvard professor Philip Drinker, a featured guest at such gatherings and a member of I.H.F.'s Board of Trustees, agreed that any codes should be advisory, otherwise they would be "a severe burden on industry and an unfair one."[18] The industrial physicians' group (at that time called Industrial Medical Association) clearly agreed that they should not be subjected to what they characterized as the arbitrary and ignorant tyranny of mandatory workplace standards enforced by the government.[14]

The history of physicians in industry, certainly in the asbestos industry, indicates that they were a self-select, management-oriented group. They served at the pleasure of higher management for the purpose of controlling employers' costs for injuries and illness at work. They also gave respectability to the primacy of the physician's role as maintaining the individual in good *working* order—a view that became more widely accepted during the Second World War but did not end with the armistice. The physicians in industry either understood or learned on-the-job about the limits of management receptiveness to health-promoting recommendations not cost-effective *to management.* The asbestos story is replete with examples of management disregard for altruistic health protection ideas (employee education, warning labels, user pamphlets advising safer procedures, engineering controls in factories, removal of affected employees from exposures, publication of research, substitution of asbestos by safer materials, filing of compensation claims for employee disability by management, etc.). Corporate medical men were called upon to testify as management "expert witnesses" in compensation and legislation arenas, in addition to muddying the waters of the published scientific literature with misleadingly mild or simply unsupported, benign evaluations of the hazards in industry. Despite the continuous medical surveillance in many major U.S. industries since the 1930s, there were extraordinarily few "discoveries" published here about occupational disease problems identified by industrial physicians—prior to 1970. In this climate of corporate control of the field of industrial medicine, the industrial physician virtually had to either go along with unethical practices or get out of the specialty altogether.[19]

Only after 1970, with federal funding, research, and regulation creating an influx of independent experts in industrial medicine, was there pressure for change. Not the least dramatic indication of this change is the striking difference in content and quality between the *Journal of Occupational Medicine* (American Occupational Medical Association's official publication since 1959) and the independent *American Journal of Industrial Medicine* (started by Dr. Irving Selikoff and others in 1980).

Physicians in general practice might have been reached by well-directed, modest government medical education programs in previous decades. However, no such programs were mounted. The Public Health Service merely made Dr. Hueper available upon request as a lecturer at medical schools and issued a thin volume of unannotated references, *Outline of Lectures on Industrial Disease for Medical Students.* Given the continuing ignorance of the medical profession, state laws requiring the reporting of occupational disease to state health departments were doomed to failure. Even today, this deficit in general medical education is the cause of much unrecognized occupational disease—for only cases of *suspected* occupational disease have a chance of being referred to occupational medicine specialists.

Due to the reticence of the medical profession to confront the problem of occupational disease, an important role was played by industrial hygiene engineers and toxicologists in the years 1945-1970. Following World War II, the American Conference of Governmental Industrial Hygienists, an organization established in 1938, began to issue annual lists of Threshold Limit Values (TLVs) for toxic vapors and dusts in the workplace air. This served a vital need to set guidelines for preventing acute health effects on the job. The 1946 list included 144 limits for specific gases, vapors, dusts, fumes, and mists.

ACGIH solicited industry participation, and did not at first publish the documentary basis of its TLVs. Industry communications were sometimes held confidential, even while serving as the primary basis for setting threshold limits for some materials. Technical (i.e., essentially economic) feasibility was considered in setting TLVs from the start, so these limits were clearly not purely health-based guidelines. As local and state health and labor officials, most members of ACGIH must have been concerned about setting guidelines that their districts' industries were not achieving.

It was inevitable that some such guidelines would eventually be adopted as mandatory codes by government authorities. From industry's point of view, a pliant ACGIH committee of toxicologists, industrial hygienists, and chemists offered an opportunity to preempt more onerous possibilities. Government activity during the first years ACGIH issued annual lists of threshold limits was growing rapidly, and medical and nursing personnel made up one-third of the professional staffs in the occupational health agencies operating in 46 states.[20] Doctors, together with engineers and chemists in at least some of these agencies, had the capability to set limits on their own. California had in fact done so since 1936, and other states including Massachusetts, Oregon, and Ohio followed with exposure limits they had developed by 1946. It was very possible that, with the War over and the economy booming, unions would be able to achieve legislative changes so that some of these lists of advisory guidelines would suddenly be backed by new enforcement powers.

For the states, ACGIH's list of TLVs offered a way out of many difficulties. It allowed the individual states to avoid the economic disadvantages attendant upon having health-protective guidelines more stringent than those in other states competing for industry. It meant that medical personnel in the state programs could be eliminated, since the guidelines set for exposure—really a medical judgment—were being issued by an ongoing national organization. In fact, medical personnel declined in number from one-third to only one-sixth of the state agencies' professional staffs by 1955.[20] The Committee on Threshold Limits also had a cordial relationship with industry—and consequently a better chance of gaining access to unpublished industry data than any aggressive state industrial hygiene department could expect to have, setting limits on its own.

The TLV Committee's limited familiarity with clinical medicine and medical literature and common reliance on unpublished reports and acute-exposure animal studies might easily have caused problems in gaining *scientific* acceptance of the TLVs. The ACGIH was a voluntary organization and not an official government body. Initially, no physicians were on the ACGIH Committee on Threshold Limits. Animal data from two-week lethal-dose tests were (and still are) heavily relied upon in assigning limits for continuous worker exposure to some substances by the toxicologists on the Committee. For substances on which little was published, private communications from financially interested parties sometimes constituted the main or sole basis for the TLVs selected. But the TLVs were nonetheless quietly accepted, and no competitive effort was made by anyone. It was rare that critiques of the TLVs appeared in print, and such critiques were usually offered in general about the list rather than in particular about specific limits for substances on it.

Yet it is obvious that the Committee on Threshold Limits has never had the resources to properly support TLVs with full and up-to-date scientific documentation. The Committee's annual budget is currently less than $30,000, most of which pays travel and lodging expenses to convene Committee meetings. Extreme reliance has always been placed on the Committee members' voluntary efforts and independent access to the necessary technical resources.[21]

It was evident that many substances for which TLVs were set did not satisfy an essential theoretical requirement for safe, continual, occupational exposure: reversibility. Substances that caused cumulative, chronic, and irreversible organ injury could hardly be assigned safe limits, even if those limits were not based on inadequate short-term exposure tests on humans and/or animals.

The extreme lack of documentation of the TLVs has been criticized on this basis and others by the West Germans, who had simply accepted the U.S. values and are now cautiously starting to modify them. A review of 150 chemicals on their list showed that less than 10 percent of the limits were based on "sufficient animal tests and/or field experience." TLVs for most substances that had remained constant over more than 20 years, "in most cases" remained so because nobody had reassessed them, according to a leading German expert.[2]

As mentioned, unpublished communications from industry were accepted by ACGIH as the *sole* basis for setting some of the TLVs. The 1986 *Documentation of the Threshold Limit Values* includes 15 such examples of substances, some widely used in industry. A larger number of other compounds (89) have TLVs *mainly* based upon unpublished industry communications.[22,23] In at least some cases, these communications downplayed or ignored adverse findings. Some of these unpublished communications were never conveyed in writing but occurred over the telephone.

The lax policies of the TLV committee invited abuse, since companies could practically write their own TLVs for substances not independently and openly evaluated in the scientific literature. By the early 1950s, industry medical consultants (e.g., Dr. Arthur Vorwald) had started to find their way onto the TLV committee; this provided further reassurance to industry that the ACGIH was not a threat.

Subsequent to 1970, corporate employees became "liaison members" of the TLV committee. In recent years, much has been disclosed about the nature and extent of their activities.[23-25] Corporate employees of Dow, DuPont, Bayer, and other firms have been assigned primary responsibility for documenting TLVs for over 100 substances, including at least 70 produced by their employers.

Sheldon Samuels of the AFL-CIO Industrial Union Department has watched with rising indignation as ACGIH has opposed OSHA and NIOSH efforts to apply stricter limits than the TLVs. Samuels has urged ACGIH to disband the TLV committee, calling its members "self-appointed agents of unnecessary death and disease."[26] Other union occupational health leaders in the U.S. express similar sentiments, and the chairmen of the ACGIH and the TLV committee have both expressed hope that NIOSH will take over the task of recommending exposure limits soon.

Tarlau, in a recent editorial in the *American Industrial Hygiene Association Journal*, has critically examined the extent of corporate influence and unscientific, irregular procedures of the TLV develolpment process, and written: "This scandal leads to the inescapable conclusion that the ACGIH TLVs are tainted and unreliable."[27]

Roach and Rappaport have reviewed the TLV *Documentation* and found no relationship between the TLVs and the human experience of adverse health effects in the literature cited as the basis for the TLVs. They did, however, find a close relationship between the TLVs and the prevailing levels of exposure reported in the cited studies.[28]

No doubt some of the people who helped draft these weakly supported guidelines starting in the 1940s were amazed to see the whole list of them for 1968 grandfathered into force as U.S. federal regulatory limits in 1971. With an arduous ritual of "due process" established in the Occupational Safety and Health Act for changing these "standards," most of the ones on the 1968 list were still in effect in 1988. By 1980, ACGIH had revised 160 of the limits on its 1968 list, but OSHA had issued regulations for only about 20 substances.[29] OSHA acknowledged in 1983 that its health standards were based on industry guidelines, and that employers "might have to be 20 years behind the times" to be in violation of them.[30]

Thus it turned out that the TLVs have presented few difficulties for industry as advisory guidelines, and they have not been particularly onerous as enforceable federal limits (1971 to date), either. Most of these limits were, after all, designed to prevent immediate effects that would disable the worker on the job. Whatever the motivations of the original TLV committees may have been, their work was conveniently timed and managed in a way that industry could accept and critically influence. As a close examination of the asbestos case study shows, industry's leading experts placed no credence in the safety of the TLV readopted year after year for decades by ACGIH. Nor did industry practice appear to be affected by the publication and adoption of the TLV as a guideline. Disregarded in practice until the imposition of federal standards in the 1970s, the old TLV for asbestos is raised in a curious way in defending against current lawsuits. Manufacturers being sued today say they didn't know or suspect that the use of their products was a danger, claiming that they believed product use entailed exposures less than the TLV.

STANDARDS FOR ASBESTOS

Defendants in asbestos litigation today point out that a Threshold Limit Value (TLV) was proposed in a 1938 report by the U.S. Public Health Service, and this was adopted as a good practice guideline over the next 30 years before stricter limits were established. Manufacturers of asbestos products and asbestos mining companies now claim that they believed the TLV advised in 1938 was a safe level during the succeeding three decades.

An associated claim is that the Public Health Service study (and an earlier one in England) involved asbestos textile plant workers, whose exposure was to "pure asbestos"; and therefore the findings from such studies could not be directly applied to workers using asbestos products whose asbestos content was only 15 to 25 percent (magnesia insulation, asbestos cement products, etc.). Since the early air sampling data included *total* particle counts, it would certainly have made a big difference if the particle counts in one process contained pure asbestos fibers and the counts from another process contained only a minute fraction of asbestos fibers. But were the workers in the textile plants exposed to an airborne dust consisting of such high fractions of asbestos fibers? At least two investigations from the 1930s and a confidential industry study in 1947 show that the vast majority of the airborne particles in asbestos textile plants were not asbestos fibers. In the factories, as in the field, the fraction of asbestos in the airborne dust varied widely and depended upon the particular task being done by the worker and by those nearby.

An issue not raised to justify adherence to the TLV is that the TLV was aimed at controlling asbestosis, and subsequent to its proposal in 1938 it became clear that asbestos was also carcinogenic. The additional hazard of cancer rendered any TLV based on preventing asbestosis alone particularly unreliable as an index of safety.

Ever since the survey of Merewether and Price in England 60 years ago, scientists have grappled with the question, "what level of asbestos dust in the air is safe?" Statements purporting to answer this question were for the most part unsupportable at the time they were made and some admitted as much. The Public Health Service's tentative recommendation in 1938 was quantitatively discredited by an earlier study in Pennsylvania, which the P.H.S. study described.

Our current deficit of knowledge on the dose-response relationship for occupational asbestos exposure is a legacy of past failures to investigate hazards in the industry (and to fully publish the work that was done). The pleas of Hoffman, Donnelly, Hueper, and others for occupational disease studies in the growing asbestos industry document the longstanding recognition of the problem.

Early British Factory Surveys and Standards

Merewether and Price found a less severe asbestosis problem in the least dusty asbestos textile process areas. These processes were "spinning, braiding, and plaiting without local exhaust ventilation." Dustiness of other processes was expressed relative to these least dusty processes, but no absolute dust concentrations were given. The authors showed that persons with fibrosis in these "spinning" type processes had an average of 18.7 years in the industry, compared with 10.9 to 13.8 years for asbestotics found working in the more dusty processes.[25]

The apparently less severe incidence of asbestosis found among "spinners" (term used for the collective minimally dusty processes) was emphasized.[31]

> (I)n order to prevent the full development of the disease amongst asbestos workers within the space of an average working lifetime, it is necessary to reduce the concentration of dust in the air of the workrooms to a figure *below* that pertaining to spinning at the time over which these cases were exposed. (emphasis added)

Following the large-scale survey by government inspectors, Merewether and Price, the British authorities moved to establish standards for dust control. Central to this process was the question, "what concentration of airborne dust would not damage the health of workers after a working lifetime in the industry?" A government-industry committee took up the dust control question.

The committee consisted of Mr. Price and another government engineer, and one representative each from Cape Asbestos, Turner Brothers Asbestos, and British Belting and Asbestos. The committee acknowledged that the dust from some processes "appears to be too small in the light of present knowledge to warrant recommendations being made for its suppression..."

> The opinion is necessarily based on one important assumption, namely, the existence of a critical limit of dust below which workers may be employed without injury to health. As the Committee rightly observe, the only working basis that can be adopted at present is a finding of the previous Report which suggests that the conditions in "flyer spinning" carried on without exhaust may be regarded as the "dust datum"; it is however desirable to emphasize that this limit is clearly provisional and is subject to alteration in the light of further medical experience.[32,33]

Thus, the government-industry committee in effect said that flyer spinning was provisionally acceptable uncontrolled.

This report, like the government report of Merewether and Price, contained not a single dust measurement.

Merewether did publish 51 dust measurements in his 1930 paper in *Journal of Industrial Hygiene*.[34] They ranged from 14.3 (braiding) to 179 million particles per cubic foot (MPPCF). Exposure levels for "spinning" were 17.6, 27.0, 30.4, 41.2, and 171 MPPCF. [Note that the air sampling instruments and analysis used at this time counted all sorts of microscopic particles in the air, not only asbestos fibers.] In virtually all cases other processes were carried on in the same room, rendering it extremely difficult to interpret the data in terms of dustiness by process. Quite likely, the exposure of "spinners" in these plants had as much to do with their proximity to other more dusty processes than to the dust from spinning per se. Merewether said only that the figures for spinning, plaiting, and braiding were "believed to be rather too high, owing to contamination of dust from neighboring and more dusty processes, and further investigation is required here."

Merewether had seen 10 cases of asbestosis in spinning, plaiting, and braiding workers, among 47 with ten or more years' employment in the industry.[31] Apparently, he hoped that control of dust from other processes would suffice to protect these "spinners" in the future.

The Asbestos Industry Regulations were framed in 1931 and resulted from meetings between the government officials and representatives of the asbestos industry. These work practice and engineering control requirements took effect in March of 1933, and covered:

- application of local exhaust ventilation, coupled with effective process enclosure
- substitution of enclosed mechanical methods for hand conveyance and for dusty hand work in general
- substitution of wet methods for dry
- elimination of certain dust-producing devices
- separation of processes and isolation of storage chambers to prevent unnecessary "bystander" exposure to dust within the factory
- use of sacks of close texture material for internal handling in the plant with cleaning of them by machinery (not hand shaking)
- regular maintenance of the ventilation system
- prohibition of employment of persons under age 18 in the most dusty processes

The industrial hygiene measures were coupled with the Silicosis and Asbestosis (Medical Arrangements) Scheme, which had come into force in 1931. This authorized a full-time medical board to manage the medical examination of asbestos factory workers upon hire and periodically thereafter. The same board conducted examinations in claims for disablement, and granted appropriate certificates in connection with occupation-related disablement and death.

Together with the extended Workmen's Compensation (Silicosis and Asbestosis) Act, 1930, which created a scheme of disability compensation for asbestosis, the above measures constituted the first comprehensive national regulatory response to the asbestosis threat.[35]

U.S. Reports Relating Degree of Exposure to Degree of Disease Risk

Within a year, Dr. Harold L. Stewart and coworkers reported another case of asbestosis in a spinner.[36]

> The patient had worked as a spinner in an asbestos mill for nine years. Although the atmosphere was not very dusty, he wore silver dust protectors in his nostrils.

This individual had left the asbestos job 5 years before his death, and asbestosis was found at autopsy. The report notes, with respect to prevention:

> The exposure was for nine years in a comparatively well ventilated factory in which precautionary appliances were used, and yet the patient developed a minor grade of the disease. It would seem that further precautionary means are necessary in this occupation to obviate a disease itself so preventable.

In the other case reported by Stewart, *et al.* the asbestosis was severe. This individual had worked in an asbestos factory for only 9 months in 1921, and had taken no precautions against the inhalation of dust. Commenting on the second case, the authors illustrated the connection between short-term, heavy exposure and longterm, brief exposure. They concluded that respiratory protection should be very widely used in work with asbestos:

> This demonstrates that the symptoms of a pneumoconiosis may come on years after a short exposure *and emphasizes again the absolute necessity for wearing masks in even the less dusty atmospheres.* (emphasis added)

At the other extreme, Aetna Life Insurance Company physician Roscoe Gray, in his *Attorneys' Textbook of Medicine,* threw caution to the wind in interpreting the literature:

> Since asbestosis practically does not occur with spinning, unless there has been previous exposure to more dusty processes, it is considered that the dust concentration of the spinning room is *safe.* Merewether found the dust count in this department to be as low as 506 to the cubic centimeter, equal to about 13,500,000 to the cubic foot. (emphasis added)*[37]

Such reasoning may have been useful in contesting asbestosis compensation claims; but it is doubtful that it was used by Aetna to justify the sale of life insurance to asbestos workers.

In 1935, the state of Pennsylvania published the results of a medical and engineering survey of four asbestos plants.[38] Table 1 shows the distribution of 14 cases of asbestosis among the 56 people examined.

The data show an increasing prevalence and severity of the disease at 4.64, 16.9, and 44.3 million particles per cubic foot.** The data indicate that the "safe" level is less than any in the

*The correct equivalent of 506 particles per cubic centimeter is 14.3 MPPCF, as previously noted.

**Here again, all types of particles captured by the sampling instrument were counted, not just asbestos fibers.

Table 1[38] Incidence and Degree of Asbestosis with Relation to Occupation, Dust Concentration, and Years of Exposure

Occupation	Average Concentration Millions of particles per cubic foot	Years of Exposure	Total Number Examined	Asbestosis				
				Negative	Slight	Moderate	Advanced	Doubtful
Preparers		0-5	3	2	—	—	—	1
and		6-10	3	—	—	3	—	—
Carders	44.26	11-15	5	1	1	3	—	—
		16-20	2	1	1	—	—	—
		over 20	1	1	—	—	—	—
		Total	14	5	2	6	—	1
Weavers		0-5	3	2	—	—	—	—
and		6-10	4	3	1	—	—	—
Spinners	10.87	11-15	4	3	—	1	—	—
		16-20	5	3	2	—	—	—
		over 20	2	2	—	—	—	—
		Total	18	14	3	1	—	—
Winders,		0-5	4	4	—	—	—	—
Twisters,		6-10	7	6	1	—	—	—
Warpers,	4.64	11-15	8	6	1	—	—	1
etc.		16-20	1	1	—	—	—	—
		over 20	4	4	—	—	—	—
		Total	24	21	2	—	—	1
Totals			56	40	7	7	—	2

range reported. An abstract of this study in *Journal of Industrial Hygiene and Toxicology* concluded that, "The study was too limited to permit the formulation of permissible standards of dustiness, but a reduction in the asbestos dust concentration in the operations studied is shown to be necessary."[39]

Lanza and coworkers at the Metropolitan Life Insurance Company conducted the first industry-sponsored study of asbestosis published in the United States.[40] X-ray evidence of asbestosis was found in over half the workers examined (and in 87 percent of those with over 15 years in the plants). A total of 121 dust counts for various processes in five plants were tabulated. Most of the values were below 5 MPPCF, and only a few were as high as 40-82 MPPCF. The authors declined to recommend any level of asbestos exposure as a guideline, saying, "It is not practicable as yet to establish standards for the asbestos dust content of air."

Plant Surveys by the U.S. Public Health Service

The Public Health Service employed engineers, doctors, and chemists who performed studies on hazardous industries. While the P.H.S. had no enforcement authority, its *Public Health Bulletins* and reports in scientific periodicals advanced the state of knowledge in many industries. These studies were widely cited and commented upon; they also were directed toward determining what degree of exposure was acceptable and what was not.

In the years 1935-1937 two separate investigations were conducted. The smaller one was published first, and consisted of an industrial hygiene engineering survey of an asbestos textile plant. This facility was not described as having the best available control technology; but it was believed to be "representative of the best practice in this country at this time."[41]

A table of dust counts taken with and without the exhaust ventilation in operation showed that exposures were reduced 90 percent and more by the controls in most operations. Most impressive was the rise from 1.7 MPPCF to 62.4 MPPCF in the carding process after one hour's operation without exhaust. An abstract of this paper by Dr. Philip Drinker at Harvard concluded, "A final table shows clearly that the industry can keep dustiness well below 10 MPPCF."[42]

Dreessen and others from the U.S. Public Health Service were meanwhile conducting a medical and engineering survey of three North Carolina asbestos textile plants. However, prior to the arrival of the Service, the mills discharged more than one fourth of their employees.[43] Public Health Service researchers later noted,

> The incidence of frank disease was so great that prior to the beginning of the study out of a total of less than 600 employees the plants discharged 150 workers suspected of having asbestosis.[44]

The reports of the Public Health Service and local chest physicians leave no doubt that most of the people discharged had asbestosis.[43-47] Shull, for example, wrote:

> During the latter part of 1934 it was my privilege to examine the chests of 71 of 100 workers who had been dismissed from local asbestos plants. All had undergone physical examination before they were referred for roentgenologic study and were found to be physically disabled.

Most of the people diagnosed with asbestosis by Dr. Shull had worked for the Southern Asbestos Company, Carolina Asbestos, and Raybestos-Manhattan.[48] Of the fired employees that the Service was able to locate, 43 of 69 had asbestosis. No attempt was made to assess their exposures based on their former jobs in the plants.[43]

Some dismissals resulted from acts of the North Carolina government, following the *McNeely* decision, in which the state supreme court held that asbestosis was covered under workers' compensation. In 1935, North Carolina set up an industrial hygiene division, with a doctor and an engineer, and required that all workers in the three asbestos plants in the Public Health Service study be examined by the state doctor. Dr. Hammond Easom, who performed this task from 1935-1939, recalled that he did not issue "work cards" for some workers because they had asbestosis. However, his recollection was that "probably less than 5 percent" were dismissed because of his actions in any of those years.[49]

The average age of the asbestos workers in the 3 plants studied was only 32.1 years. This was the youngest work force in any of the 14 industries that had been investigated by the Public Health Service. The plants themselves had only been in operation for 6 to 16 years. There were *very* few workers employed in the plants with medium-term service (10 years or more) in the lower-exposure production jobs. "Personnel not exposed to appreciable quantities of asbestos dust"—including 27 seeking employment and about four dozen office workers—were examined as "controls"; and if any of them had asbestosis it was not mentioned. Previously, asbestosis had been reported in long-term (30-40 year) clerical employees in asbestos plants.[50,51]

By firing employees with long-term exposure, especially in the less dusty processes, the companies wiped out most of the data base the Public Health Service needed in order to develop any good dose-response data on asbestosis. Only 5 workers in the study who were considered at risk of disease had been exposed to levels under 5 MPPCF for over 10 years. For those with the lowest exposure jobs, the investigators were almost apologetic about drawing conclusions:

> None of the 39 persons exposed to dust concentrations below 2.5 MPPCF had a case of asbestosis, although as a matter of fact only 6 persons had been employed more than five years.

Three "doubtful" or borderline cases of asbestosis were found among the workers whose exposure was measured at 2.5 to 4.9 MPPCF.

Among those exposed to 5.0 to 9.9 MPPCF, with more than ten years in the industry, 13 of 19 had asbestosis. Others exposed to the same dust concentrations for only 5 to 10 years had also developed asbestosis (6 out of 37).

The symptoms of asbestosis were most prevalent among the workers who had sustained the highest lifetime exposures. For workers with a cumulative exposure product of more than 100 MPPCF-years, obtained by multiplying the number of years of exposure at each job by the level of exposure in MPPCF, then adding it all together to give an estimate of life-time cumulative exposure,

- 61% had cough vs. 8% of the control group
- 61% had dyspnea (shortness of breath) vs. 7% of the control group
- 20% blood-streaked sputum vs. none in the control group
- 50% had impaired diaphragmatic movement vs. 2% of the controls

One of the four workers with the most severe grade of diaphragmatic fixation had only been exposed for less than 50 MPPCF-years (the others had had 100+). "Severe forms of diaphragmatic fixation accompanied advanced stages of lung fibrosis."

Asbestosis prevalence was related to cumulative dust exposure: 5 of 196 with less than 25 "million particle years" had early asbestosis. Three out of 84 with 25-49 million particle-years' exposure had early to moderate asbestosis. Thirteen out of 56 with 50-99 million particle years of exposure had asbestosis ranging in grade from minimal to moderately advanced. Of those with over 100 million particle years, half had asbestosis.

Nine case histories were presented, including: (Figure 49) a spinner with total exposure of 103.8 million particle years and advanced asbestosis; a weaver with 109.2 million particle years and moderately advanced asbestosis; and a spinner (Figure 51) with asbestosis and a total cumulative exposure of only 88.5 million particle years. At 5 million particles per cubic foot, these exposures would have been sustained in 21, 22, and 18 years, respectively. These data showed that a teenager going to work in the asbestos industry, exposed to 5 MPPCF on the average, could develop asbestosis before age 40.

Nonetheless, the Public Health Service investigators were

determined to set some level of dustiness which could serve an an interim guideline in the asbestos industry.

> Because of the importance of the problem, it seems to be desirable to use such data as are at hand to define tentative safe working conditions that may serve as standards for the guidance of factory managers and engineers until more complete data are available...
>
> Ideally, a threshold concentration of dust should be the highest dust concentration that would not produce pneumoconiosis in originally healthy workmen during their entire working life.
>
> Because clean-cut cases of asbestosis were found only in dust concentrations exceeding 5 million particles per cubic foot, and because they were not found at lower dust concentrations, 5 million particles per cubic foot may be regarded tentatively as the threshold value for asbestos dust exposure until better data are available ...
>
> In order to find out the levels to which asbestos dust concentrations have been reduced in practice, an engineering study was made in an asbestos textile factory in which dust control equipment has been recently installed. This shows that means are already available for reducing the dust exposure of a majority of asbestos textile workers to less than 5 million particles per cubic foot.

A very attractive feature of the 5 MPPCF limit was that it could be achieved, and in fact was being achieved, in every process except "picking" at one of the North Carolina asbestos textile mills in the study. The use of pitchforks to feed the picker machine was also described. However, the exhaust equipment used in that plant could not get dust concentrations below 2 MPPCF for most of the processes. The exhaust fan flow rates were by no means large, handling air flows of only 625-2570 cubic feet per minute (CFM). A 2570 CFM fan would have a power rating of only about 2 horsepower. The use of more high-powered exhaust fans than had been voluntarily applied by this textile mill was clearly technologically feasible, but would have raised capital and operating costs.

It is clear that the government investigators, who had no power to even enter plants, much less order the industry to clean up, sought to prescribe minimally burdensome guidelines. Though they frequently characterized the 5 MPPCF threshold as a *tentative* guideline, they also offered less guardedly optimistic statements, such as the closing sentence of the report:

> It would seem that if the dust concentration in asbestos factories could be kept below 5 million particles (the engineering section of this report has shown how this may be accomplished) new cases of asbestosis probably would not appear.

The Public Health Service report even cited the 1935 Pennsylvania study showing the incidence of asbestosis increasing with the concentration of airborne dust, with no level of exposure free from disease risk:

> In their report of a similar study carried on in Pennsylvania asbestos textile factories, Fulton, Dooley, Matthews, and Houtz found that 8 percent of the workers exposed to an average dust concentration of 5 million particles per cubic foot had asbestosis; 22 percent of the 17 million particle group; and 57 percent of the 44 million particle group had asbestosis.

The conflict between the Pennsylvania findings and the 5 MPPCF threshold recommended by the Public Health Service was not resolved in the Service's report.

Sayers and Dreessen republished the P.H.S. findings in abbreviated form in the *American Journal of Public Health* in March, 1939.[52] Apparently, this was promptly passed on by A.S. Rossiter, Editor of *Asbestos*, to Sumner Simpson, President of Raybestos-Manhattan. Simpson, in his reply, acknowledged the feasibility of a 5 MPPCF limit:[53]

> (H)e [the Public Health Service authors] does say that where the air can be kept down to five million microns, (sic) there is no danger, and I can tell you confidentially, but am not willing to make it public, that the air can be kept below five million microns, with proper controls, but I am not willing to start a controversy with my competitors.

Though it may sound like a high concentration, 5 MPPCF of dust in air is not even visibly dusty. Some idea of how little asbestos or silica can be harmful was evident from comparisons of dustiness in industrial environments and other places. Hurlbut at Harvard reported air sampling analyses as follows in Rochester, New York:[54]

Lobby of Hotel Rochester	39-49 MPPCF
Riviera Theatre	69-78 MPPCF
Court house, courtrooms	30-43 MPPCF

Asbestos Fiber Fraction of Inhaled Dust

One of the more serious problems with the limit of 5 MPPCF arose from the limitations of using the impinger air sampling method, which counted total particles and not just fibers (or, even more specifically, *asbestos* fibers). Obviously, different processes entailed different exposures to asbestos particles as a fraction of total airborne dust particles. Workers unloading sacks of asbestos fiber might be exposed to much higher fractions of airborne asbestos than others in the same plant grinding brake linings, for example. Yet with the total respirable dust as the sole index of exposure, even large variations in the asbestos exposure itself were not taken into account.

The Public Health Service found that (*asbestos and cotton*) *fibers* made up only 1 to 26 percent of the dust particles in the air, 8 percent and below in most operations. (Table 2) This was in rough agreement with mineralogists Hurlbut and Williams (the latter from Liberty Mutual Insurance Co.), who found that asbestos made up 8 to 15 percent of rafter dust particles in

Table 2. Relation of Fibers to Particles in Various Owens Jet Samples

Activity	Number of fibers counted	Total count of fibers and particles	Percent fibers
Weaving[1]	83	316	26
Weaving[2]	35	286	12
Picking[2]	24	303	8
Carding[1]	22	315	7
Twisting[1]	14	289	5
Twisting[1]	14	280	5
Crushing[2]	5	407	1

[1]Plant B.
[2]Plant A.
(From Dreessen *et al.* 1938)

asbestos textile plants, and no more than 3 percent in other asbestos manufacturing processes.[55,56] A confidential survey of asbestos textile plants also showed that non-fibrous particles comprised 80 to 95 percent of total airborne dust.[57]

At the Saranac Laboratory, Dr. Leroy Gardner was aware of the shortcomings of the standard measurement technique and guidelines based on it. He hoped to develop an improved device for sampling asbestos fibers using an electrostatic precipitator, and by 1943 had work in progress on the device. Gardner's views were expressed in his outline of a monograph he intended to write on industry-sponsored studies at the Laboratory. The outline, sent to Vandiver Brown at Johns-Manville, included a section entitled "Recommendation for a New Standard of Safe Atmospheric Concentration of Asbestos Dust." Here Gardner said,[58]

- While there is no official standard, the tentative one of 4 or 5 (MPPCF) is frequently quoted.
- This is probably unreliable because it is based upon sampling with a standard impinger which we have shown does not collect most of the fibres that are the source of the hazard.

- We now think that a standard should be based upon samples collected with an electrostatic precipitator if it is feasible to determine readily the relative proportion of fibres in such materials.

Fleischer and co-workers analyzed exposures in various shipyard insulation tasks for total airborne dust and for the percentage of asbestos fibers. The average air sample contained less than 2 percent asbestos, and there was considerable variation even for the same task in the same shipyard. Asbestos fractions as high as 10 percent and more were reported for layout and cutting, band saw cutting, and cement mixing. Dust sampling was done with the Konimeter sampling device.[59] (More detailed discussion of sampling devices appears in an early report of the Public Health Service and a more recent one by Walton.[60,61])

It was recognized within the industry that standard dust counting measurements were a poor surrogate for analyses of the asbestos *fiber* concentrations in the workplace air. Asbestos Textile Institute minutes of 1953 noted that animal research at Saranac pointed to fibers longer than 10 microns as the principal agent causing asbestosis.[62,63] "(T)he Industrial Hygiene surveys that have been made in the past, and in which only dust particles were measured, are practically without value," the member companies concluded.[63] In 1958, the sampling methods in use still did not distinguish between "rock dust" and "asbestos fiber dust."[64]

Dust Control Measures in Germany

One trade journal founded in Germany in the nineteenth century, *Gummi Zeitung* (Rubber News), became a journal for asbestos products as well. It carried an article in 1938 on medical and technical measures used to prevent asbestosis.[65] Technical precautions such as ventilation, use of dust masks in the most dusty jobs, and plant construction using smooth (easily cleaned) surfaces were recommended.

By this time, Regulations for Accident Prevention required that all workers in asbestos manufacturing be given pre-employment physical examinations, including X-ray and clinical examination. The employment of any individual was contingent upon the physician's recommendation. Those employed in the more dusty jobs were required to have follow-up medical examinations some time after hire. In the state of Saxony, beginning in 1937 all asbestos manufacturing plant workers were examined annually by the medical factory inspector.[66]

Prockat and Windel published two lengthy articles on engineering protection against asbestosis in the journal *Staub* (Dust).[67,68] Abstracts in the U.S. and England noted the German investigators' belief that the danger from asbestos dust could be eliminated in practically all processes by well-designed equipment enclosures and exhaust ventilation.[69-71]

The government followed Prockat and Windel's recommendations very closely. In 1940, the *Gummi Zeitung* published "Guidelines for the Prevention of Health Hazards from Dust in Asbestos Manufacturing Plants. Effective as of 1 August 1940."[72] Some of the provisions were:

- extensive enclosure of dust-producing operations; use and maintenance of effective vacuum systems where working conditions result in substantial dust formation; no recirculation of air from the dust collectors back inside the plant; and use of adequate dust collectors so the dust-laden air is sufficiently well-filtered to protect the health of the population outside
- vacuuming of working areas after closing time, by properly protected workers
- design of new plants with smooth surfaces that can be easily cleaned of accumulated dust and elimination of window sills and similar projections where dust can settle
- use of enclosed conveyor belts and tightly covered containers for moving and storing asbestos
- preparing and manufacturing (e.g., sawing, grinding, filing) of products from asbestos-cement only under thoroughly vacuumed conditions
- plant officials required to contact the government industrial

hygiene authorities before making substantial remodeling changes in the system (service free of charge)

- taking meals or remaining in dust-hazardous work areas during rest periods prohibited
- street garments not worn during work not to be left in the working area; dust retained on work clothes to be removed at regular intervals

Kuhn reported that in a German shipyard, workers were rotated out of asbestos insulation handling after two years of such work. He also described industrial hygiene measures used to protect shipyard insulators.[73]

In 1939, Baader in Germany wrote that,

> (I)nsurance companies have unhesitatingly recognized and indemnified as occupational disease even mild asbestosis with fatal lung cancer.[74]

Thus, the state insurance carriers in Germany recognized that life could be cut short by the development of lung cancer in a worker whose asbestosis had not become severe. It is possible that such a worker would have later died of asbestosis, and that it had taken no less asbestos exposure to cause lung cancer than to produce an ultimately fatal asbestosis. But the more likely inference is that the German authorities recognized that workers who had not been exposed to enough asbestos to die from asbestosis had nonetheless been exposed to enough asbestos to develop lung cancer (and die from it).

Unsteady Movement Toward Numerical Exposure Limits

The Public Health Service study had clearly failed to determine an asbestos dust concentration that would not produce pneumoconiosis in originally healthy workers during their entire working lives. The inadequacy of dose-response information was acknowledged in 1940 by Lanza.[75] Nonetheless, nine state industrial hygiene units recommended a 5 MPPCF limit for asbestos-containing dust in workplace air (California, Ohio, Oregon, Colorado, Michigan, North Carolina, Oklahoma, Illinois, and Pennsylvania). South Carolina alone officially condoned exposures up to 15 MPPCF.[76-79] A government manual for physicians in Canada first noted that Canada was a principal producer of asbestos and went on to recommend a maximum of "5 to 10" MPPCF.[80]

Hutchinson, an engineering professor writing in 1944 about dust hazards in the monthly trade journal, *Heating and Ventilating,* said:[81]

> Very few data are available on the relation of (asbestos-containing) dust concentration to the incidence of disease. No minimal safe concentrations have yet been set up and information is scant as to the conditions in those plants where a hazard is known to exist.

In 1947, the members of the Asbestos Textile Institute commissioned a confidential medical and dust sampling survey of their plants.[57] This work was reported by engineer W.C.L. Hemeon of the Industrial Hygiene Foundation. Hemeon's report summary underscored the inadequacy of the 5 MPPCF "threshold":

> The maximum permissible dustiness for asbestos is commonly taken to be five million particles per cubic foot. This represents good attainment in the dust control program. It is emphasized, however, that dust elimination to this extent does not positively insure that no asbestosis will develop in some workers after a long working life (greater than 20-25 years). Scientific evidence is obscure on this point. It is recommended, therefore, that studies be initiated aimed to develop another yardstick, because it is suggested that when control below five million is attained, present dust count methods may not properly measure the remaining hazard.

This point is repeated throughout the text. Some examples:

> ...dust count investigations cannot, in the present state of knowledge, give us assurance as to the extent of our success in eliminating the hazard.
>
> ...in the U.S. Public Health Service study, there were abnormally few who had been exposed for more than 15 years and practically none over 20 years. These facts seriously affected the conclusions that could be drawn.
>
> The information available *does not* permit assurance that five million is thoroughly safe nor has information been developed permitting a better estimate of safe dustiness.

But was the lack of scientific basis for the asbestos "threshold limit" understood by the executives in the asbestos companies? The businessman's question was succinctly put by Vandiver Brown, top corporate counsel for Johns-Manville, at the Sixth Saranac Symposium in 1947:[82]

> What is the so-called "threshold limit," on one side of which the concentration can be considered harmless and on the other side dangerous?

He went on,

> Maximum limits are prescribed for a great variety of materials with which I have no familiarity, but it is my earnest hope that these limits have been arrived at on the basis of a better factual and scientific background than exists in the case of asbestos. The allowable limit (proposed in New Jersey) for industries using this material is a "mandatory" requirement of not more than 5 million particles per cubic foot...
>
> ...So far as I have ever been able to ascertain, no one can state with certainty what is the maximum allowable limit for asbestos dust. I am certain no study has been made specifically directed toward ascertaining this figure and I question whether there exists sufficient data correlating the disease to the degree of exposure to warrant any determination that will even approximate accuracy.

Referring to then-unpublished research by Dr. Gardner at Saranac Laboratory indicating that long asbestos fibers were more important in producing fibrosis than the shorter fibers, Brown lamented:

> Meanwhile, the drafters of industrial codes will presumably continue to provide us with standards which have no root in experience but which take their sustenance, like orchids, from the air and, in the case of asbestos, will relate their standards to the innocuous sizes of dust and leave unmentioned those of the character that presumably can have some ill effects.

Rutherford Johnstone's 1948 book, *Occupational Medicine and Industrial Hygiene,* lists the "allowable concentration" for asbestos dust as 10 million particles per cubic foot of air.[83] No authority or reference is given in support of this value. In California, where Johnstone was a "consultant in industrial health," the "suggested maximum permissible concentration (toxic threshold)" for asbestos had been 5 MPPCF since 1945.[84] A 10 MPPCF limit had previously been recommended by the state Industrial Accident Commission, in 1936.[85]

The American Conference of Governmental Industrial Hygienists TLVs

The American Conference of Governmental Industrial Hygienists (ACGIH) was primarily a group of city, state and federal government health officials, although not itself an official government body. The ACGIH began to issue an annually revised list of threshold limits in 1946.[86] The first list contained over 140 industrial gases, vapors, dusts, fumes, and mists. The committee of volunteers who issued this list included industrial hygienists, chemists, and toxicologists, but not one physician. The Maximum Allowable Concentration for asbestos-containing dust was given as 5 MPPCF from that time on, year after year, and this figure continued to be adopted and retained by state and local health agencies.

As Chairman Fairhall, a chemist, noted in the 1948 Report of the Committee on Threshold Limits,

> (I)t has been the purpose of the conference to seek values which, on the one hand protect the individual workman, and on the other would impose no impossible burden on the manufacturer.[87]

Added words of caution were offered on the interpretation of the Committee's Threshold Limit Values (TLVs):

> People vary greatly in response to drugs and toxic substances. Therefore, it is a figment of the imagination to think that we can set down a precise limit below which there is complete safety and immediately above which there may be a high percentage of cases of poisoning among those exposed.

Later that year, W. P. Yant, who had been the first President of The American Industrial Hygiene Association, spelled out some more of the shortcomings of the TLVs at the annual meeting of the Industrial Hygiene Foundation.[88]

- averaging exposures based on limited sampling can overlook peak exposures which are harmful
- the presence of more than one potentially harmful substance may result in synergistic effects that are more serious than the separate hazards ascribed to each substance
- strenuous work involves the breathing of 10 or more times as much air as sedentary activity, creating a "large factor of unsafety"; hot environments also increase respiration and circulation

He concluded,

> The situation becomes very complex when all factors are considered. It requires that more attention be given to all important agents and factors of industrial environment and occupational activity in the development and use of standards; it supports the necessity of including an ample

> factor of safety in standards...and it emphasizes an existing inadequacy of knowledge...

Recognizing that some states would adopt the TLVs as legal standards, Yant expressed mixed sentiments.

> Mandatory requirements are usually minimum requirements or representative of the worst permissible conditions. From one viewpoint such requirements are a necessary aid to code administration for dealing with recalcitrants; from another viewpoint, they tend to stifle progress and freeze endeavor at the established minimum.

Dr. Vorwald at the Saranac Laboratory was particularly skeptical of the reliability of the TLVs for asbestos and silica. In an industrial hygiene report to Owens-Illinois on the Sayreville, New Jersey, plant where "Kaylo" insulation was manufactured, Vorwald wrote:[89]

> The maintenance of the working environment in a condition which conforms to regulations promulgated by local health agencies or which is in accord with accepted standards of good practice should not be considered as a complete protection for a worker from acquiring a disease as the result of his occupation.

Vorwald had also conducted experimental animal tests on the Kaylo insulation product made by Owens-Illinois. Referring to Saranac studies done for a group of asbestos companies, he reported to O-I that "a seemingly negligible proportion of fibrous asbestos is sufficient to produce (fibrosis)." Further emphasizing this point, Vorwald wrote:[90]

> (I)t appears that very small numbers of fibers are capable of producing asbestosis, although the development of the lesions is delayed. The present experient with Kaylo is also an example of this fact.

One shortcoming of the TLVs was that they were set by a committee comprised almost exclusively of industrial hygiene engineers and toxicologists, and in some years not a single physician was on the committee. This provoked increasing outrage among the more established industrial doctors as the TLVs came to enjoy wider recognition. At an April 24, 1952 meeting of the Industrial Medical Association (now American Occupational Medical Association), Dr. Frank Princi said:

> (M)ost of the(TLVs) are picked out of a hat, 95 percent are on the basis of animal experiments only, incorporated into state codes, and we are faced with ridiculous standards. Is there a doctor among the group that puts out these standards?

Industry contractor Vorwald replied that a main obstacle in the setting of TLVs was the lack of data on "precise concentrations of dust in an atmosphere in which the industrial worker is exposed." Dr. Vorwald did not acknowledge his own involvement with the ACGIH Committee on Threshold Limits. And no one present suggested that the members of the Industrial Medical Association either emphasize in-plant air monitoring programs or propose their own medical guidelines on ceiling exposure concentrations.[14]

Reaction in Other Countries to U.S. Numerical Guidelines for Asbestosis

The British had elected to prescribe controls for asbestos dust through engineering and work practice requirements. Looking at the limited basis for the Americans' TLVs and the great variability of human response under the conditions of work, Medical Inspector of Factories McLaughlin scorned the numerical limits:[91]

> The (TLVs) seem to be based on the assumption that man is a standardised machine, which clearly he is not.

His countryman Meiklejohn expressed satisfaction that the old "practical standard" of flyer spinning had lengthened the average exposure time for the development of asbestosis since its implementation 23 years before.[92]

Turner & Newall official David W. Hills compared various approaches to air monitoring in 1955. By then, T & N in Britain was refining thermal precipitator sampling methods to analyze workplace air for fibers, not just count dust particles in general. Concluding a lengthy review, Hills turned to the question of a "safe" level of asbestos exposure (and the TLV):[92a]

> A very pertinent question, and a very difficult one to answer, is what is the maximum asbestos dust concentration that is safe? The American literature quotes 5 million particles per cubic foot. There is no significance to be attached to this figure at all. In the first place, 5 MPPCF is meaningless unless the particle size distribution is given, in the second place this figure was based on results from Greenburg-Smith impingers, which have been shown above to be grossly inaccurate, and in the third place, due to the wide variations in dust concentration at any point . . . and also the difficulty of knowing the total effect of exposure to high concentrations for short times and vice versa, it is almost impossible to determine the integral for any one person of dust concentration and time.
>
> The answer to this question is really a negative one, and is that adopted by the Factory Inspectorate, namely that complete safeguard to health is only obtained by having no dust at all.

Hills was assistant to the executive director of Turner Brothers Asbestos Company (John Waddell).[92a]

Whatever guidelines and standards existed in theory, there was *in practice* a greater degree of worker protection afforded in the United Kingdom than in the United States. This striking disparity was recorded by Dr. John Knox, medical officer for Turner & Newall in notes of his 1960 visit to his company's U.S. subsidiary, Keasbey & Mattison Company:[93]

> The legislative framework under which industries operate in the U.S.A. makes it difficult for me here to follow the lines of thought which prompt action over there in the matter of standards of industrial practice. In many industries, the employers seem so far in front of legislation as to have created a special code of practice for themselves.

Authorities in New South Wales, Australia, interpreted the "American experience" as suggesting that,

> clinical asbestosis is unlikely to develop unless the cumulative exposure exceeds 25 MPPCF-years.

This clearly suggests a rejection of the 5 MPPCF limit, since 25 MPPCF-years would be exceeded after 5 years of work at that level.[94]

Length of Fibers and Asbestosis

The shortcomings of the 5 MPPCF threshold limit were reiterated in 1954 by Johns-Manville safety executive Hugh Jackson.[95] In a memorandum to an official at the firm's Waukegan (Illinois) plant, Jackson said:

> It must be emphasized that neither the threshold limit nor the methods of sampling and counting are absolutes. The threshold limits are not established on the basis of providing an absolutely safe-exposure level for every individual, but rather a level within which most individuals will not be harmed. There is so much variation in the reaction of individuals to a particular type of material that no guarantee of full protection can be assumed at any level of exposure.

In this note, Jackson informed the plant official that J-M's "tentative M.A.C." (Maximum Allowable Concentration) had been changed to 1 million *fibers (10 microns and longer)* per cubic foot of air. This was an internal company change to reporting in terms of fibers per cubic foot instead of total particles. It appears that the company was converting to a more precise measure of the presumed most hazardous air contaminant (long fibers)—although not imposing any greater degree of control than that entailed by the 5 MPPCF "threshold limit" for total airborne dust.

By 1946, industry-supported research at the Saranac Lab had produced "typical asbestosis" in guinea pigs breathing ball-milled asbestos. The airborne concentration of total asbestos dust was 138 MPPCF, *but the concentration of fibers longer than 10 microns was only 0.8 million per cubic foot.*[96] At the same time, British researchers had produced lung damage in rabbits with asbestos fibers shorter than 10 microns in length. Replying to Gardner's general comments on his early findings, King and coworkers said:

> Our results differ from those of Gardner in that asbestos fibers as short as 2.5 microns have produced an interstitial fibrosis.[97]

Johns-Manville was thus using a fiber *size* cutoff inferred from one set of animal studies and at odds with a different test on another animal species. Moreover, the *level of exposure* to the (10 micron) long fibers sanctioned in J-M's factories was greater than that which had produced asbestosis in guinea pigs at the Saranac Lab. This was done despite J-M's awareness of King's findings and Gardner's insistence that he had *not* shown short asbestos fibers to be safe in the workplace.[98]

The state of New Jersey had considered in 1946 applying its industrial hygiene code to control only long asbestos fibers. However, Dr. Gardner incurred the annoyance of Vandiver Brown by refusing to support this idea by testifying that short asbestos fibers were innocuous.[99]

Gardner's successor Vorwald, on the other hand, made an effort to apply the findings of the Saranac studies as *additional* guidelines in industrial hygiene. As a member of ACGIH's Threshold Limits Committee in 1952, Vorwald proposed that the 5 MPPCF limit for asbestos-containing dusts be augmented by a companion limit of 1 MPPCF for the concentration of airborne fibers longer than 10 microns.[100] This should have been no added trouble from the standpoint of compliance, since the total fiber fraction of the airborne dusts in asbestos handling was usually recorded at well under 20 percent.[43,55-59] Nonetheless, this modest proposal was not adopted by ACGIH.

The Added Threat of Cancer

The carcinogenicity of asbestos added a new dimension to the question of whether a safe threshold for asbestos exposure existed. Dreessen and coworkers had included reference to the few pre-1938 articles on asbestosis and lung cancer, but necessarily limited their prescribed threshold to the problem of asbestosis.

By 1952, however, the Chairman of the New York State Occupational Cancer Committee observed that asbestosis was "very probably" associated with lung cancer.[101] Mayers went on to suggest that:

> Maintenance in a factory workroom of Maximum Allowable Concentrations will not necessarily insure safe working conditions, if a potential carcinogen happens to be present.

A review of the literature on lung cancer and asbestos was published in 1953. This paper reported that pipecoverers were among the people dying from asbestosis and lung cancer, and concluded that asbestos workers faced a cancer hazard.[102] The article's introduction also contained this unreferenced sentence: "Experience has led to the acceptance of 5 million particles of asbestos per cubic foot of air, of small enough size to be respirable, to be the safe working concentration." The third author of that paper, Dr. Harriet Hardy, is the most well known in the field of industrial medicine. Scientists have recently brought it to her attention that her work is being "used in court continually and currently against the worker." Dr. Hardy considers it erroneous to infer that *she* relied on the TLV: "I did not say Harriet Hardy considers this the safe limit, and that is what the lawyers are stating."[103]

Hueper also expressed doubt that the TLV for asbestos would be adequate to protect against "asbestosis cancer in man."[104] Members of the Asbestos Textile Institute observed that Hueper's works were quoted by the referee in a Pennsylvania workers' compensation case lost by the company involved. ATI members understood that what Hueper called "asbestosis cancer of the lung" in fact relied on a microscopic pathological definition of the extent of "asbestosis" required:[105]

> One particle of asbestos with the physical condition surrounding it can be diagnosed as Asbestosis.

By any fair standard, the question of asbestos' carcinogenicity was settled by Doll's study, published in 1955.[106-107] Later that year, a "Symposium on Threshold Limits" was jointly held by the ACGIH and the American Industrial Hygiene Association.

The Symposium was introduced by the chemist, Warren Cook, whose 1945 article had supplied 118 of the 144 limits recommended by ACGIH in 1946.[108] He seemed to agree with Oettel, whose correspondence he quoted, in referring to the "known cancerogenicity of...asbestos." Oettel had maintained that, "no man can say today which concentration of the several industrial substances is actually required to be cancerogenic." Cook credited Stokinger with offering the first remarks on setting TLVs for cancer-causing substances.

Toxicologist Herbert Stokinger admitted that the question of establishing safe limits for industrial carcinogens had been "sidestepped completely." He proposed a remedy for that:[109]

> As a suggested method of approach, the following is offered: To the level judged safe for other types of systemic injury add a safety factor for carcinogenicity. The magnitude of the safety factor is suggested to be from 100 to 500...This manner of approach has been used for nickel carbonyl. A tentatively safe level for systemic effects from repeated daily exposure has been set at 0.1 ppm; one-hundredth this level, or 0.001 ppm was set (as the TLV) for nickel carbonyl on the basis that nickel poisoning gives

> rise to a substantial increase in the incidence of lung cancer...
>
> There are undoubtedly substances to which the suggested procedure may not strictly apply, but imperfect as it may be, the suggested method is felt to be a step in the right direction and serves better to curb exposures to industrial carcinogens than considering the problem too difficult to cope with at the present time.

Incidentally, Stokinger was skeptical about the carcinogenicity of asbestos, placing him in the minority of those writing by the 1950s.[110]

Stokinger was a member of the Threshold Limits Committee of the ACGIH for the next twenty years. But his idea for setting carcinogen limits was quietly left behind. By 1966, only three substances (aside from nickel carbonyl) were explicitly tagged as carcinogens by ACGIH, and no limits at all were prescribed for them. The *Documentation of the Threshold Limit Values* published by ACGIH in 1966 includes a page on asbestos with three paragraphs of text and 11 references, none more recent than 1955. The word "cancer" does not even appear on the page.[111]

Sure, the TLV Committee knew asbestos caused cancer. But if the committee hadn't the faintest idea of how little asbestos it took to cause cancer, Chairman Stokinger, who was employed by the Public Health Service, had his own view of who was responsible:

> The TLVs are industry's values...industry has the sole responsibility to develop data on its own products; government is not in a position to develop enough facilities to handle the problem *in total,* nor should it, when reliable toxicologic consultants are now available...There is no question that inability to obtain industrial hygiene data is one of the greatest problems facing the committee today.[112]

Criticism of the TLV and Delayed Response

ACGIH's slowness to change its adopted TLV for asbestos can

hardly be attributed to a lack of criticism. The TLV's inadequacies were thoroughly discussed at the New York Academy of Sciences conference, Biological Effects of Asbestos, held in 1964 (Volume 132 of the Academy's Annals, pp. 1-765).[113-115] Addingley of British Belting and Asbestos in England stated that,

> We do not believe there is any safe limit. We have our ideas as to how low we can get and we are always striving to get right down to zero. We also have our ideas about the American limit of 5 MPPCF as a safe limit. We know that there is no scientific basis for that limit whatever...

A Turner & Newall representative privately criticized U.S. asbestos companies for their lacking appreciation of the medical problems caused by asbestos. He believed that 5 MPPCF was "too high and it should be reduced."[115] Similarly, Union Carbide's I.C. Sayers privately reported from Britain that there was a growing sentiment that the TLV was "no longer tenable."[116]

John Wells, of the U.S. Rubber Company in Georgia, agreed. He reported that workers with cumulative exposure of 50 to 60 MPPCF-years began to develop asbestosis, and as exposures mounted so did the number of workers with the disease.

> In terms of what has been considered a safe dust count in the area, we started out with a theory—because everybody said it was so—that 5 MPPCF was a safe figure. Our own conclusion, as we began seeing what was happening in our own process, was that the only safe amount of asbestos dust exposure was zero... The safe level is nil and anything above the safe level represents certain risk.[114]

An Owens-Corning official questioned the validity of the old TLV in an internal company memorandum in 1966. "Dr. Selikoff has stated that only one fiber in the body can cause cancer," he wrote.[117] Other asbestos product manufacturers, such as Fibreboard, were less aware of debates about the TLV and appear to have never relied on any TLV to determine the safety or danger of asbestos dust concentrations in their factories.[118]

Dr. Clark Cooper, in a 1967 critique of the TLV for asbestos, characterized it as resting on "shakier evidence than most (of the other TLVs recommended by ACGIH)."[119] Cooper told the Chairman of the Committee on Threshold Limits, "When it comes to tumor prevention, I think we are in real trouble."[120] Cooper's colleague J.L. Balzer, who had conducted studies on asbestos exposure of insulation workers, noted:

> Anyone looking at the present basis for the (TLV) of 5 MPPCF as recommended by the (ACGIH) in 1946 realizes that it is not based on solid evidence.[121]

As indicated by the example of Dr. Vorwald, the ACGIH Threshold Limits Committee included members outside of government employment. Notable in this regard was Dr. Paul Gross, a pathologist hired in 1954 by the Mellon Institute, parent organization of the Industrial Hygiene Foundation. In the years 1954-1960, Dr. Gross was sent 6 to 8 lungs and portions of lungs by the Johns-Manville Corporation. As a result of his examinations of these tissues, in which cancer was almost always present in addition to asbestosis, Dr. Gross recalls that he came to the opinion that asbestos was carcinogenic.[122]

In 1964, Dr. Gross became a member of the ACGIH Threshold Limits Committee, and he was promptly made chairman of the subcommittee responsible for recommending TLVs for mineral dusts including asbestos.[123,124] Until 1983, Gross played a central role in the TLV committee's handling of asbestos and other dusts as a member of the committee. During the early part of this time, he performed confidential studies for Johns-Manville on the asbestos content of brake drum dust.[125] As a member of a U.S. Public Health Service committee in 1969, Gross secretly provided draft copies of a report to three asbestos companies. Robert de Treville, President of the Industrial Hygiene Foundation, inviting comment, explained:[126]

> We will attempt to see that needed corrections are introduced by Dr. Paul Gross, a member of the Committee.

And in 1976, Gross resigned from the Safe Drinking Water Committee of the National Academy of Sciences, amid charges of improperly sharing information with a company he consulted for—the issue was asbestos in drinking water.[127]

ACGIH's Committee on Threshold Limits briefly toyed with the idea of a separate, stringent standard for crocidolite, the blue asbestos primarily mined in South Africa. A 1968 Notice of Intent was circulated, "so that industry-connected individuals principally, but others also, may have an opportunity to help shape the deliberations of the Committee prior to its recommendation of tentative changes in the 1967 Threshold Limits List." Commenters were asked to write either to Dr. Stokinger at the Public Health Service, or to the "Repository of Anonymous Occupational Health Data" in care of Dr. de Treville at the Industrial Hygiene Foundation.[128] "Revisions under consideration... proposed for 1968 List (of TLVs)" included the following for asbestos:

> A limit of 5 MPPCF, based on impinger samples counted by light-field technics (sic), is satisfactory to control exposures to most forms of asbestos. Crocidolite, however, has been shown to produce, in addition to the asbestotic inflammation, also mesothelioma. Since no safe limit can be established for this form of asbestos at this time, until more definitive data are obtained, *it is recommended that workers exposed to crocidolite be equipped with air-supplied helmets.* (emphasis added)

Certainly such a proposal would have been problematic for the large asbestos-cement (A-C) pipe industry, which consumed virtually all the crocidolite used in the United States. The industry had found that a blend of chrysotile and crocidolite asbestos worked best in the manufacture of (about 15 percent by weight) asbestos-reinforced cement pipes. (In 1982, for example, about 16,000 metric tons of crocidolite asbestos and 21,600 metric tons of chrysotile were used in the manufacture of A-C pipes.[129]) A representative of Certain-teed Products Corporation, a manufacturer of asbestos-cement pipe, promptly and "strongly" objected to the proposed change on crocidolite; and he requested to attend the Threshold Limits Committee's discussion of the matter.[130] The main market for asbestos-cement pipe was in drinking water supply systems, and at least as far back as 1968 questions had been raised by Dr. Irving Selikoff and among U.S. public health officials, including Dr. Stokinger, about the wisdom of using A-C pipes in water supply systems.[131] (Stokinger recommended that the further use of A-C pipes for water supply systems be discontinued, based on the information available in 1969.[132]) Electron-microscope studies completed by Johns-Manville in 1970-1971 showed that water flowing through A-C pipes picked up some asbestos.[133] Thus, the industry faced eventual scrutiny both on occupational and environmental health grounds, which would have been hastened by an official recognition in 1968 of the crocidolite constituent as a cancer threat at even low levels of exposure.

This idea, which was a parallel development to the British workplace standards approach then being developed for different types of asbestos, was questioned by medical researchers in the U.S. Drs. Selikoff, Lieben, and Cooper all expressed doubts about whether crocidolite was really more dangerous than chrysotile and amosite asbestos. Selikoff and Lieben had reported cases of mesothelioma in workers which the doctors attributed to other varieties than crocidolite.[131,134,135] Wrote Dr. Selikoff:[131]

> If, as the proposed 1968 revision suggests, air helmets be supplied in the presence of crocidolite, some might suggest similar precautions in the presence of other fibers, equally fatal and more common.

Nothing was published by ACGIH along the lines of special stringent measures for working with crocidolite asbestos.

In 1968, ACGIH did list a "Notice of Intended Change" for asbestos, to set the TLV at 12 fibers per cubic centimeter (f/cc) of air, or 2 MPPCF.[136] (f/cc includes only fibers; MPPCF includes all particles.) Both measures are limited to counting microscopic, but not submicroscopic, dusts. This rule-of-thumb, that 6 f/cc = 1 MPPCF, was necessarily used as a bridge from the old measurement system to the new. But it seems to have been well recognized that one could not simply convert measurements for many diverse processes, with any precision, using a single conversion factor.[137]

In 1970, ACGIH's notice of intended change for asbestos was lowered further, to 5 f/cc (fibers longer than 5 microns in length, counted by phase contrast microscopy at 430X). The formally adopted value remained at 5 MPPCF in 1970. No such value was listed in 1971, only the notice of intended change to 5 f/cc. And in 1972, ACGIH acknowledged the carcinogenicity of asbestos and three other substances for which TLVs had been prescribed (also 6 chemical carcinogens for which no TLVs were proposed).[136]

Finally, in 1974, ACGIH listed an adopted TLV of 5 f/cc for all varieties of asbestos.[136] Using ACGIH's conversion factor of 1 MPPCF = 6 f/cc, this amounted to a reduction of less than one order of magnitude in the TLV for a recognized human carcinogen, from the old 5 MPPCF tentative threshold for asbestosis advised by Dreessen *et al.* in 1938.

The TLVs listed by ACGIH in 1968 were almost all adopted nationwide in the U.S. as mandatory workplace exposure limits under the Occupational Safety and Health Act in 1971. These TLVs have been criticized in general as inadequately safe and weakly supported.[2,23,25,27,28] Samuels, of the AFL-CIO, has described early ACGIH efforts as "voluntary private acts by government officials, acting as individuals in alliance with management specialists." He went on to say:

> Review of the documentation of ACGIH values indicates that little attention was given to chronic effects. The selected studies were, at best, sources of data critical in

> the selection of exposure limits which when exceeded meant that most workers would experience acute effects that would disrupt production.[138]

DEVELOPMENT OF THE CURRENT U.S. ASBESTOS STANDARD

The Public Health Service had begun another study in 1964 "to determine the concentration of asbestos dust to which workers can be exposed throughout their working career, without any adverse effect on their health." Medical and environmental evaluations, augmented by available records on previous exposures, were conducted in asbestos textile plants. Reduced Forced Vital Capacity (FVC) turned out to be the most sensitive indicator; and contrary to the British experience, positive chest X-rays (for small, irregular opacities) were more frequently observed than rales (crackling lung sounds). FVC is one of many measurements possible in lung function testing. Abnormally low FVC can be caused by a reduced lung volume from pulmonary fibrosis (lung scaring), an effect not caused by smoking. Reporting on their findings in 1971, P.H.S. researchers said the "cumulative exposures below 50 fiber/cc-years cause no reduction in FVC, and exposures greater than 200 f/cc are usually associated with reduction in FVC... The present mandatory standard of 12 f/cc (first applicable to government contractors in 1969, under the Walsh Healy Public Contracts Act and then incorporated generally under the Occupational Safety and Health Act) appears to be at least twice and, more likely, four to six times the value it should be to prevent any health effect."[139] They were, of course, only referring to asbestosis and not to cancer.

In 1971, cases of pleural mesothelioma and extensive pleural calcification were reported in two men who had worked as installers of vinyl-asbestos and asphalt-asbestos flooring. These men had often sanded old floors before installing new floor coverings. Simulated work conditions yielded exposures of 1.2-1.3 f/cc as measured by a personal sampler worn by the operator (who wore a respirator). Considering that floor sanding was not the continuous work activity of these patients, it was especially worrisome that the daily average exposure limits later adopted for asbestos were above 1.2 f/cc.[140]

The next year, a Vice President of Armstrong Cork objected to the idea of mandatory labels for flooring products containing the phrase "May Cause Asbestosis and Cancer." He proposed instead a warning to go only to professional flooring installers reading:[141]

> Caution to Installer: If subfloor preparation requires machine sanding of previously installed floor tile or an asbestos-type sheet backing, *do not breathe the resulting dust.* (emphasis added)

The Occupational Safety and Health Act established a new federal authority over workplace safety in the U.S. as of April 28, 1971. The asbestos industry knew it would be one of the first regulatory targets of the Occupational Safety and Health Administration (OSHA). On October 7, 1971, the concerns of Clifford Sheckler of Johns-Manville were communicated to the Board of Governors of the Asbestos Textile Institute:[142]

> Mr. Sheckler is very apprehensive that an impossibly low TLV will be adopted for asbestos and so make it impossible for manufacturers to stay in business if it is to be enforced.

Johns-Manville officials had told a Canadian government physician in 1969 that the company's internal standard was 6 f/cc; they said the company had no difficulty meeting this limit in most mining and manufacturing operations.[143]

A 5 f/cc limit was adopted as an "emergency standard" by OSHA on December 7, 1971.[144] Following this, hearings were held to develop a permanent standard which would incorporate medical exams, warning signs in the plants, labeling and disposal of wastes, retention of medical records, provision of separate clothes lockers separated by showers, laundering of work clothes, and the use of respirators whenever a variance from the exposure limits of the standard is granted.[145,146] On

June 7, 1972, OSHA decided to retain the 5 f/cc limit and gave industry until July 1, 1976 to control exposures to no more than 2 f/cc on an 8-hour, time-weighted-average basis. Peak exposures up to 10 f/cc for 15-minute intervals were allowed.[147] This remained the U.S. standard for occupational exposure to asbestos until OSHA issued an emergency temporary standard on November 4, 1983.[148]

The 1983 emergency standard lowered the permissible workplace exposure limit for asbestos to 0.5 f/cc. It permitted employers to comply through "any feasible combination of engineering controls, work practices, and personal protective equipment." Primary reliance on respirators as a means of compliance had been rejected in OSHA's standards for cotton dust and other materials. Union health experts were understandably upset that OSHA would consider allowing employers to simply make workers wear respirators rather than engineer better controls for asbestos dust in their workplace. Under the emergency rule and the proposed permanent standard that followed it, a workplace with 2 f/cc need not be further controlled for the dust; it was just as acceptable for the employer to hand respirators of questionable value to the workers. The control limit of 0.1 f/cc had been urged earlier in 1983 by the International Association of Machinists.[149]

The Asbestos Information Association immediately filed suit in the U.S. Court of Appeals for the Fifth Circuit, which issued a stay of the emergency rule.[149] OSHA also pursued a permanent asbestos standard through more lengthy rulemaking procedures. A proposal to consider limits of 0.2 and 0.5 f/cc was published in the *Federal Register* on April 10, 1984, and hearings were held a few months later. The final standard issued June 20, 1986 set 0.2 f/cc as the exposure limit and allowed use of respirators only as a last resort in achieving compliance.[150] In response to a suit brought by the AFL-CIO, OSHA has been ordered by the U.S. Court of Appeals (D.C.) to make the rules more stringent. It now appears that the permissible exposure limit will be set at 0.1 f/cc, the lowest concentration at which standard monitoring methods can be used reliably.

How Many Fibers a Day is 2 Fibers per Cubic Centimeter?
It is important to note that 1 f/cc is equivalent to 1 million fibers per cubic meter of air. In the course of an 8-hour work day, a worker would breathe in at least 5 cubic meters of air, perhaps much more for heavy work. So, in one day, someone exposed to the 1976–1986 OSHA limit of 2 f/cc (and the current TLV for chrysotile asbestos) is breathing in over 10,000,000 microscopic asbestos fibers. This does not take into account those fibers smaller than 5 microns in length and those which are 5 or more microns long but too small in diameter (0.1 micron or less) to be seen under phase contrast with an optical microscope. Electron microscope analysis of duplicate samples viewed by optical microscopy shows that only one asbestos fiber in 100 to 1000 is seen by optical fiber counting.[151] Assuming the small fibers are 100 times as abundant as the ones seen under the optical microscope using the OSHA method, the *daily* inhaled burden of asbestos at 2 f/cc in air comes to over 1,000,000,000 (one billion) fibers in all.

And though it may be the lower limit of detection using optical microscopic analysis, the lowest proposed standard of 0.1 f/cc equates to an inhalation burden of over 50 million total fibers *per day,* for sedentary work.

The small size of most airborne fibers and their ability to break down into submicroscopic sizes makes dust control most difficult. The settling speed of an asbestos fiber visible under phase contrast optical microscopy is on the order of 30 centimeters (one foot) per hour. It is easy to appreciate that this dust is slow to settle, once suspended; and once it settles, it is easily resuspended by air currents along surfaces, etc.

Unlike most man-made fibrous materials, asbestos fibers tend to break longitudinally rather than cross-sectionally, so that a larger fiber ("bundle") may break down to numerous thinner "fibrils" of comparable length. This is especially worrisome in view of animal studies suggesting that, at least for mesothelioma, long, thin fibers are the most carcinogenic.[152]

Standards in the United Kingdom and Sweden 1960-1970

The 2 f/cc limit was in effect as the chrysotile asbestos standard in Great Britain from 1970-1983. This control limit was initially believed by some authorities to reduce the risk of asbestosis to one percent among those who have a lifetime's exposure (i.e., 50 years' exposure at 2 f/cc).[153] "By asbestosis this committee means the earliest demonstrable effects on the lung due to asbestos." The British Occupational Hygiene Society (BOHS) sub-committee on asbestos had reviewed clinical and X-ray data on 290 men at work in a Turner Brothers Asbestos Company factory in 1966. The analysis of the data but not the chest X-ray films was provided to BOHS by the company medical director. Eight of the workers were said to have X-ray evidence of asbestosis and 16 had rales. The men had started work after January, 1933 (when factories were first required to control dust exposures), and the company had some air monitoring data on their exposures. One problem was, only 118 had worked for longer than 20 years.

Turner Brothers' medical officer, Dr. Knox, was succeeded by Dr. Hilton Lewinsohn around the time the U.K. asbestos standard was issued. Lewinsohn presented his own report of the health status of men employed at the company's main plant in 1971. The prevalence of abnormal chest X-rays was around 35% among those employed for 10-19 years and about 55% among those with 20-29 years since first exposure. The prevalence of pulmonary fibrosis reported for these two cohorts was 30-35%. Since these men were also in the group examined by Dr. Knox a few years before, it appeared that Dr. Lewinsohn had found at least several times as many cases of asbestosis on X-ray than the eight reported to BOHS by his predecessor.[154] The publication of Lewinsohn's paper in 1972 greatly disturbed Dr. Irving Selikoff and others in the United States, where OSHA was developing a standard largely based on the British standard (which had in turn been based on Dr. Knox's evaluation of X-rays at the large Turner Brothers plant).

In recommending a 2 f/cc standard for chrysotile asbestos, BOHS admitted that it was only proposing to address the hazard of asbestosis, which it claimed was "the primary danger of inhaling asbestos dust." The Society claimed that for cancer, "it is not possible at this time to specify an air concentration which is known will be free of risk."[153] Subsequently, cases of lung cancer and mesothelioma occurred among workers at the Turner Brothers Rochdale plant.[155]

Other researchers had already pointed out that, as asbestos workers lived longer without dying from asbestosis, more would reach the cancer age and die from malignant diseases.[156,157] This was well documented by German physicians, who reported that cancers of the lung and pleura had replaced asbestosis as the leading cause of death among asbestos workers in Dresden by the early 1960s.[158] It was also widely accepted that asbestos caused mesothelioma in persons who did not have asbestosis. So in setting a standard for the most commonly used variety of asbestos based on asbestosis alone, it was to be expected that the British erred in the direction of insufficient worker protection.

The standards required also that the Factory Inspectorate be informed whenever crocidolite asbestos was handled. Personal protection was required whenever air concentrations exceeded 0.2 f/cc. This included insulation work where the blue asbestos was handled, too.[159]

In fairness to the British, it must also be noted that specific regulations were issued in 1960 (effective March 31, 1961), requiring that respiratory protection be provided to shipyard workers employed in:

- the application of asbestos by means of a spray
- the breaking down for removal of asbestos lagging
- the cleaning of sacks or other containers which have contained asbestos

- the cutting of material containing asbestos by means of portable power driven saws

The employment of young persons in these activities was forbidden.[160] In 1960, the 5 MPPCF threshold adopted by ACGIH was accepted by the Industrial Health Advisory Committee in Great Britain.[161]

In was also recognized that a more substantial response to the asbestos problem was warranted. Leathart and Sanderson, writing about the asbestosis hazard in the insulation trade in 1963, urged that the asbestos industry hygiene and medical regulations (already long in use for asbestos factory workers) be extended to cover "laggers" as well.[162] They questioned the adequacy of a 5 MPPCF threshold, and suggested that the long-term solution was the substitution of asbestos in insulation by safer alternatives.

Sweden issued regulations for protection of workers handling asbestos in March of 1964.[163] Included were specific practices required in asbestos insulation work. Discussions of more recent regulatory efforts in Great Britain, Sweden, and other countries, are included in Selikoff and Lee's *Asbestos and Disease*.[159] (See also "Efficacy of Current Standards and Proposals to Change Them," later in this chapter.)

Exposure to Asbestos in Insulation Work

Case reports of asbestosis among insulation workers first appeared in the early 1930s.[164,165] Fatal asbestosis was reported in an insulation worker in 1940 by Kuhn.[73] It would appear, therefore, that measurement of the insulator's exposure could have contributed toward determining appropriate protective standards for asbestos exposure.

Beginning with Fleischer and co-workers, a number of reports have included measurements of the asbestos dust exposures in the insulator's trade.[59,162,166-179] An overview of these reports leads to several conclusions:

> A given insulation task (installation of a particular product, mixing of boiler cement, hand-sawing lengths of

> pipecovering to fit the bends of the pipes, pounding into place, stripping old insulation off of pipes, etc.) might give a wide range of possible exposures depending on the size of the working space and the amount of air movement and mixing in it. In the engine room of a ship, for example, spaces may be small and the need for exhaust ventilation, respiratory protection, etc. is thus especially urgent. Identical tasks performed on a breezy day out of doors at an oil refinery would result in lower breathing zone exposures than they would in a cramped, unventilated working space.
>
> The percentage of asbestos in a product could certainly influence the amount of airborne asbestos fiber created in working with the product. However, there is tremendous variation in dustiness from the same use of comparable products with an equal fractional content of asbestos.[178] For this reason, one cannot make very quantitative estimates of worker exposure to asbestos based simply on ratios of the asbestos fractions in the products handled.

It is important to bear in mind some limits on the interpretability of the data in these reports. First, the method of measurement varies from one report to another. The impinger (used by Dreessen and his co-workers for total dust measurements in the 1938 Public Health Service study), Konimeter, and thermal precipitator are dust trapping devices that have long been in use. The membrane filter has been used in more recent times because of its ability to trap asbestos fibers as small as 0.1 micron in diameter.

Once the airborne dust particles are settled on the cover slip of a Konimeter or a thermal precipitator, they may be examined using optical microscopy at 400× or more. Dust particles settled at the bottom of an impinger's collecting cell could only be viewed at the magnification of 100×. Optical microscopic counting of asbestos fibers on a millipore filter is now routinely done with the phase contrast technique, which can reveal asbestos fibers down to the limit of resolution of the light microscope (about 0.1 micron in diameter).[159]

Table 3. Insulators' Exposures to Asbestos

Reference	Data Reported	Comment
Fleischer *et al.*[59]	7.6-32 MPPCF total dust in four Navy yard shops; 11-142 MPPCF avg. exposures on ship. Lower values also reported in units of "MPPCF asbestos dust."	1) processes: layout and cutting, band saw cutting, sewing and fabrication, cement mixing, grinding, general room air 2) no data on rip-out 3) recommends exhaust ventilation for: band saw cutting, grinding, cement mixing, on-ship installation 4) analysis by Konimeter
Asbestos Dust.[166]	"dust count . . . upward of 5 m/cu. ft." (Sic) - no more information given	1) in-shop airborne insulation dust at Portmouth, N.H. Naval Yard 2) recommends: confinement of dusty operations, ventilation, and use of respirators
Occupational Health Hazards[167]	aboard ship: -installation of asbestos cloth - 5.5 MPPCF -installation and sawing block - 20.0 -installation of insulation block - 3.9 -sawing block insulation - 11.7 -mixing magnesia cement - 5.6 -sweep-up after insulating boiler - 92.5	1) "dust counts for cutting and installing insulation block and ripping out old insulation usually exceed the safe concentration . . . when installing pre-fabricated insulation and asbestos cloth, dust counts are generally within acceptable limits." 2) respirators and wet handling

	-rip out of pipe insulation - 6.8 MPPCF	recommended 3) fiberglass substitute sought for amosite insulation 4) method of analysis not given
Peele, R.E.[168]	band saw cutting of insulation block: 13.1-101.4 MPPCF for Johns-Manville "Thermobestos" and 3.1-17.1 MPPCF for Owens-Corning "Kaylo."	Union Carbide report
Ayers, O.[169]	band saw, with local exhaust ventilation, cutting: J-M "Thermobestos" - 16, 34, 104 MPPCF (average: 51); and same size Owens-Corning "Kaylo" insulation blocks - 36, 52, 98 MPPCF (avg: 62)	Johns-Manville report
Leathart, G.L. and J.T. Sanderson[162]	*asbestos fiber* counts in a well-ventilated corridor reached 5-10 MPPCF during mixing (reported in "particles per cc" - 5 MPPCF = 177 particles per cc). Lower values found while sweeping up stripped lagging in a narrow duct (less than 1 MPPCF).	1) fibers counted were 5 to 50 microns in length 2) data limited to one trial in a hospital 3) Hickish commented after the paper, in discussion, that the M.A.C. of 5 MPPCF applied to total dust, and a value of 0.85 MPPCF (30 per cc.) was "more realistic" for fibrous particles only. (p. 72) 4) sampling by thermal precipitator

Reference	Data Reported	Comment
Construction Health Hazards[170]	spraying asbestos: 14-59 MPPCF	1) sampling 15 to 30 feet from asbestos spraying 2) respirators provided to sprayers and others working in the area 3) method of analysis not stated
Marr, W.T.[171]	Most values between 1 and 5 MPPCF total dust, several installation processes done wet. Removal also monitored, for six asbestos products and one of fiberglass. "amosite . . . seldom applied in our shipyard because of the excessive dust it causes during removal." (Long Beach Naval Shipyard)	1) "The low counts on sampling do not appear to give an adequate indication of the actual hazard. During sawing of blocks and pipe sections and removal of old insulation, the work environment appears extremely dusty. Respirator filters often clog after an hour's work removing insulation." 2) Bausch and Lomb particle counter used
Balzer, J.L.[121]	1) Tabulated wide ranges of measurements for six operations, 0.5 to over 30 MPPCF; mean values of three operations between 5 and 10 MPPCF, the other three means were between 1-5 MPPCF	1) processes: pre-fabrication, application, finishing, tearing out, mixing, general
Ahlman, K. and E. Siltanen[172]	1) breathing zone and general air concentrations for mixing insulation	1) no time intervals for exposures noted

	and installing it on pipes ranged from 34-92 f/cc (fibers longer than 5 microns); total counts of particles ranged from 26 to 50 MPPCF 2) Sawing asbestos calcium silicate boards in a shipyard: breathing zone exposures 86-220 f/cc; 45 to 97 MPPCF	2) single monitoring only for these construction and shipyard tasks, 5 measurements for each 3) membrane filter method of analysis for fibers, midget impinger for particles
Murphy, R.L. *et al.*[173]	1) shipyard insulation tasks ranged up to 10 MPPCF (band saw cutting) and gave a weighted average of 5.2 MPPCF, by the impinger method of analysis, in 1965; 2) Konimeter counts for fabrication and on-ship work were higher; 8 to 62 MPPCF, with a weighted average of 32.7 (percent fiber reported as 0.1 to 3.8), for the years 1945 and 1965–66	1) Konimeter gave values nearly 5 times as high as midget impinger on matched counts 2) one third of the Konimeter measurements were made in 1945
Ferris, B.G. *et al.*[174]	1) average values for 1952-1966: general shop - 2.8 MPPCF layout area - 4.8 MPPCF cutting - 19.0 MPPCF opening bulk material - 7.2 MPPCF mixing cement - 57.3 MPPCF tear-out on ships - 29.2 MPPCF 2) samples taken in 1969:	1) fiberglass substituted for amosite asbestos "on major portions at work" in 1965 2) method of analysis for old data not given; membrane filter method useá for fiber counts

Reference	Data Reported	Comment
	in shop - up to 3.1 f/cc, mean 0.3. on ship - up to 25 f/cc, mean 2.9.	
Harries, P.G.[175]	1) processes: removal of sprayed asbestos (avg. 226 f/cc), removal of pipecovering (avg. 152 f/cc), applying pipecovering (avg. 8.9 f/cc); 2) tables of data in the second report describe exposures in a very wide range of processes.	membrane filter technique, some data also reported in mg/m^3 (mass fraction instead of a fiber count)
Barboo, S.H.[176]	1) installation and shop handling tasks generally controlled to under 5 MPPCF, except for fitting block on the sides of steam generators (12-19 MPPCF) 2) rip-out exposures were 9-81 MPPCF, and 0.85-51.0 MPPCF, for various materials	1) greatest dust control achieved in shop handling and least control in rip-out 2) substitution of asbestos ongoing 3) impinger method used
Cross, A.A.[177]	processes monitored: -three rip-out processes (159-353 f/cc) and adjacent exposures (83 f/cc) These are mean values, maximum of all was 3815 f/cc for sweeping and bagging debris	1) sources of data were government and industry in the U.K. 2) wider range of values shown in tables for each process than in initial summary table

	-spraying, undamped (150-1500 f/cc) spraying damped (1-4.7 f/cc) -application of 15% asbestos pipecovering (11.2-61 f/cc) -hand sawing incombustible board without exhaust (14-58 f/cc); with exhaust (1.1 - 3.4 f/cc); cutting incombustible board with power saws, without exhaust (63 to over 200 f/cc); with exhaust (1.4-4.5 f/cc) -drilling incombustible board without exhaust (1.0-5.4 f/cc); with exhaust (0.7-0.9) -cutting and fitting asbestos cloth (5-10); cutting "dust-suppressed" asbestos cloth (0.2-3 f/cc)	3) all data appear to employ membrane sampling method
Balzer, J.L., D.P. Fowler, and W.C. Cooper[178]	personal and area sampling for pipe covering, tear-out, band saw cutting, scoring, and pounding (simulated). Highest exposures were from the 65% asbestos product, with personal sampling for most operations between 100-800 f/cc, 2600 f/cc for scoring. Wide range of scatter for exposures from the three 10-15% asbestos (and calcium silicate) products, with up to ten-fold differences among them for given test conditions.	1) use of one asbestos-free mineral fiber product and four asbestos insulation products (one 65% asbestos, the others 10-15%) in a closed room. 2) 578 analyses in all 3) one of the calcium silicate (10-15% asbestos) insulations seemed consistently least dusty and one seemed most dusty of the three tested 4) membrane filter method.

Reference	Data Reported	Comment
Nicholson, W.J., D.A. Holaday, and H. Heimann[179]	average exposures: mixing and applying cement and cloth covering, 2.5-4.6 f/cc; cutting and applying block and pipe insulation, 5.2-11.5 f/cc; cutting materials for later use 7.6 f/cc; spraying turbines with asbestos 67 f/cc. Electron microscopy showed that low fractions of the airborne fibers were longer than 5 microns: cutting block, 3.5%; mixing cement, 1.2%; fabrication of amosite blankets, 29%; removal of pipecovering, 5.9%.	1) based on over 200 samples 2) authors believed time-averaged exposures of insulators while working with asbestos were 6 f/cc. 3) authors believed exposures could be kept to 0.7 f/cc and below with the use of improved industrial hygiene practices and appropriate respiratory protection. 4) membrane filter method

In comparisons of the impinger and Konimeter under identical sampling conditions, Murphy and his co-workers came up with a weighted average for shipyard insulation exposures of 5.2 and 24.4 MPPCF, respectively.[173] Although these values might not have been obtained in the same shipyard back in the 1940s it was recognized that the higher magnification used on Konimeter samples would yield higher dust counts than the impinger method.

Aside from variations in the methods of sampling and analysis, there was the problem that the work of the insulators varied from day to day in the short term, and underwent more gradual changes over the years. Even observations made at the same time were limited in applicability by differences in the work done by insulation workers at different locations. For example, a ship repair yard would have insulation rip-out work, but a purely ship-building yard would not (except in rare cases, perhaps). One yard might discriminate for or against the use of particular materials for health or performance reasons—another shipyard might not. The degree of exhaust ventilation used and availability of respiratory protection also varied widely, for common processes (e.g., band sawing of insulation).[59]

Over the years, wetting to keep down the dust and other work practice changes were sporadically implemented. The fact that most of the available measurements date from 1965 on should thus be kept in mind. For by this time, the hazards of asbestos insulation were very widely recognized, and measurements of exposure might well reflect some improvement over conditions decades earlier.

Though there was little change in the materials used by insulators for many years, some researchers have reported on early efforts to phase out asbestos insulations and use insulations with lower percentages of asbestos in them.[171,173,176]

The effect of such changes in lowering exposures could be obscured by fluctuations in the total volume of material handled, the extent of power tool use in machining it, and other factors mentioned already.

Murphy compared dust counts using the Konimeter in 1945 and 1965-1966 in the same shipbuilding facility. Total dust concentrations for sewing and fabrication (on-shore shop) operations were twice as high in the more recent years, and the reported "% Fiber" also ranged much higher in the 1965-1966 measurements. On ship, the opposite situation was found, with the data showing both total concentrations and percent fiber higher in 1945 than in 1965-1966.[173]

The I.L.O. conference proceedings (published in 1972) presented many papers on the subject of asbestos exposure and substitution in shipyard insulation work. Perhaps the most startling and complete range of data were presented by Cross, of the British industry's Asbestosis Research Council.[177] However, with all the data that have been compiled, the exposure history of an insulator is still not something that can be described quantitatively on a generic basis. Fleischer and his co-workers noted that, to obtain data on a worker's dust exposure over a period of years,[59]

> Daily dust counts at each specific job in each ship compartment and in the shop together with the time spent on each job would have to be compiled separately for each worker.

It is clear that many phases of insulation work entailed intense exposure to asbestos and other dusts. And even an operation of less than 30 minutes, if it entailed exposure upwards of 50 MPPCF, would make a sizable contribution toward an 8-hour work day average exposure. Looking back in 1972, Johns-Manville medical consultant George Wright suggested that these intermittent peak exposures might have accounted for the disastrous mortality experience of insulation workers, which was worse than that for some other types of asbestos workers.[180]

It is probable that in past decades insulation workers were exposed, on a daily average basis, to more than 5 MPPCF some days and (probably more often) to less on others, depending on the work they were doing. Thus, even if the 5 MPPCF "threshold" was a safe limit, asbestosis should have been anticipated in insulators based on their exposures.

Nicholson notes that three separate U.S. laboratories reported average asbestos fiber concentrations in insulation work in the 3-6 f/cc range in 1968-1971. Harries in England measured an average exposure of 8.9 f/ml for insulation application aboard ship. Nicholson factored in a reported decline by half in the asbestos content of insulation materials, and came up with crude estimates of historic *average* insulator exposure of 10-15 f/cc for construction and 15-20 f/cc for shipyard work.[181] Actual measurements of fiber concentrations by the membrane filter technique were not conducted until the 1960s, however.

The high exposure from even the best-controlled uses of asbestos insulation and the substitutability of asbestos have led to the virtual abandonment of asbestos insulation products. Efforts to replace asbestos for health reasons began in 1954 in Rhodesia (now Zimbabwe) and in 1958 in Sweden.[182,183] Denmark banned asbestos in insulation in 1972. The U.S. Environmental Protection Agency banned the use of asbestos in molded insulation as an air pollution hazard in 1975; but nevertheless, a market of 600 metric tons of asbestos per year in thermal insulation persisted here through 1981.[129,184] This appears to have been used in "air-cell" insulation, a corrugated asbestos paper used for wrapping low-temperature steam pipes (an eminently substitutable use).

Cancer from Asbestos in the Absence of Asbestosis

The early literature linking cancer with asbestos consisted of reports of workers who also had asbestosis. Hueper even referred to such tumors as asbestosis cancers, acknowledging that as of 1955 the literature did not show whether a cancer risk existed in the absence of pre-existing asbestosis.[104] However, some early reports did suggest that lung cancer and mesothelioma appeared not only in asbestos workers with no clinical and radiological signs of asbestosis, but even among chrysotile asbestos miners whose lungs were not asbestotic when examined at autopsy.[185-187]

Wagner's landmark report of mesothelioma in a crocidolite mining district involved mainly patients with only non-occupational (environmental) exposure.[188] Practically since 1960, it has been widely accepted that mesothelioma occurs among people who have not had sufficient asbestos exposure to develop asbestosis.[189-192]

Both mesothelioma and lung cancer have been induced in rats inhaling asbestos dust for a total of seven hours only, at concentrations of 10-15 milligrams per cubic meter of air. Positive results occurred with chrysotile, crocidolite, and amosite.[193] By way of comparison, the Soviet Union's official limit for asbestos-containing dust in the workplace air is 1 milligram per cubic meter, or about 20 f/cc.[159]

Other reports further indicate that exposure to asbestos insufficient to produce asbestosis of the lungs may nonetheless cause lung cancer in humans.[191,192,194-198] In view of the fact that so much of the supporting data comes from Great Britain, it is disappointing that that country's compensation law until 1985 had no provision for recognizing occupational disablement from lung cancer in asbestos-exposed workers who were not also diagnosed as having asbestosis of the lungs.[199,200] The Industrial Injuries Advisory Council reported on the subject of compensation for asbestos-related lung cancer accompanied by pleural changes in November, 1982. It concluded, "Accordingly, we suggest the terms of prescription should be on the following lines:

> Pulmonary carcinoma of the lung where there is accompanying evidence of one or more of the following:
>
> (a) Asbestosis;
>
> (b) Bilateral diffuse pleural thickening;
>
> (c) Bilateral pleural plaques.

Lung cancer in combination with only pleural asbestosis finally became a compensable disease in Britain in 1985.[200]

Efficacy of Current Standards and Proposals to Change Them

U.S. government authorities on asbestos have rated the old 2 f/cc standard "grossly inadequate" to protect against disease.[192] They attributed this largely to be "dramatic evidence of asbestos-related disease (particularly mesothelioma) in members of asbestos-worker households and in persons living near asbestos-contaminated areas." It was concluded that the standard should be set down at the limit of reproducibility of optical microscopic monitoring, for 8-hour sampling (0.1 f/cc). Moreover, non-essential uses of asbestos should be eliminated, the government's task force recommended in 1980:

> The committee also reiterates its judgment that even where exposure is controlled to levels below (0.1 fiber/cc), there is no scientific basis for concluding that all asbestos-related cancers would be prevented.

The NIOSH-OSHA panel went on to say that, while there were debates about the hazards posed by different mineral varities of asbestos and different size distributions of respirable fibers, the evidence lacked sufficient scientific basis for setting differing standards by fiber type. U.S. government regulation has continued to be the same for all commercially used asbestos fiber types, despite urgings by industries using chrysotile asbestos that this variety is less harmful.[150,201]

The British have taken a different view, setting tougher standards for crocidolite than for chrysotile and amosite asbestos. The Advisory Committee on Asbestos recommended in 1979:[202]

1. a ban on the import of crocidolite and products containing it; work necessitating exposure to crocidolite should have a control limit of 0.2 f/cc.
2. the control limit for chrysotile asbestos should be reduced from 2 f/cc to 1.0 f/cc by December 1, 1980.
3. the control limit for amosite asbestos should be reduced from 2 f/cc to 0.5 f/cc by December 1, 1980.

Media investigative reports about asbestos and cancer in Great Britain and pressure from trade unions prompted the government to finally put these recommendations into effect in 1983. A list of asbestos products which would be banned was

Table 4. Adopted Limits for Daily Average Exposure to Chrysotile Asbestos in Workplace Air

	1946–1969	1970	1971	1972	1974	1975	1976	1980	1982	1983	1984	1986	1987
OSHA (U.S.)			12 f/cc				2 f/cc					0.2 f/cc	
				5 f/cc									
ACGIH	5MPPCF				5 f/cc			2 f/cc*					
United Kingdom		2 f/cc*								1 f/cc*	0.5 f/cc*		
South Africa**			?—45 f/cc—			12 f/cc			5 f/cc	———	—2 f/cc		1 f/cc

*More stringent limits were simultaneously set for crocidolite and/or amosite asbestos

**South Africa has set a 2f/cc standard for mines only (chrysotile, crocidolite, and amosite are all mined there). Until 1987 there were no government standards for non-mine occupational exposure to asbestos. The Factory Inspectorate now has set a 1 f/cc limit for all colors of asbestos, limited to factories where asbestos is a main product component.

also reportedly being developed.[203,204] When asked about the adequacy of a 1 f/cc standard, Dr. Richard Doll replied:[205]

> A level of one fibre is too much. I doubt if the (government's advisory committee report of 1979) has got its estimates of the effect of this amount correct.

In August of 1983, the U.K. announced that stricter rules would take effect in August 1984. The new control limits are as follows: chrysotile, 0.5 f/cc; amosite and crocidolite, 0.2 f/cc. Importation and the use in manufacturing of amosite and crocidolite are banned under the new rules; exposures will continue due to the amounts of these materials already in place from past years.[206]

Intensive study of asbestos in particular, and carcinogens in general, has convinced most scientists in this field that no level of exposure can be presumed free from cancer risk.[150,191,192,201,207] Dr. William Nicholson of the Mount Sinai School of Medicine in New York has suggested that the term "risk limitation value" is more appropriate in setting limits for asbestos exposure in the workplace.[208]

Dr. Doll's associate Julian Peto has calculated that 10 percent of asbestos workers exposed to 2 f/cc for 50 years would die from asbestos diseases. His estimates were based on the excessive incidence of lung cancer and mesothelioma in the same Turner Brothers plant used in setting the BOHS standard.[155] More recently, Dr. Nicholson evaluated literature on asbestos "dose-response" relationships for Sweden's National Board of Occupational Safety and Health.[181] He found that,

- *six studies* indicate that an asbestos exposure of 2.5 f/cc for 40 years will *at least* double the risk of lung cancer and increase total mortality by 10% (original emphasis)
- three of these studies suggest that such increased mortality may result from exposures as low as 0.5 f/cc for 40 years
- at least four epidemiological studies of asbestos workers demonstrated a linear dose-response relationship with no evidence of a threshold below which disease does not appear

On the basis of observations such as these, Sweden has virtually eliminated all uses of asbestos from its economy.[209]

OSHA's emergency standard for asbestos included estimates of cancer risk to the workers associated with various levels of exposure under consideration. OSHA estimated the mortality from asbestos-related cancer from 45 years of exposure as: 0.3 percent of those exposed to 0.1 f/cc; 1.7 percent of those exposed to 0.5 f/cc; and 6.4 percent of those exposed to 2 f/cc.[149] Apparently, the Reagan administration considered 0.1 f/cc excessively burdensome for employers, even though the intent to regulate at that level had been expressed by OSHA in 1980.[192]

Stokinger's old idea of a 100 to 500-fold reduction of the TLVs for carcinogens, if applied to asbestos textile plants (and asbestos in general), would have been 30 years ahead of its time. The 5 MPPCF value equates roughly to 30 fibers per cc in such facilities, and OSHA proposed to lower the limit first to 0.5 and then 0.1 fibers per cc before issuing a 0.2 fiber limit in 1986.[149,150,192,210]

CONCLUSION

The hazards of asbestos were described by the Roman historian, Pliny, shortly after the time of Christ. Modern recognition of asbestosis was recorded in the last years of the nineteenth century and after 1900 in the annual reports of the Factory Department in Great Britain.

Merewether and Price conducted a survey of dust exposure and disease in the asbestos textile industry in England, providing a basic analysis of the need for both a fibrosis-producing quantity of dust in the lungs and a fibrosis-producing ("maturation") period necessary for the disease to become manifest. These authors suggested that since spinners were less severely affected by asbestosis than other textile workers with comparable durations of exposure, that the spinners' exposure level might be considered a "dust datum." Merewether's data were inadequate for quantitative prescription of the dust datum.

By 1930, asbestosis was also reported in the United States, and within a few years three large-scale surveys were conducted under industry and government sponsorship. The state of Pennsylvania found asbestosis in workers exposed to airborne dust counts averaging as low as 4.64 MPPCF.

The U.S. Public Health Service conducted a survey of three asbestos textile plants and produced a lengthy report on medical and industrial hygiene conditions. Unfortunately, the mill owners fired 150 out of fewer than 600 workers prior to the P.H.S. survey, most of whom had asbestosis. Government inspectors found 3 "doubtful or borderline" cases of asbestosis among the few remaining workers who had been employed for 5 or more years in less dusty conditions, and proposed a tentative threshold limit of 5 MPPCF. Dreessen and co-workers cited the findings of the state of Pennsylvania, but did not attempt to reconcile their proposed TLV with this earlier finding of asbestosis at a lower exposure level than 5 MPPCF. Nor did they acknowledge the implications of their own finding of advanced asbestosis in workers with cumulative exposures equal to only 20-22 years at 5 MPPCF.

Most regrettably, Dreessen's recommendation was accepted by the American Conference of Governmental Industrial Hygienists as a good practice guideline, despite the mounting evidence of asbestos' carcinogenicity through the 1940s. While ACGIH was reporting its first lists of TLVs for industrial dusts and gases, the asbestos textile industry in the United States was surveyed by the Industrial Hygiene Foundation. Hemeon, in his confidential report to the industry, repeatedly criticized the 5 MPPCF level as potentially unsafe and requiring further study. In the meantime, writers less familiar with the literature on asbestos disease (e.g., Sax) placed unwarranted confidence in the safety of the 5 MPPCF limit, and some states adopted this limit in industrial codes and guidelines.[211]

The publication of guidelines by ACGIH and state agencies did not assure that such limits would be observed in actual practice, however. Few state agencies had the authority and resources to enforce standards for worker exposure to toxic substances. This regulatory vacuum persisted nationwide until the passage of the Occupational Safety and Health Act of 1970.

In earlier decades, there was no requirement imposed on

manufacturers to monitor employee asbestos exposures (except perhaps by workers' compensation insurance carriers). Very scant data have been published from the years 1930-1970, and it appears that very little effort was made to monitor worker exposures to see if they exceeded 5 MPPCF. This was true despite the fact that 5 MPPCF was, "a very small concentration, so small in fact that the condition may look good even to the critical eye and still present an exposure greater than this low limit." As Warren Cook went on to explain in 1942,

> In the case of asbestos dust... the toxic limit is so low that the only safe procedure is to have recourse to actual dust determinations.[212]

In actual practice, asbestos mining and manufacturing firms appear to have commonly exceeded the TLV in their own operations. Eight of the 10 asbestos textile plants surveyed by Hemeon in 1947 had dust counts over 5 MPPCF.[57] Unpublished monitoring data from Johns-Manville's plant in Manville, New Jersey show that concentrations commonly exceeded 5 MMPCF in the years 1952-1954. Measurements several times that level were common, and a number of values upwards of 50 MPPCF were recorded.[213] The Quebec Asbestos Mining Association observed that the ACGIH Committee on Threshold Limits had "potent legal standing in theory, but not in practice." The QAMA members, mostly multinational corporations based in the U.S. and the U.K., also emphasized the fact that adequate information was not always available to the Committee, and that in 1968 the TLV for asbestos was "not up-to-date."[214] Other examples of non-compliance with the TLV are given in Chapter 9 (See "Raybestos-Manhattan, Inc.", Owens-Illinois," "Owens-Corning Fiberglass Corp.," "Asbestos Corporation, Ltd.").

Stokinger suggested that the ACGIH set definite exposure limits for carcinogens in industry, utilizing a large safety factor below the level where toxic non-malignant effects were thought to occur. However, this proposal was not adopted for asbestos. The concept was applied to one substance only, nickel carbonyl, and that at the time of Stokinger's presentation. That same year, 1955, epidemiological evidence firmly established asbestos' carcinogenicity.

Between 1960 and 1965, a number of articles showed that asbestos caused malignant mesothelioma both in asbestos workers and people with "bystander" exposure. The cancer hazard from asbestos dust was thus shown to extend to workers in all the shipyard and construction trades, family members of asbestos workers, and neighbors of asbestos plants.

Despite all this, the value recommended by ACGIH in the U.S. was still 5 MPPCF until 1969. At that time, a federal standard of 12 fibers per cubic centimeter of air was adopted under provisions of the Walsh Healy Public Contracts Act (this applied only to government contract jobs costing $10,000 or more). The Occupational Safety and Health Administration set an emergency asbestos standard for all U.S. workplaces in 1971, with an exposure limit of 5 f/cc. This remained the U.S. standard until 1976, when a reduction to 2 f/cc took effect. Proposals were made by OSHA to further lower the 8-hour time-weighted limit for asbestos exposure to 0.1 and 0.5 f/cc (100,000 and 500,000 fibers per cubic meter of air). Eight years after the first of these proposals was published, OSHA finally issued an emergency temporary standard of 0.5 f/cc but broke with precedent by allowing the use of respirators as an alternative to engineering controls to achieve compliance. The emergency standard would have remained in effect for 6 months had it not been stayed by the courts in response to the industry's challenge. In the meantime, a permanent standard was developed by OSHA. The permissible exposure limit was set at 0.2 f/cc, and the courts have subsequently ordered OSHA to set even lower limits wherever feasible.

In Great Britain, workplace asbestos standards were issued in the late 1960s which admittedly were not set so low that they would protect against the risk of cancer. Even this purported protection from asbestosis was postulated on an optimistic appraisal of a limited study of actively employed workers at an asbestos textile plant. Independent scientists were refused access to the chest X-ray films, whose interpretation by Turner

Brothers' medical director provided the basis of the standard.[208,215] The 2 f/cc standard for chrysotile asbestos had been thoroughly discredited by 1978, and a 1 f/cc standard was finally adopted in 1983. Britain then cut the control limit for chrysotile to 0.5 f/cc in 1984.

Additional human experience coming to light has offered further opportunity to quantify the relationship between asbestos exposure and the risk of disease. Yet the crucial low end of the dose-response curve remains a matter of scientific dispute, with a wide range of uncertainty.

Consumption of asbestos fiber in the U.S. peaked in 1973 (795,000 metric tons) and had dropped by more than one fourth by 1979 (to 560,500 m.t.). A one-year plunge of 35% occurred in 1980 (to 358,700 m.t.), followed by a further decline in 1982 (to 246,500 m.t.).[129] The Bureau of Mines figure for 1986 was 120,000 metric tons, the lowest since 1934.[216] The Bureau's estimate for 1989 is 55,000 metric tons, as U.S. asbestos consumption continues its steep decline.[216] This trend is largely attributable to public concern over the hazards of asbestos, and liability considerations by companies who used to use asbestos in brake linings, fire-resistant textiles, etc. Specific product bans by government regulators also played a part, as did EPA and OSHA standards that raised operating and fixed production costs.

It is tragic that only after so much death and disease have occurred and been set in motion are industrial nations turning away from the use of asbestos. The opportunity to take direct preventive action by the establishment of and adherence to truly health-based standards had hardly been given a chance.

REFERENCES

1. Lehmann, K.B., "Experimentelle Studien über den Einfluss Technisch und Hygienisch Wichtiger Gase und Dämpfe auf den Organismus," *Archiv Hyg. 5:* 1-126 (1886).

2. Henschler, D., "Exposure Limits: History, Philosophy, Future Developments," *Ann. Occup. Hyg. 28:* 79-92 (1984).

3. Paull, J.M. "The Origin and Basis of Threshold Limit Values," *Amer. J. Indust. Med. 5:* 227-238 (1984).

4. Henderson, Y., and H. Haggard, *Noxious Gases,* New York: Chemical Catalog Co. 1927.

5. Bowditch, M., *et al.* "Code for Safe Concentrations of Certain Common Toxic Substances Used in Industry," *J. Indust. Hyg. Tox. 22:* 251 (1940).

6. Heimann, H. and V. Trasko, "Evolution of Occupational Health Programs in State and Local Governments," *Pub. Health Rep. 79:*942-947 (1964).

7. Hueper, W.C. *Adventures of a Physician in Occupational Cancer: A Medical Cassandra's Tale* (unpublished) National Library of Medicine, Bethesda, MD, 1976, pp. 218-236.

8. Hueper, W.C., letter to W.E. Smith dated July 18, 1957, in *Food Additives,* hearings before a subcommittee of the House of Representatives Committee on Interstate and Foreign Commerce, 85th Congress, Washington, 1958, pp. 188-189.

9. Schepers, G.W., personal communication to the author.

10. Phelan, J., and R. Pozen, *The Company State,* New York: Grossman Pub., 1973.

11. Zilg, G.C., *DuPont: Behind the Nylon Curtain,* Englewood Cliffs, N.J.: Prentice-Hall, 1974.

12. Hayes, A.J., "Labor's Stake in Safety," *1957 National Safety Congress,* Chicago: National Safety Council, 1958, pp. 16-21.

13. McCord, C., "Health Hazards in the Foundry," *Trans. 22d National Safety Congress,* Chicago: Nat. Safety Council, 1933, pp. 320-324.

14. American Occupational Medical Association, Chicago, archives reviewed by the author in 1984.

15. Robinson, T. (Chairman, Ethics Committee, American Occupational Medical Association), personal communication to the author, 1984.

16. "Annual Congress on Industrial Health," *J.A.M.A. 151:*646 (1953).

17. Felton, J., "Occupational Medicine in the United States," *Clinical Medicine for the Occupational Physician* (M. Alderman and M. J. Hanley, Eds.), New York: Marcel Dekker, 1982, pp. 1-23.

18. *Transactions Bulletin No. 28,* Pittsburgh: Industrial Hygiene Foundation, 1955, p. 167.

19. Irwin, T., "On the Job Cancer—The Killer They Won't Track Down," *Cavalier* (Jan. 1962).

20. Trasko, V., "Industrial Hygiene Milestones in Government Agencies," *Amer. J. Pub. Health 45:*39-46 (1955).

21. Kelly, W. (Exec. Dir. of ACGIH), personal communication to the author.

22. *Documentation of the Threshold Limit Values,* (5th ed.), Cincinnati: American Conference of Governmental Industrial Hygienists, 1986.

23. Castleman, B.I. and G.E. Ziem, "Corporate Influence on Threshold Limit Values," *Am. J. Indust. Med. 13*:531-559 (1988).

24. Elkins, H.B., "Response to 'Corporate Influence on Threshold Limit Values'," *Am. J. Indust. Med. 14*:737-740 (1988).

25. Ziem, G.E. and B.I. Castleman, "Threshold Limit Values: Historical Perspectives and Current Practice," *J. Occup. Med. 31*:910-918 (1989).

26. Samuels, S.W. "Ethical and Metaethical Criteria for Emerging Technologies," *Ann. N.Y. Acad. Sci. 534*:920-927 (1988).

27. Tarlau, E.S., "Industrial Hygiene Without Limits," *Am. Indust. Hyg. Assoc. J. 51*:A-9 (1990).

28. Roach, S.A. and S.M. Rappaport, "But They Are Not Thresholds: A Critical Analysis of the Documentation of Threshold Limit Values," *Am. J. Indust. Med. 17*: 727–753 (1990).

29. Stokinger, H.E., "Threshold Limit Values," *Dangerous Prop. Indust. Mater. Rep. 1(5)*:8-13 (May-June, 1981).

30. Occupational Safety and Health Administration, "Compreshensive Health Policy," *Fed. Register 48*:54546-54548 (Dec. 5, 1983).

31. Merewether, E.R.A., and C.W. Price, *Report on Effects of Asbestos Dust on the Lungs and Dust Suppression in the Asbestos Industry* London: H.M. Stationery Ofc., 1930.

32. *Report on Conferences between Employers and Inspectors Concerning Methods For Suppressing Dust in Asbestos Textile Factories* London: H.M. Stationery Ofc., 1931.

33. *Annual Report of the Chief Inspector of Factories and Workshops for the Year 1930*. London: H.M. Stationery Ofc., 1931, p. 50.

34. Merewether, E.R.A., "The Occurrence of Pulmonary Fibrosis and other Pulmonary Affections in Asbestos Workers," *J. Indust. Hyg. 15:* 198-222, 239-257 (1930).

35. Merewether, E.R.A., "A Memorandum on Asbestosis," *Tubercle 15:* 152-159 (1934).

36. Stewart, H.L., Bucher, C.J., and E.H. Coleman, "Asbestosis, Report of Two Cases," *Arch. Path. 12:* 909-916 (1931).

37. Gray, R.N., *Attorney's Textbook of Medicine* Albany, N.Y.: Matthew Bender & Co., 1934, pp. 36-37. Also, Gray, (enlarged Asbestosis chapter) *op. cit.*, 2 ed., 1940, pp. 913-925.

38. Fulton, W.B. *et al., Asbestosis,* Harrisburg, PA: Commonwealth of Pennsylvania, 1935.

39. Fulton, *et al., op. cit., Abstract of the Literature of Industrial Hygiene and Toxicology* suppl. to *J. Indust. Hyg. Tox. 18:* 26-27 (1936).

40. Lanza, A.J., McConnell, W.J. and J.W. Fehnel, "Effects of the Inhalation of Asbestos Dust on the Lungs of Asbestos Workers," *Publ. Health Rep. 50:*1-12 (1935).

41. Page, R.T. and J.J. Bloomfield, "A Study of Dust Control Methods in an Asbestos Fabricating Plant," *Publ. Health Rep. 52:* 1713-1727 (1937).

42. Page and Bloomfield, *op. cit., Abstracts of the Literature of Industrial Hygiene and Toxicology* suppl. to *J. Indust. Hyg. Tox. 20:*89 (1938).

43. Dreessen, W.C. *et al., A Study of Asbestosis in the Asbestos Textile Industry,* Public Health Bull. No. 241, Washington, D.C.: U.S. Public Health Service, 1938, esp. pp. 23, 90-95.

44. Lynch, J.R. and H.E. Ayer, "Measurement of Asbestos Exposure," *J. Occup. Med. 10:* 21-24 (1968).

45. Donnelly, J., "Pulmonary Asbestosis: Incidence and Prognosis," *J. Indust. Hyg. 18:* 222-228 (1936).

46. McPheeters, S.B., "A Survey of a Group of Employees Exposed to Asbestos Dust," *J. Indust. Hyg. 18:* 229-239 (1936).

47. Shull, J.R., "Asbestosis: A Roentgenologic Review of 71 Cases." *Radiology 27:* 279-292 (1936).

48. Fabel, G.S. (President, Southern Asbestos), letter to S. Simpson (President, Raybestos-Manhattan), Dec. 18, 1936.

49. Deposition of Dr. H.F. Easom, *In Re Asbestos Litigation,* c/p No. 77-1, United States District Court for E. Dist. of Virginia, Norfolk and Newport News Div., taken Dec. 29, 1982.

50. Wood, W.B. and S.R. Gloyne, "Pulmonary Asbestosis, A Review of One Hundred Cases," *Lancet 2:*1383-1384 (1934).

51. Page, R.C., "A Study of the Sputum in Pulmonary Asbestosis," *Amer. J. Med. Sci. 189:* 44-55 (1935).

52. Sayers, R.R. and W.C. Dreessen, "Asbestosis," *Amer. J. Publ. Health 29:*205-214 (1939).

53. Simpson, S. letter to A.S. Rossiter (*Asbestos* magazine), March 22, 1939. Sumner Simpson papers.

54. Hurlbut, C.S., "Report of the Petrographic Examination of Dust Samples Taken by R.M. Freer at the Foundry of the American Laundry Machinery Company During Shake-Out Operations on Nov. 22, 1933," and "Report of the Petrographic Examination of Non-Industrial Dusts Collected by R.M. Freer in the City of Rochester" (Jan. 30, 1935).

55. Hurlbut, C.S. and C.R. Williams, "The Mineralogy of Asbestos Dust," *J. Indust. Hyg. 17:* 289-293 (1935).

56. Hurlbut, C.S., "Petrography in the Study of Occupational Diseases," *Safety Eng. 68:*73-74 (1934).

57. Hemeon, W.C.L. *Report of Preliminary Dust Investigation for Asbestos Textile Institute.* Pittsburgh: Industrial Hygiene Foundation, 1947. (Unpublished. Sumner Simpson papers.)

58. Gardner, L.U. letter to V. Brown (Johns-Manville) and attached "Outline of Proposed Monograph on Asbestosis" (Feb. 24, 1943). Unpublished, Turner & Newall documents.

59. Fleischer, W.E. *et al.*, "A Survey of Pipecovering Operations in Constructing Naval Vessels," *J. Indust. Hyg. Tox. 28:*9-16 (1946).

60. Bloomfield, J.J., and J.M. Dallavalle, *The Determination and Control of Industrial Dust,* Public Health Bulletin No. 217, Washington: U.S. Treasury Dept., 1935.

61. Walton, W.H., "The Nature, Hazards and Assessment of Occupational Exposure to Asbestos Dust: A Review," *Ann. Occup. Hyg. 25:*117-247 (1982).

62. Asbestos Textile Institute, Air Hygiene Committee Mtg. (Mar. 11, 1953).

63. Asbestos Textile Institute, Hygiene Committee Mtg. (June 10, 1953).

64. Minutes of the Asbestos Textile Institute, Air Hygiene and Manufacturing Comm. (Sept. 1958).

65. Windel, T., "Asbestose und ihre Verhütung," *Gummi Zeitung 52:*309-310 (1938).

66. Brachman, "Asbestosis in Grinders and Drillers of Brake Bands", *Arbeitsschutz* pp. 172-174 (1940). Summary in *Abstract of the Literature of Industrial Hygiene and Toxicology* suppl. to *J. Indust. Hyg. Tox. 23:*76-77 (1941).

67. Prockat, F. "Zur Verhütung der Asbestose in der Industrie," *Staub 5:*133-162 (1937).

68. Prockat, F. and T. Windel, "Asbestose und Ihre Bekämpfung," *Staub 10:*264-283 (1939).

69. Prockat (article 67). Abstract in *Bull. Hyg. 13:* 272-273 (1938).

70. Prockat and Windel (article 68). In *Abstract of the Liter. Ind. Hyg. Tox.* suppl. to *J. Indust. Hyg. Tox. 23:*14 (1941).

71. Prockat and Windel (article 68). Abstract in *Bull. Hyg. 15:*346 (1940). Abstract reprinted in *Pneumoconiosis Abstracts II:*409-410 (1954).

72. "Richtlinien für die Bekämpfung der Staubgefahr in Asbest Verarbeitenden," *Gummi Zeitung 54:*796 (1940).

73. Kuhn, A., "Erkrankungen der Werftarbeiter der Kriegsmarinewerft Wilhelmshaven unter besonderer Berucksichtigung der Betriebsunfalle und Berufskrankheiten," *Arch. Gewerbepath. Gewerbehyg. 10*:133-150 (1940). Abstract in *Bull. Hyg. 17*:819-821 (1942); reprinted in *Pneumoconiosis Abstracts Vol. II* London: I. Pitman and Sons, 1954, pp. 4-5.

74. Baader, E.W., "Asbestose," *Deut. Med. Woch. 65*: 407-408 (1939).

75. Lanza, A.J., "Pneumoconiosis," *Minnesota Med. 23*:776-780 (1940).

76. *Useful Criteria in the Identification of Certain Occupational Health Hazards.* Division of Industrial Hygiene, Utah State Dept. of Health, p. 68 (1945).

77. *Rules and Regulations for the Prevention and Control of Occupational Diseases.* Oregon State Board of Health (1945).

78. *Legal Requirements for the Prevention and Control of Industrial Public Health Hazards.* Ohio Dept. of Health (1946).

79. "Wartime Operations Emphasize Industrial Hygiene Problems of Asbestos Industry," *Illinois Labor Bull. 3*:10-22 (1943). In *Abstract Lit. Indust. Hyg. Tox.* supplement to *J. Indust. Hyg. Tox. 25*:137 (1943).

80. Ministry of Health and Welfare, *A Guide to the Diagnosis of Occupational Disease,* Ottawa: The King's Printer, 1949, pp. 106-107.

81. Hutchinson, F.W., "Dust as an Industrial Health Hazard," *Heating and Ventilating 41*:57-61 (1944).

82. Brown, V., "Discussion," *Pneumoconiosis* New York: Paul B. Hoeber, Inc., 1950, pp. 567-572.

83. Johnstone, R.T., *Occupational Medicine and Industrial Hygiene* St. Louis: C.V. Mosby Co., 1948, pp. 368-372.

84. *Dusts, Fumes, Vapors, and Gases Safety Orders,* Division of Industrial Safety of the State of California, San Francisco, 1945, p. 16.

85. Sappington, C.O., *Medicolegal Phases of Occupational Diseases,* Chicago: Industrial Health Book Co., 1939, pp. 6-7, 76.

86. Report of the Sub Committee on Threshold Limits. *Proceedings of the Eighth Annual Meeting of the American Conference of Government Industrial Hygienists,* Chicago, 1946, pp. 54-56.

87. Report of the Committee on Threshold Limits. *Transactions of the Tenth Annual Meeting of the American Conference of Governmental Industrial Hygienists,* Boston, 1948, pp. 29-32.

88. Yant, W.P., "Industrial Hygiene Codes and Regulations," *Transactions of Thirteenth Annual Meeting,* Pittsburgh: Industrial Hygiene Foundation of America, Inc., 1948, pp. 48-61.

89. Vorwald, A.J., *Kaylo Division Plant, Owens-Illinois Glass Company,*

Sayreville, N.J. Industrial Hygiene Survey by the Saranac Laboratory (May 29, 1951).

90. Vorwald, A.J., *Interim Report Regarding the Biological Activity of Kaylo Dust,* to the Owens-Illinois Glass Co. (Oct. 30, 1948).

91. McLaughlin, A.I.G., "The Prevention of the Dust Diseases," *Lancet 2:*49-53 (1953).

92. Meiklejohn, A., "Asbestosis." *Industrial Medicine and Hygiene,* Vol. III (Ed. E.R.A. Merewether), London: Butterworth & Co., 1956, pp. 116-117.

92a. Hills, D.W., "Subcommittee on Dust Sampling" T&N memorandum and report (Nov. 21, 1955). Deposition of D. Hills in *Prudential Insurance Co. v. Turner & Newall et. al.* U.S. Dist. Court for Dist. of Mass. Civ. No. 85-2179-MA (Feb. 17, 1987).

93. Report of Visit by Dr. J.F. Knox to Keasbey & Mattison Company August 4-5. 1960. Turner & Newall, Ltd. (U.K.) document.

94. Roberts, C.G. and H.M. Whaite, *Studies in Industrial Hygiene.* No. 24, N.S.W. Dept. of Health (1953). Cited in Telleson, W.G., "Rheumatoid Pneumoconiosis (Caplan's Syndrome) in an Asbestos Worker," *Thorax 16:*372-377 (1961).

95. Jackson, H. (Johns-Manville General Headquarters). Memorandum to R.G. Smith (Waukegan plant)-Hygienic Dust Control/Your Letter September 27th (December 3, 1954).

96. Vorwald, A.J., T.M. Durkan, and P.C. Pratt, "Experimental Studies of Asbestosis," *Arch. Indust. Hyg. 3:*1-43 (1951).

97. King, E.J., J.W. Clegg, and V.M. Rae, "The Effect of Asbestos, and of Asbestos and Aluminum, on the Lungs of Rabbits," *Thorax 1:*188-197 (1946).

98. Brown, V. (Johns-Manville), letter to M. Bowditch (Saranac Laboratory), March 12, 1947; and enclosed abstract of ref. 97 from the *Industrial Hygiene Digest,* Feb., 1947. Archives of Dr. Kenneth M. Lynch.

99. Brown, V. (Johns-Manville) letter to T.L. Gatke (President, Asbestos Textile Co.) May 9, 1946. Copy sent to Keasbey & Mattison Co. (U.S. subsidiary of Turner and Newall, Ltd. of England).

100. Vorwald, A.J. (Saranac Lab) letter to A.L. Coleman (Chief Industrial Hygienist, State of Connecticut and Chairman of ACGIH Threshold Limits Committee), April 1, 1952.

101. Mayers, M.R., "Industrial Cancer of the Lungs," *Compensation Med. 4:* 11-18 (1952).

102. Isselbacher, K.J., Klaus, H. and H.L. Hardy, "Asbestosis and Bronchogenic Carcinoma," *Amer. J. Med.* *15*:721-732 (1953).

103. Hardy, H.L., letter to Dr. Grace Ziem (Feb. 7, 1990).

104. Hueper, W.C., "Silicosis, Asbestosis, and Cancer of the Lung," *Am. J. Clin. Path.* *25*:1388-1390 (1955).

105. Minutes of Asbestos Textile Institute, Air Hygiene Comm. Mtg. (Mar. 7, 1956).

106. Doll, R. "Mortality from Lung Cancer in Asbestos Workers," *Brit. J. Ind. Med.* *12*: 81-86 (1955).

107. Editorial. "Lung Cancer in Asbestosis," *Lancet 1*:1163 (1955).

108. Cook, W.A., "Symposium on Threshold Limits/Present Trends in MAC's," *Am. Ind. Hyg. Assoc. Quarterly 17*:273-274 (1956). And, Cook, W.A., "Maximum Allowable Concentrations of Industrial Atmospheric Contaminants," *Indust. Med.* *14*:936-946 (1945).

109. Stokinger, H.E., "Prepared Discussion," *Am. Ind. Hyg. Assoc. Quarterly 17*: 284-286 (1956).

110. Stokinger, H.E., "Recent Industrial Hygiene Developments—A Symposium/In the Field of Toxicology," *Am. Ind. Hyg. Assoc. Quarterly 17*:340-345 (1956).

111. *Documentation of the Threshold Limit Values* American Conference of Governmental Industrial Hygienists, (Cincinnati, 1966), p. 15.

112. Stokinger, H.E., "Current Problems of Setting Occupational Exposure Standards," *Arch. Environ. Health 19*:277-281 (1969).

113. Schall, E.L., "Present Threshold Limit Value in the U.S.A. for Asbestos Dust: A Critique," *Ann. N.Y. Acad. Sci. 132*: 316-322 (1965).

114. Addingley, C.G., "Discussion," *Ann. N.Y. Acad. Sci. 132*: 335 (1965). And Wells, J. *Ibid.*, pp. 335-336.

115. Horowitz, L.D. (Turner & Newall) memorandum to M.S. Davis, Jr. on Conference on Biological Effects of Asbestos/New York Academy of Sciences (Nov. 10, 1964).

116. Sayers, I.C. (Union Carbide, U.K., Ltd., Alloys Div.) *Asbestos as a Health Hazard in the United Kingdom* (1967).

117. Edwards, F.H., "Kaylo Dust—Bath Iron Works", OCF internal memorandum to J.M. Briley (Aug. 8, 1966).

118. Deposition of E. Torbohn, *J. Dartez v. Owens-Illinois et al.* C.A. No. B-81-227, U.S. Dist. Court, E. Dist. TX, Beaumont Div. (Feb. 6, 1989).

119. Cooper, W.C., "Asbestos as a Hazard to Health," *Arch. Environ. Health 15*:285-290 (1967).

120. Cooper, W.C. (University of California School of Public Health), letter to H.E. Stokinger (Chairman of ACGIH Committee on Threshold Limits), Jan. 17, 1968.

121. Balzer, J.L., "Industrial Hygiene for Insulation Workers," *J. Occup. Med. 10*:25-31 (1968).

122. Deposition of Paul Gross. In *Dolibois v. Raybestos-Manhattan et al.* U.S. Dist. Court, Middle Dist. TN Nashville Div. No. 80-3550.

123. "Minutes of Meeting of Threshold Limits Committee, ACGIH," Washington, D.C. (Nov. 5-6, 1964).

124. "Minutes of Meeting of Threshold Limits Committee, ACGIH," Washington, D.C. (Mar. 11-12, 1965).

125. Gross, P., "The Pulmonary Response to Brake-Drum Dust: A Preliminary Investigation," document No. 3071 and file card on it at Institute for Occupational and Environmental Health (successor organization, Asbestos Institute), 1968.

126. de Treville, R., "To IHF Fibrous Dust Study Sponsors," memorandum to Hugh Jackson (Johns-Manville), Lee Grant (PPG Industries), and Joseph Goodman (Raybestos-Manhattan), Sept. 10, 1969.

127. Wade, N., "NAS Committee on Asbestos: Discovery of a Special Relationship," *Science 193:* 661-664 (1976).

128. *1968 Notice of Intent,* Committee on Threshold Limits of the American Conference of Government Industrial Hygienists.

129. Clifton, R.A., *Asbestos* Preprint from the 1982 *Bureau of Mines Minerals Yearbook* Washington: U.S. Dept. of Interior, 1983.

130. Horowitz, L.D. (Certain-teed Products Corp.), letter to H.E. Stokinger (Jan. 22, 1968).

131. Selikoff, I.J. (Mt. Sinai School of Medicine, New York), letter to H.E. Stokinger (Jan. 16, 1968).

132. Stokinger, H.E. *Evaluation of Health Hazards-Asbestos, in Drinking Water* (2-pp memorandum to Chief, Water Supply and Sea Resources Program), March 4, 1969. From Toxicology Files of NIOSH, Cincinnati, Ohio.

133. American Water Works Assoc. Research Foundation, "A Study of the Problem of Asbestos in Water," *J. Amer. Water Works Assoc. 66:*Part 2, Appendix D-2 (Sept. 1974).

134. Cooper, W.C., letter to H. Stokinger (Jan. 30, 1968).

135. Lieben, J. (Penna. Div. Occ. Health), letter to R.T.P. de Treville (Industrial Hygiene Foundation), copy to H. Stokinger (Jan. 29, 1968).

136. *Threshold Limit Values of Airborne Contaminants adopted by ACGIH* (for 1966, 1968, 1969, 1970, 1971, 1972, 1974) *and Intended Changes.*

Published yearly by American Conference of Governmental Industrial Hygienists, Cincinnati, Ohio.

137. Ayer, H.E., J.R. Lynch, and J.H. Fanney, "A Comparison of Impinger and Membrane Filter Techniques for Evaluating Air Samples in Asbestos Plants," *Ann. N.Y. Acad. Sci. 132*:274-287 (1965).

138. Samuels, S.W., "The International Context of Carcinogen Regulation: Benzidine," *Banbury Report 9: Quantification of Occupational Cancer.* Cold Spring Harbor (N.Y.) Laboratory, 497-512 (1981).

139. The Asbestos Worker Study of the National Institute for Occupational Safety and Health—A Progress Report. Presented at Western Industrial Health Conference. Oct. 1, 1971. From Toxicology Files of NIOSH, Cincinnati.

140. Murphy, R.L. *et al.*, "Floor Tile Installation as a Source of Asbestos Exposure," *Amer. Rev. Resp. Dis. 104*:576-580 (1971).

141. Bibri, L.J. (Armstrong Cork). Testimony in *Standard for Exposure to Asbestos Dust,* O.S.H.A., U.S. Dept. of Labor, Washington, pp. 426-427 (March 17, 1972).

142. Minutes of the Board of Governors, Asbestos Textile Institute (Oct. 7, 1971).

143. Mastromatteo, E. (Ontario Dept. of Health), letter to H.E. Stokinger (Chairman ACGIH Threshold Limits Committee), June 13, 1969.

144. U.S. Occupational Safety and Health Administration. "Emergency Standard for Exposure to Asbestos Dust." *Federal Reg. 36:* 23207-23208 (1971).

145. Brodeur, P., *Expendable Americans* New York: Viking Press, 1974, pp. 115-140.

146. *Criteria for a Recommended Standard: Occupational Exposure to Asbestos,* HSM-10267 Washington: U.S. Dept. of Health, Education, and Welfare, 1972.

147. U.S. Occupational Safety and Health Administration. "Standard for Exposure to Asbestos Dust." *Federal Reg. 37*:11318-11322 (1972).

148. "Occupational Exposure to Asbestos: Emergency Temporary Standard," *Federal Reg. 48:* 51086-51140 (Nov. 4, 1983).

149. "Asbestos/Emergency Standard of 0.5 Fiber Issued by OSHA: Industry Files Suit," *Occup. Safety and Health Reporter* Nov. 10, 1983, pp. 587-588, 596-650.

150. U.S. Occupational Safety and Health Administration, "Occupational Exposure to Asbestos, Tremolite, Anthophyllite, and Actinolite; Final Rules," *Fed. Reg. 51*:22612-790 (1986).

151. Rohl, A.N. *et al.*, "Exposure to Asbestos in the Use of Consumer Spackling, Patching, and Taping Compounds," *Science 189*:551-553 (1975).

152. Stanton, M.F. *et al.*, "Relation of Particle Dimension to Carcinogenicity in Amphibole Asbestoses and Other Fibrous Minerals," *JNCI 67:* 965-975 (1981).

153. British Occupational Hygiene Society Sub-committee on Asbestos, "Hygiene Standards for Chrysotile Asbestos Dust," *Ann. Occup. Hyg. 11:* 47-69 (1968).

154. Lewinsohn, H.C., "The Medical Surveillance of Asbestos Workers," *Roy. Soc. Health J. 92:* 69-77 (1972).

155. Peto, J., "The Hygiene Standard for Chrysotile Asbestos," *Lancet 1:* 484-489 (1978).

156. Linzbach, A.J. and H.W. Wedler, "Beitrag zum Berufkrebs der Asbestarbeiter," *Virchows Arch. Path. Anat. 307:* 387-409 (1941).

157. Hueper, W.C., *A Quest into the Environmental Causes of Cancer of the Lung,* Public Health Monograph No. 452, Washington: U.S. Public Health Service, 1955.

158. Jacob, G. and M. Anspach, "Pulmonary Neoplasia among Dresden Asbestos Workers," *Ann. N.Y. Acad. Sci. 132:* 536-548 (1965).

159. Selikoff, I.J. and Lee, D.H.K., *Asbestos and Disease,* New York: Academic Press, 1978, pp. 75-79, 450-462.

160. The Shipbuilding and Ship-repairing Regulations, 1960 (1960 No. 1932) paragraphs 76 and 77. *Statutory Instruments 1960 Part II,* London: H.M. Stationery Ofc., 1961, pp. 1427-1456.

161. Michaels, L. and S.S. Chissick, *Asbestos Vol. I,* Chichester, England: J. Wiley & Sons, 1979, p. 7.

162. Leathart, G.L. and J.T. Sanderson, "Some Observations on Asbestosis," *Ann. Occup. Hyg. 6*:65-74 (1963).

163. "Regulations Respecting Protection against Occupational Hazard in Work with Asbestos," Royal Worker-Protection Commission's Regulation No. 52. Issued March, 1964 in Stockholm.

164. Russell, A.E., "Address," *Proceedings of Conference Concerning Effects of Dusts Upon the Respiratory System,* Wisconsin: Democrat Press (conference held Nov. 16-17, 1932), pp. 167-187.

165. Ellman, P., "Pulmonary Asbestosis: Its Clinical, Radiological, and Pathological Features, and Associated Risks of Tuberculous Infection," *J. Indust. Hyg. 15*:165-183 (1933).

166. U.S. Navy Department, "Asbestos Dust," *Safety Review 4*:13 (January, 1947).

167. *Occupational Health Hazards.* Release No. 27, U.S. Navy, 1961, p. 104.

168. Peele, R.E. (Union Carbide Chemicals Co.), "Industrial Hygiene Survey Construction Insulation Shop, Bldg. 511-2018," Reports 62-1-H-1-G-1 and 62-1-H-2-G-1 (March and July, 1962).

169. Ayers, O., "Delamination Free Thermobestos by Pan Casting Progress Report No. 2—Dustiness During Fabrication," Johns-Manville Research and Engineering Center Report No. 432-257-51 (Nov. 6, 1962).

170. "Construction Health Hazards," *Michigan's Occupational Health 8*:1-5 (1963).

171. Marr, W.T. "Asbestos Exposure during Naval Vessel Overhaul," *Amer. Indust. Hyg. Assoc. J. 25*:264-268 (1964).

172. Ahlman, K. and E. Siltanen, "Exposure of Insulation Workers to Asbestos Dust," *Work-Environment-Health 8*:1-5 (1971).

173. Murphy, R.L. *et al.*, "Effects of Low Concentrations of Asbestos," *New Engl. J. Med. 285*:1271-1278 (1971).

174. Ferris, B.G. *et al.*, "Prevalence of Chronic Respiratory Disease: Asbestosis in Ship Repair Workers," *Arch. Environ. Health 23*:220-225 (1971).

175. Harries, P.G., "A Comparison of Mass and Fibre Concentration of Asbestos Dust in Shipyard Insulation Processes," *Ann. Occup. Hyg. 14*:235-240 (1971), and Harries, P.G., "Asbestos Dust Concentrations in Ship Repairing," *Ibid.*, pp. 241-254.

176. Barboo, S.H., "Recent Developments in Asbestos Control Measures in United States Naval Shipyards," *Safety and Health in Shipbuilding and Ship Repairing*, Geneva: International Labour Office, Occupational Safety and Health Ser. No. 27, 1972, pp. 85-92.

177. Cross, A.A. "Practical Methods for Protection of Men Working with Asbestos Materials in Shipyards," *Ibid.*, pp. 93-101.

178. Balzer, J.L., D.P. Fowler, and W.C. Cooper, "Dust-Producing Potential of Construction Materials," *Ibid.*, pp. 107-122.

179. Nicholson, W.J., D.A. Holaday, and H. Heimann, "Direct and Indirect Occupational Exposure to Insulation Dusts in United States Shipyards," *Ibid.*, pp. 37-47.

180. Wright, G.W., Testimony in *Standard for Exposure to Asbestos Dust*, Washington: O.S.H.A., March 14, 1972, p. 247.

181. Nicholson, W.J., *Criteria Document for Swedish Occupational Standards: Asbestos and Inorganic Fibers*, 1981, pp. 17-67.

182. Mostert, C. and R. Meintjes, "Asbestosis and Mesothelioma on the Rhodesia Railways," *Central Afr. J. Med. 25*:72-74 (1979).

183. Sunstedt, N., "Introduction of Asbestos Substitutes in a Swedish Shipyard," *Safety and Health in Shipbuilding and Ship Repairing*, Geneva: International Labour Office, 1972, 27-30.

184. National Emission Standards for Hazardous Air Pollutants. *Federal Register 40*:48292-311 (Oct. 14, 1975).

185. Cartier, P., "Abstract of Discussion," *Arch. Indust. Health 5*: 262-263 (1952).

186. Cartier, P., Presentation at the Seventh Saranac Symposium, Saranac Lake, New York, 1952 (unpublished). Similar report published in less complete form in Cartier, P., "Some Clinical Observations of Asbestosis in Mine and Mill Workers," *Arch. Indust. Health 11*: 204-207 (1960).

187. Keal, E.E. "Asbestosis and Abdominal Neoplasms," *Lancet 2*: 1211-1216 (1960).

188. Wagner, J.C., Sleggs, C.A., and P. Marchand, "Diffuse Pleural Mesothelioma and Asbestos Exposure in the North Western Cape Province," *Brit. J. Ind. Med. 17*:260-271 (1960).

189. Smither, W.J., J.C. Gilson, and J.C. Wagner, "Mesotheliomas and Asbestos Dust," *Brit. Med. J. 2*:1194-1195 (1962).

190. Newhouse, M.L. and H. Thompson, "Mesothelioma of Pleura and Peritoneum following Exposure to Asbestos in the London Area," *Brit. J. Indust. Med. 22*:261-269 (1965).

191. *IARC Monographs on the Evaluation of Carcinogenic Risk of Chemicals to Man/Asbestos*, Volume XIV, Lyon, France: International Agency for Research on Cancer, 1977, pp. 75-81.

192. NIOSH-OSHA Asbestos Work Group. *Workplace Exposure to Asbestos/Review and Recommendations*, U.S. Dept. of Health and Human Services DHHS (NIOSH) Publication No. 81-103 (1980).

193. Wagner, J.C., G. Berry, J.W. Skidmore, and V. Timbrell, "The Effects of the Inhalation of Asbestos in Rats," *Brit. J. Cancer 29*:252-269 (1974).

194. Kannerstein, M. and J. Churg, "Pathology of Carcinoma of the Lung Associated with Asbestos Exposure," *Cancer 30*:14-21 (1972).

195. Fletcher, D.E., "A Mortality Study of Shipyard Workers with Pleural Plaques," *Brit. J. Indust. Med. 29*:142-145 (1972).

196. Becklake, M.R., "State of the Art," *Amer. Rev. Resp. Dis. 114*:187-227 (1976).

197. Edge, J.R., "Asbestos Related Disease in Barrow-in-Furness," *Environ. Res. 11*:244-247 (1976).

198. Martischnig, K.M. *et al.*, "Unsuspected Exposure to Asbestos and Bronchogenic Carcinoma," *Brit. Med. J. 1*:746-749 (1977).

199. Davies, D., "Asbestos-Related Diseases without Asbestosis," *Brit. Med. J. 287*:164-165 (July 16, 1983).

200. "Lung Cancer and Bilateral Diffuse Pleural Thickening," 1985

No. 159 *The Social Security (Industrial Injuries) (Prescribed Diseases) Amendment Regulations 1985.*

201. U.S. Environmental Protection Agency, "Asbestos: Manufacture, Importation, Processing and Distribution in Commerce Prohibitions, Final Rule." *Fed. Register 54*:29460-29513 (July 12, 1989).

202. Health and Safety Committee, *Asbestos. Volume I: Final Report of the Advisory Committee* London: H.M. Stationery Ofc., 1979, pp. 97-100.

203. Greenberg, M. (Health and Safety Executive) personal communication to the author, Sept. 21, 1982.

204. Singer, A., "Asbestos Dust Health Rules to Be Tightened," *The Guardian*, July 31, 1982.

205. Singer, A. "Asbestos Masks Were Only of Cosmetic Value, Says Firm," *The Guardian*, Aug. 5, 1982.

206. Asbestos (News Release), Health and Safety Commission, London, Aug. 24, 1983.

207. Saffiotti, U. *et al.*, *Evaluation of Environmental Carcinogens/ Report to the Surgeon General April 22, 1970*, National Institutes of Health, Bethesda, MD, 20 pp.

208. Nicholson, W.J., "Case Study 1: Asbestos—the TLV Approach," *Ann. N.Y. Acad. Sci. 271*:152-169 (1976).

209. Åhlberg, R. (Swedish Metalworkers Union), personal communication to the author, November 5, 1982.

210. U.S. Occupational Safety and Health Administration, "Occupational Exposure to Asbestos/Notice of Proposed Rulemaking," *Federal Reg. 40*: 47652-47665 (1975).

211. Sax, N.I., *Handbook of Dangerous Materials*, New York: Reinhold Publishers, 1951, p. 34.

212. Cook, W.A., "The Occupational Disease Hazard," *Indust. Med. 11*: 193-198 (1942).

213. Notebooks recording dust counts in the Manville plant of John-Manville, 1952-1954, in possession of Karl Asch, Elizabeth, N.J.

214. Quebec Asbestos Mining Assocation, "Special Meeting—Grand Bahama Hotel and Country Club, G.B." (Mar. 29, 1968).

215. Wagoner, J.K. (U.S. Public Health Service, retired), personal communication to the author, 1982.

216. Clifton, R.A. (U.S. Bureau of Mines), *Asbestos* preprint from the 1984 *Bureau of Mines Minerals Yearbook*, Washington: U.S. Dept. of the Interior, 1985. Also, personal communications from R. Virta, U.S. Bureau of Mines, 1978, 1990.

5
Asbestos Product Use

"As with the rest of industry, we are also aware of our responsibilities to the consuming public. Today, the products of industry are designed to promote the health and comfort of the public. Industry is constantly striving to bring about more pleasant living through improved products as better values to the consumer. Moreover, every effort is made nowadays to protect the consumer with safer products and better methods of handling them.

Years ago industrial research was unconcerned about problems of health and safety that might be involved in a product. When the product was developed, it was put on the market. Today our industrial research organizations probe into every health hazard. And every safeguard is insisted upon before the product is marketed to the consumer...

And industry has inspired, to a very great extent, the movement to label properly certain types of products that might harm the consumer if he were not forewarned."

A.R. Fisher, President of Johns-Manville Corporation, Address to Industrial Hygiene Foundation 20th Annual Meeting 1955 (Trans. Bull. No. 29, pp. 12–18, I.H.F. Pittsburgh)

This chapter will discuss issues which arise in personal injury suits brought by asbestos insulation workers and others exposed through asbestos product use.

The Charges: Failure to Test, Failure to Warn

In the personal injury suits brought by U.S. asbestos product users, the manufacturers are being sued for their failure to do these things:

1. test the products for potential dangers to consumers
2. label the products with appropriate warnings about the dangers and means to minimize them; and
3. use other available means to safeguard users of the products against the hazards involved

U.S. Mineral Products Company considered affixing health warnings to packages of its sprayed asbestos products in 1962 and claims to have started using such labels in late December of that year. Johns-Manville considered and rejected applying health warning labels on sacks of asbestos in Canada (1952, 1965), "Marinite" asbestos-containing boards (1958), and "J-Spray" asbestos spray-on fireproofing (1960). The usual reasons for not using warning labels were the expected loss of sales, the implications for having to label other product lines, and damage to J-M's competitive position unless the other members of the industry agreed to take identical action. The reasons warning labels were considered were dust created in product use, legal protection from liability, and (in 1952) compliance with generally stated Illinois law and regulations. In 1958, the failure to warn of health concerns in addition to advising dust control was seen as a "good business answer" but not a good "legal" answer!

A pivotal year was 1964, when some but not all of the manufacturers of asbestos insulation products began to affix the first generation of caution labels. The Johns-Manville Corporation placed this warning label on packages of its asbestos insulation products:

> This product contains asbestos fiber. Inhalation of asbestos in excessive quantities over long periods of time may be harmful. If dust is created when this product is handled, avoid breathing the dust. If adequate ventilation

> control is not possible, wear respirators approved by the U.S. Bureau of Mines for *pneumoconiosis-producing* dusts. (emphasis added)

Not until 1969 were the first warnings also placed on sacks of asbestos fiber; other products, such as asbestos-cement panels and brake linings, do not appear to have borne warning labels until the 1970s.

In 1964, the epidemiologic studies of Selikoff, Hammond, and Churg were published, showing that insulation workers had a startlingly high likelihood of dying from occupationally caused diseases such as asbestosis, lung cancer, mesothelioma, and gastrointestinal cancer.[2] Later in the year, a large conference on asbestos disease was held by the New York Academy of Sciences. The proceedings were published in the Academy's *Annals* (V. 132) in 1965. At this meeting, Dr. Selikoff and his co-workers reported that radiological evidence of asbestosis was seen in 86 percent of the 392 insulators they had examined who had started in the trade more than 20 years before. "In half of these, the asbestosis was moderate or extensive."[3]

Most asbestos insulation workers swear they never saw a warning label until the late 1960s or early 1970s. They also testify, with rare exceptions, that they were unaware of the health threat of their work in the years prior to 1965.

In the precedent setting *Borel v. Fibreboard* case, the U.S. Fifth Circuit Court of Appeals concluded that "a duty to warn attaches, *whenever a reasonable man would want to be informed of the risk in order to decide whether to expose himself to it*." (emphasis added) In this case, the trial judge instructed the jury that the manufacturers had no duty to warn of the danger from the use of their products unless and until the state of knowledge was such that a reasonably prudent manufacturer would have been aware of the danger.[5]

The court held the manufacturer to "the knowledge and skill of an *expert*" regarding scientific discoveries and, "even more importantly, a manufacturer has a duty to test and inspect his product."[4] The court explained,

> The extent of research and experiment must be commensurate with the dangers involved. A product must not be made available to the public without disclosure of those dangers that reasonable foresight would reveal. Nor may a manufacturer rely unquestioningly on others to sound the hue and cry concerning a danger in its product. Rather, each manufacturer must bear the burden of showing that its own conduct was proportionate to its duty.

The trial judge in *Borel* defined, "unreasonably dangerous" as dangerous to an extent beyond that contemplated by an insulator with knowledge available to him. The manufacturers' claim that it was the insulation contractors' responsibility to warn the insulators was rejected.

> The sellers' warning must reasonably be calculated to reach (the ultimate consumers) and the presence of an intermediate party will not by itself relieve the seller of this duty.

Each of the fifty states imposes its own laws, precedents and peculiarities on product liability. This introduction is intended only to basically frame the issues involved. Several volumes on this subject by attorneys are already in print.[6,7,8]

Basic "State of the Art" Defense Arguments

Subsequent to the verdict in *Borel* being upheld on appeal, it was clear that many similar lawsuits would be filed by other workers. A meeting of 18 insurance company representatives in 1976 concluded with a decision to do research on the state of the art defense and identify doctors who would be willing to testify in maintaining it.[9]

The defendants in asbestos disease litigation today contend that they had no actual knowledge of a hazard to the users of their products before 1964, nor did they have sufficient cause to conduct studies to see whether their products posed health dangers for the users. They claim the risk of developing an illness from breathing asbestos dust was thought to be limited to mining, milling, and manufacturing plant workers between 1930 and 1964.

The principal defendants acknowledge that the disease, asbestosis, has been known since 1930. They point out that it was the asbestos industry that had approached Dr. Lanza in 1929 and cooperated in the plant surveys described in Lanza's 1935 article.[10]

They note that the broad-scale surveys published by Merewether and Price, Fulton *et al.*, Lanza *et al.*, and Dreessen *et al.* in the 1930s all involved asbestos factory workers, and asbestos textile workers in particular.[10-13] They claim that a hazard to users of asbestos products could not be assumed nor necessarily anticipated based on reports of asbestosis among textile workers. As Selikoff and his co-workers had acknowledged, the asbestos textile plants were chosen in early surveys as the best places to observe the uncomplicated effects of asbestos dust:[3]

> The textile industry was selected for study since only here was there pure or almost pure asbestos exposure. Since it was urgent to investigate the effect of this dust, limiting the investigation to this branch of the industry avoided the possible complications which might be introduced by the presence of other potentially fibrogenic dusts.

These authors noted that fibrous glass products had come into increasing use over the preceding 30 years; moreover, the molded products frequently used by insulators were approximately 15 percent asbestos. The authors characterized the insulators' asbestos exposure as "limited and intermittent."

Much is made of the reference above to "pure asbestos" in the factories versus "limited" asbestos exposure in insulation work. Some defendants in asbestos litigation today contend that they had believed that the daily exposure level of 5 MPPCF was a safe level until the late 1960s, and that insulators were exposed to lower levels of asbestos-containing dust. Some defendants further suggest that asbestos textile workers were exposed to much purer asbestos exposure in the airborne dust breathed than were insulation workers, i.e., that the asbestos fiber fraction of the dust was much greater in the textile plants than in insulation work.

The contention that insulation installers were presumed to

be exposed to less than 5 MPPCF—and hence were considered, until well into the 1960s, to be within the "safe" zone of exposure to asbestos—is very open to question on both grounds (see Chapter 4). The "asbestos" and "total fiber" fractions reported in the airborne dust for both asbestos textile factory and insulation exposures lend little if any support to the "all versus nearly nothing" account of textile plant workers' vs. insulators' fractional asbestos fiber exposure. (See "Asbestos Fiber Fraction of Inhaled Dust" in Chapter 4).

Knowledgeable lawyers representing asbestos companies and former asbestos companies have posed the question: "State of the art as a defense—is it real?" While no clear answer to that question was offered, it was concluded that, "(T)he threshold limit value concept is probably the best thing the defense has in its arsenal."[14] Though this may be, few defendants have documented any historic awareness of the TLV before the 1970s; and fewer, if any, offer a persuasive record of evidence that it was corporate policy to assure conformance with the TLV in their own operations. No insulation manufacturer ever conducted product testing to see if customers' exposures were above or below the TLV; and no testing was done before Selikoff came along that even suggested that normal use of asbestos insulation could be expected to yield exposures below the TLV (See Table 3, Chapter 4). No company ever issued a warning label stating that exposure during product use should not be allowed to exceed 5 MPPCF or any other specific concentration (and if so, what disease risks would then exist and what should be done to eliminate them).

In view of the factual record, the author submits that the answer to the question posed by the knowledgeable defense attorneys at their strategy meeting is obvious, at least from a scientific point of view.

The Published Literature on Asbestos Disease from Product Use

In fact there wasn't ever any necessity to rely on interpretations of the plant worker studies' import for insulators, analyze Dr. Selikoff's restrospective remarks, or await the publication of data showing whether insulators were exposed daily to 5 MPPCF of sufficiently asbestiform airborne dust. The reason is simple: *There were dozens of reports of asbestosis among insulators published before 1964.*

Asbestosis is a distinctive disease, both radiologically and pathologically. The clinical findings are also distinctive enough that the diagnosis can usually be made on the basis of an adequate occupational history and chest X-ray, other causes having been ruled out with reasonable medical certainty. Asbestosis is caused by one thing only—breathing asbestos. When an asbestosis patient who worked as an insulation worker is described in the literature, there are only three possible inferences:

1. the worker didn't really have asbestosis; his condition was misdiagnosed;
2. the asbestosis was contracted from an unrecognized and unreported asbestos exposure; or
3. the asbestosis was contracted as a consequence of doing insulation work.

One or two such early reports, especially if not verified pathologically, might be open to doubt. However, autopsy reports confirming the early observations were available by the early 1940s. The two insulators described by Holleb and Angrist (1942) had lung cancer as well as asbestosis. Kuhn's 1940 report appears to document the first case of fatal asbestosis in an insulation worker. Pathologists at Massachusetts General Hospital reported asbestosis and mesothelioma in an insulation worker in 1947. (See Tables 1–3).

In addition to primary reports of asbestosis in product users, review articles and medical textbooks existed that mentioned the asbestosis hazard to insulators and/or asbestos product users starting in the 1930s. Other sources listed only asbestos textile processes as the occupations at risk of asbestosis. But certainly many of the doctors who authored those writings never even thought they were providing all-inclusive lists of the occupations at risk. They were, after all, more interested,

Table 1.

Recognition of Asbestosis Hazard Among Insulators and Other Asbestos Product Users

Country	Year of Recognition	Year Reported	Author(s)	Reference
USA		1932	Russell	in Table 2
Germany	1937	1940	Kuhn	in Table 2
Finland	1938	1971	Ahlman & Siltanen	Exposure of Insulation Workers to Asbestos Dust. *Work-Environment-Health 8:* 1-5 (1971).
United Kingdom		1933	Ellman	in Table 2
Norway		1940–41	Wolff, Schrumpf	in Table 2

Italy		1948	Canepa	in Table 3
Denmark		1950	Frost	in Table 2
Switzerland		1952	Sroka	in Table 5
Sweden	1950	1956	Ahlborg & Hansson	in Table 3
Netherlands	1939	1988	Swuste, et al.	*Asbest, het Inzicht in de Schadelijke gevolgen in de Periode 1930–1969 in Nederland* Delft Univ. Press
Australia		1957	Thomas	in Table 5

Table 2. Asbestos Disease in Insulation Workers and Other Asbestos Product Users Medical Literature: Cases of Disease Reported Before 1964

Year	Author(s)	Reference	Occupations	Diseases
1932	Russell	*Proceedings of Conference Concerning Effects of Dusts Upon the Respiratory System* (held by the Industrial Commission of Wisconsin; p. 180), Democrat Press	insulator	asbestosis
1933	Ellman	*J. Indust. Hyg. 15:* 165-183	insulator	asbestosis
1934	Ellman	*Brit. J. Radiol. 7:* 281-295	insulator	asbestosis
1934	Wood & Gloyne	*Lancet 2:* 1383-1385	boiler riveter	asbestosis
1935	Jacobson	*Acta Med. Scand. 78:* 482-488	welder	"early acute asbestosis"
1936	Ellman	*Seventh International Congress of Occupational Accidents and Illnesses,* Jean Vromans, Brussels, pp. 409-423	insulator	asbestosis
1939	Arnold, Beal and Cookson	*Brit. J. Tuberc. 33:* 45-48	asbestos handler in a chemical plant	asbestosis

1940	Wolff	*Nord. Med. 5:* 535-541	3 asbestos handlers in a chemical plant	asbestosis
1940	Kuhn	*Arch. Gewerbepath. Gewerbehyg. 10:* 133-150	shipyard insulator	asbestosis
1941	Schrumpf	*Nord. Med. 9:* 704-706	asbestos handler in a chemical plant	asbestosis
1942	Williams	*Med. Bull. Vet. Admin.* 18:250-253	aluminum plant worker wearing asbestos apron and gloves	asbestosis
1942	Holleb & Angrist	*Amer. J. Path. 18:* 123-131	2 insulators	asbestosis & lung cancer in both
1947	Kennaway & Kennaway	*Brit. J. Cancer 1:* 260-297	insulator	asbestosis & lung cancer
1947	Mallory, Castleman, and Parris	*New Eng. J. Med. 236:* 407-412	insulator	asbestosis & mesothelioma
1949	Franchini & Canepa	*Med. Lavoro 40:* 161-172	insulator	asbestosis
1950	Frost	*Ugeskr. Laeger 112:* 1284-1289	shipyard insulator	asbestosis

(continued)

Table 2. Asbestos Disease in Insulation Workers and Other Asbestos Product Users Medical Literature: Cases of Disease Reported Before 1964 *(cont.)*

Year	Authors	Reference	Occupations	Diseases
1951	Stoll, Bass, & Angrist	*Arch. Internal Med. 88:* 831-834	plumber/insulator	asbestosis & lung cancer
1953	van Luyt	*Third International Conference of Experts on Pneumoconiosis, Sydney, Feb.–March, 1950, Record of Procceedings,* pp. 169-171	"some" insulators	asbestosis
1953	Isselbacher, Klaus, & Hardy	*Amer. J. Med. 15:* 721-732	contractor's helper sawing asbestos board	asbestosis & lung cancer
1953	Weiss	*Medizinische 3:* 93-94	shipyard insulator	asbestosis & pleural mesothelioma
1955	Sander	*Arch. Industr. Health 12:* 208-211	plumber's helper sawing pipecoverings	asbestosis
1956	Hampe	*Ned. Tijdschr. Geneesk. 100:* 2965-2966	insulator	asbestosis & lung cancer
1956	Molfino & Zannini	*Folia Med. 39:* 525-539	6 shipyard insulators	asbestosis
1957	Marks *et al.*	*Am. J. Med. 22:51-73*	pipefitter	asbestosis

1958	Pendergrass	*Am. J. Roent. 80:* 1-41	insulator	asbestosis
1958	Pendergrass	*The Pneumoconiosis Problem* Charles C. Thomas, Springfield, pp. 97-100	insulator	asbestosis
1958	Van der Schoot	*Ned. Tijdsch. Geneesk. 102:* 1125-1126	3 insulators	asbestosis & mesothelioma
1959	Hertz & Reinwein	*Ärztliche Woch. 14:* 361-365	3 insulators	asbestosis (and lung cancer in one case)
1960	*Whitmore, et al.*	*Armed Forces Med. J. 11:* 203-216	bricklayer	asbestosis & lung cancer
1960	Anderson & Campagna	*Arch. Environ. Health 1:* 27-32	insulator	asbestosis & lung cancer
1960	Ahlmark, Bruce, and Nyström	*Silicosis and Other Pneumoconioses in Sweden* Svenska Bokförlaget, Stockholm, pp. 353-357	8 to 11 insulators and two asbestos sprayers (including cases reported by Ahlborg and Hansson in 1956)	asbestosis (and lung cancer in one case)
1960	Keal	*Lancet 2:* 1211-1216	5 insulators	asbestosis & cancer
1960	Wagner, Sleggs, & Marchand	*Brit. J. Industr. Med. 17:* 260-271	3 insulators	mesothelioma and asbestosis
1960	Eisenstadt & Wilson	*Journal-Lancet 80:* 511-514	2 insulators	asbestosis & mesothelioma

(continued)

Table 2. Asbestos Disease in Insulation Workers and Other Asbestos Product Users Medical Literature: Cases of Disease Reported Before 1964 *(cont.)*

Year	Authors	Reference	Occupations	Diseases
1961	Ambrosi & Cavallo	*Riv. Infort. Mal. Prof. 48:* 818-827	2 insulators	asbestosis
1961	Castleman & Kibbee	*New Eng. J. Med. 265:* 745-751	shipyard worker	asbestosis
1961	Heárd & Williams	*Thorax 16:* 264-281	carpenter, insulator	asbestosis & lung cancer; asbestosis & peritoneal mesothelioma
1961	Frenkel & de Jager	*Yearbook of Cancer Research & The Fight Against Cancer in the Netherlands 11:* 99-106	insulator	peritoneal mesothelioma
1961	Telischi & Rubenstone	*Arch. Path. 72:* 116-125	plaster mixer	asbestosis & lung cancer
1961	Brugsch & Bavley	*New Eng. J. Med. 265:* 375-381	automobile undercoater	asbestosis
1961	Sleggs, Marchand, and Wagner	*S. Afr. Med. J. 35:* 28-34	3 insulators	mesothelioma
1962	Thomson	*S. Afr. Med. J. 36:* 759-760	1 builder	mesothelioma

1962	Eisenstadt	*Amer. Practitioner 13:* 573-578	1 insulator, 2 refinery foremen	mesothelioma & asbestosis
1962	McCaughey, Wade, and Elmes	*Brit. Med. J. 2:* 1397	5 shipyard workers, 1 engine room fitter	mesothelioma
1962	Cordova, Tesluk, and Knudtson	*Cancer 15:* 1181-1187	hod carrier, iron worker, shipyard worker, bricklayer, 3 insulators, carpenter	asbestosis & lung cancer
1963	Bogetti	*XIVth International Congress of Occupational Health*, Madrid, Spain, Sept. 16, 1963, Vol. 4, Abstracts of Free Communications, Excerpta Medica Foundation, Amsterdam, page E52.	10 insulators	asbestosis
1963	Castleman & Kibbee	*New Eng. J. Med. 269:* 747-753	1 plumber	asbestosis & mesothelioma
1963	Farina & Mazzanti	*Lavoro Umano 15:* 276-281	1 insulator	asbestosis & lung cancer
1963	Leathart & Sanderson	*Ann. Occup. Hyg. 6:* 63-74	18 insulators	asbestosis

Table 3. Epidemiological Reports on Insulation Workers and Related Trades

Year	Reference	Disease
1946	Fleischer, Viles, Gade, and Drinker *J. Industr. Hyg. Tox. 28:* 9-16	asbestosis in 3 of 51 active workers with more than 10 years experience in the insulation trade; no cases found in over 1000 with shorter exposure
1948	Canepa, *Lavoro Med. 2:* 18-20	summary report of asbestosis in a cohort of 52 Genoa insulators
	Canepa, *Zacchia, 12:* 188-205	definite asbestosis in 5 cases and early asbestosis in 10 others — in a survey of 52 insulators in Genoa
1954	Breslow, *et al., Amer. J. Publ. Health 44:* 171-181	an excessive rate of lung cancer among "steamfitters, boilermakers, and asbestos workers" in an epidemiologic study of relation between occupation, smoking, and lung cancer
1955	Breslow, *Dis. Chest 28:* 421-430	
1956	Ahlborg and Hansson, *Svenska Läkartidningen 53:* 1376-1383	7 insulators and 2 asbestos sprayers with asbestosis in a group of about 60 workers examined
1956	Frost, Georg, and Møller. *Danish Med. Bull. 3:* 202-204	9 asbestosis cases, and 19 with pleural abnormalities among 31 workers examined with 20 or more years in the insulation trade
1961	Hetzel, "Long Beach Naval Shipyard Study of Asbestos Workers in Relation to Asbestosis" 3-16, June, 1961. U.S. Navy document	17 cases of asbestosis in about 80 shipyard insulators

Table 3. Epidemiological Reports on Insulation Workers and Related Trades (*con't*)

1964	Selikoff, Hammond, and Churg. *J.A.M.A. 188:* 22-26	Follow-up mortality study on 632 insulators (255 deaths) showing excessive incidence of lung cancer and gastrointestinal cancer; also 4 deaths from mesothelioma and 12 from asbestosis.

in general, in manifestations of the disease process than in the myriad industrial aspects of asbestos use and control.

Usually the hazard was described as, "breathing asbestos dust." In many cases the authors were more or less explicit in including as at risk the asbestos product users as well as asbestos miners and plant workers.[15-18] What one does *not* see expressed repeatedly in the literature is the view that: mining, milling, and manufacturing workers are at risk of asbestosis, but asbestos product users are not.

There is one article only that contains qualified statements along these lines: "Survey of Pipecovering Operations in Constructing Naval Vessels," by W.E. Fleischer and co-workers.[19]

The Fleischer, Viles, Gade, and Drinker Report

Fleischer and his co-workers conducted chest X-ray examinations and dust surveys at four Naval shipyards at the close of World War II. As shown in their report, there were 51 workers with "10 plus" years in the pipecovering industry, out of 1,074 workers examined. Fully 948 had had less than 5 years in the trade. Three cases of moderate and advanced asbestosis were found, all in men with more than 20 years of asbestos work.

Dust counts for individual tasks ranged from 0 to 250 MPPCF, and no attempt was made to estimate an "average" daily exposure for insulation work. Removal of old insulation for replacement, probably the dustiest job, was not monitored at all in this survey of new ship construction sites. (See

"Exposure to Asbestos in Insulation Work," in Chapter 4, for more details.) The authors noted that the TLV recommended in 1938 by Dreessen and co-workers was based on total dust analyses. Although the sampling data tabulated in this study included figures for total dust and "asbestos dust," only the total dust figures were discussed in the text of the paper.

The findings of these authors were fully consistent with previous reports on the time needed for development of asbestosis. What distinguishes the Fleischer report is the authors' analysis of their findings. While recommending exhaust ventilation for the dustiest processes, these investigators gave the pipecovering trade a rather clean bill of health. Because of the importance lately attributed to this report, the authors' conclusions are included here in full:

1. The character of asbestos pipecovering industry on board naval vessels is such that conclusions drawn from other asbestos industries such as textiles, cannot be applied.
2. The operations of band saw cutting, grinding, cement mixing, and installation on board a ship should be equipped with exhaust ventilation to keep the total dust concentration low.
3. The incidence of asbestosis among pipe coverers in the shipyards studied was low, *0.29 percent or 3 cases out of 1074*. In view of the nature of shipyard pipe covering work, this low incidence is not surprising. (emphasis added)
4. Since each of the 3 cases of asbestosis had worked at asbestos pipe covering in shipyards for more than 20 years, it may be concluded that such pipecovering is not a dangerous occupation.

This report is unusual in its absence of any discussion of the disease asbestosis. Whether the authors carefully read the radiology chapter in Dr. Lanza's book (... "no appreciable number of cases of asbestosis are discovered until the second five years of employment. Relatively few cases mature in this minimum period of seven years; many, even in the more dusty processes, require eleven years.") which they cited, is questionable.[20] The inclusion of 277 workers with 0–2 years' experience in their survey is understandable. But fully 88 percent of the workers in this study had had less than five years of employment as insulators in the shipyards. The inclusion of these workers as a dilution factor in conclusion No. 3 indicated considerable ignorance about the "maturation period" for the development of asbestosis. The only medical reference cited besides Lanza's book was the Dreessen survey.[13]

It is not even clear how the authors determined whether some of the men had asbestosis. The text and one of the tables (4) clearly indicate that diagnosis was based solely on the reading of 1074 chest X-rays. But in Table 5, on the "relationship between length of exposure and incidence of asbestosis," a total of 1124 subjects are included. For one of the yards (B), the number of men included in this table far exceeded the number X-rayed. For two other yards, the number X-rayed was greater than the number included in Table 5. If some of the latter yards' X-rays were of such poor quality that they couldn't be read for asbestosis, this was nowhere acknowledged. So there are questions both about men included in the analysis in Table 5 for whom there were no X-rays, and men excluded from it for whom there were chest X-rays taken.

The article published by Fleischer, Drinker, and co-workers in 1946 appears to conflict with earlier, unpublished reports by some of these writers. In 1944, Fleischer and Dr. W.C. Dreessen found radiologically well-established asbestosis in 2 men and considered the X-rays of 4 others "consistent with a diagnosis of asbestosis." In all, they examined chest X-rays of 38 pipecoverers in Bath, Maine.[21] Local exhaust ventilation, respiratory protection, and yearly chest X-rays of the workers were advised. "The conditions in this shop present a very real asbestosis hazard and immediate steps should be taken to segregate the most dusty processes into a well-ventilated area," the doctors wrote. Similarly strong recommendations were made in a 1942 survey of the Oregon Shipbuilding Corporation. In this, Drinker and his co-workers urged that the union be told about the hazards of breathing asbestos and instructed in proper preventive measures.[22] In 1944, Drinker voiced concern about high peak exposures where men worked with amosite asbestos.[23] Dust counts were "very much higher than anyone would recommend—they ran up to 25 million." Given the above data and expressions of concern over the industrial hygiene aspects of insulation work during the War, it is especially difficult to understand how these investigators could then write that pipecovering was "not a dangerous occupation."

It is almost impossible to find any comment on the Fleischer report in the medical literature during the fifteen years after its publication. The 1956 paper by Molfino and Zannini is the only such reference the author has located. It credited Fleischer and co-workers with being the discoverers of the asbestosis hazard in shipyard insulation work.[24] It is very hard to believe that anyone who was knowledgeable about asbestosis was misled by the Fleischer study's naive conclusions.

The author has seen counsel for asbestos product manufacturers go to great lengths to impress juries through strained readings of this 1946 article. The implication, at least, is that this article was read by corporate management, and that it influenced corporate policy. However, when pressed, no defendant, with the possible exception of Johns-Manville, has been able to produce documentation or testimony to show that this article was even read by anyone in management in the asbestos industry in the 1940s and 1950s. And no defendant has produced documentation or testimony to the effect that this article was relied upon by management for any purpose during that era. On the other hand, corporate officials of some companies (e.g., E. Torbohn of Fibreboard, Dr. K. W. Smith of Johns-Manville) have acknowledged that they had never heard of this report, much less relied upon it in making business decisions.

Other Early Population Studies of Asbestosis in Insulators

Earlier "case reports" of asbestosis in insulators and other asbestos product users contained no data on the prevalence of the disease in the work force at risk. The Fleischer study was the first survey of a defined population of insulators (prevalence study). During the next 10 years, reports from Italy, Sweden, and Denmark showed a consistently high prevalence of asbestosis in insulation workers (see Table 3).

Table 4. Abstracts of Articles (in Tables 2-3) Which Cite Asbestosis and Cancer Hazards to Asbestos Product Users

Wood, W.B. and S.R. Gloyne (1934) — *Bull. Hyg. 10:* 219-220 (1935). Reprinted in *Pneumoconiosis Abstr. I;* 143 (1953).

Kuhn, A. (1940) — *Bull. Hyg. 17:* 819-821 (1942). Reprinted in *Pneumoconiosis Abstr. II:* 4-5 (1954).

Fleischer, W.E. *et al.* (1946) — *Indust. Hyg. Digest 10:* 12 (April, 1946).

Franchini, A. and G. Canepa (1949) — *Bull. Hyg. 25:* 150 (1950). Reprinted in *Pneumoconiosis Abstr. II:* 169-170 (1954).
- –*Arch. Indust. Hyg. Occup. Med. 1:* 362-363 (1950).
- –*Indust. Hyg. Digest 14:* 28-29 (March, 1950).

Stoll, R., R. Bass, and A.A. Angrist (1951) — *Bull. Hyg. 27:* 444 (1952). Reprinted in *Pneumoconiosis Abstr. III:* 177 (1959).

Breslow, L. (1955) — *Chest Diseases Section XV of Excerpta Medica 9:* 257 (1956).

Frost, J., J. Georg, and P.F. Møller (1956) — *Indust. Hyg. Digest 21:* abstract no. 761 (June, 1957).
- –*Bull. Hyg. 32:* 260 (1957).
- –*Abstr. World Med. 21:* 359 (1957).
- –*Public Health, Social Medicine and Hygiene Sec. XVII of Excerpta Medica 3:* 596 (1957).

Molfino, F. and D. Zannini (1956) — *Bull. Hyg. 32:* 1168-1169 (1957).
- –*Public Health, Social Medicine and Hygiene Sec. XVII of Excerpta Medica 3:* 596 (1957).
- –*Chest Diseases Sec. XV of Excerpta Medica 10:* 501 (1957).

Hertz, C.W. and H. Reinwein (1959) — *Chest Diseases Sec. XV of Excerpta Medica 12:* 674 (1959).

Ambrosi, L. and A. Cavallo (1961) — *Public Health, Social Medicine and Hygiene Sec. XVII of Excerpta Medica 8:* 837-838 (1962).
- –*Chest Diseases Sec. XV of Excerpta Medica 16:* 37-38 (1963).

Telischi, M. and A.I. Rubenstone (1961) — *Public Health, Social Medicine and Hygiene Sec. XVII of Excerpta Medica 8:* 442 (1962).
- –*Chest Diseases Sec. XV of Excerpta Medica 15:* 454 (1962).

Brugsch, H.G. and H. Bavley (1961) — *Arch. Environ. Health 4:* 114 (1962).
- –*Indust. Hyg. Digest 25:* abstract no. 997 (Oct. 1961).
- –*Chest Diseases Sec. XV of Excerpta Medica 15:* 269 (1962).
- –*Public Health, Social Medicine and Hygiene Sec. XVII of Excerpta Medica 8:* 517 (1962).

Eisenstadt, H.B. (1962) — *Indust. Hyg. Digest 26:* abstract no. 1171 (Dec. 1962).
- –*J.A.M.A. 182:* 205 (1962).

Leathart, G.L. and J.T. Sanderson (1963) — *Public Health, Social Medicine and Hygiene Sec. XVII of Excerpta Medica 9:* 988 (1963).

Note: In all the above examples, the asbestosis risk to product users is evident from the abstract itself. There are also abstracts of other papers from Tables 2-3 which do not describe the occupations of the patients, but these are not included here.

Table 5. Some Articles Noting Disease/Risk in Insulation Workers and Other Asbestos Product Users

Merewether, E.R.A. A Memorandum on Asbestosis. *Tubercle 15:* 69-81 (1933).

Asbestos. *Indust. Bull. 13:* 95 (1934).

Lanza, A.J. Dust Diseases as They Affect the Construction Industry. *Trans. 25th Nat. Safety Cong.*, Chicago: Nat. Safety Council, 1936, pp. 244-246.

Sappington, C.O. Banish the Dust Hazard. *Mill and Factory 18:* 69-71, 150-152 (1936).

Merewether, E.R.A. Dusts and the Lungs. *Industrial Medicine Symposium No. 3* Medical Press and Circular Supplement pp. 11-17 (July 20, 1938).

Brown, E.W. Industrial Hygiene and the Navy in National Defense. *Air Hygiene Foundation of America, Inc. Fifth Annual Meeting of Members,* 77-84 (Nov. 12-13, 1940).

Hueper, W.C. *Occupational Tumors and Allied Diseases,* Springfield, Ill.: C. Thomas Publ., 1942, pp. 399-405.

Dublin, L.I. and R.J. Vane. *Occupation Hazards and Diagnostic Signs.* Bull. No. 41, U.S. Dept. of Labor Standards, 1942, p. 25.

Gardner, L.U. The Pneumoconiosis. *Med. Clin. North Amer. 26*: 1239-1260 (1942).

Grämer, J. Health Injuries in Electro-welders. *Arch. Gewerbepath. Gewerbehyg. 11:* 644-685 (1942). Abstract in *Bull. Hyg. 18:* 847-848 (1943); reprinted in *Pneumoconiosis Abstracts II:* 327-328 (1954).

Minimum Requirements for Safety and Industrial Health in Contract Shipyards. *Indust. Med. Surg. 12:* 259-263 (1943).

Homburger, F. The Coincidence of Primary Carcinoma of the Lungs and Pulmonary Asbestosis. *Amer. J. Path. 19:* 797-807 (1943).

Lawrence, W.E. Fume Control in Shipyards. *Nat. Safety News* (1944), April, pp. 16-17, 90-92, and, Trans. 32nd Nat. Safety Cong., 1943, pp. 401–404.

Hutchinson, F.W. Dust as an Industrial Health Hazard. *Heating and Ventilating 41:* 57-61 (1944).

Alden, H.S. and W.H. Howell. The Asbestos Corn. *Arch. Dermatol. Syphil. 49:* 312-314 (1944).

Annual Report of the Chief Inspector of Factories for the Year 1945, London: H.M. Stationery Ofc., 1946, pp. 13-14.

Drinker, P. Health and Safety in Contract Shipyards During The War. *Occup. Med. 3:* 335-343 (1947).

Asbestos Dust. *Safety Review 4:* 13 (1947). U.S. Navy.

Brahdy, L. Discussion. *Dis. Chest. 14:* 885-888 (1948).

(Editorial) Asbestosis and Cancer of the Lung. *J.A.M.A. 140:* 1219-1220 (1949).

Asbestos Regulations. *Annual Report of the Chief Inspector of Factories for the Year 1949,* London: H.M. Stationery Ofc., 1951, pp. 144-146.

Table 5. Some Articles Noting Disease/Risk in Insulation Workers and Other Asbestos Product Users (continued)

Sroka, K.H. Occupational Disease caused by Asbestos. *Krebsarzt 7:* 167-171 (1952).

Hardy, H.L. Occupational Medicine. *New Eng. J. Med. 247:* 473-483 (1952).

McVittie, J.D. Pneumoconiosis in the United Kingdom. *Third International Conference of Experts on Pneumoconiosis, Sydney, February–March, 1950, Record of Proceedings.* Geneva: International Labor Office, 1953, p. 172.

Lung Cancer. *Safety Maint. Prod. 107:* 66 (1954).

Portigliatti-Barbos, M. Considerations on the Association between Asbestosis and Pulmonary Carcinoma. *Giorn. Acad. Med. Torino* 91-107 (1955).

McLaughlin, A.I.G. The Dust Diseases in Great Britain. *Arch. Industr. Health 12:* 83-98 (1955).

Gardiner, J.F. Occupational Diseases of the Lungs. *Nebraska State Med. J. 40:* 285-289 (1955).

Pabst, A.C. The Expanding Field of Industrial Hygiene. *Nat. Safety News 71:* 20-21, 103-111 (April, 1955).

____________. Industrial Hygiene in the Petroleum Industry. *Petroleum Eng.* E-2 to E-8 (May, 1955).

Hueper, W.C. *A Quest into the Environmental Causes of Cancer of the Lung.* Public Health Monograph No. 36, Washington: Public Health Service Publication No. 452, 1955, pp. 35-38.

Francia, A. and G. Monarca. Asbestosis and Pulmonary Carcinoma. *Minerva Med. 47:* 1950-1959 (1956).

Thomas, D.L.G. Pneumokoniosis in Victorian Industry. *Med. J. Australia 1:* 75-77 (1957).

The Protection of Workers against Occupational Diseases and Poisoning. Geneva: Chemical Industries Committee, Fifth Session, Third Item on the Agenda, International Labour Office, 1957, pp. 21-23.

Asbestos Industry Regulations, 1931. *Annual Report of the Chief Inspector of Factories for the Year 1956,* London: H.M. Stationery Ofc., 1958, pp. 141-145.

Gough, J. Discussion. *Proceedings of the Pneumoconiosis Conference held at the University of Witwatersand, Johannesburg, 9-24 Feb. 1959.* (Ed. A.J. Orenstein), Boston: Little, Brown & Co., 1960, p. 390.

Schepers, G.W.H. Pneumoconiosis. *Encyclopedia Britannica 18:* 99-100 (1960).

Occupational Health Hazards Release No. 27, U.S. Navy, p. 104 (1960).

Occupational Health Hazards Release No. 29, U.S. Navy, p. 32 (1961).

Meyer, W.H. and F.W. Church. Industrial Hygiene Aspects of Mechanical Operations in a Petroleum Refinery. *Med. Bull. 21:* 256-265 (1961).

Hueper, W.C. Carcinogens in the Human Environment. *Arch. Path. 71:* 237-267 (1961).

Hurwitz, M. Roentgenologic Aspects of Asbestosis. *Amer. J. Roent. 85:* 256-262 (1961).

Table 5. Some Articles Noting Disease/Risk in Insulation Workers and Other Asbestos Product Users (continued)

Sheinbaum, M. Some Health Hazards Associated with the Building Trades. *Amer. Industr. Hyg. Assoc. J. 23:* 353-358 (1962).

Working Conditions and Safety in Shipbuilding and Ship Repairing. Metal Trades Committee, Seventh Session, International Labour Office, 1962, pp. 85-86.

Hervieux, J. Certain Aspects de l'Asbestose. *Cahiers Méd. Inter Professionelle 7:* 41-42 (1962).

Hueper, W.C. Part 1. Environmental and Occupational Cancer Hazards. *Clin. Pharm. Therap. 3:* 776-813 (1962).

Asbestosis, *Safety Review 19:* 10 (1962).

An, S.H. and I. Koprowska. Primary Cytologic Diagnoses of Asbestosis Associated with Bronchogenic Carcinoma. *Acta Cytol. 6:* 391-398 (1962).

Thomson, J.G., R.O.C. Kaschula, and R.R. MacDonald. Asbestos as a Modern Urban Hazard. *S. Afr. Med. J. 37:* 77-81 (1963).

Construction Health Hazards. *Michigan's Occupational Health 8:* 1-5 (1963).

Editorial. *S. Afr. Med. J. 37:* 629-630 (1963).

Thermal Insulation of Pipes and Vessels EEUA Handbook 12, London: Constable & Co., 1963, p. 31.

Gault, G.A. and M.F. Adams. *Dusting Properties of Thermal Insulation Materials* Wash. State Institute of Technology Bull. 269 (1963).

Table 6. Some Textbook References to Occupational Disease Hazard of Insulation Work and Other Asbestos Product Use

Lanza, A.J. (ed.) Occupational, Preventive, and Legislative Aspects in Great Britain/Asbestosis. *Silicosis and Asbestosis,* New York: Oxford University Press 1938, pp. 385-390.

Collier, H.E. Asbestosis. *Outlines of Industrial Medical Practice.* Baltimore: Williams and Wilkins Co. Baltimore, 1941, pp. 364-368.

Sappington, C.O. Essentials of Industrial Health, Philadelphia: J.P. Lippincott Co., 1943, p. 191.

Sax, N.I. *Handbook of Dangerous Materials* New York: Reinhold Publ. Corp., 1951, p. 34.

Johnstone, R.T. Asbestosis. *Occupational Medicine and Industrial Hygiene,* St. Louis: C.V. Mosby Co., 1948, pp. 368-372.

Hinshaw, H.C. and L. H. Garland. Asbestosis. *Diseases of the Chest,* Philadelphia: W.B. Saunders Co., 1956, pp. 666-668.
–(second edition) pp. 742-744 (1963).

Merewether, E.R.A. (ed.) Pneumoconiosis and Industrial Carcinogenesis chapters *Industrial Medicine and Hygiene Vol. 3,* London: Butterworth & Co., 1956, pp. 105-117 and 215-224.

Hunter, Donald. Asbestosis. *Health In Industry,* Baltimore: Penguin Books, 1959, pp. 214-215.
DuBois, K.P. and E.M.K. Geiling. Asbestosis. *Textbook of Toxicology,* New York: Oxford University Press, 1959, pp. 105-106.
Eckhardt, R.E. Asbestos Handling. Industrial Carcinogens, New York: Grune and Stratton, 1959, pp. 132-134.
Schepers, G.W.H. (Fleming, A.J., C.A. D'Alonzo, and J.A. Zapp eds.) Asbestosis. *Modern Occupational Medicine,* Philadelphia: Lea and Febiger, 1960, pp. 463-470.
Gross, P. (A.J. Lanza, Ed.) Pathology of Asbestosis. *The Pneumoconioses,* New York: Grune & Stratton, 1963, pp. 48-53.

Table 7. Legal Literature/Cases—Asbestos Product Users

cite	issues	outcome date
Lacomastic Corp. v. Parker U.S. District Court, Distr. of Md. Admiralty — No. 2617. in *Workmen's Compensation Law Reporting Service,* Commerce Clearing House (1944), p. 1068.	aggravation of tuberculosis in an asbestos sprayer's helper in ships; decided in favor of claimant	appeal decided Feb. 9, 1941
CSI 68/49 (K.L.) *Reported Decisions of the Commissioner under the National Insurance (Industrial Injuries) Acts.* Vol. 1 1948-1952 (1955).	affirms an award of compensation for asbestosis to a man who removed insulation from old copper cables	appeal decided in 1949 (U.K.)
CWI 53/50 (K.I.) *Ibid.*	approves of a claim for pneumoconiosis by a man who had insulated pipes	appeal decided in 1950 (U.K.)
Record of Proceedings/ Third International Conference of Experts on Pneumoconiosis, Sydney, February-March 1950 Vol. 1. Geneva: International Labour Office, 1953, pp. 235-247.	workers' compensation law in France includes asbestosis from asbestos spraying; in Italy, from asbestos-cement fabrication	

(continued)

Table 7. Legal Literature/Cases—Asbestos Product Users (*con't*)

cite	issues	outcome date
Hyatt v. Armstrong Florida 121 S. 2d 793	ruling on liability limit in effect for an insulator last exposed in 1945, totally disabled by asbestosis in 1953 (at which time claim was filed)	appeal decided by Florida Supreme Court in 1960
Muldoon v. Charles S. Woods Co. New York Supreme Court Appellate Div. Third Judicial Dept. No. 1397. In *Workmen's Compensation Law Reports*, Commerce Clearing House, pp. 3048-3049 (1959).	asbestosis and tuberculosis in an insulation worker; permanent and total disability award affirmed	appeal decided June 9, 1959
The Shipbuilding and Shiprepairing Regulations, 1960 *Statutory-Instruments 1960 Part II.* 1960 No. 1932 Part VII Regulation 76, H.M. Stationery Office, London, (1961), p. 1454.	requires use of approved breathing apparatus for workers spraying asbestos, ripping out insulation, cleaning sacks that contained asbestos, and cutting asbestos-containing material with a power saw	
Northwestern Asbestos and Cork Co. v. Industrial Commission 21 Wis. 2d 554 124 N.W. 2d 628.	rejects employer's dispute over payment of compensation for asbestosis to an insulator	appeal decided by Supreme Court of Wisconsin Nov. 26, 1963

The "Downstream" Literature

One abstract written in 1957 about the Danish survey (Frost *et al.*) begins with a comment that asbestosis in insulation workers was by then nothing new:[25]

> Experience in many countries has established that workmen employed in the lagging of pipes and boilers may

> contract pneumoconiosis in the course of their employment.

More or less continuously since 1932, insulation workers and other shipyard and construction trades workers had been numbered among the cases of asbestosis and cancer reported in the literature. Increasingly, the risk of asbestos disease associated with the use of asbestos products was noted in primary medical literature, medical textbooks, and medical abstracts (Tables 2–6). Prominent medical dictionaries in the 1930s and 1940s defined "steamfitters' asthma" as asbestosis.[26-29]

Hazards of asbestos product use were reported as well in diverse engineering and safety publications, government reports, trade magazines, and publications even further removed from the medical literature (Table 5). Appealed workers' compensation claims of asbestos insulators made their appearance in legal forums and resulting legal literature at least as early as the 1940s (Table 7).

Unpublished Documentation

Aside from this publicly available literature, more than 3 dozen compensation claims have been discovered, filed in the years 1952–1963, involving workers (with asbestosis and cancer) employed by the contracting divisions of asbestos insulation manufacturers (see "Workers' Compensation Claims by Insulators against Contracting Divisions of Asbestos Product Manufacturers," in Chapter 3). Johns-Manville, Eagle-Picher, and others were also sued for product liability by insulation workers (See "Lawsuits by Product Users Against Asbestos Manufacturers," in Chapter 3).

There existed various other unpublished references to insulation workers' asbestos hazards, mainly contained in correspondence, that have come to light in discovery proceedings. Some of these add further to the demonstrable body of "actual knowledge" of specific companies that may not have read *Heating and Ventilation* in 1944 or the *Encyclopedia Britannica* in 1960 (Table 8).

Table 8. Nonpublished Reference to Asbestos Disease/Risk in Insulators and Other Product Users

Document	Contents
Bernard Dugan v. R.V. Aycock Co. et al.(1933) Kansas City, MO.	Damage suit brought by employee of a construction contracting firm (a subsidiary of Johns-Manville) alleging pulmonary disability. (See "Lawsuits by Product Users against Asbestos Manufacturers," in Chapter 3.)
General Managers Association documents, 1936-1937	Railroads in Illinois developed guidelines for the prevention of asbestosis in insulation work on locomotives (See "Railroad Companies," in Chapter 9).
E.O. Gustafson (college student in Seattle) letter to A.J. Lanza (Nov. 1, 1939)	Says Dr. George Dowling at a local clinic had seen a number of cases of lung disease "which resulted from no more than handling asbestos while wrapping steam pipes with insulation material."
C.S. Stephenson (U.S. Navy Commander of Preventive Medicine) memorandum to Rear Admiral McIntire (March 11, 1941)	Under the heading "Asbestosis" he notes that "we are not protecting the men as we should," citing reports from several Naval yards. Refers to objections by the Navy to teams of Public Health Service scientists doing health surveys at Navy yards; the writer preferred having medical officers in the yards do this. "I told (the Assistant Secretary of the Navy) that I had spoken to you and that you had indicated that President Roosevelt thought that (letting the P.H.S. inspect Navy yards) might not be the best policy, due to the fact that they might cause disturbances in the labor element." Also referred to as the "triple hearsay memo."
"Asbestos Workers Union." Ed Ames, memorandum to E.J. Marshall (Owens-Corning Fiberglas Corp.), Jan. 7, 1942.	Discusses the idea of using "the asbestosis weapon in reserve" to overcome union reluctance to work with fiberglass insulation — including U.S. Public Health Bulletin #241 (Dreessen *et al.*, 1938).

Document	Contents
"Bethlehem Steel Company, Quincy." Dr. Morris memorandum to M. Bowditch (Massachusetts Dept. of Occupational Hygiene) Jan. 7, 1943. M. Bowditch, letter to A.J. Lanza of Metropolitan Life, Feb. 13, 1942. A.J. Lanza reply to M. Bowditch, Feb. 16, 1942. H.E. Elkins letter to A.D. Brandt (Medical Division, Bethlehem Steel Co.), May 17, 1954	Report of interview with Dr. Manley, the company doctor, about a visit to the shipyard by Dr. Merewether of England. "Dr. Manley and Dr. Merewether discussed the asbestosis problem and both agreed that a definite hazard exists, especially in the removal of old asbestos in ships which are being repaired." There is also reference to an asbestosis case seen earlier, which Bowditch tells Dr. Lanza was brought to his attention by Dr. Manley — "a man who had been engaged for some twelve years in the installation of molded asbestos pipe insulation." Lanza replied "I think it is possible that this man may have asbestosis . . . We have found evidence of it in men who trim asbestos pipe moldings, shingles, and other material of this nature, with a power saw." The chest X-rays were apparently never sent in to the state officials. An inquiry by Brandt brought back a note in 1954 quoting the 1943 memorandum on Merewether's visit and concerns about asbestos.
H.M. Aber (Eagle-Picher Sales Company salesman) internal memorandum to T.C. Carter, D. Via, and C.B. Igade, April 8, 1942.	A state health officer in Texas had been asked by officials of Humble Oil and Refining Company for an opinion on the safety of handling Eagle-Picher Supertemp Block insulation. The reply placed Eagle-Picher "in an awkward and costly position," according to salesman Aber, who obtained a promise from the state official responsible (W.E. Wardlow) to "help straighten things out." Aber continued, "Wardlow will contact Humble in person to make any reasonable test on Supertemp relative to its being injurious to workmen, if requested by either Humble or ourselves. If we are sure of ourselves

Table 8. Nonpublished Reference to Asbestos Disease/Risk in Insulators and Other Product Users *(cont.)*

Document	Contents
	on this product this might be the thing to do . . ." Aber asked for further instruction on that question. "While in Mr. Wardlow's office I had the opportunity to read a section in 'Occupation and Health', as compiled by the International Labor Institute (sic), on asbestos, compiled in 1938 . . . If you think mineral wool is dangerous you should read this." Aber urged that a copy of the article by Gloyne and Merewether be secured from the I.L.O. office in Washington, D.C.
"Industrial Health Survey of the Oregon Shipbuilding Corp. Portland Oregon, Sept. 3-4, 1942" (P. Drinker *et al.*) "Industrial Health Survey of the South Portland Shipbuilding Corp. and the Todd-Bath Ironworks, South Portland, Maine, Sept. 18, 19, 22, 1942" (P. Drinker *et al.*) "Industrial Health Survey of the Bath Iron Works Corp. Bath, Maine, Sept. 22, 1942" (P. Drinker *et al.*) "Re-Inspection Report Safety and Industrial Health, Defoe Shipbuilding Co., Bay City, Michigan" Jan. 20-21, 1944" (K.W. Nelson and R.F. Clow). "Industrial Hygiene Survey of Gulf Shipbuilding Corp. Chickasaw, Alabama, March 21, 22, 23, 28, 29, 1944" (K.W. Nelson and J.P. Morgan).	Consultant reports to the U.S. Maritime Commission and Navy about industrial hygiene problems in private contract shipyards during World War II. These reports mention asbestosis hazards in pipecovering shops and on ships; many call for local exhaust ventilation, respiratory protection, and/or annual medical examination of the workers exposed to asbestos. The 1944 Bath Iron Works survey includes 6 radialogically diagnosed cases of asbestosis.

Document	Contents
"Asbestosis from Amosite Pipe Covering at Bath Iron Works, Bath, Maine, Dec. 19, 1944" (W.C. Dreessen and W.E. Fleischer)	
"Industrial Health and Safety Re-Survey of Albina Engine and Machine Works, Inc. Portland, Oregon, March 20-26, 1945" (H.G. Beck, L.O. Hughes, and L.G. Wayne)	
E. DeForest (Northwest Magnesia Association) "Copy," letter to J.E. Morgan (Washington Department of Labor and industries) June 14, 1943 A.S. Rossiter (*Asbestos* magazine) letter to S. Simpson (Raybestos-Manhattan) June 18, 1943 Vandiver Brown (Johns-Manville) letter to S. Simpson, June 24, 1943. (all from the Sumner Simpson papers)	DeForest's angry letter to the state officials (describing asbestosis as a so-called disease . . . "Since this foreign disease has not come to our attention, we feel it should be left in Europe where it belongs and not brought to our local communities and create hysteria and fear amongst the lives of our contented workmen who are now enjoying good health and living to a ripe old age, which is significant of the Pipe Coverers Union . . .") was received by the trade magazine. *Asbestos* editor Rossiter passed it on to Simpson for reply, who sent it to Brown. Brown wrote: "I am inclined to let Mr. DeForest learn the facts of life and asbestosis from the State of Washington Department of Labor and Industries, and shall merely file his letter unless you feel strongly there is something I should do about it and so advise."
Chief of the Bureau of Ships, memorandum to Supervisor of Shipbuilding, USN, Camden, N.J. "Insulation—Water Repellent Amosite for Cold Water Piping" (Aug. 12, 1943)	Announces that a mineral wool insulation is being tested which would be safer than amosite; recommends medical and hygiene measures to observe in handling the amosite. The first memorandum was transmitted to the contract shipyard by local Naval personnel.

Table 8. Nonpublished Reference to Asbestos Disease/Risk in Insulators and Other Product Users *(cont.)*

Document	Contents
G.H. Wood (Navy Dept., Camden, N.J.) memorandum to New York Shipbuilding Corp. (Sept. 24, 1943)	
Gardner, Leroy (Saranac Laboratory), letter to Dr. Ludwig Hektoen, Executive Director, National Advisory Cancer Council (Chicago) Sept. 29, 1943.	Following up an earlier request for federal funding of a cancer assay of asbestos dust, Dr. Gardner noted, "A considerable number of persons are also exposed in the electrical industries where asbestos is used not only in wiring but motor armatures. The U.S. Navy has had a real problem from the use of asbestos in insulating marine boilers, electrical installations, and other insulating work."
P. Drinker (consultant to U.S. Maritime Commission) letter to Captain Ingram (Navy Bureau of Ships), Jan 8, 1944.	Transmits union concerns about use of amosite insulation at New York Shipbuilding Co. and warns that there could be a labor "disturbance" if union questions about the hazards of amosite are not properly handled. Recommends respiratory protection, exhaust ventilation, and/or substitution of the amosite. Mentions reliance on air line respirators in a similar case on the west coast.
Asbestos Insulation Aboard Ships. Two-page notice issued by A.W. Garrett, Chief Inspector of Factories, London, August, 1945.	Factory Inspectorate expressed concern over asbestosis hazard in shipyard insulation work. Six work practices were listed, which "have been accepted by the Shipbuilding Employers' Federation and the Trade Unions concerned..."
C.W. Dawe, Thermal Insulation Contractors Association, letter to the Chief Inspector, Sept. 14, 1945.	Provisions listed included respiratory protection for asbestos sprayers and workers removing old insulation. No one was to work in same space with asbestos spraying unless equipped with a

Document	Contents
	respirator. Ventilation, damping dust, prompt clean-up were also advised. Seventy more copies of the circular were requested by Thermal Insulation Contractors Association. Sending of the notice was described in the *Annual Report of the Chief Inspector of Factories for the Year 1945.*
A.J. Vorwald (Saranac Laboratory) Letter to U.E. Bowes, Owens-Illinois Glass Co. Nov. 16, 1948 and the accompanying Interim Report Regarding the Biological Activity of Kaylo Dust, Oct. 30, 1948.	Described inhalation experiments using the dust from Kaylo insulation on guinea pigs. "In all animals sacrificed after more than 30 months of exposure to Kaylo dust unmistakable evidence of asbestosis has developed, showing that Kaylo on inhalation is capable of producing asbestosis and must be regarded as a potentially-hazardous material." The letter ends: "I realize that our findings regarding Kaylo are less favorable than anticipated. However, since Kaylo is capable of producing asbestosis, it is better to discover it now in animals rather than later in industrial workers. Thus the company, being forewarned, will be in a better position to institute adequate control measures for safeguarding exposed employees and protecting its own interests."
Willis G. Hazard. Memorandum to M.M. Olander, (both of Owens-Illinois) Oct. 5, 1955.	Hazard, who was continuously informed about the Kaylo test results, noted that they had been published by Dr. Schepers of the Saranac Lab with no mention of the names Kaylo and Owens-Illinois (Effect of Inhaled Commercial Hydrous Calcium Silicate Dust on Animal Tissues. *Arch. Indust. Health 12:* 348-360, 1955).
E.R.A. Merewether (British Factory Department) Discussion in "Pneumoconiosis and	On a panel with Drs. Hueper, Cartier, and Lynch, introduced by Dr. Vorwald, he noted the occupations of 48 workers in the UK known to have died with

Table 8. Nonpublished Reference to Asbestos Disease/Risk in Insulators and Other Product Users *(cont.)*

Document	Contents
Cancer," Seventh Saranac Symposium (unpublished), p. 404 of transcript. Sept. 24, 1952. From the archives of Dr. A.J. Vorwald, Armed Forces Institute of Pathology, Washington, D.C.	asbestosis and lung cancer. Included were "eight pipe and boiler coverers."
Conference on Environmental Carcinogens Sept. 12-13, 1955 at National Institutes of Health (from the unpublished papers of Dr. Wilhelm Hueper, National Library of Medicine, Bethesda, Md.)	Panels of specialists rated the evidence that various materials were carcinogenic. The asbestos panel consisted of Dr. William E. Smith (New York University,) Dr. Kenneth W. Smith (Johns-Manville), and Dr. Arthur J. Vorwald (Wayne State University, formerly Saranac Lab). "English reports are very suggestive" of a lung cancer risk. "Widespread hazard if a causal relationship exists due to many uses of this material under various conditions."
Kane, J.W. (International Association of Heat and Frost Insulators and Asbestos Workers) letter to Industrial Hygiene Foundation, Aug. 13, 1955 Walmer, C.R. (I.H.F.) letter to Hugh Jackson (Johns-Manville) Aug. 26, 1955.	Kane noted that "seven of the last nine of the members of our Union, the Asbestos Workers, (pipe coverers) have died of lung disorders." He expressed concern not only about asbestos but also fiberglass and mineral wool. "We would appreciate any information you could give us on these materials and what dangers they could create. I am sure that you as thoughtful human beings will help us make a deep cut in the preventable cases, by giving the proper knowledge and safety factors we may practice." Walmer passed the letter on to Jackson saying: "We did not feel we could reply in correspondence to Mr. Kane, and therefore invited him to the

Document	Contents
	Institute for a conference. We notified him of the fact that much information is available on the safe handling and use of practically all insulating materials, and we supplied him with sufficient data to allay his fears."
Frederick LeGrande (insulation worker) damage suit against Johns-Manville 1957.	See "Lawsuits by Product Users Against Asbestos Manufacturers," in Chapter 3.
D.C. Braun (Industrial Hygiene Foundation) letter to Hugh Jackson (Johns-Manville) Aug. 23, 1957.	Discusses literature search and numerous reports of lung cancer and asbestosis, "occupations given were: . . . lagger, pipecoverer . . ." Also mentions Isselbacher's case ("a contractor's helper engaged in cutting and sawing asbestos board . . .")
Dr. J.F. Knox (Turner Brothers Asbestos Co.), opening remarks at Meeting of Research Committee at Cambridge, 15th December 1958; 5 pages.	Refers to research in Denmark and Sweden showing "abnormalities in the lungs of insulating workers."
H. Jackson (Johns-Manville) letter to W.T. Marr (Long Beach Naval Shipyard) June 22, 1959.	"Your reference to asbestosis arising out of insulation operations is of considerable interest. I am aware of only two cases of asbestosis arising out of exposures involving the installation of asbestos insulations . . . Another area in which there is a lack of knowledge is that of the import of short duration massive exposures. I would assume that in shipboard installations, a part of the work, at least, would be performed in confined spaces which might result in heavy concentrations for short periods of time."

Table 8. Nonpublished Reference to Asbestos Disease/Risk in Insulators and Other Product Users *(cont.)*

Document	Contents
G. Faciane civil suit against Eagle-Picher and other manufacturers of insulation, 1961.	See "Lawsuits by Product Users Against Asbestos Manufacturers," in Chapter 3.
Fred C. Wenham (insulator) damage suit against Johns-Manville, 1961.	See "Lawsuits by Product Users Against Asbestos Manufacturers," in Chapter 3.
A. Edwards letter to L. Pechstein (Philip Carey Manufacturing Co.) Feb. 17, 1961; and Pechstein memo of Edwards' phone call, Feb. 21, 1961.	Indiana health official told Pechstein that "Careytemp insulation" contained a "toxic" material, asbestos. Complaints had been received from Carey's own contract insulation workers in Indiana.
W.E. Latto claim for workers' compensation filed against Philip Carey Manufacturing Co. in 1961 (No. OD 117 279)	Compensation for permanent and total disability awarded to Latto in 1962 by Ohio Bureau of Workmen's Compensation.
H.C. Hinshaw letter to I.A. Schwab, April 17, 1961.	Medical report on R.E. Borden's workers' compensation claim for asbestosis against Western Asbestos Co. in California. Notes that insulation workers face a risk of asbestosis, and that, "rather substantial evidence that asbestosis may predispose to lung cancer" was recorded in medical literature.
R.E. Peele (Union Carbide Chemicals Co.) Industrial Hygiene Survey Construction Insulation Shop. Building 511-2018 Reports 62-1-H-1-G-1 and 62 1-H-2-G-1 (March and July, 1962)	Report of total dust counts from bandsaw cutting of Johns-Manville "Thermobestos" and Owens-Corning "Kaylo" insulation blocks. Dust counts ranged from 13.1 to 101.4 MPPCF for Thermobestos and 3.1 to 17.1 MPPCF for Kaylo. Report advised against continued use of Thermobestos unless improvements were made in either the bandsaw exhaust ventilation or the product itself.

Document	Contents
W.E. Shoemaker (American Mutual Liability Insurance Co.) memorandum to Blaine. March 20, 1962.	Shoemaker asked J-M medical director K. Smith to testify for the defense in a compensation claim brought by an insulation worker with lung cancer. Smith declined, recommended Dr. Lanza.
R. Fisher (Chief Medical Examiner, State of Maryland) letter to A. Porth, Feb. 3, 1962.	Dr. Fisher had earlier replied to defense attorney Porth to the effect that the claimant had a strong case. (See "The Law Journals and Informal Consultation with Insurance Officials," in Chapter 3)
O. Ayers. Johns-Manville Research and Engineering Center Report No. 432-257-S1, November 6, 1962.	Band sawing (J-M) Thermobestos and (Owens-Corning) Kaylo blocks produced exposures of 15-104 MPPCF total dust. (See Table 3 of Chapter 4 for further details)
Washington Chemical Co. memorandum to A.D.N. Jones (Turner & Newall), "Asbestosis Claims" (Oct. 24, 1962) enclosing "Downward Trend in Number of Factory Accidents Last Year" (from *Belfast Telegraph*)	Confidential memorandum returning news report that 6 insulators died in 1961 "of asbestosis or lung cancer."
Thomas Mancuso consultation for Philip Carey Manufacturing Company 1962-1963	Dr. Mancuso advised Carey executives to institute a comprehensive program to advise product users about hazards and protective measures. Mancuso also recommended cessation of contracting activities due to their compensation liability. (See "The Mancuso Documents" in Chapter 3)

Epidemiology of Cancer in Asbestos Product Users

In 1954, California health officials published a report on smoking and occupational factors in lung cancer. They had interviewed 518 hospital patients with lung cancer and an equal number of "control" patients. When the researchers saw how the results were coming out, they created a special category of jobs whose common hazard was asbestos exposure:

steamfitters, boiler makers, and asbestos workers. In most, if not all of these cases, the dust hazard arose from the handling of asbestos insulation products. Ten lung cancer patients but only one of the "matched control" patients had substantial work histories in the asbestos-exposed jobs. After taking smoking habits into account, the excess lung cancer liability of these jobs was statistically significant.[30]

Of course, reports of cancer among asbestos product users didn't emerge in a vacuum. In the context of overwhelming evidence of an excessive lung cancer risk among asbestotics, it became an inescapable conclusion in the 1950s that insulation workers had an occupational cancer hazard in addition to an asbestosis one.

CONCLUSION

The epidemiologists at the Mount Sinai School of Medicine finally showed vividly the devastation to health sustained by insulation workers in 1964. The observation that insulators died from asbestosis was not new, and an excessive incidence of cancer was anything but surprising to find. But such a large number of "excess deaths" was shocking nevertheless. How many men would have knowingly entered a trade with an almost guaranteed chance of developing asbestosis in 30 years and nearly a 50 percent chance of dying from occupational cancer or asbestosis?

Dr. Selikoff and his colleagues deserve praise for their many fine works. But accolades to the Mt. Sinai group as the *discoverers* of asbestos disease in insulators should go to their predecessors instead. The 1965 article by Selikoff, Hammond, and Churg on asbestosis in insulators cites no less than 18 pre-1964 references to asbestosis and cancer among asbestos product users.

An increasing number of asbestos products have been shown to be hazardous, including industrial "protective clothing," vinyl asbestos flooring, and drywall patching compounds.[31-43]

REFERENCES

1. Verhalen, J.P. (U.S. Mineral Products Corp.), "National Accounts" internal memorandum to E.W. Fairweather (Nov. 12, 1962); Eaton, T.H., "Marinite Dust" memorandum (June 18, 1958); Eaton, T.H., memorandum to H.M. Ball (July 7, 1958); Smith, K.W., "Caution Label Marinite" memorandum (July 9, 1958); Hoffer, W.G., "Marinite Dust" memorandum to D.L. Hinmon (July 29, 1958); Koch, E.C., teletype message to Dr. K.W. Smith (Oct. 11, 1960); Hodgson, W.G. (Toronto) "Caution Labels Industrial Insulation Products Your Letter January 29" memorandum to A. Pocius (Feb. 1, 1965); Fisk, A.L. (J-M General Headquarters), "Rules and Regulations Relating to Labeling in the Use, Handling, and Storage of Substances Harmful to the Health and Safety of Employees" memorandum to J.C. Kelleher, Montreal (Mar. 6, 1952); Fisk, A.L., memorandum to W.H. Souter (Apr. 3, 1952); Fisk, A.L., memorandum to J.C. Kelleher (May 2, 1952); Kelleher, J.C., memorandum to A.L. Fisk (Apr. 23, 1952).

2. Selikoff, I.J., E.C. Hammond and J. Churg, "Asbestos Exposure and Neoplasia," *J.A.M.A. 188*:22–26 (1964)

3. Selikoff, I.J., J. Churg, and E.C. Hammond, "The Occurrence of Asbestosis among Insulation Workers in the United States," *Ann. N.Y. Acad. Sci. 132*:139–155 (1965).

4. *C. Borel v. Fiberboard Paper Products et al.* 493 Fed. 2d 1076 U.S. Court of Appeals for the 5th Circuit (Sept. 10, 1973).

5. Asch, K., "Asbestos Law/Victims' Rights and Industry's Reaction," *Ann N.Y. Acad. Sci. 330*:255–272 (1979).

6. Peters, G.A. and B.J. Peters, *Sourcebook on Asbestos Diseases* New York: Garland STPM Press, 1980. And volumes 2–4 (1986–1989). Also, *Asbestos Disease Update* (1989) and *Asbestos Abatement Update* (1990), New York: Garland Publishing Co.

7. Baron, F.M., *Handling Occupational Disease Cases* Tiburon, California: Lawpress, 1981.

8. *Asbestos Litigation* New York: Law & Business, Inc./Harcourt Brace Jovanovich, 1982.

9. Berryman, C.F. (American Mutual Insurance Alliance) and R.F. Ingegneri (American Insurance Association), "Minutes. Enterprise Liability Discussion Group, Nov. 10, 1976, 10:00 A.M., American Insurance Association, New York, New York."

10. Lanza, A.J., W.J. McConnell, and J.W. Fehnel, "The Effect of Inhalation of Asbestos Dust on the Lungs of Asbestos Workers," *Publ. Health Rep. 50*:1–12 (1935).

11. Merewether, E.R.A. and C.W. Price, *Report on the Effect of Asbestos Dust on the Lungs and Dust Suppression in the Asbestos Industry* London: H.M. Stationery Ofc., 1930.

12 Fulton, W.B. *et al.*, *Asbestosis* Commonwealth of Pennsylvania Dept. of Labor and Industry Special Publ. No. 42, Harrisburg, PA, Sept. 20, 1935.

13. Dreessen, W.C. *et al.*, *A Study of Asbestosis in the Asbestos Textile Industry.* Publ. Health Bull. No. 241 Washington, D.C., 1938.

14. Garrard, H.G., "State of the Art as a Defense—Is It Real?" *Asbestos Medicine* Chicago: Defense Research Institute (1987).

15. Hoffman, F.L. *Mortality from Respiratory Diseases in Dusty Trades* U.S. Bureau of Labor Statistics Bull. 231, Washington, D.C., 1918, pp. 176–180.

16. Asbestos. *Occupation and Health* International Labour Office Encyclopedia of Hygiene, Pathology and Social Welfare, Vol. 1, Geneva, 1930, pp. 189–191.

17. Soper, W.B., "Pulmonary Asbestosis: A Report of a Case and a Review," *Amer. Rev. Tuberc. 22*:571–584 (1930).

18. Willson, F., "The Very Least an Employer Should Know about Dust and Fume Diseases," *Safety Eng. 52*:317–318 (1931).

19. Fleischer, W.E. *et al.*, "A Survey of Pipecovering Operations in Constructing Naval Vessels," *J. Industr. Hyg. Tox. 28*:9–16 (1946).

20. Lanza, A.J. (ed.) *Silicosis and Asbestosis* New York: Oxford University Press, 1938, p. 175.

21. Dreessen, W.C., and W.E. Fleischer, "Asbestosis from Amosite Pipe Covering at Bath Iron Works," Bath, Maine (Dec. 19, 1944). Unpublished Navy document.

22. Drinker, P., *et al.*, "Industrial Health Survey of the Oregon Shipbuilding Corporation, Portland Oregon, Sept. 3–4, 1942," report to U.S. Maritime Commission.

23. Drinker, P. (Consultant, U.S. Maritime Commission), letter to Captain Ingram, U.S. Bureau of Ships (Jan. 8, 1944).

24. Molfino, F. and D. Zannini, "Pulmonary Diseases Caused by Dust among Dockworkers," *Folia Med. 39*:525–539 (1956).

25. Meiklejohn, A., "Abstract 1156 (Asbestosis with Pleural Calcification among Insulation Workers," *Abstracts World Med. 21*:359 (1957).

26. Dorland, W.A.N. and E.C.L. Miller, *The American Illustrated Medical Dictionary* (17th Ed.) Philadelphia: W.B. Saunders Co., 1937, p. 158.

27. Taylor, N.B., *Stedman's Medical Dictionary* (17th Rev. Ed.) Baltimore: Williams & Wilkins Co., 1949, p. 112.

28. Taylor, N.B. and A.E. Taylor. *Stedman's Practical Medical Dictionary* (16th Rev. Ed.) Baltimore: Williams & Wilkins Co., 1946, p. 107.

29. Jones, H.W., Hoerr, N.L., and A. Osol. *Blackiston's New Gould Medical Dictionary* Philadelphia: Blackiston Co., 1949, p. 103.

30. Breslow, L. *et al.*, "Occupations and Cigarette Smoking as Factors in Lung Cancer," *Amer. J. Publ. Health 44:*171–181 (1954).

31. Williams, H.B., "Pneumoconiosis: A Study of 379 Cases," *Med. Bull. Vet. Admin. 18:*250–253 (1942).

32. Bamber, H.A. and R. Butterworth, "Asbestos Hazard from Protective Clothing," *Ann Occup. Hyg. 13:*78–79 (1970).

33. Lumley, K.P.S., "Asbestos Dust Levels Inside Firefighting Helmets with Chrysotile Asbestos Covers," *Ann. Occup. Hyg. 14:*285–286 (1971).

34. Gibbs, G.W., "Fibre Release from Asbestos Garments," *Ann. Occup. Hyg. 18:*143–149 (1975).

35. Sors, C. *et al.*, "Pathologie de l'Amiante et Vêtements de Protection," *Arch. Malad. Prof. 40:*987–995 (1979).

36. Samimi, B.S. and A. Williams, "Occupational Exposure to Asbestos Fibers Resulting from the Use of Asbestos Gloves," *Amer. Indus. Hyg. Assoc. J. 42:*870–875 (1981).

37. Murphy R.L. *et al.*, "Floor Tile Installation as a Source of Asbestos Exposure," *Amer. Rev. Resp. Dis. 104:*576–580 (1971).

38. Sebastien, P., J. Bignon and M. Martin, "Indoor Airborne Asbestos Pollution From the Ceiling and the Floor," *Science 216:*1410–1413 (1982).

39. Rohl, A.N. *et al.*, "Occupational and Community Asbestos Exposure from Wallboard Finishing Compounds," *Science 189:*551–553 (1975).

40. Nicholson, W.J. *et al.*, "Occupational and Community Asbestos Exposure from Wallboard Finishing Compounds," *Bull. N.Y. Acad. Med. 51:*1180–1181 (1975).

41. Fischbein, A., *et al.*, "Carcinoma of the Lung in a Drywall Taping Worker—Report of a Case," *Toxicology Letters 2:*231–236 (1978).

42. Fischbein, A. *et al.*, "Drywall Construction and Asbestos Exposure," *Amer. Indus. Hyg. Assoc. J. 40:*402–407 (1979).

43. Verma, D.K., and C.G. Middleton, "Occupational Exposure to Asbestos in the Drywall Taping Process," *Amer. Indus. Hyg. Assoc. J. 41:*264–269 (1980).

6
Alternatives to Asbestos Insulation

Stephen L. Berger, P.E.

INTRODUCTION

Of all uses of asbestos that have achieved widespread application, none can rival the toll of death and disease resulting from the use of thermal insulations. Used in the presence of millions of workers in shipyards, construction sites, oil refineries, and chemical and power plants, the dust from insulation wafted onto surrounding communities in an ever-widening radius of destruction. In light of the long-standing recognition of the hazards of asbestos and the essential role of insulation in modern times, the necessity of using asbestos was brought into question:[1]

> (M)any doctors have asked whether the properties of asbestos are as unique as the salesmanship of the asbestos companies appears to indicate. There are many other mineral fibers such as glass wool, rock wool or slag wool, which have useful inherent fire-proofing properties but not the fibrogenic or carcinogenic effects on the lungs. Is it certain that the properties of asbestos justify the risks of asbestosis, carcinoma of the lung and mesothelioma which are entailed by its use?

There were three main categories of asbestos-containing thermal insulation. Each had its own range of uses, mainly determined by the temperature limits of its composition. In each category, asbestos substitution was achievable, as attested to by numerous patents and scientific articles. Many of these patents were held by companies manufacturing asbestos insulation or companies purchased by asbestos insulation manufacturers.

An extensive patent and technology investigation was necessary to resolve the question of available alternatives. It has shown that, first of all, asbestos played a limited role in thermal insulation products. Moreover, the acceptability of alternative materials in place of asbestos has been a fixture in this technology since the 19th century. As the technology developed, increasing numbers of substitutes emerged even while the use of asbestos in heat insulation soared.

Patents and Government Publications

Before a detailed analysis of possible alternatives to asbestos-containing thermal insulations can be undertaken, a few words should be mentioned about patents because they preponderate all references disclosing these alternatives.

Patents contain the history of technological advances. A patent is actually a nonrenewable grant by the United States government for a term of 17 years giving the patentee the right to exclude others from making, using or selling the invention. A full disclosure of the invention is given by the patentee in exchange for this limited monopoly. The application for a patent contains a specification, which is a written description of the invention; drawings, if necessary; and an oath. The specification ends with claims that particularly point out the subject matter which the applicant regards as the invention. Patents are considered intellectual property and can be assigned, sold or licensed. However, inventors employed by companies usually have prior contracts stating that any patents issued to them would be automatically assigned to their employers.

The issue date of the patent is the day of public disclosure, but the patentee or the assignee would have had knowledge of the disclosure on or before the filing date of the application.

Moreover, if the patent is a division, continuation, or continuation-in-part from an earlier (parent) application, the disclosure will not usually contain much new matter, and the patentee or assignee would have had knowledge of the bulk of the disclosure on or before filing date of the parent application. Typically, several years elapse between the filing date of a patent application and the granting of a patent.

Although patents reveal the technological advances behind the development of the various thermal insulations, they only occasionally state that a specific invention was used or available commercially. These revelations are best found in references such as journal articles, books and government publications. Journal articles inform the insulation engineer, distributor or user of recent developments and disclose the commercial availability of insulation. Books generally compare the physical properties and uses of various types of insulations. Government publications deal with reviews of current and past insulations, and also establish industry standards or specifications.

Three specific government publications were particularly useful in reviewing thermal insulating materials. First, a 1929 Bureau of Mines Information Circular provided a history of mineral wool in the United States, manufacturers and processes of making it, and its uses including pipe covering.[2] Second, a 1943 Bureau of Mines Information Circular surveyed the available industrial insulations, including mineral wool, asbestos, magnesia, vermiculite, diatomaceous earth, silica aerogel, and Foamglas.[3] Third, a 1955 Bureau of Mines Bulletin was directed to asbestos and its uses, but contained a section devoted to substitutes for asbestos.[4]

In 1949, the United States Department of Commerce promulgated a Commercial Standard entitled *Mineral Wool Insulation for Heated Industrial Equipment* which revised the original 1944 standard for mineral wool insulation.[5] One of the purposes of this standard was "to establish minimum specifications for insulating heated surfaces with mineral wool for the guidance of manufacturers, distributors, installers, contractors, engineers, and users. . . ." As with many other government specifications, the basis for developing this standard originated with the manufacturers, distributors, and users. A standing committee was formed to review any proposed revisions. This committee included representatives from Eagle-Picher, Owens-Corning, National Gypsum and Baldwin-Hill. Also, the acceptors of the standard are listed, all of whom must have had knowledge of the many uses for mineral wool.

Government and military specifications for thermal insulations disclosed available types and, more importantly, demonstrated that asbestos was not a necessary constituent of many of these insulations. The asbestos industry has asserted that the government insisted on the use of asbestos through its military procurement specifications. This argument, referred to by some plaintiffs' attorneys as the "Devil-Made-Me-Do-It defense," has been used by defendants' attorneys in litigation. In fact, Asbestos Textile Institute minutes of Sept. 11, 1953 and Industrial Hygiene Digest news items of May 1945 indicate that industry's role in drafting specifications may have been dominant. It is true that some government specifications were written specifically for asbestos insulation and, therefore, necessitated the use of asbestos. However, the major specifications covering pipe and block insulations were performance specifications and did not specify a particular insulating material, only that the material meet the required physical properties. For example, the 1953 specification for pipe covering, MIL-I-2781A, stated, "The thermal pipe insulation shall be composed of heat-resisting compounds suitable for the temperature conditions and the purpose intended." Others mention specific material such as asbestos and/or alternative materials. In its book, *Specifications for Construction of a Twin Screw Passenger and Cargo Vessel,* the U.S. Maritime Commission stated, "The insulating materials for temperatures below 600°F shall be 85% magnesia, fibrous asbestos, rock wool, or fibrous glass; except that for temperatures below 200°F, 85% magnesia or asbestos shall not be used."[6] Another military specification, 32P5b, in force in the 1930s, was entitled "Rock Wool; Pipe Covering, Blanket, Cement and Fiber."

The Role of Asbestos

Before this question of substitutability can be answered, the role of asbestos in thermal insulation must be examined. Although asbestos insulations were also made in the form of blankets, felts and paper, the great majority of asbestos-containing insulations were either "85% magnesia" or calcium silicate molded compositions. These latter two were especially dangerous to installers and their co-workers because frequent sawing of the insulation, necessary to produce correct fittings, created much airborne dust. Asbestos was also used in insulating cements that were troweled into place.

The major function of asbestos in all three of the above types of insulation was to reinforce the finished product so that it would not crack or disintegrate at the temperature of use. Two kinds of substitution were possible to maintain this reinforcing property of the insulation. First, alternatives to asbestos-containing insulations were feasible if other reinforcing fibers or materials could directly replace the asbestos in magnesia, calcium silicate, or cement. Second, if completely different products without asbestos could withstand the same temperature conditions as asbestos-containing insulations, substitution would also be possible.

A secondary function of asbestos was to suspend the initial reacting materials that form calcium silicate. If other fibers or materials could suspend these initial reactants, asbestos would be obviated.

Magnesia Insulation

From the late nineteenth century until the mid 1960s, a common and popular insulation was "85% magnesia." The common source material used to prepare magnesia was dolomite, a mineral consisting of calcium and magnesium carbonate. First it was heated and then mixed with water to form a suspension. Pressurized carbon dioxide was bubbled through this suspension to separate the insoluble calcium carbonate from the soluble magnesium carbonate. The solution of magnesium carbonate was then boiled down and concentrated to produce magnesia. This product was commonly mixed with asbestos fiber and then molded into the desired shape. *Asbestos acted merely as a reinforcing fiber and added little to the insulating value of the magnesia.*[7]

The limitations of magnesia insulation were numerous. It could be used only for temperatures up to 550–600 degrees F.[8] It had a poor resistance to water and lost strength when wet. One patent noted: "At high temperatures its thermal conductivity is excessive; its breaking load is low; its shrinkage is unduly severe; and its loss in weight is notable."[9] Increasing the amount of asbestos in magnesia insulations only made it more dense and reduced its insulating value.[10]

There are two ways in which asbestos substitution could have been accomplished in these products. If other reinforcing materials could have directly replaced the asbestos in magnesia, the problem of substitution was solved. Similarly, if different products without asbestos could withstand the same temperature conditions as the asbestos-magnesia products, then this would offer another means for eliminating asbestos-reinforced magnesia insulations.

Beginning with the first magnesia pipe insulation patent issued in 1886, the major manufacturers were granted patents that disclosed substitute reinforcing agents.[11] (See Table 1.) Keasbey & Mattison, the assignee of this first patent, included as choices of the fibrous material animal hair, wool, asbestos, and various other fibers not readily affected by heat.[12]

Other companies, including Philip Carey and Johns-Manville listed in their patents specific fibers as alternatives for the asbestos in magnesia.[13,14,15] In a patent application filed in 1945, for example, Johns-Manville stated that "satisfactory and useful products" could be made using raw cotton, spun glass (a type of fiberglass), fine rock wool (a type of mineral fiber formed from melted rock), and steam-treated wood as the reinforcing fibers.[16] Additional patents assigned to these and other manufacturers suggested that there were other suitable fibers without naming them specifically.[17,18,19,20,21]

Not only major insulation manufacturers but independent inventors have suggested substitutes for asbestos fiber in

Table 1. Patents Describing Alternatives to Asbestos Fiber in Magnesia Insulation

Year	Company (unless otherwise noted)	Reference Number
1886	Keasbey & Mattison	11
1930	Philip Carey	17
1940	Plant Rubber & Asbestos Works	18
1942	Philip Carey	13
1943	Philip Carey	14
1946	Armstrong Cork	19
1947	Johns-Manville	20
1947	Johns-Manville	15
1952	James D. Akins*	22
1952	Johns-Manville	26
1957	Keasbey & Mattison	21

*assignee of patent by inventor M. Baxter

magnesia insulations. One of the best examples of this is a 1952 patent issued to Mason Baxter. He used a mixture of fiberglass and slag wool pellets (a type of mineral fiber derived from melted blast-furnace slag, a steel industry by-product) to bind and strengthen magnesia and calcium silicate compositions. Comparing the magnesia product with conventional 85% magnesia, the patent states "a product using [slag] wool and magnesia would have a lower "K" factor, a better temperature range, lower costs of production, and less shrinkage in the manufacture and when used at high temperatures."[22] ("K" factor is thermal conductivity; the greater the K factor, the poorer a heat insulator the substance is.)

Product alternatives to asbestos-containing magnesia insulation also existed. (See Table 2.) These were completely different types of thermal insulating materials whose useful temperature range approximated that of magnesia. The most common of these was fiberglass insulation, which was used in Europe since before World War I and was substituted for asbestos thermal insulation in factories, power stations, locomotives and ships.[23] A 1923 article remarked, "Due to its lightness and high qualities this material is absolutely without peer for insulation on shipboard...."[24] The advantages of fiberglass over 85% magnesia thus included lower thermal conductivity, lower density, and higher resistance to water, acids and alkalies.

The first types of fiberglass insulation were in the form of "blankets" and were good up to 1000 degrees F.[25] Later developments included molded fiberglass pipe insulation.[26,27,28] Many of the molded insulations were formed by mixing fiberglass with a resin binder and then molding into a semi-rigid pipe insulation. (Resins used in these products were synthetic plastic-like polymers such as nonvolatile organic compounds.) Because the resin would smolder and char at higher temperatures, these types were generally good only up to 600 degrees F.[29,30]

Also of interest historically is a report by the British Intelligence Objectives Sub-Committee (B.I.O.S.) which stated that Owens-Illinois licensed its patented process for making glass fiber, covered by a German Patent, to Germany in 1934.[31] The report further stated that during World War II, "Glass fibre has been used extensively as an asbestos substitute."[32]

Fiberglass insulation was not the only product capable of substituting for magnesia insulation. As will be discussed later, molded mineral wool pipe insulation had a temperature limit of at least 600 degrees F. Exfoliated vermiculite insulation had even higher temperature limits.[33] (Vermiculite is a mineral, and exfoliated vermiculite is the lighter product resulting from

Table 2. Patents Describing Product Alternatives to Magnesia Insulation

Year	Company (unless otherwise noted)	Main Constituents	Reference Number
1928	Babor et al.*	vermiculite	33
1953	Baldwin-Hill	fiberglass or mineral wool	35
1957	Gustin-Bacon	fiberglass	26
1959	Pittsburgh Plate Glass	fiberglass	27
1962	Johns-Manville Fiber Glass	fiberglass	28

*inventor

heat expansion of the mineral.) This was molded into brick, slab or pipe covering shapes and found use aboard ships, among other places. Rigid glass insulating material made of thousands of glass bubbles was suitable for temperatures up to 800 degrees F. and available in both blocks and pipe coverings.[34] Another insulating sheet material, suitable for use on ships, contained an inorganic fiber, such as asbestos, fiberglass, or mineral wool (the latter was preferred). This product was "utilized with a minimum of dusting and breakage and, therefore, with practically no industrial health hazard."[35] This 1953 Baldwin-Hill patent may have been the first patent to acknowledge a health hazard in the use of thermal insulation products.

Calcium Silicate Insulation

Although calcium silicate insulation was first patented in 1912, it did not gain widespread use until the 1940s. Briefly, a typical manufacturing process included reacting a lime (a mineral containing calcium) and a silica (naturally occurring silicon dioxide, such as sand, quartz, or diatomaceous earth) under certain conditions.[36] The silica was usually diatomaceous earth (a silica composed of fossils of microscopic algae). The reaction was conducted in heated water and in the presence of a suspending agent, commonly asbestos. Additions, such as clay and other bonding agents, were made and then the product was shaped and hardened by steam treatment under pressure. *Here again, asbestos served not as an insulator, but rather as a suspending agent during the reaction period and reinforcing agent to prevent cracking in the final product.*[37]

Calcium silicate has replaced magnesia because it overcomes some of the deficiencies of magnesia and could withstand higher temperatures. The need for insulation that could withstand temperatures above 600 degrees F. grew steadily with the increased scale and advances of technology in power generation, oil refining, and numerous other industries. Calcium silicate could be used up to a temperature of 1200 degrees F., and in the case of high-temperature calcium silicate, up to

Table 3. Patents Describing Alternatives to Asbestos Fibers in Calcium Silicate Insulation

Year	Company (unless otherwise noted)	Reference Number
1912	Armstrong Cork	36
1924	Celite	41
1926	Celite	42
1941	Johns-Manville	43
1947	Paraffine	62
1949	Paraffine	63
1950	Owens-Illinois	49
1951	Owens-Illinois	50
1952	James D. Akins*	22
1955	Johns-Manville	44
1955	Insulex Mineral Products	65
1956	Owens-Illinois	55
1956	Columbia-Southern Chemical	66
1959	Fibreboard Paper Products	64
1963	Owens-Corning	56
1965	Owens-Corning	57
1966	Joseph Crosfield & Sons	67
1969	Owens-Corning	58
1971	Owens-Corning	59
1971	Owens-Corning	60
1975	Owens-Corning	61

*assignee of patent by inventor M. Baxter

1800 degrees F. It has good resistance to water, moisture and abrasion. Also, its shrinkage is low at high temperatures. On the other hand, its breaking load is low and its thermal conductivity slightly higher than that of magnesia.[38]

An analysis will show that alternatives existed to asbestos-containing calcium silicate thermal insulations since their initial development. The first part of this analysis is on a company-by-company basis for the major manufacturers and, as with magnesia, examines direct replacements for the asbestos fibers in the product. (See Table 3.) The second part of the analysis will discuss other types of thermal insulating materials whose useful temperature ranges approximated that of calcium silicate.

The earliest calcium silicate insulation patent, obtained in 1912 by Armstrong Cork, could have substituted either spun glass or mineral wool for the asbestos.[39]

Johns-Manville's knowledge of possible substitutes became proprietary in 1928 when it purchased, under the guidance of J.P. Morgan & Company, the Celite Company, owner of the largest and purest deposit of diatomaceous earth that had been discovered.[40] Among its many patents, Celite had at least two that mentioned substitutes for asbestos in calcium silicate heat insulating compositions.[41,42] The first was a 1924 patent which noted that for blocks not requiring refractory properties, "the use of asbestos fiber may be dispensed with and a cheap manila or cellulose fiber substituted therefor."[41] (*Refractory* means extremely high temperature applications, usually over 2000 degrees F., such as furnace walls).

A Johns-Manville patent, applied for in 1936, described a sheet or block material useful as a ship panel and containing calcium silicate and wood fibers.[43] This sheet product was similar to and served the same purpose as Marinite® asbestos insulation. In addition, a 1955 Johns-Manville calcium silicate pipe insulation patent listed glass and mineral wool as alternatives to asbestos reinforcing fiber.[44]

Johns-Manville had timely knowledge of other companies' patents. John McKinney, former Chairman of the Board and patent attorney for the company, has testified that Johns-Manville automatically received copies of their competitors' new patents from the Patent Office.[45] McKinney and Johns-Manville received and acknowledged other information concerning patents and their disclosures. During the prosecution of a typical patent application, correspondence will be exchanged between the applicant, or more likely applicant's attorney, and the patent examiner. This correspondence, usually in the form of a rejection of the proposed claims by the examiner and a response by the applicant, is placed in the application file. After a patent is issued, this exchange is not printed with the patent specification but is only available by inspecting the patent file at the Patent Office in Arlington, Virginia. Johns-Manville thus received not only copies of the patents cited by the examiner in rejecting the claims, but also comments by the examiner relating these patents to the proposed invention.

For example, in the file of a 1962 Johns-Manville patent directed to hydrated calcium silicate, the 1951 and 1954 Kalousek patents (see Owens-Illinois patent list at end of chapter) are cited by the examiner in his rejection of the pending claims.[46] Johns-Manville's attorney acknowledged in his response to the rejection that the 1954 patent resulted "in a porous insulation which has found wide application in the art." Another example involved an exchange of correspondence between the patent examiner and Johns-Manville's attorney during prosecution of a patent application which was eventually issued in 1976.[47] The examiner pointed out that both the 1959 Hoopes et al. and the 1947 Abrahams et al. patents (see Fibreboard patent list at end of chapter) contemplated the use of inorganic mineral fibers equivalent to asbestos. The examiner quoted directly from the Hoopes et al. patent: "other suitable non-combustible reinforcing fibers may be employed, such as mineral fiber or glass fibers." In both examples, McKinney was one of the attorneys of record.

Owens-Illinois developed the Kaylo® line of calcium silicate insulations starting in the 1940s.[48,49,50] One of these patents disclosed the utility of cellulosic fibers, such as paper pulp, both as suspending agents during mixing of the reactants and reinforcing agents in the final product.[49]

Although an organic fiber such as cellulose might not seem suitable as a reinforcement in thermal insulation, there is ample evidence to suggest the opposite. First, the use of cellulose continued to be recommended in later patents as well as the earliest ones. Second, a 1947 report from Arthur D. Little, Inc. to Owens-Illinois evaluated the combination of Kraft paper, a common type of strong paper made from a specific kind of wood pulp, and heat-treated clay in calcium silicate insulations, and recommended pilot plant experimentation.[51] Third, Everett Shuman, the Kaylo® Division director of research at that time, has testified that bagasse (fiber derived from dried sugar cane), wood or other organic fibers could have been used because only within a short radial distance from the hot pipe would the fibers in a pipe covering be altered.[52] The temperature in a covering, measured outwardly from the pipe, drops very quickly, so the integrity of the covering as a whole would not be affected by the use of cellulose.

One of the patents in the Kaylo® series, applied for in 1949, described a product so strong it needed no asbestos or other fibers to reinforce it. Its crystalline structure, called xonotlite, was superior in terms of heat insulation, strength, and resistance to shrinkage and corrosion.[50] It also had "freedom from shrinkage and cracking wherein no reinforcement, such as asbestos fiber, need be utilized for increasing strength or preventing cracking in the finished product."[53] The patent further mentioned that paper pulp or starch could be used as suspending agents. A 1948 report on xonotlite Kaylo®, which was the basis for the above patent, stated that xonotlite would be cheaper to make and perform better than the then-present Kaylo® and would have eliminated the fuzzy appearance that asbestos fibers gave Kaylo®.[54] In further refinements, even the above non-asbestos suspending agents were rendered unnecessary by using discrete particles of the calcium silicate product to suspend the initial reactants.[55]

Owens-Corning Fiberglas was formed in 1938 by Owens-Illinois and Corning Glass Works, each initially holding an equal percentage of the common stock. During the 1980s, Corning Glass sold its share in Owens-Corning. In 1958, Owens-Corning bought the Kaylo® Division from Owens-Illinois and continued the research on this type of insulation. Several patents assigned to Owens-Corning gave examples using fibers other than asbestos.[56,57,58,59,60,61] These fibers included cotton and coated fiberglass.

Another company active in manufacturing calcium silicate insulation was Fibreboard Corporation, whose former names included The Paraffine Companies, Inc., Pabco Products, Inc. and Fibreboard Paper Products Corporation. Two patents, issued in the late 1940s and assigned to Paraffine, described calcium silicate insulation using either asbestos, mineral wool, glass or metallic fiber.[62,63] A 1959 Fibreboard Paper Products patent also disclosed asbestos, mineral wool, or fiberglass as usable for reinforcement.[64]

In addition to these larger manufacturers, other companies and independent inventors had patents which formed calcium silicate insulation without the need of asbestos. The previously mentioned 1952 Baxter patent disclosed a mixture of fiberglass and slag wool pellets as a reinforcement for insulating materials, such as magnesia or calcium silicate. A similar invention was disclosed in a 1955 British patent to Insulex Mineral Products Limited.[65]

An important 1956 patent to Columbia-Southern Chemical Corporation, at that time a subsidiary of Pittsburgh Plate Glass Company, listed asbestos, fiberglass, or rock wool as the possible reinforcement.[66] In two out of three examples given, acceptable products were obtained using fiberglass.

A significant advance was disclosed in a 1966 patent to Joseph Crosfield & Sons Limited, a British company.[67] By including certain metals, aluminium, nickel, or zirconium, in the reaction mixture, the pressurized steam treatment was obviated. This treatment tended to weaken fiberglass reinforcement. Examples 54 through 58 replaced the asbestos with either fiberglass or rock wool.

Perhaps the most widely used product alternative to as-

Table 4. Patents Describing Mineral Wool Product Alternatives to Calcium Silicate Insulation

Year	Company	Reference Number
1926	Banner Rock	73
1931	General Insulating and Manufacturing	75
1933	Coast Insulating	76
1960	Eagle-Picher	77
1962	Eagle-Picher	78
1964	Johns-Manville	79
1971	Keene	80

bestos was mineral wool insulation. (See Table 4.) Mineral wool was first produced commercially in Wales in 1840.[68]

The source of the raw material determined the type of mineral wool product. Rock wool was made from natural rock, primarily a calcareous shale, a type of rock shale mineral containing calcium, whereas slag wool was made from blast-furnace slag. Glass wool or fiberglass can also be classified as a type of mineral wool. Mineral wool was manufactured by first melting the raw materials, then blowing or drawing the resultant molten mass into fine fibers. The wool was fabricated into blankets, felts and molded coverings.

The advantages of mineral wool were its flexibility and lower heat conductivity than calcium silicate and magnesia. Felts and molded coverings were generally good up to 600 degrees F.; however, one type of high-temperature bonded mineral wool had a limit of 1700 degrees F.[69] Blankets had a temperature limit of 1200 degrees F. and found extensive use in the petroleum refining industry.[70] Mineral wool was also employed aboard ships.[71]

Rock wool was probably first made in 1897 by Charles Hall who later formed the Banner Rock Products Company.[72] This company developed rock wool pipe insulation in the 1920s.[73] In 1928, Banner Rock was purchased by Johns-Manville. In view of the fact that Johns-Manville derived a large amount of its profits from the sale of asbestos, it is possible that competitive considerations adversely affected the advance of rock wool for pipecovering and other applications. Other patents for mineral wool insulations were issued in the early 1930s, including one

Table 5. Patents Describing Fiberglass Product Alternatives to Calcium Silicate Insulation

Year	Company	Reference Number
1939	Owens-Corning	85
1960	Owens-Corning	86
1960	Owens-Corning	84
1962	Johns-Manville Fiber Glass	87

each to General Insulating and Manufacturing Company and to Coast Insulating Co.[75,76]

Later representative patents for mineral wool pipe insulation included two assigned to Eagle-Picher Company (1960, 1962); one to Johns-Manville (1964); and one to Keene Corporation (1971).[77,78,79,80] In general, the above patents described products good up to 1200 degrees F. From 1931 to 1957, Eagle-Picher made an asbestos-free pipe insulation called 77 Pipe Covering, which contained mineral wool and metal fabric.[81] Baldwin-Hill Company was also active in manufacturing mineral wool insulation products.[82]

A 1964 article in *Thorax,* a medical journal, mentioned that glass wool and rock wool could be used as substitutes for asbestos in insulation. This article also reported that exposure to glass wool or rock wool dust did not lead to fibrosis of the lungs or impairment of cardiopulmonary functions.[83]

Superior high-temperature fiberglass pipe insulations were developed by both Owens-Corning and Johns-Manville. (See Table 5.) The molded type patented by Owens-Corning could withstand temperatures of up to 1200 degrees F.[84,85,86] The product patented by Johns-Manville in 1962 had a temperature limit of about 2000 degrees F. Comparing it with several other insulations, including calcium silicate, Johns-Manville concluded that a greater resistance to thermal transmission "has been achieved by an insulation unit of the present invention over all of the known similar insulation materials which had the same or even greater density."[87]

As with the case of rock wool (Banner Rock) and calcium silicate (Celite), Johns-Manville entered the fiberglass business by acquisition; in this case, of L.O.F. Glass Fibers Company in 1958.[88] Within months, another competitor in the insulation field, F.E. Schundler & Co., Inc., was also purchased by Johns-Manville.[88]

Another category of insulation useful at high temperatures was composed mainly of expanded perlite, a volcanic ore. (See Table 6.) The ore was ground, mixed with water and then expanded by heating in a furnace. An interesting 1952 patent, to independent inventor Harold Thomas, combined a specific

Table 6. Patents Describing Perlite Product Alternatives to Calcium Silicate Insulation

Year	Company (unless otherwise noted)	Reference Number
1952	Thomas*	89
1959	Philip Carey	91
1962	Johns-Manville Perlite	94
1963	Johns-Manville Perlite	95
1972	Panacon	93
1973	E.I. du Pont de Nemours	96

*inventor

grade of expanded perlite with a binder.[89] The mixture was formed into a pipe covering in compression molds and applied immediately to pipes without drying. The insulation had a 1200 degree F. temperature limit and "has been found to be cheaper and to provide better insulation than compositions heretofore used."[90]

In 1959, the Philip Carey Manufacturing Company patented an insulating material comprising expanded perlite, binders, and fiber, such as asbestos or mineral fiber.[91] The material withstood temperatures up to 1700 degrees F. In 1970, the Panacon Corporation, into which Philip Carey Manufacturing Company merged in 1970, filed a patent application for an-

Table 7. Patents Describing Miscellaneous Product Alternatives to Calcium Silicate Insulation

Year	Company	Main Constituents	Reference Number
1934	Johns-Manville	reacted mineral wool	98
1943	Asbestos Limited	cement plus mineral fibers	9
1947	Johns-Manville	mineral wool or fiberglass	99
1948	F.E. Schundler	cement plus metal fiber	102
1952	Johns-Manville	mineral wool or fiberglass	100
1957	Johns-Manville	silica	101

other expanded perlite insulation containing fiberglass.[92] Moreover, this application acknowledged the health hazards of asbestos, stating that the result of asbestos inhalation "in many cases is the lung disease termed 'asbestosis,' which often develops eventually into lung cancer."[93]

Johns-Manville became involved with perlite insulation after it purchased, in 1959, F.E. Schundler & Co., Inc. which mined and processed perlite. Two 1960s patents were obtained by Johns-Manville Perlite Corporation for expanded perlite insulation, usable to 1200 degrees F., in which the fiber was asbestos, fiberglass or rock wool.[94,95] A du Pont patent filed in 1971 for asbestos-free perlite insulation referred to "the serious health hazards in handling asbestos. . . ."[96]

Other miscellaneous insulating materials (see Table 7) patented by Johns-Manville and other companies might also have substituted for calcium silicate in at least some applications.[97,98,99,100,101] An example is the previously mentioned fiberglass blanket, whose temperature limit was 1000 degrees F.[25] Another type, disclosed in a 1948 patent assigned to F.E. Schundler, contained light-weight refractory particles, a dispersing agent and, if necessary, asbestos or metal fiber rein-

Table 8. Patents Describing Alternatives to Asbestos-Containing Insulating Cements

Year	Company (unless otherwise noted)	Reference Number
1905	Hayde*	108
1920	Winkley**	109
1925	Celite	103
1925	Celite	104
1934	Jenkins*	105
1939	Blokh*	111
1950	Baldwin-Hill	106
1951	Randall et al.*	107
1963	Quigley***	110

*inventor
**assignee of patent by inventor R. MacDonald
***assignee of patent by inventor R. Demaison

forcement. The product was superior to both 85% magnesia and calcium silicate in insulating efficiency. It was superior to the former in strength, hardness, and resistance to abrasion and vibration, and was capable of resisting temperatures up to 1400 degrees F. "Its cost of manufacture is less than that of 85% magnesia."[102]

Insulating Cements

Insulating cements were used as protective coverings and in situations in which an odd-shaped insulation was necessary or advantageous. To apply them, water was added to a mixture of ingredients to form a trowelable mass. Typical uses included filling joints and seams, covering pipe bends, and covering the outside of pipe insulation. Insulating cement was sometimes applied to pipes and boilers as the sole insulation. It was also used to bond blocks of refractory material. Insulating cements commonly contained a fibrous material, such as mineral wool, and any of various cements or binding agents. When used, the purpose of asbestos was to strengthen these formulations. Other types of insulating cements were composed almost totally of asbestos or ground up 85% magnesia.

Various patents described insulating cements or related compositions (see Table 8) in which asbestos was not included in the composition or was not an essential ingredient. Two 1925 patents assigned to Celite combined diatomaceous earth with other ingredients.[103,104] One of these patents used a binding agent, such as Portland cement, and a fibrous material, such as "asbestos, manila fiber, hair, wood fiber, or any kind of fiber which may assist in giving mechanical strength to the composition."[104]

A plaster composition patented in 1934 was comprised mainly of rock wool and diatomaceous earth. Rock wool was included because it could withstand temperatures over 1500 degrees F. On the other hand, materials such as asbestos were specifically excluded because they had "a critical point of about 1400 degrees F., that is, at this temperature they break down and become of practically no use as a fire-proofing material."[105]

A corrosion-resistant insulating cement, patented in 1950 by Baldwin-Hill, contained mineral wool and an inorganic binder.[106] Although asbestos could have been included, it was not deemed essential.

A weather-resistant insulating cement used as an outer layer covering other layers of insulating cements, was patented in 1951. This had no asbestos and was composed primarily of cement, clay, and mineral wool.[107] Other asbestos-free insulating cements were patented in the United States and the Soviet Union.[108,109,110,111]

CONCLUSION

In summary, many alternative materials were capable of substituting for asbestos-containing thermal insulation throughout the history of asbestos use in such products. Asbestos was used in magnesia and calcium silicate insulations not for its insulating property, but only as a reinforcing agent in the finished product and a suspension aid in processing.

Not only were magnesia products disclosed in numerous patents using alternative fibers such as animal hair, mineral wool, fiberglass, wood and cotton; but also other types of insulation, such as fiberglass, vermiculite, and rigid glass, could have replaced asbestos-reinforced magnesia insulations.

Asbestos-free calcium silicate compositions, now widely used, appear to be based essentially on technology that was available long before asbestos was banned in molded insulations in the 1970s (1972 in Denmark, 1975 in the U.S.). Examples of substitute fibrous reinforcement in calcium silicate insulations included fiberglass, mineral wool, cellulosic fiber, and paper pulp. Moreover, xonotlite, a particular calcium silicate developed in the late 1940s by Owens-Illinois, needed no reinforcement. Various materials, such as cellulose, paper pulp, or starch, were usable as suspending agents in the initial slurry of lime and silica reactants. Certain types of fiberglass, mineral wool and expanded perlite insulations, whose useful temperature ranges approximated that of calcium silicate, could have replaced calcium silicate (and thus magnesia as well).

Several patents disclosed insulating cements and related compositions in which asbestos was not included in the composition or was not essential.

Once the dangers of asbestos, and specifically the use of asbestos in insulation, became known, the manufacturers could have vigorously developed and used the above alternatives to eliminate the asbestos hazard in manufacturing, product application, and removal. Over the decades that the tragedy of asbestos unfolded, an increasing number of technological alternatives were available but underutilized. The substitution of less hazardous products would have been preferable to the use of warning labeling by manufacturers or the use of partially effective control measures by workers exposed to asbestos insulation dust.

REFERENCES

1. Hunter, D., *The Diseases of Occupations,* 4th ed., Boston: Little, Brown & Co., 1969, pp. 1023–1024.

2. Thoenen, J.R., *Mineral Wool,* Bureau of Mines Information Circular No. 6142, June 1929.

3. Bowles, O., *Industrial Insulation With Mineral Products,* Bureau of Mines Information Circular No. 7263, Dec. 1943.

4. Bowles, O., *The Asbestos Industry,* Bureau of Mines Bulletin 552, 1955.

5. *Mineral Wool Insulation for Heated Industrial Equipment,* Commercial Standard CS117-49, United States Department of Commerce, June 1, 1949.

6. *Specifications for Construction of a Twin Screw Passenger and Cargo Vessel,* United States Maritime Commission, Jan. 1945, p. 75-1.

7. Abrahams, S.A., "Better Magnesia Insulation by New Process," *Chemical Engineering,* 58:141 (Sept. 1951).

8. *Ibid.,* p. 140.

9. Newman, N.E. (to Asbestos Limited Inc.), U.S. Patent 2,309,206 (Jan. 26, 1943), col. 1, lines 1-7.

10. Saborsky, A.D., "Glass Wool Heat Insulation in Europe," *J. Amer. Ceram. Soc.*, 6:674 (May, 1923).

11. Hanmore, H.M. (to Keasbey and Mattison), U.S. Patent 345,843 (July 20, 1886).

12. *Ibid.*, p. 1, lines 65-69.

13. Greider, H.W. et al. (to The Philip Carey Manufacturing Company), U.S. Patent 2,275,032 (Mar. 3, 1942), col. 1, lines 30-34.

14. Greider, H.W. et al. (to The Philip Carey Manufacturing Company), U.S. Patent 2,335,242 (Nov. 30, 1943), col. 3, lines 50-54.

15. Cummins, A.B. et al. (to Johns-Manville Corporation), U.S. Patent 2,428,555 (Oct. 7, 1947), col. 3, lines 29-33.

16. Honnig, R.W. (to Johns-Manville Corporation), U.S. Patent 2,609,733 (Sept. 9, 1952), col. 13, lines 54-59.

17. Greider, H.W. (to The Philip Carey Manufacturing Company), U.S. Patent 1,782,384 (Nov. 18, 1930).

18. Abrahams, S.A. et al. (to Plant Rubber & Asbestos Works), U.S. Patent 2,209,754 (July 30, 1940).

19. McGarvey, A.R. (to Armstrong Cork Company), U.S. Patent 2,409,297 (Oct. 15, 1946).

20. Dinkfield, A.M. et al. (to Johns-Manville Corporation), U.S. Patent 2,413,958 (Jan. 7, 1947).

21. Seipt, W.R. (to Keasbey & Mattison Company), U.S. Patent 2,800,415 (July 23, 1957).

22. Baxter, M. (to James D. Akins), U.S. Patent 2,598,102 (May 27, 1952).

23. de Dani, A., "Glass Fibres. Their Manufacture, Properties and Uses," *Chemistry and Industry,* April 30, 1955, p. 482.

24. *Op. cit., J. Amer. Ceram. Soc.*, p. 676.

25. Rase, H.F. and Barrow, M.H., *Project Engineering of Process Plants,* New York: John Wiley & Sons, Inc., 1957, pp. 476-7.

26. Stephens J.F. et al. (to Gustin-Bacon Manufacturing Co.), U.S. Patent 2,778,759 (Jan. 22, 1957).

27. Keyes, M.W. (to Pittsburgh Plate Glass Company), U.S. Patent 2,906,317 (Sept. 29, 1959).

28. Labino, D. (to Johns-Manville Fiber Glass Inc.), U.S. Patent 3,063,887 (Nov. 13, 1962).

29. *Op. cit., Project Engineering of Process Plants,* p. 475.

30. Product Pamphlet for Micro-Lok 650, Johns-Manville, Jan. 1979.

31. *The German Mineral Wool and Heat Insulation Industries,* British

Intelligence Objectives Sub-Committee Final Report No. 916, copy received at U.S. Patent Office May 10, 1955, p. 21.

32. *Ibid.* p. 24.

33. Babor, J.A. et al., U.S. Patent 1,693,015 (Nov. 27, 1928).

34. *Op. cit., Project Engineering of Process Plants,* p. 475.

35. Hollenberg, Jr., F.H. (to Baldwin-Hill Company), U.S. Patent 2,633,433 (Mar. 31, 1953), col. 5, lines 25-40.

36. Belknap, C.H. (to Armstrong Cork Co.), U.S. Patent 1,045,933 (Dec. 3, 1912).

37. Taylor, W.C. (to Owens-Corning Fiberglas Corp.), U.S. Patent 3,116,158 (Dec. 31, 1963), col. 1, lines 55-65.

38. *Op. cit., Project Engineering of Process Plants,* p. 476-7.

39. *Op cit.,* U.S. Patent 1,045,933, p. 2, lines 60-65.

40. Haynes, W., ed., *American Chemical Industry The Chemical Companies,* vol. VI, New York: D. Van Nostrand Company, 1949, p. 237.

41. Teitsworth, C.S. (to The Celite Company), U.S. Patent 1,520,893 (Dec. 30, 1924), p. 3, lines 7-14.

42. Teitsworth, C.S. (to The Celite Company), U.S. Patent 1,590,132 (June 22, 1926), p. 3, lines 29-35.

43. Brown, G.B. (to Johns-Manville Corporation), U.S. Patent 2,247,355 (July 1, 1941).

44. Binkley, M.E. (to Johns-Manville Corporation), U.S. Patent 2,699,097 (Jan. 11, 1955), col. 2, lines 43-46.

45. Deposition of John McKinney, St. Jacque vs. Johns-Manville Corporation et al., Nov. 25, 1980, p. 232.

46. Vander Linden, C.R. (to Johns-Manville Corporation), U.S. Patent 3,033,648 (May 8, 1962).

47. Noll, C.H. et al. (to Johns-Manville Corporation), U.S. Patent 3,965,020 (June 22, 1976).

48. Shuman, E.C., "Hydrous Calcium Silicate Heat Insulation," *The Petroleum Engineer,* 24:C-55 (April 1952).

49. Fraser, L.H.D. (to Owens-Illinois Glass Company), U.S. Patent Re. 23,228 (May 9, 1950), col. 14, lines 13-37.

50. Kalousek, G.L. (to Owens-Illinois Glass Company), U.S. Patent 2,547,127 (Apr. 3, 1951), col. 2, lines 40-47.

51. Arthur D. Little, Inc., *Tenth Progress Report on Studies of Kaylo,* Oct. 9, 1947, p. 4.

52. Deposition of Everett Shuman, St. Jacque vs. Johns-Manville Corporation et al., Mar. 4, 1981, pp. 73-74.

53. *Op. cit.*, U.S. Patent 2,547,127, col. 3, lines 7-13.

54. Kalousek, G.L., *The System CaO-SiO$_2$-H$_2$O Xonotlite Kaylo*, General Research & New Development Division of Owens-Illinois Glass Company, Nov. 26, 1948, pp. 7-8.

55. Kalousek, G.L. (to Owens-Illinois Glass Company), U.S. Patent 2,748,008 (May 29, 1956).

56. *Op. cit.*, U.S. Patent 3,116,158.

57. Pfeifer, O.W. et al. (to Owens-Corning Fiberglas Corporation), U.S. Patent 3,216,881 (Nov. 9, 1965).

58. Pfeifer, O.W. et al. (to Owens-Corning Fiberglas Corporation), U.S. Patent 3,472,668 (Oct. 14, 1969).

59. Shannon, R.F. (to Owens-Corning Fiberglas Corporation), U.S. Patent 3,562,084 (Feb. 9, 1971).

60. Shannon, R.F. (to Owens-Corning Fiberglas Corporation), U.S. Patent 3,574,113 (Apr. 6, 1971), col. 5, lines 44-50.

61. Shannon, R.F. (to Owens-Corning Fiberglas Corporation), U.S. Patent 3,923,674 (Dec. 2, 1975).

62. Abrahams, S.A. et al. (to The Paraffine Companies, Inc.), U.S. Patent 2,432,981 (Dec. 23, 1947).

63. Lewon R. et al. (to The Paraffine Companies, Inc.), U.S. Patent 2,483,498 (Oct. 4, 1949).

64. Hoopes, H.P. et al. (to Fibreboard Paper Products Corporation), U.S. Patent 2,904,444 (Sept. 15, 1959).

65. Smith, E.C.W. et al. (to Insulex Mineral Products Limited), British Patent 722,015 (Jan. 19, 1955).

66. Allen, E.M. (to Columbia-Southern Chemical Corp.), U.S. Patent 2,754,547 (July 17, 1956).

67. Burak, N. et al. (to Joseph Crosfield & Sons Limited), U.S. Patent 3,238,052 (Mar. 1, 1966).

68. Stewart, J. and Richardson, C.D., "One Hundred Years of Mineral Wool," *Industrial and Engineering Chemistry News Edition*, 18:997 (Nov. 25, 1940).

69. *Op. cit., Project Engineering of Process Plants*, pp. 476-9.

70. "Insulation and Application Methods for Heated Piping," *The Petroleum Engineer*, 23:C-44 (Oct. 1951).

71. *Op. Cit., Industrial Insulation With Mineral Products*, p. 5.

72. *Op. cit., Mineral Wool*, p. 2.

73. Hall, C.C. (to Banner Rock Products Company), U.S. Patent 1,611,907 (Dec. 28, 1926).

74. *Moody's Industrial Manual*, New York: Moody's Investors Service, Inc., 1981, p. 3755.

75. Mottweiler, O.F. et al. (to General Insulating and Manufacturing Company), U.S. Patent 1,827,035 (Oct. 13, 1931).
76. Smith, H.C. (to Coast Insulating Co.), U.S. Patent 1,907,307 (May 2, 1933).
77. Losse, P.L. (to The Eagle-Picher Company), U.S. Patent 2,950,225 (Aug. 23, 1960).
78. Losse, P.L. (to The Eagle-Picher Company), U.S. Patent 3,030,250 (Apr. 17, 1962).
79. Hahn, W.P. et al. (to Johns-Manville Corporation), U.S. Patent 3,128,503 (Apr. 14, 1964).
80. Eriksen, H.N. (to Keene Corporation), U.S. Patent 3,577,889 (May 11, 1971).
81. Answers to plaintiff's interrogatories to Eagle-Picher dated April 30, 1982.
82. *Moody's Industrial Manual,* New York: Moody's Investors Service, Inc., 1958, p. 73.
83. Bjure, J., Soderholm, B., and Widimsky, J., "Cardiopulmonary function studies in workers dealing with asbestos and glass-wool," *Thorax,* 19:22-27 (1964).
84. Stalego, J.P. (to Owens-Corning Fiberglas Corporation), U.S. Patent 2,941,904 (June 21, 1960).
85. Plummer, J.H. (to Owens-Corning Fiberglas Corporation), U.S. Patent 2,184,316 (Dec. 26, 1939).
86. Stalego, J.P. (to Owens-Corning Fiberglas Corporation), U.S. Patent 2,941,899 (June 21, 1960).
87. Labino, D. (to Johns-Manville Fiber Glass Inc.), U.S. Patent 3,053,715 (Sept. 11, 1962), col. 7, lines 66-75.
88. *Op. cit., Moody's Industrial Manual,* 1981, p. 3755.
89. Thomas, H.K., U.S. Patent 2,600,812 (June 17, 1952).
90. *Ibid.,* col. 3, lines 20-22.
91. Cook, H.A. et al. (to The Philip Carey Manufacturing Company), U.S. Patent 2,884,380 (Apr. 28, 1959).
92. *Moody's Industrial Manual,* New York: Moody's Investors Service, Inc., 1972, p. 2897.
93. Mueller, A.P. (to Panacon Corporation), U.S. Patent 3,639,276 (Feb. 1, 1972), col. 6, lines 4-6.
94. Denning, P.S. (to Johns-Manville Perlite Corporation), U.S. Patent 3,042,578 (July 3, 1962).
95. Becker, N.V. (to Johns-Manville Perlite Corporation), U.S. Patent 3,095,347 (June 25, 1963).

96. Yates, P.C. (to E.I. du Pont de Nemours and Company), U.S. Patent 3,718,491 (Feb. 27, 1973), col. 1, lines 10-14.

97. *Op. cit.*, U.S. Patent 2,309,206.

98. Drill, D.C. (to Johns-Manville Corporation), U.S. Patent 1,956,377 (Apr. 24, 1934).

99. McDermott, P.F. (to Johns-Manville Corporation), U.S. Patent 2,425,293 (Aug. 12, 1947).

100. Farrell, E.A. (to Johns-Manville Corporation), U.S. Patent 2,609,312 (Sept. 2, 1952).

101. Bruno, A.J. et al. (to Johns-Manville Corporation), U.S. Patent 2,808,338 (Oct. 1, 1957).

102. Napier, H. (to F.E. Schundler & Co., Inc.), U.S. Patent 2,456,643 (Dec. 21, 1948), col. 1, lines 26-32.

103. Caldwell, L. (to The Celite Company), U.S. Patent 1,544,215 (June 30, 1925).

104. Teitsworth, C.S. (to The Celite Company), U.S. Patent 1,544,196 (June 30, 1925), p. 2, lines 120-4.

105. Jenkins, S.M., U.S. Patent 1,968,489 (July 31, 1934), p. 1, lines 40-44.

106. Hollenberg, Jr., F.M. (to Baldwin-Hill Company), U.S. Patent 2,509,599 (May 30, 1950).

107. Randall, M.C. et al., U.S. Patent 2,574,843 (Nov. 13, 1951).

108. Hayde, S.J., U.S. Patent 803,285 (Oct. 31, 1905).

109. MacDonald R.B. (to W.H. Winkley), U.S. Patent 1,332,348 (Mar. 2, 1920).

110. Demaison, R.J. (to Quigley Company, Inc.), U.S. Patent 3,092,505 (June 4, 1963).

111. Blokh, L.E., U.S.S.R. Patent 54,360 (Jan. 31, 1939). See *Chemical Abstracts* 35:col. 3007 (1941).

ANNOTATED LIST OF THERMAL INSULATION PATENTS

The following are lists of patents that suggest alternatives to asbestos-containing thermal insulations. There is a separate list for each of the major manufacturers. These are followed by a single list combining other companies and independent inventors. Collectively, these patents contain claims directed towards methods and apparatus for forming insulating compositions, in addition to the compositions themselves.

To better understand the development of each company's

knowledge, the former names of the companies, their subsidiaries, and the companies purchased by them are given below.

Manville Corporation
Johns-Manville Corporation
Johns-Manville Perlite Corporation
F.E. Schundler & Co., Inc.
Johns-Manville Fiber Glass Inc.
L.O.F. Glass Fibers Company
Banner Rock Products Company
The Celite Company
Johns
Manville

Jim Walter Corporation
Panacon Corporation
The Celotex Corporation
The Philip Carey Manufacturing Company

Nicolet, Inc.
Keasbey & Mattison Company

Fibreboard Corporation (merged into Louisiana-Pacific Corporation)
Fibreboard Paper Products Corporation
Pabco Products Inc.
The Paraffine Companies
Plant Rubber & Asbestos Works

Armstrong World Industries, Inc.
Armstrong Cork Company

Bairnco Corporation
Keene Corporation
Baldwin-Ehret-Hill, Inc.
Baldwin-Hill Company

PPG Industries, Inc.
Pittsburgh Plate Glass Company
Pittsburgh Corning Corporation (50% owned)
Columbia-Southern Chemical Corp.

UNR Industries, Inc.
Unarco Industries, Inc.
Union Asbestos & Rubber Company

Raymark Corporation
Raybestos-Manhattan

Most of the assignees in the lists are given as shortened names of the above companies.

Patent Number	Issue Year	Patentee (Assignee)	Description
Manville Corporation			
433,471	1890	Johns	Covering containing wood pulp plus sawdust and chopped cork, sponge, hay, straw or hair
441,165	1890	Johns	Covering containing wood pulp plus binder and sawdust, straw, hay, cork, sponge, hair or asbestos
465,701	1891	Manville	Covering containing clay, graphite, glue, and wool dust
1,520,893	1924	Teitsworth (Celite)	Calcium silicate with manila, cellulose or asbestos fibers
1,544,196	1925	Teitsworth (Celite)	Insulating composition containing

Patent Number	Issue Year	Patentee (Assignee)	Description
Manville Corporation (cont.)			
			diatomaceous earth, a vegetable gum, and manila fiber, hair, wood fiber or asbestos
1,544,215	1925	Caldwell (Celite)	Insulating mortar comprising diatomaceous earth and a vegetable gum
1,569,755	1926	Irvin (Celite)	Calcium silicate with hemp, hair or asbestos
1,590,132	1926	Teitsworth (Celite)	Calcium silicate with manila fiber, hair or asbestos
1,611,907	1926	Hall (Banner Rock)	Rock wool jacket for pipe insulation
1,613,137	1927	Seigle (Johns-Manville)	Method for making insulation containing diatomaceous earth, bentonite, and asbestos; asbestos not essential
1,734,209	1929	Huffine (Banner Rock)	Rock wool or asbestos jacket for pipe insulation
1,824,430	1931	Hall (Banner Rock)	Process for treating mineral wool
1,948,395	1934	Powell (Banner Rock)	Apparatus for producing rock wool products
1,956,377	1934	Drill	Molded insulation

Patent Number	Issue Year	Patentee (Assignee)	Description
Manville Corporation (cont.)			
		(Johns-Manville)	formed with reacted mineral wool
1,972,500	1934	Toohey et al. (Johns-Manville)	Wool scrap plus wood pipe insulation
1,982,542	1934	Seigle (Johns-Manville)	Magnesia with hemp, jute, organic wool or asbestos
2,019,021	1935	O'Brien (Johns-Manville)	Moisture-resistant mineral wool heat insulation
2,055,446	1936	Powell (Johns-Manville)	Mineral wool felt
2,077,720	1937	Seigle et al. (Johns-Manville)	Mineral wool felt pipe insulation
2,116,303	1938	Coss (Johns-Manville)	Mineral wool composition
2,190,271	1940	Powell (Johns-Manville)	Apparatus and process for manufacturing mineral wool
2,192,524	1940	Powell (Johns-Manville)	Apparatus for the manufacture of mineral wool
2,247,355	1941	Brown (Johns-Manville)	Calcium silicate ship panel with wood fibers or asbestos; example with wood fibers given
2,282,230	1942	MacAlpine (Johns-Manville)	Mineral wool insulation mat

Patent Number	Issue Year	Patentee (Assignee)	Description
Manville Corporation (cont.)			
2,348,614	1944	Dinkfeld (Johns-Manville)	Magnesia shingle, wallboard or other shape with jute, cotton or asbestos
2,413,958	1947	Dinkfeld et al. (Johns-Manville)	Magnesia with asbestos or other reinforcing fibers and fillers
2,425,293	1947	McDermott (Johns-Manville)	Method and apparatus for making asbestos, mineral wool or glass fiber blanket or tape
2,428,555	1947	Cummins et al. (Johns-Manville)	Magnesia with mineral wool, diatomaceous silica or asbestos
2,456,643	1948	Napier (F.E. Schundler)	Portland cement or calcium silicate containing metal fiber or asbestos
2,554,934	1951	Ayers (Johns-Manville)	Thermal insulation in which part of the asbestos can be replaced with wood fibers
2,584,300	1952	Simmers (Johns-Manville)	Liquid binder for mineral wool bats
2,609,312	1952	Farrell (Johns-Manville)	Tubular pipe covering containing glass, mineral wool or asbestos fibers

Patent Number	Issue Year	Patentee (Assignee)	Description
Manville Corporation (cont.)			
2,609,733	1952	Honnig (Johns-Manville)	Magnesia products made using raw cotton, spun glass, fine rock wool, steam treated wood, or asbestos fibers
2,699,097	1955	Binkley (Johns-Manville)	Calcium silicate with mineral wool, glass fibers or asbestos
2,699,397	1955	Hahn (Johns-Manville)	Mineral wool composition
2,808,338	1957	Bruno et al. (Johns-Manville)	Heat insulation comprising silica aerogel plus fibers such as asbestos, mineral, glass, cotton, acetate, rayon or acrylic fibers
2,904,453	1959	Labino (L.O.F. Glass Fibers)	Glass fiber pipe wrap
3,012,930	1961	Labino (Johns-Manville Fiber Glass)	Silica glass fiber mats
3,017,318	1962	Labino et al. (Johns-Manville Fiber Glass)	Thermal insulation board comprising siliceous fiber, mineral filler and collodial silica
3,042,578	1962	Denning (Johns-Manville Perlite)	Expanded perlite insulation containing vegetable, glass or asbestos fibers

Patent Number	Issue Year	Patentee (Assignee)	Description
Manville Corporation (cont.)			
3,050,106	1962	Pusch et al. (Johns-Manville)	Apparatus for forming pipe insulation containing rock wool, glass or asbestos fibers
3,053,715	1962	Labino (Johns-Manville Fiber Glass)	High temperature glass fiber pipe insulation
3,055,831	1962	Barnett et al. (Johns-Manville)	Heat insulation comprising silica aerogel plus fibers such as asbestos, mineral, glass, cotton, acetate, rayon or acrylic fibers
3,063,887	1962	Labino (Johns-Manville Fiber Glass)	Method and apparatus of forming glass fiber pipe insulation
3,081,207	1963	Fox (Johns-Manville Fiber Glass)	Glass fiber mats
3,092,531	1963	Labino (Johns-Manville Fiber Glass)	Siliceous glass fiber bats
3,095,347	1963	Becker (Johns-Manville Perlite)	Expanded perlite insulating board containing newsprint, rock wool or asbestos
3,118,807	1964	Holcomb (Johns-Manville)	Refractory mineral wool felts and blankets
3,128,503	1964	Hahn et al.	Apparatus for forming

Patent Number	Issue Year	Patentee (Assignee)	Description
Manville Corporation (cont.)			
		(Johns-Manville)	mineral wool and fiberglass pipe insulation
3,162,895	1964	Pusch (Johns-Manville)	Apparatus for forming pipe insulation containing rock wool, mineral wool, glass, asbestos, or synthetic fibers
3,331,669	1967	Sinclair (Johns-Manville)	Apparatus and method for forming felted products containing mineral and glass fibers
3,346,016	1967	Blau et al. (Johns-Manville)	High temperature laminated insulation containing glass, mineral, rock wool, asbestos, or alumina-silica fibers
3,816,149	1974	Zettel (Johns-Manville)	Calcium silicate with glass fiber, rock wool, rayons, cellulosic fiber, nylons or asbestos
3,856,544	1974	Benner et al. (Johns-Manville)	Calcium silicate with poly(ethylene terephthalate) fibers (Dacron®) plus glass fibers
3,965,020	1976	Noll et al. (Johns-Manville)	Calcium silicate with glass, polyester and cellulosic fibers

Patent Number	Issue Year	Patentee (Assignee)	Description
Manville Corporation			
4,111,712	1978	Pusch (Johns-Manville)	Calcium silicate (tobermorite form) with wollastonite and organic fibers (kraft paper, newsprint fiber, polyester or cotton)
4,128,434	1978	Pusch (Johns-Manville)	Calcium silicate (tobermorite form) with wollastonite, mineral wool and organic fibers (kraft paper, newsprint fiber, polyester or cotton)
4,131,638	1978	Whitaker et al. (Johns-Manville)	Calcium silicate with asbestos, rock wool, glass fiber, cellulosic fiber, rayons, nylons or polyesters
Owens-Corning Fiberglas Corporation All of the patents in this list were assigned to Owens-Corning Fiberglas Corporation.			
2,160,009	1939	Walker	Spring clip for glass wool pipe insulation
2,184,316	1939	Plummer	High temperature glass wool felt pipe insulation
2,189,840	1940	Simison et al.	Method for applying coatings on glass fiber mats
2,206,059	1940	Slayter	Glass wool felt useful as pipe insulation

Patent Number	Issue Year	Patentee (Assignee)	Description
Owens-Corning Fiberglas Corporation (cont.)			
2,252,157	1941	Bergin et al.	Glass wool, slag wool or rock wool insulating bats
2,288,072	1942	Collins	Method and apparatus for making glass or mineral wool insulation mats
2,331,146	1943	Slayter	Method for producing glass wool pipe coverings
2,335,102	1943	Bergin et al.	Method of producing glass wool, slag wool or rock wool insulating bats
2,350,996	1944	Atkinson et al.	Method for producing glass wool pipe coverings
2,528,091	1950	Slayter	Glass fiber thermal insulating mats
2,566,619	1951	Lyon et al.	Glass wool, slag wool or rock wool thermal insulations and method for forming them
2,640,784	1953	Tiede et al.	Glass fiber compositions
2,694,025	1954	Slayter et al.	Heat-insulating panel containing gypsum cement and glass fibers
2,702,069	1955	Lannan	Method for forming glass fiber mats

Patent Number	Issue Year	Patentee (Assignee)	Description
Owens-Corning Fiberglas Corporation (cont.)			
2,703,762	1955	Slayter	Heat resistant products containing magnesium oxide and glass fibers
2,731,066	1956	Hogendobler et al.	Glass fiber sheets useful as electrical, sound or heat insulation
2,941,899	1960	Stalego	High temperature glass fiber pipe insulation
2,941,904	1960	Stalego	High temperature glass fiber pipe insulation
3,002,857	1961	Stalego	Binder for glass fiber insulation
3,104,196	1963	Shannon	Board made from expanded polystyrene
3,116,158	1963	Taylor	Calcium silicate with asbestos or wollastonite fibers; examples 4 and 5 use wollastonite fibers
3,151,633	1964	Shuman	Disclosed shaped glass fiber pipe insulation
3,216,881	1965	Pfeifer et al.	Calcium silicate with resin coated glass fibers
3,227,570	1966	Bishop	Calcium silicate slurries including asbestos or other fillers

Patent Number	Issue Year	Patentee (Assignee)	Description
Owens-Corning Fiberglas Corporation (cont.)			
3,239,369	1966	Glaser	Heat-insulating silica glass fibers
3,286,785	1966	Shannon et al.	Thermal insulating board containing siliceous fibers
3,317,643	1967	Denny	Calcium silicate with or without asbestos
3,348,994	1967	Rees et al.	Glass fiber insulation board
3,472,668	1969	Pfeifer et al.	Method for forming calcium silicate with resin coated glass fibers
3,562,084	1971	Shannon	Calcium silicate with cotton fibers
3,574,113	1971	Shannon	Calcium silicate with asbestos or resin coated silica glass fibers (example 12)
3,794,505	1974	Helser et al.	Calcium silicate with cellulose plus zirconia glass fibers
3,923,674	1975	Shannon	Calcium silicate with asbestos, bagasse or glass fibers
4,015,994	1977	Hill	Coated glass fibers as replacement for asbestos in calcium silicate, cement, mortar or gypsum compositions

Patent Number	Issue Year	Patentee (Assignee)	Description

Owens-Illinois, Inc.

All of the patents in this list were assigned to Owens-Illinois Glass Company.

Patent Number	Issue Year	Patentee (Assignee)	Description
2,133,236	1938	Slayter et al.	Apparatus and method for making glass wool useful for insulation
2,469,379	1949	Fraser	Calcium silicate with spiculated cellulose or asbestos; disclosed use of cellulose fiber as a suspending agent
Re. 23,228	1950	Fraser	Reissue patent of and same disclosure as 2,469,379
2,540,354	1951	Selden	Calcium silicate with asbestos or cellulose such as paper pulp
2,547,127	1951	Kalousek	Calcium silicate (xonotlite form) without the need of reinforcement; disclosed starch or highly pulped and beaten paper as suspending agents
2,665,996	1954	Kalousek	Calcium silicate (lepisil form) with cellulose or asbestos; disclosed use of cellulose as a suspending agent and to prevent the "hinging effect" (cracking)
2,748,008	1956	Kalousek	Method of making calcium silicate using

Patent Number	Issue Year	Patentee (Assignee)	Description
Owens-Illinois, Inc. (cont.)			
			lepisil or xonotlite to suspend the initial reactants
Jim Walter Corporation			
1,782,384	1930	Greider (Philip Carey)	Magnesia with asbestos or other suitable fibrous materials
1,882,810	1932	Greider (Philip Carey)	Magnesia with asbestos or other suitable fibrous materials
2,262,953	1941	MacArthur et al. (Philip Carey)	Magnesia with asbestos or other mineral fibers
2,275,032	1942	Greider et al. (Philip Carey)	Magnesia with asbestos or other mineral fibers or substances
2,335,242	1943	Greider et al. (Philip Carey)	Magnesia with mineral wool, glass wool, cellulose or asbestos
2,348,829	1944	MacArthur et al. (Philip Carey)	Disclosed hydraulically set heat insulation composed of gypsum and diatomaceous earth, and a molded insulation of mineral wool and a binder
2,348,898	1944	Greider et al. (Philip Carey)	Magnesia with asbestos or other mineral fibers or substances

Patent Number	Issue Year	Patentee (Assignee)	Description
Jim Walter Corporation (cont.)			
2,354,593	1944	Greider et al. (Philip Carey)	Plastic composition useful for fire-resistant floor or pavement, conduits for electrical wires, or coatings for oil pipes; contained fibers such as asbestos, rock wool or glass
2,396,915	1946	Greider et al. (Philip Carey)	Magnesia with asbestos or other mineral fibers or substances
2,884,380	1959	Cook et al. (Philip Carey)	Expanded perlite insulation with mineral fibers
2,971,878	1961	Heilman et al. (Philip Carey)	Expanded perlite insulation containing asbestos or other mineral fibers
3,639,276	1972	Mueller (Panacon)	Expanded perlite insulation containing glass fibers; described health hazards of asbestos
Nicolet, Inc.			
345,843	1886	Hanmore (One-half to Keasbey & Mattison)	Magnesia with animal hair, wool, asbestos or various other materials
Re. 22,952	1947	Miller (Keasbey & Mattison)	Magnesia with fibrous matter such as asbestos
2,486,050	1949	Miller et al. (Keasbey &	Method for forming heat insulation

Patent Number	Issue Year	Patentee (Assignee)	Description
Nicolet, Inc. (cont.)			
		Mattison)	containing asbestos, rock wool or glass wool
2,574,652	1951	Miller (Keasbey & Mattison)	Process of producing magnesia containing asbestos and/or other suitable ingredients
2,800,415	1957	Seipt (Keasbey & Mattison)	Magnesia with asbestos or similar fibers
4,244,781	1981	Heckman (Nicolet, Inc.)	Nonasbestos millboard refractory composition; also acknowledged various nonasbestos insulating compositions, including those disclosed in U. S. Patents 3,042,578 and 3,658,564, both perlite insulations
Fibreboard Corporation			
2,209,754	1940	Abrahams et al. (Plant Rubber & Asbestos Works)	Magnesia with asbestos or other suitable fiber
2,339,041	1944	Abrahams et al. (Plant Rubber & Asbestos Works)	Magnesia with asbestos or other suitable fiber
2,432,981	1947	Abrahams et al. (The Paraffine Companies)	Method of making calcium silicate containing mineral fiber, glass fiber, or asbestos

Patent Number	Issue Year	Patentee (Assignee)	Description
Fibreboard Corporation (cont.)			
2,483,498	1949	Lewon et al. (The Paraffine Companies)	Method of making calcium silicate containing mineral fiber, glass fiber, metallic fiber or asbestos
2,517,001	1950	Lewon et al. (The Paraffine Companies)	Molding apparatus for magnesia or calcium silicate containing asbestos or other fibers
2,904,444	1959	Hoopes et al. (Fibreboard Paper Products)	Method of making calcium silicate containing mineral fiber, glass fiber or asbestos

Armstrong World Industries, Inc.

All of the patents in this list were assigned to Armstrong Cork Company.

Patent Number	Issue Year	Patentee (Assignee)	Description
1,045,933	1912	Belknap	Calcium silicate with asbestos, mineral wool or spun glass
2,367,093	1945	Brown, Jr. et al.	Method of manufacturing insulating firebrick or block
2,409,297	1946	McGarvey	Process for making magnesia suitable alone, or with fibers such as asbestos
2,423,839	1947	McGarvey et al.	Method of making magnesia suitable alone, or with fibers such as asbestos

Patent Number	Issue Year	Patentee (Assignee)	Description
Armstrong World Industries, Inc. (cont.)			
2,476,306	1949	King	Heat-insulating block using mineral wool
British 766,428	1955	Armstrong Cork Company	Heat-insulating board containing mineral wool and kraft pulp
Bairnco Corporation			
2,509,599	1950	Hollenberg, Jr. (Baldwin-Hill)	Mineral wool insulating cement; asbestos not necessary
2,633,433	1953	Hollenberg, Jr. (Baldwin-Hill)	Insulating sheet containing mineral wool, glass wool or asbestos; characterized by ease of handling, minimum of dusting and breakage, with practically no industrial health hazard
2,732,295	1956	Hollenberg, Jr. (Baldwin-Hill)	Same disclosure as 2,633,433
3,577,889	1971	Eriksen (Keene)	Method and apparatus for slitting and trimming mineral wool pipe insulation

The Eagle-Picher Company

All of the patents in this list were assigned to The Eagle-Picher Company.

Patent Number	Issue Year	Patentee (Assignee)	Description
2,950,225	1960	Losse	Method of producing mineral wool insulation

Patent Number	Issue Year	Patentee (Assignee)	Description
The Eagle-Picher Company (cont.)			
3,030,250	1962	Losse	Mineral wool blanket pipe insulation
3,336,951	1967	Huelster	Mineral fiber pipe insulation
PPG Industries, Inc.			
2,620,513	1952	Cryor et al. (Originally assigned to Union Asbestos & Rubber, but records in the U.S. Patent Office show this patent was later sold to Pittsburgh Corning)	Method and apparatus for forming rigid pipe insulation containing glass, mineral or asbestos fibers
2,754,547	1956	Allen (Columbia-Southern Chemical)	Calcium silicate with rock wool, glass fiber or asbestos
2,906,317	1959	Keyes (Pittsburgh Plate Glass)	Method for forming glass fiber pipe insulation
UNR Industries, Inc.			
2,468,589	1949	Cryor et al. (Union Asbestos & Rubber)	Insulating tape containing asbestos or glass rovings
2,620,513	1952	Cryor et al. (Union Asbestos & Rubber)	Method and apparatus for forming rigid pipe insulation containing glass, mineral or asbestos fibers

Patent Number	Issue Year	Patentee (Assignee)	Description
Raymark Corporation			
2,514,170	1950	Walter et al. (Raybestos-Manhattan)	Composite blanket pipe insulation filled with asbestos, glass wool, mineral wool or slag wool
Other Companies and Independent Inventors			
148,972	1874	O'Hara	Covering consisting of ashes and sodium silicate
308,516	1884	Ordway	Pipe covering containing charcoal and water glass (sodium silicate)
570,634	1896	Hicks	Pipe insulation containing mica flakes
775,541	1904	McConnell (McConnell Asbestos & Covering Co.)	Pipe covering containing hair, asbestos, mineral wool, plastic magnesia, or similar fibrous or granular material
803,285	1905	Hayde	Insulating cement comprising Portland cement, burnt clay, and mineral wool
1,228,609	1917	Schmid ("Lipsia" Chemische Fabrik, Actien-Gesellschaft)	Process of making magnesia containing asbestos, coconut fiber, hairs or fibrous peat
1,332,348	1920	MacDonald (W.H. Winkley)	Insulating mortar or plaster consisting of

Patent Number	Issue Year	Patentee (Assignee)	Description
Other Companies and Independent Inventors (cont.)			
			diatomaceous earth, alkali, starch and water
1,427,014	1922	von Pazsiczky	Apparatus for producing spun glass useful as insulation
1,693,015	1928	Babor et al.	Insulation containing exfoliated vermiculite and a binder
1,827,035	1931	Mottweiler et al. (General Insulating and Manufacturing Company)	Rock wool jacket pipe insulation
1,907,307	1933	Smith (Coast Insulating Co.)	Mineral wool pipe insulation
1,939,329	1933	White	Mineral wool pipe insulation
1,968,489	1934	Jenkins	Insulating cement containing rock wool, diatomaceous earth, lime and flour
2,047,187	1936	Becher (The Agasote Millboard Company)	Insulation comprising exfoliated vermiculite and gelatinized cellulose
2,101,921	1937	Shaver	Mineral wool pipe insulation
Russian 54,360	1939	Blokh	Thermal insulation for hot pipes containing

Patent Number	Issue Year	Patentee (Assignee)	Description
Other Companies and Independent Inventors (cont.)			
			calcium hydrosilicate; troweled into place
2,309,206	1943	Newman (Asbestos Limited Incorporated)	Process of producing insulation containing cement, silica and fibers such as rock wool, mineral wool or asbestos
2,460,848	1949	Rover (Foster Wheeler Corporation)	Mineral wool, rock wool or asbestos insulating blanket useful as a furnace wall
2,491,761	1949	Parker et al. (The H.I. Thompson Company)	Silica glass fiber insulation
2,574,843	1951	Randall et al.	Insulating finishing cement comprising mineral wool, fly ash, aluminous cement, and bentonite
2,598,102	1952	Baxter (James D. Akins)	Magnesia, diatomaceous earth or calcium silicate insulation with glass fiber and slag wool pellets
2,600,812	1952	Thomas	Insulation containing expanded perlite, sodium silicate and sodium chloride
British 722,012	1955	Insulex Mineral Products Limited	Calcium silicate with rock wool and glass fibers

Patent Number	Issue Year	Patentee (Assignee)	Description
Other Companies and Independent Inventors (cont.)			
2,778,759	1957	Stephens et al. (Gustin-Bacon Manufacturing Co.)	Glass fiber pipe insulation
3,015,626	1962	Kingsbury	Insulating board containing expanded perlite, vermiculite particles, a binder, and a fiber, such as newsprint pulp, kraft paper pulp, bagasse, asbestos or glass fibers
3,025,176	1962	Herrington	Premolded insulation jacket for pipe fittings
3,092,505	1963	Demaison (Quigley Company, Inc.)	Refractory insulating cement comprising mineral wool, fireclay, Portland cement, and porous particles
3,238,052	1966	Burak et al. (Joseph Crosfield & Sons Limited)	Calcium silicate with glass fiber, mineral wool or asbestos; examples 54–58 without asbestos
3,501,324	1970	Kubo (Kabushiki Kaisha Osaka Packing Seizosho)	Calcium silicate with rock wool, glass fiber or asbestos
3,718,491	1973	Yates (E.I. du Pont de Nemours and Company)	Process for producing perlite-silicate insulation; mentioned the health hazards of asbestos

Patent Number	Issue Year	Patentee (Assignee)	Description
Other Companies and Independent Inventors (cont.)			
3,769,072	1973	Echerd et al. (H.K. Porter Company, Inc.)	Pipe lagging with mineral, glass, ceramic or asbestos fibers
4,144,121	1979	Otouma et al. (Nippon Asbestos Co., Ltd.)	Calcium silicate board with fibrous wollastonite and wood pulp

ANNOTATED LIST OF CEMENT PATENTS

This list contains patents that disclosed various fibers useful as replacements for asbestos in cement products such as asbestos-cement pipe.

Patent Number	Issue Year	Patentee (Assignee)	Description
3,736,162	1973	Chvalovsky et al. (Ceskoslovenska Akademie Ved.)	Corrosion-resistant mineral fibers coated with polysiloxane resin; replaced asbestos in a cement medium
3,854,986	1974	Chvalovsky et al. (Ceskoslovenska Akademie Ved.)	Corrosion resistant mineral fibers coated with polysiloxane resin; replaced asbestos in a cement medium
4,040,851	1977	Ziegler (GAF Corporation)	Cement articles reinforced with cotton fibers
4,064,307	1977	Lajoie	Urea-formaldehyde

Patent Number	Issue Year	Patentee (Assignee)	Description
		(L. Lajoie Inc.)	fibers useful in cements, sealants and paints
4,085,001	1978	Fukuwatari et al. (Asahi Glass Company, Ltd.)	Process of preparing fiberglass-reinforced cement sheets
4,095,986	1978	Matsuda et al. (Director-General of the Agency of Industrial Science and Technology)	Alkali-resistant glass composition useful in cement products
4,118,239	1978	Gagin (Johns-Manville Corporation)	Alkali-resistant glass composition useful in cement products
4,140,540	1979	Caspar et al. (Societe Anonyme dite: Lafarge)	Ettringite fibers useful in cement products
4,153,439	1979	Tomić et al. (Rockwool Aktiebolaget)	Method for producing mineral wool useful in a basic medium such as cement
4,191,585	1980	Jaunarajs (Johns-Manville Corporation)	Alkali-resistant glass fibers coated with zinc stearate, and useful in cement products
4,199,366	1980	Schaefer et al. (Inventa AG fur Forschung und Patent-verwertung)	Cement-like material reinforced with polyvinyl alcohol fibers

This list contains patents which have disclosed asbestos-free friction elements, such as brake linings, disc brakes, and clutch facings.

Patent Number	Issue Year	Patentee (Assignee)	Description
1,950,262	1934	Norton (Bendix Brake Company)	Brake facing containing asbestos or cellulose
2,110,571	1938	Elerath	Brake or clutch; asbestos not necessary
2,158,337	1939	Rasmussen (General Motors Corporation)	Brake linings containing glass fibers
2,239,134	1941	Wellman (The S.K. Wellman Company)	Brake linings or clutch facings comprising mainly metals
2,369,502	1945	Walker (Raybestos-Manhattan, Inc.)	Clutch facings or brake linings comprising metal powder and binder; asbestos not necessary (Ex. 2)
2,408,430	1946	Lowey et al. (The S. K. Wellman Company)	Metallic brakes and clutches containing molybdenum sulphide
2,784,105	1957	Stedman et al. (Bendix Aviation Corporation)	Asbestos-free aircraft brake containing metal and mullite
2,861,964	1958	de Gague et al. (Johns-Manville)	Railroad brake block with organic

Patent Number	Issue Year	Patentee (Assignee)	Description
			reinforcing fibers instead of asbestos
2,938,790	1960	Stedman et al. (Bendix Aviation Corporation)	Aircraft brakes containing mullite, and metal, but no asbestos
2,945,291	1960	Ankeny et al. (General Motors Corporation)	Clutch or brake containing iron, graphite and molybdenum disulfide
2,945,292	1960	Luther, Jr. et al. (General Motors Corporation)	Clutch or brake containing iron powder, graphite and bismuth powder
3,033,326	1962	Byers (The S.K. Wellman Company)	Aircraft brakes containing iron and graphite, but no asbestos
3,184,001	1965	Reinsch et al. (General Motors Corporation)	Brake lining (as in 2,945,291 or 2,945,292) and brake drum, wherein the drum contained no ferrite
3,210,303	1965	Biggs (American Brake Shoe Company)	Asbestos-free passenger car brake linings containing iron, graphite, and resin binder
3,269,976	1966	Ueda	Railroad brake containing graphite, copper, aluminum, and resin
3,494,884	1970	Kraft (Jurid-Werke GmbH)	Brake or clutch composition

Patent Number	Issue Year	Patentee (Assignee)	Description
			containing metal, an abrasive, a binder, and a filler, such as asbestos, glass, metal, barytes, or metal oxides
3,552,533	1971	Nitz et al. (Abex Corporation)	Structural part, including facing, made with carbonized filaments
3,743,069	1973	Barnett et al. (Johns-Manville Corporation)	Clutch facings containing glass fibers, cement, and brass wire
3,756,910	1973	Peters et al. (Johns-Manville Corporation)	Process of preparing clutch facings containing glass fibers, brass wire, and cement
3,835,118	1974	Rhee et al. (The Bendix Corporation)	Brake linings comprising metallic powder, sponge iron, ceramic powder, rubber particles, steel fibers, graphite particles, and a binder
3,870,581	1975	Afflerbach et al. (Johns-Manville Corporation)	Method of making clutch facings containing glass fibers and metal chips
3,896,075	1975	Longley (BBA Group Limited)	Brake lining or clutch in which basalt fibers are substituted for conventional asbestos fibers

Patent Number	Issue Year	Patentee (Assignee)	Description
3,967,037	1976	Marzocchi et al. (Owens-Corning Fiberglas Corporation)	Asbestos-free brake linings or pads containing glass fibers
4,118,528	1978	Lowry (Raybestos-Manhattan, Inc.)	Clutch facings containing glass fibers, carboxy nitrile rubber, phenol formaldehyde resin, and furnace black
4,119,591	1978	Aldrich (The Bendix Corporation)	Brake linings comprising at least one of steel, cellulose, glass, mineral and rayon fibers, thermosetting resin, cashew nut particles, elastomeric modifiers, and inorganic modifiers
4,197,223	1980	Bartram (Ferodo, Ltd.)	"Asbestos-free" clutch facing using a wide range of organic and inorganic fibers
4,217,255	1980	Griffith (Abex Corporation)	Lead-free, asbestos-free railroad brake
4,244,994	1981	Trainer et al. (Raybestos-Manhattan, Inc.)	Clutch facings containing aramid fibers

ANNOTATED LIST OF MISCELLANEOUS ASBESTOS SUBSTITUTE PATENTS

Patents in this list disclosed products that could have replaced asbestos for various applications. These included textiles, filters, electrical insulations, plaster compositions, and roofing felt.

The 1,730,609, 1,807,178 and 2,018,478 patents claimed to have made synthetic or chemical asbestos, but the products were really forms of mineral or rock fibers and, therefore, would not have exposed the product user to the dangers of asbestos.

Patent Number	Issue Year	Patentee (Assignee)	Description
1,730,609	1929	Grossman	Process for producing synthetic mineral fibers useful as a replacement for asbestos
1,807,178	1931	Seil	Synthetic "amphibole" products useful for the same purposes as amphibole asbestos
1,913,242	1933	McClure (Gustin-Bacon Manufacturing Co.)	Mineral fiber blanket useful in gas or electric stoves, or refrigerators
2,018,478	1935	Whittier	Apparatus for making chemical "asbestos-like" fibers useful for the same purposes as natural asbestos, including textiles
2,461,841	1949	Nordberg (Corning Glass	Methods for making refractory glass fibers

Patent Number	Issue Year	Patentee (Assignee)	Description
		Works)	useful as substitutes for asbestos fabrics and textiles, thermal insulation, and electrical insulation
2,494,259	1950	Nordberg (Corning Glass Works)	Refractory glass fibers useful as substitutes for asbestos fabrics and textiles, thermal insulation, and electrical insulation
2,503,454	1950	Quinn (Johns-Manville Corporation)	Roofing felt containing asphalt and wood fibers
Dutch 65,729	1950	Algemeene Kunstvezel Maatschappij N.V.	Refractory glass fibers useful as absorbents, or insulation of wires and electrical conductors
2,681,863	1954	Croce et al. (Certain-Teed Products Corporation)	Gypsum plaster composition with glass fibers
2,685,527	1954	Labino (Glass Fibers, Inc.)	Glass fibers useful in the preparation of paper for electrical insulation, heat insulation, and filters
2,756,158	1956	Hahn et al. (Johns-Manville Corporation)	Glass fibers useful as thermal insulation or as plastic reinforcement
2,871,134	1959	Loechl (The Celotex Corporation)	Gypsum plaster and other products containing

Patent Number	Issue Year	Patentee (Assignee)	Description
			individualized mineral wool fibers
3,062,670	1962	Marzocchi et al. (Owens-Corning Fiberglas Corporation)	Gypsum plaster and other products reinforced with glass fibers
3,080,247	1963	Slayter (Owens-Corning Fiberglas Corporation)	Glass-reinforced article useful as a high temperature gasket
3,366,001	1968	Meserole (Johns-Manville Corporation)	High temperature yarns consisting of silica fibers encased in synthetic plastic
3,634,250	1972	Commons, Jr. (United States of America as represented by the Secretary of Commerce)	Process of producing an insulation useful as a fill for roofs and walls of furnaces, tunnel kilns, and muffles, and as a reinforcing additive for plastics and resins
3,904,579	1975	Braddicks (Union Carbide Corporation)	Vinyl floor-tile without asbestos

ANNOTATED LIST OF OTHER ASBESTOS SUBSTITUTE REFERENCES

This list contains references, other than patents, that disclosed various substitutes for asbestos.

Reference	Description
Saborsky, A.D., "Glass Wool Heat Insulation in Europe," *J. Amer. Ceram. Soc.*, 6:674–684 (May, 1923).	Glass wool thermal insulation used in Europe before World War I and useful for pipes, boilers, etc., especially aboard ships, in chemical factories, and in power stations
Thoenen, J.R., *Mineral Wool*, Bureau of Mines Information Circular No. 6142, June 1929.	Mineral wool useful as high temperature pipe insulation, and linings for furnaces and stoves
"Glass Silk for Heat Insulation," *Engineering*, 131:613 (May 8, 1931).	Glass silk insulation for steam pipes; heat loss lower than same thickness of 85% magnesia
"Glass Silk as a Heat Insulator," *The Engineer*, 152:150 (Aug. 7, 1931).	Glass silk insulation for boilers on ships and steam pipes
"Chance Brothers and Co., Ltd.," *The Engineer*, 156:229–230 (Sept. 8, 1933).	Glass silk insulation for boilers and steam pipes
Gurley, R.R. and Sinclair, W.P., "Pipe Covering Materials for High Temperatures," *Journal of the American Society of Naval Engineers*, 47:247–256 (May 1935).	High temperature pipe coverings for naval use included felted mineral wool and aluminum foil
Schaeffer, J.A., "Mineral Wool and Vermiculite as Insulation," *Industrial and Engineering Chemistry*, 27:1298–1303 (Nov. 1935).	Mineral wool pipe covering superior to 85% magnesia
Cox, O.L., "Heat Insulation," *The Society of Naval Architects and Marine Engineers Transactions*, 44:470–486 (1937).	Naval heat insulations included rock wool and aluminum foil; procedures for testing insulations; table of physical characteristics and chart of conductivities for various insulations

Reference	Description
"Fibrous Glass Insulation," *Marine Engineering and Shipping Review,* 42:653 (Dec. 1937).	Owens-Illinois glass fiber insulation useful "in stoves, ovens, for pipe covering, in ships, in refrigerator truck bodies, residences, factories and many other fields"
"Glass Fiber Enters Electrical Insulation Field," *Electrical World,* 110:40–42, 110 (Nov. 19, 1938).	Glass fiber electrical insulation; advantages listed and compared to asbestos
Ferris, R.E. and Moses, G.L., "Fibrous Glass for Electrical Insulation," *Electrical Engineering,* 57:480–483 (Dec. 1938).	Glass fiber electrical insulation; compared to asbestos
Moses, G.L., "Fiber Glass Compared With Asbestos," (Letter to the Editor), *Electrical World,* 111:39 (Apr. 8, 1939).	Advantages of glass fiber electrical insulation over asbestos included greater tensile strength, and higher resistance to vibration and moisture
Slayter, G., "A New Marine Insulating Material," *Marine Engineering and Shipping Review,* 45:60–65 (Feb. 1940).	Uses of glass fiber insulation aboard ships
Phillips, C.J., "Glass as an Electrical Insulator," *Journal of Applied Physics,* 11:173–181 (Mar. 1940).	Glass fiber electrical insulation; compared to asbestos
Cope, E.T. and Kinney, W.F., "A Study of Heat-Insulation in Steam Power Plants," *Mechanical Engineering,* 62:465–470 (June 1940).	Heat insulation, including glass wool, for the power plant
Slayter, G., "Fiberglas A New Basic Raw Material," *Industrial and Engineering Chemistry,* 32:1568–1571 (Dec. 1940).	Uses for glass fiber heat and electrical insulation in houses, ships, trains, and aircraft

Reference	Description
Saginor, S.V., "Thermal Insulation for Industry," *Chemical & Metallurgical Engineering,* 48:82–86 (Jan. 1941).	Physical and thermal characteristics of some commercial insulations
"Woven-Glass Insulation for Electrical Windings," *The Engineer,* 171:38–39 (Jan. 10, 1941).	Glass fiber electrical insulation; compared to asbestos
"Fiberglas on Shipboard Its Uses in Merchant and Naval Vessels," *The Nautical Gazette,* 131:14–17 (Oct. 1941).	Uses of glass fiber heat and electrical insulation aboard ships
Allcut, E.A., "Properties of Heat Insulating Materials," *The Engineering Journal,* 24:514–523 (Nov. 1941).	Comparisons of various pipe insulations, including 85% magnesia, rock wool, and glass wool
Saginor, S.V., "Thermal Insulating Materials for Industrial Equipment," *Product Engineering,* 13:494–497 (Sept. 1942).	Physical and thermal characteristics of some commercial insulations
Tooley, F.V., "Fiberglas: Some Properties and New Applications," *Bulletin of The American Ceramic Society,* 22:60–64 (Mar. 15, 1943).	Fiberglass useful as thermal and electrical insulation
"Glass Fabric for Electrical Insulation," *Engineering,* 155:452 (June 4, 1943).	Glass fiber electrical insulation; compared to, and used as a replacement for, asbestos
Allcut, E.A., "Tests of Steam-Pipe Insulation," *Transactions of the American Society of Mechanical Engineers,* 65:407–419 (July 1943).	Comparison tests of various pipe insulations, including rock wool, glass fiber, 85% magnesia, and corrugated asbestos

Reference	Description
Bowles, O., *Industrial Insulation with Mineral Products*, Bureau of Mines Information Circular 7263, Dec. 1943.	Survey of various insulating materials, including mineral wool, asbestos, magnesia, vermiculite, diatomaceous earth, silica aerogel, and Foamglas
"Insulation—How to Install It," *Power Plant Engineering*, 48:96–100, 162, 164 (Sept. 1944).	How to install mineral wool thermal insulations
Specifications for Construction of a Twin Screw Passenger and Cargo Vessel, United States Maritime Commission, Jan. 1945.	"The insulating materials for temperatures below 600°F. shall be 85% magnesia, fibrous asbestos, rock wool or fibrous glass . . . "
" 'Fiberglas' Insulation—A Most Versatile Material," *Machinery*, 51:163 (Jan. 1945).	Owens-Corning fiberglass insulation useful "as insulation in stoves, ranges, ovens, refrigerators, water heaters, industrial boilers, trucks, trailers, buses, railroad cars, merchant ships, etc."; also useful for pipe insulation, electrical insulation, and welding curtains
"Cellulated Glass Blocks for Insulation," *Heating and Ventilating*, 42:63–65 (Feb. 1945).	Cellulated glass thermal insulation blocks for temperatures up to 1000 degrees F.
"Glass Fibers for Insulation," *Heating and Ventilating*, 42:59–61 (Mar. 1945).	Owens-Corning glass fiber insulation in rigid, blanket or block form useful for pipes, boilers, etc.
"Fiberglas in Post-War Ships Will Go Beyond War-Time Insulation Uses," *Marine News*, 32:48, 53–54, 159–164 (Jan. 1946).	Uses for glass fiber insulations
Hogendobler, H.R., "Fibrous Glass in the Power Plant," *Power*	Glass fiber thermal and electrical insulations for the power plant

Reference	Description
Plant Engineering, 50:88–90, 122 (July 1946).	
"Glass Fibers as an Engineering Material," *Steel,* 120:96–99, 127–128 (Mar. 10, 1947).	Glass fiber thermal, sound and electrical insulation useful in homes, railroad cars, and ships
Parker, S.S., "Insulation Technique for Oil-Refinery Structures," *The Oil and Gas Journal,* 45:160–162 (Apr. 26, 1947).	Mineral wool insulation at an oil refinery
Dutton, G.R., "Mineral Fiber Insulations & Textiles For Marine Service," *Marine News,* 33:62,64,66,68,70 (May 1947).	Rock wool, glass wool, and asbestos fiber insulations and textiles used aboard ships
"Heat Insulation Solves Breeching and Boiler Troubles," *Power Plant Engineering,* 51:88–89 (May 1947).	Mineral wool insulation at a power plant
Otto, F.C., "Estimating Mineral Wool Insulation," *Chemical Engineering,* 54:102–106 (July 1947).	Mineral wool blankets, pipe insulation, blocks, and cement; lists prices and conductivities
"Modern Boiler, Tank and Line Insulation," *Power Plant Engineering,* 51:84–86 (Sept. 1947).	Mineral wool thermal insulation for a boiler
"Mineral Wool Insulation of Ducts Cuts Plant Operating Costs," *Sheet Metal Worker,* 38:100,102 (Sept. 1947).	Installation of mineral wool duct insulation
"What the Power Engineer Needs to Know About Heat Insulation," *Power Plant Engineering,* 51:77–79 (Oct. 1947).	Mineral wool insulation in the power plant
Minutes of the General Meeting of the Asbestos Textile Institute, p. 2,	Glass cloth, laminated with aluminum or silver foil, as

Reference	Description
Apr. 7, 1949.	protective clothing for firefighting purposes
Mineral Wool Insulation for Heated Industrial Equipment, Commercial Standard CS117-49, United States Department of Commerce, June 1, 1949.	Commercial standard for mineral wool products, including pipe and block insulation; lists members of the standing committee for revisions and acceptors of the standard
Stone, J.F., "Thermal Insulation in Refineries," *The Petroleum Engineer,* 22:C-11 to C-16 (Jan. 1950).	Various insulating materials, including cellulated glass, useful in refineries
Swain, P., "Insulation Handbook: Part 2 – Types and Shapes of Heat Insulation," *Power,* 94:118–119 (Mar. 1950).	Types of thermal insulation and their uses
Swain, P., "Insulation Handbook: Part 5 – How To Apply Mineral Wool Heat Insulation," *Power,* 94:86–90 (Sept. 1950).	Installation of different kinds of mineral wool heat insulations
Specifications for Construction of a Single Screw Cargo Vessel, United States Department of Commerce Maritime Administration, Nov. 1950.	Insulating materials for piping systems and machinery, including 85% magnesia, amosite asbestos, fibrous glass pipe insulation, fibrous glass sheet insulation, calcium silicate, and diatomaceous silica; high temperature insulating cement composed predominately of mineral wool; lagging of asbestos or fibrous glass
"Insulation and Application Methods for Heated Piping," *The Petroleum Engineer,* 23:C-44 to C-46 (Oct. 1951).	Mineral wool pipe insulation in both blanket and molded forms as used in the petroleum refining industry

Reference	Description
Asbestos A Summary of Information on Uses, Production, Trade, and Supply, Industrial Materials Series Report No. M-3, United States Tariff Commission, Dec. 1951.	Glass fiber electrical and high temperature thermal insulation as a substitute for asbestos
"Insulating Papers Vs. Asbestos," *Chemical Engineering,* 59:248 (July 1952).	Quartz paper and ceramic paper as electrical insulation; developed by the U.S. Navy
Lewis, H.E. and Young, C.E., "Application Methods for Mineral Wool Pipe Insulation," *Heating, Piping & Air Conditioning,* 24:106–108 (July 1952).	Installation of mineral wool pipe heat insulation
"Ceramic Fiber Resists 2,300°F," *Chemical Engineering,* 59:198 (Sept. 1952).	Carborundum Co. alumina-silica fiber useful for heat insulation and filters
"Manufacture of Heat Insulating Sections for Pipes," *The Engineer,* 195:512 (Apr. 3, 1953).	Molded glass fiber pipe insulation
Thomas, R. and Turner, W.C., "Insulation for Heat and Cold," *Chemical Engineering,* 61:221–225 (June 1953).	Characteristics of thermal insulation materials, including their advantages and disadvantages
"Pipe Wrapped in Glass Blanket," *Chemical Engineering,* 61:250 (June 1953).	Glass fiber pipe insulation
"Snap-Around Pipe Insulation Cuts Labor Costs 20%," *Factory Management and Maintenance,* 111:132–133 (Nov. 1953).	Gustin-Bacon glass fiber pipe insulation
"Owens-Corning Improves Fibered Pipe Insulation," *Marine Engineering,* 58:136 (Nov. 1953).	Glass fiber pipe insulation

Reference	Description
Hadley, J.B., "Improved Hull Board For Marine Use," *Marine Engineering and Shipping Review,* 59:65–66 (Oct. 1954).	Glass fiber hull board developed by Glass Fibers, Inc.
Bowles, O., *The Asbestos Industry,* Bureau of Mines Bulletin 552, 1955.	Soda-lime-silica glass fibers useful in stoves, refrigerators, electrical insulation, cable coverings, filters, gas masks, and pipe insulation; high-silica glass fibers useful as high temperature insulation; fiberglass replaced amosite asbestos in 85% magnesia; during World War II, Germany developed cardboard with an organic plastic as a substitute for asbestos packings in steam and water pipe flanges; during this same time they also developed a polyvinyl chloride diaphragm as a substitute for the asbestos cloth diaphragm in a Siemens-Billiter cell in the manufacture of NaOH by the electrolysis of NaCl solution
"Thermal Conductivity of Pipe Coverings," *Electrical World,* 143:142 (Mar. 21, 1955).	Thermal conductivity of seven types of pipe insulations
"Inorganic Fiber Insulation," *Materials & Methods,* 42:152, 154 (Nov. 1955).	Two high temperature glass or quartz fiber insulating materials developed by L.O.F. Glass Fibers Co.
Mansergh, R.A., "Thermal Insulation Materials – I," *Power and Works Engineering,* 51:257–260 (July 1956).	Survey of thermal insulations available

Reference	Description
Klingholz, R., "Materialien fur Thermische und Akustische Isolierungen," *Schiff und Hafen,* 8:845–849 (Oct. 1956).	Types of thermal and acoustical insulation aboard ships
Waller, E.L. and Humes, H.L., "Tidewater Insulates Refinery," *The Oil and Gas Journal,* 55:166,169 (Feb. 18, 1957).	Felted block type of mineral fiber insulation used in a refinery
"Prefabricated Metal Insulation Offers New Features," *Marine Engineering/Log,* 63:128 (Dec. 1958).	Reflective type all-metal thermal insulation for marine use
"Piping Insulation Costs," *Chemical Engineering,* 66:128 (Feb. 9, 1959).	Costs of Foamglas, Kaylo, and Fiberglas pipe insulation (including weatherproof covering)
McGinnis, E.J., "Reflective Blankets Cut Welding Costs," *American Machinist,* 103:109 (Nov. 2, 1959).	Insulating blanket for welding operations replacing ones made with asbestos
"Fiberfrax Production: Carborundum's Versatile Ceramic Fiber," *Ceramic Age,* 78:37-40 (Feb. 1962).	Ceramic fiber useful as high temperature insulation and textiles
Williams, A.E., "Refractories and Insulation for Steam Raising Plant – III," *Steam Engineer,* 32:232–237 (Apr. 1963).	Types of thermal insulations, including glass fiber, mineral wool, and asbestos
Roberts, J.C.H., "Reducing Costs of Thermal Insulation of Marine Machinery & Piping Systems," *Insulation,* 8:108–111,117 (May 1964).	Advantages of glass cloth over asbestos cloth to wrap pipe insulation
"Search for Composites Spurs Growth in Inorganic Refractory Fibers," *Chemical & Engineering News,* 45:28–29 (Oct. 2, 1967).	Babcock & Wilcox alumina-silica welding blanket as a substitute for asbestos blanket

Reference	Description
Bewsher, M.R., "Cost-Effectiveness Evaluation of Thermal Insulation in Naval Vessels," American Society of Mechanical Engineers Paper 67-WA/Mgt-10, Nov. 1967.	Cost comparisons between thermal insulations for marine use
Aldrich, F. W., "Semi-Metallics: A New Type of Friction Material," *Society of Automotive Engineers Transactions*, Paper 710591, 1972.	Asbestos-free semi-metallic brakes compared favorably to conventional organic brakes
Kwolek, J. P., "Friction Materials for Small Car Solid Rotor Applications," *Society of Automotive Engineers Transactions*, Paper 750874, 1976.	Advantages of semi-metallic brakes as compared to conventional organic brakes
"Friction Modifiers Tailor Brake and Clutch Characteristics," *Automotive Engineering*, 87:74-76, June, 1979.	New friction modifier for asbestos-free semi-metallic brake
Loken, H. Y., "Asbestos Free Brakes and Dry Clutches Reinforced with Kevlar® Aramid Fiber," *Society of Automotive Engineers Transactions*, Paper 800667, 1981.	Kevlar® aramid fiber as a replacement for asbestos in friction materials

7
"Bystander" Asbestos Disease

"However one assesses the hazard of inhaling asbestos fibres, as it exists today, as a trifling matter or as a potentially significant one, it must become greater with years. The half-life of strontium 90 is 28 years, but the half-life of the asbestos fibre is an infinity of years. The 2,400,000 tons of asbestos used each year are added to the millions of tons used in previous years, and even if a small portion becomes available as an air-contaminant in towns, the actual amount will increase, as more asbestos accumulates on the surface of the earth.

(A) lurid picture could be painted of what conditions might be in 30 years' time, when the accumulations of so much asbestos in towns would lead to much higher concentrations of asbestos fibres in the air. The results of life-long inhalations of these fibres might be...a frequency of mesothelioma of pleura or peritoneum higher than that of bronchial carcinoma today. It could be added that even if the hazard were then appreciated, and all mining and utilization of asbestos ceased, there might be no significant reduction of the air contamination, owing to the indestructibility of the asbestos already mined and used, and its inevitable weathering and disintegration with time."

J.G. Thomson, R.O.C. Kaschula, and R.R. MacDonald. Asbestos as a Modern Urban Hazard. S. *Afr. Med. J.* 37:77-81 (1963).

INTRODUCTION

We now recognize that the threat to life from breathing asbestos extends in some degree even to individuals only slightly exposed to the dust. We also know that levels of exposure insufficient to produce asbestosis can nonetheless cause cancer; moreover, the exposures that can cause asbestosis are not as great as once imagined. On the continuum of risk were, roughly speaking, the asbestos handling workers ("direct" occupational exposure), others who worked nearby but did little or no work with asbestos themselves ("indirect" occupational exposure), asbestos workers' family members (household contact exposure), and neighbors of sources of asbestos air pollution and solid wastes. This section will trace the historic recognition of environmental asbestos contamination as a menace to people other than those we would think of as asbestos workers.

Earliest Recognition of the Potential for Bystander Asbestos Disease

The idea that industrial air pollutants could cause chest diseases and death among factory neighbors is nothing new. Ramazzini in 1713 described a "violent dispute" culminating in a lawsuit against an Italian factory owner demanding the relocation of a plant releasing sulfuric acid ("vitriol") fumes.[1]

> Various cleverly worded documents were produced by both sides, and this dispute which was literally 'about the shadow of smoke,' as the saying is, was hotly argued. In the end the jury sustained the manufacturer, and vitriol was found not guilty. Whether in this case the legal expert gave a correct verdict, I leave to the decision of those who are experts in natural science.

Environmental exposure to carcinogenic dye intermediates was attributed as the cause of bladder cancer among persons residing in the vicinity of dye factories as early as 1919.[2]

Asbestos air pollution was unlikely to provoke neighborhood complaints, because asbestos caused no irritation or immediate breathing problems in the way an acid mist did. Yet as early as 1929 medical authorities were commenting on "asbestos bodies" in the lungs of an asbestos factory neighbor who never went inside the plant.[3] While it doesn't appear that this person had asbestosis, still the characteristic "signature" of asbestos in the lungs was recognized as a result of exposure to the dust.

The idea that workers next to those with dusty jobs were also endangered by the asbestos dust created was expressed by Collis in 1911 (quoted by Hoffman in the U.S. in 1918).[4,5] Watchmen and shipping clerks at the Manville, New Jersey plant of J-M were among the plant's many employees diagnosed as having asbestosis in 1932, in an unpublished survey by Lanza and Fellows of Metropolitan Life Insurance Company.[6] A 1934 review by British physicians Wood and Gloyne of 100 cases of asbestosis described the disease in an asbestos factory employee with about 40 years of "clerical and administrative work."[7] This man had serious lung damage ("fibrosis involving all but the apical regions of the lungs"). A U.S. report less than a year later described "mild" asbestosis in an asbestos plant cashier with 30 years' exposure.[8] A former bookkeeper in an asbestos plant filed a claim for disability from asbestosis against U.S. Gypsum Company in 1937 (See "United States Gypsum Comnpany," in Chapter 9). Railroad companies in Illinois recognized the potential for bystander exposure from the handling of asbestos insulation by 1937 (See "Railroad Companies," in Chapter 9). So it was evident by the mid-1930s that "bystanders" such as clerical workers in asbestos plants could develop asbestosis from years of relatively light exposure.

Similar results arose from brief but intense exposure. Wood and Gloyne saw asbestosis in patients with as little as 6 months of asbestos factory work.[7] Pathologists in Philadelphia reported fatal asbestosis in one man who had worked only nine months in an asbestos plant. They also reported that another man developed "a minor grade of the disease" from 9 years of work "in a comparatively well ventilated factory in which precautionary appliances were used" (he wore "silver dust protectors" in his nostrils). These authors concluded from their two cases and the literature that there was an "absolute necessity for wearing masks in even the less dusty atmospheres."[9]

If the production workers in the asbestos plants of that era should have all been wearing respirators and even office workers were contracting asbestosis, could the danger not also extend further out, into the community? If people could develop advanced asbestosis from brief, intense exposure, was there not a grave potential for an equal lung burden accumulated over a period of decades to also produce disease? Despite some differences in the physiology of lung clearance and deposition for heavy and light exposures, Stewart and his coworkers in Philadelphia clearly were concerned about individuals with long-term, low-level exposure to the airborne mineral fibers.[9]

It was recognized by 1933 that asbestos breathed in normally reached all the way to the alveoli, the tiny air sacs of the lung. Here, the pathologist S.R. Gloyne discovered that removal of asbestos from the lungs into the lymph system was much more limited than such clearance of minute coal and silica dusts (which are not fiber-shaped). Moreover, the relative inability of scavenger cells to engulf and carry off the asbestos fibers in the lung was readily apparent under the microscope. Gloyne also described foreign body giant cells which formed as "an attempt on the part of the tissues to protect themselves against an irritant...." Gloyne believed that significant retention of asbestos fibers occurred in the lung:[10]

> With this question (of scavenger cells as a lung defense) is bound up that of the 'cleansing action' of the lung in removing from its tissues foreign particles whether harmless, such as carbon, or deleterious, such as silica.... In view of the size and shape of the asbestos particle it is difficult to believe that much cleansing action can take place.

The lung defenses were thus especially ill-prepared to deal with these tiny mineral fibers. It followed that there was probably no concentration of asbestos dust in air so low that retention of some fibers in the lung could not occur. Whether there was much or little asbestos in the inspired air, some of it was likely to lodge in the lungs and remain there to provoke cell damage. Simply put, it was known by 1933 that inhaled asbestos fibers got into the lung tissues, were partly retained there, and caused scarring there.

Asbestosis and Cancer in Bystanders in the 1940s

Asbestosis and lung cancer in non-production asbestos factory workers (machine adjuster, plant manager, departmental manager) were reported in the 1940s by Canadian and British writers.[11,12] In 1947, Johns-Manville Waukegan plant foreman Dominic Bertogliat died with asbestosis, and arrangements were made to compensate his widow after she approached the company. It was acknowledged by J-M safety engineer Hugh Jackson that Bertogliat had only been exposed to the general atmosphere in the plant (See "Saranac Compensation Reviews for Manufacturers" in Chapter 3 for further details).[13]

The British Factory Inspectorate sent a notice to the Thermal Insulation Contractors Association in 1945, recommending that, during asbestos spraying aboard ships, no person be allowed in the compartment unless provided with a respirator.[14] Here, the bystander shipyard workers' risk was explicitly acknowledged, with its potential for widespread disease which has since occurred.

The Thetford Industrial Clinic provided medical services to asbestos mining companies in Quebec in the 1940s. One of the clinic's patients who was diagnosed as having pleural mesothelioma was the Treasurer of Asbestos Corporation, Ltd. The cause of death was verified at autopsy. This man's exposure history was recorded as "only office work from 1920 to 1949."[15] Quebec asbestos miners were also dying from pleural mesothelioma at that time, according to a published report of Thetford clinic director Dr. Paul Cartier.[16]

Asbestos Air Pollution in the Community

The threat of asbestos air pollution was recognized in different ways in the U.S., Germany, and Canada. Cause for concern increased with the growing recognition that asbestos was carcinogenic.

In 1936, North Carolina health officials examined asbestos textile employees at the Thermoid Company and found varying degrees of asbestosis in about half of the workers. The dust inside the plant was so thick at times that one could not see across the room. Of 11 dust counts reported by health officials, the *lowest* was 45 MPPCF. Some of the dust was sucked out by a few fans in the plant and drifted over to nearby homes.[17] In the wake of the health officials' survey, the company was sued by some of the neighbors of the factory:

> (S)urrounding property owners were entering suits for damage claimed as the result of air pollution. All of this was attended with the newspaper publicity that might be expected to accompany such disclosures.

German guidelines for asbestos plant hygiene in 1940 called for filtering systems to be used before releasing the exhaust air into the environs. The expressed concern was that it could otherwise pose health hazards to the population outside.[18,19] Unfortunately, compliance in at least one asbestos plant in Hamburg was delayed until after World War II, at which time so much material was recovered that the installation of dust collectors was ascribed to economic reasons.[20]

Dr. Kenneth W. Smith, who went to work for Canadian Johns-Manville in 1944, recalled a discussion he had had with his chief, Dr. R.H. Stevenson, about community asbestos hazards in the 1940s:

> Metropolitan Life was conducting personnel studies of employees and non-employees in Thetford and, to a lesser degree, in our town. And, walking through the town of Asbestos on a dry August day, you could see little rolls of asbestos fiber rolling along the street like tumbleweed, and you just assumed that anybody walking the streets—the storekeepers or policeman walking his beat, or anybody in the house—would be exposed to that airborne dust.... We were standing on the edge of the open pit (Johns-Manville's huge asbestos mine) on the eastern side.

> The whole town of Asbestos was behind us, and, of course, the winds are constantly from the west, blowing across the mine, across the mill, and into the town. And Stevenson said, 'What a shame the town wasn't built on that hill over there on the western side of the pit. There would have been no dust in the town.'

A.R. Fisher, who was then a corporate Vice President and would in 1951 become President of Johns-Manville Corporation, was also present at this discussion.[21]

In Quebec, LeDoux's scathing exposé of the asbestos industry publicly called attention to the air pollution threat to the communities.[22] Medical surveys showing disease among Johns-Manville asbestos mine and mill workers (millwrights and electricians were also examined) and a lengthy, bitter strike induced the corporate management to spend more than $5 million for dust controls in 1949. It was understood that the ventilation system was designed to "improve the dust situation in and outside of the mills."[23,24]

The installation of some early asbestos plant ventilation systems may have even *increased* the neighborhood pollution by respirable fibers. In some cases, dust withdrawn from the workplace air was vented directly to the atmosphere. In other cases, settling chambers and "cyclone" type dust collectors were used that recovered only the largest particles from the exhaust air. Such devices were able to recover most of the *mass* of material that would otherwise have been blown away, but were useless in controlling the most abundant tiny, respirable-sized particles polluting the neighborhood of the plants. The advantages and limitations of various dust collectors were discussed in the early 1950s by members of the Asbestos Textile Institute. Ralph Smith of Raybestos-Manhattan was especially critical of the cyclone type collectors.[25]

> This type was effective in collecting the dust, but the top outlet would discharge very fine particles of dust to the atmosphere. This would create a problem to the Plant Property and adjoining community.

Residents and scientists visiting communities where asbestos was mined, milled, and processed have commented on the large amount of dust emitted by the old asbestos mills and factories.[20,26-28] This was true as well in the Soviet Union, which was second only to Canada in the production of asbestos. One study attributed an increase in children's respiratory infections to ambient dust in the city of Asbest, where three plants processed asbestos ore.[26] "It may be wise to consider" the possible existence of environmental cancer in the "fume zones" of asbestos plants and other sources, advised Dr. Hueper in 1950.[29]

In a report of an air pollution conference in Washington in 1950, *Newsweek* cited Dr. Hueper as referring specifically to air pollution with asbestos and other carcinogenic agents as the "probable cause of increased lung and respiratory tract cancer" in the general public.[30] This was noted by officials of Johns-Manville.[31]

Hueper noted in 1955 that, "since asbestosis, like berylliosis, presents a characteristic histologic lesion, there should be no serious difficulty in identifying 'neighborhood' cases of asbestosis and asbestosis cancer of the lung."[32] Neighborhood cases of berylliosis had been identified some years earlier, and at least to Dr. Hueper this suggested the need for and feasibility of investigations of potential environmental asbestos disease.[33]

Hueper's message was immediately picked up by members of the asbestos industry. His remarks on asbestos as a carcinogen in U.S. Public Health Monograph No. 36 and the above-quoted editorial were the subjects of intense discussion at meetings of the Asbestos Textile Institute in March, 1956.[34-36] The minutes of one meeting attribute to Johns-Manville's Dr. Kenneth W. Smith the conclusion,

> Dr. Hueper also infers that Asbestosis-Cancer may be determined in an autopsy performed on persons living in the area of a plant.[35]

Hueper's editorial was cited in an insurance claim adjuster's memorandum of March 13, 1956. It was paraphrased as saying "that anyone living near an asbestos plant can get lung cancer."[37] (See "Cancer," in Chapter 3).

Had anyone acted on Hueper's challenge, there should have been little difficulty identifying asbestosis among people living in the neighborhoods of asbestos plants. For many neighbors were doubly exposed, both by pollution released to the community and by accumulated household contamination carried home on the clothes of family members employed in the factories.[38,39]

Hueper himself was unable to conduct such studies, despite his position as Chief of the Environmental Cancer Section of the National Cancer Institute. Following 1951 "lobbying activities" by Dr. Anthony J. Lanza, representing industrial concerns, Hueper was forbidden by his supervisors in the government to do industrial cancer epidemiology research. Hueper was even ordered to have no further contact with industry and state health departments on matters of environmental and occupational cancer.[40]

But if Hueper had been a voice in the darkness, he did not remain so for long. By the end of the 1950s, the threat of asbestos air pollution was becoming more generally recognized. Even Rosato's book on asbestos technology, no medical reference, mentioned that neighborhood asbestos air pollution "could become harmful to the people who are constantly exposed to it."[41]

A Mesothelioma Epidemic Forces the Issue of Environmental Asbestos Cancer

In the late 1950s, a large number of mesothelioma cases were found in a crocidolite asbestos mining district of South Africa.[38] It was soon confirmed that rare mesothelioma was a "signal tumor" for asbestos exposure, simplifying the task of tracking the mortal asbestos hazard into the community. The histories taken from mesothelioma patients and their survivors (as well as "matched controls" where appropriate) readily showed these patients all too commonly had had prior residence in the households of asbestos workers and in asbestos-polluted neighborhoods.[38,39,42,43]

Then, in 1963, the South African pathologist Thomson discovered asbestos bodies occurring routinely in the lungs of urban dwellers at autopsy, and he feared the worst. It might be dismissed as pathological curiosity, he said, since none of these urban dwellers had mesothelioma. But it alarmed Thomson that ordinary urban dwellers had asbestos in their lungs, and that every year several million more tons of asbestos was being added to the vast quantity already in place in the world's cities.[44,45] There could eventually be a frequency of mesothelioma "higher than that of bronchial carcinoma today," he wrote.[44]

The period 1953-1962 also saw a number of reports of "bystander worker" asbestosis, lung cancer, and mesothelioma, as well as secondary reports citing the bystander risk from exposure to asbestos.[46-62] And in 1963, Philip Carey Manufacturing Company executives were pointedly warned of the firm's potential liability for cancers attributable to the firm's community asbestos air pollution[63,64] (See "The Mancuso Documents," in Chapter 3).

Household-Contact Asbestos Disease

The families of asbestos workers have sustained significant exposure over the years, due to dust brought home by the workers on their clothes, shoes, hair, toolboxes, lunch boxes, and more recently, automobiles.

In 1897, the first physician in modern times to comment on lung disease in asbestos workers (weavers) also observed ill health among the members of their families.[65] But, in general, there is little explicit commentary on a hazard to asbestos workers' families in the early literature.

Nonetheless, it has long been an internationally recognized good practice to provide washing accommodations and cloakrooms separated from process areas in industries with dust hazards.[66-69] American specialists in industrial medicine, writing in 1924, advised that street clothes not be worn at work, and added that provisions for changing clothes and washing were needed in all dusty occupations:[66]

> It is desirable, in all dusty occupations, that the workmen should take off all their street clothing before beginning work, and this is absolutely essential when the work involves exposure to poisonous dust. For this purpose suitable dressing-rooms, provided with lockers for street suits and separate compartments for overalls, are necessary. Facilities for washing and bathing, brushes, soap and individual towels should be furnished. In most of the civilized countries statutory provisions have been made for these sanitary requisites, in all establishments in which poisonous substances are manufactured or used and the result has been most beneficial.

Asbestos insulation was not the first insulation product to be definitely associated with illness in the households of workers handling it. "Cable rash," or "Halowax acne," was reported during World War II among electricians handling electrical cables and some of their wives, who had had contact with the men's work clothes and laundered them. Halowax, a wax-like gray powder, was used to insulate cables on ships, and it was made by a subsidiary of the Union Carbide and Carbon Company.[70]

The Germans, in their 1940 industrial hygiene guidelines for asbestos plants, established the practice that, "outdoor clothes were not to be kept in workrooms and work clothes had to be cleaned at regular intervals."[18,19,71,72]

But little attention was paid directly to the families of asbestos workers until the 1960s. Researchers in Finland reported cases of pulmonary asbestosis in the households of asbestos workers at the large conference held in 1964 by the New York Academy of Sciences. These investigators and others in Germany had previously called attention to pleural changes they had observed in chest X-rays of populations with environmental asbestos exposure.[73]

In compiling histories of 76 deceased mesothelioma patients and 76 hospital patient "controls" in London, British investigators indentified 9 mesothelioma patients as having had "domestic" exposure to asbestos.[42] Only one of the control series had had household-contact asbestos exposure, a highly significant difference.

> The most usual history was that of the wife who washed her husband's dungarees or work clothes. In one instance, a relative said that the husband, a docker, came home 'white with asbestos' every evening for three or four years and his wife brushed him down. The two men in this group, when boys of 8 or 9 years old, had sisters who were working at an asbestos factory. One of these girls worked as a spinner from 1925 to 1936. In 1946 she died of asbestosis. The press report of the inquest states, 'she used to return home from work with dust on her clothes.' Her brother had apparently no other exposure to asbestos...He died in 1956 of a pleural mesothelioma.

The authors concluded,

> There seems little doubt that the risk of mesothelioma may arise from both occupational and domestic exposure to asbestos...Among these with no evidence of occupational or domestic exposures, 30.6% of the mesothelioma patients and 7.6% of the in-patients with other diseases lived within half a mile of an asbestos factory ($p<0.01$). [$p<0.01$ means that there is more than a 99 percent chance that the difference observed in the two groups was real, and not a random chance event such as flipping a true coin and having "heads" come up seven or more times in a row.]

It is noteworthy that these authors considered household exposure predominant in importance over neighborhood exposure, in cases where both types occurred.

Between 1960 and 1976, there were seventeen reports published including 37 household-asbestos-exposure mesothelioma cases. Anderson and his co-workers at the Mt. Sinai School of Medicine in New York conducted examinations of 326 members of the households of former amosite asbestos insulation manufacturing workers. Fully 35 percent showed (pleural and/or lung) chest X-ray abnormalities characteristic of asbestos exposure. Among the total household cohort under observation, four persons were diagnosed with pleural mesothelioma.[74]

Dr. Paul Kotin of Johns-Manville vividly described the insidious hazard of asbestos accumulating inside the home.[75]

> I would suggest, however, that once asbestos gets into the home, carried home by the workmen, which in itself is a tragedy, it shouldn't happen, it is asbestos that is there virtually permanently—it gets into the rugs, into the carpets, it gets suspended by movement and actually you are getting 24 hour/day exposure, relatively speaking, rather than a partial exposure. But even worse than that is the fact that you are exposing the population of the family which includes the very young and very old. And in the induction of cancer, it is the very young that are always the most susceptible. We use the fact that it is the young that are the most susceptible in the laboratory when we want to test agents for their ability to induce cancer.

The thrust of Dr. Kotin's presentation to an OSHA advisory committee was that household cases of mesothelioma resulted from substantial exposure, and thus their occurrence did not necessarily imply that current workplace asbestos standards were unsafe.

Anderson and co-workers eventually examined 679 individuals with household-contact asbestos exposure. The subjects' family members handling asbestos had been employed at the same amosite asbestos manufacturing plant just mentioned (Unarco in Paterson, N.J.). The exposures in all cases had begun at least 20 years prior to the study. In many cases the periods of asbestos employment of members of these households were brief—several months.[76]

Some of the findings are shown in Tables 1-2. In summary, they show that asbestosis was not a rare occurrence among the spouses, children, and siblings of asbestos workers.

While it may be curious that no reports of asbestosis in the workers' families appeared until relatively recently, one has to consider the repercussions for the community practitioner who discovered such a thing and had the courage to announce it in a public manner. Workers may have expected to have to run some risk of getting an occupational illness. But as sensitive as the matter of the job hazards may have been, the recognition that the health of workers' whole families was endangered might have had an even greater impact. Such reports do not long remain unnoticed in medical journals. The discoverer of such a scourge coming from a mainstay of the town's livelihood might, in the words of Ibsen and Selikoff, find himself branded "an enemy of the people."[77] In the 1970s, a man didn't have to be a doctor to face death threats (for himself and his children) and violence in Quebec for questioning the safety of asbestos.[28]

It is surprising that more early medical reports were not published documenting the hazard of asbestosis and cancer to the workers' families. But the gross contamination of asbestos-exposed workers' homes largely grew out of a more obvious neglect: the lack of industrial hygiene protection afforded to the workers themselves.

CONCLUSION

Since the 1930s, it has been known that, even with low levels of exposure to asbestos, the lung defenses were inadequate to totally remove the inhaled fibers. By then, it was also obvious that the dust in the workplace atmosphere did not respect job classifications in claiming its victims. Reports of "bystander" workers with asbestosis and cancer continued to appear despite the lack of any apparent effort to look for them.

Meanwhile, in practice, environmental contamination with asbestos continued to be generally treated as a mere nuisance by those mining asbestos, and those manufacturing and using asbestos products. This went on despite official guidelines to control asbestos air pollution in Germany, official expressions of concern about bystander asbestosis in shipyards in England, and very pointed alarms raised in the U.S. by Dr. Hueper of the National Cancer Institute.

The full horror of asbestos contamination of the environment suddenly became apparent in 1960, with the report that a rare form of cancer (pleural mesothelioma) was rampant in the

Table 1. Prevalence of Asbestos-Associated Radiographic Abnormalities among Household Contacts of Amosite Asbestos Workers and Controls[76]

Group	Total Examined	Small Irregular Opacities	Pleural Thickening	Pleural Calcification	Pleural Plaques	One or more Abnormalities
Household contacts	678	114 (17%)*	128 (19%)*	54 (8%)*	57 (8%)*	239 (35%)*
Controls	325	10 (3%)	4 (1%)	0	2 (0.6%)	15 (5%)

*Prevalence of all types of abnormalities significantly higher in the household contacts than the controls, p<.001.

* * *

Table 2. Distribution of Profusion of Combined Small Opacities among Household Contacts and Controls[76]

Group	Total Examined	Combined Small Opacities						Combined Opacities
		0/0	0/1	1/0	1/1	1/2	2/2	1/0 or Greater
Household contacts	677	398 (59%)	165 (24%)	47 (7%)	61 (9%)	4 (1%)	2 (0.3%)	114 (17%)
Controls	325	288 (89%)	27 (8%)	8 (3%)	2 (0.6%)	0	0	10 (3%)

crocidolite asbestos mining region of South Africa. Worldwide attention immediately focused on this rare disease, which became known as a "signal tumor" for asbestos exposure generally. Many of the victims of this disease had worked directly with asbestos. But even more frequently, these people got their exposures in general shipyard and construction trades or from the contamination of their homes and communities. Thus it occurred that the virtually unrestrained use of asbestos gradually broadened the population at risk from a few thousand asbestos workers to millions of people in the general population. This tragedy is best understood as an outgrowth of the failure to take the appropriate precautions in the workplaces where asbestos was used and long known to be a mortal threat to those using it.

REFERENCES

1. Ramazzini, B. *Diseases of Workers* Translated by W.C. Wright, New York: Hafner Publ. Co., 1964, p. 51

2. Nassauer, M., 1919. In Hueper, W.C., *Occupational Tumors and Allied Diseases* Springfield, IL: C.C. Thomas Publ., 1942, pp. 525-526.

3. Haddow, A.C., *Lancet* 2:231 (1929). Also, Stewart, M.J., N. Tattersall, and A.C. Haddow, "On the Occurrence of Clumps of Asbestosis Bodies in the Sputum of Asbestos Workers," *J. Path. Bact.* 35:737-741 (1932).

4. Collis, E.C., *Annual Report of the Chief Inspector of Factories and Workshops for the Year 1910*, London: H.M. Stationery Ofc., 1911, p. 188.

5. Hoffman, F.L., "Asbestos," *Mortality from Respiratory Diseases in Dusty Trades*, Washington: U.S. Bur. Labor Statistics Bull. No. 231, 1918, pp. 176-180.

6. Physical Examinations at Manfille Factory (1932). Manville document.

7. Wood, W.B. and S.R. Gloyne, "Pulmonary Asbestos/A Review of One Hundred Cases," *Lancet* 2:1383-1385 (1934).

8. Page, R.C., "A Study of the Sputum in Pulmonary Asbestosis," *Amer. J. Med. Sci.* 189:44-55 (1935).

9. Stewart, H.L., C.J. Bucher, and E.H. Coleman, "Asbestosis/Report of Two Cases," *Arch. Path.* 12:909-916 (1931).

10. Gloyne, S.R., "The Morbid Anatomy and Histology of Asbestosis," *Tubercle* 15:445-451, 493-497, and 550-558 (1933).

11. Desmeules, R. *et al.*, "Amiantose et Cancers Pulmonaires," *Laval Med.* 6:97-108 (1941).

12. Kennaway, E.L. and N.M. Kennaway, "A Further Study of Cancer of the Lung and Larynx," *Brit. J. Cancer* 1:260-298 (1947).

13. Dominic Bertogliat file, Arthur J. Vorwald Archives, Armed Forces Institute of Pathology, Walter Reed Hospital, Washington, D.C.

14. Garrett, A.W. (Chief Inspector of Factories), "Asbestos Insulation Aboard Ships (2 pp)," August, 1945. C.W. Dawe (Thermal Insulation Contractors Assoc.), letter to the Chief Inspector, Sept. 14, 1945 (procured from files of the U.K. Health and Safety Executive).

15. Vorwald archives patient file IM573, Armed Forces Institute of Pathology, Washington, D.C.

16. Cartier, P., "Abstract of Discussion," *Arch. Indus. Hyg. Occup. Med.* 5:262-263 (1952).

17. Mitchell, J., "Health Programs in an Asbestos Textile Works," *Arch. Environ. Health* 3:37-41 (1961).

18. "Richtlinien fur die Bekañpfung der Staubgefahr in Asbest Verarbeitenden Betrieben," *Gummi Zeitung* 44:796 (1940).

19. "Richtlinien fur die Bekañpfung der Staubgefahr in Asbest Verarbeitenden Betrieben," *Staub* 13:147-150 (1940).

20. Bohlig, H. *et al.*, "Epidemiology of Malignant Mesothelioma in Hamburg," *Environ. Res.* 3:365-372 (1970).

21. Deposition of K.W. Smith, *DeRocco v. Forty-Eight Insulations, Inc.*, Nos. 2880, 2881, Allegheny Co., PA, Court of Common Pleas, taken Jan. 13, 1976; and Brodeur, P., *Outrageous Misconduct: The Asbestos Industry on Trial*, New York: Pantheon Books, 1985, pp. 100-102.

22. LeDoux, B. *Asbestosis* (Jan. 1949). Originally printed in *Le Devoir* (Montreal).

23. Smith, K.W., "Industrial Hygiene—Survey of Men in Dusty Areas," unpublished report forwarded to V. Brown and J.P. Woodard by A.R. Fisher with confidential memorandum dated Feb. 3, 1949.

24. Woodard, J.P. Memorandum to "C.M. McGaw—Asbestos" (Aug. 18, 1949).

25. Asbestos Textile Institute Minutes of the Air Hygiene Committee (Dec. 15, 1953).

26. Bobyleva, A.T., *et al.*, "The Amount of Dust in Residential Districts of the City of Asbest and Its Effect on the Children's Health," *Gig. Sanit.* (Moscow) 23:9-12 (1958). Abstract in *Arch. Environ. Health* 2:727 (1961).

27. Kowalski, T. (Manville, New Jersey), Personal communication to the author.

28. *Alice, A Fight for Life.* Yorkshire Television, London (July 14, 1982).

29. Hueper, W.C., "Environmental Cancer Hazards Caused by Industrial Air Pollution." *Arch. Indust. Hyg. Occup. Med.* 2:325-328 (1950).

30. "Small Studies," *Newsweek*, p. 53 (May 15, 1950).

31. Foster G. (Johns-Manville) memorandum to J.P. Woodard (July 28, 1950).

32. Hueper, W.C., "Silicosis, Asbestosis, and Cancer of the Lung." *Amer. J. Clin. Path.* 25:1388-1390 (1955).

33. Eisenbud, M. *et al.*, Non-Occupational Berylliosis. *J. Indust. Hyg. Tox.* 31:282-294 (1949).

34. Hueper, W.C., *A Quest into the Environmental Causes of Cancer of the Lung.* Public Health Monograph No. 36, Public Health Service Publication No. 452, Washington, 1955, pp. 35-38.

35. Asbestos Textile Institute, Air Hygiene Committee, Minutes of Meeting (March 7, 1956).

36. Asbestos Textile Institute, General Meeting minutes (March 18, 1956).

37. Shoemaker, W.E. Memorandum to N. Kley (American Mutual Liability Insurance Co.) "Asbestos Textile Institute 3-7-56 Air Hygiene Committee Meeting" (March 13, 1956).

38. Wagner, J.C., C.A. Sleggs, and P. Marchand, "Diffuse Pleural Mesothelioma and Asbestos Exposure in the North Western Cape Province," *Brit. J. Industr. Med.* 17:260-271 (1960).

39. Lieben, J. and H. Pistawka, "Mesothelioma and Asbestos Exposure," *Arch. Environ. Health* 14:559-563 (1967).

40. Hueper, W.C., Letter to W.E. Smith dated July 18, 1957 in *Food Additives.* Hearings before a Subcommittee of the House Committee on Interstate and Foreign Commerce, 85th Congress, Washington: 1958, pp. 188-189.

41. Rosato, D.V., *Asbestos: Its Industrial Applications,* New York: Reinhold Publ. Corp., 1959, pp. 21-22.

42. Newhouse, M.L. and H. Thompson, "Mesothelioma of the Pleura and Peritoneum following Exposure to Asbestos in the London Area," *Brit. J. Industr. Med.* 22:261-269 (1965).

43. Borow, M., *et al.*, "Mesothelioma and Its Association with Asbestos," *J.A.M.A.* 201:587-591 (1967).

44. Thomson, J.G., R.O.C. Kaschula, and R.R. MacDonald, "Asbestos as a Modern Urban Hazard," *S. Afr. Med. J.* 37:77-81 (1963).

45. Thomson, J.G., "Exposure to Asbestos Dust and Diffuse Pleural Mesotheliomas," *Brit. Med. J.* 1:123 (1963).

46. Isselbacher, K., H. Klaus, and H.L. Hardy, "Asbestosis and Bronchogenic Carcinoma," *Amer. J. Med.* 15:721-732 (1953).

47. Ziemke, P.C., "A Second Look at Welding Hazards," *Safety Maint. Prod.* 108:22-23, 86-87 (1954).

48. Breslow, L. *et al.*, Occupations and Cigarette Smoking as Factors in Lung Cancer," *Amer. J. Publ. Health* 44:171-181 (1954).

49. Breslow, L., "Industrial Aspects of Bronchiogenic Neoplasms," *Dis. Chest* 28:421-430 (1955).

50. Todd, T.C., H.E. MacDermot, and W.H. Matthews, "Clinico-Pathological Conference. VII." *Canad. Med. Assoc. J.* 75:757-760 (1956).

51. Francia, A. and G. Monarca, "Asbestosis and Pulmonary Carcinoma," *Minerva Med.* 47:1950-1959 (1956).

52. Bohme, A. "Asbestosis and Carcinoma of the Lung," *Arch. Gewerbepath. Gewerbehyg.* 17:384-395, 457-462 (1959).

53. Williams, R. and P. Hugh-Jones, "The Significance of Lung Function Changes in Asbestosis," *Thorax* 15:109-119 (1960).

54. Keal, E.E., "Asbestosis and Abdominal Neoplasms," *Lancet* 2:1211-1216 (1960).

55. Telischi, M. and A.I. Rubenstone, "Pulmonary Asbestosis Associated With Primary Carcinoma of the Lung, Bronchial Adenomas, and Adenocarcinoma of the Stomach," *Arch. Path.* 72:116-125, 234-243 (1961).

56. Whitmore, J.T. *et al.*, "Clinicopathologic Conference," *Armed Forces Med. J.* 11:203-216 (1960).

57. Thomson, J.G., "Mesothelioma of Pleura or Peritoneum and Limited Basal Asbestosis," *S. Afr. Med. J.* 36:759-760 (1962).

58. Sleggs, C.A., P. Marchand, and J.C. Wagner, "Diffuse Pleural Mesotheliomas in South Africa," *S. Afr. Med. J.* 35:28-34 (1961).

59. Sheinbaum, M., "Some Health Hazards Associated with the Building Trades," *Amer. Ind. Hyg. Assoc. J.* 23:353-358 (1962).

60. McCaughey, W.T.E., O.L. Wade, and P.C. Elmes, "Exposure to Asbestos Dust and Diffuse Pleural Mesotheliomas," *Brit. Med. J.* 2:1397 (1962).

61. Cordova, J.F., H. Tesluk, and K.P. Knudtson, "Asbestosis and Carcinoma of the Lung," *Cancer* 15:1181-1187 (1962).

62. An, S.H. and I. Koprowska, "Primary Cytologic Diagnosis of Asbestosis Associated with Bronchogenic Carcinoma, Case Report and Review of Literature," *Acta Cytol.* 6:391-398 (1962).

63. Mancuso, T.F. letter to L.J. Knippa (Lockland, Ohio plant manager, Philip Carey Manufacturing Co.) May 23, 1963.

64. Mancuso, T.F. *The Philip Carey Manufacturing Company Occupational Health Program.* 11 pp. (Sept. 23, 1963).

65. Netolitzky, A., "Hygiene der Textilindustrie," *Handbuch der Hygiene* (Th. Weyl, Ed.) Vol. 8, Industrial Hygiene, Jena: G. Fischer Publ. 1897, pp. 1102-1103.

66. Kober, G.M. and E.R. Hayhurst, *Industrial Health,* Philadelphia: P. Blackiston's Son, 1924, p. 24.

67. *Standard Codes of Industrial Hygiene,* International Labour Office. Ser. F. (Industrial Hygiene) No. 14, Geneva, Part 41 (1934).

68. Sappington, C.O., *Essentials of Industrial Health,* Philadelphia: J.P. Lippincott, 1943, pp. 308-309.

69. Brandt, A.D., "Plant Sanitation," *Manual of Industrial Hygiene* (Ed. W.M. Gafafer), Philadelphia: W.B. Saunders Co., 1943, p. 350.

70. Good, C.K. and N. Pensky, "Halowax Acne ('Cable Rash')," *Arch. Dermatol. Syph. 48:* 251-257 (1943)

71. Board of Trade, "German Industry," *Technical and Scientific Developments Related to the Asbestos Industry in Germany,* F.I.A.T. Final Report No. 1070. London: H.M. Stationery Ofc., 1947, Abstract in *Bull Hyg.* 23:783-784 (1948).

72. Board of Trade, *op. cit.,* abstrated in *Pneumoconiosis Abstracts* Vol. II, London: Sir Isaac Pitman & Sons, 1954, pp. 167-168.

73. Kiviluoto, R., "Pleural Plagues and Asbestos: Further Observations on Endemic and Other Nonoccupational Asbestosis," *Ann. N.Y. Acad. Sci.* 132:235-239 (1965).

74. Anderson, H.A. *et al.,* "Household Contact Asbestos Neoplastic Risk," *Ann. N.Y. Acad. Sci.* 271:311-323 (1976).

75. Kotin, P. Presentation before OSHA Advisory Committee on Construction Safety and Health, U.S. Department of Labor, Washington, January 22, 1976.

76. Anderson, H.A. *et al.,* "Asbestosis among Household Contacts of Asbestos Factory Workers," *Ann. N.Y. Acad. Sci.* 330:387-399 (1979).

77. Selikoff, I.J. Personal communication to the author, 1977.

8

Asbestos Disease in Brake Repair Workers

> "Only recently did I learn that when a vehicle is taken in for brake work, the mechanic cleans the drums and wheels by blowing the dust with a high-pressure air hose. The volume of dust raised is unbelievable, and it drifts about in the shop for a long time before it floats out or settles down in the shop. The mechanic inhales this during the blowing procedure and again when dusting. I understand that many mechanics are not aware that there is asbestos as well as metallic dust in the air."
>
> Mrs. Arthur G. McLeod. Asbestos and Cancer (Letter). *Canad. Med. Assoc. J.* 93:278 (Aug. 7, 1965).

Automotive brake linings, brake shoes, and clutch facings have contained asbestos since the beginning of this century. Brake linings containing asbestos cloth were first made in 1906, and rigid molded linings were developed in the early 1930s. The type of asbestos used in the United States has been chrysotile, and in general it has made up roughly 50 percent of the composition of brake linings and brake shoes. "Friction products," as they are called, have been a major U.S. market for asbestos, consuming 50,000 metric tons or more of fiber annually, until the latter half of the 1980s.The government estimates that about 900,000 workers in the U.S. are regularly exposed to asbestos in brake servicing.

In the wake of epidemiological reports identifying environmental exposure to asbestos as a cause of mesothelioma, the

Public Health Service analyzed brake lining decomposition products and identified a small fraction of surviving asbestos fiber (Lynch, 1968). Subsequent studies showed that brake mechanics were exposed to appreciable quantities of asbestos dust. Work histories of mesothelioma patients published in the literature have periodically included automotive brake servicing. However, the lack of any large, unionized, traceable work force with longterm (30 years or so) exposure has impeded the collection of quantitative data on the occupational disease risks of brake repair workers.

Measurements of the exposure of brake mechanics were practically high enough to include some of them under the 2 f/cc workplace standard for chrysotile asbestos issued in Britain in 1969. Air sampling in brake shops in the U.S. showed that with the commonly used technique of blowing out dust from brakes with compressed air jets, peak levels of exposure could exceed the 15-minute ceiling of 10 f/cc allowed by the 1972 OSHA standards. In addition to the high fiber counts monitored under conventional optical microscopy, a much larger number of the asbestos fibers released were so small they could only be detected by tedious electron microscopy.

It is evident from visual observation that immense dust exposures are sustained by mechanics blowing out brake drums. The presence of 50% asbestos in the brake linings whose disintegration products made up that dust cloud should have been reason enough in itself for testing to have been done. Tests reported by Lee in England (1970) showed that when total dust counts were made on the exposures during "blow-out," the old (1938 U.S.) guideline of 5 Million Particles Per Cubic Foot (MPPCF) of air could be exceeded.

The author, first surveying the asbestos literature in 1970-1971, promptly developed a concern for the health of brake mechanics. And despite their apparent lack of recognition under either the U.K. standard or the 1972 OSHA asbestos standard, a warning was sent to brake repair workers in Baltimore County in 1972 advising the use of vacuum methods. As the results of local attempts to warn brake mechanics of an occupational cancer risk and advise safer work practices were published in the literature, the federal government (NIOSH) sent out a lengthy notice of its own (Castleman *et al.*, 1975; Lloyd, 1975).

This was soon followed by the publication of additional measurements of brake mechanics' exposures and clinical studies on brake repair workers by the Mount Sinai (N.Y.) research team. Lorimer and co-workers (1976) identified signs and symptoms of asbestosis in a limited survey of workers who had been doing brake repair for more than 10 years and were actively employed at the time. Nicholson and co-workers estimate that over the next 40 years there will be 20,000 "excess deaths from asbestos-related cancer" among automobile maintenance workers in the United States.

It appears that the first warning labels on asbestos friction products appeared in 1972. The Annual Report of the largest U.S. manufacturer (Raybestos-Manhattan) for 1976 evidenced a corporate decision to substitute asbestos-containing friction products as soon as possible. Similar assertions by Bendix and General Motors soon followed.

Friction products manufacturers, beset with mounting asbestos disease damage suits and increasing government regulation in the 1970s, have developed alternative formulations using "semimetallic" compositions with steel fibers and conventional organic compositions reinforced with non-asbestos fibers. However, with the non-regulatory posture of the Reagan Administration, U.S. manufacturers appear to have set back their asbestos replacement investment schedules. U.S. consumption of asbestos in friction products remained unchanged in the period 1978-1982, while consumption of asbestos in every other major use declined dramatically. (R. Clifton, "Asbestos" preprint from the 1982 Bureau of Mines *Minerals Yearbook*, 1983).

U.S. manufacturers have seemed willing to gradually make new cars with asbestos-free brakes, but were more "pessimistic" about providing competitively priced, asbestos-free replacement brakes for older cars. It is certain that U.S. brake repair workers will be exposed to asbestos for many years to come before government regulations force the conversion to safer materials. Asbestos-free replacement brakes are commercially available for a large number of cars and larger vehicles. Sweden requires asbestos-free brakes for replacement on older cars; and since 1987, new cars have not been allowed for sale in Sweden unless they had asbestos-free brakes. Similar steps have been taken in Denmark and Austria.

But recent developments suggest that simply banning asbestos in brakes will not suffice to protect mechanics, and other additional options warrant consideration. The carcinogenicity of inhaled aramid fibers in rats raises concern over similar risks to mechanics servicing brakes made with these synthetic fibers. And even after the imposition of a ban on asbestos in friction products, millions of vehicles still in use will eventually have to be serviced after their asbestos brakes wear down.

Fortunately, at least 4 manufacturers are now offering enclosed systems for doing brake repairs. Two of the enclosed systems have been tested and shown to involve little or no exposure to the dust. The best solution to the immediate problem may be to require licensing of brake repair shops by government health, environmental, or labor agencies. (Barber and beauty shops, far less hazardous, have been licensed for decades.) The shops should have to provide government-approved training for the workers and use approved equipment for repairs (to be maintained regularly in an approved manner). This would provide immediate protection to workers doing brake repairs, their shop-mates, and the general public. Brake repair would become a specialty business with relatively fewer shops for the regulators to monitor.

The U. S. Environmental Protection Agency published *Guidance for Preventing Disease among Auto Mechanics* in 1986. This summed up the state of knowledge about the hazards of asbestos in brake servicing and the available protective measures.

The E.P.A. proposed a ban on most uses of asbestos on January 29, 1986, and the final rules were published in the *Federal Register* July 12, 1989. Manufacture and importation of some friction products will be banned on August 25, 1993. The balance of friction product categories face a ban on manufacture and importation as of August 26, 1996. E.P.A. declined to complement its ban with a brake shop licensing program as described above and urged by the Natural Resources Defense Council.

A trade magazine poll of key friction product suppliers "produced nothing but yawns" in response to the E.P.A. ban. "At least one major supplier has completely eliminated asbestos already, and a couple of others said they could do so tomorrow if necessary." *Brake and Front End* predicts that the brake industry will have new products available in plenty of time to meet the 1996 deadline ("Was Ban Foreseen by All," Aug. 1989).

OSHA, which issued an asbestos workplace standard on June 20, 1986, has been ordered to further lower the permissible exposure limit from 0.2 fibers/cc in those industries where feasible, including brake repair. Responding to a challenge from the AFL-CIO, the U. S. Court of Appeals in Washington, D.C. ordered OSHA to make major changes to the rules in a February, 1988 decision. On July 20, 1990 OSHA proposed to lower the permissible exposure limit for asbestos in all workplaces to 0.1 f/cc. The 1986 standard did ban the use of compressed air to remove asbestos unless it is done within a system that captures the dust cloud so produced.

The following annotated bibliography chronicles the developing awareness of asbestos health hazards from friction product manufacture, fabrication, and replacement. Virtually all of this material is drawn from public sources. Very limited discovery has been conducted so far from the standpoint of friction materials. The bibliography is divided into 8 parts:

1. Brake lining manufacture
2. Grinding and Drilling Brake Linings—Early Papers
3. Compensation

4. Asbestos Air Pollution Hazard from Brake Wear
5. Remaining Chronology of Papers Relating to Asbestos Hazard in Brake Repair (through 1985)
6. Commercial Substitution of Asbestos in Friction Products
7. Control Technology for Brake and Clutch Work
8. Case Reports of Mesothelioma in Brake Repair Workers

ANNOTATED BIBLIOGRAPHY OF HEALTH HAZARDS FROM FRICTION PRODUCT MANUFACTURE AND REPAIR

Brake Lining Manufacture

1. Lanza, A.J., W.J. McConnell, and J.W. Fehnel. "Effects of the Inhalation of Asbestos Dust on the Lungs of Asbestos Workers," *Publ. Health Rep. 50*:1-12 (1935).

   High prevalence of asbestosis among workers with "more than 3 years of employment in the industry" at five plants including one where molded brake band and clutch friction materials were manufactured.

2. Fulton, W.B. *et al., Asbestosis.* Harrisburg, Pennsylvania: Department of Labor and Industry, Commonwealth of Pennsylvania, 1935.

   Report of 25 percent prevalence of asbestosis among selected workers at four asbestos fabricating plants, including three where brake linings were manufactured.

3. George, A.W. and R.D. Leonard. "An X-ray Study of the Lungs of Workmen in the Asbestos Industry Covering a Period of Ten Years," *Radiology 33*:196-209 (1939).

   Documents asbestosis in brake lining manufacturing workers since 1928, with compensation. Explains that the asbestosis cases seen by Hawes (*New Engl. J. Med. 216*:162-165, 1937) were brake lining manufacturing workers. Discusses switch from dry to wet methods of processing.

4. Stone, M.J. "Clinical Studies in Asbestosis," *Amer. Rev. Tuberc. 41*:12-21 (1940). Also, "Studies in Asbestosis," *Dis. Chest 6*:170-171 (1940).

Asbestosis in 148 brake lining manufacturing workers seen by Drs. Stone and Hawes.

Grinding and Drilling Brake Linings—Early Papers

1. Osborn, S.H. *Forty-Ninth Report of the State Department of Health,* State of Connecticut Public Document No. 25, Hartford, CT, 1934, pp. 507-511.

   Describes the grinding of molded asbestos brake and clutch parts under varying degrees of local exhaust ventilation. Total dust counts ranged from 0.6 to 17 MPPCF. The need for dust sampling and analysis to evaluate these exposures was stressed, as the visual appearance of the worst grinding exposure was unremarkable.

2. *Memorandum on the Industrial Diseases of Silicosis and Asbestosis,* London: H.M. Stationery Ofc., 1935.

   Lists under "Industries and Processes in which asbestosis occurs...the sawing, grinding, and turning in the dry state of articles composed wholly or partly of asbestos such as motor car brake and clutch linings..."

3. Brachmann. "Asbestosis in Grinders and Drillers of Brake Bands," *Arbeitsschutz* 172-174 (1940). Abstract in the *Abstracts* supplement to *J. Indust. Hyg. Tox. 23*:76-77 (1941).

   Clinical and X-ray examination showed asbestosis in nearly all workers employed 5 years or more as grinders and drillers of brake linings.

4. Castrop, V.J. "Fume and Dust Exposure," *Nat. Safety News* (Feb. 1948).

   By General Motors industrial hygienist. Section on asbestos noted that brake lining grinding and "surfacing" operations were equipped with local exhaust ventilation systems.

5. Thomas, D.L.G. "Pneumokoniosis in Victorian Industry," *Med. J. Australia 1*:75-77 (1957).

   > The following occupations (involve asbestosis hazards)...sawing, cutting and finishing any product containing asbestos—for example, brake linings, asbestos sheeting, and various insulating materials...

6. Patty, F.A. *Industrial Hygiene and Toxicology,* New York: Interscience, 1963 (2d ed.), pp. 2243-2244.

Written by former director of Industrial Hygiene Dept., General Motors.

> The sawing, filing, drilling, and grinding of brake linings is ordinarily well controlled... It is desirable in asbestos exposures to keep the dust count down to 5 million particles, or less, per cubic foot of air.

Compensation

1. McVittie, J.C. "Asbestosis in Great Britain," *Ann. N.Y. Acad. Sci. 132*:129-138 (1965).

   Describing the occupations of workers diagnosed with asbestosis (and compensated for disability) in the years 1955-1963, he lists "brake lining" workers with an average of 14 years' exposure.

2. Smither, W.J. "Surveillance of High-Risk Groups—A Survey of Asbestos Workers: The Present Position in the United Kingdom," *Ann. N.Y. Acad. Sci. 330*:525-532 (1979).

   Updates McVittie's figures through 1969, showing that the four U.K. Pneumoconiosis Panels diagnosed 10 cases of asbestosis in "brake lining" workers in the years 1963-1969.

Asbestos Air Pollution Hazard from Brake Wear

1. Thomson, J.G., R.O.C. Kaschula, and R.R. MacDonald. "Asbestos as a Modern Urban Hazard," *S. Afr. Med. J. 37*:77-81 (1963).

   Expresses fear of public cancer hazard from asbestos released into the air of cities by brake wear. (See opening quote in Chapter 7)

2. "Pulmonary Asbestosis," *S. Afr. Med. J. 37*:629-630 (1963).

   Editorial expresses similar concerns to Thomson's.

3. Lynch, J.L. "Brake Lining Decomposition Products," *J. Air. Pollut. Contr. Assoc. 18*:824-826 (1968).

   Electron micrograph showed no free fibers in accumulated brake drum dust. Testing was then done on dust released by braking, using equipment of a brake lining manufacturer. The apparatus permitted simulation of stopping using complete brake assemblies.

> In all but a few tests the automobile drum brake linings showed less than 1% free fiber in the decomposition product. . . In those tests where a *significant* mass of free fiber was released, the temperature was in an extremely high range for the lining in question as evidenced by the rapid drop in the coefficient of friction. . . (under which conditions the brakes would have failed). . . Similar results were obtained in the bus and truck drum brake tests. . . (emphasis added)

(Subsequent studies would confirm the presence of asbestos in brake emissions and also demonstrate that asbestos is retained in accumulated brake drum dust.)

Remaining Chronology of Papers Relating to Asbestos Hazard in Brake Repair (through 1985)

1. Hueper, W.C. "Carcinogens in the Human Environment," *Arch. Path. 71*:237-267 (1961).

   Lists brake linings under, "operations and products with contact to asbestos for producers, processors, users, consumers, residents." Lists as a population with occupational and environmental exposure, in italics, "brake linings producers."

2. Enterline, P.E. and M.F. McKiever. "Differential Mortality from Lung Cancer by Occupation," *J. Occup. Med. 5*:283-290 (1963).

   A study of the relation of lung cancer rates and occupation in the U.S. One group with significantly high lung cancer mortality was, "mechanics and repairmen, automobile." The authors suspected automobile exhausts as a cause.

3. Newhouse, M. and H. Thompson. "Mesothelioma of Pleura and Peritoneum following Exposure to Asbestos in the London Area," *Brit. J. Indust. Med. 22*:261-269 (1965).

   Major study linking asbestos exposure (household, neighborhood, etc.) to mesothelioma in England. Listed in table at end as "no history of contact with asbestos" is case #66: "garage hand, chauffeur, mechanic." The basis for stating no exposure appears to simply have been that there was no household or occupational asbestos exposure as the authors had defined such exposures.

4. Hueper, W.C. "Occupational and Nonoccupational Exposures to Asbestos," *Ann. N.Y. Acad. Sci. 132*:184-195 (1965).

Table lists "garage attendants" under the heading of groups occupationally exposed to asbestos and lists brake linings as a source of general environmental asbestos exposure.

5. Gross, P. "The Pulmonary Response to Brake-Drum Dust: A Preliminary Investigation." Indust. Hyg. Foundation—Report for Johns-Manville (July 1968). Unpublished.

   The index card for document no. 3071 at the Institute for Occupational and Environmental Health, library of the Quebec Asbestos Mining Association in Montreal, recorded the authors' summary: "Brake-drum dust has evoked a pulmonary response which suggests that this dust is biologically 'inert.' Brake-drum dust is capable of producing ferruginous bodies in the lungs of hamsters that are indistinguishable from asbestos bodies." Handwritten on the card are the phrases, "Not to circulate!" and "Scientific Committee only." The library is now part of the Asbestos Institute in Montreal.

6. Gross, P. and R.T.P. de Treville. "Pulmonary Ferruginous Bodies/Studies on Their Origin," *Pneumoconiosis Proceedings of the International Conference Johannesburg 1969*. H.A. Shapiro, Ed. Cape Town, South Africa: Oxford University Press, 1970, pp. 86-91.

   > (O)f the 6 ferruginous bodies isolated from hamster lungs injected with brake drum dust, all gave an electron diffraction pattern characteristic of chrysotile; this, in spite of the relative paucity of fibers in the dust by optical microscopy and the negative X-ray diffraction pattern of the powder. These 6 ferruginous bodies were, therefore, asbestos bodies.

7. Sullivan, R.J. and Y.C. Athanassiadis. *Preliminary Air Pollution Survey of Asbestos*. Litton Systems, Inc. report prepared for the National Air Pollution Control Administration, 1969, p. 32

   Refers to Newhouse and Thompson's report of mesothelioma "in a mechanic."

8. McDonald, A.D. *et al.* "Epidemiology of Primary Malignant Mesothelial Tumors in Canada." *Cancer 26*:914-919 (1970).

   In a retrospective review of the potential asbestos exposures of a series of mesothelioma patients in Canada,

> Men employed in...the installation of brake linings...were responsible for most of the excess of cases over controls.

In a tabulation of the "occupations classified under definite or probable exposure to asbestos," are 21 cases of mesothelioma, including 2 who did "brakelining installation" and one more who worked in brake lining manufacture. (Table 6). This study attributes the main risk of mesothelioma to asbestos exposure in manufacturing and product use, as opposed to the mining of chrysotile asbestos. Funded by Quebec Asbestos Mining Association.

NEXT: Papers (9-17) from the Conference on Exposure to Asbestos During Brake and Clutch Maintenance, held at Ford's Central Office, Brentwood, Essex, England, March, 1969. Published in *Annals of Occupational Hygiene,* Volume 13, 1970.

Chairman of the conference was Dr. G.H. Channing, Chief Medical Officer, Ford of Britain. In the "Preface," Ford's D.E. Hickish explains that the motor industry was concerned about whether it was affected by the British government's promulgation of an asbestos standard.

9. Smither, W.J. "Asbestos and Asbestosis." *Ibid.* 3-5.

   The medical advisor to Cape Asbestos opens with discussion about the different mineral varieties of asbestos, then notes that all "current" friction materials contain 50% chrysotile asbestos. This figure he expected to gradually decline to as little as 30%.

10. Roach, S.A. "Hygiene Standards for Asbestos." *Ibid.* 7-15.

    Describes standard-setting committees in U.K. as containing industry representatives in order to "take into account the economic consequences of any recommendations made." Describes variable susceptibility:

    > In a real population the threshold dose will vary from one individual to another...

    Admits that regulators accept standards that do not assure the protection of all workers from asbestos disease (implying a need to warn workers so that they, too, can knowingly accept or reject such risks):

> An air quality standard is still associated with a small but non-zero probability of men being affected by the contaminant in question. The risk of people being affected can be made as small as one wishes. Zero risk is the ultimate target and an air quality standard has to be a compromise between the costs of bearing a health risk and the costs of air contaminant control.

He went on to cite a paper (pub. 1965) by Schall criticizing the inadequacies of the TLV in the U.S., which was roughly "17 times higher" than the British standard scheduled to take effect in 1970. He noted that the British standards committee "has not decided whether their chrysotile standards... give sufficient protection against lung cancer or mesothelioma."

The reader gets a glimpse of the Committee's internal disputes over how much safety could be afforded in setting a limit for asbestos exposure. Of major concern to the industry was the number of workplaces covered by the standard. The government must also have shuddered at the thought of enforcing a standard for asbestos in thousands of brake repair shops as well as the asbestos plants and shipyards, etc.

> Our present information is very imprecise, particularly in terms of the practical consequences of specific hygiene standards. In developing recommendations for a hygiene standard *the (committee) found that knowledge of the relationship between exposure and risk was not the greatest area of uncertainty.* A much more difficult and contentious problem was to decide on what, in fact, was an acceptable level of dust control. (emphasis added)

The balance of the article discloses the uncertainties of the economics of dust controls to meet the standards. It looks as though Roach and the others on the standards committee accepted the fact that chrysotile asbestos caused cancer. However, this risk to workers breathing asbestos was weighed against the cost to employers and the asbestos companies in protecting workers from the dust.

11. Hickish, D.E. and K.L. Knight. "Exposure to Asbestos During Brake Maintenance." *Ibid.* 17-21.

This paper contains data on the asbestos dust exposure of brake mechanics reported by the Medical Services of Ford of Britain.

The first car servicing tests were done using Cortina and Anglia vehicles, which presumably had smaller brakes than American cars of this era. Sampling was done in the dust cloud generated by blow-out of the accumulated dust in brake drums. This yielded an average value of 2.55 fibers per cc of air (Table 1). Other tests were done beside the car when the repairs were in progress, yielding somewhat lower values averaging 1.25 f/cc (Table 1). Personal samples were also taken, to get the best measure of the workers' actual exposure to airborne asbestos. The average exposure during brake servicing was 0.68 f/cc (Table 2).

Truck brakes generated more dust. Sampling was done in an adjacent bay and two bays away from the service bay where brake repairs were performed. The values recorded were lower in these bystander locations. The bystander fiber counts ranged from 0.17 to 0.49 f/cc in the mornings, during which time only 1.5-2 hours was devoted to brake cleaning. Personal sampling for mechanics doing truck brake repair showed concentrations of 7.09 f/cc, declining to 0.08 after cleaning and averaging 1.75 f/cc over the time sampling interval. The duration of this interval could easily have been adjusted to yield an average value on either side of the new British asbestos standard, 2 f/cc. Even clutch repair in the adjacent bay was recorded as 2.25 f/cc "during cleaning." Samples from bays adjacent to truck brake repair showed 0.79 f/cc as a time-averaged exposure (for cleaning and a post-cleaning combined interval). (Table 4) The authors conceded that "personal exposures in the vicinity (of truck brake repair) do exceed the standard."

Brake drum dust was analyzed by Holmes, of Turner & Newall, who found chrysotile asbestos present at up to 1 % in it. The authors advised safeguards during brake repair:

> It is however recommended that care should be exercised during brake cleaning to avoid inhalation of dust produced, and the development of cleaning procedures that would reduce air contamination is desirable.

They also noted that their studies did not include sampling during such procedures as "filing or grinding brake lining," but they assumed that these were hazardous processes "with the attendant need for strict precautions to prevent the inhalation of fibres."

12. Luxon, S. "Technical Implementation of the New Asbestos Regulations." *Ibid.* 23-24.

    Representative from the Factory Inspectorate says the 2 f/cc limit should be applied to 4-hour sampling periods, "and it seems reasonable to expect that a concentration of say 12 fibers/cc should not be exceeded during any period of 10 minutes."

    Brake drum dust analyses showed a content of 1 to 3 percent chrysotile asbestos. Expresses concern over the "increasing tendency to carry out brake overhauls on an assembly line basis."

13. Hatch, D. "Possible Alternatives to Asbestos as a Friction Material." *Ibid.* 25-29

    Representative of Ferodo, a manufacturer. Begins with history on the development of friction products and the technical role of asbestos in the products. For brake linings the author said "there is no substitute for asbestos which would not result in a deterioration of performance and strength." For disc brake pads the picture was brighter:

    > (I)t cannot be said that the use of asbestos in disc brake pads remains a technical necessity, and it is in this field of friction materials that some departure from resin-asbestos based composites could occur in the next few years on technical and performance grounds.

    On the subject of clutches, he said the spider clutch being used in the U.S. for "heavy duty manual shift gear boxes" could use asbestos-free materials such as sintered metals or ceramic-metal composites.

    Towards the end, he said: "the wear products from friction materials are probably no more dangerous to health than many other dusts and can be treated as merely dirty." But this is balanced by an earlier remark, "I am not suggesting for a minute that the practice of blowing out brake drums with a compressed air line is to be recommended, merely that an intense dust cloud of this composition is a lot less harmful than one might think."

Data from compressed air brake cleaning showed a preponderance of fibers in the 2-5 micron range (the asbestos standard applied only to fibers 5 microns and longer).

14. Bentley, M.L. "Control of the Use of Asbestos-Containing Friction Materials." *Ibid.* 31-32.

The author was employed by Mintex, a manufacturer of friction materials in Britain. He noted that the Asbestosis Research Council (ARC) was set up by the industry in England (in 1957), after it had become apparent that "cases of asbestosis were occurring (among) certain users of asbestos products, such as ...laggers..."

A working group of the ARC's Environmental Control Committee was devoted to friction products. Constituent members were Small and Parkes (now part of Cape Industries), Ferodo, and Mintex. "The Group (which has been formed recently) is concerned with the users of friction materials...in the replacement and service field."

Bentley also said the ARC work group on friction materials was preparing "two codes of practice for users of asbestos based friction materials which will be used by (ARC). One of these is for...the guidance of those engaged in servicing brakes and clutches."

He called the codes of practice "Notes of Guidance."

15. Lee, G.L. "Removing Dusts from Brake Assemblies During Vehicle Servicing—Alternative Cleaning Methods." *Ibid.* 33-36.

The author worked for the auto manufacturer British Leland. He noted that a technique for cleaning brakes that would reduce dust emissions would also involve an increase in time and effort involved (hence an increase in cost). He commented:

> When viewed under normal lighting conditions, the result of applying a compressed-air line to remove brake dusts is very dramatic.

Lee provided data (Konimeter sampling) in units one can convert for comparison with the old asbestos TLV. He showed that at the beginning of brake blow-out, there were 5000 brake dust particles per 5 cubic centimeters of air; this declined within minutes to 580 particles per 5 cc. Converting the units of these measurements to millions of particles per cubic foot of air:

(1 cu. ft. = 28,317 cc),

$$\frac{5000 \text{ particles}}{5\text{cc}} = 28.3 \text{ Million particles/cu. ft. (MPPCF)}$$

$$\frac{580 \text{ particles}}{5\text{cc}} = 3.3 \text{ MPPCF}$$

Though it was only for brief periods of exposure that these high values were measured, it is still conceivable that the exposures would be kept high in a shop where numerous and continuous brake repairs were being done. The old TLV for asbestos exposure was 5 MPPCF, and it applied to dusts containing asbestos fibers (i.e., all particles were counted, not just the asbestos fraction of the particles). So peak exposure levels would have exceeded 5 MPPCF in brake repair although daily-average exposures were unlikely to have been that high in most shops, according to this report.

For 5-minute samples of *fibers* only,

> ...Asbestos fibers counted on membrane filter samples gave a concentration on the order of 3-5 fibers/cc.

A "modified technique" for cleaning brakes used a portable vacuum unit to extract dust raised by brushing out the brake dust with a paint brush. Damp rag wiping followed. This eliminated visible dust emissions, vastly reduced airborne particle counts, and no fibers were detected in the airborne dust samples.

16. Knight, K.L. and D.E. Hickish. "Investigations into Alternative Forms of Control for Dust Generated During the Cleaning of Brake Assemblies and Drums." *Ibid.* 37-39.

Notes that when the brake dust is blown off with a compressed air hose, the dust cloud in which the operator works is "proportionate in size to the drum assembly being cleaned."

Vacuum funnel and vacuum brush cleaning methods were tested. The peak exposures for both of these were way below that observed for "blow-off"—1.04 f/cc for the funnel, 0.57 f/cc for the brush, and 87 f/cc for blow-off. The vacuum brush method was preferred for its ease of use as well as the lowering of exposures.

17. Luxon, S. "Respirators for Protection against Asbestos." *Ibid.* 41.

He was with the Factory Inspectorate and discussed British respirator standards.

For "ordinary respirators" the "protection factor is of the order of 20, that is, the external concentration is reduced to one twentieth that inside the face piece." Mentioned that "High Efficiency Dust Respirators" (of the full facepiece or positive pressure type) provide a protection factor of 400.

> Respiratory protection should in general be regarded as providing protection for work where control is difficult or where the work is intermittent and of short duration. It is hoped that the control of the dust will be achieved by the methods indicated earlier and that respiratory protection will therefore only be needed for special work not of a routine nature.

18. *Asbestos.* Washington, D.C.: National Academy of Sciences, 1971, p. 22

This report on asbestos air pollution notes that "an appreciable percentage (1-3%)" of the asbestos in brake linings survives the heat of friction and remains as fibrous asbestos.

19. Oels, H.C. *et al.* "Diffuse Malignant Mesothelioma of the Pleura: A Review of 37 Cases," *Chest 60*:564-570 (1971).

One mesothelioma patient with a history of "probable occupational exposure to asbestos" was a "service station operator."

20. Harwood, C.F. "Asbestos Air Pollution Resulting from the Wear of Brake Linings," Supplementary Notes Supplied to the Attendees of Seminar on Asbestos, Illinois Institute of Technology Research Institute, Chicago, pp. 65-74 (April, 1972).

> (A)n estimate is presented which indicates that the asbestos emission from brake linings is significant.

He assumes that 1% of brake dust is asbestos fiber, that 80% of this dust is emitted and 20% remains lodged within the brake system.

This paper contains a several-page discussion, "Alternatives to Asbestos," in which sintered metals, ceramic metal, fiberglass, and sealed systems are discussed.

> At the present time, no alternative to asbestos containing friction products is developed to the stage of finesse required by the industry. It is difficult to believe that modern technology cannot overcome the problems presented by the use of alternates.

This was a several-day seminar attended by a number of industry representatives and the author (BC).

21. Newman, B. "Perilous Particles," *Wall Street J.* (June 8, 1972).

Article on asbestos begins with description of some mechanics blowing dust out of brake parts:

> What the mechanics don't seem to know—like thousands of other mechanics—is that the brown dust is dangerous. And if a mechanic breathes in enough dust from worn out linings it could eventually kill him.

22. Moertel, C.G. "Peritoneal Mesothelioma," *Gastroenterology 63:*346-350 (1972).

Explaining that mesothelioma is caused by asbestos, he says, "Particularly vulnerable occupations are... brake lining installation..."

23. *Control Techniques for Asbestos Air Pollutants* Research Triangle Park, N.C.: U.S. Environmental Protection Agency Office of Air and Water Programs, (Feb. 1973), pp. 3-48 and 3-49.

> "In the course of servicing and overhauling motor vehicle brakes and manual clutches, the accumulated asbestos-containing dust is frequently dislodged from drums and housings by directing a compressed air jet against the deposits." Expressed concern over environmental air pollution.

24. Boillat, M.A. and M. Lob. "Risk of Asbestosis among Workers Replacing Brake Linings," *Schweiz. Med. Woch. 103:*1354-1359 (1973).

English summary:

> Thirty nine workers with the job of replacing automobile brake linings (asbestos) have been investigated. The working conditions and clinical findings, including radiology and spirometric studies, are discussed. In view of the comparatively brief exposure during the working day, the

> maximum permissible concentration of asbestos fibers, according to the norms indicated by American health workers, does not appear to be exceeded. No cases of asbestosis were detected, but in one instance the diagnosis is open to discussion. Despite the satisfactory outcome of this study, periodic examinations of workers in this type of occupation are indicated.

Subjects of the study averaged only 8 years of brake repair experience at ½ to 2 hours per day of work. Fiber concentrations from drilling holes for rivets and grinding ranged up to 29.2 f/cc; four of nine measurements exceeded 5/cc.

25. Jacko, M.G., R.T. DuCharme, and J.H. Somers. "Brake and Clutch Emissions Generated during Vehicle Operation." Society of Automotive Eng. meeting, Detroit (May 14-18, 1973).

The first two authors were with Bendix Corp., the other worked for the U.S. Environmental Protection Agency. Tests of brake wear emissions from braking showed 14.4 percent of total car asbestos emissions were "retained in brake" of test vehicle. The corresponding figure for trucks was 9.2%. The overall figure for all vehicles in U.S. was 11.2% brake retention.

26. Davis, J.M., and S.W. Coniam. "Experimental Studies on the Effects of Heated Chrysotile and Automobile Brake Lining Dust Injected into the Body Cavities of Mice," *Exper. Molec. Pathol.* *19*:339-353 (1973).

Automobile brake lining dust was provided by Turner & Newall from a test vehicle. The dust produced "very small granulomas and little fibrosis" when injected into the pleural cavities of mice. The study was terminated after only one year, and sponsored by the Asbestosis Research Council.

> It is planned to undertake a new series of experiments that will test the long-term effects of brake lining dust in conditions where normal chrysotile is known to produce tumors. [Davis says no such studies were done—1986.]

27. Greenberg, M. and T.A. Lloyd-Davies. "Mesothelioma Register 1967-68," *Brit. J. Ind. Med.* *31*:91-104 (1974).

Lists "Industry or Job Title in 167 'Definite' Mesotheliomas with Definite Occupational Exposure to Asbestos" (Table 5)—includes one "motor mechanic."

28. Castleman, B.I. *et al.* "The Hazards of Asbestos for Brake Mechanics," *Publ. Health Rep. 90*:254-256 (1975).

    Review of literature and report of efforts to warn brake mechanics about cancer risks from blowing out brake dust with a compressed air hose. Surveys starting in 1972 found that the blow-out method was most commonly used, that most mechanics seemed unaware of a cancer risk (or other serious health risk). Follow-up surveys found that some establishments and mechanics acted on the warning but most did not. Concluded that asbestos regulations needed to be stricter so that brake repair by the "blow-out" method would be forbidden.

    > The manufacturers of automotive friction materials could easily attach a clear hazard warning to every item sold.

29. Lloyd, J.W. "Dear Colleague..." Hazard Alert letter, National Institute for Occupational Safety and Health, Rockville, MD (Aug. 8, 1975).

    Reports on July 21, 1975 NIOSH meeting with industry, labor, and academic attendees to discuss brake repair asbestos hazards. Data generated by the Mt. Sinai Environmental Sciences Laboratory included 1) blowout of automobile drum brakes, 2) grinding used truck brake linings, and 3) bevelling new truck brake linings. "Average peak asbestos air concentrations for these three activities based on personal samples taken within 10 feet of the operation were, respectively, 10.5, 3.75, and 37.3 fibers (greater than 5 microns in length)" per cc. of air.

    > The present findings indicate that enough asbestos is preserved to produce significant exposures during certain brake servicing procedures.

    Earlier reports of mesothelioma among persons with jobs involving automobile brake servicing were cited. NIOSH estimated that 833,535 auto mechanics, 67,679 garage workers, and 6,657 (original and rebuilding) manufacturing employees made up a workforce "potentially exposed to asbestos."

    "Recommended (Interim) Procedures for Asbestos Brake and Clutch Servicing" were attached. These procedures included: 1) posting signs in the work area warning people not to stay there unless their work required it ("...May Cause Asbestosis and Cancer"); 2) use of industrial vacuum cleaners (with high efficiency filters) for removing dust from brakes; 3) use of respirators; 4) use of local exhaust ventilation and high efficiency dust collection on grinding machines; 5) adherence to OSHA asbestos regulations' provisions regarding special clothing and change rooms.

30. "HEW Warns of Asbestos Hazard in Work with Brake Linings, Spackling Mixtures," *Wall Street J.* (Aug. 15, 1975).

    Summarizes the NIOSH alert notice (previous item).

31. Marsh, J. (Raybestos-Manhattan) letter to B. Castleman. (Oct. 29, 1976).

    Announces that "work practice instructions are included with every package of brake lining shipped from our factories."

    > When inquiries are received from the field, we routinely supply the (Asbestos Information Association) booklet, "Recommended Work Practices in the Fabrication and Use of Asbestos Friction Materials."

32. *Asbestos and Brake Linings.* Asbestos Information Association, Washington (1976).

    Pamphlet on asbestos air pollution from brake decomposition:

    > Emissions from brake lining wear are *not* a significant source of asbestos in the environment. (original emphasis)

33. *Fabrication and Use of Asbestos Friction Materials.* Asbestos Information Association, Washington (1976).

    Summary and text of 1972 OSHA asbestos standard.

34. Menck, H.R. and B.E. Henderson, "Occupational Differences in Rates of Lung Cancer," *J. Occup. Med. 18*:797-801 (1976).

    This study on occupation and lung cancer rates in California shows a statistically significant Standard Mortality Ratio (146, meaning 46 percent higher than expected) for "Auto Repair" workers. This figure is based on eight deaths from lung cancer in the years 1972-1973.

35. Alste, J., D. Watson, and J. Bogg. "Airborne Asbestos in the Vicinity of a Freeway," *Atmos. Environ. 10*:583-589 (1976).

    Chrysotile asbestos fibers from new and worn brake linings and from the air near a freeway were examined by electron microscopy and electron diffraction. The major effect of braking appears to be in separating bundles of fibers and reducing their average length but not altering their crystal structure. The majority of particles had a maximum linear dimension of 2 microns or less.

36. Rohl, A.N., A.M. Langer, M.S. Wolff, and J. Weisman. "Asbestos Exposure during Brake Lining Maintenance and Repair," *Environ. Research* 12:110-128 (1976).

Unaltered chrysotile asbestos was found in garage air samples and brake drum dust. "(E)xposure of garage mechanics during brake lining maintenance and repair show that fiber concentrations frequently in excess of regulated limits are common." (optical microscopy)

Blowing out automobile brake drum dust yielded exposures of 6.6 to 29.8 f/cc with measurable exposure 50-75 feet away. Some of the other data had been summarized in the NIOSH alert of Aug. 8, 1975.

Electron microscopy showed most of the fibers were too small to be seen by optical microscopes. The authors warned that exposure to these very small and numerous asbestos fibers could have adverse effects.

37. Lorimer, W.V. *et al.*, "Asbestos Exposure of Brake Repair Workers in the United States," *Mount Sinai J. Med.* 43:207-218 (1976).

Tabulates exposures previously measured by others, includes their own data in great detail for all types of brake work.

Clinical study of 90 men with ten or more years of brake repair work and no other history of occupational exposure to asbestos. Most of the general mechanics examined did brake lining more than once weekly. Parenchymal fibrosis was seen on X-ray in 18 (20%) and pleural thickening in 5 (6%). Those who started work before 1946 had twice the prevalence of abnormal X-rays as those starting in 1946-1955. One quarter of the workers had restrictive pulmonary function test findings.

> (T)he findings suggest that asbestos disease will be present among (brake maintenance) workers and that appropriate control measures should be urgently instituted.

38. Rohl, A.N. *et al.*, "Asbestos Content of Dust Encountered in Brake Maintenance and Repair," *Proc. Roy. Soc. Med.* 70:32-37 (1977).

Another report from the Mt. Sinai group on the presence of chrysotile asbestos in brake drum dust from all over the world, the submicroscopic size of most of the asbestos fibers, and comparison of brake mechanics' asbestos exposure with OSHA standards (optical microscopy). Authors call for implementation of industrial hygiene practices and for epidemiological mortality studies of garage mechanics.

39. Bruckman, L., R.A. Rubine, and B. Christine. "Asbestos and Mesothelioma Incidence in Connecticut," *J. Air Pollut. Contr. Assoc. 27*:121-126 (1977).

Reports a case of mesothelioma in a toll booth operator. These investigators found increased asbestos exposure at toll booths compared to ambient air of Connecticut cities.

40. Seshan, K. "On the Utility of Dark-Field Electron Microscopy in the Determination of the Degree of Deformation in Chrysotile Asbestos: An Environmental Research Application" *Environ. Research 16*:383-392 (1978).

New technique of analysis verifies that "chrysotile asbestos in various stages of deformation" survives in brake drum dust.

41. Rohl, A.N., A.M. Langer, and I.J. Selikoff. "Airborne Asbestos in the Vicinity of a Freeway," *Atmos. Environ. 12*:2030-2031 (1978).

Adds a number of unpublished reports confirming the presence of chrysotile in disintegrated brake linings from Great Britain (F. Pooley), France (P. Sebastien), and South Africa (M.S. Kikine). Refers to findings of asbestosis among automotive maintenance workers.

42. "Friction Materials Work Practices Guide." Friction Materials Standards Institute, Paramus, N.J. (Oct. 1978), 12 pp.

> When removing worn friction materials remove the accumulated dust in the assembly with an industrial vacuum cleaner equipped with a high efficiency filter system. If such equipment is not available, dust can be removed with a damp cloth. Do not use compressed air or dry brushing for cleaning. Use a NIOSH approved respirator when removing worn friction materials, or cleaning brake or clutch assemblies.

Local exhuast ventilation is recommended for machining of friction materials. Machining and repair areas "should be isolated from other work areas in a restricted area to prevent unnecessary exposure of other workers." Warning signs are suggested to limit access to brake work areas.

Work clothing should not be taken home.

Disposal of vacuum cleaner waste in marked, impermeable bags is also covered in this pamphlet by the industry trade group.

43. Kagan, E. *et al.* "Asbestos-Associated Neoplasms of B Cell Lineage," *Amer. J. Med. 67*:325-330 (1979). And, Kagan, E., and R.J. Jacobson. "Lymphoid and Plasma Cell Malignancies: Asbestos-related Disorders of Long Latency," *Amer. J. Clin. Path. 80*: 14-20 (1983).

    Reports one case of pleural mesothelioma in a man who had installed automotive brake linings for 25 years.

44. de Lajartre, M. and A.Y. de Lajartre. "Mesothelioma on the Coast of Brittany, France," *Ann. N.Y. Acad. Sci. 330*:323-332 (1979).

    "Certain" occupational exposure to asbestos was identified in 51 cases of mesothelioma, including 4 "mechanics." Exposure characterized as "probable" for 6 "construction mechanics."

45. McDonald, A.D. and J.C. McDonald. "Malignant Mesothelioma in North America," *Cancer 46*:1650-1656 (1980).

    A review of mesothelioma cases included 11 with occupational histories of garage work. A series of matched controls without mesothelioma included 12 with such histories. Individuals with histories of asbestos mining and manufacturing, or construction and shipyard work in addition to garage work were not counted as garage workers.

46. Roberts, D.R., and R.D. Zumwalde. "Industrial Hygiene Summary Report of Asbestos Exposure Assessment for Brake Mechanics." NIOSH Report #32.4, Cincinnati (1982).

    Time-weighted average exposures for mechanics using various brake repair techniques were generally in the range of 0.1 to 0.3 f/cc. General area air samples were 0.01-0.13 f/cc.

47. Williams, R.L., and J.L. Muhlbaier. "Asbestos Brake Emissions," *Environ. Research 29*:70-82 (1982).

    Report of brake asbestos emissions from General Motors Research Laboratories.

> The ratio of small fibers which can be seen with an electron microscope (less than 5 microns in length) to large fibers as determined with an optical microscope (more than 5 microns in length) was about 460 for disc brakes and 230 for drum brakes.

The authors conclude that over 99.9% of the asbestos in the brake materials is destroyed in braking. They calculate that concentrations of asbestos at toll booths from braking could be 19 nanograms per cubic meter of air. Comparing this to a published report of 25 ng/cm at a Connecticut toll booth, the authors deduce that "a significant fraction...could arise from braking."

48. Selikoff, I.J. *et al. Disability Compensation for Asbestos-Associated Disease in the United States,* U.S. Dept. of Labor Contract No. J-9-M-8-0165 (June, 1981). Printed by the Mt. Sinai School of Medicine. Similar data and analysis in Nicholson, W.J., G. Perkel, and I.J. Selikoff. "Occupational Exposure to Asbestos: Population at Risk and Projected Mortality 1980-2030," *Amer. J. Indust. Med. 3*:259-311 (1982).

Projects a risk of asbestos cancer for a number of occupations compared with insulation work. "Automobile maintenance" is estimated to carry 4% as much risk as insulation work. Projected number of deaths from asbestos-related cancer among automobile maintenance workers estimated to be rising steeply, from 400/year in 1983 to a peak of 500-600/year during the years 1990-2015. Quotes Weston as saying that 900,000 workers are continually exposed and 1,070,000 are exposed occasionally or infrequently.

49. Langer, A.M. and W.T.E. McCaughey. "Mesothelioma in a Brake Repair Worker," *Lancet* 1103-1104 (Nov. 13, 1982).

Finds asbestos fibers in the lung tissue of a mesothelioma patient whose occupational exposure consisted of many years of brake servicing work.

50. Glickman, L.T., *et al.* "Mesothelioma in Pet Dogs Associated with Exposure of Their Owners to Asbestos," *Environ. Res. 32*:305-313 (1983).

Over a five-year period, 18 pet dogs were diagnosed with mesothelioma at a veterinary hospital. The owners of 2 were car and truck mechanics by occupation, and the hobby of a third was automobile servicing. Two of the other dogs' owners were an automobile body repairer and a used automobile parts supply worker.

51. Mancuso, T.F., "Mesothelioma Among Machinists in Railroad and Other Industries," *Amer. J. Indust. Med.* 4: 501-513 (1983).

    Report of pleural mesothelioma in an auto mechanic.

52. Guillon, F., *et al.* "A Case of Association of Myoproliferative Syndrome and Pleural Mesothelioma after an Asbestos Exposure," *Arch. Malad. Prof. Med.* 45:119-121 (1984).

    Case report of mesothelioma in a man who worked 45 years in automobile repair shops.

53. "Asbestos Fact Book." U.S. Environmental Protection Agency, (Feb. 1985), 11 pp.

    > (P)eople who work directly on brake maintenance are widely exposed to exceptionally high levels of asbestos. This occurs when brakes are cleaned and serviced during routine maintenance activities. EPA is establishing a Brake Mechanics Program to provide information and education on asbestos problems to vocational/technical students, working mechanics, and brake repair and maintenance specialists. The program will alert these specialists to the presence of asbestos in brakes and to methods that will minimize the release of asbestos fiber into the workplace.

Commercial Substitution of Asbestos in Friction Products

U.S. Patents of asbestos-free friction products—see "Annotated List of Friction Elements Patents," in Chapter 6. This list includes a molded composition brake block for railroad cars (No. 2,861,964) patented in 1958 by a former patent attorney of Manville Corporation who later became Chairman of the Board of Directors. More recent developments are noted here:

"ICI Asbestos-Free Brake Shoe," *Asbestos* 12-14 (Sept. 1976).

Announces immediate production and worldwide marketing of a railroad brake shoe that contains no lead or asbestos. Called Tiger, the product was developed by Abex Corporation, subsidiary of IC Industries, Inc.

Kwolek, J.P. "Friction Materials for Small Car Solid Rotor Applications," *SAE Transactions*, paper no. 750874, (1976).

Gives history of development of semimetallic brakes, starting with their use in police cars, taxi cabs, and "a few vehicles sold to the general public." Notes that semimetallic front disc brakes achieved success in meeting standards of the Los Angeles Police Department, and displayed a number of advantages over conventional asbestos-organic brake compositions by 1970. Increased cost was a major obstacle to widespread usage at that time. Author worked for Bendix Corporation.

1976 Annual Report, Raybestos-Manhattan, Inc.

> The escalating costs associated with handling this raw material and the uncertain consequences of future government asbestos regulations, however, have necessitated our decision to work toward the elimination of asbestos from all our friction products and this eventuality has become an essential part of our long term product and manufacturing plans.

1978 Annual Report, Raybestos-Manhattan, Inc.

> Although from a social and political standpoint, publicity concerning asbestos has not adversely affected our business nor do we expect it to in the near future, from a long-range standpoint, we are planning to eliminate asbestos from our friction materials products by 1982 in order to minimize the effect of any further government regulations in this area.

Castleman, B.I. and M.J. Vera. "Impending Proliferation of Asbestos," *Internat. J. Health Serv. 10:*389-403 (1980).

Paraphrases a communication from General Motors to the U.S. Environmental Protection Agency (Sept. 7, 1979), called "General Motors Programs on Non-Asbestos Friction Materials for Brake Systems." Approximately 60 percent of all passenger car disc brakes manufactured and used by G.M. had non-asbestos friction materials in 1979. G.M. projected that all its 1983-model passenger cars with disc brakes would have asbestos-free brakes, and all cars with drum brakes and light trucks would have asbestos-free brakes by the 1985 model year.

Norman, J.C. "Synthetic Fibers Find Applications in Transportation," *Indust. Research and Development* (July, 1981).

DuPont marketing specialist for "Kevlar" aramid fiber presents test results and describes performance of this product as an asbestos substitute in brakes. Cost of use initially higher but longer service life expected to offset the 25 percent initial cost premium in the life-cycle cost of the product. Excels in heavy duty applications, compared with conventional asbestos brakes.

Jacko, M.C., M. Brunhofer, and F.W. Aldrich. "Non-Asbestos Friction Materials," *Proceedings of the National Workshop on Substitutes for Asbestos. Arlington, VA, July 14-16, 1980*. Contract No. 68-02-3168. Washington: U.S. Environmental Protection Agency, 1981, pp. 9-34.

Bendix researchers report on the company's efforts to manufacture asbestos-free brakes. Excerpts:

> Semimetallic development began in 1962... General acceptance came in the mid-1970s with the second generation of semimetallic formulations. Today, semimetallic disc brakes are utilized on the disc brakes of approximately 50 percent of the new vehicles built in the U.S., and projections approach 100 percent utilization by 1985...
>
> The initial generation of asbestos-free organic drum-brake linings is in the final development stage at Bendix, and initial evaluations are underway at vehicle manufacturers. Some asbestos-free blocks are available commercially for heavy truck applications. While it is too early to tell whether these formulations will achieve commercial success, the first significant production release would probably be in 1982...
>
> (I)t may not be possible to substitute the asbestos-free materials directly in older vehicles without compromising safety...
>
> As stated in the Bendix Corporation's 1979 annual report, ...Bendix early in the 1980s will offer its automotive customers brakes made with long-wearing, high-performance friction materials that are asbestos-free.' We intend to meet that commitment.

Environmental Tidbits. *Working Environment 1982 in Sweden.* Stockholm: Swedish Work Environment Association, p. 24

> During 1982, asbestos-free (brake) linings will be introduced in all Saab models. The asbestos is replaced by so-called semi-metallic linings.

Ählberg, R. (Swedish Metalworkers Union, Stockholm) letter to B. Castleman, June 8, 1982.

Reports that in Sweden only brake linings still use asbestos. "We are now at the end of the fight for a total ban on asbestos." He continued:

> The Swedish car Saab has now completely changed over to asbestos-free brake linings, even when they are exchanging linings on older Saab cars. Today there are asbestos free brake linings for nearly all cars.

Ählberg enclosed leaflets advertising asbestos-free brake products from the Hesselman, Bennetter, and Rydahls companies in Sweden. Hesselman "Metal Master" asbestos-free brakes were offered for dozens of different models of cars by Audi, BMW, Fiat, Ford, Mercedes, Opel, Peugot, Renault, Saab, Toyota, Volkswagen, Volvo, and others.

Tombs, F. (Chairman of the Board), *Turner & Newall 1982 Report and Accounts.*

Announces progress on the introduction of asbestos-free brakes in Europe and the United States (including original-equipment drum linings in Ford Sierra models).

Reinhardt, C.F. (DuPont), certified letter to the Environmental Protection Agency, Docket WH-557 (Apr. 4, 1985).

Report of a two-year inhalation study of aramid fibers in rats. Animals exposed to the highest concentrations developed "cystic keratinizing squamous cell carcinomas": 6 of 56 females and 1 of 36 males exposed to 400 fibrils/cc; 4 of 69 females and 0 of 68 males exposed to 100 fibrils/cc; no tumors in animals exposed to 25, 2.5, and 0.

> DuPont has adopted a workplace exposure limit of 5 fibrils/cc (8 hr. time weighted average) for its operations and is suggesting this limit to its customers.

No data were provided for exposures from machining aramid-fiber-reinforced brakes. DuPont has invested $500 million in aramid ("Kevlar") fiber, which is used in many applications including canoes and bomber planes. Other chemical companies also make aramid fibers.

Castleman, B., certified letter to Robert Nelson (Nuturn Corp., subsidiary of Turner & Newall, U.K.), Apr. 26, 1985. No reply received.

Informs the leading U.S. producer of aramid-fiber-reinforced brake and clutch parts about the above report from DuPont. Urges analysis of brake drum dust, animal exposure tests of such dust, and air monitoring of worker exposures to aramid fiber from working with brakes made with aramid fibers.

Swedish Ministry of Labor, General Agreement on Tariffs and Trade Notification (May 13, 1985). Based on Government Resolution March 21, 1985.

> (Sweden) intends proposing a ban on the sale of newly manufactured passenger cars and motorcycles with brake linings containing asbestos... to take effect on 1st January, 1987.

The government announced that extension of a similar ban to cover larger vehicles was under consideration. Its actions on asbestos became an issue in the 1985 elections, in which the Social Democrats retained control in Sweden.

Following the petition of the Natural Resources Defense Council, a leading environmental group, asking for a ban on asbestos in brakes, the U.S. Environmental Protection Agency published a notice in the *Federal Register* on December 19, 1984. Several companies responded with comments that they were developing asbestos substitutes for use in brakes, among other applications.

American Kynol, Inc., New York (agent for Nippon Kynol, Inc., Osaka, Japan)—commercially markets novolid fibers for use in friction materials: "generally used in conjunction with other materials including aramid and/or glass fibers and inorganic filler materials."

Jim Walter Corp., Tampa, Florida—commercially markets one type of processed mineral wool fiber now used in friction materials (PMF 204) and is developing another (PMF 1104). The latter is of non-respirable size, about 1100 microns long and 4 microns in diameter.

Ashland Petroleum Co. (Ashland, KY)—manufactures carbon fibers "as a suitable substitute for asbestos in automobile and truck brakes."

Engelhard Corp. (Edison, NJ)—manufactures a mineral composition based on attapulgite clay for use in friction products.

Monsanto Co. (St. Louis, MO)—developing a calcium sodium metaphosphate fiber for use in friction products.

Enka AG Product Group Industrial Fibers (Wuppertal, West Germany)—manufactures aramid fibers.

Control Technology for Brake and Clutch Work (by Dr. Grace Ziem)

1. *Asbestos Dust Control in Brake Maintenance.* PEI Associates, Inc., P.O. Box 46100, Cincinnati, OH 45246 (July 22, 1985). Prepared for the U.S. Environmental Protection Agency, Office of Pesticides and Toxic Substances.

   This report reviews exposures with a variety of improvised control techniques which have emerged as alternatives to the compressed air hose. Their performance was generally poor: damp rag use permitted peak asbestos exposures up to 2.6 f/cc with time-weighted averages (TWAs) up to 0.28; a liquid squirt bottle created a 10-minute peak of 0.54 f/cc with TWA over five hours of 0.21; the use of stoddard solvent flowing through an air gun caused peak levels up to 0.68 f/cc and TWAs slightly under 0.1; dry rag and brush generated peaks up to 0.81 f/cc with TWAs up to 0.2.

   Wetting methods not using a collection system simply disperse the fibers, and when the liquid dries, fibers remain in the shop ready to enter the room air with minimal motion. Background contamination from such methods, therefore, would not necessarily be less than with the compressed-air cleaning method.

   A wet method system with a collection tray was also evaluated (Ammco Brake Assembly Washer). Unfortunately, 15-minute peaks were 1.1 f/cc.

2. *Asbestos Product Test Results.* GCA Corp., Bedford, MA 01730 (1980). Prepared for the U.S. Environmental Protection Agency, Office of Pesticides and Toxic Substances.

   Widespread garage contamination is illustrated by worker exposure measurements during compressed air use of 0.85 f/cc with levels of 0.1 f/cc 25 feet away. When the mechanic removed the brake housing and cleaned it by repeatedly striking it with a hammer, his 14-minute exposure was measured as 1.29 f/cc. In these tests, a scanning electron microscope was used to analyze the air samples, so this would not be comparable to measurements using conventional optical techniques.

3. Nilfisk of America, Inc., 201 King Manor Dr., King of Prussia, PA 19406.

   This manufacturer was the first developer of a brake enclosure system, the Asbesto-Clene system. Nilfisk was also the first to obtain transmission electron microscopic analysis of exposure levels during equipment use (by Dr. Arthur Rohl of the Mt. Sinai School of Medicine, NY). Essentially zero exposure levels were monitored during use. The enclosure size did not permit internal drum removal and hammer use.

4. Clayton Associates, Inc., P.O. Box 589, Farmingdale, NJ 07727

   The Clayton enclosure system has been tested by Dr. Rohl during use and also during coarse filter change, with zero exposure measured by transmission electron microscopy. Vacuum suction within the filter enclosure pulls released dust away from the mechanic during coarse filter change, toward the High Efficiency Particulate Air filter (HEPA filter). The manufacturer offers the service of changing the HEPA filter at cost.

   A clutch enclosure system has also been recently developed by this manufacturer. Exposure measurements during the system's use are not yet available.

5. Hako, 111 S. Route 53, Addison, IL 60101.

   The Hako "Minuteman" asbestos brake drum vacuum system is a newly developed, relatively inexpensive but somewhat flimsy appearing enclosure system. Like other brake enclosure systems, it surrounds the brake assembly and uses a compressed air jet for cleaning inside the enclosure.

   No air measurements are available during use of the Hako equipment. Such measurements are essential, since if the enclosure does not provide a tight seal (such as against the backing plate), leakage can occur, with fiber release.

6. Control Resource Systems, Inc. P.O. Box 421, Michigan City, IN 46360.

This company produces the "Brakemaster" enclosure unit. Unlike Hako, non-permeable gloves are offered as an optional feature to prevent hand contamination (and the resulting ingestion hazard). The unit allows both hands inside the enclosure for two-handed work, but is not large enough to accommodate a hammer for use on sticking drums. No air measurements are available to verify the claim of "100% safe."

Note: The brake enclosure systems offered by Nilfisk, Hako, and Control Resource Systems can be purchased without the vacuum/HEPA filter attachments. Clayton will not sell an enclosure unless the whole system is obtained. The use of one of these enclosures with hook-up to an ordinary shop vacuum would render the enclosure largely ineffective, since the filter in an ordinary vacuum cleaner is incapable of capturing most of the tiny asbestos fibers—which would be re-released by the vacuum into the shop air.

7. National Loss Control Service Corp., Long Grove, IL 60049. *Report of Industrial Hygiene Study for Ammco Tools, Inc. North Chicago, IL* (1978).

   A 15-minute exposure peak of 1.1 f/cc was found with brake washing using the Ammco Model 1250 brake assembly washer after use of a hammer. A "poorly maintained" Model 880 created operator exposures during grinding of 1.4 f/cc, but the "well maintained" Model 880 also created operator exposure of 1.4 f/cc for grinding brake linings.

   This system uses a solvent which dries into a gel in the collection tray, trapping the fibers, according to verbal communication from the manufacturer. Nonetheless, measured asbestos levels using optical microscopy are excessive and allow shop contamination to occur.

8. U.S. Sales Co., 17 Nepperhan Ave., Elmsford, NY 10523

   This company makes a wet method brake cleansing system with a wet brush attachment. No air measurement data are available to evaluate this equipment. Until proven otherwise, it must be assumed to create potentially hazardous asbestos exposures to the mechanic and others generally present in the shop, as do all of the "wet" approaches thus far evaluated.

Case Reports of Mesothelioma in Brake Repair Workers

These case reports were compiled in 1984-86 by a review of medical records and legal depositions or occupational history interviews by Dr. Grace Ziem. One of these cases was the subject of tissue analyses reported by Langer and McCaughey (*Lancet*, 1982). Subsequent cases have been reported (e.g., E.S. Hansen, "Mortality of Auto Mechanics." *Scand. J. Work Environ. Health 15*:43-46, 1989).

* * *

T.Y. was a 60-year-old man diagnosed by pleural biopsy in 1980 as having a left pleural mesothelioma (later confirmed by autopsy). He had worked as an electric arc welder for 6 months in 1942. He used no asbestos blanket and primarily did tack or spot welding, using few welding rods each day. He worked in a shipyard building new ships. At the time of his work, insulation had not been installed in the ships. He never recalls seeing any insulation crews or jobs nor did he ever weld near or handle any insulation material.

From 1946 to 1953 he worked as a mechanic on trains in a public transportation system. All brakes were steel-to-steel without asbestos, and there was no other known asbestos exposure during this time. In 1953 he was transferred to do brake and mechanical work on buses. He did 4 to 5 brake jobs weekly, each lasting about 3 hours, in a very large garage with a 30-foot ceiling. The brake debris was blown out with an air hose, forming a visible cloud of dust. No local ventilation, respirators, or wet methods were utilized, nor was he warned of any hazard.

Brake linings were rounded on a grinder to improve contact, without exhaust ventilation. Approximately 10-12 other mechanics worked in the same garage, each doing approximately the same number of brake repairs. He was not aware of any other exposure to asbestos than described above.

* * *

J.M. was a 55-year-old man who was diagnosed in 1975 as having a right pleural mesothelioma, with metastasis to the liver, diagnosed surgically by biopsy.

He worked for a military supply company in 1940 for 18 months as a lathe machine operator on shells. In 1942 he worked for a year as a maintenance mechanic installing diesel motors in LST boats. In 1943 he went into the army for 18 months. In none of these positions was he aware of any asbestos exposure.

From 1945 to 1965 he worked as a brake repair mechanic for a general contractor. He had almost daily exposure to asbestos during those 20 years, on truck, crane, and other large vehicle brakes.

In 1965 he operated a service station for a year doing frequent brake repair. In 1967 and 1968 he worked on call through an operating engineers' local union with no brake repair exposure. From 1969 until 1975 he worked for a vehicle service contractor as an operator-mechanic, including brake repair duties.

Brake dust was blown out of the drum with an air hose. No local exhaust, respirators, or wetting procedures were utilized at any time. He was unaware of any hazards from asbestos until after his diagnosis.

* * *

C.H. was a 54-year-old man diagnosed by biopsy in 1980 as having a right pleural mesothelioma. His diagnosis was confirmed at autopsy in 1981. At age 19 he began to work in his father's used car business, changing brakes about once a week. In 1963 at about age 37 he bought a service station and did frequent brake repair work for the next three years. In 1966 he bought a used car business and again was involved regularly in brake repair. The last several years prior to his diagnosis he was able to work only intermittently due to health reasons unrelated to asbestos exposure.

He removed debris from the drums with a compressed air hose. No wet methods, respirator or local ventilation was utilized. He was unaware of the hazards of asbestos exposure. He did not recall ever seeing a warning label on either the brake lining material or the shipping boxes. He had no other known exposure to asbestos.

* * *

R.H. was diagnosed at the age of 78 as having mesothelioma involving the right pleura after a thoracotomy procedure with biopsy. His first exposure to brake dust was in 1924 working with an auto dealership in Los Angeles. For about 7 years he averaged about 3 brake jobs daily and sometimes did as many as 25 or 30 in a day. After that he worked in smaller garages for another 20 years or more, averaging one or two brake procedures daily. He used a compressed air hose for all brake work and was unaware of the hazard.

For a twelve-year period somewhat later, this man worked as a supervisor for maintenance operations in buildings in a professional center. However, all insulation repair procedures were subcontracted, and Mr. H. was never around these jobs during their implementation nor afterward until clean-up was complete. (Such activities were fairly uncommon.) He does not recall seeing any insulation products left behind after clean-up. He does not recall ever being exposed to asbestos in any other manner, such as from sprayed insulation, ceilings, roofing jobs, construction, shipyard work, etc.

* * *

C.T., a 45-year-old woman, was diagnosed with right pleural mesothelioma by open-chest biopsy in 1982. She was the wife of an auto mechanic, and several times a week beginning in 1959 she went to the garage at lunch time. She also laundered her husband's work clothes, placing them into the washer without shaking. The garage was a 3-bay station servicing an automobile dealership. Her last exposure to his work-clothes or the garage was in 1964. During those 5 years there were several long intervals with neither garage nor clothing exposure, so that the total exposure duration she estimates as not longer than a full year. She had no other known asbestos exposure, either as a child or as an adult.

This case is an illustration of the critical importance of occasional bystander exposure, thus re-emphasizing the potential for disease among customers and others not directly conducting brake repair, nor even having regular ongoing bystander exposure. This may be the first published report of mesothelioma in the spouse of a brake mechanic.

Two additional cases of mesothelioma from brake and clutch repair have been seen by Dr. Susan M. Daum (J.Z., 59-years-old and C.J., 37-years-old). Both had frequent brake dust exposure for over 20 years, one as a bystander (an automobile salesman) and the other as a mechanic. Dr. Daum personally obtained the occupational history from both and is satisfied that friction products constituted the only known source of asbestos exposure. (Personal communication to Grace Ziem from Susan M. Daum, River Edge, New Jersey)

9
Company Knowledge

"I'll never forget, I turned to Mr. Brown, one of the Browns made this crack (that Unarco managers were a bunch of fools for notifying employees who had asbestosis), and I said, 'Mr. Brown, do you mean to tell me you would let them work until they dropped dead?' He said, 'Yes. We save a lot of money that way.'"

> Testimony of Charles H. Roemer about the meeting of Unarco officials with Johns-Manville President Louis Brown and his brother, Vandiver, in 1942 or 1943. (Deposition taken April 25, 1984, *Johns-Manville Corp. et al. v. the United States of America,* U.S. Claims Court Civ. No. 465-83C.)

CONTENTS

Raybestos-Manhattan, Inc..	484
Owens-Illinois	492
Armstrong Cork	500
Fibreboard Corporation	500
Owens-Corning Fiberglas	502
Unarco	509
Pittsburgh-Corning Corporation	511
Eagle-Picher Industries	513
United States Gypsum Company	516
Southern Textile (HK Porter)	519
Keene Corporation	521

Union Carbide Corporation 523
W.R. Grace & Company 526
GAF Corporation 530
Companies Mining Asbestos in Quebec 532
Philip Carey Manufacturing Company 537
Asbestos Corporation, Ltd. 540
Johns-Manville Corporation 542
National Gypsum Company 549
Turner & Newall, Ltd. 554
CSR 559
Railroad Companies 561

Much could be said to further acquaint readers unfamiliar with the U.S. judicial system for resolving civil claims. However, this section is focused on the utility of legal discovery as a tool for doing historical research on asbestos disease.

To encourage fair settlement of damage suits, the U.S. legal system allows each side to ask the other questions (Interrogatories) which must be answered in writing under oath. By means of Interrogatories, the plaintiff may verify that a defendant asbestos company manufactured certain products and sold them to the shipyard where the plaintiff worked, for example. The defendants, on the other hand, can fully inquire about the nature of the damages claimed, and about the plaintiff's medical and occupational history—did the man smoke cigarettes, did he work with other carcinogens, who is the treating doctor, and so on. Some questions will be directed toward legal matters: When did the manufacturer begin to put warning labels on his products; how long ago did the plaintiff learn he had asbestosis (i.e., does the statute of limitations prevent the case from being prosecuted)?

The Interrogatories are supplemented by the right of each side to take depositions and examine documents in the other side's possession. This also takes place in advance of the trial. The plaintiff wants to know when and how the manufacturers became aware of the product dangers, and what was the subsequent conduct by each manufacturer. This "actual knowledge" is not ascertainable by merely reading the published literature that may have been *available* to the manufacturer. Reports *published* by the manufacturers and their employees cannot be relied upon as complete or valid statements of the firms' internal knowledge.

For the purpose of legal "discovery," as it is called, corporate employees and former employees can be deposed. The deposition is a scheduled questioning session where the person deposed is under oath and every word said is recorded. Statements made in a deposition may then be used in trial, if an out-of-court settlement or dismissal of the case does not intervene. The deponent might be a company executive, medical director, industrial hygienist, or a clerk who has been the custodian of records of interest (and can thus testify that the records are "authentic").

It is not usually difficult to find out who the principal people in the company were who had responsibility for plant and product safety. This can be gleaned from company answers to interrogatories, inquiries to "old timers" in the health and safety field, and sources like the historical publications of the Industrial Health Foundation (previous to 1971, Industrial Hygiene Foundation). The old IHF Transactions list members of numerous committees, and note the companies where these people were employed.

Under the discovery rules, defendants are required to produce the relevant corporate documents upon request. Other persons or institutions, such as research bodies that did contract work for the companies, may also be subjected to discovery proceedings. Concealment of vital evidence can result in the granting of a new trial (if the case was lost by the disadvantaged party) or, even more rarely, in disciplinary action against the offending lawyer by the state licensing authority or the court.

Documentation obtained from sources other than the asbestos companies and their employees is, for the most part, discussed elsewhere in the book. This chapter will attempt to at least note the possible knowledge specific companies had of such information and provide fuller discussion of documentation obtained in discovery from the companies themselves. The role of company doctors will also be noted here.

(For reference to specific companies not included in sections in this chapter, the reader may find the Index helpful).

RAYBESTOS-MANHATTAN, INC
(Renamed "Raymark" in 1982)

This company has been a leading manufacturer of asbestos friction products (brake linings, etc.) and textiles since the 1920s. It has more recently diversified into additional lines of business not involving asbestos.

In Answers to Interrogatories, this company has acknowledged paying compensation for disability from asbestosis to employees since the 1930s. The first employees compensated for "asbestosis-carcinoma" worked at the Manheim, Pennsylvania plant. One of these individuals was paid compensation in 1950 (R. Gelder) and another apparently was compensated before 1946 (K. Hilton, no date given). The company acknowledges paying compensation for mesothelioma to another worker at the same plant, in 1962 (H. Frey).

Raybestos-Manhattan produced what have become the best-known discovery documents in the history of asbestos litigation. These are known as the "Sumner Simpson Papers." Popularly dubbed the "Pentagon Papers of the Asbestos Industry" in news reports, this is the single most revealing cache of corporate documents found in these legal proceedings. The documents are the correspondence and file reports retained by Sumner Simpson, President of the company in the 1930s and 1940s. Many of these documents are discussed in Chapter 3 in greater detail, and the most important documents are letters exchanged with attorney Vandiver Brown of Johns-Manville Corporation.

A measure of the importance of these documents is the decision by South Carolina Circuit Judge James Price to grant a new trial in an asbestos damage suit won by the defendant companies. The after-discovered evidence, as it was called, would likely have led the jury to an opposite verdict—and on this basis a new trial was granted.

Judge Price characterized the documents as follows:

> The correspondence very arguably shows a pattern of denial and disease and attempts at suppression of information which is highly probative.

The correspondence

> reveals written evidence that Raybestos-Manhattan and Johns-Manville exercised an editorial prerogative over the publication of the first study of the asbestos industry which they sponsored in 1935.
>
> (It) further reflects a conscious effort by the industry in the 1930s to downplay, or arguably suppress, the dissemination of information to employees and the public for fear of the promotion of lawsuits.
>
> (Amended Order. *Barnett v. Owens-Corning Fiberglas Corp. et al.*, State of South Carolina, County of Greenville, Court of Common Pleas, Aug. 23, 1978).

Federal Judge Harold Ackerman of New Jersey has agreed to grant plaintiffs trial by jury in negligence, fraud, and conspiracy claims against Metropolitan Life Insurance Company (*Anna Billetz et al. v. Johns-Manville,* Civ. No. 80-2976). The judge found that the study as published by Lanza and co-workers was altered, "apparently in accordance with the asbestos industry's wishes." One of the "most glaring alterations" was the deletion from conclusion 4 of the sentence: "However, it is possible for uncomplicated asbestosis to result fatally."

There are thousands of pages of documentation, but the highlights only are given below:

1. Asbestos Magazine Letters

Sept. 25, 1935	Rossiter to Simpson
Oct. 1, 1935	Simpson to Brown
Oct. 3, 1935	Brown to Simpson
March 23, 1939	Rossiter to Simpson
Nov. 3, 1941	Brown to Simpson

These describe ongoing pattern of non-publication of articles on asbestosis in the trade magazine, *Asbestos,* at the direction of industry executives. (See "The Asbestos Magazine Letters," in Chapter 3, and Appendices 1-2)

2. Editing of the Metropolitan Life study (by Lanza and co-workers)—letters

Dec. 10, 1934	Brown to Lanza
Dec. 15, 1934	Hobart to Brown
Dec. 18, 1934	Brown to Judd
Dec. 21, 1934	Brown to Lanza
Dec. 24, 1934	Brown to Judd
Jan. 2, 1935	Judd to Brown

Key changes asked by Johns-Manville lawyers of Dr. Lanza, in consultation with Judd of R-M (See "Industry Editing of Medical Publications: Lanza's Surveys," Chapter 3).

3. Industry Sponsorship of Saranac Lab Research—letters.

Nov. 10, 1936 Simpson to Schluter—calls meeting of Schluter (Thermoid Rubber Co.), Blagden (Keasbey & Mattison Co.), Lamont (Asbestos Manufacturing Co.), Williams (Russell Manufacturing Co.), and Brown (Johns-Manville).

> The idea of Mr. Brown and myself would have to have four to five (or even more if we could get them) Asbestos manufacturers take over this study by subscribing an equal amount per year, for three years, and then we could determine from time to time after the findings are made, whether we wish any publication or not. My own idea is that it would be a good idea to distribute the information among the medical fraternity, providing it is of the right type and would not injure our companies.

Nov. 20, 1936	Brown to Gardner
Nov. 23, 1936	Gardner to Brown

The asbestos companies authorized commencement of animal studies.
Brown:

> It is our further understanding that the results obtained will be considered the property of those who are advancing the

> required funds, who will determine, whether, to what extent, and in what manner they shall be made public. In the event it is deemed desirable that the results be made public, the manuscript of your study will be submitted to us for approval prior to publication.

Gardner agreed to those terms.

Feb. 27, 1937	Brown to Simpson

Lists contributors:

American Brake Block Corp.
Gatke Corp.
Union Asbestos and Rubber Co. (Unarco)
United States Gypsum Co.
Russell Manufacturing Co.
Asbestos Manufacturing Co.
Johns-Manville Corp.
Keasbey & Mattison Co.
Raybestos-Manhattan, Inc.
Thermoid Company
Southern Asbestos Co.

May 3, 1939	Brown to Simpson
May 4, 1939	Simpson to Brown
May 10, 1940	Brown to Simpson

Brown and Simpson expressed alarm that Dr. Gardner had published information on his research in violation of the 1936 funding agreement.

4. Chest X-rays at R-M Plants—letters

Oct. 30, 1936	Lanza to Mitchell
Oct. 31, 1936	Simpson to Jeffords
Nov. 5, 1936	Simpson to Jeffords

R-M President wrote to his general manager in Charleston, S.C. that the Public Health Service can take X-rays on conditions that they not be given to "shyster lawyers" etc. Lanza assured that Public Health Service records are confidential, lauded P.H.S. investigator Sayers.

5. Founding of Air Hygiene Foundation

Jan. 22, 1935	Brown to Judd

Jan. 15, 1935	Memorandum Re: Mellon Institute of Industrial Research Symposium on Dust Problems.
Dec. 4, 1935	Brown to Stover
Dec. 8, 1936	Stover to "Members Asbestos Industry"

Vandiver Brown represented the Asbestos, Cork, and Non-Metallic industries. He and six other representing industries with dust hazards advanced the idea of forming an industry center for research and consultation. This was passed on to Stover, publisher of *Asbestos,* who sent the word out industry-wide:

> I have before me a list of the officers and trustees of the Air Hygiene Foundation, and it certainly is a cross-section of the very finest American industries, insurance companies, chemists, attorneys, and others interested in the prevention of silicosis and the protection of industries from unreasonable claims of workers.

6. Dr. Lynch's Criticisms of the Saranac Research

May 6, 1938	Lynch to Mitchell
May 17, 1938	Simpson to Mitchell
May 18, 1938	Brown to Simpson
May 19, 1938	Gardner to Simpson
May 23, 1938	Simpson to Gardner

Simpson was sent a letter from Dr. Kenneth Lynch concerning the work at Saranac and referred it to Brown. Brown said he thought Lynch was saying that no conclusions could yet be drawn from the Saranac tests. But Gardner responded defensively to Lynch's implication of the questionable value of his animal studies:

> I am of course sorry that he feels that our experiments have no practical bearing on whether there is such a thing as asbestosis... This is a matter of opinion...

Simpson encouraged Gardner:

> I want to say I am pinning my faith on you, and am quite positive it will not be very long before you convince Dr. Lynch that your findings, whatever they be, are correct.

7. Northwest Magnesia Association letter

June 14, 1943	DeForest to Morgan
June 18, 1943	Rossiter to Simpson
June 29, 1943	Brown to Simpson

DeForest expressed concern about Washington state standards for workers using insulation to be protected against asbestosis. Also complained that asbestosis was a "foreign disease" and discussion of it could arouse hysteria among insulators. Letter passed on by *Asbestos* magazine to Simpson, and thence to Brown. Brown decided "to let Mr. DeForest learn the facts of life and asbestosis from the State of Washington Department of Labor and Industries."

8. Air Sampling for R-M and Other Members of the Asbestos Textile Institute

May 2, 1944	Cilley to Simpson

Provides record of dust counts in various processes. With a range of 1.7 to 9.9 MPPCF, three of the fourteen values were over 5 MPPCF.

June, 1947. *Report of Preliminary Dust Investigation for Asbestos Textile Institute.* By W.C. Hemeon, Industrial Hygiene Foundation.

Shows continuing occurrence of asbestosis industry-wide, with 20 percent prevalence of asbestosis in two of five plants where employees were regularly examined. Criticizes the 5 MPPCF guideline as requiring additional scrutiny and urges industry-wide investigations.

Raybestos-Manhattan was associated with the Industrial Hygiene Foundation from its start in the late 1930s, and hence received the *Industrial Hygiene Digest* containing abstracts of medical articles on asbestosis. The Sumner Simpson Papers indicate that Simpson was also aware even earlier of articles on asbestosis appearing in "British trade magazines," and he expressed his appreciation that this material was not being reprinted by *Asbestos* magazine in the United States (Oct. 1, 1935 letter to Brown). These letters show that Simpson was familiar with Public Health Service studies on asbestosis in the

1930s. The company was also a member of the Asbestos Textile Institute, whose minutes include reference to discussions about asbestosis and lung cancer starting in the 1940s. (See "Industry Trade Associations and Research Organizations," in Chapter 10).

More recent documentation has also been produced by this company in discovery:

Nov. 7, 1966.—M. Scowcroft (R-M) letter to R.L. Lebel (Bath Iron Works, purchasing agent). Referring to Lebel's concern over asbestos cloth, the writer arranges to have a sample of treated cloth sent in which "the fibers have been coated and brushed so that they will not tend to migrate." Scowcroft also says:

> We feel that the recent unfavorable publicity over the use of asbestos fibers in many different kinds of industries has been a gross exaggeration of the problems. There is no data available to either prove or disprove the dangers of working closely with asbestos.

July 12, 1971.—Scowcroft letter to R.E. Wartham (Newport News Shipbuilding and Drydock Co.).

> You will recall that we were the unsuccessful bidder on your inquiry...because your Pipe Shop reported that our original samples exhibited a higher degree of fiber fall-out according to their test procedures.

Discusses efforts to provide free samples to the customer.

March 7, 1973	I. Weaver memorandum to J. Marsh
Jan. 29, 1974	G.W. Gibbs (McGill Univ.) letter to J. Marsh
March 1, 1974	J.H. Marsh memorandum to P.G. Dolan and four others
March 4, 1974	J.J. Magenheimer memorandum to J. Marsh
March 6, 1974	J. Hawkins memorandum to J. Marsh
June 17, 1974	J.J. Magenheimer memorandum to J. Trainor
July 15, 1974	J.J. Magenheimer memorandum to J. Marsh
July 24, 1974	J. Marsh memorandum to M.Q. Scowcroft

Discusses studies of asbestos exposures from wearing asbestos "safety clothing," conducted by Gibbs at McGill. Gibbs reported that men wearing asbestos garments at a plant were exposed to average concentrations of more than 5 f/cc and 15-minute peak concentrations above 10 f/cc, in violation of OSHA standards. Various modifications of the fabric were made and suggested, including surface treatment with an adhesive, without apparent success. The last memo by Marsh acknowledges that,

> The McGill study confirms earlier British studies showing that in normal use asbestos safety garments can release concentrations of asbestos fibers in excess of permissible limits.

(Gibbs' findings were published the next year: "Fibre Release from Asbestos Garments," *Ann. Occup. Hyg. 18*:143-149, 1975)

May 5, 1975	J. Marsh memorandum to F.D. Bauce and 7 others
Nov. 24, 1976	J. Marsh memorandum to G. Ferrucci
Feb. 16, 1977	J. Marsh memorandum to M.Q. Scowcroft

The first of these memos from the chief of environmental affairs acknowledges the danger of "high dust levels" in brake repair and the need to assure that warnings reach the small shops. The second, marked "CONFIDENTIAL," notes that, "exposure to excessive levels (of asbestos) for a few months or even a few weeks can result in the appearance of disease many years later." This memo also stresses the importance of preventing workers from taking dust home on their clothes. The last memo advises against telling customers that asbestos products can be used safely. "(W)e cannot use the word safe simply because we do not know what a safe level of exposure is."

Nov. 24, 1976	J. Marsh memorandum to F.S. Daly
Mar. 31, 1978	J. Marsh memorandum to R.B. Sims

These refer to the hazard of surface dust on asbestos-containing friction materials, and the use of caution labels on packages of automatic transmission plates.

July 14, 1978. Plant Manager memorandum to "All RMFM Employees"

Refers to recent televised publicity about asbestos.

> It is important for you to understand that workers in shipyards and on construction sites were exposed to extremely high dust concentrations. In most instances dust control equipment and respiratory protection were not provided and work was frequently carried on in confined spaces which greatly increased the risk. In contrast, in our manufacturing plants you are protected by extensive dust control systems, respiratory equipment, and medical surveillance programs.

Raymark Annual Report 1984.

Notes that the company had continuously purchased products liability insurance coverage since 1941, totaling $395 million. As of December 31, 1984, $360 million of this amount had still not been used. The company had won suits making its insurers liable for all defense costs until the limits of coverage are exhausted.

This company was also a party to the censorship of all references to cancer in the report of industry-sponsored asbestos research at Saranac, published by Vorwald in 1951 (See "Early Saranac Laboratory Cancer Tests with Asbestos" in Chapter 2). Raymark was forced into bankruptcy court in 1989, after trying to restructure to protect assets from liability in asbestos claims (See "Asbestos Litigation" in Chapter 11).

OWENS-ILLINOIS (O-I)

Animal testing of dust from the insulation product "Kaylo" was initiated at Saranac in 1945, following discussions which took place as commercial introduction of Kaylo was proceeding. Note: Items 1,2,4,5,7,9 and 10 were in the Kaylo file of the old Saranac Laboratory, retained at the Trudeau Institute, Saranac Lake, New York.

1. Feb. 12, 1943 U.E. Bowes (O-I Director of Research) letter to L.U. Gardner (Saranac Laboratory).

> (The health hazard) should be considered from the standpoint of employees working in the plant where the material is made or where it may be sawed to desired dimensions, and also considered from the standpoint of applicators or erectors at the point of use.

2. Mar. 12, 1943 Gardner letter to U.E. Bowes.

> The fact that you are starting with a mixture of quartz and asbestos would certainly suggest that you have all the ingredients for a first class hazard.

3. *Ninth Progress Report On Studies of Kaylo* to Owens Illinois Glass Co. from Arthur D. Little, Inc. (May 16, 1947); including letter of transmittal (p. 1) to U.E. Bowes, same date. From the Introduction:

> Since from a merely sales point of view there may be a resistance towards the inclusion of an organic material in Kaylo, it is assumed that the use of paper pulp is contemplated as a substitute only when and if the amount of suitable asbestos grades available are insufficient. Accordingly, it was endeavored to develop formulae for the incorporation of paper pulp which will not necessitate any change of the present plant procedure, as well as the least possible change in slurry characteristics and batch formulation. It is believed that we have achieved this aim for Kraft pulp as a substitution material, even though we are fully aware of the fact that the final test will reside in pilot plant tests. (p. 3)

4. Nov. 16, 1948. A.J. Vorwald (Saranac) letter to U.E. Bowes on animal (guinea pig) inhalation tests of Kaylo dust.

> In all animals sacrificed after more than 30 months of exposure to Kaylo dust unmistakable evidence of asbestosis has developed, showing that Kaylo on inhalation is capable of producing asbestosis and must be regarded as a potentially-hazardous material.

The letter ends,

> I realize that our findings regarding Kaylo are less favorable than anticipated. However, since Kaylo is capable of producing asbestosis, it is better to discover it now in animals rather than later in industrial workers. Thus the company,

> being forewarned, will be in a better position to institute adequate control measures for safeguarding exposed employees and protecting its own interests.

5. Attached to the Nov. 16, 1948 letter was a report, *Interim Report Regarding the Biological Activity of Kaylo Dust* to the Owens-Illinois Glass Company, Toledo, Ohio by A.J. Vorwald, Saranac Laboratory (Oct. 30, 1948).

   From the Introduction:

   > ...Kaylo is capable, on prolonged inhalation, of producing asbestosis in the lungs of guinea pigs (and) it should be handled industrially as a hazardous dust.

   The experimental conditions:

   > The animals were exposed to atmospheric suspensions of Kaylo dust for eight hours daily, five and one half days a week throughout the experiment. The dust concentration, which varied somewhat from time to time, has averaged 116 million particles per cubic foot of air over the entire course of the experiment to date.

   Results:

   > (All) nine animals sacrificed subsequent to thirty months in the present experiment...have developed true fibrosis of a type characteristic of the response of guinea pigs to asbestos.
   > While the lesions up to 30 months showed no fibrosis, certain aspects of them were compatible with a preliminary stage in the development of asbestosis. These aspects were masked by the inert type of reaction to the materials other than asbestos in the dust.

   Conclusions:

   > Kaylo, because of its content of an appreciable amount of fibrous chrysotile, is capable of producing asbestosis and should be handled as a hazardous industrial dust.

   This report also noted that "very small numbers of fibers are capable of producing asbestosis" (See "The American Conference of Governmental Industrial Hygienists TLVs," in Chapter 4).

Over the next few years, subsequent studies on Kaylo were reported to Owens-Illinois, and the above results were repeatedly referred to in overall summations of the work by Saranac.

6. "New Thermal Insulating Material Combines Light Weight and High Strength." *Materials and Methods 29*:63 (April, 1949).

   "New materials preview" showing a man wearing a respirator using a power saw to cut a block of Kaylo insulation. (Not an advertisement.)

7. Dec. 12, 1950. Willis G. Hazard (industrial hygienist, Owens-Illinois) letter to A.J. Vorwald.

   > Some time ago we mentioned to you that our Kaylo Division wants to gather together in brochure form material on the health aspects of Kaylo dust, and wants to consider the possibility of publishing some of your experimental findings.

8. Dec. 9, 1952. C.W. Howard, intra-company correspondence to George White (O-I).

   Attaches draft of proposed pamphlet "on the health aspect of Kaylo," acknowledges the assistance of Mr. Hazard and Dr. Shook as well as "people in Sales." Describing the Saranac experiments, the proposed pamphlet says:

   > (T)here is no danger of developing Asbestosis with normal handling of Kaylo products. Test showed that continued exposure to concentrated Kaylo dust inhaled over a long period of time was capable of producing in animals increased tissue growth typical of Asbestosis. The reaction was milder than what pure asbestos dust would produce.

   General Conclusions:

   > Experience in the factories and field and research findings have proven that normal handling of Kaylo products is safe from a health standpoint. The usual precautionary measures taken for any product containing asbestos are needed in a continued exposure to heavily concentrated Kaylo dust.

   No brochure about Kaylo's health hazards was ever issued by O-I.

Author's Comment (BC):

It is very significant that Dr. Vorwald's guinea pig experiments were not construed *by him* as showing that *any* level of exposure to Kaylo dust was safe for *humans.* Exposure at only one test concentration doesn't even provide dose-response information for the guinea pigs; i.e., perhaps an adverse reaction would have occurred at half the dose tested or less, but there is no way of knowing from the results of experiments at one dose level. Equally important is the impossibility of quantitatively extrapolating from guinea pigs to humans, given the possibility that humans could be the more susceptible species to the adverse effects of a given concentration of asbestos in air.

9. *Report, Kaylo Division Plant Owens-Illinois Glass Co. Sayreville, New Jersey* by Saranac Laboratory (May 29, 1951).

 Total dust counts in various areas of the plant where Kaylo was produced ranged from 2.2 to 8.3 MPPCF—with a high percentage of asbestos and free silica (most samples had an asbestos content in the 10-50% range).

 > Although the dust counts of the seven impinger samples were all below 10 million, and therefore relatively low, the rather high quartz or asbestos content of the air-suspended material tended to create in certain areas a condition which might be hazardous, or at least one which approached the maximum allowable limit established by code... Also, the concentration of asbestos dust inside the boxcars probably exceeded safe limits. (estimated concentration of airborne dust in boxcars being loaded with Kaylo material: 50 MPPCF)

 Respirators were recommended for workers loading boxcars. Vorwald advised against reliance on compliance with government and industry standards as complete protection against the threat of occupational disease (See also "The American Conference of Governmental Industrial Hygienists TLVs," in Chapter 4).

10. Feb. 7, 1952 A.J. Vorwald letter to W.G. Hazard

Encloses final report (Jan. 30, 1952) on *The Capacity of Inhaled Kaylo Dust to Injure the Lung*. Four copies enclosed, and a note that another had gone to Dr. Shook (the Corporate Medical Director of O-I).

> ...Kaylo dust is capable of producing a peribronchiolar fibrosis typical of asbestosis. The dust also has a slightly unfavorable influence upon a tuberculous infection. Although extrapolation from animal to human experience is difficult, nevertheless the results of the study indicate that every precaution should be taken to protect workers against inhaling the dust.

Vorwald expressed desire to publish the findings, first sending the final manuscript to O-I.

> Reference will be made only to hydrous calcium silicate and not to 'Kaylo'; thus the interest of your company will be safeguarded.

The enclosed final report observed (p. 2):

> (S)ince experiments with animals have shown that both amosite and chrysotile are causing asbestosis, it is unlikely that the substitution of one mineral for the other in Kaylo would cause a significant change in the toxic properties of the final product.

11. E.C. Schuman. "Hydrous Calcium Silicate Heat Insulation." *Petroleum Eng.* C-55 to C-62 (April, 1952). Schuman was Director of Research at O-I. The article generally promoted Kaylo for use in refineries and similar plant applications.

> The story of how this company researched and developed the non-glass insulating material... is an inspiring example of the American Way. Without the vision, resources, and technical know-how of 'big business,' this material would not be on the market today.

Photograph shows insulator sawing a length of molded pipe insulation using a shipping carton as a bench. There is dust on the carton and floor, and the man wears no respirator. The carton reads: Handle With Care. The article comments:

> Applicators appreciate the fact that hydrous calcium silicate is non-toxic and 'easy on the hands.'

An advertisement in the same magazine also described Kaylo as "non-toxic."

12. Deposition of Everett C. Shuman, State College, Pennsylvania, in the *Gilmore* case, Aug. 19, 1980. (attorney for the plaintiff: Conard Metcalf of Boulder, Colorado.)

Mr. Shuman had only recently seen copies of reports to his company from the Saranac Laboratory on the adverse effects of inhaled Kaylo dust. However, he had been told something about the tests by Mr. Hazard in 1952 or 1953. He worked at the company's Berlin, N.J. plant in research and development of calcium silicate thermal insulation, during which time (1944-1949) he was not told of any health hazard from inhaled asbestos.

Owens-Illinois got all of its asbestos from Johns-Manville and had concerns about long-term availability of asbestos raw material.

Explaining his use of the expression, "non-toxic," in the 1952 *Petroleum Engineer* article, Shuman said:

> (T)he word toxic as I was brought up in chemistry was poison and there was no known poisons in the lime and silicate and the silica had reacted so that they were a calcium silicate, not either a lime or silica. So there was no known poison substances in the material.

The Berlin, N.J. plant was insulated with Kaylo, and workers applying it in "closed areas" were provided with respirators. Kaylo contained 18 percent (chrysotile and amosite) asbestos.

13. May, 1952. Seventh Saranac Symposium (unpublished).

This was attended by Willis Hazard of Owens-Illinois. There was considerable discussion of asbestosis and cancer at this conference. (See also "The Seventh Saranac Symposium," in Chapter 2; "Archives and Collected Papers of Scientific Researchers," in Chapter 10.)

14. Oct. 5, 1955 W.G. Hazard to M.M. Olander and Dr. C. F. Shook (Owens-Illinois).

Dr. Vorwald's successor at Saranac, Dr. Schepers, had just published the Kaylo findings without first showing the report to Owens-Illinois officials ("Effect of Inhaled Commercial Hydrous Calcium Silicate Dust on Animal Tissues." *Arch. Indust. Health* 12:348-360, 1955). The article was written in highly technical language and did not identify the substance tested as a common thermal insulation product.

> We had felt (publication of the research) would be the proper procedure for the long run, even though the experiments did *not* show Kaylo to be lily-white. They showed, to be specific, that Kaylo dust could cause asbestosis, an uncurable lung condition; and they showed the dust could reactivate tuberculosis...

Hazard commented that Kaylo was not more hazardous than universally used heat insulation, and noted:

> The names 'Kaylo' and 'Owens-Illinois' appear nowhere in the article. It's completely anonymous.

Hazard said he was glad to see this research reported in the open literature and was ordering 50 reprints.

15. F.W. Sehl and J.M. Robinson, "Special Hazards Survey/Dust Survey," Apr. 28 and May 2, 1958, prepared for Owens-Illinois Kaylo Division, by Aetna Life Affiliated Companies.

Impinger dust counts in the Berlin, N.J. plant ranged from 4.0 to 91.8 MPPCF, with all but one of the 12 samples over 5 MPPCF, half the values exceeding 10 MPPCF. The authors considered 10 MPPCF the maximum acceptable concentration of dust. Recommendations were given to bring the respirator program "up to Owens-Illinois' standards" and bring about the other industrial hygiene improvements.

On May 1, 1958, Owens-Illinois sold substantially all assets of the Kaylo Division to Owens-Corning Fiberglas Corp. Owens-Corning had been the primary purchaser of Kaylo since 1953. Documentation of Kaylo testing at Saranac was also provided to Owens-Corning. Owens-Illinois Vice President F.W. Sherwood and attorney A.C. Hirth were instrumental in organizing the Industrial Hygiene Foundation (V. Brown, cover letter and memorandum of Jan. 15, 1935, to S. Simpson). Hirth served on the I.H.F. Board of Trustees at least until 1957. OCF President Harold Boeschenstein, who received a memorandum referring to asbestosis in 1942, was then also on the Board of Directors of O-I, which owned half of OCF. O-I's public relations director from 1954-1958 was Edward C. Ames, who had learned about asbestos hazards in a similar job at OCF (See "Owens-Corning Fiberglas Corp.," this chapter).

ARMSTRONG CORK
(now Armstrong World Industries)

Armstrong was in the insulation contracting business and manufactured asbestos-containing insulation products starting in the first decade of this century. Starting in about 1939, Armstrong also sold and installed many asbestos-containing insulation products made by other companies. There were numerous contract unit workers' compensation claims for occupational asbestosis and cancer against Armstrong and other companies. The main list of such claims against firms manufacturing asbestos insulation products was produced by Armstrong in legal discovery. (See "Claims by Insulators Against Contracting Divisions of Asbestos Product Manufacturers," in Chapter 3.)

FIBREBOARD CORPORATION
(formerly Paraffine Companies, Pabco Products, Fibreboard Paper Products Corporation, and Plant Rubber & Asbestos)

This company obtained the entire capital stock of Plant Rubber and Asbestos Works in 1928. In addition to manufacturing asbestos insulation products (and gaskets, packings, shingles, and other products), the company was in the insulation contracting business. Compensation claims for asbestosis were filed against Fibreboard by the following individuals employed by the company as insulators (or their survivors):

H. Kish	1953
J. Cuthbertson	1954
J.W. Riley	1957
E. McCarrell	1959
L. Streithorst	1960
S. Gilivich	1961
J. Wyss	1962
E. Meyer	1962
A. Miller	1962
P. Greischar	1962
E. Novak	1963
R. Goans	1963
J. Faulkner	1963

All these claims were filed with offices of the California Industrial Accident Commission (See "Claims by Insulators Against Contracting Divisions of Asbestos Product Manufacturers," in Chapter 3). Mr. Meyer was diagnosed with asbestosis and lung cancer, and his physician filed a report listing many medical papers on cancer from asbestos (L. Lewis, Apr. 23, 1963, IAC Claim No. SF-199-141).

Another claim for compensation for asbestosis was filed against Fibreboard by John Peretti, a foreman at the insulation manufacturing plant in Emeryville, California, in 1961. Compensation for partial disability was awarded in 1962.

Former Emeryville plant manager Edmond Torbohn has testified that he never relied upon Threshold Limit Values to determine whether asbestos dust conditions were safe or unsafe. He never heard of the "Fleisher-Drinker report" published in 1946, until it came up in litigation decades later. Fibreboard did not test products for harmfulness before 1966, he said (deposition in *Dartez v. Owens-Illinois et al.*, U.S. Dist. Court, E. Dist. of Texas, Beaumont Div., C.A. No. B-81-227, Feb. 6, 1989).

Pabco Products was a member of the Magnesia Insulation Manufacturers Association in the 1950s, and Fibreboard was a member of the National Insulation Manufacturers Association in the 1960s.

OWENS-CORNING FIBERGLAS CORPORATION (OCF)

OCF was organized in 1938 and initially manufactured fiberglass ("Fiberglas") insulation, a competitor of asbestos-containing insulation materials. OCF used asbestos and fiberglass to make insulating cement from 1940-1951. OCF made a number of other products with asbestos, including coating for acoustical tile (in the 1960s) and roofing cements. In the mid-1950s, OCF was a major customer for "Kaylo," an asbestos-containing insulation made by Owens-Illinois. In 1958, OCF bought the Kaylo business outright and continued to use asbestos in Kaylo until 1972. OCF was also active in the insulation contracting business. The following material consists of internal communications produced by OCF in discovery and contract unit workers' compensation claims (filed by insulation workers).

Internal Communications, Etc.

Jan. 20, 1941. Legal and Patent Dept. letter to L.U. Gardner (Saranac Lab).

> It is indeed good news to hear that you do not feel you will encounter any evidence of an asbestos-like reaction since none of the (glass) fiber reaches the interior of the lungs.

May 23, 1941. "Trip Report." (memorandum to Harold Boeschenstein, who later became President of OCF).

Describes meeting of OCF representatives with Mr. Bartley, a union attorney and consultant, who was interested in the health effects of fiber-glass, particularly respiratory dangers. Mentions a meeting with union representatives in which the low workers' compensation insurance rate for fiber-glass manufacturers was contrasted with the rates for asbestos manufacturers, magnesia manufacturers, etc. At the meeting with Asbestos Workers Union (union of insulation installers) representatives, OCF officials read from Gardner's report on fiber-glass ("These findings may allay any skepticism as to the theoretical hazard involved from the handling of a glass wool . . ."). This memorandum also discusses meetings at American Industrial Hygiene Association and interest expressed by the National Safety Council in fiber-glass safety.

June 16, 1941. E.C. Ames memorandum to H. Boeschenstein, "Investigation of Health Aspects of Fiberglas by Dr. W.J. Siebert."

Discusses research and writing by Dr. Siebert in St. Louis, a pathologist considered reliable by the Asbestos Workers Union. Dr. Siebert questioned Gardner's implication that there was no health hazard because the glass fibers were too large to get into the lungs, and wanted to see Gardner's slides.

1941. OCF brochure featuring a letter from J. Hill (Aetna) saying workers' compensation insurance for fiber-glass was cheaper than coverage for asbestos, etc. (Industrial Health Foundation files)

Sept. 8, 1941. OCF legal and patent department letter ordering government reprints of the asbestos industrial hygiene reports of Page and Bloomfield, Lanza *et al.* from *Public Health Reports.*

Jan. 7, 1942. Ed Ames memorandum to Harold Boeschenstein, President of OCF.

Jan. 7, 1942. Ed Ames memorandum to E.J. Marshall.

These describe a plan to "take the offensive" in 1942, by going to the Asbestos Workers Union with documentation on asbestosis. To further make fiber-glass an attractive alternative to asbestos, OCF considered offering the assurance that product safety was, in effect, "certified," by low-cost product liability coverage purchased by OCF from the insurer, Aetna (See "The Owens-Corning Fiber-glass Itch Documents" in Chapter 3).

Mar. 13, 1943. L.U. Gardner letter to E.C. Ames.

Reports on examination of pre-employment chest X-rays, notes that R. Smock "shows a reaction strongly suggestive of asbestosis," urges rejection for employment at OCF.

Dec. 27, 1943. Ed Ames memorandum to C.E. Gregory. "Public Relations Angles in Branch and Division Post War Survey."

> In formulating our policy on admixtures with asbestos, we should keep on the alert because otherwise *we will run the risk of smearing Fiberglas with the hazards of exposure to asbestos."* (original emphasis)

Talks about premium rates charged by insulators to handle fiber-glass, discusses "the itch" as a marketing obstacle.

Nov. 21, 1944. Dr. A.E. Canfield letter to Ed Ames

Nov. 22, 1944 Ed Ames letter to Dr. Canfield.

Undated letter from Dr. Canfield to Ed Ames

Jan. 21, 1946. Don Hanna letter to Medical Department (copy from OCF files).

Discusses asbestosis in insulation worker Albert Baumgardner. After a claim was filed, Ohio state officials attributed the man's dust hazard to asbestos, with exposures in the "range of from 5 to 10 M."

Aug. 29, 1945. Ed Ames memo to J.A. McKay. "Todd Ship Yard Erie Basin." Says in part:

> The asbestos fiber is the only silicate that has been determined by lung pathologists to involve a lung hazard . . . The asbestos fibers of certain particle size and in certain concentrations can penetrate into the respiratory passages and cause havoc when they reach the alveoli of the lungs where they set up a chemical reaction with body fluids, similar to that found in silicotics.

April 7, 1947. A.R. Morrison (OCF Laboratories, Newark, OH). Memorandum for the Record. "Dust Counts".

Reports on dust counts in OCF Insulation Cement Dept. taken for the purpose of determining the "extent of an asbestos dust hazard." Total dust counts were made and reduced to account for average asbestos fractions, with the result that the "asbestos concentrations' calculated were 7 to 12 MPPCF (first floor) and 12 to 25 MPPCF (2d floor). This was contrasted by the OCF laboratory author with the 5 MPPCF limit for asbestos set by the Ohio Dept. of Health. Possible control options listed were substitution of asbestos, installation of exhaust ventilation, and continual use of respirators by the workers.

Dec. 6, 1955. T.S. Rogers memorandum to H. Boeschenstein. "New Health Hazard Research Fine Fibered Fiberglas Products."

Describes Schepers' report of old Saranac studies ("An Experimental Study of the Effects of Glass Wool on Animal Lungs." *Arch. Indust. Health 12*:276-279, 1955) commenting on adverse effects of small-diameter fibrous glass. Memo warns of potential resulting liability and advises that $15,000 is available for a "defensive" research contract.

Feb. 6, 1956. G.W.H. Schepers (Saranac Laboratory) letter to M. Burch (OCF Director of Personnel and Industrial Relations).

Feb. 8, 1956. John D. Black memorandum to Dr. Charles Bishop.

Schepers urges OCF to sponsor research to see if fiber-glass is carcinogenic. Asbestos "fairly well incriminated as a carcinogen." Attorney Black disappointed that the requested letter was "certainly nothing that we could show customers or a union."

July 27, 1956. G.W.H. Schepers (Saranac Laboratory) letter to M. Burch (OCF Director of Personnel and Industrial Relations). Informs OCF that fiber-glass does not produce fibrosis of the lungs as asbestos does.

Oct. 11, 1956. W.L. Bowes memorandum to John Black (OCF). "Asbestos Workers Union."

Oct. 16, 1956. J.D. Black memorandum to W.L. Bowes. "Asbestos Workers Union."

Nov. 20, 1956. Ira I. Brought (consultant) letter to M.D. Burch (OCF).

These documents discuss union concerns about occupational lung disease hazards, and OCF officials' fears that fibrous glass may be implicated as a cause.

May 9, 1957. Brought letter to H. Boeschenstein (President of OCF).

Quotes minutes of western states conference of the Asbestos Workers Union, mailed out to thousands of union members. The minutes announced that due to the recognition that "a large number of men" in the trade had definite symptoms and concern that a number of deaths in one local might be job-related, the international union was "compiling facts and figures on this matter." The diseases asbestosis and silicosis were named and lung ailments were blamed on "fibrous materials."

May 23, 1957. K.S. Johnson (OCF) memorandum to M.D. Burch (OCF). "Asbestosis."

Refers to notice in *Asbestos Worker* that a motion carried at the union's western states conference to "investigate the causes of Asbestosis and allied lung ailments caused by fibrous materials..." Expresses concern that the union may again ask a premium to handle Fiberglas. "I am sure that everyone in our company is conscious of the interest of the Asbestos Workers in the problems of Asbestosis and allied diseases."

1960-1963. Union-Management Committee meetings, monthly, Berlin, N.J. plant.

Frequent and repeated mention is made of excessive dust from mechanical saws in the plant making Kaylo insulation. Almost every month, the union complained about the dust, and various control options were discussed.

May 11, 1961. B. Roy (Aetna). Special Hazards Survey, Owens-Corning Fiberglas, Berlin, NJ.

Reports that the TLV for "mineral dusts containing asbestos" of 5 MPPCF was not exceeded on a daily average basis, although exposures in some non-continuous operations were 8.4 and 11.2 MPPCF.

Sept. 17, 1963. William A. Lots (OCF, Newark Product Devel. Lab) memorandum to A.J. Pearson, "Health Hazard Kaylo vs. GPL-400."

Acknowledges that asbestos in Kaylo "when breathed into the lungs causes asbestosis which often leads to lung cancer." Notes that "all insulations are dusty and insulators seldom complain except when the dust is particularly irrritating to them."

August 12, 1964. F.H. Edwards memorandum to C.G. Staelin. "Labeling of Asbestos-Containing Products by Johns-Manville Company."

This acknowledges advance notice from Dr. K.W. Smith at Johns-Manville that his company had decided to begin using warning labels on shipping cartons of thermal insulation products containing asbestos.

> The question before us is whether or not Fiberglas' Kaylo should protect itself against more stringent and punitive health laws and the possibility of third party actions by following the J-M lead.

Aug. 8, 1966. F.H. Edwards memorandum to J.M. Briley. "Kaylo Dust—Bath Iron Works."

After noting that Kaylo is 12-18% asbestos, he says:

> Asbestos is recognized as a health hazard causing asbestosis. The threshold limit value set by ACGIH is 5 million particles per cubic foot. However, Dr. Selikoff has stated that only one fiber in the body can cause cancer... At

> this point, I believe there is reason to question the ACGIH threshold limit... Again, I suggest that we consider the labeling of our Kaylo products in the same general way that J-M labels their Thermobestos...

Feb. 9, 1968. Dr. J.L. Konzen memo to Robert L. Logan (OCF Corporate Legal Dept.)

Refers to interrogatories sent to Dr. Selikoff in the lawsuit brought by Claude Tomplait in Texas. After noting that Tomplait had been an insulation installer for 25 years, Konzen confronted the implication that "asbestosis was a well-known entity to industrial medical practice over the entire period that Mr. Tomplait handled asbestos insulation." He concluded, "the condition was well known and well documented in the literature during the entire time that Mr. Tomplait used the insulation." No distinction was made between asbestosis from product use and product manufacture by the OCF Corporate Medical Director.

Apr. 10, 1968. W.C. Taylor memorandum to M. Hardwick. "Crocidolite Asbestos."

Notes the use of crocidolite in Kaylo on rare occasions either because it was accidentally included in an amosite shipment or purchased at a good price. Passes on request from Dr. Konzen that crocidolite not be used because of its prominence as a cancer causing agent.

Apr. 30, 1968. R. F. Shannon memorandum to W.R. Hibbard, Jr. "Corporate Planning."

Reports that program to replace asbestos in calcium silicate insulation "is temporarily on the shelf" due to shortage of manpower.

> Asbestos, the current reinforcing fiber for calcium silicates, is reported to cause cancer. Because of adverse publicity, possible court actions, and for the protection of our position in the calcium silicate market, it is necessary for OCF to eventually remove asbestos fibers from Kaylo.

May 29, 1969. D. Bradshaw memorandum to L. W. Saxby. "Asbestos-Free Insulation."

> It appears that it should be possible to go to non-asbestos insulation systems at about present costs... Let's get rid of

> asbestos in the insulation industry and we can then get rid of other costly problems which are beginning to develop.

Oct. 30, 1969. E.B. Engel (Aetna). Special Hazards Survey, Owens-Corning Fiberglas, Berlin, NJ.

Notes that 8 of 12 samples taken exceed the current TLV (5 MPPCF of total dust, "regardless of the amount of asbestos present") and all 12 exceeded the proposed TLV (2 MPPCF). Control of asbestosis hazard possible through asbestos replacement or environmental controls.

Aug. 13, 1970. G.D. Clayton (Clayton & Associates) letter to Dr. Jon Konzen (OCF Medical Director). And attached report.

Reports excessive explosure to asbestos fiber and isocyanate vapor at OCF's Bloomington, IL plant, recently purchased from Unarco. ACGIH and British standards were described as based on data that was "not ideal." Construction of an entirely new plant was recommended.

September 21, 1970. J.P. Kern memorandum to Dr. John Konzen. "Asbestos-Labeling."

> Reference is made to your memo of September 15 regarding the warning label that should appear on Kaylo. Are you saying that *we have* to do this now? I naturally would like to delay this requirement as long as possible. Please advise. (original emphasis—entire text of memorandum).

September 25, 1970. J.L. Konzen reply to J.P. Kern. "Asbestos-Labeling."

> From a health standpoint I feel that we should label the product at this time. By copy of this letter I suggest Mr. Logan comment concerning the legal need for such a label. (entire text).

It appears that identical warning labels were put on packages of all OCF thermal insulation products in 1970, acknowledging explicitly that the dust could be harmful.

Workers' Compensation Claims Brought by Insulation Workers Against OCF and its Subsidiary Contracting Divisions. OCF was joined as a defendant in claims filed by Fred Strickland (1957), James Whitcomb Riley (1958), E.O. McCarrell (1959), Clifford

Harding (1961), John Gronenthal (1961), John Wyss (1962), John Staples (1962), Paul Greischar (1963), and Robert Goans (1963) (See also "Claims by Insulators Against Contracting Divisions of Asbestos Product Manufacturers," in Chapter 3).

In addition to these claims, OCF and Johns-Manville were defendants in a claim brought by insulator Dean Templeton. The claim was filed with the Michigan Workmen's Compensation Department in 1960, and a settlement was approved in 1961 (produced in discovery by R.B. Von Wald, Corporate Counsel of Johns-Manville Sales Corp., in 1982).

In 1990, OCF acknowledged that it had records of hitherto undiscovered compensation claims by contract insulation workers alleging injury from asbestos. Those predating 1964 were:

Paul Gratishire	1962	Oakland, CA
Burton Kramer	1960	Washington (state)
Leroy C. Winters	1959	Albuquerque, NM

Another 20 such claims were filed by OCF employees in the years 1966–1970 (Amended Answers to Interrogatories, U.S. Dist. Court, Dist. S.C., Columbia Div., Mar. 13, 1990).

OCF was also named as a defendant in 1961 in the product liability suit brought against insulation manufacturers by G. Faciane (See "Lawsuits by Product Users Against Asbestos Manufacturers," in Chapter 3).

Joint advertisements by OCF and O-I in October, 1956, continued to describe Kaylo insulation as "non-toxic," in the manner previously introduced by O-I (See "Owens-Illinois," this chapter).

UNARCO
(formerly Union Asbestos & Rubber Company; since 1980, UNR Industries)

This company made "Unibestos" insulation initially at a plant in Cicero, Illinois in 1936. Another Unibestos manufacturing plant was opened in Paterson, New Jersey, in 1941; this was moved to Tyler, Texas in 1954. Unarco also operated a Unibestos manufacturing plant in Bloomington, Illinois, starting 1951.

Amosite asbestos from South Africa used by Unarco was supplied by Cape Asbestos.

In 1942 or 1943 officials of Unarco became aware that employees of their firm were developing asbestosis. A meeting was then set up with top executives of Johns-Manville Corporation to discuss the problem and measures taken to deal with it (See "A Lobster Lunch with Vandiver Brown" and "Saranac Compensation Reviews for Manufacturers" in Chapter 3, and opening quote to this chapter). Unarco Vice President R.E. Cryor received a report from the Saranac Laboratory in 1948 concerning an employee who had died with moderately advanced asbestosis and lung cancer. Dr. Vorwald at Saranac reviewed other cases for the company around that time (Vorwald patient files P-48-430, P-48-435, P-49-445, and IM-10).

In April, 1950, Unarco's Texas plant was inspected by the Safety and Claims Service, Inc. of Chicago. "The dust hazard there was described as serious although an exhaust system is in operation. Until a satisfactory dust collection system could be installed, the inspection report recommended the use of respirators by all employees in dusty areas." (from "Proposed Findings of Fact" submitted by the U.S. Department of Justice to U.S. District Court Judge William Steger in Civ. No. TY-78-104-CA, *Asbestos Litigation Reporter* June 24, 1983)

In 1952 Unarco paid the widow of a longtime employee compensation, after the man died with asbestosis and intestinal cancer (See "Cancer" in Chapter 3).

Unarco was one of the sponsors of Dr. Gardner's asbestosis research at the Saranac Laboratory starting in 1937 and was a member of the Asbestos Textile Institute in the 1950s, attending meetings where carcinogenicity of asbestos was discussed. E.A. Hayes, Unarco Personnel Director, attended the Seventh Saranac Symposium in 1952 (See "The Seventh Saranac Symposium" in Chapter 2). In September, 1952, Unarco sent a number of chest X-ray films of Illinois employees to Saranac for review (in "Proposed Findings of Fact," cited above).

This company was also a party to the censorship of all references to cancer in the report of industry-sponsored asbestos research at Saranac, published by Vorwald in 1951 (See "Early Saranac Cancer Tests with Asbestos" in Chapter 2).

PITTSBURGH-CORNING CORPORATION

Pittsburgh-Corning began manufacturing amosite asbestos insulation (Unibestos) after purchasing the business from Union Asbestos and Rubber Company (Unarco) in 1962. The manufacturing plants were in Tyler, Texas, and, starting in 1964, Port Allegany, Pennsylvania.

Previous to acquiring this business, in 1961, Pittsburgh-Corning officials met with Dr. Richard Gaze, chief scientist of Cape Asbestos and seller of the amosite raw material. Dr. Gaze described the manufacturing process and the precautions that ought to be taken to protect employees from the asbestos dust hazard. To further acquaint the Pittsburgh-Corning people with the manufacturing process and engineering controls, Dr. Gaze arranged to take them for an immediate plant tour. They flew to Canada and observed the plant owned by Holmes Foundry, another customer of Cape Asbestos making amosite asbestos insulation. Dr. Gaze has testified that he consulted with Pittsburgh-Corning "continually" over the next ten years (Deposition of Richard Gaze, in *H. Yandle et al. v. PPG Industries, Inc. et al.* U.S. Distr. Court, Eastern Dist. Texas, Tyler Div. Civil Action No. TY-74-3-CA, June 4-5, 1975).

Upon its purchase of the Unibestos business, Pittsburgh-Corning turned to the Pittsburgh Plate Glass Company (which, together with Corning Glass, had set up Pittsburgh-Corning as a joint venture in 1937) for information on asbestos hazards. In all, 10 such articles were sent to Pittsburgh-Corning Vice President Karl Baumler by PPG Manager of Plant Safety Clyde C. Ruddick (attached to letters dated May 16 and 25, 1962). Ruddick also offered to obtain information from PPG's occupational medicine consultant, Carey McCord. Dr. McCord had described asbestos dust as "a menace to health and life" in the 1930s ("Hazards of Industry," *Modern Home Medical Adviser*, M. Fishbein, Ed., Garden City Publ. Co., 1937).

Ronald K. Francis, assistant works manager at the Port Allegany plant, visited the Cape Asbestos manufacturing plant and met the company physician in England in 1965. When he returned to Pennsylvania urgently recommending the installation of engineering dust controls to prevent asbestosis and cancer, he was personally turned down by Pittsburgh-Corning President Russell Brittingham. Brittingham said the plant was already making a poorer return on capital investment than money deposited in a bank (Videotape deposition of R. Francis, in *T.D. Lyons and D. Lyons v. GAF Corp. et al.*, Civ. No. 83-1634, U.S. Dist. Court, W. Dist. of PA, taken in Pittsburgh, Sept. 28, 1983).

In the years 1964 to 1971, Pittsburgh-Corning and Pittsburgh Plate Glass hired industrial hygiene engineering consultant Morton Corn to examine conditions at both the Port Allegany and Tyler plants. In both cases, Corn identified extremely hazardous asbestos exposures and recommended specific engineering control measures (sometimes in combination with the use of respirators). Corn's recommendations were mostly not followed. At Port Allegany, where a ventilation system was eventually installed, no steps were taken to provide an enclosed conveyor to remedy the practice of workers continuously shoveling asbestos scrap from a collection bin (Depositions of Morton Corn in *H. Yandle et al. v. P.P.G. Industries, Inc., et al.* Civ. No. TY-74-3-CA, U.S. District Court for Eastern District of Texas, Tyler Div., taken in Washington D.C. Sept. 21, 1976; and *A. Barber et al. v. United States of America* Civ. No. 80-321, U.S. District Court for Western District of Pennsylvania, taken in Baltimore, Dec. 1-2, 1983).

The equipment in the Tyler plant was dismantled and buried following the plant closing. A book was written by *New Yorker* journalist Paul Brodeur about the hazardous conditions in this plant (*Expendable Americans,* Viking Press, 1974). The class action brought by 445 Tyler plant employees was settled out of court for $20 million in 1977. Pittsburgh-Corning paid $8.1 million, Union Asbestos and Rubber Co. paid $1.0 million, Cape Industries paid $5.2 million, and the U.S. government paid $5.7 million. Pittsburgh-Corning had previously made non-asbestos insulations, and was a member of the National Insulation Manufacturers Association during the years 1960–1964.

EAGLE-PICHER INDUSTRIES

Eagle-Picher began producing "Super 66" asbestos-containing insulating cement in 1938. Another product line, "One-Cote Cement," was added in 1950. The company also manufactured asbestos-free, mineral wool insulation products.

As early as 1932, the hazards of asbestos were pointedly noted in a report to the company by the U.S. Bureau of Mines. In a report of lung fibrosis among employees at the company's plant in Joplin, Missouri, where rock wool and asbestos were used, the mixing room was described as "a particularly dusty place." The report continued, "It is now known that asbestos dust is one of the most dangerous dusts to which man is exposed." Dust control was recommended throughout the plant by the author of the report, Dr. F.V. Meriwether (F.V. Meriwether report and letter of transmittal to Dr. R. R. Sayers, March 11, 1932; Bureau Director Scott Turner letter to Erbon Mahon, Safety Engineer, Eagle-Picher Co., Picher, OK, March 21, 1932. U.S. National Archives documents). Glen Christner, who began work for Eagle Picher in 1931 and retired as Vice President of the insulation division in 1963, recalls having heard about the early Bureau of Mines report at the plant when it arrived (testimony in *Kitsap Co. Cases of Shroeter, Goldmark, and Bender,* No. 81-2-00669-0, Port Orchard, WA, Nov. 1, 1984).

In 1942, a salesman reported from Texas that health officials had made unfavorable comments about "Supertemp" to a customer, Humble Oil and Refining Company. The salesman, H.M. Aber, also reported that a 1938 article, "Asbestos" (written by Gloyne and Merewether and published in the 1938 *Supplement* to the encyclopedia, *Occupation and Health,* by the International Labor Office) showed asbestos to be more dangerous than mineral wool. (See also Table 8 in Chapter 5) Aber communicated a state health official's offer to "make any reasonable test on Supertemp relative to its being injurious to workmen." (H.M. Aber. "Texas State Board of Health." Eagle-Picher Sales Co. Industrial Contact Report, April 8, 1942)

Eagle-Picher advertised its "Super 66" in the same issue of *Southern Power and Industry* that carried the article "Industrial Hygiene Importance of Dust" (Nov. 1946). The article, by N.V. Hendricks of the Georgia Dept. of Public Health, repeatedly referred to asbestos as a threat to health warranting engineering controls and exposure monitoring.

The Research Library of the Eagle-Picher firm accumulated the following documents relating to asbestosis:

Document	Year Received	Comments
Drinker, P. and T. Hatch. *Industrial Dust* New York: McGraw-Hill Book Co., (1936).	1938	section on asbestosis pp. 32-34
Johnstone, R.T. *Occupational Medicine and Industrial Hygiene* St. Louis: C.V. Mosby Co., (1948).	1953	Chapter 30 on asbestosis notes that occupational exposure occurs in the insulation trade
Sax, N.I. *Handbook of Dangerous Materials* New York: Reinhold Publ. Co., (1951).	1951	notes that occupational exposure occurs in insulation work, p. 34

Eagle-Picher was the primary defendant in the product liability case filed by the widow of insulator C. Faciane in 1960 (See "Lawsuits by Product Users Against Asbestos Manufacturers," in Chapter 3).

Correspondence of officials of the company also dealt with the subject of health hazards of Eagle-Picher insulations.

July 8, 1960. R. Beaudry letter to Eagle Picher Sales Co., and July 21, 1960 reply from Glen Christner (V.P. Insulation Div.).

Insurance claims adjuster writes that E-P mineral wool products used in 1946–1948 are suspected of contributing to asbestosis in an insulator. Christner reply says products sold in those years contained no asbestos.

April 6, 1965. P.L. Losse letter to R. Alexander (Sun Shipbuilding and Drydock Co. Chester, PA).

> Notes that "minor amounts" of asbestos and other materials were used in the products. "(W)hile each of these added ingredients could be a health hazard if exposure were to a high concentration, such is not the case." After mentioning occasional dermatitis problems, Losse concluded: "In view of the above relative minor hazard potential for the materials we manufacture, we do not have any medical reports relative to this matter."

May 22, 1968. P.K. Maitre letter to F.J. Hess (Shell Oil Co. Wood River, Illinois.)

> The above Eagle-Picher products (Super 66 and One-Cote cements) do not contain any toxic ingredients. Therefore, no antidotes are needed.

Subsequent to the filing of a civil claim against Eagle-Picher in 1963, attorneys employed by and representing the company met with Johns-Manville Medical Director K.W. Smith. A memorandum of these discussions observed that:

> Dr. Smith gave us an example of samples taken of a man who was exposed approximately 5 minutes an hour who sustained a serious asbestosis in a working period of only a few months.

The use of warning labeling was also discussed. This memorandum was withheld for years under the claim of attorney-client privilege ("Conference Feb. 19, 1964, Eagle-Picher Insulation Plant, Joplin, Missouri"; and Affidavit of E-P Vice President James Ralston in *Heathman*, Case No. 87-C-1934, Brazoria Co., TX, March 25, 1988; and videotaped deposition of E-P corporate representative, R. Bochstaller, by former insulation worker, attorney Lawrence Madeksho, of Houston, TX, in *Heathman* case, Mar. 2, 1989). The document's existence was revealed after it was inadvertently produced by E-P in discovery, in a lawsuit E-P had filed against the U.S. government.

An internal memorandum about the size of printing to use in labeling product hazards reflects the dominance of commercial considerations over concern for the consumer's awareness of health risks. Placement and design of health warnings predictably prevented their notice by many workers handling labeled insulation products.

> This is large and clear enough type face to be completely legible, yet does not 'shout CAUTION from the roof tops.'
>
> (W.F. McCarthy, E-P Advertising Dept. memorandum to Alton L. Jones, Joplin Insulation Plant, "Type Face for 'Caution' Notice, June 19, 1964.")

In a letter July 20, 1970, Dr. Irving Selikoff urged Eagle-Picher President W. Atteberry to market asbestos cement products in plastic bags to facilitate lower worker exposures by enclosed mixing (as opposed to mixing in open troughs).

Retired Eagle-Picher engineer Herman Lee Huelster has testified that, although asbestos was used in the company's insulating cements from 1942 to 1971, it was never needed. He attributed the use of asbestos to pressures from the company sales department, and characterized this as a "sales gimmick." Huelster had always objected to spending "big money for an ingredient that we did not manufacture ourselves and (which) did nothing to improve the insulating qualities of the product." He attributed the requirement for asbestos in some Naval specifications for insulating cements not to technical purposes, but rather to "clout" of firms with major interests in asbestos (deposition taken Aug. 28, 1980 in *Zsamba v. State Insulation Corp. et al.* Superior Court of New Jersey, Middlesex County, No. L-32392-770).

Eagle-Picher was a member of the Industrial Hygiene Foundation during the years 1936–1961, and thus received the *Industrial Hygiene Digest* abstracts on industrial medicine and hygiene. The company was also a member of the National Insulation Manufacturers Association in 1960, when NIMA considered the possibility of a health program and rejected it.

UNITED STATES GYPSUM COMPANY

U.S. Gypsum has manufactured a wide range of building products in which asbestos is used. These include trowel-applied and sprayed acoustical plasters, sprayed insulation, block insulation, ceiling tiles, and paints.

The company was associated with the Saranac Laboratory from the early 1930s, when tissue samples from employees were examined for pathological effects of gypsum dust. After purchasing the National Asbestos Co. plant (in Jersey City, NJ), USG had the Saranac Laboratory conduct a survey. Loading and packing asbestos cement were among the most hazardous jobs, with exposures of 261 MPPCF. Asbestosis was diagnosed in 5 workers and suspected in the cases of 5 others. The findings were transmitted to USG Vice President W.L. Keady ("Report of Dust Survey at National Asbestos Co. Plant of United States Gypsum Co. at Jersey City, NJ," by L.U. Gardner, Saranac Laboratory, May 25-June 2, 1936; and "Dust Survey—Jersey City," 3-pp. memorandum to W.L. Keady from General Service Manager, Aug. 13, 1936). The memorandum characterized the asbestos dust hazard as "serious."

USG was one of the contributors to the series of asbestos experiments started at Saranac in 1937 (See "Raybestos-Manhattan, Inc.," this chapter.) The company received progress reports on Saranac asbestos experiments from Vandiver Brown at Johns-Manville. USG was also a party to the censorship of all references to cancer in the report of industry-sponsored asbestos research at Saranac, published by Vorwald in 1951 (See "Early Saranac Laboratory Cancer Tests with Asbestos" in Chapter 2).

On September 16, 1937, sales manager C.G. Scharwath wrote that a suit had been filed by a "former assistant bookkeeper of the old National Asbestos Company, whose desk (was) at least more than 200 feet away from any machinery; as well as being segregated in the office from the factory." USG's Assistant to the President, J.S. Offutt, responded by letter September 29, 1937, that General Counsel attorney Charles Price would be in touch regarding the alleged asbestosis suit. Further details were included in a note to Price from Jersey City lawyer J.J. Cuneo on October 8, 1937. Mr. Wetzel, the plaintiff, had worked for 3 or 4 years and on occasion entered the area of the plant where manufacturing took place. Price replied on Oct.

28, 1937 that USG had never defended a case brought for asbestosis and recommended that Saranac be requested to conduct a physical examination with chest X-ray and render an opinion.

An internal operations bulletin of the company listed substances to which excessive exposure was hazardous, including asbestos (1948). In 1954, a similar company document noted, "Operations involving manual handling of asbestos in any plant shall be considered an area in which employees shall be required to wear adequate respiratory equipment" ("Elimination of Dusty Conditions," No. 2-5, Feb. 11, 1954).

Published literature accumulated at the company's research center library in Libertyville, Illinois, includes: *The Pneumokonioses (Silicosis),* Vol 1 (see "Abstracts," in Chapter 10); the 1938 Public Health Service Bulletin on asbestosis by Dreessen and co-workers; and the text *Industrial Dust* (1954 edition), by Drinker and Hatch, with the British statistics linking asbestosis and cancer of the lung in the chapter on asbestosis.

In 1949, a former employee at a shingle plant of USG died from asbestosis. His son, Ben Miriello, wrote a bitter letter to the company (June 8, 1950) describing his father's suffocating terminal condition and his mother's illness following the death of his father. He enclosed a copy of his father's death certificate naming asbestosis as the cause of death. In December of 1950, Mr. Miriello wrote again and received a reply (Dec. 27, 1950, signature illegible) acknowledging receipt of both his letters. The reply, from corporate headquarters in Chicago, assured that it was company policy and practice to safeguard the health of employees. Mr. Miriello was invited to visit the Jersey City USG plant where his father had worked in the Thirties and see for himself.

USG manufactured "Spraydon," a spray-applied acoustical plaster, for Sprayon Research Corporation. In 1969, the Sprayon firm applied warning labels because of the asbestos hazard from this product, and in 1970 the product was reformulated to eliminate asbestos. In the meantime, USG continued to manufacture "Audicote," another spray-applied acoustical plaster with asbestos it had sold since the 1950s but which did not carry warning labels until 1973. In that year, this class of products was, in effect, banned by the U.S. Environmental Protection Agency as an air pollution hazard (*Fed. Reg.*, April 6, 1973).

USG was represented at a Sept. 19, 1967 meeting of the Gypsum Association where a report of "lung cancer" cases in the neighborhood of an asbestos plant was discussed. In 1970, USG was among the members of the Asbestos Cement Products Association willing to warn the public that sawing asbestos-cement products would create a "health risk"—if agreement could be reached within the industry (See "National Gypsum Company" later in this chapter).

In view of its history, jurors were surprised by USG's sworn Answers to Interrogatories to the effect that the company's first awareness of a relationship between asbestos and asbestosis dated from 1975 (signed by J. Hernan, *Lexington County, South Carolina School District v. U.S. Gypsum*, No. 82-2072-0, trial in April, 1984).

SOUTHERN TEXTILE CORPORATION
(Southern Asbestos, H.K. Porter, Thermoid)

The original Southern Asbestos Company was incorporated in 1927 in Charlotte, N.C. A manufacturer in Charleston, S.C., Thermoid Corporation, purchased the fixed assets of Southern Asbestos in 1941. H.K. Porter Company acquired Thermoid Corporation by merger in 1958. A few years earlier (1954), Porter had acquired the Laclede Christy Works in St. Louis, where high-temperature insulating cements and blocks were made. In the early 1960s, Porter also took over Carolina Asbestos Company and Russell Manufacturing Company. H.K. Porter formed a subsidiary, Southern Asbestos Company, in 1974, and this was renamed Southern Textile Corporation in 1979 (Thomas H. Hart, III, Blatt and Fales, Barnwell, S.C.).

Southern Asbestos was the object of an exposé in the *Philadelphia Record* in 1935 (See "Newspaper Articles," Chapter 10). Thermoid Corporation and Southern Asbestos were two of the original industrial sponsors of Dr. Gardner's asbestos experiments at Saranac. Thermoid was also a party to the censorship of all reference to cancer in the report of industry-sponsored asbestos research at Saranac, published by Vorwald in 1951 (See "Early Saranac Laboratory Cancer Tests with Asbestos" in Chapter 2).

"Many" of the asbestotics described in Shull's report ("Asbestosis: A Roentgenologic Review of 71 Cases," *Radiology 27*:279-292, 1936) were Southern employees (G. Fabel, President of Southern Asbestos, letter to Sumner Simpson, Raybestos-Manhattan, Dec. 18, 1936). The company was also an active member of the Asbestos Textile Institute starting in the mid-1940s, and had no medical monitoring program for its employees at the time of the Hemeon report to A.T.I. in 1947 See "Industry Trade Associations and Research Organizations," in Chapter 10).

Dr. O.A. Sander was the medical consultant representing Southern Asbestos Company at the Oct. 6, 1954 meeting of the Asbestos Textile Institute at which Dr. Schepers presented a review of the literature on asbestos and cancer. Sander also authored a report in which "moderately well developed asbestosis" was described in a plumber's helper. The man's work history involved less than 10 years of this work, sawing pipe coverings, "usually in confined basement rooms." But the emphasis of this presentation was that doctors should be careful to not scare workers, producing "doctor-induced disability." ("Asbestosis as Differentiated from Other Pneumoconioses." *Arch. Indust. Health 12*:208-211, 1955) In an article for surgeons, Sander reported:

> The pessimism of the past is being replaced by the realization that a diagnosis of silicosis or asbestosis is compatible with good health and a feeling of well-being. ("Silicosis and Asbestosis." *Amer. J. Surg. 90*:115-119, 1955)

Shortly after H.K. Porter acquired Thermoid Company, the manager of the Thermoid plant in Charleston, S.C. published an article about their historic problem with asbestosis and efforts in dust control (J. Mitchell, "Health Progress in an

Asbestos Textile Works," *Arch. Environ. Health* 3:37-41, 1961). Conditions in 1936 and 1960 were compared, including narrative descriptions and dust counts for both periods. The 1936 figures were all in the 45-210 MPPCF range, and the 1960 ones were all less than 5 MPPCF (See also "Asbestos Air Pollution in the Community" in Chapter 7).

Documents obtained in discovery describe reactions at the time of the New York Academy of Sciences conference on asbestos in 1964.

Nov. 6, 1964. John A. Brown (President, Asbestos Textile Institute) letter to J.T. Griffis (H.K. Porter Company).

> I am attaching three copies of news releases A, B, and C which were supposed to have been released to the press during the conference on the Biological Effects of Asbestos at the Waldorf Astoria several weeks ago. Fortunately, due to the alertness of Mr. Edward Shuman of J-M and Mr. Robert Cryor, of North American Asbestos Company, these releases were discovered before their release, and the resultant objections that arose in the meeting, because of the sensationalism of the material held up their issuance...
>
> I also feel that this subject should not be brought to the attention of other than management of our several companies, as any discussion on this situation by sales personnel with users of our products could possibly aggravate the situation and result in individual opinions which could be damaging.

Nov. 4, 1964. Dr. Hillis L. Seay (chest physician and plant physician to H.K. Porter in Huntersville, N.C.) letter to J.T. Griffis.

> Notes that Seay had attended the international conference on asbestos disease at the request of H.K. Porter Company. This 4-page report includes findings, quotes from presentations, and recommendations.

KEENE CORPORATION
(Ehret Magnesia, Baldwin-Hill, Baldwin-Ehret-Hill)

Insulation manufacturers Ehret Magnesia and Baldwin-Hill merged to form Baldwin-Ehret-Hill in 1959, which in turn was taken over by Keene Corporation in 1968.

In 1930, Ehret ran monthly advertisements in *Asbestos* magazine on the inside back cover. In the March issue, there was also an article on pulmonary asbestosis. The company hired a sales clerk in 1936 named Dwight Satterthwaite, and within one month he learned that asbestos was a dangerous dust (Deposition of D.L. Satterthwaite, *In Re: All Asbestos Cases*, C.P. 77-1, U.S. Dist. Court E. Dist. VA, Aug. 29, 1983).

In 1952, Ehret Magnesia hired chemist John D. McAllister, who had worked for Owens-Illinois, to develop a calcium silicate insulation product. Employees in the pilot plant set up in the 1950s were required to wear respirators, and dust control equipment was used in the process. When the process was expanded and a commercial scale plant built, McAllister examined respirators on the market and bought enough to make them available plant-wide. Around this time, the company's insurer conducted air sampling in the plant. In the late 1950s, McAllister recalls that there was considerable discussion over the deaths of three Ehret workers from lung cancer and nonmalignant lung conditions (Deposition of J.D. McAllister, same case as Satterthwaite deposition).

E.R. Stevens, President of Baldwin-Ehret-Hill from 1959-1968, has testified that the use of asbestos in insulating cements was unnecessary, and the use of a small fraction of asbestos in "Monoblock" (1940-1968 or later) was just a "sales gimmick." Stevens was among industrialists attending presentations by Dr. Selikoff in 1964, where hazards to insulators were discussed (E.R. Stevens deposition in *Bade et al. v. Armstrong World Industries et al.* Superior Court of NJ, Middlesex Co. Docket No. W-000026-87, Jan. 24, 1989).

Baldwin-Hill patents in the 1950s stressed that insulations whose use entailed "a minimum of dusting" would have "practically no industrial health hazard." These patents also demonstrated that mineral wool could be used instead of asbestos (Patent No. 2,633,433, granted in 1953; and No. 2,732,295, granted in 1956).

On February 9, 1976, within months after the U.S. Environmental Protection Agency banned asbestos-containing molded insulation, Keene's Joseph Saville wrote to a Miami firm about liquidating Keene's inventory of calcium silicate insulation. He offered to discount material with a "list value" of $70,000, for export "outside of the continental United States." (letter to Edgar Gerber, Multi-Trades Inc.)

In 1982, samples of warehoused insulation at Amerada Hess' giant oil refinery in St. Croix were analyzed to see if they contained asbestos. A sample of Thermacil calcium silicate from Keene Corporation, labeled asbestos-free on the bag, was found to have 20-25% amosite asbestos. Orders were sent to the refinery to remove the material and dispose of it (O.W. Henderson memorandum to W. Jones, "Asbestos Samples," Jan. 19, 1983).

Ehret Magnesia was a member of the Magnesia Insulation Manufacturers Association in the 1950s, and Baldwin-Ehret-Hill belonged to the National Insulation Manufacturers Association in the 1960s.

UNION CARBIDE CORPORATION

Union Carbide operated chrysotile asbestos mines in California from 1963 until 1985. So-called "Calidria" asbestos is short grade fiber, and has been used as a filler, reinforcing agent, opacifier, and thickening agent in such products as drywall patching compounds, plastics, and paints.

One country where sales resistance was soon encountered was the United Kingdom. Media stories and anticipated pressures from unions and government inspectors prompted "over 20 potential customers" to request assurance that Carbide's material would not endanger their employees. Dockers were refusing to handle imported sacks of asbestos in London and Liverpool.

Union Carbide's New York headquarters issued at least two internal communications on asbestos hazards in 1966. A rather thorough 19-page report was then prepared by I.C. Sayers of the Alloys Division of Union Carbide U.K. Limited (*Asbestos as a Health Hazard in the United Kingdom*, 1967). This last report was located at the library of the Quebec Asbestos Mining Association in Montreal (now called Asbestos Institute; document no.

3095), where the index card on it read, "Confidential—not circulated."

Sayers' review describes the 1965 mesothelioma epidemiology study of Newhouse and Thompson. It has separate sections on asbestosis, lung cancer, and mesothelioma. Mesothelioma is described as the "most disturbing" effect because it could occur after only brief exposure. The 1938 TLV of 5 MPPCF is described as an arbitrary choice having no experimental foundation. "There is a growing feeling that the quoted 'Threshold Limit Value' is no longer tenable." In a section entitled "Moral Issues" the report states:

> On the basis of present evidence we are not entitled under any circumstances to state that our material is not a health hazard. What is more, if it is believed that a potential customer would use our material 'dangerously,' and that he is unaware of the toxicity question, then it must surely be our duty to caution him and point out means whereby he can hold the asbestos air float concentration to a minimum.

Union Carbide sacks of asbestos did not bear warning labels until late 1971 or 1972.

On August 15, 1975, Dr. Arthur Rohl and co-workers at the Mt. Sinai School of Medicine published a report in *Science* on the high levels of airborne asbestos exposure entailed by mixing, sanding, and sweeping up after applying drywall spackling and joint compounds. The Natural Resources Defense Council then petitioned the Consumer Product Safety Commission to ban asbestos in such products. Throughout 1977, Union Carbide led the opposition to the ban. The day before the ban order was published in the *Federal Register,* Union Carbide reiterated its objection, on the basis that "consumer" exposure (as distinct from occupational exposure) did not entail an "unreasonable risk" (H.B. Rhodes and J.F. Collings, Union Carbide Corp. Metals Div. letter to R.D. Pittle, Consumer Product Safety Commission, Dec. 14, 1977).

Union Carbide hired Dr. Hans Weill, longtime asbestos industry consultant and chest physician, to fly to Bhopal, India, in the wake of the catastrophic chemical release in that city on December 3, 1984. Dr. Weill, who also serves as an expert witness in asbestos product liability suits, has testified (*Timm v. Raymark* Solano County, CA Case No. 85911, Jan. 14-15, 1985) that he was correctly quoted in the *New York Times*, which reported on December 15, 1984:

> Dr. Weill said that the victims who had survived to this point "have an encouraging prognosis" and that most would probably recover fully.

This extraordinarily optimistic outlook was not shared by the editors of the prestigious journal, *Lancet*, who stated that longterm lung effects "can be expected" (Dec. 15, 1984). Nor has it been borne out by experience. In March, 1985, Indian doctors reported that pulmonary fibrosis had developed in approximately 20,000 people, diagnosable by chest X-ray and pulmonary function tests.

Even before the purchase of the asbestos mines, Union Carbide (Chemicals Co.) was aware that asbestos dust was hazardous and conducted tests to determine the relative exposures from Johns-Manville and Owens-Corning thermal insulation products (See 1962 Peele study in Table 8, Chapter 5).

Union Carbide played a leading role in the National Safety Council in the 1930s and in the Industrial Hygiene Foundation in the 1940s, having representatives on the executive boards of these organizations. Carbide sent three representatives to the Seventh Saranac Symposium in 1952, where asbestosis and cancer were discussed repeatedly (See "The Seventh Saranac Symposium" in Chapter 2). As a major chemical company, Carbide would have made use of *Chemical Abstracts*, which contained numerous citations on asbestos disease (See "Abstracts," in Chapter 10).

W.R. GRACE & COMPANY

W.R. Grace bought Dewey & Almy Chemical Co., which had made asbestos brake linings, in 1954. In 1963, Grace purchased the Zonolite Company, which operated the world's largest vermiculite mines (in Libby, Montana). Zonolite made "Mono-Kote" fireproofing cement and asbestos-containing acoustical plaster.

The Dewey & Almy Chemical Company had numerous compensation claims brought by employees of its "Multibestos" plant, which closed in Massachusetts in 1936. Bradley Dewey, the firm's president, was interested in the subject of asbestosis and corresponded with a state official and others about it (See "Rising Tide of Compensation in the 1930s" in Chapter 3). Some asbestosis cases at the Multibestos plant were reviewed at the Saranac Laboratory in the mid-1930s (Vorwald Patient Files, Nos. P-31-37, P-35-85, P-34-101, P-35-129, and P-36-124, Armed Forces Institute of Pathology, Washington, DC).

The Montana operation was originally called the Vermiculite and Asbestos Corporation when mining began in 1919 (both minerals were present in the deposit). Large-scale production began in the 1930s, as vermiculite-expanding factories were built in Spokane, Chicago, and Detroit. The vermiculite was used just in insulation at first, then in concrete mixes in the 1950s.

Montana State Board of Health industrial hygienist Benjamin Wake visited the Libby mine and mill in 1956 and took atmospheric dust samples. Total dust counts averaged 40 MPPCF. Relying on company records saying the dust was 8-21% asbestos, Wake estimated that the maximum concentration of total dust should not exceed 25-30 MPPCF. Numerous recommendations were made to management to improve dust control in the mill.

Wake returned to the plant in 1958, again taking air samples (average total dust: 23.8 MPPCF) and making even more extensive recommendations for dust control. He again called attention to asbestos as a respiratory hazard. Conditions were still poor in 1962, with 20 dust counts averaging 43.3 MPPCF. Based on an analysis indicating that 40% of the airborne dust was tremolite asbestos, Wake suggested a maximum of 12 MPPCF to limit the pure asbestos exposure to 5 MPPCF. There was no improvement in 1963, either.

Wake's reports were all marked, "This report is confidential and is not for distribution except to the management of the Zonolite Company." The reports were all titled "Report on an Industrial Hygiene Study of the Zonolite Company Libby, Montana" (Aug. 8-9, 1956; Jan. 12, 1959; Apr. 19, 1962; and Apr. 11, 1963. Montana State Board of Health reports).

Documents produced in discovery relate to conditions from the standpoint of management:

June 14, 1961. Letter from E. Lovick (Libby plant manager) to C.A. Pratt (VP, Western Mineral Products Co.) acknowledges that asbestosis is a matter of concern based on "many studies." The 1956 report from the Montana State Board of Health is quoted as saying asbestos dust is "of considerable toxicity." A 19-year mill employee was very disabled and sent to a TB sanitarium where he was diagnosed as having "questionable asbestosis." Montana's inclusion of occupational disease coverage in the workers' comp. law in 1959 was accompanied by the company's decision to institute an employee X-ray program. Doctors' reports are said to have been inconclusive on the question of whether there was a lung disease hazard in the plant. Asbestos in concentrates shipped to vermiculite expanding plants should give rise to "very small" amounts of it in the dust in expansion plants. "Dust Foe" respirators provided.

Aug. 11, 1961. Letter from Pratt to Lovick states that Western Mineral Products (WMP) also has pre-employment X-rays and appreciates any effort to lower the asbestos content of the ore.

Sept. 15, 1961. Letter from Pratt to J.A. Kelley (Zonolite) mentions that Minneapolis Health Dept. has expressed concern about dust in vermiculite plants.

Apr. 2, 1964. Letter from Pratt to Kelley mentions a claim for total disability compensated in Minneapolis; and another worker seen by a Dr. Park who was advised to leave the employ of WMP.

Aug. 25, 1964. Letter from Dr. W. Nelson in Libby to J. Kelley (President, Zonolite Div. of W.R. Grace) asks for expenses to go to a medical center and obtain clinical training in occupational lung diseases. He notes that his 1959 X-ray study showed "an unusually high incidence of basilar fibrosis," at Zonolite. The survey was repeated in 1964, and "the consensus of local medical opinion was that an important increased incidence of chronic respiratory disease existed in Zonolite employees who had prolonged exposure to dust." Preliminary analysis showed "distinct and important change in respiratory function and pathology." He had not charged for his services but now requested assistance to consult and make time for a competent analysis of his data.

Oct. 21, 1964. Letter from Dr. Siemens (Alberta Dept. Pub. Hlth.) to T.A. Williams (Grant Industries) reports that 7/9 workers examined had abnormal forced breathing curves and 2 had fibrosis, recommends respirators. Attached is a note from H. Buchwald (16 Sept. 1964) calling attention to the use of asbestos in "Mono-Kote." Asbestos is described as a "well known cause of lung fibrosis...It is most important that dust respirators be worn when any work is done with ground asbestos."

Dec. 3, 1964. Letter from Williams to Dr. Siemens assures that no adverse health effects had been seen among U.S. Zonolite plant workers. It does acknowledge a danger from asbestos and the need to use respirators.

Dec. 8, 1964. Letter from N. Bushell (Grant Industries) to J.A. Kelley encloses all the above Williams-Siemens correspondence.

Dec. 29, 1964. Letter from L. Park (MD Casualty) to F.W. Rupp (WRG-Zonolite) suggests respirator use and maintenance program to follow.

Jan. 2, 1965. Memo from R.A. Bleich (Libby plant) to J.A. Kelley (WRG headquarters) comments on reports from Montana State Board of Health and says, "I can only say it presents a very sorry record."

Jan. 2, 1965. Memo from Lovick (Libby) to J.A. Kelley, "Dust at Libby," reviews events. The doctors' findings in the 1959 health survey were described as equivocal. A 1964 follow-up exam had pulmonary function tests in addition to chest X-rays: 30/143 showed emphysema or fibrosis, and in 14 there was progression in the serial X-rays since 1959. Of 39 hourly workers with over 10 yrs. employment, 18 were classed as abnormal. One 19-yr employee with severe impairment was ultimately diagnosed as having "questionable asbestosis." In 1962 a Wyoming doctor said his patient, a former employee, had progressive fibrosis resembling asbestosis. In 1961, a Spokane doctor told the company that another former employee had extensive bilateral pneumoconiosis with definite progression. "These cases were referred to Chicago and handled by our insurance carrier." There had been other cases, too. Attachments listed included a survey report by Dr. Nelson and medical reports on 4 employees with 7-19 years' employment.

Feb. 4, 1965. Bushell asks Kelley if Zonolite had contacted the Alberta health dept. and notes that 2 employees were being sent to a chest clinic at the dept.'s recommendation.

Feb. 9, 1965. O.F. Stewart (WRG headquarters) reply to Bushell acknowledges that the presence of asbestos in Libby vermiculite, and says there have been reports of "men having pulmonary trouble," at Libby and WMP. Letter details steps being taken to control dust and disease at WRG plants. Attachments speak to growing public concern, and letter says to anticipate increasing government regulation in designing dust control into plants.

Oct. 4, 1965. Report by Dr. Wiley (Los Angeles Co. Div. Occup. Health) says CA Zonolite plant had no apparent hazard—even though breathing zone of operator "mixing Mono-Kote, asbestos side" was 7.7 MPPCF.

Jan. 5, 1968. "Personal and confidential" memo from P. Kostic to R.W. Sterrett (WRG Zonolite Div.) summarizes meetings with Johns-Manville environmental specialists E. Fenner and C. Sheckler. The main focus is on 32 Libby workers with abnormal chest X-rays, and the need to attain exposures in the plant of no more than 5 MPPCF total dust. "Fenner and Sheckler emphasized that Threshold Limits should be used as guides... and should not be regarded as fine lines between safe and dangerous conditions."

Nov. 28, 1969. Memo from T.F. Egan to R.W. Sterrett describes a presentation by Dr. Irving Selikoff on the hazards of sprayed asbestos insulation. "The officials of the international unions were there along with the contractors and I know it landed like a bomb. We must go all out to get asbestos out of Mono-Kote at once."

July 15, 1970. Report by W.C. Cooper, J.L. Balzer, and D.P. Fowler, *Asbestos Fiber Concentrations in Air from Spray Fireproofing Operations Using Zonolite Products,* Tabershaw-Cooper Associates, Berkeley, CA. Samples of exposures to workers applying sprayed fireproofing of vermiculite-asbestos cement were taken at several construction sites. The highest exposures were spray gun operators', 2.5 to 8 f/cc. Other members of spray crews were exposed to 0.5 to 1.9 f/cc. Exposures on other floors than those being sprayed and in the neighborhood of buildings where spraying was being done were less than 0.01 f/cc.

As a major chemical company, WRG would have made use of *Chemical Abstracts*, which contained numerous citations on asbestos disease (See "Abstracts," in Chapter 10).

GAF CORPORATION
(Ruberoid)

Ruberoid Company operated asbestos mines in Vermont starting in 1936 and also made asbestos insulation and shingles. Ruberoid also manufactured asbestos-cement panels and siding. It was taken over by GAF Corporation in 1967.

Ruberoid had a full-page advertisement in the March, 1930, issue of *Asbestos* magazine that carried an article on asbestosis.

In the 1930s, employees of a Ruberoid plant in St. Louis sued the company, claiming they suffered respiratory impairment from their exposures to dust. The plaintiffs charged that management had been negligent in not posting warnings of the dangers, not installing exhaust ventilation equipment, and failing to provide respirators and medical examinations to the workers (Samuel Robertson and Alexander Smith suits against Eternit, U.S.A., which became part of Ruberoid in 1930, and Ruberoid Co., Circuit Court of City of St. Louis, both filed in 1934). The outcomes of these cases are not known. GAF has acknowledged that 3 more similar cases were filed against

Eternit and Ruberoid in 1935, and has stated that these cases were dismissed.

In 1952, a workers' compensation claim was filed against Ruberoid by another worker at the Missouri plant, Fee James, who claimed he was totally disabled with asbestosis and silicosis. The workers' compensation claim was then withdrawn and a damage suit filed in its place. James' deposition recounted the extremely dusty conditions he worked in as a "beaterman" at Ruberoid's shingle plant, dumping asbestos and other materials into mixing tanks, etc. A settlement was reached in the case in 1953 (*Fee James vs. Ruberoid Co.*, U.S. Dist. Court, E. Dist. MO, Cause No. 8864).

In 1954, a damage suit was filed against Ruberoid following the death of another worker in the St. Louis plant. Opil B. Reed had worked in the asbestos room and warehouse from 1944 until his death in 1953 from a respiratory condition. Damages were sought by his family, which charged the company with negligence along similar lines as Robertson and Smith had done twenty years earlier. The outcome of this case is not known (*Gloria D. Reed et al. vs. Ruberoid Co.*, U.S. Dist Court, E. Dist. MO, No. 9875).

Ruberoid was also named as a defendant in the product liability suit brought by the widow of Clarence Faciane in 1961-62 (See "Lawsuits by Product Users against Asbestos Manufacturers" in Chapter 3).

GAF President Jesse Werner was personally invited to join a "working group" on asbestos insulation industry hazards by Dr. Irving Selikoff (letter dated April 12, 1968). At a May 19, 1970 meeting of the Asbestos Cement Products Association, GAF was in the majority on a 4-3 vote against including explicit acknowledgement of a health risk from sawing, drilling, or machining asbestos-cement products (in a brochure for the public—See "National Gypsum Company" later in this chapter). Former Ruberoid chemist and research chief Phillip Bettoli has testified that GAF never put a warning on asbestos-cement products (*Baltz v. Johns-Manville et al.*, deposition Apr. 25, 1980).

Ruberoid joined the Industrial Hygiene Foundation in 1953. The *Industrial Hygiene Digest* listed the 1953 Threshold Limit Values published by ACGIH in the October, 1953 issue, giving 5 MPPCF as the TLV for asbestos dust. In December of 1953, the *Digest* published a table of state occupational disease statistics, including one case of "Asbestosis—cancer (dust, asbestos)" occurring in Connecticut in October of 1953.

Ruberoid was also a member of the National Insulation Manufacturers Association. A Ruberoid representative participated in discussions wherein a NIMA health program was rejected in 1960, and the text of the Johns-Manville insulation shipping carton warning label was presented in 1964. On June 4, 1970, GAF insulation marketing manager R.W. Henry wrote to NIMA executive secretary J.M. Barnhart that caution labels would be printed on "Calsilite" insulation products.

Primarily a chemical company, GAF would have made use of *Chemical Abstracts*, which contained numerous citations on asbestos disease (See "Abstracts," in Chapter 10).

COMPANIES MINING ASBESTOS IN QUEBEC, CANADA

There is a body of knowledge that may be ascribed to Canadian asbestos mining companies, generally. The largest asbestos mining operation in Quebec was that of Johns-Manville (sold by Manville Corporation to former employees in 1983), in the town of Asbestos. Others are located not far away, most near the town of Thetford Mines. These others include, or in the past years have included:

Company	Relevant History
Bell Asbestos Mines	Subsidiary of Keasbey & Mattison Co. which itself was bought by Turner & Newall, Ltd. (U.K.) in 1934. Sold in 1980 to the Quebec government company, Société National de l'Amiante.

Asbestos Corporation, Ltd.	Formed by the consolidation of many smaller mines in 1925; General Dynamics Corp. (U.S.) obtained a 54% interest in 1969 and sold it to Société National de l'Amiante in 1981.
Johnson's Company	Obtained by Asbestos Corp. Ltd. in 1964.
Nicolet Asbestos Mines, Ltd.	Operated by Nicolet Industries, Inc. (U.S.) from 1939-1969.
National Asbestos Mine	Operated by National Gypsum Company from 1958-1973 and sold to Lake Asbestos.
Lake Asbestos (Lac d'Amiante du Quebec, Ltee.)	Subsidiary of Asarco, Inc. (U.S.) in operation since 1958.
Flintkote Mines, Ltd.	Subsidiary of Flintkote Company (U.S.), in operation from 1946 until around 1970.
Quebec Asbestos Corp.; Carey Canadian Mines	Subsidiaries of Philip Carey Manufacturing Company (U.S.), which in turn has become part of Jim Walter Corp. (U.S.). The first of these operations closed and the second began in the late 1950s.

Cooperation among asbestos mining companies in Quebec dates from 1930 or before, on the subject of asbestosis. In that year, an article on asbestosis appeared in *Asbestos* magazine amidst advertisements by Philip Carey Manufacturing Company, Johns-Manville, Keasbey & Mattison, Asbestos Corporation Ltd., and others. Other material on asbestos hazards known to mining firms in Quebec includes the following items:

1. Health surveys were undertaken under the auspices of the Metropolitan Life Insurance Company in 1930 by Drs. Frank

Pedley and A.J. Lanza. Their findings were contained in a report by Dr. Geroge Wheatley, medical director of Metropolitan Life. This obscure 1944 report, *Tuberculosis and Asbestosis,* included data from a 1930 survey of 195 asbestos miners in Asbestos and Thetford Mines. Of this number, 42 had asbestosis. The Wheatley report also noted that asbestosis was a compensable disease in the Province. According to a memorandum by Quebec Asbestos Mining Association lawyer I. Sabourin (attached to the back of the report), the report had been sent to compensation officials and pulmonary experts in Quebec at the time it was prepared (See also "Other Events of 1930" in Chapter 1).

Another report produced by Metropolitan Life Insurance Company identifies the companies surveyed in Thetford Mines as Asbestos Corporation, Keasbey & Mattison, and Johnson's Mine (Frank Pedley. *Report of the Physical Examinations and X-ray Examinations of Asbestos Workers in Asbestos and Thetford Mines, Quebec,* 15 pages, Nov. 1930).

2. Burton LeDoux report, "Asbestosis," and the asbestos strike of 1949.

Pierre Elliott Trudeau's book, *The Asbestos Strike* (Toronto: J. Lorimer & Co., 1974) says that LeDoux had previously written exposés of silicosis in Quebec, creating a scandal in 1948 (pp. 241-242, 274). His investigation of the asbestos mines was written entirely about Quebec Asbestos Corp., Ltd. a subsidiary of Philip Carey. LeDoux' account was printed in the newspaper *Le Devoir,* an indictment that filled several full pages of the newspaper. It was entitled, "Asbestosis at East Broughton—A Village of 3,000 Suffocated by Dust," and appeared in print on January 12, 1949.

LeDoux' account was also printed in English. It describes case histories of workers disabled by asbestosis, local doctors who were afraid to tell them so, estimates of how much profit Carey mined out of the town, descriptions of asbestos air pollution in town, commentary on the "ample and authoritative medical literature... that the disease is incurable and fatal"; and culminates with what LeDoux called "proof of company and government responsibility" starting in 1944. This was a thorough, piercing, investigative report.

Le Devoir let hardly a day pass for the next month without adding reports and editorials on asbestosis. One of the reporters of this scene, Gerard Pelletier of *Le Devoir,* is the raconteur of the chapter of Trudeau's book about press coverage of the strike. He described the workers of Carey's East Broughton mining operation as "preeminently the victims of asbestosis," and yet the only unionists who did not join the five-month strike in the asbestos mines that began in February, 1949.

3. F. Lathe, "Associate Committee on Asbestos" (Aug. 11, 1936); and D. Wolochow, "Asbestos" (June 3, 1938).

   Canadian government officials who attended meetings of the Quebec Asbestos Producers Association in the 1930s referred to discussions of asbestosis by the industry trade association (renamed Quebec Asbestos Mining Assocation in 1948).

4. O.C. Smith (Bell Asbestos Mines, subsidiary of Turner & Newall, U.K.), "Report to Quebec Asbestos Mining Association re Pulmonary Cancer and Supplementary Memorandum re Cancer Research" (Dec. 19, 1950).

   Memorandum enclosing review by Dr. John Knox of T & N about the U.K. Factory Inspectorate's statistics linking asbestosis and pulmonary cancer. Addressed to representatives of the following companies: Asbestos Corporation Ltd., Flintkote Mines, Canadian Johns-Manville, Nicolet Asbestos Mines, and Quebec Asbestos Corp.

5. A.J. Vorwald, *First Interim Report Asbestosis and Pulmonary Cancer.* Saranac Laboratory, report to Q.A.M.A. (May 7, 1952).

   The Saranac Lab was commissioned by the Quebec Asbestos Mining Association to test Canadian chrysotile asbestos in mice by inhalation. By May 1952, this preliminary report of 14 months' testing appeared, showing a trend toward positive findings, and shortly thereafter the study was apparently halted (See "The Saranac Lab's Cancer Studies for the Quebec Asbestos Mining Association," in Chapter 2).

6. P. Cartier, Reports of Cancer among Asbestos Miners at Thetford Mines, 1952-1955.

   Pathology reviews of tissues were done at the Saranac Laboratory for the mining companies starting in 1942, and a number of pulmonary cancer cases were already recorded by 1949 (See "Dr. Schepers' Visit to America," in Chapter 2). Dr. Cartier, of the Thetford Industrial Clinic, periodically reported on these cancer cases (See "More Reports and Reviews" and "The Seventh Saranac Symposium," in Chapter 2).

7. D.C. Braun, *An Epidemiological Study of Lung Cancer in Asbestos Miners* prepared by Industrial Hygiene Foundation for Quebec Asbestos Mining Association (Sept. 1957). D.C. Braun and T. Truan, "An Epidemiological Study of Lung Cancer in Asbestos Miners," *Arch. Indust. Health 17:* 634-652 (1958).

   These and other documents describe research sponsored by Q.A.M.A. on lung cancer in asbestos miners (See "The Industrial Hygiene Foundation Cancer Study," in Chapter 2).

8. "Minutes of the 89th Meeting of the Quebec Asbestos Mining Association," held Oct. 14, 1964 at the St. George's Club, Sherbrooke, Quebec.

   Q.A.M.A. decided to contribute toward the expenses for the international conference on asbestos sponsored by the New York Academy of Sciences.

9. "Minutes of the Special Meeting of the Quebec Asbestos Mining Association Held on March 28 and 29, 1968, at the Grand Bahama Hotel and Country Club, G.B." And "Special Meeting, Grand Bahama Hotel and Country Club, G.B."

   The first of these mentions a proposed health warning label for bags of asbestos "to release the producers from possible legal responsibility." The text was to be checked by "member company counsels" for review at the next Q.A.M.A. meeting.

   The second refers to the TLV Committee of the American Conference of Governmental Industrial Hygienists.

   > The Committee has potent legal standing in theory, but not in practice. It was emphasized that adequate information is not always available to this Committee; for instance, standards for the asbestos industry are not up-to-date.

10. *Montreal Star* (March 20, 1975).

    Contains two front-page stories about the Thetford clinic's failure to inform asbestos miners that they had asbestosis, over a period of decades.

The minutes of the Quebec Asbestos Mining Association (founded in 1931) have never been made available for inspection in discovery proceedings.

PHILIP CAREY MANUFACTURING COMPANY
(later Celotex, Panacon, Jim Walter Corp.)

The Philip Carey Company of Cincinnati, Ohio, boasted that it had been supplying asbestos and asbestos products for over 50 years in an ad appearing in *Asbestos,* in March, 1930 (this issue also carried an article about asbestosis). Carey was in the insulation contracting business as well.

Publicity over asbestosis among Carey's Quebec mine employees led to a historic asbestos strike in the Province (See "Compensation at the Asbestos Mines in Canada," in Chapter 3, and "Companies Mining Asbestos in Quebec, Canada," this chapter). Carey's ownership of the Quebec Asbestos Corporation was recorded in *Moody's Manual of Investments* (1950). Q.A.M.A. lawyer Ivan Sabourin communicated the initial report and findings of the industry-sponsored cancer epidemiology study to Ed Broadway of Quebec Asbestos Corp. on Nov. 11, 1957 (See "The Industrial Hygiene Foundation Cancer Study," in Chapter 2).

The following documentation relates directly to Carey:

1. National Industrial Recovery Administration, Hearing on Code of Fair Practices and Competition, Presented by Asbestos Industry, Oct. 19, 1933.

   Carey President George Crabbs and Johns-Manville President Lewis Brown, accompanied by representatives of 3 other asbestos companies, testified at hearings on a proposed code that would have excluded minors under age 18 from employment in occupations with exposure to "asbestos dust . . . in injurious quantities." Brown presented a list of companies that had signed the proposed code (including American Brakeblok, Carey, Ehret, Garlock, J-M, Keasbey & Mattison, Ruberoid, Southern Asbestos, Theromoid, Union Asbestos & Rubber) and a list of "members of the asbestos industry which have not signed the proposed code" (including Armstrong Cork & Insulation, Plant Rubber & Asbestos Works, and Firestone Tire & Rubber Co.). Brown and Crabbs were followed by Waldo C. Holden of the AFL-CIO, who expressed concern about children exposed to a health hazard from asbestos dust (See also "1931-1935: Taking Account of Asbestosis," in Chapter 1).

2. *Heating and Ventilating* magazine, June, 1944.
   Contained an article by Hutchinson ("Dust as an Industrial Health Hazard") noting the asbestosis hazard to insulation workers and others; also an advertisement by Philip Carey Manufacturing Company for "all-asbestos" Careyduct. (See "Trade Journals," in Chapter 10.)

3. In late 1944, a Carey plant worker in Ohio died, and Dr. Robert Ritterhoff diagnosed asbestosis at autopsy. This was pathologically confirmed by Dr. Gardner at the Saranac Laboratory. When Gardner requested details about the man's exposure to dusts, Ritterhoff replied that the company had been "uncooperative." He explained, "They have not permitted me to visit the plant, nor have they given in detail his occupational history" (letter dated Dec. 23, 1944). Dr. Ritterhoff eventually did visit the company and discuss this case with a company official. "The purpose of the visit was to tell someone at Philip Carey that their employee, Mr. Scobie, died of asbestosis," Dr. Ritterhoff recalls. He was informed by his co-worker, Dr. John Skavlem, that the company had "privately" compensated Mr. Scobie's widow. (Deposition of Dr. Ritterhoff, *State of Maryland v. Keene Corp. et al.*, Civ. No. 1108600. Circuit Court Anne Arundel Co., MD, taken Jan. 30, 1986; and Vorwald Patient File No. P-44-326, Armed Forces Institute of Pathology, Washington, DC.)

4. Following the death of Carey employee Len R. Hope in 1953, a workers' compensation claim was filed in Ohio by his widow. This went through various appeals and was ultimately resolved by pathologist Kenneth M. Lynch's report in 1956, to the effect that the man's death was caused by asbestosis. Compensation was awarded on Jan. 24, 1957 (Len Hope file from archives of K.M. Lynch, Ohio Industrial Commission No. OD 79998).

5. Contracting Division Compensation Claims by Insulation Workers.
   Carey was named as a defendant in claims brought by Swartout, Riley, Gilivich, and Onofrio, with notice to Carey dated from 1956-1963 (See "Claims by Insulators against Contracting Divisions of Asbestos Product Manufacturers," in Chapter 3); and Latto in 1961-1962 (See "The Mancuso Documents," in Chapter 3).

6. Carey was named as a defendant in 1961 in the product liability suit brought against insulation manufacturers by G. Faciane (See "Lawsuits by Product Users Against Asbestos Manufacturers," in Chapter 3).
7. The Mancuso Documents, 1962-1964

   Carey's medical insurance carrier, Metropolitan Life, tallied numerous death claims due to lung cancer and other respiratory conditions during the years 1957-1962 (J.R. Lynch, letter to Karl Krieg, Philip Carey, April 16, 1963).

   At the direction of actuaries, Carey hired Dr. Thomas Mancuso as Consulting Medical Director for the entire company. Mancuso reported directly to top management about the urgent need for measures to protect employees, customers for Carey asbestos products, and neighbors of Carey facilities exposed to asbestos air pollution (See "The Mancuso Documents," in Chapter 3). Dr. Mancuso's services were terminated by Carey in 1964, following his report on the New York Academy of Sciences conference on asbestos disease (T.F. Mancuso, letter to J.T. Cantlon, Oct. 26, 1964; and L.A. Pechstein, letter to Cantlon, Dec. 8, 1964).
8. L.A. Pechstein (Secretary and General Counsel, Philip Carey Corp.), letter to T. Lindsey (John T. Cantlon & Associates), Nov. 4, 1969.

   Notes that Carey was a defendant in a common law asbestosis suit in Texas, in which the plaintiff had posed interrogatories. One asked, "Do you agree that the State of Ohio had a Workmen's Compensation Law covering the occupational disease of asbestosis beginning in the year 1939?" Pechstein wrote,

   > We would appreciate your suggestion for a short, somewhat evasive answer to the interrogatory.
9. Harold Plate (Sales Mgr., Carey Canadian Mines, Quebec), letter to Kermit Hayden (California Portland Cement Co.), May 8, 1970.

   Responds to health concerns about asbestos.

   > We've been in the asbestos business since 1918 and can find no reported conditions of asbestosis or lung disease claims they have been trying to associate with asbestos.

The Philip Carey Manufacturing Company apparently never did place health warning labels on its asbestos products, which contained amosite and chrysotile asbestos (deposition of

Arthur P. Mueller in *Goad v. Johns-Manville Corp. et al.* U.S. Dist. Court for S. District of Ohio, Western Div., Case No. C-1-82-127, Feb. 13, 1985). Upon incorporation by merger into Celotex at the time that (OSHA) workplace asbestos standards were issued in the United States, newly required warnings were placed on asbestos products by the company in mid-1972. Celotex had been in the asbestos business starting in the 1940s or earlier, manufacturing such products as "Cemesto" structural insulating panels and "Acousti-Celotex Perforated Asbestos Board." These products were described in Celotex annual reports in the 1940s and 1950s, as well as in *Moody's Manual of Investments*, etc. Celotex also made asbestos-containing products in the United Kingdom in the 1950s (deposition of Donald Gibson, *In re Master Asbestos File*, Civ. Action M.A.D. 100, U.S. Dist. Court, Southern Dist. of TX, Houston Div., Feb. 6, 1987).

Complete information on product lines may be contained in *Celotex' History of Insulation Products* and *Philip Carey's History of Asbestos Products*, which were sent by Jim Walter Corporation's Legal Department to Celotex defense counsel in Texas in 1978. The letter of transmittal noted that information handled between corporate lawyers and outside defense counsel offered "less chance of this information being supoenaed or subject for production." (Dec. 26, 1978). Sure enough, the histories described were not produced to plaintiffs until 1990, under order of Judge Neil Caldwell of Brazoria County, TX. The judge declared that the company had committed "a fraud upon the Plaintiffs and this Court." (Order of Feb. 14, 1990 in *Searls v. Owens-Corning et al.* Dist. Court of Brazoria Co., TX, Case No. 88-C-0615)

ASBESTOS CORPORATION LIMITED (ACL)

This company was set up in 1925 and nationalized in the 1980s (incorporated into the Quebec government company, Société Nationale de l'Amiante).

A dust survey of the firm's King mine and mill was conducted in 1944 by Metropolitan Life Insurance Company, and the brief report of the findings was on file (Document No. 1178) at the Institute of Occupational and Environmental Health, in Montreal (I.O.E.H. was a part of the Quebec Asbestos Mining Association until its library was merged into the Canadian Asbestos Information Centre in 1982, now the Asbestos Institute). The report notes that a similar survey had been conducted in 1930. Dust concentrations ranged from 11.6 to 26.6 MPPCF in the five operations evaluated. The plant was not running at full production, and the windows were open in most areas at the time samples were taken. Improved housekeeping and the covering of conveyors, in addition to the above factors, were given as reasons for the "much lower" dust concentrations measured in 1944 than in 1930. In terms of plant design, very little had changed:

> No changes have been made in the mill operations since the first survey. The only effort at dust suppression consisted in covering some conveyors.

The Metropolitan Life report recommended that efforts be made to lower exposures to a maximum concentration of 5 MPPCF. In this connection, the report of the U.S. Public Health Service (Dreessen *et al.*, 1938) was cited. Reprints of two papers by Dr. Lanza and his co-workers at Met Life (1935, 1936) were attached to the King Mine survey report.

Starting in 1943, numerous cases in which asbestosis was suspected among ACL employees were referred to the Saranac Laboratory. Many of these people had been seen by Dr. Cartier's Thetford Industrial Clinic, and compensation claims had been filed in at least 17 of the cases reviewed by Dr. Gardner and Dr. Vorwald between 1943 and 1957. In a 1946 case where a death claim had been filed, the asbestosis was extensive and was accompanied by lung cancer (Vorwald Patient File P-46-372). The Treasurer of ACL, whose exposure consisted of office work only starting in 1920, died from pleural mesothelioma in 1949 (Vorwald Patient File IM-573). Details of these cases beyond those in the Vorwald files are unavailable from the Quebec government and the mining companies in Quebec, due to the Quebec Records Concerns Act, which bars the transfer of certain types of records out of the Province, even as photocopies.

ACL was a member of the Industrial Hygiene Foundation from Dec. 1, 1953 until Dec. 31, 1960. ACL was an "associate member of the Asbestos Textile Institute from June, 1952 until ATI was dissolved in the 1970s.

On January 5, 1970, ACL Vice President I.C. Campbell wrote to representatives of other asbestos mining companies that caution labels would be placed on future ACL asbestos shipments. These labels were being placed on shipments "to Canadian and American customers *only*" (original emphasis):

> This bag contains chrysotile asbestos fibre. Persons exposed to this material should use adequate protective devices as inhalation of this material over long periods may be harmful.

JOHNS-MANVILLE CORPORATION
(renamed Manville in 1981)

This company was the asbestos industry leader in the United States, with mines in Canada. Its founder was Henry Ward Johns, who patented inventions for roofing and insulation products. Johns started his own company at the age of 21, and died 40 years later of a chronic lung condition, in 1898. (His death certificate lists the cause of death as "phthisis pulmonalis.")

The company's continuous concern about the problem of asbestosis apparently dates from the late 1920s. Lanza, in his 1935 publication, acknowledged that "officials representing the asbestos industry in the United States" had approached him to conduct a health survey in 1929.

J-M also presumably knew that Lanza and Pedley examined workers at their mine in Asbestos, Quebec, and identified 18 cases of asbestosis there in 1930 (see "Other Events of 1930," in Chapter 1).

A 1930 report by J-M Sales Promotion Department (Market Analysis Section) contained factual summaries of British medical reports published in 1929. This is one of the few documents of interest produced in discovery by Johns-Manville to plaintiffs in civil litigation (from files of the J-M Waukegan, Illinois plant). Discovery conducted by the U.S. Department of Justice in the mid-1980s, in connection with a suit brought by J-M against the government, unearthed files of Vandiver Brown and others that had been preserved on microfilm.

Lawsuits were filed against Johns-Manville by employees claiming disability from lung diseases at least as early as 1929. The corporation's Board of Directors approved of a settlement of asbestosis lawsuits in New Jersey in 1933 (See "Asbestos Compensation in the Early Years," in Chapter 3).

Aided by Dr. A.J. Lanza of Metropolitan Life Insurance Company, J-M found that 29 percent of its Manville, NJ plant employees, including 2 watchmen and 2 shipping clerks, had pneumoconiosis (See "1931-1935: Taking Account of Asbestosis," in Chapter 1). Lanza advised against putting up health warning signs in J-M's Waukegan, IL plant in 1933, because of concern over lawsuits (See "Asbestos Compensation in the Early Years: Damage Suits," in Chapter 3).

Johns-Manville's early involvement in matters relating to the health hazards of asbestos seems to have been handled primarily by corporate attorney Vandiver Brown in the years 1930-1950. Shortly after 1950, Brown was summarily retired, and until his death in 1983 he resided alternatively in Scotland and Waco, Texas. Plaintiffs' attorneys were surprised to discover that he was still living, having been told in Johns-Manville's Answers to Interrogatories that Vandiver Brown was dead. Brown's doctor and banker (financial guardian) then testified that he was completely senile and in such poor health that he could not safely undergo a deposition. Brown never was prevailed upon to add to the documentary record of his years at Johns-Manville.

Brown's activities in the 1930s are known largely through the Sumner Simpson Papers (See "Raybestos-Manhattan," this chapter; and Chapter 3). These activities included making editorial suggestions to Dr. Lanza on galley proofs of his paper published in 1935; discouraging the trade magazine *Asbestos* from running stories on asbestosis and dust control; and representing asbestos companies sponsoring research at the Saranac Laboratory. In this last capacity, Brown vigilantly watched for any violation of the laboratory director's contract forbidding publication without approval of the industry sponsors. He also received in 1943 an annotated outline of a monograph that Dr. Gardner intended to write. This contained evaluations of human and unpublished Saranac animal test data, to the effect that in both cases the evidence was suggestive but not conclusive that asbestos was a carcinogen. Brown and representatives of other companies pressed Saranac to omit all mention of cancer in the published report of Gardner's research (See "Early Saranac Laboratory Cancer Tests with Asbestos," in Chapter 2).

Vandiver Brown was the asbestos industry representative who joined with representatives of other industries to launch the Air Hygiene Foundation, soon after renamed Industrial Hygiene Foundation.

Brown and the Johns-Manville president (Lewis Brown) met with Charles Roemer and officials from the Union Asbestos and Rubber Company in 1942 or 1943. According to Mr. Roemer, Brown explained that it was company policy to not tell employees their medical examinations showed they had asbestosis. Brown went on to explain the financial reasoning behind this policy (See "A Lobster Lunch with Vandiver Brown," in Chapter 3, and opening quote to this chapter).

In 1947, Brown criticized the lacking of scientific basis of the tentative threshold limit first proposed for dust in asbestos plants by the U.S. Public Health Service (See "Unsteady Movement Toward Numerical Exposure Limits," in Chapter 4).

In 1950, Brown demanded that Dr. Gerrit Schepers suppress a report Schepers had prepared for the South African government about the asbestos problem in the U.S. and Canada. Brown objected particularly to Schepers' reference to cancer at the Canadian mines and the extreme dustiness of two Johns-

Manville asbestos plants (See "Dr. Schepers' Visit to America," in Chapter 2).

In late 1950, Page Woodard, another J-M executive, met with Dr. Vorwald, Dr. A.J. Lanza, and Quebec Asbestos Mining Association attorney Ivan Sabourin to negotiate terms for an animal inhalation test on the carcinogenicity of asbestos. The test was apparently interrupted before completion, and none of the findings were published (See "The Saranac Lab's Cancer Studies for the Quebec Asbestos Mining Association," in Chapter 2).

Another key figure in the Johns-Manville response to the health threat of asbestos was Dr. Kenneth W. Smith. At the company's large mine and mill complex at Asbestos, Quebec, he conducted a survey of 708 employees in the late 1940s and considered 59 "probable compensation claims." None of the employees were informed that they had asbestosis (See "Compensation at the Asbestos Mines in Canada," in Chapter 3). Even before 1949, Smith recalled that Johns-Manville's top medical official at Asbestos, Quebec was concerned that the town was downwind of J-M's mining activities (See "Asbestos Air Pollution in the Community," in Chapter 7).

In 1950, Dr. Gerrit Schepers met Dr. Smith and discussed with him the pathological records of cancer on file at the Saranac Laboratory from eleven Canadian asbestos mine and mill workers (See "Dr. Schepers' Visit to America," in Chapter 2). But even before 1950, Dr. Harriet Hardy recalls, Dr. Smith was discreetly trying to interest doctors at the Massachusetts General Hospital in the issue of asbestos carcinogenesis. Even though this suggestion was well received, Smith later told Hardy he was not allowed to follow up because of J-M executives' objections.

Smith recommended warning labels for asbestos as early as 1952, the year he became corporate medical director. He testified as follows shortly before his death about the fate of that recommendation:

> The reason why the caution labels were not implemented immediately, it was a business decision as far as I could

> understand. Here was a recommendation, the corporation is in business to make, to provide jobs for people and make money for stockholders and they had to take into consideration the effects of everything they did and if the application of a caution label identifying a product as hazardous would cut into sales, there would be serious financial implications. And the powers of be (sic) had to make some effort to judge the necessity of the label versus the consequences of placing the label on the product.
>
> (K.W. Smith deposition in *Louisville Trust Co. v. Johns-Manville, Corp.* Jefferson Circuit Court, Common Pleas Br. 7th Div. of Kentucky, Case No. 174-922, April 21, 1976.)

Labels warning that breathing asbestos was dangerous were not placed on J-M asbestos (insulation) products until 1964; on sacks of J-M asbestos fiber from Canada until 1969 (See also "The Charges: Failure to Test, Failure to Warn," in Chapter 5). Apparently, most if not all others in the industry did not begin to label their products as hazardous until Johns-Manville did so; and some lagged years behind.

The company policy of not informing J-M employees when their medical examinations revealed asbestosis has also been described by Wilbur Ruff, former manager of the company's Pittsburgh, California manufacturing plant. Ruff testified that this "hush-hush condition" persisted as company policy at the plant he managed until 1971 or 1972. Ruff himself had been told asbestos caused lung disease in the late 1940s from C.B. Burnett, who went on to become the company's president in 1960 (Sworn Statement of Wilbur L. Ruff, Jan. 11, 1978, at law offices of Marrs A. Craddick, Walnut Creek, California).

At the corporate level, safety engineer Hugh Jackson worked closely with medical director Dr. Kenneth Smith. Even before Smith arrived at the corporate offices in New York, Jackson dealt with health problems at the plants, even arranging for lung tissue slides to be sent to Saranac Laboratory. In 1948, he verified that a plant foreman had died of asbestosis from breathing the general atmosphere in the plant, and expressed concern to Dr. Vorwald at Saranac that such exposure could produce such severe lung disease (See "Saranac Compensation Reviews for Manufacturers," and "Cancer," Chapter 3).

In 1954, Jackson wrote to an official at the Waukegan plant that compliance with threshold limit values for employee exposure to asbestos did not assure protection for all the workers: ". . . no guarantee of full protection can be assumed at any level of exposure." (See "The American Conference of Governmental Industrial Hygienists TLVs," Chapter 4).

A management "compensation committee" held regular meetings at the large Manville, New Jersey, manufacturing plant in 1957-1958. Kenneth Smith, Clifford Sheckler, and others decided whether to inform workers whose medical examinations had turned up lung disease, whether to transfer affected workers to less dusty areas of the plant, and how to handle the affected individuals so that they would not file workers' compensation claims. Similar practices were followed by J-M management elsewhere, in the 1960s (See "Corporate Compensation Meetings at Manville," in Chapter 3).

A construction contracting firm owned by J-M was sued in 1933 by a workman, Bernard Dugan, who said he was totally disabled with lung disease from mixing asbestos-containing materials used in construction. In 1957 and 1961, Johns-Manville was named in damage suits in New Jersey by insulators Frederick LeGrande and Fred Wenham. Both plaintiffs received out-of-court settlements. Johns-Manville was also named in the product liability suit filed by G. Faciane in 1961 (See "Lawsuits by Product Users Against Asbestos Manufacturers" in Chapter 3).

Workers' compensation claims were also filed against Johns-Manville by insulation workers employed in J-M construction contracting divisions in the 1950s. Based mainly on a list of claims involving Armstrong Cork, it was possible to ascertain that J-M was joined as a co-defendant in the following cases:

Harry Kish (1953)
Edward Campbell (1954)
James Riley (1957)
Harry Haake (1957)

John Swartout (1958)
Ervey McCarrell (1959)
Lewis Munger (1959)
Harvey Curtis (1961)
Anthony Onofrio (1962)
Robert Goans (1963)

(See "Workers' Compensation Claims by Insulators against Contracting Divisions of Asbestos Product Manufacturers," Chapter 3.) J-M was also a defendant in the claim of Dean Templeton in Michigan in 1960 (See "Owens Corning Fiberglas," this chapter).

Johns-Manville also referred a number of asbestosis cases to the Saranac Laboratory for review. In the case of one worker who had asbestosis and died from lung cancer, Safety Engineer Hugh Jackson at corporate headquarters arranged to have the plant documents and chest X-rays sent to Saranac. He wrote to Dr. Vorwald on July 28, 1950, "As you know, Johns-Manville is considerably interested in the relationship of asbestosis and lung carcinoma" (Vorwald Patient File P-49-455). Two other cases of lung cancer and asbestosis were reviewed by Saranac for Johns-Manville in 1950 and 1951; one of these men had worked at the Waukegan, Illinois plant, and the other had worked at the company's Quebec asbestos mine (Vorwald Patient Files P-50-495, P-51-542).

By 1954, Johns-Manville operated a clinic in Asbestos, Quebec, with the capability to perform microscopic analyses of airborne dust samples. In addition, an annual survey was conducted with dust samples shipped to the Travelers Insurance Company for analysis (H. Rozovsky. "Air Handling and Dust Control at the Jeffrey Mine of Canadian Johns-Manville Company." *Canad. Mining J. 75:*59-65, 1954).

Johns-Manville was a member of the Asbestos Textile Institute, the National Insulation Manufacturers Association, Industrial Hygiene Foundation, Quebec Asbestos Mining Association, and the Asbestosis Research Council, among others. Through special studies, meetings, and publications of these organizations Johns-Manville was continually dealing with the problem of asbestos disease (See "Industry Research and Trade Associations," in Chapter 10).

In 1968-1970, J-M was among the members of the Asbestos Cement Products Association willing to warn the public that sawing asbestos-cement products would create a health risk (See "National Gypsum Company," next in this chapter)—if others in the industry would also do so.

NATIONAL GYPSUM COMPANY

National Gypsum owned interests in asbestos mining (National Asbestos Mine in Quebec) and manufacturing (plants in Louisiana and New Jersey). This company made "Gold Bond" drywall joint compounds and asbestos-cement panels.

Another product under development at the firm's research labs in 1949 was a sprayed acoustical treatment. Several different compositions were tested using various combinations of mineral wool, asbestos fibers and "floats," etc. The test materials were applied to the ceiling of a school auditorium in Ohio and evaluated. The first recommendation in the report was:

> The floats should be removed from the formula since the increase in dust and the possibility of Asbestosis out-weigh the slight increase in surface smoothness.

It was also recommended that the amosite asbestos content be raised to offset the effect of removing the short fibers (floats). (F.M. Stumpf and B.O. Stewart, "On the Job Application of Spraying Wool for Acoustical Treatments," File No. 6a-6004, Rept. No. 391, June 28, 1949).

On March 11, 1953, National Gypsum Director of Safety M. Pollard wrote to Dr. L.W. Spolyar, Director of the Indiana Division of Industrial Hygiene. He listed amosite asbestos as a constituent of "Thermacoustic" spray-applied insulation, and recommended that operators mixing it for use wear a respirator approved for pneumoconiosis-producing dusts "because of the asbestos used in the product." Pollard suggested that respirators might be necessary for applicators, too, "if there is dust present." The same day, Pollard also sent an internal memorandum to others in the company, saying that asbestosis was a respiratory disease "with results usually worse than those produced by silicosis."

One recipient of these communications was G.W. Handy, who replied to Pollard that his letter was "full of dynamite." He speculated that if respirators were required for the job, the contractor would not be able to find men to apply the product. He concluded by urging that the letter be retrieved before mailing and reference to respirators be deleted.

> I am concerned that the National Gypsum Company is on record to Dr. Spolyar that Thermacoustic is hazardous business. If this snowballs, we are out of the Thermacoustic business.

A handwritten note on this (Mar. 12, 1953) memorandum states, "Handy succeeded in stopping ltr to Spolyar. Will be modified."

Pollard had further discussions with company officials and mailed the letter, explaining (Mar. 16, 1953) to Handy:

> I very much appreciate your thinking in this matter and I want to reassure you that the Indiana State Division of Industrial Hygiene uses no information to the detriment of any manufacturer. I purposely kept my reply on an objective basis because Mr. Willis thought this would be to our greatest advantage.

During the years 1953-1972, employees' chest X-rays were regularly examined by Dr. George Wright, a radiologist formerly employed at the Saranac Laboratory. In at least one case, Dr. Wright went beyond the traditional physician's role and offered advice to the company on a matter of personnel policy.

> I suspect that (he) has more of a problem with his heart than he either knows about or is willing to talk about. In all probability the abnormalities in the basal portions of his lung are related to the heart disease but the possibility

> that he may have inflammation and changes in the pleura of the lung which might be related to asbestos exposure should be kept in mind. I don't believe that at this point it should be pointed out to him.
>
> It is my impression that you have done as much as management needs to do since you have called to his attention the fact that he has an abnormal film. From my own past experiences I would not advise making a stronger approach to either (him) or his physician.
>
> (G.W. Wright letter to Timothy D. Tolin, National Gypsum Personnel and Safety Supervisor, Millington, N.J. "Re: Film No. 27530 Taken on 10/4/68.")

Other documents, most of them obtained in discovery from National Gypsum, describe a meeting by asbestos-cement producers on April 3, 1968, and subsequent events.

1. March 27, 1968 C.L. Sheckler (Manager, Occupational Environmental Control, Johns-Manville) letter to Frank Zimmerman (Director of Safety, National Gypsum).

   This was an invitation to a meeting of representatives from Johns-Manville, Certain-teed, General Aniline and Film (GAF had just purchased the Ruberoid Co.), Flintkote, and Owens-Corning. The letter noted that contact had been made already between the President of J-M (C.B. Burnett) and a Vice President of National Gypsum (A.H. Fay). "We are currently preparing a booklet entitled 'Recommended Health and Safety Practices for Handling and Applying Asbestos-Cement Products'."

2. April 17, 1968 F.H. Zimmerman letter to Clifford L. Sheckler.

   > In the Council meeting of April 3, 1968 held in your conference room, it was agreed that I would advise you by April 19, 1968 of National Gypsum Company's position relative to the printing and distribution of the booklet entitled, "Recommended Health and Safety Practices." Our position is that we strongly oppose the publication and distribution of the booklet. Our reasons are:
   >
   > a) No risk has been shown to the general public from exposure to asbestos cement products manufactured for use in the building and construction industry.

> b) The proposed booklet points to dangers to health from the handling of corrugated and flat asbestos sheets when there is no scientific evidence of such dangers.
> c) The booklet creates fear in the minds of buyers, users, and workers without justification. These fears would be damaging to the entire industry.

The letter affirmed that,

> This strong opposition to the publishing of the booklet has the full concurrence of the top executives of our company, including the Chief Executive Officer.

3. May 8, 1968 Sheckler letter to Zimmerman.

> I have received tentative approval of the booklet as written in draft form from Certain-teed, General Aniline and Film, and Johns-Manville. It would be extremely advantageous to have unanimous agreement of the council members concerning any publications dealing with health. This is especially desirable in view of the continuous adverse publicity and attacks on various materials.

Sheckler proposed that Mr. Faý come to another meeting in June, 1968, to try to work out points of disagreement concerning the booklet.

4. November 7, 1968 Zimmerman memorandum to A.H. Fay (Vice President, National Gypsum), entitled "Recommended Practices Booklet."

The memorandum summarized changes recommmended by Zimmerman in the draft booklet. This was provided to Fay in advance of the first meeting of the Asbestos Cement Products Association, Health and Safety Council, on Nov. 14, 1968. The gist of the recommended changes was to downplay the language and narrow the content of the draft version of the booklet.

> *COVER SHEET:* Title changed from 'Recommended Health and Safety Practices' to 'Recommended Practices.'
> *CONTENTS* Page 2—Removed section headline, 'For Health and Safety's Sake'...
> *INTRODUCTION* Page 3—Did considerable rewriting in this area to change statements which could be used against the industry in compensation or law suits. Have attempted to take 'scare' wording from the booklet.

The rest of the recommended changes followed the lines of the first three, above.

5. April 10, 1969 Zimmerman memorandum to E.J. Killian (Vice President).

   This reviewed the situation, indicating that Johns-Manville wanted to print the booklet about asbestos-cement products but apparently had not yet done so. At this time, the development of a booklet that would be acceptable industry-wide had been passed on to a committee of the new Asbestos Cement Products Association. Zimmerman anticipated, "many federal regulations controlling the health and safety aspects of asbestos workers."

6. May 19, 1970, Minutes of the Seventh Meeting of Health and Safety Council/ACPA.

   The company representatives discussed 9 publications on asbestos health hazards and regulation. The revised pamphlet, now called *Recommended Practices for Fabricating, Handling, and Applying Asbestos Cement Products in the Building and Construction Industries*, had been held up pending votes from Supradur, U.S. Gypsum, Cement Asbestos Products Company, and Philip Carey (which was going out of the business). A representative from Supradur, K. Schwarz, revived the idea of a health warning by proposing to add this sentence:

   > The handling and installation of solid pieces of asbestos-cement products do not normally present a health risk unless sawing, drilling, or other machining of the product is required.

   This was voted down by 4 to 3, with Johns-Manville, Supradur, and U.S. Gypsum in favor and Certain-teed, Flintkote, GAF, and National Gypsum against. The brochure published later that year recommended dust controls and discussed respiratory protection without making any explicit statement that breathing the dust could cause lung disease.

National Gypsum was also a member of the Gypsum Association, whose minutes of Sept. 19, 1967 include reference to "lung cancer" causes that had been reported in the neighborhood of an asbestos plant.

National Gypsum Vice President Albert Fay invited William Hunt, President of Georgia Pacific Corporation, to a meeting of the Asbestos Information Association on Sept. 15, 1971, to discuss state and federal government regulation. After the meeting, which Hunt did not attend, Fay wrote:

> Our tests indicate that sanding of joint treatment products and particularly the spraying of wall finishes offers some substantial potential hazards.

In 1980, a "Region Report" stated that the year's sales of asbestos products exceeded $12 million. The memorandum concluded by emphasizing that the company was "still in the business of making and selling asbestos products . . . The sales dollars are good as long as they last!" (J.E. Jones, "Asbestos Sales," memorandum, Jan. 16, 1981).

Most of the above documents have been identified by National Gypsum representative Russell Ward in deposition (*Athens City Board of Education v. National Gypsum et al.* U.S. Dist. Court, E. Dist. TN, D. Div., C.A. No. 1-85-355, Jan. 23, 1987).

TURNER & NEWALL, LTD.

Turner & Newall was founded in 1920 by the merger of four companies primarily in businesses using asbestos. Soon afterward the company obtained asbestos mines in southern Africa. In 1934, Turner & Newall purchased the Keasbey & Mattison Company, in Ambler, Pennsylvania. The American company made asbestos-cement products, shingles, and insulation, using fiber from its Bell Mine in Quebec. Bell in turn acquired an interest in Cassiar Asbestos Corporation, which owned chrysotile mines in western Canada. With the liquidation of Keasbey & Mattison in 1963 and sale of its asbestos-cement operations to Certain-teed Products Corporation, Turner & Newall became the largest single stockholder in Certain-teed. Though mainly an "asbestos giant" in the 1960s, the firm was diversifying into plastics, fiber-glass, and mineral wool products as well (Corporate history in *Turner & Newall Limited/The First Fifty Years 1920-1970,* copyright by Turner &

Newall; and a series of articles on the British asbestos industry in *Asbestos* magazine, 1966-1967)

According to Robert R. Porter, President of Keasbey & Mattison from 1957 to 1962:

> T & N had 100 percent control over decision making on policy matters for Keasbey and were in no sense passive stockholders. T & N possessed and exercised the ultimate control and dictated the manner in which the company's capital and resources should be employed... T & N had complete control over Keasbey asbestos fiber supply and control as to which products Keasbey made at its various plants... Because T & N operated other companies in Canada, including Atlas Asbestos Company, Keasbey was prevented from selling asbestos-containing products in Canada.
>
> (Affidavit of Robert R. Porter, filed with Commonwealth of Pennsylvania, County of Philadelphia, April 5, 1983)

The woman described in Cooke's 1924 case report was an employee of T & N (See "Case Reports in Medical Journals," in Chapter 1).

In 1943, Leroy Gardner reported his studies and opinions to the asbestos industry in an outline which went to T & N via Porter's predecessor Ernest Muehleck at Keasbey & Mattison Company. The report contained unpublished animal data on asbestos carcinogenicity, and Gardner's repeated assertion that both human and animal data were "suggestive but not conclusive." Attached letters indicated concern about the cancer issue. Muehleck was a party to the censorship of all references to cancer in the report of industry-sponsored asbestos research at Saranac, published by Vorwald in 1951 (See "Early Saranac Laboratory Cancer Tests with Asbestos," in Chapter 2).

The company defrayed a 1949 review and animal research on asbestos disease by J. MacLean-Smith, E.J. King, and I.D.P. Wooton of the Postgraduate Medical School in London ("Asbestosis"—unpublished). The review included numerous references to cancer and concluded that the reports were "suggestive of an etiological relationship between asbestosis and carcinoma."

J.W. Roberts, Ltd., a Turner & Newall Company, initially marketed "Limpet" sprayed asbestos in the 1930s in both the U.K. and U.S. (through Keasbey & Mattison Company). Presumably, this company knew of the Factory Inspectorate's 1945 notice to insulation contractors expressing concern over the hazards of sprayed asbestos in shipyards (See Table 8 in Chapter 5). By 1946 the Roberts company ran a "Limpet Asbestos Spray School" in Leeds, England, where use of respirators by sprayers was advised.

T & N subsidiary Atlas Asbestos Company Ltd. sold sprayed Limpet asbestos in Canada. In 1949, a claim for asbestosis was filed by a worker who had applied Limpet on ships. The Vancouver Workmen's Compensation Board wrote to the federal government for further information, expressing concern about the growth of asbestos use in western Canada. The inquiry was passed on to engineer S.R. Plamondon of the Ministry of Health in Montreal. He wrote that, "From the companie's official, we are informed that they have never had any claim regarding asbestosis here in Canada." (Letter to Dr. K.C. Charron, Dept. National Health and Welfare, Ottawa, June 29, 1949)

A number of employees of T & N's Bell Asbestos Mines in Quebec were diagnosed as having asbestosis in the 1940s and 1950s. At least 5 former Bell employees or their survivors were identifiably involved in workers' compensation proceedings starting in 1946. Lung cancer in combination with asbestosis was seen in Bell workers in 1950, and at least one of these was the subject of a workers' compensation claim in which Dr. Lanza testified for the company to "debunk" British data linking asbestos to cancer (Vorwald Patient Files P-50-475 and P-550-500). These cases were generally referred by QAMA attorney Sabourin or Dr. Cartier to the Saranac Laboratory, where pathologic materials were examined and reports rendered.

Doll's 1955 study showing an excessive incidence rate of lung cancer in asbestos textile manufacturing workers was based on experience at a Turner & Newall plant. Though the company had originally asked Doll to analyze the data, it was displeased with the findings and tried to block their publication. The company medical officer, J.F. Knox, did not dispute the positive association demonstrated in Doll's report (See "1955: Doll's Study and Other Events," in Chapter 2).

T & N executive assistant David Hills observed in 1955 that the American TLV of 5 MPPCF of dust was groundless ("There is no significance to be attached to this figure at all."); and that "complete safeguard to health is only obtained by having no dust at all." ("Subcommittee on Dust Sampling," Nov. 21, 1955)

Turner & Newall subsidiary Keasbey & Mattison was named as a defendant in 1961 in the product liability suit brought against insulation manufacturers by G. Faciane (See "Lawsuits by Product Users Against Asbestos Manufacturers," in Chapter 3).

The major conference of the New York Academy of Sciences in 1964 took place after the asbestos-cement manufacturing facilities of Keasbey & Mattison had become the property of Certain-teed Corporation. Plant officials met with representatives of Turner & Newall at the New York conference, at which time they were told that the British firm was "years ahead of the U.S. in awareness of the medical problems associated with asbestos." A memorandum of this discussion continues,

> Dr. Knox (T & N medical officer) said that U.S. Industry, in general, does not want to accept the fact that asbestos is very hazardous and they will accept any doctor's view if he intimated that it is not hazardous.

The memorandum also notes that Turner & Newall officials were convinced that the 5 MPPCF guideline cited in the U.S. was "too high" (Memorandum from L.D. Horowitz to M.S. Davis, Jr. on Conference on Biological Effects of Asbestos/New York Academy of Sciences, Nov. 10, 1964).

Keasbey & Mattison was a member of the Asbestos Textile Institute from its founding in 1944, and was a member of Industrial Hygiene Foundation from 1937–1962.

Following highly publicized reports that mesothelioma was occurring in the neighborhoods of asbestos plants and the households of asbestos workers, concern arose about the hazards of asbestos products in buildings, particularly sprayed "Limpet," ceiling tiles, and asbestos insulation generally. The Northern Ireland Hospitals Authority had issued a directive in July, 1966, to the effect that the use of asbestos should be avoided, since even light and occasional contact entailed a cancer risk. Turner & Newall representatives, meeting with the Belfast hospital people (including Dr. Elmes) in 1968, were able to allay concerns over "possible air contamination in buildings," with new survey data (J.F. Knox and S. Holmes, "Visit to Northern Ireland Hospitals Authority, Belfast, 29th May, 1968").

The survey, conducted by T & N and Cape Asbestos employees, had utilized optical microscopy only. The report as published concluded:

> In our present state of knowledge, the dust concentrations found in completed buildings incorporating asbestos-based products in their construction are not considered likely to constitute a hazard to the health of the occupants. (J.C. Byrom, A.A. Hodgson, and S. Holmes. "A Dust Survey Carried Out in Buildings Incorporating Asbestos-Based Materials in Their Construction." *Ann. Occup. Hyg. 12:* 141-145, 1969).

Johns-Manville environmental control chief, wrote to Stephen Holmes at T & N to inquire if any sample evaluations had been done using the more powerful electron microscopy (Nov. 18, 1969). Holmes replied (Jan. 19, 1970) that only phase-contrast optical analyses had been done on the building samples. He admitted:

> It is reasonable to assume that those asbestos fibers which remain airborne in the general atmosphere are very fine indeed and may well be individual fibrils. The elect-

> ron microscope is therefore our only means of looking at them...

CSR

Colonial Sugar Refinery, as CSR used to be known, has become one of Australia's dozen largest corporations. One of its subsidiaries was a crocidolite asbestos mine and mill that operated at Wittenoom, in remote Western Australia, from 1943-1966. The mining business was called Australian Blue Asbestos (ABA), and, after 1959, Midalco. This operation had commercial dealings with Johns-Manville, whose operations were visited by managers of the Australian mine in the 1940s and 1950s.

Internal company documents evidenced an awareness of asbestos dust as a health hazard as early as 1943, and signs of asbestosis in a mill foreman were discussed by management in 1946. In 1948, Eric Saint, a British-educated "Flying Doctor," began to visit Wittenoom, and repeatedly warned the management about the dangers of uncontrolled asbestos dust. Dr. Saint deplored conditions at the mine, which he predicted would yield "the richest and most lethal crop of cases of asbestosis in the world's literature." His notes of meeting with the mine manager, Joe Broadhurst, recorded criticism of the manager as having the mentality of Goebbels and Mussolini.

In 1949, CSR received the *Annual Report of the Chief Inspector of Factories for the Year 1947*, containing powerful evidence of a cancer hazard in Britain's asbestos industry.

CSR's Dr. Rennie attended an I.L.O. pneumoconiosis conference in Sydney in 1950, where international authorities discussed asbestosis and cancer from asbestos.

Dust in the underground mine and the mill were, from an industrial hygiene point of view, essentially uncontrolled. One of the immigrant workers lured to the mine from war-devastated Europe, Carlo Finnamore, was hospitalized from an injury he received walking into machinery he could not see through the dust in the air. The immigrants recruited to work in the hot desert gorge came mostly with expectations of better working conditions; and the average employee worked there less than 6 months. Bagging of fiber was done by workers scooping asbestos in their arms and then packing it down with mallets.

Government mine and health inspectors repeatedly called attention to the dust hazard at the mine and mill in the 1940s and 1950s. In the late 1950s, health official James McNulty came to again advise managment to control asbestos dust. Dr. McNulty soon afterward reported that one of the asbestos miners had developed mesothelioma (*Medical Journal of Australia 2:* 953-954, 1962).

Mesothelioma as an occupational cancer received worldwide attention after Wagner's presentation at the I.L.O. conference on pneumoconiosis in Johannesburg in 1959. South Africa was one of the few places besides Australia where blue asbestos was mined. Starting in 1959 and continuing until the mine closed, CSR's mining operation purchased liability insurance coverage applicable for employees' occupational disease claims from the State Government Insurance Organization in Western Australia. The State Government Insurance Commission reacted to 1988 court decisions by declaring its policy covering CSR subsidiary Midalco inoperative.

Victims of asbestos disease do not include only (approximately 7000) former mine employees and their families, but also such people as a man who delivered meats to Wittenoom and carried back sacks of asbestos in his truck.

Australia is perhaps the only country where negligence on the part of an employer is grounds for a civil suit by an injured worker in general industry (i.e., workers' compensation is not an exclusive "remedy" for injured workers to recover damages against their employers). In 1988, a judge in Western Australia and a jury in Melbourne held the mining company responsible in separate cases.

The Perth trial held both CSR and its paper subsidiary mining company Midalco responsible. This case took the better part of a year to try, during which time one of the two plaintiffs (both had mesothelioma) died, precipating a massive street demonstration by unions in Perth. One of the witnesses for CSR was Dr. Robert Murray, who had worked with Dr. Merewether at the U.K. Factory Inspectorate from 1947-1956. Murray's challenge in this case was to help justify what was politely referred to as an extremely conservative approach. The judge found it "rather difficult to understand" that Murray said he would not have called attention to the cancer risk, if asked for advice on asbestos, prior to the publication of Doll's report in 1955.

The jury in the Melbourne case, in an unprecedented decision, assessed punitive damages against the mining subsidiary, whose robust defense was underwritten by CSR. On appeal, the Full Court of Victoria said a strong case had been made supporting a finding of recklessness and continuing, conscious, and contumelious disregard for the employee's right to be free from risk of disease.

A number of books have been written that describe the tragedy at Wittenoom, most recently Ben Hills' *Blue Murder* (Macmillan Co. of Australia, 1989) and Jock McCulloch's *Asbestos/Its Human Cost* (Univ. of Queensland Press, 1986).

RAILROAD COMPANIES

In the United States, some transportation industries including railroads never made legal provision for workers' compensation. As a result, employees who develop occupational diseases must bring suit against their employers in an appropriate legal forum. In the case of railroad workers, there has been intense exposure to asbestos insulation dust in roundhouses where locomotives were overhauled. The old steam locomotives were equipped with large quantities of asbestos insulation. Severe asbestos exposure in railroad maintenance work is apparently a thing of the past in the United States, with the replacement of steam locomotives by diesels and the substitution of asbestos-free railroad brake shoes. However, the toll of disease from past years is great (T.F. Mancuso. "Mesothelioma among Machinists in Railroad and Other Industries," *Amer. J. Indust. Med* 4:501-513, 1983).

Medical directors of the railroad companies held annual meetings starting in 1921 under the auspices of the Association of American Railroads. The meetings of the Medical and Surgical Section, as the group was known (or simply the Medical Section in later years), were often concerned with occupational health and safety, and proceedings of the working sessions were published and distributed to the membership. The members of various committees and the attendees of each meeting were duly recognized in the proceedings, with each doctor's company affiliation designated.

The following notes of the meetings through 1958 relate to the forseeability of asbestos hazards by the medical officers of the railroad companies. The documents were located in the library of the Interstate Commerce Commission in Washington, D.C. (Proceedings of the Medical and Surgical Section of the Association of American Railroads). Relevant page numbers are noted in parentheses.

1932 Committee on Occupational Diseases and Rehabilitation reported on "Dust as an Industrial Hazard" (60-62), discussing pneumoconiosis at length. It was noted that chest X-rays were diagnostic of fibrous tissue. Many symptoms of pneumoconiosis are cited, hypersusceptibility to infection in the lung is noted. Wetting and ventilation are offered as control methods. Asbestos not explicitly mentioned.

1933 Report of the same committee by same title, recommends respirators in addition to the above measures as controls. Asbestos not mentioned. (72,77).

1935 Report of the same committee now has a subtitle "Pneumoconiosis" (89-90). "Asbestosis is not a common condition but it causes extensive pulmonary fibrosis and takes on a more rapid course than does silicosis." Following, "(A)s railroad surgeons (we) are undoubtedly more interested in silicosis and asbestosis than in the other types." Examinations upon hire were advised to include complete history and physical, with chest X-ray "for diagnosis and future record."

> For old employees with a history of working in dust and having the classical clinical symptoms, we suggest:

1. To make a change in his occupation.
2. To make an X-ray of his chest for lung tissue.

In the way of prevention it becomes necessary

1. To educate all concerned.
2. Get rid of dust.
3. Sprinkle the working area with water.
4. Have employees wear inhalers. (sic)
5. Have frequent analyses made of the dust content of the air at different times during the working hours.

1937 Discussion of occupational disease (compensation and prevention) laws enacted in Illinois, with mention of extended statute of limitations for asbestosis and silicosis claims. (19) Concern expressed that state distribution of pamphlets would "create a fear complex" with resulting unjustified workers' compensation claims (20).

> Silica, asbestos, and lead are the principal substances generating toxic dusts to which railway employees may be exposed. (20)

Pre-employment physicals and histories are again recommended, as well as periodic physical examinations of employees "in occupations in which known hazards exist." (21) Control measures discussed include: exhaust ventilation of dusty processes, substitution of safer materials and methods of handling, and use of personal protective equipment such as respirators approved for the intended use by the U.S. Bureau of Mines. (21-22) It is reiterated at the end that asbestosis and silicosis are dust diseases and can be contracted only by breathing asbestos or silica dust. (22)

Report of the Committee on Disability and Rehabilitation has a lengthy section, Pneumoconiosis. (72-76) This is almost entirely on silicosis, until the mention of the Illinois law provisions where asbestosis is mentioned.

1939 Report of Committee on Disability and Rehabilitation (CDR) noted the emergence of the Air Hygiene Foundation (name changed to Industrial Hygiene Foundation in 1941) with its interest in pneumoconiosis, noted that (37) CDR Chairman had attended AHF meetings and summarized AHF presentations. Summaries deal with industrial hygiene, compensation laws;

Lanza quoted as saying that instead of removing men from dust hazards the dust should be removed. (38)

1940 CDR report again consists of review of presentations at AHF meeting. (28) "(M)any details are brought out at (AHF's) annual meetings which can be made of immense value to the Railroads." (29) Nothing on asbestosis here, but such items as Drinker's presentation on preventive engineering clearly had broad application.

1941 CDR Chairman again attended the AHF meeting but had nothing new to report on pneumoconiosis. (37,46)

1951 CDR report section on Pneumoconiosis contains the same
1952 language all three years. Opens with, "The Committee...
1953 mentioned silicosis and asbestosis as forms of the disease most interesting to railroad surgeons." (38 in 1951; 35 in 1952; 34 in 1953) Exam at time of hire to include history and chest X-ray, "particularly in those occupations where unusual quantities of silica or asbestos dust have been encountered or are contemplated as a routine occupational exposure." Periodic exams of such workers also recommended, with X-ray, and those presenting symptoms to be considered for removal and counseling.

Indexes in 1952 (42) and 1953 (41) list all years (of Medical Section published proceedings) in which the Committee previously discussed pneumoconiosis.

1957 CDR adds to and deletes some of its previous statements, adding that periodic X-ray examinations should be done "annually" on employees exposed to dust. (24)

1958 The entire Medical Section of the Association of American Railroads hosted Dr. Alton Ochsner, a lung cancer surgeon from New Orleans. He had been affiliated with Illinois Central and Southern Pacific. (81)

> There is very good proof that asbestos is a cause of carcinoma. This is seen in individuals working with asbestos, particularly miners. It is also seen among plumbers who work with asbestos, seamfitters (sic) particularly. (81)

He said "Heuber" (Hueper) did a study "in which he showed there was a higher incidence of cancer among the operating

> staffs of the railroads than among the non-operating staffs." Ochsner attributed this finding to a preponderance of males in operations and females in offices (there was a well-recognized difference in incidence of the disease between the sexes).
>
> He said people in these occupations with which an increased risk of cancer has been shown—who develop cancer themselves—are usually heavy smokers, and the smoking is the cause, not occupation. He noted that the only doctors who doubted smoking caused cancer worked for tobacco companies or smoked themselves. (84) Railroad doctors were advised to check smoking histories and tumor cell types of workers filing for compensation for lung cancer.
>
>> If they have an adenocarcinoma, it has not been produced by smoking because it is not related to smoking.

Hueper had reported that lung cancer cases were more than three times as numerous among "operating" railroad workers (engineers, firemen, brakemen, conductors, switchmen, and roundhouse personnel) than "non-operating" workers. Yet the former group made up only about 25 percent of the work force. Hueper suspected oil and coal combustion products as a cause of occupational cancers (*A Quest Into the Environmental Causes of Cancer of the Lung* Washington: Public Health Service Publ. 452, 1955, p. 16).

Railroad companies operating in Illinois looked into the industry's asbestos problem and other occupational disease threats following enactment of workers' compensation legislation in Illinois in 1936. A group of management representatives called the General Managers Association developed these guidelines in 1937 (documents produced by Illinois Gulf Central Railroad Co. in 1987):

REVISED RECOMMENDATIONS COVERING RULES AND INSTRUCTIONS FOR PREVENTION OF ASBESTOSIS. THESE RULES TO SUPERSEDE THOSE ADOPTED BY THE SHOP AND ENGINEERING COMMITTEE ON JAN. 18, 1937.

1. Respirators should be furnished by the Company and they should be worn at all times by employees handling asbestos.

Attention is called to some of the specific instances where respirators are required:

Loading or unloading shipments of asbestos.
Mixing asbestos.
Removing lagging from boilers.
Removing lagging from pipes.
Breaking up or grinding asbestos.

2. Before removing lagging from a boiler, either locomotive or stationary, asbestos must be sprayed with water sufficiently to lay the dust.
3. Removal of lagging from locomotive boilers should be done when there is the least number of men working in the vicinity, and all such men should be protected by wearing approved respirators.
4. Grinding asbestos causes excessive dust. Where such operations are performed and facilities are equipped with exhaust systems, employees should also be required to wear approved respirators. When exhaust systems are not provided, employees so engaged should be required to wear air masks or helmets with clean dry air furnished from an outside source.
5. Each employee required to wear a respirator should be furnished one for his individual use or one that has been sterilized if previously used by any other person.
6. To insure maximum protection from respirators, only those that have the approval of the U.S. Bureau of Mines should be furnished.
7. Foremen should make periodical checks to see that respirators fit properly, and to note that they are in good condition.
8. Foremen should be held responsible for seeing that respirators are worn in accordance with instructions.
9. It is suggested that the above recommendations be communicated directly to the foremen involved. Publicity on the above might suggest the making of claims.

Railroad claims agents also discussed asbestosis at meetings and in their journals in the 1930s (P. Folger, "Legal and Other Aspects of Dust Hazards," *Minutes of the 45th Annual Meeting of the Association of Railway Claim Agents,* held in May, 1934, pp.

27-48; O.G. Browne, "Silicosis," *The Bulletin 19*:281-284, April, 1935; E.R. Hayhurst, "Common Occupational Diseases and Their Differential Diagnosis," *Minutes of the 48th Annual Meeting of the Association of Railway Claim Agents* held in May, 1937, pp. 31-41). In 1960, asbestos was listed as one of 7 materials which had been "suspected as lung carcinogens" in an article by Dr. I. Kaplan of the Baltimore and Ohio Railroad ("Relationship of Noxious Gases to Carcinoma of the Lung in Railroad Workers," *J.A.M.A. 171*:2039-2042, Dec. 12, 1959, reprinted in *The Bulletin 44*:511-520, 1960).

At least one railroad, the Norfolk & Western, had an asbestosis claim decades ago. The man had worked in the engine shop of the railroad, frequently handling insulation materials made with asbestos. He claimed he was totally disabled with asbestosis and had suffered pleural effusion as well (*Ancel Wheeler v. Norfolk & Western*, U.S. Dist. Court S. Dist. Ohio, W. Div., Civ. No. 2740; and Dr. Allen Barker's letter to Dr. W. R. Whitman, Chief Surgeon for N & W, Aug. 18, 1951 describing the X-ray findings as "compatible with asbestosis").

10

Historical Research on Toxic Substances

INTRODUCTION

This research on asbestos disease history is more extensive than any ever done on a toxic substance. It has involved thousands of hours of library and patent searches, translations, depositions, and examinations of corporate and government records. Access to corporate files and sworn testimony could only have been gained in the context of litigation.

The basic historical picture about asbestos disease was assembled and summarized by the author in 1977. This required only a few months' time, and a minimum of clerical and editorial assistance (*The Development of Knowledge about Asbestos Disease*, 93 pp., unpublished, 1977). The more complete historical mosaic since assembled still follows the chronology pictured in the 1977 report. The motivation to "leave no stone unturned" arose largely as a consequence of finding such an extensive and accessible published body of medical literature.

Legal discovery has documented the perception of the historical medical literature held by various people and companies. Only corporate documents and testimony of the individuals involved could recreate events as they emerged "from the inside." This inside story was developed at enormous expense by attorneys representing plaintiffs in asbestos litigation. It could not have emerged as fully by any other means. Though many of the attorneys involved are motivated by "the pot of gold at the end of the rainbow," nonetheless their work has vitally informed the public on major issues of public policy and social justice. This is invaluable for legislators and society at large, facing the aftermath of past failures to control asbestos.

Just as the asbestos litigation has broken new ground in setting legal precedents, the scientific research on asbestos disease history has wide applicability. There is a similarly vast body of knowledge on other substances such as lead and benzene, which have also been foci of occupational and environmental damage suits in the United States.

Synthetic chemicals have not been used as pesticides for quite so long, but their power as human poisons has been far better recognized by manufacturers than by some users of these products. Long-delayed, deadly diseases are steadily following society's increasing use of toxic substances. As the chronic effects of excessive exposure to these products becomes increasingly manifest as clinical disease, the question will be asked: could this reasonably have been foreseen and prevented?

In the context of historical research on toxic substances several questions are posed: what was scientifically known about the health effects and means of preventing them; when was the knowledge available; and what was actually known and done by the producers of these hazardous products? The process of seeking answers to these questions will be described, using the asbestos research experience as a guideline.

Index Medicus

A classical method of searching the medical literature is to use the *Index Medicus.* This has been in existence since 1879, and lists articles from periodicals by author and subject from all over the world. It has also been called *Quarterly Cumulative Index* (1916-1926) and *Quarterly Cumulative Index Medicus* (1927-1956). This source has proved to be far from all-inclusive on the subject of asbestos disease; but it is nonetheless quite comprehensive and useful for doing searches for the years in which an industrial health hazard first began to achieve recognition. The *Index Medicus* is particularly helpful for the era before the development of computerized medical retrieval services.

Computerized Indexes

Computerized indexing of medical articles is a relatively recent occurrence. Until the 1960s, there was no such means for gaining access to the literature. The National Library of Medicine in the U.S. has introduced a number of computerized literature retrieval services including:

Name of Service	Years Covered	Type of Service
Toxline/Toxlit	1965 on	toxicology, epidemiology, mutagenesis, teratology (2.5-3.0 million citations)
Medline	1966 on	contains over 6 million citations to biomedical journals
Cancerlit	1963 on	Carcinogenesis: articles, proceedings, monographs, theses, government reports (over 700,000 citations)

Use of these services is reasonably inexpensive and widely accessible in the United States. Through the use of appropriate key words, computer retrieval services can be used to summon citations and, in some cases, summaries of the contents of each article.

This sort of access is helpful for learning the current state of knowledge and its recent origins. However, more tedious and conventional methods must be used to reach back to the earliest published origins of the knowledge if these pre-date the 1960s.

Reviews—NIOSH Criteria Documents and Other Reports

It is best to start a search with an exhaustive review article on the hazards of the substance or occupation in question. The

National Institute for Occupational Safety and Health (Cincinnati, Ohio) has published a large series of Criteria Documents on particular substances, as well as special reports of other kinds. NIOSH Criteria Documents make excellent starting points for historical research on most substances covered. Although the main purpose of these documents is to justify and recommend a standard to OSHA, these documents typically trace the recognized hazards of a substance from the principal early reports and usually include at least some mention of all the adverse effects that have been attributed to the material.

Alphabetical Listing of NIOSH Criteria Documents

NIOSH Publication Number	Subject
76-195	Acetylene
77-112	Acrylamide
78-116	Acrylonitrile
77-151	Alkanes
76-204	Allyl Chloride
74-136	Ammonia
78-216	Antimony
74-110	Arsenic, Inorganic
75-149	Arsenic, Inorganic (Revised)
72-10267	Asbestos
77-169	Asbestos (Revised)
78-106	Asphalt Fumes
74-137	Benzene
+ (1976)	Benzene (Revised)
77-166	Benzoyl Peroxide
78-182	Benzyl Chloride
72-10268	Beryllium
77-122	Boron Trifluoride
76-192	Cadmium
77-107	Carbaryl
78-204	Carbon Black
76-194	Carbon Dioxide
77-156	Carbon Disulfide
73-11000	Carbon Monoxide
76-133	Carbon Tetrachloride

Alphabetical Listing of NIOSH Criteria Documents

NIOSH Publication Number	Subject
76-133	Carbon Tetrachloride (Revised)
76-170	Chlorine
75-114	Chloroform
+ (1976)	Chloroform (Revised)
77-210	Chloroprene
73-11021	Chromic Acid
76-129	Chromium (VI)
78-191	Coal Gasification Plants
81-131	Coal Liquefaction Volume I - Summary
81-132	Coal Liquefaction Volume II - Assessment
78-107	Coal Tar Products
82-107	Cobalt
73-11016	Coke Oven Emissions
80-106	Confined Spaces, Working in
75-118	Cotton Dust
78-133	Cresol
77-108	Cyanide, Hydrogen, and Cyanide Salts
77-193	Decomposition Products of Fluorocarbon Polymers
78-115	Dibromochloropropane
78-215	Diisocyanates
78-131	Dinitro-ortho-cresol
77-226	Dioxane
76-128	Emergency Egress From Elevated Work Stations
76-206	Epichlorohydrin
77-221	Ethylene Dibromide
76-139	Ethylene Dichloride (1,2 Dichloroethane)
78-211	Ethylene Dichloride (1,2 Dichloroethane) (Revised)
77-152	Fibrous Glass
76-103	Fluorides, Inorganic
77-126	Formaldehyde
79-133	Furfuryl Alcohol
78-166	Glycidyl Ethers
72-10269	Hot Environments
78-172	Hydrazines
76-143	Hydrogen Fluoride
77-158	Hydrogen Sulfide
78-155	Hydroquinone
75-126	Identification System for Occupationally Hazardous Materials

(continued)

Alphabetical Listing of NIOSH Criteria Documents

NIOSH Publication Number	Subject
76-142	Isopropyl Alcohol
+ (1976)	Kepone
78-173	Ketones
73-11010	Lead, Inorganic
78-158	Lead, Inorganic (Revised)
76-188	Logging-From Felling to First Haul
76-205	Malathion
73-11024	Mercury, Inorganic
76-148	Methyl Alcohol
77-106	Methyl Parathion
76-138	Methylene Chloride
77-164	Nickel, Inorganic
76-141	Nitric Acid
78-212	Nitriles
76-149	Nitrogen, Oxides
78-167	Nitroglycerin and of Ethylene Glycol Dinitrate
73-11001	Noise
77-115	Organotin Compounds
76-190	Parathion
78-174	Pesticides Manufacturing and Formulation
76-196	Phenol
76-137	Phosgene
77-225	Polychlorinated Biphenyls
77-192	Refined Petroleum Solvents
75-120	Silica, Crystalline
76-105	Sodium Hydroxide
83-119	Styrene
74-128	Sulfuric Acid
74-111	Sulfur Dioxide
77-121	1,1,2,2-Tetrachloroethane
76-185	Tetrachloroethylene (PERC)
78-213	Thiols: N-Alkane, Mono, Cyclohexane, and Benzene
78-179	o-Tolidine
73-11023	Toluene
73-11022	Toluene Diisocyanate
76-184	1,1,1-Trichloroethane (Methyl Chloroform)
73-11025	Trichloroethylene
77-227	Tungsten and Cemented Tungsten Carbide
73-11009	Ultraviolet Radiation
77-222	Vanadium
78-205	Vinyl Acetate

Alphabetical Listing of NIOSH Criteria Documents

NIOSH Publication Number	Subject
+ (1974)	Vinyl Chloride
77-140	Waste Anesthetic Gases and Vapors
75-168	Xylene
76-104	Zinc Oxide

+ No NIOSH Publication Number is assigned.

(See also "U.S. Government Documents," this chapter, for more on NIOSH)

Abstracts

Not only were there journals specializing in industrial hygiene and medicine since the early years of this century, but there were also periodicals offering abstracts of the literature. In the United States, the *Journal of Industrial Hygiene* first appeared in 1919. After 1935, it was called the *Journal of Industrial Hygiene and Toxicology,* and it continued until 1949 (at which time it was replaced by the *AMA Archives of Industrial Hygiene and Occupational Medicine*).

A regular feature of this journal was a very lengthy supplement (at the end of each volume, with separate numbered pages) called *Abstract of the Literature of Industrial Hygiene.* Here appeared excellent summaries of key European and U.S. reports on asbestosis and other occupational diseases. The Annual Reports of the Chief Inspector of Factories (U.K.) were also summarized, as were legislative developments in industrial hygiene and compensation. The journal also benefited from the flight of Dr. Ludwig Teleky from Germany in the late 1930s. Teleky had been an editor of the *Archiv fuř Gewerbepathologie und Gewerbehygiene* published in Berlin. See, for example, his abstracts of the articles on asbestosis and cancer by Nordmann and Hornig (*Abstr. Literature Indust. Hyg. Tox.* Suppl. to *J. Industr. Hyg. Tox. 20*:184, 1938). The articles and abstracts sections of this journal were continuously indexed. In 1947 the publisher issued a cumulative index for the years 1936–1945, which contained reference to more than 50 abstracts on asbestos disease (*Cumulative Index/Journal of Industrial*

Hygiene and Toxicology. Williams and Wilkins Co., Baltimore, MD, p. 60, 1947).

From England, there was the *Bulletin of Hygiene* during the years 1926 to 1967. It was afterwards incorporated into *Abstracts of Hygiene.* This journal included only abstracts of articles, and was perhaps the best single source of abstracts in English on non-English European publications dealing with asbestos diseases. Abstracts were contributed by renowned figures in the field of industrial medicine not only in Great Britain but elsewhere in Europe. In 1956, for example, large-scale reports on asbestosis in insulation workers were published in Denmark, Italy, and Sweden. Abstracts of all three promptly appeared in the *Bulletin of Hygiene.*

Abstracts of 1956 Reports of Asbestosis in Insulation Workers

Authors of report, journal	Bull. Hyg. cite	Abstract Author
Frost, Georg, and Møller (Danish Medical Bulletin)	*32:* 260 (March, 1957)	E.L. Collis
Molfino and Zannini (Folia Medica)	*32:* 1168 (December, 1957)	E. Vigliani
Ahlborg and Hansson (Svenska Läkartidningen)	*31:* 1115-1116 (November, 1956)	C. Lillingston

One of the most remarkable achievements of this journal was the timely and uninterrupted publication of abstracts during World War II. One might expect that British pathologist S. Roodhouse Gloyne would have had some difficulty obtaining and reading current German asbestosis articles during the war. Yet the 1942 articles on asbestosis by Böhme and on asbestosis/cancer by Welz in *Archiv für Gewerbepathologie und Gewerbehygiene* were abstracted by Gloyne in the *Bulletin of Hygiene* the following year (Vol. 18, p. 651). And Wedler's landmark report on cancers of the lung and pleura with asbestosis, published in the *Deutsche Medizinische Wochenschrift* in August of 1943, was summarized by Gloyne nine months later in the *Bulletin of Hygiene* (Vol. 19, p. 362).

The *Bulletin of Hygiene* abstracts of the papers by Welz, Böhme, and Wedler were reprinted in full in the abstracts section of *Journal of Industrial Hygiene and Toxicology* (Vol. 26, pp. 8, 183, 1944). The 1941 paper by Linzbach and Wedler, "Occupational Cancer among Asbestos Workers," was abstracted in *Journal of Industrial Hygiene and Toxicology* by Teleky (Vol. 24, p. 40, 1942).

Pneumoconiosis Abstracts was an offshoot of *Bulletin of Hygiene*. Volume I was comprised of reprinted *Bulletin of Hygiene* abstracts for the years 1926 to 1938. It was published in London (by Sir Isaac Pitman & Sons, Ltd.) in 1953. Volume II covered the years 1939 to 1950 and was published in 1954. Volume III covered 1951-1955 and came out in 1959. Each volume had a special section on articles that dealt primarily with asbestosis.

The *Bulletin of Hygiene* was not the only source of medical abstracts from Great Britain. The British Medical Association began to issue *Abstracts of World Medicine* after World War II. This carried a few abstracts of literature on asbestos, including one of the article, "Asbestosis with Pleural Calcification among Insulation Workers" (by J. Frost and co-workers, *Dan. Med. Bull. 3*:202-204, Nov. 1956). The abstract opens by describing the pneumoconiosis hazard to insulators as having been "established" by "experience in many countries." (A. Meiklejohn, *Abstr. World Med. 21*:359, May, 1957). So, occasionally, an abstract contained commentary that went beyond the mere summarizing of individual research findings.

In the Netherlands, Excerpta Medica Foundation began publishing a range of abstracting periodicals in 1948 in the English language. Excerpta Medica publications were subdivided into numerous "sections" covering different types of medical subjects. Abstracts of papers on asbestosis prior to 1965 appeared most often in the *Excerpta Medica* sections on 1) Chest Diseases and 2) Public Health, Social Medicine, and Hygiene. It was common for abstracts appearing in one section of the *Excerpta Medica* series to later be reprinted in another section with overlapping interests. *Excerpta Medica* sections on Cancer, Occupational Health and Industrial Medicine, and Pharmacology and Toxicology are among the 50 sections of *Excerpta Medica* now produced. Since 1959, these abstracts have also been published in New York and other cities in addition to Amsterdam.

A remarkable source of articles on dust diseases was *The Pneumoconioses (Silicosis),* issued as three volumes in 1934-1937 (by G.G. Davis, E.M. Salmonsen, and J.L. Earlywine, Chicago Medical Press). This compilation includes well-indexed citations of over 80 scientific articles on asbestosis from all over the world. Included as well are abstracts of then-current articles from insurance industry and engineering publications. These offer a fascinating glimpse of the ferment existing at that time over civil suits and the applicability of workers' compensation statutes for occupational diseases. In addition, there are extensive descriptions of applicable laws in the various states of the U.S. and provinces of Canada.

The Industrial Hygiene Foundation, founded as the Air Hygiene Foundation in 1936 and renamed in 1941 (called Industrial Health Foundation since 1971), has published *Industrial Hygiene Digest* monthly since 1937. Copies were automatically sent to member industrial and insurance companies, which numbered 300 by the end of 1946 (the published *Transactions* in these years listed member firms and "special subscriber" institutions). Thus, in 1946, asbestos companies including American Brake Shoe Company, Eagle-Picher Company, Johns-Manville Corporation, Keasbey & Mattison Company, Owens-Corning Fiberglas Corporation, Owens-Illinois Glass Company, Raybestos-Manhattan, and Union Asbestos and Rubber Company, obtained current abstracts of worldwide literature on workplace illnesses. Ruberoid Co. and Asbestos Corporation, Ltd. joined I.H.F. in 1953. The Decennial Index of the *Digest* for 1945-1954 had 43 entries under the headings asbestos and asbestosis. As of 1944, I.H.F.'s *Digest* regularly reviewed more than 200 medical journals from around the world, and a comparable number of trade, engineering, and science journals. By 1958 this *Digest* provided more than 1500 abstracts annually to subscribers.

The *Asbestos Bulletin/Abstracts of Recent Articles and Patents* was available by subscription starting in 1960 from Astex

Publishing Company in England. Under the heading, "Miscellaneous" appeared a very brief abstract of the case report on asbestosis and cancer in an insulation worker by Anderson and Campagna (Vol. 1, p. 96, 1960), and mere references to other titles by Keal and others in England and Germany (Vol. 2, p. 96, 1961).

Less specialized sources of medical abstracts on subjects like asbestosis contain less information. The *Journal of the American Medical Association* periodically carried abstracts on industrial medicine, as did the *American Review of Tuberculosis*, but the specialty journals (as opposed to general medical journals) were clearly the main repositories of such abstracts.

Chemical Abstracts, which is mainly about technology, not medicine, nonetheless carried several dozen abstracts of early articles on the pathology and other aspects of asbestosis. The earliest of these were writings of Stewart and Haddow in 1929 (*CA 23:* 2482) and Gloyne in 1930 (*CA 24:* 2791) and 1931 (*CA 26:* 2499). The U.S. Public Health Service reports of Page and Bloomfield (*CA 32:* 1009) and Dreessen *et al.* (*CA 33:* 6471) were also reviewed. A number of pre-1960 articles describing the cancer hazards of asbestos were also summarized in *Chemical Abstracts*:

Author (Year) of Article	Chemical Abstracts Cite
Nordmann (1938)	*32:* 711
Teleky (1938)	*35:* 3732
Nordmann and Sorge (1941)	*36:* 2006
Mottura and Fagiano (1940)	*36:* 3581
Linzbach and Wedler (1941)	*37:* 2844
Boemke (1947)	*42:* 9002
Hueper (1949)	*44:* 5037
Perry (1947)	*45:* 9773
Owen (1950)	*46:* 6291
Boemke (1953)	*47:* 4471
Doll (1955)	*49:* 9195
Schmähl (1958)	*53:* 22414

Citations of articles on asbestos and asbestosis were easily accessible, using decennial indexes published by *Chemical Abstracts* since the 1930s.

Other technical abstracts also included references to writings on asbestosis. *Ceramic Abstracts*, for example, included summaries of the historic government publication in Britain of Merewether and Price (*Cer. Abstr. 10*:531, 1931); articles on pneumoconioses by Drinker and by Clark (*16:* 137, 1937), McConnell and Middleton (*16:* 138, 1937), Gardner (*19:* 205, 1940; *23:* 132, 1944), Williams (*20:* 135, 1941), and others; asbestosis papers of Sayers and Dreessen (*18:* 168, 1939), Stone (*19:* 149, 1940), Vigliani (*19:* 226, 1940), and Noro (*26:* 190, 1947); Lanza's 1938 text, *Silicosis and Asbestosis* (*19:* 81, 1940); also reference to government reports in the U.S. and elsewhere on the subjects of air sampling, industrial hygiene engineering, etc. The British counterpart, *Transactions of the Ceramic Society Abstracts*, similarly reported on the seriousness of the health hazard from asbestos dust (*36:* 51A, 1937; *39:* 89A, 1940). This appears to have been succeeded by *British Ceramic Abstracts*, which noted publications on dust diseases in the 1950s by McLaughlin, Holt, and others.

Medical Textbooks

Downstream of the primary medical literature are specialized medical textbooks. For asbestos diseases, one finds mention in books on chest diseases, preventive medicine, pathology, industrial hygiene/toxicology, occupational medicine, and, of course, pneumoconioses. Some of the earlier books on occupational health are shown in the table (See also "Other Sources of Information on Asbestos and Cancer," in Chapter 2).

EARLY TEXTBOOKS ON OCCUPATIONAL HEALTH (In English)

1. Ramazzini, Bernardino. *Diseases of Workers (De Morbis Artificum).* Translated from Latin original (1713). New York: Hafner Publ. Co., 1964.

2. Thackrah, C.T. *The Effects of the Principal Arts, Trades and Professions, and of Civic States and Habits of Living, on Health and Longevity, with Suggestions for Removal of Many of the Agents which Produce Disease and Shorten the Duration of Life.* London: Longman, Rees, Orme, Brown, and Green, 1831.

3. McCready, B.W. *On the Influence of Trades, Professions, and Occupations in the United States, in the Production of Disease* (1837). Baltimore: Johns Hopkins Press, 1943.

4. Arlidge, J.T. *The Hygiene, Diseases, and Mortality of Occupations.* London: Percival, 1892.

5. Oliver, Thomas. *Dangerous Trades.* London: E.P. Dutton, 1902.

6. Kober, G.M. *Industrial and Personal Hygiene.* Washington: President's Homes Commission, 1908.

7. Oliver, T. *Diseases of Occupation.* London: Methuen & Co., 1908 and 1916.

8. Greer, W.J. *Industrial Diseases and Accidents.* London: J.W. Arrowsmith, 1909.

9. Price. G.M. *The Modern Factory.* New York: J. Wiley & Sons, 1914.

10. Thompson, W.G. *The Occupational Diseases.* New York: D. Appleton & Co., 1914.

11. Hayhurst, E.R. *A Survey of Industrial Health Hazards and Occupational Diseases in Ohio.* Columbus, Ohio: F.J. Heer Printing Co., 1915.

12. White, R.P. *Occupational Affections of the Skin.* New York: Paul Hoeber, 1915, 1920, 1923, and 1934.

13. Mock, H.B. *Industrial Medicine and Surgery.* Philadelphia: W.B. Saunders Co., 1920.

14. Collis, E.L. and M. Greenwood. *The Health of the Industrial Worker.* London: J. & A. Churchill, 1921.

15. Clark. W.I. *Health Service in Industry.* New York: Macmillan Co., 1922.

16. Hope, E.W., W. Hanna and C.O. Stallybrass. *Industrial Hygiene and Medicine.* New York: W. Wood & Co., 1923.

17. Kober, G.M. and E.R. Hayhurst. *Industrial Health.* Philadelphia: P. Blackiston's Son & Co., 1924.

18. Hamilton, Alice. *Industrial Poisons in the United States.* New York: MacMillan Co., 1925, 1929.

19. Hackett, J.D. *Health Maintenance in Industry.* Chicago: A.W. Shaw Co. Chicago, 1925.

20. Henderson, Y. and H.W. Haggard. *Noxious Gases,* New York: Chemical Catalog Co., later Reinhold Publ. Corp., 1927, 1943.

21. Price, G.M. *Labor Protection in Soviet Russia.* New York: International Publishers Co., 1928.

22. Haslam, J.F.C. *Recent Advances in Preventive Medicine.* London: J. & A. Churchill, 1930.

23. Goldberg, R.W. *Occupational Diseases.* New York: Columbia University Press, 1931.

24. McCord, C.P., and Allen, F.P. *Industrial Hygiene for Engineers and Managers.* New York: Harper & Bros., 1931.

25. Bristol, L.D. *Industrial Health Services.* Philadelphia: Lea & Febiger, 1933.

26. Legge, Thomas. *Industrial Maladies.* London: Oxford University Press, 1934.

27. Hamilton, A. *Industrial Toxicology.* New York: Harper & Bros., 1934.

28. Clark, W.I. and P. Drinker. *Industrial Medicine.* New York: National Medical Book Co., 1935.

29. Browning, Ethel. *Toxicity of Industrial Organic Solvents.* London: H.M. Stationery Office, 1937.

30. Drinker. P., and T. Hatch. *Industrial Dust.* New York: McGraw-Hill, 1936 and 1954.

31. Ling, T.M. and J.A. Nixon. *Recent Advances in Industrial Hygiene and Medicine.* Philadelphia: P. Blackiston's Son, 1937.

32. McNally, W.D. *Toxicology.* Chicago: Industrial Medicine Publishing Co., 1937.

33. Gonzales, T.A., *et. al. Legal Medicine and Toxicology.* New York: D. Appleton-Century, 1937.

34. Chenoweth, L.B. and W. Machle. *Industrial Hygiene: A Handbook of Hygiene and Toxicology for Engineers and Plant Managers.* New York: F.S. Crofts & Co., 1938.

35. Lanza, A.J. (ed.) *Silicosis and Asbestosis.* London: Oxford University Press, 1938.

36. Lanza, A.J. and J.A. Goldberg (eds.) *Industrial Hygiene.* New York: Oxford University Press, 1939.

37. Vernon, H.M. *Health in Relation to Occupation.* London: Oxford University Press, 1939.

38. Sappington, C.O. *Medicolegal Phases of Occupational Diseases.* Chicago: Industrial Health Book Co., 1939.

39. Schwartz, L. and L. Tulipan. *Occupational Diseases of the Skin.* Philadelphia: Lea & Febiger, 1939 and 1947.

40. Collier, H.E. *Outlines of Industrial Medical Practice.* London: Edward Arnold & Co., 1940.

41. Eilmann, H.J. *Medicolegal and Industrial Toxicology.* Philadelphia: The Blakiston Company, 1940.

42. Fickler, J.B. *Manual of Industrial Health Hazards.* West Hartford, Connecticut: Service to Industry, 1940.

43. Johnstone, R.T. *Occupational Diseeases.* Philadelphia: W.B. Saunders Co., 1941.

44. Reed, J.V. and A.K. Harcourt. *The Essentials of Occupational Diseases.* Springfield, Ill.: C.C. Thomas, 1941.
45. Amor, A.J. *An X-ray Atlas of Silicosis.* Baltimore: Williams & Wilkins, 1941.
46. Jacobs, M.B. *The Analytical Chemistry of Industrial Poisons, Hazards, and Solvents. New York: Interscience Publ., 1941.*
47. Hueper, W.C. *Occupational Tumors and Allied Diseases.* Springfield, Ill.: C.C. Thomas, 1942.
48. Gafafer, W.M. (ed.) *Manual of Industrial Hygiene and Medical Service in War Industries.* Phialdelphia and London: W.B. Saunders Company, 1943.
49. Rosen, G. *The History of Miners' Diseases.* New York: Schuman's, 1943.
50. Hamilton, A. *Exploring the Dangerous Trades.* Boston: Little, Brown & Co., 1943.
51. Weiss, J.E. (ed.) 1021 *Answers to Industrial Health and Safety Problems.* Cleveland: Occupational Hazards, Inc., 1943.
52. Sappington, E.O. *Essentials of Industrial Health.* Philadelphia: J.P. Lippincott Co., 1943.
53. Wampler, F.J. *The Principles and Practice of Industrial Medicine.* Baltimore: Williams and Wilkins, 1943.
54. Lehmann, K.B. and F. Flury. *Toxicology and Hygiene of Industrial Solvents.* Baltimore: Williams & Wilkins, 1943.
55. Rolliston, H. and A. Moncrieff. *Industrial Medicine.* London: Eyre and Spottiswoode, 1944.
56. Hunter, D. *Industrial Toxicology.* Oxford at the Clarendon Press, 1944.
57. Hamilton, A. and R.T. Johnstone. *Industrial Toxicology.* New York: Oxford Univ. Press, 1945.
58. Stern. B.J. *Medicine in Industry.* New York: The Commonwealth Fund, 1946.
59. Brandt, A.D. *Industrial Health Engineering.* New York: J. Wiley & Sons, 1947.
60. Brodman, K. *Men At Work: The Supervisor and His People.* Chicago: Cloud, Inc., 1947.
61. Hazlett, T.L. (ed.) *Introduction to Industrial Medicine.* Chicago: Industrial Medicine Publ. Co., 1947.
62. Teleky, L. *History of Factory and Mine Hygiene.* New York: Columbia University Press, 1948.
63. Dallavalle, J.M. *The Industrial Environment and Its Control.* New York: Pitman Publ. Corp., 1948.

64. Patty, F.A. *Industrial Hygiene and Toxicology.* New York: Interscience Publ., 1948 and 1962.

65. Lloyd-Davies, T.A. *The Practice of Industrial Medicine.* London: J. & A. Churchill, 1948 and 1957.

66. Johnstone, R.T. *Occupational Medicine and Industrial Hygiene.* St. Louis: C.V. Mosby Co., 1948.

67. Hamilton, A. and H. Hardy. *Industrial Toxicology.* 2nd ed. New York: Paul Hoeber Inc., 1949.

68. Fairhall, L.T. *Industrial Toxicology.* Baltimore: Williams & Wilkins, 1949 and 1957.

69. Industrial Health Division, Canada Department of National Health and Welfare, and the Division of Industrial Hygiene, Department of Health for Ontario. *A Guide to the Diagnosis of Occupational Diseases.* Ottawa: Minister of National Health and Welfare, 1949.

70. Schoenleber, A.W. *Doctors in Oil.* New York: Standard Oil Co. (New Jersey), 1950.

71. McGee, L.C. *Manual of Industrial Medicine.* Philadelphia: Univ. of Pennsylvania Press, 1950, 1954, 1956.

72. Passmore, R., and C.N. Swanston. *Industrial Health.* Edinburgh: E. & S. Livingstone, 1950.

73. Sax, N.I. *Handbook of Dangerous Materials.* New York: Reinhold Publ., 1951, 1957...

74. von Oettingen, W.F. *Poisoning: A Guide to Clinical Diagnosis and Treatment.* Philadelphia: W.B. Saunders Company, 1952, 1958.

75. Goldman, F.H. and M.B. Jacobs. *Chemical Methods in Industrial Hygiene.* New York: Interscience Publishers, Inc., 1953.

76. Davies, C.N. *Dust is Dangerous.* London: Faber and Faber, 1954.

77. Fleming, A.J., C.A. D'Alonzo, and J.A. Zapp. *Modern Occupational Medicine.* Philadelphia: Lea and Febiger, 1954, 1960.

78. Hunter, D. *The Diseases of Occupations.* Little Brown & Co. 1955, 1957, 1962, 1969...

79. Hinshaw, H.C. and L.H. Garland. *Diseases of the Chest.* Philadelphia: W.B. Saunders & Co., 1956, 1963...

80. Merewether, E.R.A. (ed.) *Industrial Hygiene and Medicine.* London: Butterworth & Co., 1956.

81. Wershub, L.P. *Urology in Industry.* Springfield, Ill.: Charles C. Thomas, 1956.

82. Jennings, B.H. *Hazardous Vapors and Dusts in Industry.* Chicago: Ventilating and Air Conditioning Contractors Association of Chicago, 1957.

83. Locket, S. *Clinical Toxicology: The Clinical Diagnosis and Treatment of Poisoning*. St. Louis: The C.V. Mosby Company, 1957.

84. Holt, P.F. *Pneumoconiosis: Industrial Diseases of the Lung Caused by Dust*. London: E. Arnold & Co., 1957.

85. Pendergrass, E.P. *The Pneumoconiosis Problem*. Springfield, Ill.: Charles C. Thomas, 1958.

86. DuBois, K.P. and E.M.K. Geiling. *Textbook of Toxicology*. New York: Oxford University Press, 1959.

87. Eckart, R.E. *Industrial Carcinogens*. New York: Grune & Straton, 1959.

88. King, E.J. and C.M. Fletcher (ed.) *Industrial Pulmonary Diseases*. Boston: Little, Brown & Co., 1960.

89. Schilling, R.S.F. (ed.) *Modern Trends in Occupational Health*. London: Butterworth & Co. (Publishers) Ltd., 1960.

90. Johnstone, R.T. and S.E. Miller. Occupational Diseases and *Industrial Medicine*. Philadelphia: W.B. Saunders, 1960.

91. Gerarde, H.W. *Toxicology and Biochemistry of Aromatic Hydrocarbons*. New York: Elsevier, 1960.

92. Maisel, A.Q. (Ed.) *The Health of People Who Work*. New York: National Health Council (1960).

93. Browning, E. *Toxicity of Industrial Metals*. London: Butterworths, 1961.

Carcinogens—See Hueper, IARC

The subject of industrial carcinogenesis was encyclopedically reviewed continuously by Dr. Wilhelm C. Hueper for nearly three decades starting in 1942. Hueper's monumental book, *Occupational Tumors and Allied Diseases* (Charles C. Thomas, Publishers), came out in early 1942. From that time on, Hueper published hundreds of medical articles, editorials, books, and experimental reports announcing the emerging knowledge on asbestos, arsenic, benzene, chromates, beryllium, nickel, aromatic amine dye intermediates, and numerous synthetic materials whose industrial use was soaring. His experimental work covering a wide range of materials is not included in the list which follows.

Though Hueper was considered by some to be quick to designate a substance as carcinogenic, it is noteworthy that he was several years behind some German writers in coming to the conclusion that asbestos definitely caused lung cancer. And well into the 1950s, Hueper referred to "asbestosis lung cancer," noting that the literature had not shown that lung cancer from asbestos occurred unless asbestosis had developed first. Hueper was extremely accurate in identifying industrial carcinogens, and there is little if any evidence that he raised false alarms by unjustified pronouncements.

His Public Health Monograph No. 36 on environmental cancer of the lung was sent to Turner & Newall in 1957, and this reply came back from the English firm:

> It seems to us that (Hueper) is very fair in stating the views of those authorities who still doubt the relationship between asbestosis and lung cancer, as well as those who consider the connection to be established.

(Letter from "J.W." to R.R. Porter, Keasbey & Mattison Co., Oct. 28, 1957)

REVIEWS ON ENVIRONMENTAL CANCER BY DR. WILHELM HUEPER

"Cancer in Its Relation to Occupation and Environment." *Bull. Am. Soc. Control Cancer 25:*63-69, 1943.

"Environmental Causes of Occupational Cancers." *Mod. Med. 11:*159, 1943.

"Environmental Cancer." *J. Am. Med. Ass. 126:*826, 1944.

"Industrial Management and Occupational Cancer." *J. Am. Med. Ass. 131:*738-741, 1946.

"Significance of Industrial Cancer in the Problem of Cancer." *Occup. Med. 2:*190-200, 1946.

"The Significance of Industrial Cancer in the Cancer Problem." *Cancer Res. 7:*47-48, 1947.

"Environmental and Occupational Cancer." A Monograph. Suppl. 209, *Public Health Rep.* 1948.

"Cancer of the Urinary Bladder." *J. Am. Med. Ass. 137:*1320, 1948.

"Estrogens and Cancer." *J. Am. Med. Ass. 141:*334, 1949.

"Cancers Due to Industrial Tar and Arsenic." *J. Am. Med. Ass. 140:*408, 1949.

"Asbestosis and Cancer of the Lung." *J. Am. Med. Ass. 140*:1219-1220, 1949.
"Problems in the Control of Occupational Cancer." *Indust. Med. 18*:163-166, 1949.
"Present and Potential Occupational Cancer Hazards and Carcinogenic Operations in Modern Industry." *South. Med. J. 43*:118-124, 1950.
"Carcinogens and Carcinogenesis." *Am. J. Med. 8*:355-371, 1950.
"The Role of Environmental Agents in the Causation of Human Cancer." *Acta Unio Internat. contra Cancrum 6*:1295-1324, 1950.
"The Significance of Occupational Cancer for Industry and Public Health." *Acta Unio Internat. contra Cancrum 6*:1351-1358, 1950.
"Environmental Lung Cancer." *Industr. Med. & Surg. 20*:49-62, 1951
"Environmental Cancers: A Review." *Cancer Res. 12*:691-697, 1952.
"Industrial Aspects of Cancer of the Skin." *CA-A Bull. Cancer Progress 2*:195-198, 1952.
"Air Pollution and Cancer of the Lung." *Rhode Island Med. J. 36*:24-30, 34-36, 52, 1953.
"Occupational Cancers: A Challenge." *Health News 31*:4-16, 1954.
"Recent Developments in Environmental Cancer: A Review." *Arch. Path. 58*:360-399, 475-523, 645-682, 1954.
"Silicosis, Asbestosis and Cancer of the Lung." *Am. J. Clin. Pathol. 25*:1388-1390, 1955.
"Lung Cancer and the Tobacco Smoking Habit." *Industr. Med. & Surg. 23*:13-19, 1954.
"Occupational Cancer Hazards. Safety Standards." *Workmen's Compensation Problems 1954*. Washington: U.S. Bureau of Labor Standards Bull. 180, 1955, pp. 126-144.
"Environmental Lung Cancer." *Proc. 1st Canad. Cancer Conf. 1954*. New York: Academic Press, Inc., 1955, pp. 186-236.
"Medicolegal Aspects of Cancer." *Am. J. Clin. Pathol. 25*:116-125, 1955.
"Lung Cancers and Their Causes." *CA-Bull. Cancer Prog. 5*:95-100, 1955.
"Environmental Causes of Lung Cancer." *Publ. Health Rep. 71*:94-98, 1956.
"Environment and Cancer." *J. Am. Med. Ass. 157*:679, 1955.
A Quest Into the Environmental Causes of Cancer of the Lung. Publ. Health Monograph No. 36. PHS Publ. No. 452, 1955.
"Environmental Causes of Cancer of the Lung Other than Tobacco Smoke." *Dis. Chest 30*:141-159, 1956.
"Causal and Preventive Aspects of Environmental Cancer." *Minnesota Med. 39*:5-11, 1956.

"New Environmental Diseases Resulting from Modern Industrialism." *Med. Sci. 1*:8-9, 1957.

"Potential Role of Non-Nutritive Food Additives and Contaminants as Environmental Carcinogens." *Acta Unio Internat. contra Cancrum 13*:220-252, 1957.

Environmental Cancer of the Lung." *Acta Unio Internat. contra Cancrum 13*:97-140, 1957.

"Environmental Cancer Hazards: Problem of Community Health." *South. Med. J. 50*:923-933, 1957.

"Newer Developments in Occupational and Environmental Cancer." *Arch. Int. Med. 100*:487-503, 1957.

"The Role of Occupational and Environmental Air Pollutants in the Production of Respiratory Cancers." *Arch. Pathol. 63*:427-450, 1957.

"Prevention of Occupational Cancer Hazards." *CA-Bull. Cancer Progress 9*:88-97, 1959.

"Luftverunreinigung und Krebs." *Krebsforsch. u. Krebsbek. 3*:162-189, 1959.

"Potential Cancer Hazards from Cosmetics to Producers and Consumers." *Drug Research Rep. 3* (Suppl. 16): 430S-446S, 1960.

"Occupational Cancers With Special Reference to Occupational Cancer Hazards to Laboratory Personnel." *Am. J. Med. Technol. 27*:157-164, 1961.

"Environmental Carcinogenesis and Cancers." *Cancer Res. 21*:842-857, 1961.

"Lung Cancer. Air Pollutants as a Cause." *Am. J. Nurs. 61*:64, 66-68, 1961.

"Carcinogens in the Human Environment." *Arch. Pathol. 71*:237-267; 335-380, 1961.

"Environmental and Occupational Cancer Hazards and Cancers." *Clin. Pharm Ther. 3*:776-813, 1962.

"Environmental Carcinogenesis in Man and Animals." *Ann. New York Acad. Sci. 109*:963-1038, 1963.

Chemically Induced Skin Cancers in Man. Nat. Cancer Inst. Monograph No. 10, pp. 377-391, 1963.

"Environmental Cancer." *Connecticut Med. 27*:465-472, 1963.

"The Environment in Relation to Cancer." *Arch. Environ. Health. 7*:737-738, 1963.

"Cancer in Industry." *Proc. 1964 Conv. Internat. Ass. Industr. Accident Boards & Commissions.* 20-75, 1964.

"Cancer Hazards in Foods and Consumer Products." *Nat. Health Fed. Bull. 12*:25-32, 1966.

"Public Health Hazards from Environmental Chemical Carcinogens, Mutagens and Teratogens." *Health Physics 21*:689-707, 1971.
"Environmental Cancer Hazards." *J. Occup. Med. 14*:149-153, 1972.
"Environmental Cancer Risks in an Industrialized Economy." *Industrial Pollution* (N.I. Sax, ed.) New York: Van Nostrand Reinhold, 1974, pp. 118-149.

Current information on carcinogens is available from the International Agency for Research on Cancer (IARC). The IARC is a part of the World Health Organization and is located in Lyon, France. IARC publications are locally sold in 70 countries. IARC has published monographs on the evaluation of the Carcinogenic Risk of Chemicals to Humans and separately numbered Scientific Publications. The monographs have been published since 1971, and number 42 to date. They summarize the state of knowledge on carcinogenicity of selected substances. Volume 14, on asbestos, is quite good, and the IARC Monographs are of high quality in general. Separate IARC "Scientific Publications" now number more than 40, and cover a wide range of topics in cancer epidemiology, experimental pathology, environmental occurrence, carcinogenic screening tests, methods of chemical analysis, etc. Two of the Scientific Publications deal with asbestos (No. 8, 1973; and No. 30, a two volume collection of brief reports in 1980).

Anyone who has read this far cannot help but be impressed with the degree to which public health scientific literature is deformed by the stresses imposed by commercial interests. The recognition and regulation of carcinogens is the most bitterly contested area of occupational health field today. The IARC consensus Monographs on cancer have been widely acclaimed for their quality, but they also "receive serious consideration by regulatory agencies and courts throughout the United States and indeed the rest of the world," according to a "leading chemical industry consultant."

The consultant was concerned about an in-press IARC Monograph evaluating benzene. The chemical industry had just fought a brutal battle to the Supreme Court to maintain OSHA's allowable concentration of benzene in the workplace air at 10 parts per million (ppm). The IARC scientific panel

International Agency for Research On Cancer—Monographs

Vol.	Subjects
1	Inorganic Substances, Chlorinated Hydrocarbons, N-Nitroso Compounds, Aromatic Amines, Natural Products
2	Some Inorganic and Organometallic Compounds
3	Certain Polycyclic Aromatic Hydrocarbons and Heterocyclic Compounds
4	Some Aromatic Amines, Hydrazine and Related Substances, N-Nitroso Compounds and Miscellaneous Alkylating Agents
5	Some Organochlorine Pesticides
6	Sex Hormones (I)
7	Some Anti-Thyroid and Related Substances, Nitrofurans and Industrial Chemicals
8	Some Aromatic Azo Compounds
9	Some Aziridines, N-, S- & O-Mustards and Selenium
10	Some Naturally Occurring Substances
11	Cadmium, Nickel, Some Epoxides, Miscellanous Industrial Chemicals, and General Considerations on Volatile Anaesthetics
12	Some Carbamates, Thio-Carbamates and Carbazides
13	Some Miscellaneous Pharmaceutical Substances
14	Asbestos
15	Some Fumigants, the Herbicides 2,4-D and 2,4,5-T Chlorinated Dibenzodioxins and Miscellaneous Industrial Chemicals
16	Some Aromatic Amines and Related Nitro Compounds—Hair Dyes Colouring Agents and Miscellaneous Industrial Chemicals
17	Some N-Nitroso Compounds
18	Polychlorinated Biphenyls and Polybrominated Bipenyls
19	Some Monomers, Plastics and Synthetic Elastomers, and Acrolein
20	Some Halogenated Hydrocarbons
21	Sex Hormones (II)
22	Some Non-Nutritive Sweetening Agents
23	Some Metals and Metallic Compounds
24	Some Pharmaceutical Drugs
25	Wood, Leather and Associated Industries
26	Some Antineoplastic & Immunosuppressive Agents
27	Some Aromatic Amines, Anthroquinones, and Nitroso Compounds and Inorganic Chlorides used in Drinking Water and Dental Preparations
28	Rubber Industry
29	Industrial Chemicals and Dyestuffs
30	Miscellaneous Pesticides
31	Some Food Additives, Feed Additives, and Naturally Occurring Substances
32	Polynuclear Aromatic Compounds, Part 1, Environmental and Experimental Data.
33	Polynuclear Aromatic Compounds, Part 2, Carbon Blacks, Mineral Oils, and Some Nitroarenes

International Agency for Research On Cancer—Monographs

Vol.	Subjects
34	Polynuclear Aromatic Compounds, Part 3, Industrial Exposures in Aluminum Production, Coal Gasification Coke Production, and Iron and Steel Founding
35	Polynuclear Aromatic Compounds, Part 4, Bitumins, Coal Tars and Derived Products, Shale-oils and Soots
36	Allyl Compounds, Aldehydes, Epoxides and Peroxides
37	Tobacco Habits Other than Smoking; Betel-Quid and Areca-Nut Chewing; and Some Related Nitrosamines
38	Tobacco Smoking
39	Some Chemicals Used in Plastics and Elastomers
40	Some Naturally Occurring and Synthetic Food Components, Furocoumarins and Ultraviolet Radiation
41	Some Halogenated Hydrocarbons and Pesticide Exposures
42	Silica and Some Silicates

report contained a sentence to the effect that workers exposed to 10 ppm of benzene would have three times the normal rate of leukemia. But then pressures were brought by a main source of IARC's funding, the U.S. National Cancer Institute (NCI), after a meeting with distraught industry representatives. IARC dropped the offending sentence from the Monograph published in July, 1982 (No. 29). The deletion was made by IARC Director Lorenzo Tomatis without informing the expert scientific panel that wrote the Monograph. Dr. Tomatis may still have been shaking after rejecting an NCI proposal that would have allowed NCI to select the researchers invited and the chemicals to be studied in IARC's carcinogenic risk assessment program ("Benzene and 'Risk Assessment'—One Little Sentence was Deleted," *The Sun*, Baltimore, Aug. 6, 1982; also M. Sun, "Risk Estimate Vanishes from Benzene Report," *Science 217*:914-915, 1982).

This incident should serve as a reminder that even the best public health scientific documents cannot be uncritically relied upon.

Medical Conference Proceedings

Conferences on occupational diseases are not always published in the scientific periodicals. Sources of information on asbestos and other toxic substances include these conferences, the proceedings of which appeared as unique publications:

Industrial Commission of Wisconsin—1932
Effects of Dust upon the Respiratory System

International Labor Office-1930, 1938, 1950, 1971
Pneumoconiosis conferences in South Africa, Switzerland, Australia, Romania

South African Council for Scientific and Industrial Research—1959, 1969, 1977
Pneumoconiosis conferences.

American Cancer Society and National Cancer Institute 1949, 1952, 1956, 1960...
National Cancer Conferences

Permanent Commission on Occupational Health (Accident Medicine, Occupational Diseases, etc.)
—fourteen held between 1906 and 1963
International Congresses on occupational health (exact title varies) held in European cities.

Saranac Laboratory for Research on Tuberculosis (Trudeau Institute)
—seven held by 1952
Symposia on pneumoconioses and other occupational diseases held in New York. Seventh Saranac Symposium (1952) never was published.

Association of American Railroads, Medical Section, 1921 on
Annual meetings on subjects of interest to railroad industry physicians.

Transcribed discussions at these conferences sometimes contain anecdotal material not found in carefully prepared medical journal reports. Meiklejohn, for example, described some of his experiences in maintaining that "asbestosis is a clinical condition, not a pathological or radiological one." He told of wartime complaints by asbestos workers, who were persuaded not to strike by the government. Doctors then came to visit the plant every month to conduct some exams and to be available for consultation. The doctors always came on pay days when there was a band and dancing. "The doctors danced with the girls and incidentally learned whether they were short of breath."

Further emphasizing the clinical aspects of asbestosis, Dr. Meiklejohn explained how he learned about finger clubbing from a worker:

> A workman refused to be examined. He said he knew quite well how to diagnose asbestosis. He took me to the factory and asked the workers to hold out their hands. He picked out those with 'clubbing' and said that these had the disease. I followed this up and found it to be correct. (*Proceedings of the Pneumoconiosis Conference, Held at University of Witwatersrand, Johannesburg,* A.J. Orenstein, ed. Boston: Little, Brown & Co., 1960, p. 389.)

Additional information could also be found in conferences on more general medical subjects (e.g., cancer).

International Labor Office Publications

The I.L.O. is headquartered in Geneva, Switzerland, and is constituted as a tripartite organization: management, labor, and government from a large number of countries are represented. Since its founding in 1919, the I.L.O. has been a source of documentation on the effects of toxic substances.

The two-volume I.L.O. Encyclopedia of Occupational Health and Safety was first issued in 1930 and has undergone revision ever since. A supplement to the encyclopedia from 1938 and the original encyclopedia were good state-of-the-art documents on asbestosis. Early editions of the encyclopedia were published in English and French. In 1932, the I.L.O. published a bibliography including 70 references to asbestos (*Pneumoconiosis/Essai Bibliographies* Études et Documents Série F, Hygiène Industrielle, No. 15, pp. 34-37).

Over the years, the I.L.O. has published conventions and recommendations dealing with occupational diseases and their prevention (lead poisoning, 1919-1921; occupational diseases, 1925 and 1934; medical exams, 1946; ionizing radiation, 1960; benzene, 1971). Various reports of I.L.O. Industrial Committees covered coal mining, the petroleum industry, chemical industries, iron and steel industries and textiles. The early chemical committee reports included remarks on the subject of warning labeling. At least one such report has been illustrative of the recognition of an asbestosis risk in shipyard insulation work (Metal Trades Committee, Seventh Session, "Working Conditions and Safety in Shipbuilding and Ship Repairing," 1962).

Starting in 1960, I.L.O. has issued abstracts on occupational safety and health literature at the rate of about 2000 per year in English, French, and German. The service was computerized in 1974, and these ("CIS") abstracts cover books, journal articles, regulations, guides, manuals, dissertations, and conference proceedings. This abstracting resource, with its annual index, offers one of the shortest routes to current scientific literature in occupational health.

There is also an "Occupational Safety and Health Series" of over 40 titles which has emerged since around 1960. Information on asbestos is contained in the following:

No. 22 *ILO/UC International Classification of Radiographs of Pneumoconioses* (1971)

No. 27 *Safety and Health in Shipbuilding and Ship Repairing* (1972)

No. 30 *Asbestos: Health Risks and Their Prevention* (1974)

Historic I.L.O. pneumoconiosis conference proceedings (1930, 1938, 1950, and 1971) also contain valuable information on asbestos.

Unfortunately, I.L.O.'s recent activities on asbestos are disappointing compared with the organization's past record. In October of 1983, I.L.O. convened an "Experts' Meeting on the Safe Use of Asbestos." The draft I.L.O. "Code of Practice" infuriated leading trade unionists and government authorities in Sweden and Finland. One of the panelists, Ms. Nancy Tait of the Society for the Prevention of Asbestosis and Industrial Diseases, walked out in protest over the dominant presence of the asbestos industry on the panel. I.L.O. published its code of practice, called "Safety in the Use of Asbestos," in 1984.

INDUSTRY TRADE ASSOCIATIONS AND RESEARCH ORGANIZATIONS

Industry trade associations and the periodicals, reports, and other documentation they produce are surprisingly numerous. Over the years there have been about a dozen trade groups representing the asbestos industry in the United States, and similar groups have long existed in other countries. In recent years, the world asbestos industry has been formally united through the Asbestos International Association, headquartered in London with member firms in more than 30 countries.

Aside from published reports, the larger industry trade and research groups have spawned committees on such topics as industrial hygiene, workers' compensation, and warning labeling. The minutes of committee meetings, and the recollections of those who were present, can offer candid glimpses into the historic awareness and attitudes of the various members of the industry. Manufacturers' groups have also sponsored research that in many cases was not all published or even alluded to in the published literature. Here, again, the recollections of "old timers" along with whatever documentation can be unearthed is of enormous value.

The principal research contractors used by the asbestos industry were the Saranac Laboratory for Research on Tuberculosis and the Industrial Hygiene Foundation. The Saranac Laboratory was started as an adjunct to the sanitorium of Edward Trudeau in the Adirondack Mountains of upstate New York. Having set up facilities for animal experimentation on dusts to study the synergistic effects of silicosis and tuberculosis in 1921, the laboratory was well prepared to investigate the effects of other dusts as well. The earliest published work on asbestos at Saranac (published 1931) was supported by the asbestos industry (Testimony of Johns-Manville executive J.B. Jobe at 1972 OSHA hearing on workplace asbestos standard). The "Sumner Simpson Papers" contain correspondence showing that a research contract was arrived at in 1936 involving a number of asbestos firms, and this was re-funded every year for about ten years. Positive experimental findings on asbestos carcinogenicity were reported to the industry in 1943. Other animal studies to investigate asbestos' carcinogenicity were initiated at the end of 1950 for the Quebec Asbestos Mining Association. Saranac did pathologic and radiologic consultation on pneumoconiosis cases for asbestos companies starting in 1942. The Saranac Lab also tested the dust from the Owens-Illinois thermal insulation, "Kaylo," for nearly a 10-year period starting in 1943. The Saranac Lab was closed in 1956, but the Trudeau Institute still remains and has made available for inspection the surviving records of the Saranac Laboratory.

The Industrial Hygiene Foundation, as it is called throughout this book, was founded in 1936 under the auspices of the Mellon Institute by a cross-section of large industrial companies. In the effort to launch this organization, Vandiver Brown promoted it as "the creature of industry and the one institution upon which employers can rely completely for a sympathetic appreciation of their viewpoint." (Brown letter to C.J. Stover, publisher of *Asbestos*, Dec. 4, 1936. Sumner Simpson Papers) It was first called Air Hygiene Foundation (1936-1941), then Industrial Hygiene Foundation (1941-1971), and is presently called Industrial Health Foundation (1971-present). I.H.F. is located in Pittsburgh and has been induced in the course of legal discovery to open its surviving records for inspection.

I.H.F. conducted industrial hygiene and medical surveys for Raybestos-Manhattan in 1944 and the members of the Asbestos Textile Institute in 1947. I.H.F.'s proposal to conduct a cancer epidemiology study for the Asbestos Textile Institute was refused in 1957, but a similar proposal was funded by the Quebec Asbestos Mining Association and completed in 1957. The findings were edited and reviewed by Q.A.M.A. and Johns-Manville, and published in 1958.

The Industrial Hygiene Foundation also arranged closed informal medical meetings among members in particular

May, 1945 Industrial Hygiene Foundation Trustees' meeting held in the Board Room of the Johns-Manville Corporation in New York.

Seated, left to right, are: Dr. C.D. Selby, General Motors; A.C. Hirth, Owens-Illinois Glass; J.W. McLaughlin, Bakelite and Union Carbide & Carbon; Dr. A.J. Lanza, Metropolitan Life; Andrew Fletcher, St. Joseph Lead and Chairman of the Foundation's Board; John F. McMahon, Managing Director. *Standing are:* W.E. Mack, Carborundum Co.; T.C. Waters, Mullikin, Stockbridge & Waters; Dr. L.U. Gardner, Saranac Laboratory; Vandiver Brown, Johns-Manville; W.C.L. Hemeon, Foundation engineer; Joseph Dilworth, Westinghouse Electric; J. Dewey Dorsett, Assn. Casualty & Surety Executives; Dr. R.R. Sayers, U.S. Bureau of Mines; and W.P. Yant, Mine Safety Appliances.

industries. The proceedings contain only fleeting mention of such meetings, such as one planned for 1948 "for physicians associated with the asbestos industry." (*A Better Place to Work,* I.H.F. Transactions Bull. No. 9 of Annual Meeting Nov. 20, 1947, p. 5)

There were regular published I.H.F. medical, engineering, and legal conferences. The annual legal meetings contained published discussions of workers' compensation laws and significant court decisions. Through vehicles such as confidential industrial hygiene surveys, annual conferences, and the *Industrial Hygiene Digest* (see also "Abstracts," this chapter), I.H.F. provided a full complement of services to member companies. I.H.F.'s annual meetings were not only covered by industry trade magazines, but also such prestigious newspapers as the *Wall Street Journal* and *The New York Times,* as well as the national wire services Associated Press and United Press International (*Foundation Facts,* Nov. 1947).

Industry trade groups also had overlapping memberships. In I.H.F.'s 1946 "Summary of Conference on Chemistry and Toxicology" appears a reference to warning label manuals just developed by the Manufacturing Chemists' Association. One concern was frankly stated in the I.H.F. summary:

> Under no circumstances should chemicals be overlabeled, i.e., the degree of hazard should not be exaggerated.

(*Health in Industry*, Transactions Bull. No. 8 of Eleventh Annual Meeting of Industrial Hygiene Foundation, Inc. Nov. 7, 1946, p. 36).

In the records of the following trade and research groups, valuable historical information has been found with respect to the recognition of asbestos hazards:

> *Asbestos Textile Institute* (founded 1944): Minutes of meetings describe: Air Hygiene Committee started in 1946; I.H.F. survey in 1947; U.K. firms ahead of U.S. in dust control (1949); Criticism of Conklin article naming asbestos as a carcinogen in *Scientific American* (1949); redrafting of government specifications (1953); 5 to 11 percent prevalence of asbestosis in plants, use of forced breathing therapy, air pollution control equipment (1953); health insurance used to cover asbestosis, no comp. claims (1954); recognition of cancer in the industry and concern about publicity in such popular literature as *Consumer Reports* (1955); acknowledgement of publicity on asbestos and cancer (1956); concern about Dr. Hueper's publications saying asbestosis and lung cancer could possibly occur among asbestos plant neighbors (1956); ATI's refusal to fund an animal study on carcinogenicity ("There is a feeling among certain members that such an investigation would stir up a hornet's nest and put the whole industry under suspicion"—1957); H. Jackson's discussion of various respirators (1957); advance notice of Selikoff's paper presented in 1963 on cancer among asbestos insulation workers, with increasing concern leading up to the New York Academy of Sciences Conference in 1964;

Quebec Asbestos Mining Association seeking "alliance with some university such as McGill, for example, so that authoritative background publicity can be had" (1965); ATI lawyers sent to talk to *Chemical Week* staff after "irresponsible article" in 1966; Dr. Selikoff a "dangerous" man, pressure on the Mt. Sinai School of Medicine mentioned (1971).

Minutes of Sept. 26, 1945 list the following members of ATI: Johns-Manville, Raybestos-Manhattan, Keasbey & Mattison, Carolina Asbestos, Southern Asbestos, Philadelphia Asbestos, and J. Franklin Burke & Co. By 1952, Union Asbestos and Rubber Co., Asten-Hill Manufacturing Co., American Asbestos Textile Corp. (later Amatex), and the British firm Small and Parkes, Ltd. were added.

Magnesia Insulation Manufacturers Association (founded 1944)—MIMA published the 85% Magnesia Insulation Manual in 1949 (90 pp.) and issued a revised edition in 1955 (74 pp.). The manual was originally prepared "to provide designers and users of insulation with *comprehensive* information on the use of 85% Magnesia" (emphasis added). The first edition advised that, "The material can be shipped, stored, and handled without any special precautions..." (p. 4). The second edition said that 85% magnesia insulation "is easily cut and fit... and offers no hazard to the workman" (p. 13). Members of MIMA listed on page one of the second edition were: Philip Carey Manufacturing Co., Ehret Magnesia Manufacturing Co., Johns-Manville, Keasbey & Mattison, Mundet Cork, and Pabco Products, Inc. With the increasing use of calcium silicate and other alternatives to 85% magnesia, the trade association became the National Insulation Manufacturers Association.

National Insulation Manufacturers Association (now Thermal Insulation Manufacturers Association)—Establishment of an industry health program was brought up in January, 1960, and rejected in May of that year. Represented: Mundet Cork, Keasbey & Mattison, Pittsburgh-Corning, Refractory and Insulation Corp., Baldwin-Ehret-Hill,

Johns-Manville, Pittsburgh Plate Glass, Owens-Corning, Union Asbestos and Rubber Co., Forty-Eight Insulations, Gustin-Bacon Manufacturing Co., and Eagle-Picher. The text of Johns-Manville's new warning label on shipping cartons of asbestos insulation products was quoted in the minutes of the April 14, 1964 meeting (full text of warning in Chapter 5). Several years later, NIMA issued a pamphlet, *Recommended Health Safety Practices*, which said only that excessive exposure to "any dust including mineral fiber dust may result in some respiratory irritation."

Saranac Laboratory—Files of asbestosis/cancer cases and names of persons or companies submitting the tissues for examination (1942-). Letters from Dr. Gardner describing preliminary positive cancer findings and requesting funding for studies from National Cancer Advisory Committee (Dr. Hektoen). Expresses concern over asbestos hazards in naval shipyards (1943). Correspondence between Gardner and Dr. R. Ritterhoff about asbestosis in the Philip Carey employee, Herbert Scobie (1944). Confidential report to Johns-Manville on earlier studies (1949). Reports and correspondence with Owens Illinois regarding tests for pulmonary reactions from "Kaylo" dust in animals, 1943-1952. Annual reports of Saranac lab list research sponsors and funding provided.

Industrial Hygiene Foundation—an empty file folder titled, "Preliminary Dust Investigation for Asbestos Textile Institute" (copy of the report was in the Sumner Simpson Papers); memorandum to H. Jackson (Johns-Manville) proposing epidemiological study on the connection between pulmonary carcinoma and asbestosis (1953); I.H.F. letters and proposals to ATI citing published literature on asbestos carcinogenicity and proposing to do a cancer study (1956, 1957); letter to H. Jackson of Johns-Manville passing on an inquiry received from J. Kane of the International Association of Heat and Frost Insulators and Asbestos Workers union inquiring about occupational lung disease risks in the trade (1955); statements by President A. Fisher and H. Jackson of Johns-Manville about a manufacturer's responsibility for warning consumers about safe practices for use of commercial products (1955-published); Dr. K.W. Smith's letter to Q.A.M.A. attorney I. Sabourin regarding critical changes in the pre-publication version of the I.H.F. study on lung cancer in asbestos miners, and the text of the pre-publication version of that investigation itself (1957). I.H.F. has maintained a file of its historic membership since its founding, and was ordered to produce this in litigation in Pennsylvania.

Asbestosis Research Council—Set up by the industry in the U.K. in 1957, this organization has supported research and issued codes of practice and safety guides. Its founding has been attributed to the recognition that asbestosis was occurring in "people who had joined the industry since the dust control measures were introduced and... certain users of asbestos products, such as thermal insulation..." (M.L. Bentley, Control of the Use of Asbestos-Containing Friction Materials. *Ann. Occup. Hyg. 13*:31-32, 1970). By 1969, Bentley reported, this group's Environmental Control Committee had established a "working group" concerned with the use and replacement of friction materials. No discovery has been done on the Asbestosis Research Council, and the information available has all come from published sources.

Asbestos International Association—Minutes of labeling committee on delaying the use of warning labels in countries where they are not required, because of adverse effect on sales (1978). This was produced in discovery by Raybestos-Manhattan. AIA has never been subject to discovery and has even refused to identify the members of the labeling committee (only Mr. Van der Rest of Eternit in Belgium is identified in the minutes). This organization has published position papers in recent years on asbestos-cement products and asbestos waste disposal, etc.

Quebec Asbestos Mining Association—Files (1931 to date) are retained in Quebec, Quebec: access to these records has so far been blocked. Some QAMA documents have emerged from the files of Johns-Manville and other sources (See "Companies Mining Asbestos in Quebec, Canada," in Chapter 9). The group was called Quebec Asbestos Producers Association until 1948. QAMA's library and research arm since 1966, the Institute of Occupational and Environmental Health, has been a source of some useful reports: the Wheatley report (see "Other Events of 1930" in Chapter 1); I.C. Sayers' report on the asbestos situation in Britain in 1967 (see "Union Carbide" in Chapter 9); Metropolitan Life's report on the King Mine (see "Asbestos Corporation, Ltd." in Chapter 9); and fine translations of early medical articles on asbestos from non-English journals. In 1982, resources of this institute were combined with others to create the Canadian Asbestos Information Centre, located in Montreal and involving participation by the government of Canada. In 1985, this institution was reorganized and named the Asbestos Institute.

Resilient Floor Covering Institute—Independent investigators had reported mesothelioma in a floor tile installer in 1971 (Murphy *et al., Am. Rev. Resp. Dis. 104*:576-580, 1971). The trade group R.F.C.I. hired S.R.I. International to monitor asbestos exposures when vinyl-asbestos flooring was removed by typical techniques. Time-weighted-average exposures (in f/cc) were: 0.08 to 0.16 for vinyl flooring removal; 0.41 for wet scraping of felt backing adhering to the floor; 0.83 to 2.02 for dry scraping of the floor (R.J. Walcott and J.C. Warrick, *Monitoring for Airborne Asbestos Fibers: Sheet Vinyl Floor Covering, Wet Versus Dry Scraping*, SRI International, Arlington, VA). R.F.C.I. issued a brochure, *Recommended Work Procedures for Resilient Floor Coverings*, in 1980. Members of R.F.C.I. were given as: American Biltrite, Inc.; Uvalde Rock Asphalt Co.; Congoleum Corp.; Flintkote Corp.; GAF Corp.; and National Floor Products Company.

Other trade groups of asbestos manufacturers include: Asbestos Cement Products Association (See "National Gypsum" in Chapter 9) and its successor since 1973, A-C Pipe Producers Association; Friction Material Standards Institute (1949-present); and Asbestos Information Association (1968–present). Others that existed decades ago include: Asbestos Paper Manufacturers Association, Asbestos Brake Lining Association.

In the United Kingdom, there is the Thermal Insulation Manufacturers Association, which requested 70 copies of the Factory Inspectorate's warning about asbestosis dangers in ship repair yards in 1945 (See Table 8 in Chapter 5). In West Germany, the Asbestos Trade Association has been formed in recent years. And around the world, there is one called the South Pacific Asbestos Association which has been in existence since 1979.

Also of interest are industry organizations not centered on asbestos but dealing with occupational health hazards generally. These include the National Safety Council and the Chemical Manufacturers Association.

National Safety Council—The National Safety Council was set up in 1912 as management's response to the industrial safety issue, with its associated problems of disability compensation and labor unrest (Dan Berman, *Death on the Job* New York: Monthly Review Press, 1978). Among the Council's publications dealing with asbestos were:

General Classification of Respiratory Devices. *"The Industrial Supervisor"* (July 15, 1936), pp. 12-13. Describes the three main types of respirators, including Type A for pneumoconiosis-producing dusts including asbestos.

Compounding Materials Used in the Rubber Industry. Industrial Safety Series No. RU-3 (1938). Notes that asbestos was used in packing and gasket rubber products. "Suitable exhaust systems or respiratory protective equipment are usually needed to prevent the inhalation of dust by the workers."

W.E. Lawrence. "Fume Control in Shipyards." *Nat. Safety News* (April, 1944), pp. 16-17, 90-92. Notes that a water-

> repellent asbestos insulation had become available for ship work. "For protection against dust or possible asbestosis, it is recommended that such material be dampened wherever possible, and that dust respirators be worn in addition to the provision of special ventilation. Periodic medical examination of those exposed is also necessary."

National Safety News, the main periodical of the National Safety Council since 1919, ran a number of articles dealing with asbestosis in the 1930s (C.O. Sappington, "Industrial Health," 46 and 76-77, May, 1931; C.O. Sappington, "Are All Dusts Hazardous?" 18-20, Feb. 1932; L.U. Gardner, "Inhaled Mineral Dusts," 34-36. Jan. 1933; A.S. Johnson, "No Half Way Measures in Dust Control," 17-18 and 48-51, Sept. 1935; R.B. Hunt, "Lesser Known Facts about Occupational Diseases," 34-38, Nov. 1936; H.B. Meller, "Air Contaminants that Affect Health," 43-46, Dec. 1936; R.R. Sayers, "Dusts That Harm," 51-52 and 82-84, Jan. 1938; J.M. Roche, "Settling the Dust Problem," 18-19 and 72-74, May, 1939).

The National Safety Council held annual congresses, and the published "transactions" of these meetings were automatically mailed to the industrial members of the Council. (N.S.C. originally claimed that its membership records were privileged information. Upon having to reveal the names of members, N.S.C. asserted that the surviving records indicate only the identities of present members and the years of their continuous membership to date.) Leading figures in industrial medicine and hygiene made presentations at the annual congresses. Some examples from the 1930s that relate especially to asbestos are:

> Dr. Leroy Gardner of the Saranac Laboratory described the lung tissue response to asbestos in 1932 and again in 1934. In the latter he acknowledged that asbestos was "generally recognized as a cause of severe pulmonary injury." Asbestos hazards received passing mention in discussions

by: W.S. Ash of U.S. Tire Company, on dust problems in the rubber industry (1934); R.R. Sayers of the Public Health Service, on dust disease investigations of the Service (1934); Liberty Mutual experts on exhaust ventilation systems (1934); F.R. Jones, insurance executive, on workers' compensation (1935); and E. Mayer of New York, on dust diseases (1935).

Dr. R.B. Hunt, Medical Advisor to American Mutual Liability Insurance Company, described asbestos work as offering "another type of dust which may cause fatalities among workers." He also talked about metals, benzene and chlorinated hydrocarbons. Hunt concluded with an urgent plea for employers to demand more information from the manufacturers of products they used regarding health hazards: "The manufacturer should be held responsible for the ills produced by his product and unless he can guarantee its safety, it has no place in industry." (1936)

Dr. A.J. Lanza of Metropolitan Life presented a paper called "Dust Diseases as They Affect the Construction Industry." He said, "(In) construction material, asbestos is usually combined with other substances which, by reducing the amount of asbestos in the dust, tend to mitigate the hazard." He described asbestosis. Asbestosis was also mentioned in a paper on dust control by the managing director of the newly formed Air Hygiene Foundation of America, Incorporated, H.B. Meller (1936). Papers on industrial dust hazards and control were presented by Dr. R. R. Sayers (U.S. Public Health Service), A.S. Johnson (American Mutual Liability Insurance Co.), A.D. Lazenby (Maryland Casualty Co.), and R.C. Starr (U.S. Department of Labor), at the National Safety Congress of 1937.

Henry Sayer offered an insurance executive's view on occupational disease compensation, remarking that liability for dust diseases was a matter of great controversy. He mentioned asbestosis and noted that fibrosis of the lungs was permanent and incurable. Dr. Carey McCord

> criticized the widespread practice of selling products by trade names without any indication of their hazardous ingredients (1938). A panel on occupational disease control included W.G. Hazard of Owens-Illinois and Dr. O.A. Sander. Medical surveillance, exhaust ventilation, and respiratory protection were among the subjects discussed (1939).

The Chemical Manufacturers Association and Others—The main trade group of the chemical industry is the Chemical Manufacturers Association (CMA) in Washington, until recently called the Manufacturing Chemists Association. This group issued Manual L-1 (a guide for the Preparation of Warning Labels for Hazardous Chemicals) in 1945 and revised it over the years. The label advised for harmful dusts (1946) read, "Caution! Harmful Dust/Avoid repeated breathing or skin contact. Wash thoroughly before eating or smoking. Keep away from food or food products."

In recent years, U.S. chemical manufacturers have formed increasingly specialized groups to deal with Congress and the federal regulatory agencies. Some new groups form as *ad hoc* committees and others as permanent units under the umbrellas of established trade groups. CMA has spawned about 50 "panels" of companies focused on specific chemicals, under CMA's "Chemstar" program (e.g. butadiene, diisocyanates). The Synthetic Organic Chemical Manufacturers Association has 24 groups to deal with specific interests (e.g., the Methacrylate Association), and the Society of the Plastics Industry claims 27 "operating units" (e.g., the Vinyl Institute). At the same time, other new trade groups are being formed independently (e.g., the Pesticide Producers Association). This proliferation of narrowly focused manufacturers' associations will continue.

The concerns shared and the actions taken by such groups are indicative of what member firms know about the hazards of their products and processes.

Chemical Industry Associations
Acrylamide Producers Association*
Acrylonitrile Group***
Adhesives Manufacturers Association
Adhesive and Sealant Council
Alkyl Amines Council*
American Coke and Coal Chemicals Institute
American Industrial Health Council
American Petroleum Institute
American Pharmaceutical Association
Aniline Association*
Association of Solvent Recyclers
Basic Acrylic Monomer Manufacturers Association*
Cadmium Council
Canadian Agricultural Chemicals Association
Canadian Chemical Producers' Association
Chemical Advertisers Group of New York
Chemical Coaters Association
Chemical Corps Association
Chemical Fabrics and Film Association
Chemical Market Research Association
Chemical Public Relations Associations
Chemical Specialties Manufacturers Association
Chemical Toilet Association
Chemical Warfare Association
Chlorine Institute, Inc.
Chlorobenzene Producers Association*
Coal Association of Canada
Coal Fuel Mixtures Association
Composites Institute
Compressed Gas Association, Inc.
Council of Chemical Associations
Cultured Marble Institute
Degradable Plastics Council
Diethylenetriamine Producers/Importers Alliance*
Drug Chemical and Allied Trade Association
Dry Color Manufacturers Association
Electronic Chemical Mfgrs. Association*
Epoxy Resin Formulators
Ethylene Oxide Industry Council
Fertilizer Institute
Fire Retardant Chemicals Association
Formaldehyde Institute*
Glycerine Producers Association
Halogenated Cleaning Solvent Association

Chemical Industry Associations
Halogenated Solvent Industry Alliance
Hazardous Waste Services Association
Hazardous Waste Treatment Council
Independent Battery Manufacturers Association
Independent Liquid Terminals Association
Independent Lubricant Manufacturers Association
Industrial Biotechnology Association
Industrial Specialty Chemicals Association***
Institute for Polyacrylate Absorbents*
Institute of Makers of Explosives
Institute of Paper Chemistry
International Ozone Association
International Pesticide Applicators Association
Isobutylene Task Force*
Lead Industries Association
Man-Made Fiber Producers Association Inc.
Methacrylate Producers Association*
Methyl Chloride Industry Alliance
Methyl Tertiary Butyl Ether Task Force*
National Agricultural Chemicals Association
National Association of Chemical Distributors
National Association of Solvent Recyclers
National Coal Association
National Chemical Credit Association
National Fertilizer Solutions Associations
National Lime Association
National Paint and Coatings Association
National Pest Control Association Inc.
National Petroleum Refiners Association
National Pharmaceutical Council
National Solid Waste Management Association
Nitrobenzene Association
Oxygenated Fuels Association*
Pesticide Producers Association
Phosphate Chemicals Export Association Inc.
Polystyrene Safety Group
Polyurethane Manufacturers Association
Process Equipment Manufacturers Association
Pulp Chemicals Association
Rigid Insulation Board Group
Sales Association of the Chemical Industry
Semiconductor Industry Association
Silicones Health Council*

Chemical Industry Associations
Society of American Wood Preservers, Inc.
Spill Control Association of America
Styrene and Ethylbenzene Association*
Sulphur Development Institute of Canada
Synthetic Amorphous Silica and Silicates Association
Synthetic Organic Chemical Manufacturers Association
Textured Yarn Association of America
Thermoforming Institute
United Pesticide Formulators and Distributors Association
United States Shellac Importers Association Inc.
Urethane Institute
Vinyl Institute**
Weed Science Society of America
Western Agricultural Chemicals Association

* Synthetic Organic Chemical Manufacturers Assn. project
** Society of the Plastics Industry division
***May no longer exist or may have changed names

REFERENCES

National Trade and Professional Associations of the United States and Canada and Labor Unions, Fifteenth Annual Edition, Columbia Books, Inc., Washington, (1980). And 20th Ed. (1985).

Encyclopedia of Associations Volume 1 National Organizations of the U.S. 13th Edition, Gale Research Company, Detroit, (1980).

Environmental Defense Fund, Washington, D.C. (1982)

Washington, D.C. telephone book (1982).

"Trade Groups Feel the Pinch, Too." *Chemical Week* (Jan. 12, 1983), pp. 11-12.

Chemical Manufacturers Association, Washington, D.C.

Society of the Plastics Industry, New York.

Synthetic Organic Chemical Manufacturers Association, Washington.

Chemical industry councils also exist at the state level, largely for the purpose of legislative lobbying and "industry defense" in general. By 1983, about half the states in the U.S. had chemical industry councils ("Chemical Industry Councils," *Chem. Week* June 1, 1983, pp. 28-32).

Unions

The International Association of Heat and Frost Insulators and Asbestos Workers, also known as the Asbestos Workers' union, has issued *The Asbestos Worker* magazine since the 1920s. The magazine contained a reprinted medical article on asbestosis in 1930 (see "Other Events of 1930" in Chapter 1). No subsequent mention of asbestos hazards was published in this magazine until the mid-1960s, by which time the union was assisting Dr. Selikoff in conducting epidemiologic studies of member locals in New York and New Jersey.

The Oil, Chemical, and Atomic Workers Union has been a leading force in bringing about worker safeguards in the U.S. over the past 20 years. In 1989, OCAW Secretary-Treasurer Anthony Mazzocchi established the Alice Hamilton Library at the union's headquarters in Denver. This is intended to serve as a resource in occupational and environmental health for labor and for the community. One purpose of the library is to serve as a repository for materials of historic interest.

Engineering Journals

The journal *Insurance Engineering* began in 1901, changed its name in 1913 to *Safety Engineering* and from 1950-1956 became *Safety Maintenance and Production.* It was simply called *Safety Maintenance* from 1956-1969. As concerns about health hazards from dusts and chemicals were intertwined with safety considerations, the health aspects received regular attention in *Safety Engineering.*

As early as 1931, an article for managers (Dr. F. Willson, "The Very Least an Employer Should Know About Dust and Fume Diseases," vol. 52 [November 1931]: 317-318) provided a stern assessment of the hazard of asbestos dust in "every operation in which it is used." Continuing in this vein, the journal carried a story about pneumoconiosis contracted by workers mixing asbestos and silica flour in an asphalt roofing mixture: "Had the management known what the outcome might be, not a man among them would have allowed his employee to work in such a condition." ("Silicosis in Odd Places," vol. 81 [May, 1941]: 39) In an article on welding hazards, Ziemke described the use of filter type respiratory protection for welders exposed to toxic and fibrogenic dusts ("A Second Look at Welding Hazards." *Safety Maint. Prod. 108* [Oct. 1954]: 22-24, 86-87).

Over the years, *Safety Engineering* carried articles by Dr. A.J. Lanza ("Occupational Diseases," 57 [May 1934]: 210-212), Dr. Leroy Gardner ("The Pathology of Various Dust Diseases." 57 [March 1934]: 109-112), and other authorities on occupational diseases. Annual reports of the Chief Inspector of Factories in Great Britain were also summarized for some years, including the early 1930s. There were also editorials and news articles on workers' compensation and medical supervision for occupational diseases.

Engineering and *The Engineer* are venerable British journals. At the time of the 1930 survey of the asbestos textile industry and in the years that followed, both of these journals carried articles about asbestosis and means to prevent it. Legislative actions regarding dust control standards and workers' compensation were also covered (e.g., "Miscellanea," *The Engineer 151* [October 14, 1931]: 77, and "Regulation for the Asbestos Industry," *Engineering 133* [1932]: 107). *The Engineer*, in particular, asserted the importance of educating workers to "a sane appreciation of the risk" and not having a false sense of security from reliance on the "partial... protection afforded by respirators." (*"Notes and Memoranda" 149,* [April 4, 1930]: 379, and *"Miscellanea." 154* [Oct. 14, 1932]: 381.) By using the indexes of the journals, these articles are easy to locate.

Engineering Inspector of Factories, Charles W. Price, addressed the Institute of Heating and Ventilating Engineers shortly after completing his surveys with Dr. Merewether. "(T)he men and women in the asbestos factories were not slack in the matter of wearing respirators where provided," he said. Price readily acknowledged that the controls then urged by the Factory Department were "not a complete resolution." ("Exhaust Ventilation in an Asbestos Textile Works," *Inst. Heat. Vent. Eng. Proc. 30*:158-179, 1932.)

The American Society of Mechanical Engineers' journal, *Mechanical Engineering,* carried five papers on occupational diseases and dust control presented at the Society's 1934 annual meeting (all in Vol. 57, 1935):

F.R. Jones. "Occupational Diseases/The Problems of Their Practicable Prevention in Industry." pp. 90-91.
A.S. Gray. "The Administration of Occupational Disease Control." pp. 92-94.
R.C. Stratton. "Toxic Dusts/Their Origin and Sources in Various Industries." pp. 95-98.
T. Hatch. "Dust Control." pp. 154-156.
R.R. Sayers and J.M. Dallavalle. "Prevention of Occupational Diseases Other Than Those That Are Caused by Toxic Dust." pp. 230-234.

The Stratton article contained a section on the asbestos industry and many others. Drinker contributed an article, "Uses and Limitations of Respiratory Equipment" the following year (Vol. 58: 171-176, 1936).

U.S. GOVERNMENT DOCUMENTS

This is an enormous collection of information sources. It includes both published material and unassembled information available in government files.

U.S. Department of Health and Human Services (formerly Health, Education, and Welfare)
The NIOSH Criteria Documents on specific substances have already been cited as good initial sourcebooks for historic research. NIOSH has also issued *Current Intelligence Bulletins* since 1975, on relatively new discoveries. Hazard alert notices were also issued on asbestos (brake repair work, Aug. 8, 1975) and other occupational health hazards. In addition, NIOSH publishes special reports, guidelines, occupational hazard

assessments, and conference proceedings (listed in NIOSH *Publications Catalog*, issued by Div. Standards Development and Technology Transfer, tel. 513-533-8302). Notable among these is *Workplace Exposure to Asbestos*, report of the NIOSH-OSHA Asbestos Work Group (DHHS/NIOSH Publication 81-103, 39 pp., 1980) calling for lowering the workplace asbestos limit 20-fold to 0.1 f/cc.

Prior to the establishment of NIOSH under the Occupational Safety and Health Act of 1970, a predecessor existed, the Bureau of Occupational Safety and Health, also within the U.S. Public Health Service in the Department of Health, Education, and Welfare. Reports on occupational health hazards were published by the PHS in *Public Health Bulletins* (1881-1949) and continued as *Public Health Monographs* (1950-1971). Notable among these on the subject of asbestos were *Bulletin No. 241* by Dreesen *et al.* (1938) and *Monograph No. 36* by Hueper (on lung carcinogens, 1955). Selected subjects covered by these reports are shown in the table.

One consequence of the involvement of Public Health Service employees in the American Conference of Governmental Industrial Hygienists (ACGIH) was the accumulation of documentation files on toxic substances by the government. Some of these files are still retained, and are known as the historic toxicology files. They are located in the Cincinnati Offices of NIOSH and ACGIH. Sensitive and confidential documents appear to have been filed elsewhere or retained in the personal files of members of the ACGIH threshold limits committee.

The Public Health Service also published an *Outline of Lectures on Industrial Disease for Medical Students*. The "revised edition" in 1951 listed under Asbestos, "nature of the material, sources of exposure, and clinical disease." There were 13 references provided, 5 specifically listed as cancer articles. Similarly, hundreds of references to articles on industrial diseases were included with the outline in this slender volume.

Government conferences on environmental and occupational health hazards are held often by the National Institute of Environmental Health Sciences, with the conference proceed-

Public Health Bulletins		
Bulletin No.	*Short title*	*Date*
71	Garment workers, and workshop illumination	1915
73	Tuberculosis among workers	1916
76	Health insurance	
78	Influence of occupation during adolescence	
81	Gas-heated appliances and workshop air	1917
85	Miners' consumption	1918
92	Color blindness	
99	Medical and surgical care of workers	
106	Fatigue and working capacity	1920
116	Lead poisoning in pottery trades	1921
117	Physiology of fatigue	
135	Railroad malaria surveys	1923
140	Illumination, visual defects and efficiency	.1924
144	Tests of instruments for determining atmospheric dusts	1925
150	Carbon-monoxide literature	
157	Health hazards of brass foundries	
158	Tetraethyl lead gasoline	
162	Health of ten thousand male workers	1926
163	Tetraethyl lead gasoline	
165	Economic status and health	
176	Health of workers in Portland cement plant	1928
177	Efficiency of painters' respirators	
181	Illumination, ocular efficiency and fatigue	
184	State industrial health activities	1929, 1932, 1943
185	Methyl bromide and other esters	1929
186	Automobile exhaust gas	
187	Silicious dust in granite industry	
195	Review of carbon monoxide poisoning	1930, 1936
202	Pneumonia among iron and steel workers	1932
205	Lead poisoning in storage-battery plant	1933
207	Health of workers in textile plant	
208	Health of workers in dusty trades	

Public Health Bulletins

Bulletin No.	*Short title*	*Date*
210	Mortality of coal miners	
215	Skin hazards in American industry, Part 1	1934
216	Industrial-hygiene problem in industrial area	
217	Determination and control of dust	1935
218	Daylight in buildings	
221	Anthracosilicosis among hard-coal miners	
224	Atmospheric pollution of American cities	1936
229	Skin hazards in American industry, Part 2	
234	Mercurialism in hatters' fur-cutting industry	1937
236	Industrial-hygiene problem of State	
238	Cement, clay, and pottery industries	
241	Asbestosis in asbestos textile industry	1938
244	Silicosis and lead poisoning in potteries	1939
246	Dermatitis among plate printers	
247	Manganese poisoning in ore crushing mill	1940
249	Skin hazards in American industry, Part 3	1939
250	Pneumoconiosis, mica and pegmatite workers	1940
253	Toxicity of lead and its compounds	
255	Toxicity of hydrocarbons	
259	Survey of industrial-hygiene problem in United States	1941
260	Illness among workers and housewives	
262	Lead hazard in storage-battery industry	
263	Mercurialism in felt-hat industry	
265	Fatigue of truck drivers	
266	Occupational and related dermatoses	
267	Lead arsenate exposure of orchardists and consumers	
269	Health of granite workers	
270	Soft-coal miners' health	
271	Aromatic amino and nitro compounds, toxicity	
272	Toxicity of nitrous fumes	
277	Health of nonferrous-metal miners	1942
278	Carbon monoxide in Holland tunnel	
279	Toxicity of toluene	
281	Toxicity of aliphatic alcohols	1943

Public Health Bulletins

Bulletin No.	Short title	Date
282	Toxicity of penta-erythritoltetranitrate	1944
284	Occupational and related dermatoses	
285	Toxicity of trinitrotoluene	
289	Bibliography of industrial hygiene	1945
290	Carbon monoxide, mechanism of action	1944
291	TNT in bomb and shell-loading plant	1945
293	Toxicity of molybdenum	
297	Respiratory disease and cotton dust	1947
298	Welders in steel ship construction	
299	Sodium fluoride at open hearth furnaces	1948
301	Industrial hygiene problem in Bolivia, Peru, and Chile	1949
306	Smog episode in Donora, Pa	

Public Health Bulletins

Monograph No.	Description
1.	A methodology for environmental and occupational cancer surveys. W. C. Hueper. (Public Health Service Publication No. 12) 1950. 37 pages.
36.	A quest into the environmental causes of cancer of the lung. W. C. Hueper. (Public Health Service Publication No. 452) 1955. 54 pages. Illustrated. [Published concurrently with *Public Health Reports* 71: (1); see pages 94–98 for interpretive article.]

ings published in *Environmental Health Perspectives* (about 84 volumes issued so far, starting in 1973).

In the past, such meetings were not always published as government reports. There is no system for indexing such material, and files for meetings held before 1960 can be very hard to track down. One "Conference on Environmental Carcinogens" coinciding with the 1955 American Medical Association meeting was summarized, and a mimeographed copy was found in the unpublished papers of Dr. Wilhelm C. Hueper

(National Library of Medicine, History of Medicine section). Panelists discussed the state of knowledge and compiled "score sheets" on various suspected and presumed carcinogens including asbestos (See "Other Developments in 1955" in Chapter 2), arsenic, chromates, nickel, beryllium, petroleum cutting oils, coal tar dyes and intermediates, radioactive materials, and ultraviolet radiation.

The National Library of Medicine has done relatively recent literature searches on a number of subjects, including asbestos. *Asbestos Toxicity* (LS 77-14) and its sequel, *Asbestos Toxicology* (LS 82-6) include literature published from 1970 on. Some of the literature searches offered by the Library are listed below. Notice of new searches is published in *Index Medicus.* Copies of these literature searches and updated lists of the searches available may be obtained by sending an addressed mailing label to: Literature Search Program, Reference Section, National Library of Medicine, 8600 Rockville Pike, Bethesda, MD 20209.

The Food and Drug Administration has issued regulations to prevent the contamination of intravenous drugs by fiber-releasing filters used in their preparation (*Fed. Reg. 40*:11865, March 14, 1975). Prior to the creation of the Consumer Product Safety Commission, the F.D.A. banned the use of asbestos in garments other than heat-resistant industrial textiles. This rule was precipitated by the discovery that imported coats from Italy had 8 percent asbestos to reduce import duties for wool content (*Fed. Reg. 37*:14872, July 16, 1972). F.D.A. also considered regulating asbestos contamination of foods arising from use of asbestos-containing talc in coating rice, etc.—but no final regulations were issued (*Fed. Reg. 38*:27076, Sept. 28, 1973).

U.S. Department of Labor

In the early years of this century, the Department of Labor produced valuable literature on health hazards in industry. *Bureau of Labor Statics (BLS) Bulletins* covered industrial hygiene and occupational diseases, industrial accidents, safety codes, and workers' compensation. Reviews of Labor Legislation and

Literature Searches Available from the National Library of Medicine	
No.	*Title*
77-4	Bismuth toxicology. January 1975 through July 1977. 54 citations.
77-5	Ozone toxicology. January 1975 through July 1977. 87 citations.
77-9	Saccharin. January 1970 through July 1977. 109 citations.
77-14	Asbestos Toxicity. 1970–1977. 698 citations.
78-1	Patient package inserts. January 1975 through December 1977. 38 citations.
78-22	Sarcoidosis. (Updates L.S. 76-31.) June 1976 through August 1978. 619 citations.
78-23	Smoking and reproduction, pregnancy, and the newborn. January 1972 through July 1978. 241 citations in English, French, Spanish or German.
78-24	Cadmium and the environment. January 1976 through August 1978. 94 citations.
78-27	The physician and malpractice. May 1974 through September 1978. 521 citations in English.
78-29	Adverse effects of prenatal exposure to diethylstilbestrol (DES). January 1975 through October 1978. 163 citations.
80-1	Passive smoking. January 1972 through September 1980. 162 citations.
80-8	Vinyl chloride toxicology. January 1977 through October 1980. 245 citations.
80-9	Benzene toxicology. January 1977 through September 1980. 164 citations.
80-24	Legionnaires' disease. January 1978 through December 1980. 389 citations.
80-26	Toxicology of polychlorinated biphenyl compounds. January 1975 through December 1980. 517 citations.
80-28	Diet and cancer: etiology and prevention. January 1978 through December 1980. 371 citations.
80-30	Agent Orange. January 1972 through December 1980. 99 citations.
80-32	Toxicology of polybrominated biphyenyl compounds. January 1977 through December 1980. 124 citations.

Literature Searches Available from the National Library of Medicine

No.	*Title*
81-1	Occupational neurobehavioral toxicology. January 1975 through March 1981. 282 citations.
81-4	Toxic shock syndrome. January 1979 through June 1981. 34 citations.
81-7	Lead exposure in children. January 1977 through July 1981. 354 citations.
81-16	Male reproductive toxicology. January 1977 through August 1981. 230 citations.
81-24	Chromium toxicology. January 1977 through September 1981. 250 citations.
81-25	Arsenic toxicology. January 1977 through October 1981. 354 citations.
82-4	Health effects of nuclear radiation. January 1979 through May 1982. 427 citations.
82-6	Asbestos toxicology. August 1977 through May 1982. 597 citations.
82-9	Inhalation injury. January 1977 through June 1982. 133 citations.
82-10	Zinc toxicology. January 1977 through July 1982. 204 citations.
82-11	Formaldehyde toxicology. January 1977 through June 1982. 213 citations.
82-24	Toxic shock syndrome. January 1979 through December 1982. 255 citations.
83-3	Kepone (Chlordecone) toxicology. January 1977 through March 1983. 90 citations and addendum.

Decisions of Courts and Opinions Affecting Labor continuously provided supplementary information in these fields. From 1916 to 1933, annual meetings of the International Association of Industrial Accident Boards and Commissions were published as *Bulletins* (they were then continued by the Bureau of Labor Standards). Proceedings of the annual meetings of the International Association of Governmental Labor Officials were also published as *BLS Bulletins* for a number of years from 1920 on.

Outstanding reports by Dr. Alice Hamilton and others covered lead poisoning and other specific hazards in industry. The *BLS Bulletin* (#231, 1918) by insurance statistician Frederick Hoffman had an excellent section on asbestos: citing Murray's case reported to the Parliamentary Committee, quoting Collis from an annual factory inspectors' report in England, and providing the information that asbestos workers were considered unacceptably poor risks by life insurance companies.

Asbestosis was also mentioned in the *Handbook of Labor Statistics* (1929, *BLS Bull. 491;* 1931, *BLS Bull. 541*) and in *Occupation Hazards and Diagnostic Signs* (1933, *BLS Bull. 582* revised in 1942 as the *Bureau of Labor Standards Bull. No. 41*). These articles summarized early medical reports on asbestosis. The BLS also published *Bulletins* to index its own publications as well as articles in its journal, *Monthly Labor Review (BLS Bulletins 683, 696).*

The *Monthly Labor Review* carried articles on the annual reports of state governments on industrial diseases (e.g., Massachusetts, Ohio) and reports from other countries. The *Review* also carried articles on specific hazards in industry. With respect to asbestosis, articles and summaries were published in the early 1930s covering the work of Donnelly, Merewether, Ellman, Oliver, and the International Labor Office. In addition, the annual reports of the Chief Inspector of Factories in Great Britain were also summarized, and statistics on asbestosis deaths were presented throughout the 1930s. Some of these articles and others on job hazards to health were reprinted in the *Handbook of Labor Statistics* (1929, 1931).

Some publications of the Bureau of Labor Statistics and the Bureau of Labor Standards are listed below.

Selected U.S. Bureau of Labor Statistics Bulletins

No.	*Title (Author)*	*Year Issued*
104	Lead Poisoning in Potteries, Tile Works, Porcelain Enameled Sanitary Ware Factories (A. Hamilton)	1912
120	Hygiene of the Painters' Trade (A. Hamilton)	1913
127	Dangers to Workers from Dusts and Fumes and Methods of Protection (W.C. Hanson)	1913
141	Lead Poisoning in the Smelting and Refining of Lead (A. Hamilton)	1914
157	Industrial Accident Statistics (F. Hoffman)	1915
165	Lead Poisoning in the Manufacture of Storage Batteries (A. Hamilton)	1915
179	Industrial Poisons Used in the Rubber Industry (A. Hamilton)	1915
188	Report of British Departmental Committee on the Danger in the Use of Lead in the Painting of Buildings (originally issued in U.K. in 1914)	1916
201	Report of Committee on Statistics and Compensation Insurance Cost of the International Association of Industrial Accident Boards and Commissions	1916
205 (rev.267)	Anthrax as an Occupational Disease (J.B. Andrews)	1917 (rev. 1919)
207	Causes of Death by Occupation (L.I. Dublin)	1917
209	Hygiene of the Printing Trades (A. Hamilton and C.H. Verrill)	1917
216 (rev.256)	Accidents and Accident Prevention in Machine Building (L.W. Chaney and H.S. Hanna)	1917 (rev. 1919)
219	Industrial Poisons Used or Produced in the Manufacture of Explosives (A. Hamilton)	1917
221	Hours, Fatigue, and Health in British Munition Factories (Reprints of the Memoranda of the British Health of Munition Workers Committee)	1917

Selected U.S. Bureau of Labor Statistics Bulletins

No.	*Title (Author)*	*Year Issued*
231	Mortality from Respiratory Diseases in the Dusty Trades (F. Hoffman)	1918
234	The Safety Movement in the Iron and Steel Industry 1907 to 1917 (L.W. Chaney and H.S. Hanna)	1918
236	Effect of the Air Hammer on the Hands of Stonecutters (R. Meeker)	1918
253	Women in the Lead Industries (A. Hamilton)	1919
212	Proceedings of the Conference on Social Insurance called by the International Association of Industrial Accident Boards and Commissions	1917
251	Preventable Death in the Cotton Manufacturing Industry	1919
280	Industrial Poisoning in Making Coal-Tar Dyes and Dye Intermediates (A. Hamilton)	1921
291	Carbon Monoxide Poisoning (A. Hamilton)	1922
293	The Problem of Dust Phthisis in the Granite-Stone Industry (F. Hoffman)	1922
298	Causes and Prevention of Accidents in the Iron and Steel Industry 1910–1919 (L.W. Chaney)	1922
306	Occupation Hazards and Diagnostic Signs (L.I. Dublin and P. Leiboff)	1922
339	Statistics of Industrial Accidents in the U.S. (L.W. Chaney)	1923
392	Survey of Hygienic Conditions in the Printing Trades (S. Kjaer)	1925
425	Record of Industrial Accidents in the U.S. to 1925 (L.W. Chaney)	1927
426	Deaths from Lead Poisoning (F.L. Hoffman)	1927
427	Health Survey of the Printing Trades (F.L. Hoffman)	1927

No.	*Title (Author)*	*Year Issued*
460	A New Test for Industrial Lead Poisoning (C.P. McCord)	1928
488	Deaths from Lead Poisoning 1925–1927	1929
490	Statistics of Industrial Accidents in the United States to the End of 1927 (L.W. Chaney)	1929
507	Causes of Death by Occupation (L.I. Dublin and R.J. Vane)	1930
512	Code for Identification of Gas-Mask Cannisters (National Safety Council)	1930
541	Handbook of Labor Statistics	1931
582	Occupation Hazards and Diagnostic Signs (L.I. Dublin and R.J. Vane)	1933
625	Occupational Disease Legislation in the United States, 1936	1937
667	Manual on Industrial Injury Statistics (M.D. Kossoris)	1940
700	Industrial Injury Statistics by States (M.D. Kossoris)	1942
758	Industrial Injuries in the United States during 1942 (M.D. Kossoris and F.S. McElroy)	1944
805	Injuries and Accident Causes in the Foundry Industry, 1942 (F.S. McElroy and G.R. McCormack)	1944
834	Shipyard Injuries (F.S. McElroy and G.R. McCormack)	1944
855	Injuries and Accident Causes in the Slaughtering and Meat-Packing Industry 1943 (F.S. McElroy and G.R. McCormack)	1945
884	Injury and Accident Causes in the Brewing Industry, 1944 (F.S. McElroy and G.R. McCormack)	1946
924	Injuries and Accident Causes in the Pulpwood-Logging Industry, 1943 and 1944 (F.S. McElroy and G.S. McCormack)	1947

Selected U.S. Bureau of Labor Standards Bulletins		
No.	*Title (Author)*	*Year*
7	Recent Changes in the Painters' Trade (Hamilton, A.)	1936
13	National Silicosis Conference Summary Reports Submitted to the Secretary of Labor by Conference Committees.	1937
20	Inspection Manual.	1938
21	National Silicosis Conference Final Reports of the Committees.	1938
30	Progress of State Insurance Funds under Workmen's Compensation; a Quarter Century of American Experience. (Andrews, J.B.)	1939
34	Occupational Poisoning in the Viscose Rayon Industry (Hamilton, A.)	1940
37	Protecting Eyes in Industry (National Society for the Prevention of Blindness)	1940
41	Occupation Hazards and Diagnostic Signs; A Guide to Impairments to be Looked for in Hazardous Occupations. (Dublin, L.I.)	1941, (rev. 1942)
67	Safety Subjects	1944
83	Outline of Occupational Disease Control Through Engineering (Blake, R.P.)	1946
86	Labor Management Safety Committees, How They Work.	1948
103	President's Conference on Occupational Safety, Proceedings (also Bulletins 112, 130, 153, 159, 175, 187, 196, 218, 263)	1948
122	National Conference on Workmen's Compensation and Rehabilitation, Proceedings	1950
129	Machine Tools & Their Hazards (Homan, S.)	1951
133	Reports of the Committee on Engineering 1949/50 President's Conference on Industrial Safety	1950
139	The Operation of Power-Driven Metal-Forming, Punching, and Shearing Machines	1951
197	The Principles and Techniques of Mechanical Guarding (Griffin, W.G.)	1959

Selected U.S. Bureau of Labor Standards Bulletins		
No.	*Title (Author)*	*Year*
198	Occupational Health Hazards, Their Evaluation and Control (Griffin, W.G.)	1958
207	Controlling Noise Hazards.	1959
211	Control of the Physical Environment	1960
212	State Workmen's Compensation Laws/A Comparison of Major Provisions with Recommended Standards	1958
216	Control of Electrical Shock Hazards	1960
219	Mechanical Handling of Materials	1960
222	Chemistry for the Safety Man	1960
226	Respiratory Protective Equipment	1961
227	The Operation of Circular Saws, Band Saws, and Guillotine Shears	1961
231	Personal Protective Equipment	1961
241	Chlorine Handling in Stevedoring Operations (March, Edward C.)	1962
244	Medical Care under Workmen's Compensation (Cheit, E.F.)	1962
246	Maintenance and Safety	1962
247	The Fundamentals of Accident Prevention	1962
256	Static Electricity	1963
259	The Use and Handling of Compressed Gases	1964
265	The Inorganic Acids	1964

Special Bulletin No.	*Title (Author)*	*Year*
5	Control of Welding Hazards In Defense Industries	1941
13	Wartime Working Conditions and Minimum Standards for Maximum Production	1943
14	Protecting Plant Manpower Through the Control of Air Contaminants	1944
18	Atmospheric Conditions in Cotton Textile Plants (Drinker, P.)	1945

Bureau of Labor Statistics Safety Codes

Abrasive wheels, use, care and protection of. Bull. 527 (1930); supplement, 1936.
Dust explosions, prevention of. Bull. 562 (1931); supplement Bull. 617 (1936).
Forging and hot-metal stamping. Bull. 451 (1927).
Foundries. Bull. 336 (1923).
Gas-mask canisters, identification of. Bull. 512 (1930).
Ladders, construction, care, and use of. Bull. 351 (1923).
Laundry machinery and operations. Bull. 375 (1924).
Lighting:
  Factories, mills, and other work places. Bull. 556 (1931).
  School buildings. Bull. 382 (1925).
Paper and pulp mills. Bull. 410 (1926).
Power presses and foot and hand presses. Bull. 430 (1926).
Power-transmission apparatus, mechanical. Bull. 463 (1928).
Rubber mills and calenders. Bull. 447 (1927).
Textile industry. Bull. 509 (1930).
Woodworking plants. Bull. 519 (1930).

The Occupational Safety and Health Administration (OSHA) is charged with setting standards for worker protection and enforcing them. OSHA rulemaking is a very complicated process, and comprehensive standards have been issued for only about 25 substances since 1970. The records from OSHA hearings contain 1) rather complete compilations of medical literature on health effects and 2) comments by representatives of affected parties. The literature compilations can be most helpful if the substance in question has received more study in the Soviet Union and Eastern Europe (countries whose research is less often translated or cited in English-language sources). In the case of acrylonitrile, for example, English translations of many such articles are in the docket file.

Company comments can be most interesting, especially as in the case of asbestos, where the first OSHA hearings (1972) pre-dated the main wave of product liability lawsuits. In these hearings, Johns-Manville medical consultant Dr. George Wright contended that insulation workers had been exposed to very high peak concentrations of asbestos dust. He believed such intermittent peak exposures may have been particularly dangerous. He pointed out that the mortality data showed that past exposures in the chrysotile mines and mills were less hazardous than those in the insulator's trade. This explanation runs somewhat contrary to the more current claim that product warnings were not used for years because J-M believed mining, milling, and manufacturing plant workers were more heavily exposed than users of insulating products.

The record includes a statement by J-M Vice President J.B. Jobe that he could remember personally calling on fabricators of asbestos-containing products in the early 1940s to advise them of practices to reduce or eliminate asbestos dust. Jobe, Fred Pundsack (until 1982 President of the company), and Ed Fenner (environmental affairs chief who later died with mesothelioma) vigorously objected to requirements for "unnecessarily frightening" product labels and signs in plants saying "cancer." Linked to their fear of stiff warning requirements was the expressed concern over lost sales and resulting unemployment.

Aside from standards for specific substances, OSHA has proposed (although not adopted) generic rules for regulating carcinogens and pesticides. In the wake of passage of "right to know" laws in many states, OSHA has issued a limited standard requiring identifying labeling of chemicals in the workplace. The hearing records of some of these rulemakings are quite vast.

OSHA also has advisory committees comprised of people in academia, labor unions, and industry. Transcripts of testimony heard by groups like the OSHA Advisory Committee on Construction Safety and Health may contain interesting material. This Committee has in the past considered recommending a separate OSHA asbestos standard for the construction industry, and has hosted industry representatives presenting their views (See for example, Dr. Paul Kotin's comments in "Household Contact Asbestos Disease" in Chapter 7).

In some cases, workers may need to examine company medical and industrial hygiene records relating to the hazards of their jobs. OSHA has regulations which give present or former employees or their representatives access to medical records, exposure records (including air sampling data as well as biological monitoring data—e.g., blood, urine, hair analyses for toxic substances), and company studies concerning the employee's working conditions. A simple letter invoking OSHA Standard 1910.20 is sufficient for the worker or an authorized representative to gain access to these company records. (Full details are in "Access to Employee Exposure and Medical Records." *Federal Register 45*:35212-35303, May 23, 1980).

The Department of Labor also supported research by medical authorities at the Mt. Sinai School of Medicine and economists at Syracuse University into the projected mortality and economic impact of asbestos disease in the United States (Selikoff, I.J. *Disability Compensation for Asbestos-Associated Disease in the United States* [New York: Environmental Sciences Laboratory, Mount Sinai School of Medicine, 1982]. See also "The Economic and Social Cost of Asbestos Disease in the United States," in Chapter 11.)

U.S. Navy

Various Navy documents refer to the hazard of asbestos in shipyards. These include *Minimum Requirements for Safety and Industrial Health In Contract Shipyards* (1943, republished in *Indust. Med. 12*:259-263, 1943), *Safety Review* (Vol. 4, p. 13, Jan. 1947), reports called "Occupational Health Hazards derived from Industrial Health Reports" (Releases No. 27, 1960; and No. 29, 1961), a memorandum of Cdr. V.L. Hetzel (*Long Beach Naval Shipyard Study of Asbestos Workers in Relation to Asbestosis*, June, 1961). Further information on these references is in Chapters 4 and 5.

The article by Fleischer and co-workers on asbestos health risks of shipyard insulation work was done by Navy consultants/officers, and published by permission of the Navy. However, "The opinions and assertions contained herein are the private ones of the writers, and are not to be construed as official or reflecting the views of the Navy Department or the naval service at large." (W.E. Fleischer *et al.*, "A Health Survey of Pipe Covering Operations in Constructing Naval Vessels." *J. Indust. Hyg. Tox. 28*:9-16, 1946) Marr also discussed asbestosis at a Naval shipyard ("Asbestos Exposure During Naval Vessel Overhaul." *Amer. Indust. Hyg. Assoc. J. 25*:264-268, 1964).

More recently, the Navy has taken an increasingly detailed look at both the hazards of asbestos and the availability of safer substitute materials. Some of the documents the Navy has produced are:

- Mangold, C.A., R.R. Beckett, and D.J. Bessmer. *Asbestos Exposure and Control*. Bremerton, Washington: Puget Sound Naval Shipyard, 1970.
- Asbestos Elimination/Substitution/Personal Protection Program. NAVSEA Instruction 5100.2. from Commander, Naval Sea Systems Command (4 pp.) Oct. 24, 1975.
- Winer, A. and W.D. Holtgren. *Asbestos—A Case Study of the U.S. Navy's Response to Upgraded Safety and Health Requirements*. Washington: 13th Annual Technical Symposium, Association of Scientists and Engineers of the Naval Air and Sea Systems Commands, Department of the Navy, March, 1976.

By 1978, medical surveillance was extended to 70,000 civilians and 150,000 active duty Naval personnel (*Navy Expands Asbestos Medical Surveillance Program*. News Release 394-78. Office of Asst. Secretary of Defense for Public Affairs. July 25, 1978).

A massive examination of government archives was conducted in connection with industry assertions that the government insisted on the use of asbestos through its military procurement specifications (See also "Patents and Government Publications." in Chapter 6). A related contention of the defendants is that the U.S. Navy was well aware of the hazards of asbestos—and, therefore, should have protected Naval shipyard workers despite manufacturers' failure to warn. Several industrial hygiene surveys and other World War II era government archives documents have been found which indicate Naval consultants' and officers' awareness of asbestos hazards (See Table 8 in Chapter 5).

U.S. Department of the Interior
The Bureau of Mines (in the Department of the Interior) produces statistical and technical reports on all minerals used commercially in the United States. Regular publications of the Bureau include the *Minerals Yearbook* (annual) and *Mineral Facts and Problems* (issued every 5 years). In addition, there are periodic special reports.

One of the earlier special reports, *The Asbestos Industry,* (Oliver Bowles, Bull. 552, 1955) contains a four-page discussion of "substitutes for asbestos."

U.S. Consumer Product Safety Commission
The Commission has banned asbestos in consumer drywall patching compounds and artificial fire-logs and ashes (*Federal Register* 42:63354, Dec. 15, 1977). Public concern over asbestos linings in the barrels of portable hair dryers led to a voluntary recall and replacement of these appliances by manufacturers—thus preempting regulation by the Commission. In 1983, C.P.S.C. received a report from its outside scientific expert panel responding to questions posed by the Commission. This was a summary of current information on potential hazards of asbestos in consumer products (*Report of the Chronic Hazard Advisory Panel on Asbestos,* July, 1983).

U.S. Department of Justice
The *Attorney General's Asbestos Liability Report to Congress* discussed the issue of manufacturers' liability for the cost of removing asbestos from public schools in the United States (issued by the Land and Natural Resources Division of the Department of Justice, September 21, 1981). The report included a list of 21 manufacturers of sprayed asbestos insulation and their products' names (pp. 13-14).

U.S. Environmental Protection Agency
The EPA has been in existence since 1970, and it primarily regulates air pollution, water pollution, and land disposal of

industrial wastes. The EPA has supported much research into the potential hazards of asbestos in drinking water from both natural and manmade sources (an example of the latter being asbestos-cement water supply pipes). The EPA also calls upon the National Academy of Sciences for reports on the state of knowledge about the health risks to the general public from environmental asbestos exposure (*Asbestos/The Need for and Feasibility of Controls*, 1971; *Drinking Water and Health*, Volume 1, 1977, pp. 144-168; and Volume 5, 1983, pp. 123-147; and *Asbestiform Fibers/Nonoccupational Health Risks*, 1984).

Major rulemaking by the EPA includes the following regulations:

National Emission Standards for Hazardous Air Pollutants (*Fed. Register* Apr. 6, 1973; amended October 14, 1975)—curtails asbestos use in sprayed and molded insulation, bans visible emissions from asbestos mills and manufacturing plants and waste dumps, regulates demolition of buildings containing asbestos; bans use of asbestos mine tailings for surfacing roads.

Effluent Limitations Guidelines and Standards (*Fed. Reg.* Feb. 26, 1974, Jan. 9, 1975, Feb. 11, 1975, Apr. 25, 1975, Aug. 29, 1979)—sets limits for total suspended solids in wastewater effluent from plants using asbestos in manufacturing. The "Best Available Control Technology" requirement to be achieved under the law by July 1, 1984 has been set at "no discharge of process wastewater to navigable waters."

More recently, EPA has moved to compile an inventory of commercial users of asbestos. Investigations into the presence of friable asbestos in public schools and the associated health risks have been directed by the EPA. A ban on most uses of asbestos was issued by EPA after years of delays on July 12, 1989. Brake linings and other friction products will be banned in two stages, in 1993 and 1996. The EPA' docket on the rule contains extensive material on the substitutability of asbestos in many applications.

The Asbestos Information Association (1735 Jefferson Davis Highway, Arlington, VA 22202) publishes a compilation, *Asbestos/Federal and State Regulations,* which is updated periodically.

State and Local Government Documents

As far back as the 1930s, state agencies were actively concerned about asbestosis. A major contribution to the literature was the survey by Fulton and co-workers in 1935, in Pennsylvania (See Chapter 4).

The Massachusetts Department of Labor and Industries (Division of Occupational Hygiene) issued a fact sheet on asbestos in 1949 (Bulletin No. 492). This described the dust as "VERY HARMFUL—May cause asbestosis," and advised use of exhaust ventilation and "approved type dust respirators only as a last resort." Pre-employment medical screening was also advised. A comprehensive survey might well show that other states also issued brief printed notices of this type.

The Massachusetts Division of Occupational Hygiene also retains its old records. Memoranda recording Dr. E.R.A. Merewether's visit in 1942 to Bethlehem Steel's Quincy, Massachusetts shipyard have been preserved (For more details, see Table 8 in Chapter 5).

Perhaps the most important use of state records has been in documenting the compensability of asbestos diseases. State laws on workers' compensation in some cases listed specific occupational diseases, causative agents, or hazardous industries covered. In other states, "blanket coverage" was provided for any disease that could be proven to be occupation-related. The language of these laws and their vintage is available from numerous sources, including the states themselves, Commerce Clearinghouse Inc.'s *Workmen's Compensation Law Reporter,* and proceedings of annual legal meetings held by the Industrial Hygiene Foundation.

While the language of these laws may be helpful, it has proven still more enlightening to get into the actual records of the compensation proceedings. Specific claims, brought by workers handling asbestos insulation products against the contracting divisions of the companies manufacturing those products, have been found in a number of states (for details see Table 3 in Chapter 3). The existence of these early workers' compensation claims, documenting actual knowledge of the mortal risk by the manufacturers of the products, are highly relevant to current product liability claims.

Some of the states also issued periodical publications about industry generally and hazards in industry in particular. Early examples of this are *The Industrial Bulletin* (issued monthly by the Industrial Commissioner of New York State), and *Monthly Review* (issued by the N.Y. State Dept. of Labor). The former carried an editorial warning "manufacturers or handlers of asbestos products" to take preventive measures against a risk of incurable disease ("Asbestos," in Vol. 13, [1934], p. 95). The latter carried an article on dust hazards warning about the cancer risk from asbestos (J. Silson, "Dust Inhalation in Relation to Pulmonary Disease." Vol. 30 [1951] pp. 5-8). A thorough search of state periodicals such as these has not been carried out, and there may well have been more such publications over the years.

Some state agencies issued media messages on occupational diseases, such as C.W. Chamberlain's "Asbestosis as an Industrial Disease" (Radio Talk No. 209, March 2, 1934, Illinois State Dept. of Public Health—abstract in *The Pneumokonioses Book II*, p. 35).

Government Publications in the United Kingdom

Here again, a comprehensive search has not been attempted. However, certain sources have been checked and proved most helpful.

Annual Reports of the Chief Inspector of Factories have mentioned the hazards of asbestos since the report for the year 1898. In most cases, the report for a given year was published the following year. Though these reports are cited in many places in this book, here are some notes on asbestos from the Chief Inspector's annual reports (page numbers in parentheses):

Annual Reports of the Chief Inspector of Factories, U.K.	
Year of the Report	Comment (pages)
1898	The "evil effects of asbestos" particles noted . . . "and where they are allowed to rise and remain suspended in the air of a room, in any quantity, the effects have been found to be injurious . . . " (171-172)
1899	Dust controls being developed in a plant making pipe insulation (264)
1901	Application of exhaust ventilation needed in asbestos works both textile and non-textile (174).
1906	No dusty process seen in 1906 surpassed in "injuriousness to the workers the sieving, preparing, carding, and spinning processes in the manufacture of asbestos." Five cases of illness among women working in these plants briefly described (219-220).
1907	Large asbestos factory employed local ventilation for carding and spinning machines. "In the other factories visited the conditions were not so good . . . " (173)
1908	"In a large asbestos factory the women told me that they went home 'quite clean' now" (146).
1910	Dr. Collis describes 5 deaths from "phthisis" (lung scarring) in 5 years among a staff of 40 in one factory where asbestos was woven. Local exhaust ventilation and annual medical exams of workers instituted. Two other large factories had dust control equipment in place (188).
1911	"Very defective provision for exhaust in the dusty processes in asbestos manufacture was found by Miss Whitlock in most of the factories she visited, and in some cases, no provision has yet been made" (based on visits to 24 factories employing 1,075 men and women) (149).
1930	Refers to the completed report of Merewether and Price, and to the convening of a 5-man government-industry committee to take up the matter of dust control in the asbestos industry. The law was changed to include workers' compensation coverage for asbestosis (49 -50, 94-95, 112-114).
1936	Continuing a tabulation that had run for the past few years, it is shown that overall, the average age at death for silicotics was 55.7 (avg. duration of employment 34.8 years) versus only 42.8 for asbestotics (avg. duration of employment 13.3 years). (54)
1938	"Among 103 fatal cases in which asbestosis . . . was present,

Annual Reports of the Chief Inspector of Factories, U.K.	
Year of the Report	Comment (pages)
	cancer of the lung was associated in 12 cases (11.6 percent)." The corresponding rate for lung cancer with silicosis was 23/943 (2.4 percent). (81)
1945	Concern about asbestosis hazard in shipyards led to the mailing of a letter from the Factory Department "to employers' and employees' organizations." The letter said that eventual amendment of the Factories Act Regulations was considered desirable. Deaths attributed to asbestosis averaged about 11 per year from 1940–1945 (13, 14, 79).
1947	"Thirty-one cases of carcinoma of the lungs and pleura were found at autopsy of 235 cases of asbestosis. That is 13.2%. The average age at death of those suffering from carcinoma of the lung was 52.1 years compared with 44.2 years for those with asbestosis alone. Out of 6,884 cases of silicosis at post mortem, 91 (or 1.32%) had carcinoma of the lungs and pleura." (81)
1949	• Describes the spraying of asbestos and special training of sprayers ("in view of the risks to health unless proper precautions are taken"). • Criticizes the packing of imported asbestos fiber in unlined jute bags. It was in violation of the regulations to use such sacks to transport the material *within* a factory. Use of an approved respirator "very important" when handling packages "which are not impermeable" (145–146).
1951	Deaths from asbestosis averaged just over 15 a year in 1946–1951. Fatal cases of asbestosis averaged less than 16 years' duration of exposure, with as little as a half year (155–156).
1954	Among 344 deaths in which asbestosis was involved from 1924–1954, cancer of the lung was present in 55 (16 percent). Analysis offered in three tables (190–195).
1955	"The proportion of all (365 recorded) cases of cancer of the lung was 17.8 percent compared with 13.2 percent and 16.0 percent in the cases which had come to light by 1947 and 1954 respectively" (206).
1956	"One very hazardous process, to which the Regulations do not always apply, is the removal of old heat-insulation lagging." Companies were still receiving asbestos in permeable sacks, which were often torn (142–143).

No thorough search has been made of legal literature from the U.K. However, *Reported Decisions of the Commissioner under the 1948 National Insurance (Industrial Injuries) Acts* shows that the 1948 workers' compensation law covered people handling asbestos thermal and electrical insulation. (See "Published Literature on Compensability of Asbestosis Disability in Asbestos Product Users," in Chapter 3).

Archives and Collected Papers of Scientific Researchers

Inquiries to the institutions where they worked and family members can sometimes lead to memoirs and collected papers of scientists. The "archives" of Dr. Arthur J. Vorwald are particularly informative, as they contain numerous documents which complement the published literature. Vorwald's widow donated his archives to the Armed Forces Institute of Pathology, Walter Reed Hospital, Washington, D.C. The first public reference to this material came after its discovery in the course of litigation in 1979.

Vorwald's archives include much unpublished material from his years as Director of the Saranac Laboratory for Research on Tuberculosis (1946-1953). Some examples:

- case file (about 70 pages) on Dominic Bertogliat, foreman at Johns-Manville's Waukegan, Illinois plant, whose wife inquired about compensation after he died of asbestosis (see Chapter 3).
- exchange of letters with J-M's Dr. K.W. Smith (then in Quebec) about Merewether's publication with U.K. asbestosis/cancer statistics in the *Canadian Medical Association Journal* (Feb. 1950). Vorwald mentioned a "storm which is brewing, this time concerning a case of asbestosis and cancer. I am most anxious to get on with the survey of all data available on the subject..."(April 18, 1950).
- an exchange of letters between Vorwald and J.P. Woodard (Johns-Manville executive). Vorwald noted that Dr. C.F. Shook of Owens-Illinois had complained that "shipping of asbestos in burlap bags is very troublesome as a possible source of an undue amount of dust." He suggested that paper containers would be less dusty to empty asbestos from (July 25, 1950). Woodard replied that

> The fibre packaging problem has always been a big one; and the burlap bags are a relatively large item of expense. Considerable engineering work has been done with a view toward improving this situation by using different types of containers, by bailing the material, by shipping it loose in boxcars, and by various other means. So far the burlap bag has not been eliminated; and I believe this same method is used by all producers up to this time." (July 28, 1950)

- reports on animal testing of Kaylo (thermal insulation) dust for Owens-Illinois.
- Vorwald animal study on inhaled asbestos as a cancer agent approved Nov. 7, 1950 at meeting at Saranac Lake attended by A.J. Lanza (New York University), I. Sabourin (Q.A.M.A.) and J.P. Woodard (Johns-Manville). Memorandum by Woodard.
- *Asbestosis and Pulmonary Cancer* interim (14-mo.) report on asbestos inhalation studies in mice ("there does appear to be a trend toward a greater incidence of tumors in the exposed animals than in the control animals... The experiment is not completed and it is considered likely that, if the ratios of tumor incidence at the next period when animals are killed are similar to those for the 14-month interval, the trend which is now noted may finally be shown to be statistically significant because of the larger total number of animals observed."), May 7, 1952—submitted to Quebec Asbestos Mining Association.
- letter from I. Sabourin (Q.A.M.A. to Saranac Laboratory enclosing $2,500 for research services for the *last* quarter of 1952 ("Asbestosis and Pulmonary Cancer"), Dec. 23, 1952.
- Case Folder List of patients whose X-rays were on file and an entry for each in column marked "Company or Doctor." Included here are Canadian J-M, Asbestos Corp., Union Asbestos Co., Bell Asbestos Mines, Thetford Industrial Clinic, Dr. Cartier, I. Sabourin.
- lists of workers whose tissues had been examined by Saranac pathologists.
- list of 19 cases of cancer of the lung among employees of various companies (mostly asbestos mining companies).

- correspondence between Vorwald and Dr. Samuel Keller (J-M Waukegan plant physician) and Hugh Jackson regarding possible compensation claim over the death in 1950 of Vernon Hall (lung cancer).
- guest list at Seventh Saranac Symposium, September, 1952 including Drs. Wilhelm Hueper, Paul Cartier, E.R.A. Merewether, J.F. Knox (Turner Bros. Ltd.), K.W. Smith (Johns-Manville), K. Lynch, A.J. Lanza, O.A. Sander; and Ed Ames (Owens-Corning), W. Hazard (Owens-Illinois).
- Dr. Cartier's presentation at the Seventh Saranac Symposium on asbestosis and cancer of the lung among Canadian asbestos miners at autopsy (further details in Cancer chapter).
- fragmentary transcript of the session "Pneumoconiosis and Pulmonary Cancer" with panelists W.C. Hueper, Paul Cartier, Kenneth M. Lynch, E.R.A. Merewether, and M. Levin at Seventh Saranac Symposium (Sept. 24, 1952).

Starting in the early 1930s and continuing for almost 40 years, Vorwald provided medical consultation services to many companies in connection with workers' compensation claims for occupational diseases. The records he had of these (approximately 2,000) cases were not initially made public with the rest of his papers. Because of questions of medical confidentiality, these records were not obtained until the favorable resolution of a lawsuit brought against the U.S. Army under the Freedom of Information Act.

Vorwald and his colleagues at Saranac were consulted in about 90 cases involving asbestos disease between 1931 and 1961, by mining and manufacturing firms. Pathological and radiological evaluations of suspected asbestosis and asbestos-related cancers in employees of the following firms were among the files from Saranac and Dr. Vorwald's own records after leaving Saranac in 1953: Dewey & Almy Chemical Company's "Multibestos" plant (Dewey & Almy was taken over later by W.R. Grace); Asbestos Corporation, Ltd.; Bell Asbestos Mines; Union Asbestos and Rubber Co.; Johns-Manville; Philip Carey Manufacturing Co.; and American Brake Shoe Company.

Some of the records of Dr. Kenneth M. Lynch were located in Charleston, South Carolina by plaintiffs' attorneys from California. Dr. Lynch's daughter had recovered some papers from Dr. Lynch's desk after he died. The documents relate to efforts by the Saranac Laboratory to get Lynch to write a report on Dr. Gardner's studies for Johns-Manville (See "Early Saranac Laboratory Cancer Tests with Asbestos," in Chapter 2). There was also documentation of a workers' compensation claim brought by the widow of an employee of Philip Carey Manufacturing Co. in Cincinnati. After obtaining Dr. Lynch's opinion on the case, the Industrial Commission of Ohio decided that the man's death in 1952 had been caused by asbestosis (Claim O.D. 79998 decided on appeal Jan. 24, 1957 in favor of the widow of Len R. Hope).

The unpublished papers of Dr. Wilhelm Hueper are at the National Library of Medicine, History of Medicine Section. Hueper's preference for publishing left little remaining. However, these papers do include a mimeographed review of the conference on environmental carcinogens held by the National Institutes of Health in 1955 and an address presented to labor union leaders in 1958. (See this chapter, "U.S. Government Documents," and Chapters 2 and 3 for details.)

Trade Journals and the Technology Indexes

There are innumerable trade journals in the business world. They commonly have odd names and sound obscure to the average person, but they are important sources of information within the industries they serve.

The trade magazine of the asbestos industry in the United States, *Asbestos*, was published monthly from 1919 until 1983. The magazine printed one article on asbestosis in March, 1930, before imposing a lengthy silence, apparently at the request of members of the industry (See "The Asbestos Magazine Letters," in Chapter 3).

Asbestos continuously monitored the major aspects of the industry: technology and new patents; production and international trade statistics; announcements, openings, expansions, and closings of mining and manufacturing ventures;

companies; new products; notices of trade and scientific meetings and publications; summaries of annual reports and reviews of economic conditions. The coverage on these subjects was worldwide and in no way limited to the activities of U.S.-based firms alone. In its later years, *Asbestos* committed increasing amounts of article and advertising space to industrial hygiene technology, environmental regulation, legislation, and litigation. Editor Doris Fagan was very knowledgeable about the industry and familiar with experts on every aspect of it.

It is not known to what Sumner Simpson referred when he wrote, "There have been a number of articles on asbestos dust control in the British trade magazines. The magazine 'Asbestos' is in business to publish articles affecting the trade, and they have been very decent about not reprinting the British articles" (letter to Vandiver Brown, Oct. 1, 1935). One of the articles referred to by Simpson may have been "Silicosis and Asbestosis," printed the year before in *Chemical Trade Journal.* This report stressed the seriousness of asbestosis and expressed hope that the new U.K. asbestos regulations would "at least reduce very markedly" the incidence of asbestosis (Vol. 95, p. 92, 1934—cited in *The Pneumokonioses Book III,* pp. 341-342). Other British trade publications that issued articles dealing with asbestosis in the early 1930s included *Mechanical World and Engineering Record* (Oct. 30, 1931), *The British Clayworker* (July, 1931), and *The Refractories Journal* (May, 1932 and May, 1934).

A search of the relevant U.K. trade journals of 50 years ago—even the identification of the journals—would be a very difficult task today. However, further efforts along these lines might well unearth additional articles referred to by Simpson.

Quite a few trade and even insurance journals are accessible through the *Applied Science & Technology Index,* the *Engineering Index,* the *Bibliographic Index,* and *Chemical Abstracts.* Each of these indexes monitors hundreds of scientific journals and other primary sources.

The *Applied Science & Technology Index* began in 1913 as the *Industrial Arts Index;* the name was changed in 1958. As the name suggests, its major concern is with the applications of engineering principles and other scientific research. Thus, a broad range of journals, including basic research, trade, insurance and material of general interest, is found in this index.

The *Engineering Index* was first available in 1883. This index contains many trade journals and leans toward engineering applications rather than general interest or basic chemical research.

Another source of technical and medical information is the *Bibliographic Index.* It was first published in 1945 by the H.W. Wilson Company but covers the years beginning with 1937. This index lists bibliographies and thus can be used as a source of accumulated references. As in the other indexes, the bibliography sources are listed under subject headings arranged alphabetically.

Examples of headings in the above indexes in a search on the health effects of asbestos would be: Asbestos; Dust; Workmen's Compensation; Diseases; Industrial Hygiene; and Pneumoconiosis. Examples of headings in a search on thermal insulations or substitutes for asbestos in thermal insulations would be: Asbestos; Glass Fibers; Heat-Insulating Materials; Insulation; Mineral Wool; and Pipe Coverings. The technology indexes were useful in locating articles on asbestos in U.S. trade publications:

Examples of U.S. trade magazine articles dealing with asbestosis are.

Boiler Maker and Plate Fabricator (published in Philadelphia) carried a story "Committee Reports on Dust Control" (Vol. 36, p. 343, Dec. 1936). This summarized the report of P. Drinker of the Air Hygiene Foundation preventive engineering committee. The same issue of the magazine carried an advertisement by Harbison-Walker Refractories Co.

Mill and Factory ("The National Magazine of Management, Production, and Maintenance") ran Dr. C.O. Sappington's article, "Banish the Dust Hazard," in 1936 (Vol. 18, pp. 69-71 and 150-152). The author, a specialist in industrial medicine, remarked that "asbestosis is important because of the increasing modern uses of asbestos products." He described the disease and named some of the products whose use of asbestos was on the increase.

Heating and Ventilating ("A Monthly Magazine for Engineers and Contractors Concerned with Commercial, Industrial, and Institutional Air Conditioning, Refrigeration, Piping, Heating, Ventilation") published an article on dust hazards in 1944. Written by engineering professor F.W. Hutchinson, this article noted the hazard of asbestosis in insulating and in workplaces where asbestos was used for filtration purposes ("Dust as an Industrial Health Hazard." Vol. 41 [June 1944], pp. 57-61). This same issue of *Heating and Ventilating* carried an advertisement for "Careyduct... the All Asbestos Acoustical and Insulated Duct," by Philip Carey Manufacturing Company (p. 34). The Carey ad showed pictures of the product installed in Kroger Grocery and Baking Company, Children's Hospital, and a radio station in Cincinnati. Owens-Corning Fiberglas Corporation was another advertiser in the June, 1944, issue of *Heating and Ventilating* magazine.

Modern Packaging described advances by a small manufacturer handling asbestos. "Dummy propelling charges" produced during World War II consisted of cotton bags filled with asbestos." (A) home-made machine evolved by a New York City war plant... is credited with eliminating a health hazard, increasing production 600% and saving 12½% on materials." The invention in this case was an enclosed assembly line apparatus for weighing out exact amounts of asbestos. ("Filling by Suction... an Improvised Method." *Modern Packaging 118* [September 1944] 116-117.)

Southern Power and Industry published N.V. Hendricks' "Industrial Hygiene Importance of Dust" (pp. 61-64, 80, Nov. 1946). This mentioned asbestos repeatedly as a cause of lung disease, urged air sampling and dust control measures. The same issue of the magazine contained advertisements by Eagle-Picher, Garlock Packing Company, Combustion Engineering, and Johns-Manville.

The Petroleum Engineer published A.C. Pabst's "Industrial Hygiene in the Petroleum Industry" (Management Edition,

Vol. 28, pp. E-2 to E-8, May, 1955). Compliance with threshold limit values in the industry was stressed, and the five MPPCF limit for asbestos was among those listed. "Nineteen states observe threshold limit values in their laws and regulations, and more are sure to follow."

(See also the 1952 *Petroleum Engineer* article by Shuman described in Chapter 9, in the section on Owens-Illinois.)

Patents

Patents represent the most authoritative source of technical information (for a general description of patents see Chapter 6). A patent search can be done in several ways. The easiest way is to obtain the services of a patent attorney, a patent agent, or a patent searcher. An overview of the patent search on thermal insulations and substitutes for asbestos in thermal insulations is not beyond the scope of this book, however.

If a particular company or a particular inventor is of interest, all of the patents issued to that company or inventor can be found in the inventors' index at the Patent Office.

If the chemical composition, the structure, or the use is known, patents can be searched after looking up the classification of the type of invention. This classification can be found in the Patent Office's *Manual of Classification*. This manual separates inventions into several hundred main classes, which are further divided into many thousands of subclasses. For example, calcium silicate compositions useful as thermal insulations would be found in Class 106 (Compositions, Coating or Plastic), subclass 120 (Silica-lime mixtures). If a laminated thermal insulation with a certain unique or unusual structure is of interest, Class 428, which deals with structures, would have to be searched. Heat insulations in general could be searched in Class 252 (Compositions) and subclass 62 (Heat-insulating materials). The arrangement of the patents in each subclass is in chronological order and thus details the development of that particular type of invention through the years.

One significant patent can lead to others because most patents list references cited by the patent examiner during the prosecution of the patent application. These references are usually other patents or journal articles that are close in content to the patent invention.

Besides the Patent Office in Arlington, Virginia, there are several other depositories in the United States which have copies of all or most U.S. patents. However, the only one which classifies the patents according to invention is located in Sunnyvale, California. In general, foreign patents can only be searched or copied at the Patent Office. Once a U.S. patent number is known, it can be ordered from the U.S. Department of Commerce, Patent and Trademark Office, Washington, D.C. 20231. The charge for each patent is one dollar.

Insurance Literature

Although no concerted effort has been made to search insurance industry journals, it is clear that this industry has long been concerned about the compensation costs of occupational diseases—silicosis and asbestosis in particular.

Most of the insurance industry journals have no index with which to locate articles on industrial diseases. However, *Industrial Arts Index* can be used for its indexing of articles from *The Eastern Underwriter* and *National Underwriter.*

The *National Underwriter* acknowledged the great reluctance of insurance companies to cover occupational disease risks including "wire insulation" and "asbestos goods manufacturing" on December 15, 1932 ("Occupational Diseases are Not Generally Understood." *Vol. 35*, p. 28). Asbestos was especially feared (for further details on this and other articles from insurance sources not all cited here, see Chapter 3).

At the end of 1932, the National Council on Compensation Insurance filed an occupational disease "hazard weight program" with a number of states. The extra charges assessed for insuring industries with occupational disease hazards would only be dropped upon evidence of the "entire absence of the hazard." Even then, "removal of occupational disease loading" from the rates charged would only apply for one policy period. Risks that could qualify for removal of the hazard rates included silicosis, lead poisoning, chromium poisoning, benzene poisoning, mercury poisoning, and radium poisoning.

"No risks involving asbestosis, anthrax infection, or caisson disease shall qualify for removal of (the hazard rates)." ("Send Out Rules on Disease Coverage." *Nat. Underwriter 36*:29-33, Dec. 29, 1932)

Rates for occupational disease coverage were prepared by the National Council on Compensation Insurance, upon passage of an occupational disease (workers' compensation) law in Illinois in 1936. Asbestos goods manufacturing rates were exceeded only by: stone cutting and polishing; and flint and spar grinding. Trailing asbestos manufacturing insurance rates in a list of close to 100 hazardous industries were: foundry work, cleaning outside surfaces of buildings, refractory products manufacturing, (lead) storage battery manufacturing, and "red or white lead" manufacturing ("Disease Rates Under New Illinois Laws are Given" *Nat. Underwriter 40*:29-32, June 25, 1936).

There were a number of other articles in this journal during the Thirties about the problem of occupational disease. Two which specifically referred to asbestos were published on December 1, 1932 ("New Occupational Disease Plan Out." *Vol. 36*, pp. 23 and 32) and June 21, 1934 ("Occupational Diseases—Kind and How Acquired." *Vol. 38*, pp. 37, 43).

Similarly, *The Eastern Underwriter* carried reports on the insurers' fears that "compensation for silicosis and asbestosis will greatly increase costs... This must be accomplished in a way which will not prove too crushing a blow to industry." ("Many-Sided Occupational Disease Problem Discussed by T.N. Bartlett." *Vol. 36*, pp. 45-46, Oct. 18, 1935)

Eastern Underwriter reported briefly on a decision by the Supreme Court of North Carolina to award workers' compensation for death from pneumonia of a man with "early stages of asbestosis" ("*Blassingame vs. Southern Asbestos Co.*" *Vol. 33*, p. 37, April 18, 1941).

The insurance literature contained many articles expressing concern over the compensability of "the contraction of some disease of ordinary life—...as pneumonia, common colds followed, perhaps, by tuberculosis..." ("Occupational Disease Problems Aired." *Eastern Underwriter 37*:30 and 34, Aug. 28,

1936). The insurers' fear was that without a narrowly defined schedule of compensable occupational diseases, they could not estimate the cost of providing workers' compensation insurance. And while tuberculosis was a well-known added risk of silicosis, and pneumonia was a recognized threat to those with asbestosis, these were also common diseases. Litigating numerous claims of this sort would cost the industries and their insurers a fortune, even if they weren't decided in favor of claimants.

The insurers were also keenly interested in measures to abate the hazards of occupational disease. Coupled with their expressions of concern about inestimable costs were statements to the effect that the problem itself needed to be brought under control. The responsibility of the employer was emphasized by Bartlett of Maryland Casualty, who stressed workers' unawareness of health dangers. He addressed an American Bar Association meeting in 1936:

> Many accidents do occur from carelessness of the worker...But in cases of exposure to occupational diseases there is more likelihood, because of intricate machinery, power driven tools, intensified chemical processes, with their attendant acute hazards, of the worker not having the least knowledge of the risk which he is assuming. He does not contribute to, nor is he knowingly a party to the results.

("Occupational Disease Problems Aired." Article cited above).

In 1940, Dr. A.J. Lanza wrote about "Underwriting Aspects of the Industrial Dust Hazard" in *Weekly Underwriter* (pp. 1412-1420, June 8, 1940). About asbestosis, he said, "(M)ost of the fatal cases have been complicated by other diseases such as cancer and diabetes so that the extent to which the asbestosis was responsible for death is not clear." He concluded that asbestos dust might "possibly" have a sufficient effect on the mortality of workers exposed to it as to require an extra premium charge for life insurance.

Another useful source is the Commerce Clearinghouse's *Workmen's Compensation Law Reporter.* This has been printed since the 1930s, and cited a number of early compensation cases involving asbestosis (See also Table 7 in Chapter 5). The most complete collections located by the author were at Harvard and Yale Law Libraries, and the College of Insurance Library in New York.

One article contributed to the insurance literature by the asbestos industry was written by Kenneth Smith and Hugh Jackson of Johns-Manville. There is an evident effort to downplay the problem ("Many cases with X-ray evidence of advanced asbestosis have been known to carry on their work and live very comfortable lives for several years.") There is also an interesting paragraph that says, at least "several years" before 1957,

> anyone who installed insulation materials was called an asbestos worker because asbestos was practically the only material used for this purpose.

The authors concluded that,

> Exposure to asbestos fibers does not shorten the life of the worker. Inhalation of asbestos does not predispose the worker to other pulmonary diseases which will shorten his life.

("The Asbestos Industry—Certain Health Experiences among Asbestos Workers." *Proceedings-Home Office Life Underwriters Association* 1957, pp. 187-194.)

The perspective of the insurers, who were refusing to sell life insurance to asbestos workers as early as 1918, is very helpful in understanding the history of asbestosis in society. In recent legal battles between asbestos manufacturers and their product liability insurance carriers, the insurers' contention that they were deceived by the manufacturers was an issue.

Clearly, however, the whole picture will not be available through the published sources alone. At meetings such as the

Third Conference on Occupational Diseases, held by the National Bureau of Casualty and Surety Underwriters in New York, there were both public sessions and others restricted to insurance company representatives. These conferences reportedly were "made notable by the presence of everybody of importance in the field of occupational disease." A central figure at these affairs was Dr. Anthony J. Lanza, of Metropolitan Life Insurance Company. ("Medical, Legal, and Insurance Representatives Survey the Problem of Toxic Dusts." *Spectator 134*:30-31, June 27, 1935. Abstract in *The Pneumokonioses III,* [Chicago Medical Press, 1937], p. 117)

Encyclopedias

At one point it was decided to sample the information available on asbestos disease in general subject encyclopedias. Due to their size and longevity, the *Encyclopedia Americana* and *Encyclopedia Britannica* were selected. Copies of these encyclopedias going back many years have been warehoused and were made available for inspection by the Library of Congress.

Articles on "asbestos" tended to be written by geologists and others familiar with the mineral's exploitation and use. Reference to asbestosis was therefore sought under headings like "silicosis" and "pneumoconiosis," and very often the articles on these subjects cited others on related subjects.

These popular encyclopedias carried basic information about industrial health hazards, but usually not until quite some time after the knowledge had appeared in medical journals. One exception to that rule was a full-column summary of the U.S. Public Health Service study, published in the annual supplement to the *Encyclopedia Americana* in 1939. This was listed under the heading "Asbestosis."

The 1939 and 1942 issues of *Britannica Book of the Year* carried paragraphs about asbestosis under the heading "Silicosis," written by Dr. Leroy Gardner of the Saranac Laboratory. In 1940, the *Encyclopedia Britannica* mentioned asbestosis ("a generalized fine fibrosis of the lungs which causes symptoms and disability earlier than silicosis") under the heading "Industrial Welfare and Medicine."

The 1952 *Britannica* listed "Occupational Cancers" as a subheading under "Cancer." Carcinogenicity of asbestos, chrome salts, benzene, benzidine, coal tar, and arsenical compounds was noted.

The 1953 *Britannica* described asbestosis under the heading "Respiratory System, Diseases of."

The *Encyclopedia Americana* mentioned asbestosis in 1957, under the heading "Industrial Hygiene." Here it was mentioned that "there is evidence that asbestosis may be associated with lung cancer."

The *Britannica* carried an article on "Pneumoconiosis" by Dr. Gerrit Schepers in 1960. Among other things, this included a table including insulation workers and "transite pipe workers" as groups at risk of pneumoconiosis. "Transite" was Johns-Manville's trade name for its asbestos-cement products. Two years later, the carcinogenic risk was emphasized under "Dangerous Occupations," an article by Dr. Harriet Hardy ("Evidence strongly indicates that there is a significant increase in lung malignancy in men with asbestosis.").

Newspaper Articles

Newspaper accounts offer vivid glimpses of past controversies involving toxic substances. They are often found by citation in other sources. For example, *The Asbestos Strike,* an account of the historic 1949 strikes at the Quebec asbestos mines, contains a full chapter on the role of the press at the time (Pierre Elliott Trudeau, editor, James Lorimer & Co. Toronto, 1974—translation of *La Greve de l' amiante,* 1956). With this as a source, it was then possible to go to the Library of Congress and obtain copies of the relevant stories in *Le Devoir* by Burton LeDoux and others.

In general, if health hazards were a public issue even peripherally to some controversy in a community, there is a good chance that this was mentioned in news accounts. Industry records and trade association minutes note such pressures.

The Sumner Simpson papers include a crossing of the swords in the *Philadelphia Record* between John L. Spivak, "noted liberal writer," and George S. Fabel, president of Southern Asbestos Company (Sept. 2, 1935). Spivak wrote of compensation claimants for asbestosis confronted with company doctors; dominance of the mill manufacturers over the political life of the city (Charlotte, N.C.); the employers' use of compulsorily signed papers to the effect that each worker had been provided a respirator. He also referred to life insurance company reports about asbestosis. Mr. Fabel responded that "obviously unconfirmed dramatized tommyrot would be putting it mildly," in describing Spivak's first report (Aug. 19, 1935). "We have had incalculable expense this first half because of 'walking delegates' like Spivak agitating and instilling unfounded fear in the poor Negroes' minds." It was to combat this "rather undesirable publicity" that *Asbestos* magazine approached Sumner Simpson about writing an article on asbestosis a few weeks later. (See Appendix 1)

Dr. W.A. Evans' "How to Keep Well" column described "mining and fabricating asbestos" as among the "most harmful trades" in an article on dust hazards (*Chicago Tribune*, Feb. 24, 1933).

Much more recently, exposés in *The Montreal Star* ("Asbestos clinic let sick men work," and "Chief doctor says he tried 'to be human,'" March 20, 1975) described historic practices by the asbestos industry clinic in Thetford Mines, Quebec (See also "Compensation at the Asbestos Mines in Canada," in Chapter 3). This was found at the Institute of Occupational and Environmental Health, the library of the Quebec Asbestos Mining Association in Montreal.

Individuals and unionists who worked in the asbestos industry and somehow became aware of the health hazards can also be helpful in finding news clippings, compensation claims records, etc.

11
The Legacy and the Challenge

"The medico-legal significance of dangerous dusts in industry is beginning to assume the international importance which it has long deserved... a meeting of experts is to be held at Geneva next month with the object of drawing up a preliminary charter to secure compensation for those who suffer damage due to silicosis... It is unlikely that asbestosis, another scourge whose evils have been demonstrated more recently, will as yet be granted international status."

> The Differentiation of Noxious Dusts (Editorial). *Lancet 1*:903-904 (1934).

"When life depends on it, you use asbestos."

> Asbestos Corporation, Ltd. advertisement picturing the World Trade Center in New York, whose girders were insulated with sprayed asbestos (*Asbestos*, January, 1983).

"In the Developing World asbestos is life, and we should not be shy about saying so."

> Michel Gratton, Director General of the Asbestos Institute, Canada (1990).

INTRODUCTION

In the foregoing chapters, it has been shown that the principal U.S. corporations mining asbestos and manufacturing products from it in the 1930's were aware that breathing asbestos caused a potentially fatal pneumoconiosis. American manufacturers knew of independent investigations and reports of clinicians and government agencies to this effect. Officials representing the asbestos industry in the United States initiated studies at both mines and factories starting in 1929, involving both medical evaluations and air sampling measurements. Leading industry executives, faced with disability compensation claims and civil suits beginning in the late 1920's, took a direct role in dealing with medical researchers thereafter. Through collaborative industry support of medical and industrial hygiene surveys, meetings of industry trade associations, and meetings of industry health and safety organizations, a wide range of industries were informed about the dangers of asbestos. The demonstrable knowledge of specific firms appears to have developed generally in proportion to their involvement in and dependence upon asbestos processing, their overall size, and other factors such as the manufacture of competitive products made from other materials.

The alarming publication of scientific knowledge showing that breathing asbestos caused asbestosis and cancer, during the period 1930-1964, was subject to widespread discussion and independent study by asbestos industry associations. In large part, studies conducted by individual firms, insurers, and contractors to industry trade groups in this era were either withheld from publication or published in an incomplete and misleading form. Contractors often agreed at the outset to keep their findings confidential and/or submit manuscripts to industrial sponsors prior to any publication of their findings.

Industry executives censored mention of the subject of asbestos disease in the trade journal of the industry in the United States, *Asbestos* (read by such people as industry sales representatives), through the 1930s and into the 1960s. The industry leader, Johns-Manville, followed a policy of withholding the findings of medical examinations from its own workers, as recently as the early 1970s. Johns-Manville executives told representatives of another firm (Unarco) in the early

1940s that the financial consequences of informing their workers would be great, in terms of labor unrest and claims for compensation. The existence of similar efforts by other manufacturers is indicated by the lack of historic demands for either "hazard pay" or the elimination of asbestos hazards and use, and the absence of strikes over the health hazards of asbestos by workers in the United States.

Despite the facts that asbestos had been shown to be a deadly material by 1930, and that this information was promptly available to asbestos mining and manufacturing firms generally, no warning labels were affixed to sacks of asbestos fiber or cartons of asbestos products until the years 1969 and 1964 (or at the earliest, the end of 1962), respectively. Although some manufacturers waited until the 1970s to either put warning labels on their products or eliminate the use of asbestos, the *similarity* of corporate behavior in not warning product users for so long is more striking than the differences between companies, here.

Corporate efforts to withhold knowledge from workers, the scientific community, and the public in general, were paralleled by a dramatic increase in the use of asbestos and the numbers of people endangered by it. The delay in public recognition of the dangers of asbestos caused a long delay in public efforts to regulate the asbestos industry, compensate affected members of society, and ultimately conduct independent, thorough (animal inhalation, epidemiological, and pathological) studies to determine just how deadly asbestos was.

The growth of the asbestos problem is better understood in the context of the times in which it occurred. Prior to 1970, the field of industrial medicine and hygiene was dominated by industry. Academic faculty in these areas were largely dependent upon industry grants for research and student scholarships, industry jobs for graduates, and industry consulting for themselves. General medical education was virtually devoid of training in occupational disease recognition. Government research was very limited, and state health and labor agencies had minimal expertise, laboratories, and authority to impose improved industrial hygiene in industry. Most of this has changed dramatically in the last 20 years, with the enactment of federal environmental and occupational health legislation and the establishment of research agencies at the state and federal levels. These conditions have led to an influx of independent professionals and improved public education and awareness. Public interest environmental and consumer groups, working with trade union health and safety professionals, with technical support from scientists in the government and at universities, have continued to press government agencies, in a climate of continuing strong media interest and public support.

The asbestos disease catastrophe of today resulted in part because of inadequate social measures to protect the public health. But asbestos is only one of many well-recognized, hazardous materials upon whose use the world appears increasingly to depend. What we can learn from the example of asbestos could, if implemented, save many lives jeopardized by the widespread mortal threats of which asbestos is but one representative. What we do not learn about prevention from asbestos *and put into practice,* other disasters may well call again to mind.

The grim task of appraising the present situation is therefore necessary if we are to seize a precious opportunity in prevention. This begins with a look at matters in the United States followed by some discussion of the asbestos problem in the world today.

Mortality Estimates (U.S.)

Nicholson and his co-workers have estimated that now approximately 9,500 cancer deaths a year in the U.S. are attributable to past asbestos exposure. This annual toll was projected to rise to 9,700 by the year 1992 and taper to 3,000 by around 2025.[1] (See Table 1) That averages out to about one death per hour for the next twenty years. Both higher and lower estimates have been offered, and a large degree of uncertainty confounds any attempt to make quantitative predictions of this kind.[2,3] The most recent estimate, based on mesothelioma death rates, is

TABLE 1. The Projected Annual Excess Deaths From All Asbestos-Related Cancer in Selected Occupations and Industries, 1967–2027

Industry or occupation	Number deceased in calendar year												
	1967	1972	1977	1982	1987	1992	1997	2002	2007	2012	2017	2022	2027
Primary asbestos manufacturing	237	312	385	445	494	510	491	445	367	278	187	114	60
Secondary manufacturing	236	304	403	507	610	659	674	649	584	489	367	252	149
Insulation work	266	374	497	612	705	742	723	652	578	392	279	173	94
Shipbuilding and repair	1,452	1,865	2,337	2,493	2,710	2,451	1,076	1,659	1,256	919	628	401	219
Construction trades	778	1,135	1,641	2,143	2,593	3,004	3,308	3,390	3,191	2,697	1,996	1,243	669
Railroad engine repair	129	146	162	167	147	130	91	54	28	10	2	0	0
Utility services	149	187	230	267	299	312	310	290	254	207	152	102	59
Stationary engineers and firemen	434	527	631	721	816	865	875	819	728	602	449	304	179
Chemical plant and refinery maintenance	205	269	337	404	457	482	472	437	375	301	217	142	82
Automobile maintenance	176	236	304	384	470	524	578	586	576	538	458	346	222
Marine engine room personnel	39	47	56	63	64	60	55	46	38	27	19	12	6
Totals	4,101	5,402	6,983	8,206	9,365	9,739	9,653	9,027	7,975	6,460	4,754	3,089	1,739

From Nicholson, Perkel, and Selikoff, 1982[1]

that 131,000 deaths from asbestos-associated cancer will occur in the U.S. between 1985-2009.[4]

Most of those persons expected to contract cancer from asbestos were not asbestos mining, milling, or manufacturing workers, nor were they insulation workers. They were persons whose own handling of asbestos was minimal or nil. They include in their number people exposed only as "bystanders." The *exposure* history profile of the bystander population at risk is largely guesswork, owing to the retrospective nature of our interest and the paucity and imprecise nature of historic exposure data. And it is also at the relatively low end of the dose-response curve that we know least about what the *risks* are for given levels of exposure.

Not even counted in these mortality estimates is the unknowable large population with significant histories of "miscellaneous" consumer and environmental contact. The author's own story illustrates how such exposure could occur and easily pass unrecognized or be soon forgotten. In the early 1950s, as a boy of 5 or 6, I often played in the basement of my home. The asbestos insulation on one of the pipes was torn in some places where we climbed on it. I was fascinated by the way the fine dust would fly when a certain section of pipecovering was slapped or struck with a ball. The fine dust would fly out and appear to magically hang suspended in the air. My younger sister remembers joining me for numerous and lengthy periods of slapping the pipe and standing under or beside it watching the dust cloud—which was for all appearances defying the law of gravity. There was a pile of whitish dust on the cellar floor beneath this place along the hot water pipe, which my mother periodically swept up.

This is not to criticize the projected figures for a lack of precision. On the contrary, whether the number of U.S. asbestos cancer deaths each year is 4,000 or 10,000, all the mortality risk estimates show the asbestos disease legacy to be of epidemic proportions.

With this in mind, one would hope that U.S. asbestos use would now be stringently controlled in order to keep from adding to the toll of preventable disease in future years.

Unfortunately, this is not the case. Despite commercial availability of asbestos-free substitutes in every major application, the use of asbestos continues to be permitted, even for products no longer made in the U.S. with asbestos but still imported from other countries. Equally worrisome is the lack of control over exposures from the deterioration of asbestos-containing materials already in place.

Continuing Asbestos Exposure in the United States

U.S. consumption of asbestos fiber has dropped dramatically from the peak level of 1974, most markedly in the 1980s. (See Fig. 1) Little of this has been offset by increased imports of asbestos products.

By 1980, asbestos-free brakes, packings, gaskets, fireproof textiles, and plastics were making significant penetration in historic asbestos product markets.[5-7] Asbestos use in molded insulation and drywall patching compounds had been specifically forbidden by government regulation.[8,9] Other uses such as in tobacco products, gas mask filters, dish towels, air-dropped forest fire retardants, grinding wheels, and open-heart surgery have apparently been abandoned as inappropriate. Many others among the still-numerous uses of asbestos have lost markets despite the lack of specific product bans affecting them. Local governments are turning to alternatives for asbestos-cement pipes for drinking water supplies and other uses, and at least six asbestos-cement pipe manufacturing plants in North America have been closed.[10-12] OSHA and EPA standards, workers' compensation and product liability considerations, and widespread public concern have all been factors in these market shifts.

Where stiff, durable, fibrous materials of respirable dimensions have been used in place of asbestos, there is concern about a mesothelioma risk. These apprehensions have been supported by experimental data since 1972.[13] One alternative, potassium titanate fiber, developed by DuPont, was abandoned after animal testing showed it could cause mesothelioma by inhalation.[14] Testing and prospective epidemiological study continue, and asbestos fiber substitutes

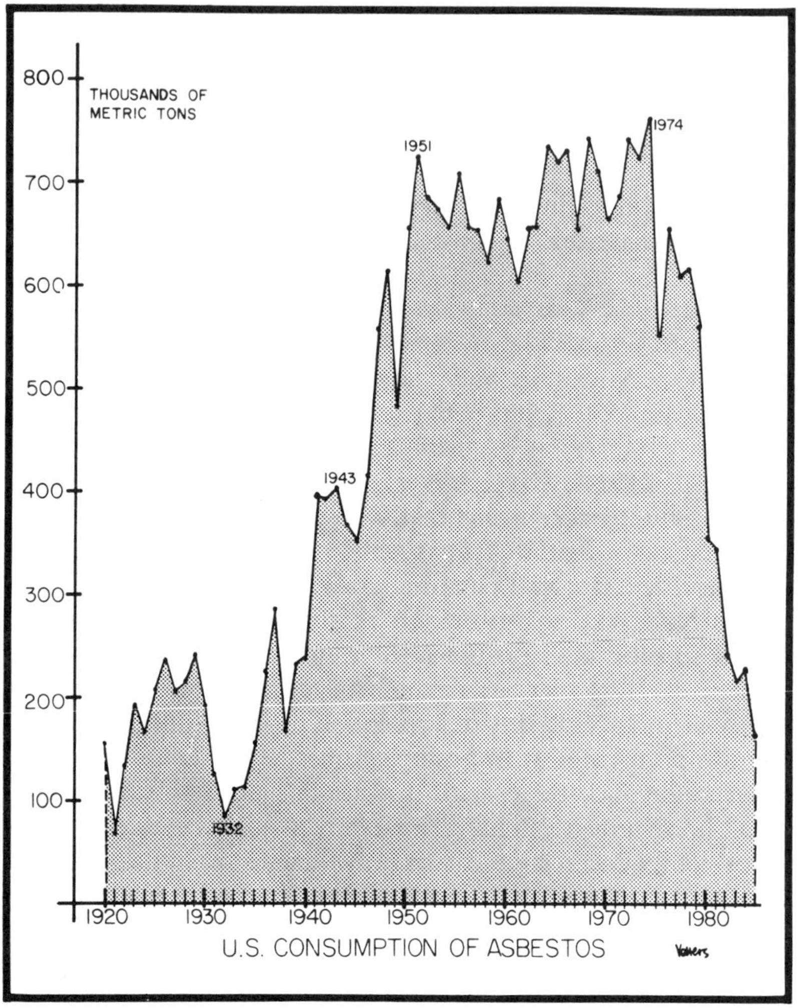

Figure 1. U.S. Asbestos Consumption

should be used with care. But it is already clear that the most widely used fibrous substitutes for asbestos cannot rival it as a health hazard, and the substitution of asbestos will have a very favorable outcome in public health terms.[15-18] Manufacturers have the capacity to make synthetic and inorganic fibers of sufficiently large diameters so that they won't be breathed into the lungs—and this would seem to be the surest way to prevent pulmonary disease.

Dr. Anthony Robbins, former Director of NIOSH and President of the American Public Health Association, has said he knows of not one application in which the use of asbestos is essential. Sweden has virtually eliminated the use of asbestos, the result of a campaign begun by the trade unions in 1975.

The continuing use of asbestos is opposed not only because of the availability of substitutes but the inadequacy of efforts to control asbestos use. Antiquated standards and discredited technologies have inertia on their side, and it is only with an effort that society replaces them. In the United States, OSHA's mandate requires that standards be "feasible" for employers to attain. In issuing a 0.5 f/cc emergency limit, OSHA also published risk estimates showing that 45 years of exposure at 0.5 f/cc would kill 1.7 percent of the work force through occupational cancer.[19] After setting a permissible exposure limit of 0.2 f/cc, OSHA was ordered by the courts in 1988 to further lower the limit wherever feasible. Brake repair is one area where more stringent safegards will be required, with the reduction of the permissible exposure limit to 0.1 f/cc proposed by OSHA on July 20, 1990.

The United States Environmental Protection Agency used its authority to summon information on asbestos use in the early 1980s.[20] Until then, there was not even a national inventory of commercial asbestos uses and users.

Consumer product regulation, food and drug regulation, and environmental regulation of asbestos (air pollution, water pollution, and waste disposal on land) have all been minimal. This is true despite highly publicized regulatory efforts aimed at asbestos in table salt, intravenous drugs, drywall patching compounds, electric hair dryers, fake fireplace logs, and some women's coats imported from Italy. The Consumer Product Safety Commission has long refused to either make a thorough inventory of asbestos in the marketplace, or ban a number of products in which asbestos is known to *have been used.* It should not be such a shock then that New Jersey schools were still using a children's modeling compound in 1982 made with

Figure 2. Snow figures made in 1982 by school children using modeling compound containing 50 percent chrysotile asbestos. "Fibro-Clay" was sold in powder form until 1976 by the Milton Bradley Company, labeled "Non-toxic." (*Courtesy of Dr. Arthur Rohl, Mt. Sinai School of Medicine.*)

at least 50 percent chrysotile asbestos (See Figure 2). Similarly, the serious and unnecessary threats to health posed by more asbestos-cement water supply pipes and asbestos-containing brakes have not been prevented by the U.S. Environmental Protection Agency. The yearly addition of fifty thousand tons of asbestos to the U.S. environment thus continues to this day.

The EPA finally did issue regulations in 1989 to eventually ban most uses of asbestos (EPA says 94% of asbestos used in products made in the U.S. in 1989). The multi-stage rules apply to manufacture and importation first, followed by a ban on sale of the products in the U.S. one year later (except for stage 1, which applies to nothing presently made in the U.S., despite EPA claims that it covered 4% of current asbestos use). The bans on distribution in commerce are:[21]

Stage 1 (Aug. 25, 1992)—flooring felt, roofing felt, pipeline wrap, asbestos-cement flat and corrugated sheet, vinyl asbestos floor tile, asbestos clothing.

Stage 2 (Aug. 25, 1994)—beater-add and sheet gaskets (except specialty industrial gaskets), clutch facings, automotive transmission parts, commercial and industrial friction products, drum brake linings and disc brake pads for light and medium weight vehicles (on new vehicles).

Stage 3 (Aug. 25, 1997)—Asbestos-cement pipe and shingles; commercial, corrugated, and specialty paper; rollboard; millboard; roof and non-roof coatings; brake blocks; drum brake linings and disc brake pads (for replacement on older vehicles of all sizes).

EPA also intended to ban another product no longer made with asbestos in the U.S.—valve and pump packings. However, this was dropped during "review" of the rule by the Office of Management and Budget. Packing manufacturers use this omission to support the claim that their products did not cause injury to plaintiffs suing them for asbestos disease. Other exemptions include missile liners and diaphragms in chlorine manufacturing plants. Given the rate at which asbestos use in the U.S. has been declining, the EPA "ban" may come to little more than closing the coffin after the industry has died from other causes. Nonetheless, EPA has been sued by the A-C Pipe Producers Association, the Asbestos Information Association, and Canadian asbestos interests.

The millions of tons of asbestos-containing materials already in place also constitute a great threat to health in the United States today. Hundreds of thousands of maintenance workers in commercial, industrial, and residential buildings are exposed to asbestos regularly. Yet because of the intermittent nature of their exposures to old asbestos thermal insulation and other materials, these people are largely overlooked by health authorities, and many have no idea their lives are threatened. Insulation is ripped out crudely, and contamination of work areas multiplies the extent of the hazard. Positive-pressure, air-supplied respirators are seldom provided for situations warranting their use; and most maintenance workers handling asbestos use no respirators of any kind.

As a result, 43 percent of janitors with 30 or more years of service have chest X-ray abnormalities consistent with asbestosis. School custodians in New York City with at least 20 years' experience have a 28 percent prevalence of similar X-ray abnormalities. New York firefighters with at least 20 years' experience have a 17 percent rate of these X-ray changes. Among construction trades like sheet metal workers and boilermakers, the figures are worse still.[22]

Equally poorly protected against occupational exposure to asbestos are nearly one million U.S. workers doing brake repair regularly. The EPA bans on asbestos in brakes, if upheld by the courts, will greatly diminish the amount of asbestos exposure from brake servicing starting in the late 1990s. However, the continuing use of asbestos in brakes and the lack of regulation of this risk by OSHA have, as of 1990, led to very little improvement in controlling brake repair asbestos exposures in the United States. For every day asbestos is used in brakes as it is now, another brake repair worker will die from cancer.[1]

The deterioration of asbestos already in place can be a hazard to the health of building occupants. Lightweight asbestos formulations have been sprayed on ceilings for acoustical, fireproofing or decorative purposes since the 1930s. Moreover, asbestos-containing sprayed fireproofing was applied to the girders of thousands of residential and office buildings from 1958 until the products were banned in the early 1970s. Recirculating air for many of these buildings passes through air plenums lined with the same friable asbestos material. Building occupants can thus be exposed to considerable indoor asbestos air pollution arising from common conditions of use.[23,24] We are starting to see reports of mesothelioma in persons whose only known history of asbestos exposure was as an occupant for years in a building with deteriorating asbestos construction materials.[25]

Public concern in the U.S. has focused sharply on the problem of asbestos in school buildings. Here, even cementitious surfaces can be damaged by harsh use coupled with the normal problems of aging buildings. Schools have been summarily closed and localities strapped with enormous expenses for asbestos removal by specialty contractors. In at least some cases, asbestos removal was not carefully performed, and a considerable effort is needed to monitor the contractors. Los Angeles alone expects to incur $40 million in costs. In 1980, Congress passed the Asbestos School Hazard Detection and Control Act, to assist states and localities in evaluating the dangers and making renovations. One requirement of the law was that the U.S. Department of Justice investigate the feasibility of recovering taxpayers' outlays by suing the manufacturers of the asbestos products. The Attorney General reported in 1981:[26]

> School authorities faced with substantial expenditures in removing or containing friable asbestos should, as a matter of the utmost urgency, consult with qualified counsel to determine whether they should file litigation on their own, as at least three school districts have already done.
>
> It is clearly in the national interest that those school districts...be able to recover from those who manufactured and sold asbestos products without warning of the dangers of breathing asbestos fibers.

States and municipalities were meanwhile left to *fund* asbestos abatement programs on their own, with the more wealthy political districts doing more and the rest doing less. On October 4, 1983, the Senate rejected a move to provide $50 million in interest-free loans for asbestos abatement. The U.S. Department of Education withheld a report that 14,000 schools were affected, leading to a cost estimate around $1.4 billion.[27] In 1984, Congress finally provided $50 million to assist localities in school asbestos removal, the first part of a planned $600 million, 7-year program. By the time the Asbestos Hazard Emergency Response Act was passed in 1986, EPA estimated that students and school employees in 35,000 schools were potentially exposed to friable asbestos material.[28]

In 1984, the first of the country's school asbestos removal

cases came to trial (*Lexington County, South Carolina School District v. U.S. Gypsum and Johns-Manville*). Both sides had presented evidence, and the judge had ruled that the issue of punitive damages would go to the jury, when a settlement was arranged. U.S. Gypsum agreed to pay the full cost of removing asbestos from a school ($377,000) plus an added sum of $298,000.

But the problem of asbestos in buildings is enormous and involves much more than schools alone. In the 26-floor Federal Building in San Francisco, for example, asbestos fibers circulated through the ventilation system and were found in the carpeting. The General Services Administration asked Congress to approve a $15 million plan to remove the asbestos from the building. The work was projected to take several years to complete. Proper removal of asbestos from skyscrapers like the Chase Manhattan Bank building in New York City will cost over $1 million per floor of height. There are an estimated 501,000 public and commercial buildings in the United States with damaged friable asbestos materials, 317,000 of which have "significantly" damaged materials, according to a 1988 EPA study.[29] And lawsuits demanding billions of dollars have been filed to recover renovation costs from companies that originally sold the asbestos materials.

The common belief that asbestos use and exposure in the U.S. is now carefully controlled thus proves to be erroneous. The disease and death toll from the past is being added to still, with a substantial amount of future disease that we are failing to prevent now.

The Economic and Social Cost of Asbestos Disease in the United States

Studies have been done to determine how the economic loss is borne by families who suffer the premature loss of a father from asbestos disease. The families involved were the survivors of 249 insulation workers who died of asbestos diseases before the end of their expected work lives. The families sustained an average net economic loss of $101,000 each (much more in cases where death occurred well before retirement age).

The economic loss to survivors here was taken as the worker's wage income, net of taxes and the consumption of the worker. The cost of medical care was not counted in these loss figures.[30]

Income in 1979 from all sources (government funds, pensions, workers' compensation, and personal injury suits) combined came to only 22.8 percent of this conservatively estimated economic loss. Fully half of the families in this survey (125) were receiving no income from any source to offset the loss of the breadwinner.[30] Thus, most of these insulation workers' families were drastically impoverished by the occupation-related deaths of the men (See Table 2).

Economists Johnson and Heler estimate the gross income loss to 420,000 workers (expected to die from asbestos diseases)

Table 2. Economic Loss Replacement Following Deaths from Asbestos Diseases*

Source	*Replacement Ratio (Total Cash Benefits: Total Net Loss)*
Social Security Survivors' Benefits	6.7%
Veterans' Widows' Benefits	0.7%
Public Assistance	0%
Government Sources, Subtotal	7.4%
Private Pensions	5.4%
Workers' Compensation	6.4%
Tort Awards and Settlements	3.6%
Total, All Sources	22.8%

*Data from Johnson and Heler[30], based on: 249 families of insulation workers whose deaths were caused by asbestos diseases. Replacement income includes cash benefits received during 1979 (base year of study) plus any income in that year that could be imputed to a prior lump sum payment.

The men who died all would *not* have reached the end of their expected work lives prior to 1979. (Loss estimates for 1979 for widows whose husbands would have stopped working by 1979 were "not possible.")

and their families at $326 billion, over the years 1967-2027. This figure does not include the cost of medical care for these people. Nor does it count the costs sustained by workers disabled with asbestosis who die from causes unrelated to asbestos. The costs to society for the administration of social agencies and courts are also not included in the above figure. Johnson and Heler did not offer any figure for pain and suffering, either, but emphasized the unquantifiable loss nonetheless sustained.[30]

Assuming a rough ratio of medical costs to lost earnings for cancer patients of 0.38, a figure of $125 billion can be added on as the cost of medical care.[31] Adding a continuing cost to society of operating social service agencies and courts at an estimated current outlay of $0.5 billion annually, the projected cost of the asbestos disease deaths comes to around $500 billion. Even this staggering amount does not include corresponding costs for persons who develop disability from asbestosis but die from causes unrelated to their asbestos exposures.

It is evident that at least the majority of the companies whose products set this tragedy in motion have unleashed bodily harm on society which, even reduced to tangible economic terms, exceeds all that these firms are worth or insured for.

Asbestos Litigation

Expanding in this virtual vacuum of compensation has been the volume of litigation over the workers' and their families' lost earnings, pain and suffering, and medical expense. In cases that actually came up for a trial by jury, punitive damages have also been awarded on occasion (in addition to compensatory damages). Damage suits have no doubt increased their share from 3.6% of recovered income loss to insulators' families in the years since 1979.

More than two hundred companies and insurers have been sued, plus a few corporate officers and doctors.[32] And in 1982, three defendant manufacturers (UNR, formerly Unarco; Manville; and Amatex) took the extreme step of seeking the protection of federal bankruptcy law, largely to at least temporarily stem the litigation costs.

By 1982, the asbestos manufacturers and their insurers had already incurred costs totaling $1 billion. The average cost to defendants and insurers per closed claim is in dispute, probably $125,000 to $150,000 in the years 1980-1982. About 39 percent was received by plaintiffs; the balance went for legal expenses, with defendants paying 1½ times as much as the plaintiff, on the average.[33] An Asbestos Claims Facility was set up in 1984 to control defense costs. This unraveled in 1988, and has been replaced by a smaller defense consortium. A representative of Lloyd's of London has predicted that asbestos litigation to cost the world insurance industry $10-30 billion.[34]

The risks of jury trials have also increased, as plaintiffs' attorneys have redirected their discovery efforts against other defendants while Manville has been in bankruptcy court. Punitive damage awards against the other defendants are an increasingly common result.

For Manville, the disposition of 1,885 claims in 1981 cost an average of $15,000 each, for a total of $28 million *excluding legal costs*.[35] The company reported that its legal expenses before the bankruptcy filing were about $2 million per month. Using such data for the purpose of rough estimation, one comes up with a total litigation expense figure of $52 million for 1981. This was about half of the company's profits in better years. After filing under Chapter 11, Manville reported a profit of $45.6 million for the first half of 1983.

Manville has paid a price for its refuge in bankruptcy court, however. To minimize the loss of business because of customers' concern about Manville's ability to stand behind long-term product warranties, Manville has had to place funds in escrow or secure special insurance for that purpose. Even then, customers have been reluctant to rely on Manville as a sole or primary supplier; and the company has had to offset this concern by cutting prices to get business. Competitors have exploited their advantage, as in the case of Owens-Corning and PPG Industries gains in the fiber-glass insulation business. The company's ability to borrow funds at competitive rates has also been affected by its Chapter 11 status. Continuity and resources for new product development were reduced. And top echelon executives have sought jobs with other companies. In the meantime, the litigation continued to dominate the attention of top management, distracting them from attending to matters on which Manville's future profitability will depend. Investment analysts saw "underperformance" attributed to the litigation.

Manville's tactic of filing under Chapter 11 in Judge Burton Lifland's jurisdiction of bankruptcy court in New York has undoubtedly achieved some of its objectives. It bought time and temporarily restored some of the profitability of the company. The judge proved willing to grant numerous delays to Manville, which filed an insulting "reorganization plan" in November of 1983. Under this plan, any asbestos disease claims that could not be paid with the cash Manville made available for them would be paid with unsecured notes redeemable within the next 50 years. Plaintiffs' attorneys' effort to then have the case thrown out of bankruptcy court for "bad faith" filing was rejected by Judge Lifland.

While this went on, thousands of asbestos victims and their families had long-awaited trials delayed for about a year on the average, while courts around the country decided to let cases involving Manville proceed against other defendants not in bankruptcy court. For plaintiffs suing Manville alone, no such option existed. By the end of 1983, heavy dockets of cases were being set for trial, and satisfactory settlements between plaintiffs and non-Chapter 11 defendants were being arrived at in most parts of the country. Defendants going to trial risked verdicts for total monetary damages, pain and suffering, and in many cases punitive damages; their claims for indemnification against Manville (for Manville's share of the liability) then had to be filed in Judge Lifland's court, where they waited.

In early 1984, Judge Lifland decided to appoint a representative for future asbestos disease claimants, placing him at odds with bankruptcy and district court judges handling the UNR and Amatex Chapter 11 asbestos cases. This introduced the need to invent a formula for setting aside funds to cover future claims, presumably at a loss to those with claims already filed. It also raised the possibility that Manville could emerge "debt-free" from Chapter 11 while a fund set aside for future claimants is rapidly consumed. Higher courts refused to get involved until 1990, after a final resolution of the future claims matter issued from Lifland's court.

On August 2, 1985, Manville's Board of Directors announced an agreement in principle with the appointed representative for future claimants. Under the plan, Manville would operate protected from asbestos lawsuits. A trust to assume all present and future liabilities would initially be funded with at least $200 million in cash and around $615 million in insurance settlement proceeds. To this would be added a $1.65 billion non-interest-bearing bond (payable at $75 million a year over 22 years beginning in the fourth year), and 50-80 percent of Manville's common stock (to be determined by the volume of claims). The trust would also be paid up to 20 percent of Manville's profits, starting in the fifth year, as long as needed to pay claims (The firm's profits were $77 million in 1984). People with health claims could sue the trust if unable to reach agreement by any other means. However, the plan as modified in late 1985 allotted only a token $5 million for punitive damages and $125 million for Manville's liability in asbestos property damage claims. The operating Manville company remaining would itself pay banks and other commercial creditors approximately $550 million owed to them within three years. Manville would reap a tax windfall of hundreds of millions of dollars, deducting its entire costs in funding the trust as a business expense.

Members of the Committee of Asbestos Health Related Litigants, the plaintiffs' lawyers' group in the Manville bankruptcy case, voted 15 to 4 to accept the plan. Dissenters feared that the trust would go through its initial $800 million or so in funds well before 1991, and would then have to dump its Manville stock at whatever price is available to pay claims. With the stock exhausted, the payments to the trust by Manville (and the U.S. Treasury), on the order of $100 million a year, would only be enough to pay 4,000 claims at $25,000 each, both low figures. New asbestos personal injury claims are currently being filed at the rate of 22,000 per year, and by March 31, 1990, the Manville Trust had received about 152,000 claims.[36,37] There may well be no way Manville could pay its future health claims; even proponents of the plan agree that its capacity won't much exceed 100,000 claims.

What it came down to was a calculated risk between fighting to liquidate Manville (value: $750 million to $1 billion) and leaving Manville viable so it can be milked as a "cash cow." The fear remains, however, that the cow will someday be both dry and bullet-proof to Johns-Manville's victims, who feel entitled to its meat if they can't milk it. Explained attorney Shepard Hoffman of Baltimore:[38]

> Financial markets will not lend Manville money if they believe the operating company can be attacked. In return for an injunction, we're saying, 'Look, you're entitled to that injunction, and to operate profitably serves our interest.' But if at some point in time, it looks like a choice ever has to be made either for the death of future claims or the death of the operating company, I'm in favor of killing the operating company.

Against this misgiving, other plaintiffs' attorneys countered that:

1. This is the best offer so far made and the best offer likely to be achieved soon. The likely payout is greater than the liquidation value of Manville, and anyway liquidation is not an option in the forseeable future.

2. The bankruptcy process is the only proceeding that can avoid endless and costly litigation over the property damage claims, which would compete against health claims for available and insufficient funds.

3. The tax windfall will better enable Manville to pay victims and maintain the value of its stock held by the trust.

4. Only by foreclosing any future suits for compensatory and punitive damages against Manville, even taking the risk that the settlement funds will run low, can the value of the company's stock which the trust owns be preserved.

5. It is unlikely that the trust will be able to administer the payment of more than 5,000 claims per year. At $30,000 per claim, it would take six years before there would be any need to sell stock to pay claims. The people with claims solely against Manville could be given priority relief and the most urgent claims could be thereby settled within the shortest time.

The Manville Personal Injury Settlement Trust was set up as a result of bankruptcy proceedings concluded in late 1988, very much along the lines described already. (A separate, smaller fund was set up for property damage claims.) Earliest-filed claims were settled first, as were cases finally coming to trial in 1989-90. In resolving 22,000 claims by paying and promising to pay a total of $935 million by the end of March of 1990, the Trust agreed to pay an average of $42,000 per case. This far exceeded the planned average settlement figure of $25,000 per case.[37]

The result was that, as the Trust's funds ran down, offers for settlement became more and more stretched out. The Trust issued a schedule for payment in the spring of 1990 that, for example, projected these dates for cases filed in 1986: estimated year for 40 percent payment, 2000; estimated date of final payment, 2005. Plaintiffs' attorneys in Virginia protested that the Trust's settlement offers were analogous to an offer to buy the judge's house for $1 million, but with payments limited to $1000 year. Administrators of the Trust were increasingly unable to come to terms with plaintiffs, and the tragic prospect of trials with the Trust as a defendant came to pass, despite virtually everyone's hope that the trust's limited funds would be used for settlement, not litigation.

In May of 1990, Federal District Judge Jack B. Weinstein and New York State Supreme Court Justice Helen Freedman held a highly unusual hearing, the immediate subject of which was 483 lawsuits arising from asbestos use at the Brooklyn Navy

Yard. The judges made it clear that they were dissatisfied with the results of the bankruptcy court's resolution of the Manville case.[37] The judges ordered the Trust to respond to questions, at the same time letting it be known that they were seeking ideas from any quarter about what should be done.

The White Lung Association held a demonstration at the Manville Trust's Washington D.C. headquarters to protest the whole idea of the Trust as a fraudulent solution. Speakers, including union representatives, called for the liquidation of Manville Corporation to compensate victims and castigated the Trust for making no real effort to seek out hardship cases and give them priority.

In the meantime, Manville Corporation reported record profits of $197 million for 1989 and was known to be holding about $1 billion in cash and unused credit lines, yet had not declared a dividend.[39] The company was now being pressed to "do more" or face the prospect of having the bankruptcy court's resolution reopened under pressure from District Court Judge Weinstein. Judges Weinstein and Freedman suggested that Manville lend the Trust $200 million to $300 million. They urged that other factors such as the severity of injury, the need for treatment, and the financial wherewithal of claimants be used for setting payment schedules, instead of the mere order in which lawsuits were filed.[40] They urged reductions in fees to the Trust's and plaintiffs' attorneys. The New York judges interpreted the law as permitting the bankruptcy court to lift its injuction barring asbestos victims from suing Manville Corporation; or, the bankruptcy court could increase the company's payments to the Trust.[39] In July of 1990 six Federal judges from around the country, including Judge Weinstein, agreed to meet to seek ways to resolve the crisis to the legal and political system posed by asbestos litigation. The trial courts made it clear that they would take action themselves if the matter was not promptly resolved in the bankruptcy court.

In 1984, Congress amended Chapter 11 of the bankruptcy law to provide that, henceforth, the "right to trial by jury that an individual has under non-bankruptcy law" would not be lost. The courts may yet interpret this as meaning that a plaintiff must still await an offer (the debtor company's reorganization plan) and reject it before being allowed to proceed with a civil suit. Since 1982, the only companies to file under Chapter 11 because of asbestos litigation have been small firms, Nicolet, Raymark, Pacor and Forty-Eight Insulation.

Manville's liabilities have not gone away or been reduced by federal legislation. The company's stock dropped in value from $34 a share when the Sumner Simpson papers were made public (in late 1978) to $2-3 in the first half of 1987, then recovered somewhat to $7 a share by mid-1990. Ultimately, the company may be liquidated entirely under pressure from Judge Weinstein if no other terms to better compensate the victims can be agreed upon. However, it is still possible if not likely that Manville and its main codefendants will come through the ordeal averting billions of dollars in liability from the sale of asbestos products. This could occur if Manville or other defendant companies succeed in:

1) winning suits against the U.S. government for indemnification on the grounds that federal specifications required asbestos, and/or the federal government had the knowledge and responsibility to assure that people handling asbestos under its direct and indirect control were protected; or
2) getting Congress to enact asbestos "compensation" legislation favorable to the industry.

Since 1977, defendants in asbestos litigation have supported some of the bills introduced in the U.S. Congress as asbestos disease compensation measures. These proposals would replace the victims' access to the courts with a federally administered system. Funding of the system would be borne by the asbestos litigation defendant companies and perhaps the government as well.

As of 1979, the government provided more than twice as much compensation as the defendants and their insurers to the families of insulators who died from asbestos disease (See Table 2). This is in addition to decreased tax revenues due to the men's premature deaths, and the enormous administrative costs to taxpayers of public programs to help the families and the operation of courts for handling the burden of litigation.

Even Manville's reorganization in bankruptcy court was designed to realize at least a half-billion dollar subsidy from U.S. taxpayers. The cost to society as a whole is thus quite high. This reality contrasts with industry demands that the government "pay its share" under new legislative proposals.

The obvious motivation for legislative proposals on the industry's part is to both limit and stretch out industry costs; however, it is doubtful whether anything so far proposed would improve the claimants' outlook, from the standpoint of eligibility, amount of compensation obtained, and length of time awaiting relief.[41] A large potential source of funding for such a system is the fortune in legal costs now borne by both sides, obviously.

But the problem lies not so much in conceiving and introducing fair, victim-oriented legislative proposals. The difficulty is in getting such bills enacted over the opposition of enormously powerful and well-organized insurance and manufacturing interests.

Legal/accounting shell games have been tried by some companies to distance their assets from asbestos-related liabilities. This has involved retaining the liable entity in name only while removing assets by a byzantine corporate restructuring scheme to a holding company owned by former shareholders of Raymark. Federal judge Panner in Oregon held the holding company responsible for Raymark's liabilities, find that "Raytech" was set up for the "improper purpose of escaping asbestos-related liabilities" (*Schmoll v. AC&S et al.*)

Leveraged buyout subterfuges have been used to separate a Fortune 500 parent corporation (Jim Walter Corp.) from the liabilities of its wholly owned subsidiaries (Celotex, Carey Canada). In this case, the Wall Street brokerage firm that arranged the deal (Kohlberg, Kravis, Roberts & Co.) has also been sued by plaintiffs with asbestosis and cancer. Other versions of liability avoidance remain to be attempted. The mettle and gullibility of the courts are being tested, and plaintiffs' attorneys have had to maneuver again and again in unfamiliar terrain to counter such moves by corporate defendants. Should any such dodge be successful, it would open a door in the legal system that corporations could pass through and close behind them on asbestos victims.

There has been some litigation over asbestos disease in other countries. In Australia, a firm that owned an asbestos mine was sued by former miners with asbestosis and mesothelioma (See "CSR" in Chapter 9). The victims' success in the first few cases where liability was addressed has led to the settlement of hundreds of other claims, largely because Australian courts discourage relitigation of issues already settled by trials. Product liability actions against James Hardie Industries have also led to many settlements, as the company evidently hopes to limit the extent of legal discovery and publicity regarding its historic policies on asbestos products sold to consumers.

In 1986, a Tokyo District Court ordered an asbestos manufacturing firm and its parent company (Asahi Asbestos Co.) to pay $1.2 million in the cases of 10 former asbestos plant employees. The defendants withdrew their appeal to a higher court, and the parent company agreed to pay the damages to prevent financial crisis at the smaller firm. After agreeing to a slight rduction in the court award with the successful plaintiffs, the defense also agreed to pay something to an unsuccessful plaintiff whose case was lost on the grounds of statute of limitations. The government had also been sued, but the court did not hold the government accoutable for damages.[42]

There has been no asbestos product liability litigation in Great Britain. Even extectations that lower thresholds of proof would be required by U.K. social security industrial injury boards in lung cancer cases have gone unfulfilled, despite changes in the law in 1985 (See "Cancer from Asbestos in the Absence of Asbestosis," in Chapter 4). Symptomatic of official attitudes, the London Medical Boarding Centre (Respiratory Diseases) appointed Dr. Kevin Browne "following his retirement as medical officer to Cape Asbestos" in 1985. The Department of Health and Social Security said Browne would not be asked to adjudicate claims by Cape employees, but he would be consulted in deciding asbestos claims involving others.

The Society for the Prevention of Asbestosis and Industrial Diseases then complained that Browne was still working for

Cape and serving as a defense medical expert in handling asbestos disease claims for others; and in addition, that Browne had access to Special Medical Board records. Pressed also by Member of Parliament Frank Dobson, the government finally admitted in 1987 that Browne was still working as a medical "consultant" to Cape up to two days weekly.[43] Nonetheless, Dr. Browne was retained on the medical board. On the whole, the medical profession in Britain has shown itself unwilling to testify in support of asbestos victims' claims.

Public Opinion and Public Health Policy

Leaders in the asbestos industry have long realized that their near-term pecuniary interests were best served by having asbestos hazards receive a minimum of publicity. The asbestos mining companies in Quebec maintained continuous public relations campaigns starting in 1954.[44] The goal of these programs was to create the public perception of asbestos as a miracle mineral and of the companies as good corporate citizens, contributing to Quebec's "prosperity, social development, and culture."

This message was conveyed through the distribution of *The Asbestos Producer*, which stated that asbestos mining was a "healthy occupation." The magazine was sent to the homes of thousands of employees, government offices and legislators, editors of Quebec newspapers, clergy, writers, broadcasters and opinion leaders in the mining communities and throughout Quebec. The Quebec Asbestos Information Service started in 1954, and the media often published the industry's news releases without alteration.[44] By 1966, it was anticipated that:

> This editorial acceptance will serve the industry well when quick and easy access to news editors and broadcasters becomes essential.

The Quebec Asbestos Information Service, QAMA, and the individual companies distributed industry literature to opinion leaders, schools, libraries, and political organizations, both within Canada and abroad. Distribution of one-minute television films was added in 1966. Also in 1966, QAMA set up a

Health Council to fund medical research, complete with advance public relations work in Canada and the U.S. Part of this was a plan to illustrate "the healthful conditions of life in the asbestos country", complete with interviews with local octogenarians and local doctors.[44]

> In all material, emphasis should be placed upon athletic prowess of asbestos youth, on healthy and energetic summer and winter activities.

As Dr. Selikoff, *New Yorker* journalist Paul Brodeur, and public interest environmental groups began to raise public awareness that asbestos was dangerous, the industry in North America had to adjust to being a focus of controversy. A turning point was approached in 1973, as asbestos use in the United States reached its zenith. Former Johns-Manville writer of position papers and executives' speeches, 30-year-old Matthew Swetonic, director of the two-year-old Asbestos Information Association (AIA), described the industry's publicity problems at a meeting of the Asbestos Textile Institute that June. He said that the industry faced a growing volume of media reports largely arising from Dr. Selikoff blowing up an essentially occupational problem into a national calamity. Swetonic went on to describe AIA's efforts to (misleadingly) publicize a World Health Organization report as saying the general public was not in danger from asbestos in the environment. Swetonic's experience was that the best he could expect of press accounts would be an inclusion of the industry's views in otherwise "negative" stories.

After acknowledging that media coverage of this type would continue until "the generation of negative news ceases," Swetonic's message to the industry brightened:

> And the good news is, despite all the negative articles on asbestos-health that have appeared in the press over the past half-dozen years, very few people have been paying attention.

He explained that a national interview survey had shown that only 22 percent of all Americans were aware that asbestos was hazardous to health. Moreover, "A mere 3 percent of those interviewed stated that they considered it a health hazard to the general public." This left open the possibility that, as public awareness of asbestos hazards grew, it could be defused as an impetus for drastic action if the public saw asbestos as a cause of disease confined to only a limited number of very heavily exposed workers (under condtions that no longer exist, now that we know . . . etc.)

For the next 16 years, the U.S. asbestos industry fought a bruising, ultimately losing battle, as medical and public opinion solidified and forced gradual regulatory action, mostly by conservative administrations in Washington. By 1989, asbestos litigation and abatement had become dominant concerns of the companies formerly active in manufacturing asbestos products. Looming large in this picture was a precipitous new deluge of lawsuits for damages exceeding $100 billion, by property owners removing and planning to remove asbestos materials that were deteriorating. The buildings at issue filled the spectrum—schools, churches, hospitals, apartment houses, legislative houses, banks, huge office buildings, everything.

In the meantime, some disturbing trends were observed by the White Lung Association, the Sheet Metal Workers union, Dr. Selikoff, and others. Asbestos abatement, despite government laws and regulations, was being done often in a shoddy manner. The resulting immediate hazards were sometimes worse that those initially intended to be removed. One contributing factor was the utter failure of the federal government to set standard criteria for asbestos abatement worker training and licensing and work practices; another was the reluctance of the insurance industry to sell coverage to asbestos removal contractors in the years that the abatement industry grew dramatically, 1985-1988.[46] There were horrible cases of untrained, illiterate, and illegal workers removing asbestos without using the required safeguards. At the same time, some contractors wre doing careful work, thereby demonstrating that asbestos removal could be done using recognized safeguards.

One response to this was local legislation to require: 1)

training of asbestos abatement workers and certification of abatement firms; and 2) advance disclosure about plans for asbestos removal jobs, even to the occupants of commercial buildings. It was reasoned that, with more people looking on, the odds were better that the proper safegards would be applied. The Sheet Metal Workers, Service Employees International Union, and other unions saw the need for aggressive regulation, including criminal prosecution of responsible individuals running businesses in violation of the law.

Another response, however, was to re-open the question of whether removing asbestos from buildings was justified. Examples could be given where removing asbestos endangered workers and building occupants more than leaving it in place probably would have, at least in the short run. And where there were examples, generalizations could be advanced in their wake.

In the midst of great concern and public frustration, the viewpoint was advanced by some that asbestos in buildings was best left alone until it was necessary to disturb, during normal building repair and maintenance. This argument had a broad appeal to powerful sectors of society: building owners, insurance companies, and former asbestos building product manufacturers, for example. The spokesmen for this view, not always willing to acknowledge whose interests it served, could affect daftness and claim that they were speaking out against the big, bad asbestos abatement contracting industry.

The view that the best asbestos abatement is none at all rests on several assumptions. Most of the asbestos now in place is chrysotile, and assumption number one is that chrysotile is far less harmful than the other (amphibole) asbestos varieties. The second assumption is that, although some asbestos abatement is carefully done, it must nonetheless be assumed that the common practice will always be in violation of laws and regulations, and nothing can be done to change this.

A product of these assumptions is that public exposure to asbestos in buildings is so low as to be essentially safe, *unless* abatement work is done. Taken all together, the public is being told the problem is now limited to only a relatively small number of heavily exposed workers, and anyway it's OSHA's job to protect them. Leave well enough alone, or the general population will be in peril! This has the cynical appeal of pitting public opinion against the most highly asbestos-exposed workers, by letting them continue to be exposed to disease-producing concentrations (mainteneance workers, janitors, firefighters, etc.). It also ignores the fact that deteriorating asbestos building materials will remain a largely invisible threat to all building occupants, not just the "blue-collar" workers.

An associated claim is that the billions of dollars needed for asbestos abatement can and should be diverted to other, more cost-effective health and environmental programs, although proponents of this view never seem to point out that such shifts would also entail a fundamental shift in *who* would pay (i.e., the public, not insurance carriers, asbestos companies, or the owners of real estate). For their part, the parties facing the cost of asbestos removal are not yet offering a "peace dividend" to society as the price of a cheaper approach to the problem of asbestos in buildings.

The principal scientific architects of the laissez-faire approach to asbestos abatement are microbiologist Brooke Mossman, physician J. Bernard Gee, and engineer Morton Corn. The first "scientific" effort to support this approach was launched by a select gathering at Harvard University in 1988. Experts on asbestos from Harvard and Mt. Sinai were not invited, as Dr. Selikoff has pointed out. Nor were unions asked to participate. The organizers of the meeting were exclusively associations representing real estate and insurance interests and defendant companies in asbestos litigation, led by the Safe Buildings Alliance.

The "Harvard Symposium report" in turn became a vehicle for media coverage worthy of a great discovery. It was followed by articles in the *New England Journal of Medicine* and *Science* magazine.[47-49] Sensationalist new terms were introduced, like "fiber-phobia", "para-toxicology", and "The Asbestos Removal Fiasco."

Britain's *New Scientist* reported on April 14, 1990:

> Plans to spend up to $150 billion to deal with dangerous asbestos in the U.S. are hanging in the balance while scientists conduct a bitter argument over just what the dangers are.

The Mossman-Gee paper in the *New England Journal of Medicine* was denounced by Dr. Orn Eliasson as subtly presenting the views of the asbestos industry:[50]

> that it is doubtful that asbestos alone can cause lung cancer, that clinical or pathological evidence of asbestosis is required before one can attribute lung cancer to asbestos exposure, that asbestos exposure does not cause gastrointestinal cancers, that pleural disease is rarely if ever associated with impairment of lung function, that chrysotile does not cause mesothelioma, and that the risk of lung cancer in workers exposed to asbestos can be accounted for by smoking and exposure to cocarcinogens.

Eliasson rightly suspected that the authors were active in defense of product liability suits, which he said would be aided by their article:

> It was not a coincidence that an attorney representing an asbestos manufacturer presented me with a copy of the article three days before I received my own copy of the *Journal* in the mail.

The *Science* paper received an extraordinary amount of media attention, despite the fact that it presented no new information, only contained an unbalanced review of the key issues, was contradicted on major points by the actions of the EPA, OSHA, and the National Academy of Sciences, and was mainly authored by people active in the defense in asbestos litigation.

A disgusted Irving Selikoff congratulated the authors of the article and the campaign carried on by the asbestos manufacturers and their advertising agencies to promote the idea that there is no hazard from asbestos in place.[51] His colleague at Mt.

Sinai, Stephen Levin, blasted the authors for putting out misinformation and cited one for talking about the "safe" form of asbestos on a radio program. New York health official James Melius criticized the attempt to overturn a social consensus based on a poor scientific review.[52]

The Service Employees International Union condemned the asbestos industry and its consultants for conducting a highly misleading disinformation campaign attempting to downplay the hazards of asbestos.[52] The Sheet Metal Workers withdrew their support for research involving Morton Corn's department at Johns Hopkins.[53]

The articles by Mossman, Gee, and co-workers were greeted with relief by politicians around the country, who wanted very much to believe that they needn't come up with millions of dollars for asbestos removal after all. Rhode Island proposed to slash all funding for the state Asbestos Control Program. Some conservative politicians were also distressed at the volume of lawsuits brought by governmental bodies against industry to recoup the costs of asbestos abatement. Senator Malcolm Wallop introduced a bill to repeal the Asbestos Hazard Emergency Response Act (requiring school districts to look for asbestos in school buildings and to remove it if it is in poor condition), while invoking an obscure news report for the first time blaming the lack of asbestos in O-ring caulk for the 1986 Challenger space shuttle disaster.[52]

Responses to the scientific and public policy issues raised in the *Science* paper were published in *Science* by Nicholson *et al.*, Brody, and EPA chief William Reilly.[54-56] Samuels of the AFL-CIO Industrial Union Department noted that at least 4 of the 5 authors of the *Science* paper had "long-term asbestos industry associations."[57]

EPA then announced that it was setting up an expert panel under the auspices of the Health Effects Institute, funded with $2 million from EPA and $2 million from real estate, insurance, and asbestos abatement interests and former asbestos manufacturers. The panel is supposed to advise EPA on scientific issues regarding asbestos in buildings. Plaintiffs' attorney Edward Westbrook promptly noted that 7 of the 15 members of the panel were listed as defense witnesses in asbestos property damage litigation (not counting Brooke Mossman, who has also been a consultant to Owens-Corning, Keene, and U.S. Gypsum). Selikoff wryly observed that the Institute was seeking to repeal the past 500 years of experience that he who pays the piper calls the tunes.

In June of 1990, a 3-day conference on asbestos, with emphasis on the problem of asbestos in place, was convened in New York. No comparable gathering had been held since the New York Academy of Sciences conference in 1978. The four authors of the *Science* paper with backgrounds in biological science were invited, but none of the authors of the controversial report came. From a safe distance, Mossman told the *New York Times* that none of the matters presented and discussed at the conference had been peer-reviewed and published.[58]

Criminal Sanctions and Personal Responsibility

Asbestos manufacturers have not been alone in facing substantial costs in damage suits. The fear of liability outweighs even regulation (to protect consumers, workers, and communities) in restraining some business practices today. But are regulation and *corporate* civil liability for damages sufficient to adequately protect the public? A strong case can be made that they are not.

This book shows that *widespread* abuse of the health of the public occurred over decades in the asbestos industry. That industry was composed of major industrial corporations, whose dominant members "knowingly and recklessly" endangered the health of their workers, their customers, and whole communities in the pursuit of profits. The fact of such business practices being so pervasive, often involving "conspiracy" in addition to misconduct within individual enterprises, stands as an indictment of our social order. This documented *breadth* of misconduct throughout an industry, unlike the comparatively scattered reports of similar acts by companies in other industries, points to a consistent legal, ethical, and corporate failure, not an aberrant one.

Ives has completed a doctoral dissertation based on interviews with the 17 largest chemical and petroleum companies in the U.S. and Great Britain. She found a high degree of consistency in the way the U.S. companies responded to regulation and other external pressures relating to occupational and environmental health. "My American consensus model of corporate response includes resistance, defiance, and loyalty to the Company and industrial colleagues," she concluded, going on to catalog the corporate mechanisms used to resist and defy external threats from environmental and societal constituencies.[59]

The truth of the cliche, "crime does not pay," is based on the real threat of severe punishment for acts that society aggressively prosecutes as crimes. The utter lack of criminal prosecution for the patently criminal conduct of some asbestos industry executives—and their counterparts in other industries—is society's unspoken invitation for continued abuses. The competitive pressure of the marketplace, the limited-term business outlook, and the short-term personal financial incentive schedules of corporate executives have left society with long-term health problems. The continuing record of abuses of power and knowledge points to the inadequacy of existing social deterrents. Moderate increases in government regulation or the cost of product liability insurance coverage (dictated by current trends in civil litigation) can hardly be expected to bring about major changes in corporate conduct.

Through litigation brought by injured persons in civil suits or by government regulatory authorities, actions highly detrimental to public health by business executives have been exposed in a wide range of industries. Wholesale endangerment of the public through the knowing sale of defective products (Ford Pinto cars; Firestone Radial 500 tires; unsafe and ineffective drugs including thalidomide; herbicides contaminated with deadly dioxin compounds; Dalkon Shield intrauterine devices, etc.), illegal environmental dumping of hazardous wastes, and falsified reporting to government agencies are the main types of such conduct to actually receive occasional criminal prosecution. "White collar crimes" by business managers are not deterred, in part because they are usually not addressed as crimes at all. When these acts *are* treated as crimes, the penalties suggest they are in a class with misdemeanors rather than felonies.[60] The following examples where charges *were* brought are illustrative.

In the trial of Ford Motor Company in 1980 on homocide charges (involving Ford Pinto car occupants' burn injuries from an exploding fuel tank), the maximum fine possible was $30,000. Defense attorneys easily sidestepped the prosecution of any *person* in the company through the force of superior resources. The prosecutor in Winamac, Indiana, had to undertake the case within his annual budget of $20,000, while Ford spent millions on litigation and public relations. The Ford Motor Company was acquitted, following the judge's ruling that key incriminating documents were inadmissable as evidence in the case. The documents showed a corporate decision to not remedy a design defect because the anticipated personal injury and death claims were projected to carry a lower cost than correcting the defect in thousands of cars.

The former president of a bankrupt chemical waste disposal firm was given a sentence of 1 to 7 years for bribery and dumping of wastes in a city creek. The firm had gone into bankruptcy after being confronted with large fines over the illegal dumping of wastes. The generators of the wastes (including Standard Chlorine, Texaco, Sullivan Asbestos, and SmithKline) were *not* subjected to any criminal or bankruptcy proceedings.[61]

In the rare case of a major corporation officer sentenced to jail on charges of conspiracy and violations of the Clean Water Act, the time served in prison was 90 days. *Chemical and Engineering News* was kind enough to withhold the Corning Fibers executive's name.[62]

Industrial Bio-Test Laboratories professionals were convicted of falsifying toxicological laboratory test results (relating to carcinogenesis of widely used pesticides) in reports to the government. They were accordingly sentenced to 6-12 months in jail in 1984. The case against the company president meanwhile ended in a mistrial.[63]

In 1985, Illinois prosecutors obtained murder convictions of the owners of a small business in a highly publicized case. At Film Recovery Systems' plant, a Polish immigrant employee had died after repeated cyanide exposures in silver reclaiming operations. Appeals courts, however, found that the convictions for both murder and involuntary manslaughter were technically inconsistent, since the underlying evidence of these intentional and unintentional crimes was the same. The case was remanded for retrial, and the state Court of Appeals declined to review the matter in 1990.

Starting in the mid-1980s, some state and local prosecutors (e.g., in Michigan and California) have begun to bring similar charges in cases where workers have died on the job. Special teams of criminal investigators have been trained to investigate every incident of death on the job within their jurisdictions. Even so, these are very limited efforts, and for the most part even they do not extend to cases of serious injury, only deaths. Furthermore, almost all such investigations involve industrial safety lapeses, not equally blatant cases of health damage to workers occurring over a longer period of time.

In most such events, of course, no criminal indictments are even brought. There have been no criminal charges filed over the conduct of anyone in the asbestos mining and manufacturing industry, though Justice Department attorneys have mused about specific actions of one firm's executives seeming rather like obstruction of justice. More extraordinary is that the commission of certain acts is not considered criminal, but an effort to conceal the facts about them in a civil suit might theoretically warrant the criminal charge, "obstruction of justice."[64]

After all, the concealment of life-threatening hazards in the pursuit of financial gains was not an isolated phenomenon in the asbestos mining and manufacturing industry. The corporate response to the hazard was, in all too many cases, knowing and reckless concealment of vital information and disregard for the health of the public. The review of corporate knowledge in this writing is a veritable encyclopedia of menacing business practices in the area of occupational health. In unusually strong language, New Jersey Superior Court Judge Sylvia Pressler wrote of the industry leader and a co-defendant mining company, "(the defendants) made a conscious, cold-blooded business decision in utter flagrant disregard of the rights of others, to take no protective or remedial action."[65]

Today's asbestos catastrophe clearly was not caused by an isolated case of a corrupt or incompetent medical director or a callous company president. It was caused primarily by the rules of a society that allows a privileged stratum to largely escape personal responsibility for acts harmful to others. The members of this privileged class decide what will be manufactured, where and how it will be made and sold. The asbestos epidemic, whose toll of preventable deaths in the U.S. alone will at least be in the hundreds of thousands, offers opportunity to see how the criminal law or lack of it relates to public health. All that is lacking is the public awareness, pressure, and political will to deal as firmly with corporate crimes as with comparably serious, generally recognized criminal offenses.

Largely inspired by revelations about the asbestos industry, Congressman George Miller proposed in 1979 to change the U.S. Criminal Code. Miller urged that until business managers were held personally accountable for their actions, civil law alone could not adequately deter financially motivated business practices from endangering the lives of unsuspecting citizens.[66] This idea of establishing in federal law provisions to punish "corporate criminal liability" with imprisonment was fiercely opposed by business interests.

Congressman Miller's bill was supported by Rev. Michael Crosby, representing 23 Midwest Roman Catholic groups. The executive director of the Interfaith Center on Corporate Responsibility testified that,[67]

> Pastors frequently hear parishoners confide that they feel morally compromised in corporations which frequently search for maximum profits despite the costs for society.

Journalist and author Morton Mintz argues that the threats of both the social stigma of a criminal trial and imprisonment itself would go a long way toward correcting the present situation. Mintz, who has been writing about corporate crime for over 20 years, deferred to Edward Ross as having described the problem long ago.[68] In the 1907 book, *Sin and Society,* Ross wrote:

> The grading of sinners according to badness of character goes on the assumption that the wickedest man is the most dangerous. This would be true if men were abreast in their opportunities to do harm...But the fact is that the patent ruffian is confined to the Social basement...He can assault or molest, to be sure, but he cannot betray. Nobody depends on him so he cannot commit breach of trust, that arch sin of our time. He does not hold in his hand the safety or welfare of the public. He is the clinker, not the live coal; vermin, not beast of prey. Today the villain most in need of curbing is the respectable, exemplary, trusted personage who, strategically placed at the focus of a spider-web of fiduciary relations, is able from his office chair to pick a thousand pockets, poison a thousand sick, pollute a thousand minds, or imperil a thousand lives.

As Economist Richard Beilock explains, "no finite system of monetary fines, as would be levied in civil offenses, would provide the same level of deterrent" as the real threat of imprisonment. He noted in 1979 that insurance and bankruptcy courts offer no way to avoid criminal prosecution and imprisonment, in contrast to their ability to insulate against civil penalties:[69]

> For all of us time is unidirectional and death is a certainty. Chunks of our lives are priceless in that there exists no market at which we can purchase a replacement. This then is the infinite cost that it is proper to impose upon executives for the crime of imposing infinite costs on others.

On October 1, 1984, Congressman John Conyers, Jr. introduced a bill (H.R. 6350) similar to that offered by Congressman Miller five years before. Mr. Conyers would erect criminal penalties under federal law for knowing failure of business managers to promptly inform appropriate federal agencies and affected employees about serious, non-obvious dangers associated with products and business practices. Penalties would include imprisonment for up to 10 years and a fine of up to $250,000 for violators (such fine not payable directly or indirectly by the business entity). In introducing this bill, Conyers said:

> This bill...is an attempt to codify respect and responsibility for human life at every level of business management, and to remove the glaring legal disparities between crime in the suites and crime in the streets. It offers business the timely opportunity to explicitly reassert its highest ethical standards and, by policing itself, to preclude or limit the need for further regulatory action.[70]

Both the idea of imprisonment and that of personally fining the responsible business executives (with the attendant publicity such proceedings would receive) go to the heart of the problem of placing personal responsibility on the decision-makers. If such legislation were enacted and enforced, there is every reason to expect that significant public health benefits would result.

Traditional Public Health Measures

Current use of and exposure to asbestos can be better controlled through a number of traditional methods. At the head of the list would be tighter workplace and environmental standards, vigorously enforced. Protection under workplace regulations can be extended to maintenance workers and brake repair workers. Contractors who do asbestos removal can be required to use proper equipment and work practices, in addition to obtaining personnel training. (This has been mandated by law in Maryland and other states.) In view of the dust exposures from uncontrolled brake and clutch repair, and continuing concern over the hazards of asbestos substitutes, brake servicing should also be licensed by health authorities. Proven, fully enclosed equipment is now available, and its use should be required.

Governments at the local, state, or federal level can take the lead by providing training and protection to state employees who do maintenance work and vehicle brake repairs. (This is being done in Maryland and New Jersey.) Product bans can also eliminate widespread exposure. In Maryland, the legislature banned the sale of asbestos-containing industrial clothing in 1984. At the federal level, grants can be offered to promote the development of safe substitutes for asbestos products, sealants for deteriorating asbestos surfaces, etc. The government can also offer tax advantages to firms developing and implementing programs that will reduce the consumption of asbestos in favor of safer materials. Workers laid off in the asbestos industry can be offered special assistance, retraining, and funds for relocation.

Public health agencies can meanwhile try to educate the public and especially those most at risk about the hazards and means to control them. Epidemiological data suggest that people with histories of occupational asbestos exposure can markedly decrease their risk of lung cancer, if they smoke, by overcoming their addiction to smoking.[71] This is certainly a matter to stress, considering the proportion of asbestos-related cancers whose risk is enhanced by cigarette smoking. Much more could also be done to hopefully improve the outlook for mesothelioma victims through increased commitment of research funds.

Victims' Groups

One reaction to the severity of the asbestos problem and the inadequacy of traditional social structures has been the formation of asbestos victims' groups. These nonprofit groups respond to public inquiries, provide counseling, promote legislation for disease prevention and compensation, and bring pressure on public officials through both administrative channels and the media. These victims' groups are weakly financed charitable organizations, which receive voluntary technical assistance by professionals in science, medicine, and law.

Association to Improve Benefits for
Retired Disabled Workers
and Their Dependents
27 N. Eleventh Avenue
Manville, New Jersey 08835 USA
(201) 722-1829

White Lung Association
1601 St. Paul St.
Baltimore, Maryland 21202 USA
(301) 727-6029

Asbestos Victims of America
P.O. Box 559
Capitola, California 95010 USA
(408) 476-3646

Society for the Prevention of Asbestosis and
Industrial Diseases
38 Drapers Road
Enfield, Middlesex EN2 8LU ENGLAND
81-366-1640

Asbestos Diseases Society
483 Charles Street
North Perth 6006
AUSTRALIA
09-444-6665

WORLDWIDE PROLIFERATION OF ASBESTOS DISEASE

Photographer Bill Ravanesi, whose father died from mesothelioma, has created an art exhibit featuring asbestos victims. Called "Breath Taken: The Landscape and Biography of Asbestos," it opened at Boston University Art Galley in March of 1990.

World asbestos consumption has plateaued at 4.3 to 4.8 million metric tons per year (See Figure 3). The trend in world asbestos use differs from that for the U.S. because of shifts in the world market for the mineral over the past decade. In general, the industrial nations are now using less asbestos while the developing countries are using more of it.

The degree of both regulation and liability attendant upon

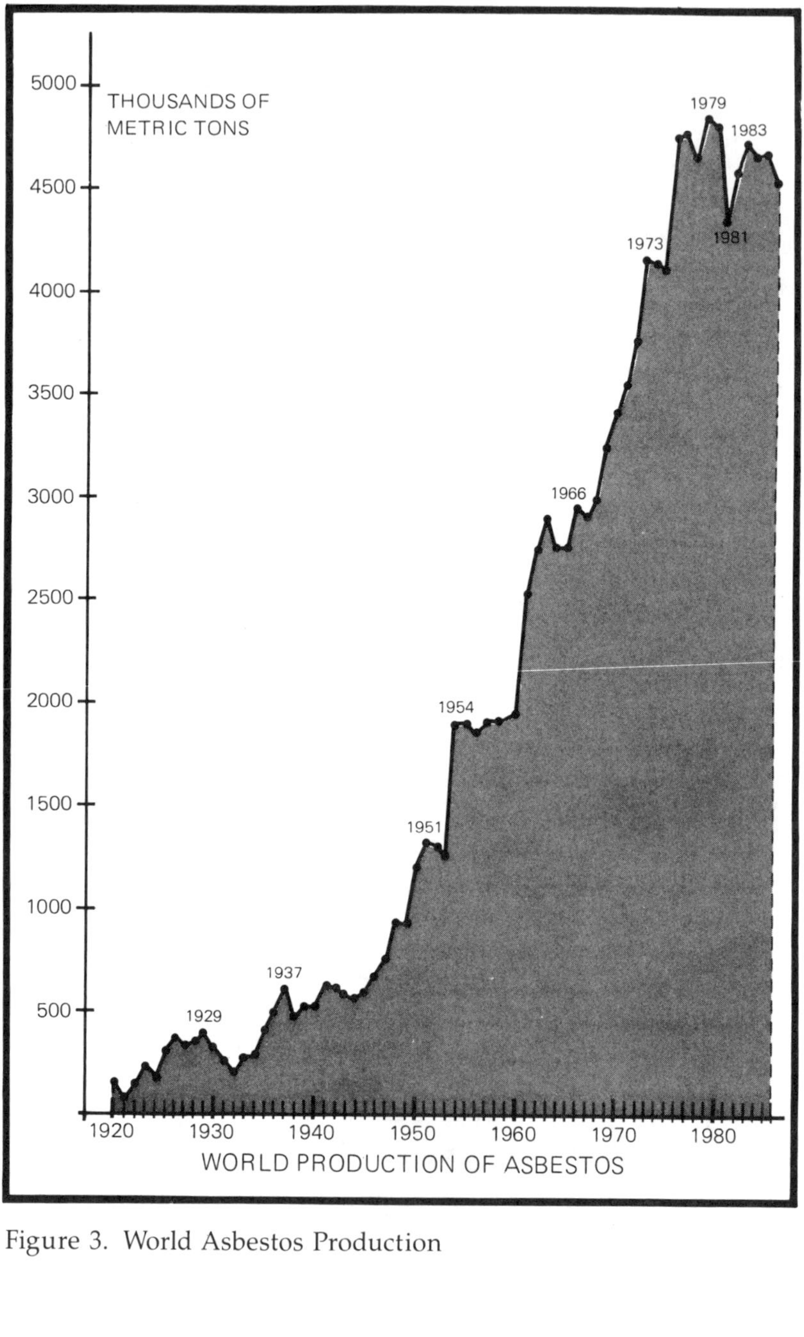

Figure 3. World Asbestos Production

the use of asbestos varies enormously from country to country. Similarly, the level of public concern about the threat of asbestos ranges from total ignorance in some countries to widespread fear in others. These conditions not only invite but assure that there will be a wide range of health protection in practice around the world.

From the time of the first asbestos regulations in England nearly 60 years ago, it was recognized that non-uniform standards internationally led to undesired economic consequences.[72] For, as dust controls and other health-related costs became more significant in some countries, manufacturers elsewhere could derive a competitive advantage by avoiding similar expenditures. It soon turned out that the "foreign competition" wasn't always owned by foreigners or competitors. In 1949, for example, one English firm (Cape Asbestos) found it unnecessary to take even minimal measures to protect the health of Black children it employed in its own mill in South Africa.[73]

And so it emerged that the threat of international "double standards" within the same enterprises grew with the dominant role played by multinationals such as Johns-Manville, Turner & Newall, Cape, and the Eternit companies (headquartered in Belgium and Switzerland).

When asked about their policies regarding asbestos and industrial hygiene, Cape Asbestos and Turner & Newall both claimed that they followed uniformly high standards everywhere in the world.[74] Johns-Manville made similar assertions, and in addition issued a policy statement that J-M asbestos fiber would not even be sold to customers who were unwilling to observe appropriate safeguards.[75] These statements have been subjected to scrutiny on occasion, however, and the level of control in practice in developing countries has been consistently poor.[7,10,75-82]

Double standards in health protection are both created and exploited by multinational corporations engaged in asbestos mining and manufacturing. The issue of warnings is illustrative. No one would question the right of a worker handling asbestos to be informed of the lethal potential of the material. Instruction in the use and maintenance of available engineering controls and respiratory protection, as well as direction in work practices to minimize dust, should be universally provided to asbestos workers. The most basic, minimal means of notifying people that a product is dangerous is through the use of a warning label.

Though the use of warning labels on sacks of asbestos had become accepted practice in Canada between 1969 and 1977, sales resistance was encountered elsewhere. An international sales representative of Carey Canada conveyed this in a memorandum to Michael Prus, the company president. He also described the manner in which Canadian asbestos companies discretely avoided both warnings and liability in Japan:[83]

> I got very strong reactions in Japan to our requirement to translate the Tampa Text Label into Japanese and print it on all the bags.
>
> Confidentially the Kakiuchi staff told me that they have deliberately left out the word cancer from the text because this must not even be mentioned in Japan in connection with asbestos. Altogether they are against a warning label because they do not wish to raise problems with the workers. They are already attaching a label on each bag according to Japanese law.
>
> Kakiuchi would prefer to sign a certificate holding us blameless from harm and would in turn get a signature from all customers on a similar disclaimer to hold themselves free of lawsuits. Asbestos Corporation and Bell have both gone this route as per attached blank forms.
>
> Kakiuchi are of the opinion that we cannot impose American law on foreign countries in general and on Japan in particular. Listening to customers around the world I second this sentiment. I do not believe that we should raise problems with people who are more primitive than we are or less educated. We cannot, in all cases, impose American standards on other people.

The salesman asked for guidance from "the lawyers in Tampa," referring to the Florida headquarters of Carey Canada's parent firm, Jim Walter Corporation, one of the 200 largest industrial corporations in the United States. The response was conveyed two months later by a vice president of Carey Canada:[84]

> Charles Wilson, V. Pres. Legal Dept. Tampa, says as far as the caution label is concerned that we must be sure to cover ourselves only where the law of the land requires. I suggest we go ahead with the new caution label in English and French only. What do you think the Japanese, Finns, Swedes, and Dutch will have to say about that?

The two Canadian mining firms named in the first Carey memorandum, like Carey Canada, were either controlled or wholly owned by multinationals in the U.S. and Britain in 1977 (Asbestos Corp. by General Dynamics, Bell by Turner & Newall). Together with Johns-Manville, they accounted for virtually all asbestos exports from the world's leading asbestos-exporting country.

The international asbestos industry's collective view of its responsibility to label its products as potentially lethal was indicated in a 1978 internal memorandum of the Asbestos International Association (AIA). The "Executive Committee" consensus was to use as little by way of warning labels as the various markets would permit:[85]

> Most participants were in favour of an action in various stages; the switching over from one stage to a further less favourable one, depending on outside pressures.

The British asbestos industry's approach to the labeling problem was apparently regarded as a model to eventually follow. In that country so famous for understatement, the government had acquiesced to the use of a label starting with the ambiguous phrase, "Take care with asbestos."

> Many of the participants were of the opinion that it was advisable to adopt the U.K label as such *if the use of a label was unavoidable.* Rediscussing the wording could bring

> along the risk of having to include the word cancer in it. (emphasis added)

The view that the best warning label was none at all appears to have had no opposition at this meeting:

> In those countries where it was felt still too early to start voluntary labeling, in fear of a negative influence on sales, steps should be taken to prepare commercial people for the idea, making clear that in the absence of an industry's initiative we could run the risk of being imposed the 'skull and crossbones' symbol for our products. It should also be pointed out to them that the fact to agree on a kind of label did not imply the agreement of starting to use it right now.

One can easily understand the apprehensions of the AIA Executive Committee regarding the inverse relationship between warnings and sales. The U.K. label stands in mute contrast to posters used by Puerto Rican teachers protesting the hazards of working in asbestos-cement schools in 1979 (See Figures 4 and 5). When Thailand wanted to label bags of imported asbestos with the skull and crossbones in 1984, the Canadian government persuaded the Thais to drop the idea as an "excessive" warning.[86] Thailand's use of asbestos is rapidly growing.

After insulation containing asbestos was banned in some countries as unnecessary and inhumane, it was hoped that the manufacture of such products elsewhere would rapidly decline. In the United States, the Johns-Manville Corporation discontinued the manufacture of Thermobestos at the end of 1973, and the use of asbestos in thermal insulation block and pipecovering was banned in the U.S. by the Environmental Protection Agency in 1975. Yet in 1976 Johns-Manville not only made Thermobestos in Brazil but was only starting to consider applying warning labels to the product. The manufacture of Thermobestos in Brazil apparently continued into the 1980s. Product brochures described Thermobestos and other Johns-

Manville insulations as reinforced with asbestos fibers, but no warnings about the health risks were given. By 1983, these insulations had been reformulated, and older stocks of asbestos-containing material had apparently all been sold.[87,88]

Some asbestos-containing insulation was shipped out of the continental United States after it was banned by the EPA. Insulation labeled asbestos-free by Keene on hand in 1982 at an Amerada Hess oil refinery on St. Croix was found to contain 20-25 percent amosite (See "Keene Corporation" in Chapter 9). Related documentation is still "under seal" in litigation, but should soon be disclosed. The practice of courts sometimes "sealing" evidence in civil cases where public hazards are at issue is coming under increasing restriction and criticism in Texas, Florida, New York, and other states.

Other aspects of international "double standards" in public protection from asbestos abound.[7,10,75-89] Flagrant occupational and environmental health abuses have been documented at a Johns-Manville affiliate in Ahmedabad, India, manufacturing asbestos-cement, and a Turner & Newall subsidiary in Bombay making asbestos textiles and friction products.[7,10,76,77,89] New and expanded asbestos-cement plants were meanwhile under construction or operating in Tunisia, Kuwait, the Sudan, the Philippines, Nigeria, Malaysia, Thailand, India, Sri Lanka, and many other countries.

The worldwide network of asbestos mining, manufacturing and distribution is largely managed by enterprises that are international in scale. By 1972, Johns-Manville shipped Canadian asbestos fiber to 58 countries. J-M was also linked to operations in many of these countries through partial ownership, licensing contracts, and marketing agreements.[90] In September, 1983, the bankruptcy judge approved the sale of Manville's Canadian asbestos mining business to individuals including former Manville employees, for $117 million. Turner & Newall mines asbestos in Swaziland and Zimbabwe, and has major holdings in asbestos manufacturing operations in India, Nigeria, Italy, Australia, Brazil, Spain, South Korea, and other countries. Even the construction of new asbestos plants in the

Figure 4. U.K. label for asbestos products.

Figure 5. Puerto Rican protest poster hung in asbestos-cement school buildings.

developing countries is dominated by engineering firms based in Europe. *Asbestos* magazine was full of their advertisements until its demise in 1983.

Asbestos has been a major revenue-producing mineral in the economies of Quebec and Zimbabwe. Both of these areas export the bulk of their output. The Soviet Union, which now leads the world in asbestos production, is second to Canada in exports of the mineral. The U.S.S.R. has continued to expand its mining capacity in recent years. (The Soviet Union's historic use of its asbestos deposits has not been paralleled by contributions to the scientific literature regarding adverse health effects.) China also mines and consumes a considerable quantity (about 150,000 metric tons per year) of asbestos.[91] It will take great political will for countries with growing economic dependence on this mineral to restrain its reckless exploitation.

The vulnerability of developing nations as sanctuaries for future asbestos mining and manufacturing is obvious. And even while Quebec's newly nationalized asbestos company claims to observe strict regulations, the title of its advertisements in *Asbestos* magazine revealed far less emphasis on regulation ("Want to Operate in a Friendly Environment?").[92] New and expanded mining ventures of the multinationals were meanwhile coming on-stream in Mexico, Zimbabwe (Turner & Newall), and Colombia (Eternit); and a government-owned mine has opened in Greece.[93] Continuing exploration in the developing nations will yield additional discoveries of ore reserves; and the result may even be the expansion of "free-fire" zones where asbestos mining, manufacturing, and product use persist virtually unrestrained from a health standpoint.

The Current Expansion of Markets for Asbestos

Canada and other asbestos-exporting countries are looking to the developing countries as the market for asbestos in the 1990s. Unfortunately, conditions of current asbestos use in Asia, Africa, and Latin America resemble those that existed in industrial nations before workers learned of the time-bomb effects of breathing asbestos dust. This exploitation of ignorance and poverty for a quick buck has the strong backing of the government of Canada, even though Canadian workers would walk off the job under the conditions of asbestos use in the poor countries. What began as a commercial lie through most of this century has thus become an official lie. Canada's Asbestos Institute proclaims, "Implementing safety in the use of asbestos is neither difficult nor expensive."

The 1990s will see growing international opposition over the export of asbestos and its use in the poor countries. Wood pulp and other safer substitutes are now used in some countries to make fiber-cement panels and roofing, the most visible market for asbestos in the Third World.

In the technological development of nations, it is widely accepted that each country would do well to choose "appropriate technology" based on its resources, its people and their needs. Public health impacts of some technologies render them undesirable for Third World country development.

For example, no one would urge that developing countries should build plants to make asbestos thermal insulation. Asbestos has been replaced by wood pulp, fibrous glass, and other materials to make insulation products far less deadly than the asbestos insulations used in the past. Thermal insulation reinforced with asbestos is an example of *discredited technology* because of its severe, unavoidable hazards and the availability of safer alternatives. The most recent manufacture of this product I know of was by Johns-Manville in Brazil in 1980; however, it may still be made by producers in Thailand and/or India.

The international asbestos industry has claimed for decades that asbestos can be used safely and that it should be used in Third World development. Corrugated asbestos-cement roofing is used worldwide, and together with other asbestos-cement sheet and pipe products accounts for over 80 percent of asbestos use. Increased use of asbestos in developing countries has offset tremendous market losses in the industrial nations over the last 10 years. Quarterly publications of the Asbestos Institute in Quebec describe aggressive sales efforts in Asia, Africa, and Latin America.

The International Labor Office has published a "Code of Practice" enumerating very basic safeguards that should be used in work with asbestos.[94] Some countries have regulations that apply to industries where asbestos hazards exist. The issuance of control instruments as published documents, however, never has and never will assure that the "mandated" controls are in fact applied. The gulf between what is advertised as "controlled use of asbestos" and the reality of manufacturing and construction work with asbestos is greatest in poor countries whose use of asbestos is on the rise.

The chief of Brazil's environmental protection agency wrote in 1986 that the labor authorities in charge of worker protection did "poor work" and were "very ineffective."[95] As of 1986, this official wrote that, "we don't make any (power tools with exhaust ventilation) in Brazil, and it is difficult to import them."[96] It is unlikely that portable saws with exhaust ventilation and dust capture are being used by any construction workers handling asbestos-cement products in countries like Brazil. When that country's authorities began to inquire about health risks in asbestos manufacturing operations in 1980, the government people depended upon the companies visited to provide and demonstrate the use of standard air monitoring equipment. As of 1986, the official workplace exposure limit for asbestos in Brazil was 4 fibers/cc, twenty times as high as the 0.2 f/cc limit in the U.S. But such comparisons hardly begin to convey the conditions of asbestos workers in the developing countries.

Uncontrolled use of asbestos continues to be the norm in the developing countries, laws and regulations notwithstanding. Dr. Rene Mendes says about 30,000 workers now are employed in Brazil's asbestos industry, most of them in small plants, and conditions are so bad that asbestosis is being diagnosed 5-10 years after workers enter the industry.[97] Mexican researchers found severe asbestosis in workers employed spraying asbestos, who were monitored as having exposures of 54 fibers/cc.[98] In Egypt, workers reportedly still empty asbestos bales and mix asbestos with cement manually.[99] In Johns-Manville's former affiliate in Ahmedabad, India, where I have been told asbestos-cement pipe was sawed without local exhaust ventilation, government hygienists measured exposures of 216-418 fibers/cc.[100]

By 1985, the Pan American Health Organization was distributing Spanish translations of the Arizona Project Module on Asbestos, to provide basic training to doctors in Latin America to diagnose asbestos disease. Dr. Robert Murray of London wrote a strong letter of protest to PAHO's Washington office, appropriately sending a copy to Neville Stack, director of the Asbestos International Association:[101]

> I hear from my contacts that this document, which we discussed last time I saw you in Washington, is still circulating. I believe it contains so many inaccurate and inflammatory comments about asbestos that it should be suppressed.

Murray wrote that a "rather more sober and scientific document" on the subject was being prepared by the World Health Organization, and that this should be used instead.

Given the historic lack of both industry product stewardship and controlled asbestos exposures, especially in the vulnerable developing countries, the operative question is: *Will* asbestos hazards be controlled? (not: *Can* asbestos hazards be controlled?) The burden is on the asbestos industry to demonstrate that it is practical to routinely use asbestos in a thoroughly controlled way in developing countries.

The record to date overwhelmingly suggests that it is unreasonable to expect that asbestos hazards will be controlled in the developing countries. Industry spokesmen acknowledge that, even now, construction contractors in the U.S. sometimes use abrasive disc saws to cut asbestos-cement pipe—despite advice against the practice by the A-C Pipe Producers Assocation and the existence of applicable OSHA standards since 1972. Lung disease has occurred in the U.S. from the uncontrolled sawing of asbestos-cement sheets in construction work in the 1970s.[102]

How then can we expect Third World manufacturers of

asbestos products and construction contractors to take on the cost of extraordinary control measures, when there typically isn't even pressure from industry or government authorities to do so? Where is the infrastructure of prevention (information, regulation, and compensation) in Third World countries? And why should developing countries submit to the likelihood of asbestos contamination and disease, when safer alternatives exist that will not warrant the unprecedented commitment of scarce public health resources?

Developing countries may also wish to consider another form of "pollution" that has frequently come along with the growth of an indigenous asbestos industry. This is the corruption of the fledgling professions of industrial medicine and hygiene, as pressures are brought to bear on health professionals in industry, government and academia to learn the "industry line" and downplay concerns about workplace and environmental exposure to asbestos. This impact on a vital sector of a society in development may pave the way for subsequent public health abuses in other industries. Again one must wonder why a developing country would want to accept the externalized costs of a growing asbestos industry, given the alternatives now available.

In the 1980s, an increasing array of asbestos-free products has become commercially available. Asbestos-containing corrugated and flat cement sheeting, valve and pump packings, roofing felts, pipeline wrap, and vinyl flooring have not even been made in the United States since the mid-1980s. In Europe, the Swiss Eternit Group, now called Nueva A.G., agreed to eliminate asbestos in fiber-cement sheet products by 1990 in Germany and Switzerland, in favor of toxicologically tested, plastic-fiber-reinforced cement sheet. The Swiss government has allowed until 1995 for asbestos use to be discontinued in making fiber-cement pressure pipes, where asbestos substitution is more difficult though research is underway.

Nueva A.G. has experimented with various plant fibers and has already been able to replace asbestos in flat and corrugated cement sheet with wood fiber and sisal substitutes in Costa Rica and other Latin American countries. Nueva does not plan to expand this business or compete with cheap domestic asbestos in Brazil and Colombia or imported asbestos in Mexico, unfortunately. Nor does the company show much willingness to share the technology with poor countries that own asbestos-cement plants, such as Vietnam and Uganda, absent the usual financial incentives (Emanuel Arni, Deputy Chief Executive Officer). Nueva's asbestos-free products carry warranties equal to those of the predecessor asbestos products and are made with locally available trees.[103] In Australia and Malaysia, James Hardie Industries and its affiliates are also making cement sheet products reinforced with wood pulp instead of asbestos.

This is at least technological, if not moral progress, when one considers that exposures from sawing asbestos-cement sheet without dust controls have been reported as hundreds of fibers per cc.[104] It is also relevant that in many countries people catch water running off their roofs for drinking and cooking. EPA researchers have reported that "asbestos fiber concentrations over 500 million fibers per liter have been found in cistern drinking waters which use asbestos-cement roofing tiles to collect water."[105]

It would be better if people had this burden of wood, sisal, coconut, or banana plant materials instead of asbestos in their drinking water.

The Role of the Canadian Government and Other Governments in Promoting Asbestos Use

When the U.S. Environmental Protection Agency proposed to ban asbestos, the Canadian government, representing both private and state-owned asbestos mines, applied considerable pressure to oppose the ban.[106] An article in the British magazine *The Economist* created a furor, for it suggested that Canada had become "a sort of merchant of death by unloading its asbestos on unsophisticated Third World clients who may not be aware of its dangers."[106,107] Canada's Energy, Mines and Resources Minister Marcel Masse in 1988 responded to the above article by writing, "(t)he risk can be managed anywhere. This includes the Third World, where governments are more aware of the risks and more capable of controlling them than your correspondent is willing to credit."[107] The *Toronto Star* went on to describe a $30 million campaign of federal and Quebec governments to "try to drag asbestos out of the doghouse."[107]

The Asbestos Institute, which is partly supported by millions of dollars from Canadian taxpayers, also worried that EPA's asbestos "ban", proposed in 1986 and issued in 1989, would impede the promotion of asbestos in countries which have little or no experience, let alone resources, in controlling industrial cancer threats. The Institute is a joint venture of the asbestos mining industry and the government, "to maximize the use of existing resources in a concerted effort to defend and promote the safe use of asbestos on a global scale." It claims to be "dedicated to promoting the proper use of asbestos."[108]

Canadian physician David Bates called in 1987 for the establishment of an independent commission ("recruited neither from industry nor from government employees") to monitor certain indicators of product stewardship in the export of Canadian asbestos and report annually to the public.[109] An appropriate topic for such an oversight panel would be the publication of lies like this by Asbestos Institute President Claude Forget: "In (Selikoff's) study of American insulation workers, asbestosis victims did not only inhale white asbestos as you state but *were exposed to mostly amosite asbestos*."[110] Or this, from Asbestos Institute's "The Real Facts on Asbestos" (1990): "(Third World) construction sites, however, tend not to be a major problem as hand-operated tools, which in general generate large particulate dust and not respirable dust, are widely used." (Hand-sawing asbestos-cement panels generates optical microscopy counts from 31 to over 200 f/cc, according to an earlier industry report.[104])

Canada's independent asbestos oversight panel, if it is ever set up, might also want to monitor the intimidation and vilification of scientists at conferences where the hazards of asbestos are discussed. For example, there is this by the Asbestos Institute Director of the Health and Environment Division, Jacques Dunnigan, at an asbestos conference in

Mexico: "It is very hard for me to abstain from expressing my feeling that what we have just heard is standard, usual, ad nauseam repeated practice of some people at Mt. Sinai."[111] One doctor's repeated efforts to inject obfuscation into the proceedings during the 1990 asbestos conference in New York led to him being referred to as a paid heckler.

Dr. Bates also called on the government of Canada to provide as much money for research into asbestos' health effects as is released for promotion of the industry. This balance, along with the creation of the oversight commission, "would help to reassure average Canadians that they could not be accused of simply cynical exploitation of other people's ignorance," he concluded.[109]

Canada's union of insulation workers and other unions feel it *is* unworthy for the Canadian people to be represented by government officials who would rather sell ever more asbestos than plan for an asbestos-free future. Canada has spent over $500 million on post-1978 government takeovers and subsidies to bail out its asbestos mining industry. Closing of this "poisonous" industry with its 3000 jobs has been compared to the government's closing of an unneeded military base by Dr. Ray Sentes, a former insulation worker with asbestosis.[112] Canadians have also been urged to close the mines by Dr. Irving Selikoff of the Mt. Sinai School of Medicine in New York, whose research on asbestos workers and courage to speak out have fueled public health efforts worldwide for over 25 years.

Nationally viewed television documentaries in Canada (CBC, Oct. 1988: CTV, Nov. 1989) critically examined the government's practice of pushing asbestos in the Third World. These programs included vivid filming of uncontrolled asbestos use in construction in Thailand and the Philippines. Canada's decision to sue the U.S. Environmental Protection Agency in a precedent-setting case, over EPA's ban/phase-down rule issued in 1989, was also criticized. In the CTV program, the Asbestos Institute spokesman was visibly upset to hear that the new Minister of Energy, Mines, and Resources had declined to be interviewed about asbestos. It is unlikely that this signaled a change in government policy, however, and seems to have been simply the extraordinary arrogance of a political leader.

The Canadian government's support of the asbestos industry in the lawsuit in the U.S. is indeed unfortunate. The EPA "ban" will not affect any U.S. industry now using asbestos as a raw material until 1994. At the rate the industry is declining, EPA's regulations may amount to nothing more than closing the coffin after the banned industry is already dead. Moreover, Canada's suit against EPA adds little or nothing of substance to the issues the asbestos industry could raise by itself, based on the rulemaking record. In other words, the good name of Canada is being dragged through the mud, so that country's taxpayers can defray $1 million or more of the legal fees that would otherwise be borne by the international asbestos industry.

Canada has displayed an inconsistent and opportunistic regard for the U.S. legal system. Canadian asbestos mining interests have repeatedly refused to honor U.S. courts' evidence requests and verdicts awarding damages for historic longterm failure to place health warnings on sacks of asbestos. Yet even as the toll of asbestos victims mounts, publicly and privately held mining interests in Canada want to be forgiven their debt to past consumers of their product while being entitled to continue creating future asbestos victims in the U.S.

It is tragic that Canada has lowered itself to become a litigant in U.S. courts, only to come in on the wrong side of a public health issue. Had Canada instead sued the EPA over the Reagan Administration's protracted refusal to regulate the sources of acid rain, Canada's use of U.S. courts would have been hailed in both countries by citizens, environmentalists, and public health workers.

South Africa is a major source and exporter of asbestos disease almost all of which is officially ignored. A management official said of asbestotic mine workers: "They are like plastic syringes. You use them, and when they are damaged you throw them back to the homelands."[113] Miners disabled equally with pneumoconiosis in South Africa are eligible to varying degrees of compensation under 1973 law, according to their *race*. But those who develop asbestosis and cancer once they go back to the so-called homelands in South Africa or return home to neighboring countries stand little chance of being correctly diagnosed or properly treated, let alone counted by the government or compensated by their former employers.

South Africa's government reports about 100 cases of mesothelioma a year, nearly half among whites, who have comprised no more than 5 percent of the total employed historically in asbestos mining and manufacturing. Even making very conservative assumptions, one can get an idea of how the actual cancer incidence contrasts with the official count of about 50 mesotheliomas a year among non-whites.

Assuming that non-white workers sustained exposures no greater than those of their white supervisors, we would expect the ratio of mesotheliomas by race to be proportional to the numbers exposed. That comes to 950 mesotheliomas a year among non-whites, if we assume the 50 cases among whites represent complete case-finding in whites. Studies elsewhere have shown that occupationally caused lung cancer may be expected to be twice as frequent among asbestos workers as mesothelioma. So we can add roughly another 2000 officially ignored deaths from lung cancer each year among non-white former asbestos workers in South Africa.

The South African government takes no responsibility for the way its exported asbestos is used in other African and Asian countries, either.[114] Most of the asbestos mines there are now owned by Hanovar Mining Holdings, set up by former managers of the Griqualand Exploration and Finance Company.

The Soviet Union's performance as a major exporter of asbestos fiber and technology is also worthy of scrutiny from a health standpoint. Reliable information on this would be most helpful, whether from the USSR, Canada, or other sources.

The eventual elimination of asbestos in favor of safer (and in some cases essentially harmless) materials is of great public health importance. The continued lack of product stewardship by companies and countries mining asbestos, in the interim, constitutues a formidable health threat. It can only be hoped that this industry will see that its credibility and near-term survival depend upon worldwide implementation of unprecedented controls. Some countries may still decide that, at least for now, the continued use of asbestos-cement water conduits, for example, is still justified in health and economic terms. But even without the demonstration that asbestos *will* be used with stringent safeguards, the industry is sure to face rapid declines as social opposition mounts. Anyone who doubts the swiftness with which such events can move should recall West Africa's revulsion and response to being used as a dumping ground for hazardous wastes from the U.S. and Europe in 1988-1989.

The world's experience with the industrial use of asbestos leads to the conclusion that the only way to assure that asbestos will stop killing people needlessly is to ban it. This approach, which has been taken in Sweden and the United States, is even more attractive in developing countries, where stringent regulation is not really a viable alternative to a ban. Developing countries that continue to use asbestos-cement pipes for water supply should consider alternative pipe materials and press for research into the use of alternative (preferably non-respirable) fibrous materials in reinforcing cement pressure pipes.

Substitution and control of asbestos are the goals expressed by the Consumers Association of Penang, Malaysia, in its international campaign against "aggressive, unethical promotion of asbestos."[115] The International Metalworkers Federation has declared the objective of a worldwide ban on the use of asbestos.[116] Unions met in Brazil in 1990 to discuss the asbestos problem, and Dr. Mario Epelman of Greenpeace/Latin America also participated. Whether a country is industrialized with much asbestos already in use and in place or just starting to develop industries where asbestos can be used, a great potential for prevention of disease exists. In the developing countries, the commitment to give health objectives great weight in technology assessment is vital if these countries are not to become the dumping grounds for discredited, deadly technologies.

CONCLUSION

The asbestos disease epidemic now taking place is the result of past events, but the seeds of future asbestosis and cancer continue to be sown worldwide. Favoring ever more asbestos disease well into the next century are two familiar conditions: lack of social integrity at the highest levels in industry, and lack of courage among politicians ostensibly in office to represent the public interest and resist the pressures of private interests.

In every industrial nation it has long been acknowledged that the social order and welfare, in fact all the advantages of civilization, exist because of the working man and woman. Great things have been said about the dignity of labor and society's obligations to people working in factories and trades. The continuing asbestos disaster reveals the depth of failure of societies both East and West to take reasonable steps to protect the health of workers against a long-recognized, insidious threat to life. This menace has carried over from the workplace to endanger society at large.

In the 1980s, with the mortal dangers well known and safer substitutes available for all uses of asbestos, it is patently criminal for some products to still be made with asbestos at all; it is no less monstrous for other asbestos products to be made and used without even minimal efforts to inform and protect the workers.

In every culture the specific social changes necessary to safeguard the worker in fact as well as in theory will vary. But at the level where the decisions are made, more weight must be given to the long-term health of the public and less to short-term economic pressures. Citizens and unions should have major participation in decisions affecting their health and lives.

An essential ingredient in making more health-oriented social decisions about technology is personal accountability on the part of the decision makers. This applies equally whether the decisions are made in corporate board rooms or the health ministries of centrally-managed economies.

REFERENCES

1. Nicholson, W.J., G. Perkel, and I.J. Selikoff, "Occupational Exposure to Asbestos: Population at Risk and Projected Mortality-1980-2030," *Amer. J. Indust. Med.* *3*:259-311 (1982).

2. Doll, R. and R. Peto, "The Causes of Cancer: Quantitative Estimates of Avoidable Risks of Cancer in the United States Today," *J. Nat. Cancer Inst.* *66*:1191-1308 (1981).

3. *Quantification of Occupational Cancer* (Banbury Report 9), Eds. R. Peto and M. Schneiderman. (Cold Spring Harbor: Cold Spring Harbor Laboratory, 1981).

4. Lilienfeld, D.E. *et al.*, "Projection of Asbestos-Related Diseases in the United States, 1985-2009, I. Cancer," *Br. J. Indust. Med.* *45*:283-291 (1988).

5. U.S. Environmental Protection Agency. *Proceedings of the National Workshop on Substitutes for Asbestos, July 14-16, 1980.* (Washington, D.C., 1981).

6. Krusell, N. and D. Cogley. *Asbestos Substitute Performance Analysis,* Draft Final Report to U.S. Environmental Protection Agency, GCA Corp. Bedford, Mass. (May, 1981).

7. Castleman, B.I. and M.J. Vera Vera. "Impending Proliferation of Asbestos," *Internat. J. Health Serv.* *10*:389-403 (1980). Includes summary of "General Motors Programs on Non-Asbestos Friction Materials for Brake Systems" (Sept. 7, 1979).

8. "National Emission Standards for Hazardous Air Pollutants/Amendments to Standards for Asbestos and Mercury," *Fed. Reg.* *40*:48292-48311 (Oct. 14, 1975).

9. "Consumer Patching Compounds and Artificial Emberizing Materials (Embers and Ash) Containing Respirable Free-Form Asbestos/Banned Hazardous Products," *Fed. Reg.* *42*:63354-63365 (Dec. 15, 1977).

10. Castleman, B.I., R. Madan, and R. Mayes, "Export of Industrial Hazards to India," *Economic and Political Weekly* (Bombay) *16*:1057-1058 (June 13, 1981).

11. Deposition of John McKinney (Chairman of the Board and Chief Executive Officer, Johns-Manville Corp.) in *Dorothy St. Jacque vs. Johns-Manville Corp. et al.* Superior Court of the State of California for the County of Los Angeles, Case No. C 137465, p. 168 (taken Oct. 29, 1980).

12. "CertainTeed Closes Two A/C Pipe Plants," *Asbestos* pp. 16, 18 (Dec. 1982).

13. Harington, J.S., "Fiber Carcinogenesis: Epidemiologic Observations and the Stanton Hypothesis," *J.N.C.I. 67*:977-989 (1981).

14. Lee, K.P. *et al.*, "Comparative Pulmonary Responses to Inhaled Inorganic Fibers with Asbestos and Fiberglass," *Environ. Res. 24*:167-191 (1981). Product discontinuance noted in letter from C.F. Reinhardt (DuPont) to D.M. Costel (Administrator, U.S. Environmental Protection Agency), Oct. 2, 1978.

15. Saracci, R. and L. Simonato, "Man-made Vitreous Fibers and Workers' Health," *Scand. J. Work Environ. Health 8*:234-242 (1982).

16. *Biological Effects of Man-Made Mineral Fibers* Euro Reports and Studies 81, Copenhagen: World Health Organization, 1983, pp. 40-44.

17. "Asbestos; Proposed Mining and Import Restrictions and Proposed Manufacturing, Importation, and Processing Prohibitions," *Federal Reg. 51*:3738-3759 (Jan. 29, 1986).

18. Enterline, P.E. "Role of Manmade Mineral Fibers in the Causation of Cancer," *Br. J. Ind. Med. 47*:145-146 (1990).

19. "OSHA Emergency Temporary Standard Reducing the Permissible Asbestos Exposure Limit" (from *Fed. Register* Nov. 4, 1983) *Occup. Safety and Health Reporter,* Nov. 10, 1983, pp. 556-560.

20. "Compiling a Data Base on Asbestos Exposure," *Chem. Week* (Aug. 4, 1982), p. 40.

21. "Asbestos: Manufacture, Importation, Processing, and Distribution in Commerce Prohibitions; Final Rule." *Federal Reg. 54*:29460-29513 (July 12, 1989).

22. Presentations of H. Anderson, P. Landrigan, S. Levin and L. Welch at conference, "The Third Wave of Asbestos Disease: Exposure to Asbestos in Place," June 7-9, 1990. And M. Jaffe, "Dangers of Asbestos Widening," *Philadelphia Inquirer* (June 8, 1990).

23. Sawyer, R.N. "Indoor Asbestos Air Pollution: Application of Hazard Criteria," *Ann. N.Y. Acad. Sci. 330*:579-586 (1979).

24. Nicholson, W.J. *et al.*, "Asbestos Contamination in United States Schools from Use of Asbestos Surfacing Materials," *Ibid.*, pp. 587-596.

25. Stein, R.C. *et al.*, "Pleural Mesothelioma Resulting from Exposure to Amosite Asbestos in a Building," *Resp. Med. 83*:237-239 (1989), and Anderson, H.A., "Mesothelioma Among Employees in Public Buildings in Wisconsin," paper presented at conference, "The Third Wave of Asbestos Disease: Exposure to Asbestos in Place," New York (June 9, 1990).

26. Wright, E.R. *et al.*, *The Attorney General's Asbestos Liability Report to the Congress,* U.S. Department of Justice (1981).

27. "Asbestos Removal Put at $1.4 Billion," *Washington Post* (Oct. 7, 1983).

28. "Asbestos Cleanup Program for Schools Set," *Chem. & Eng. News* (Nov. 3, 1986).

29. "Damaged Material in 501,000 Buildings, Potential Worker Hazard, Seen in EPA Report," *Occup. Safety & Health Reporter* (Mar. 9, 1988).

30. Johnson, W.G. and E. Heler, "The Costs of Asbestos-Associated Disease and Death," *Milbank Memorial Fund Quarterly 61* No. 2 (1983).

31. Hartunian, N.S., C.N. Smart, and M.S. Thompson, "The Incidence and Economic Costs of Cancer, Motor Vehicle Injuries, Coronary Heart Disease, and Stroke: A Comparative Analysis," *Amer. J. Publ. Health 70*:1249-1260 (1980).

32. *Asbestos . . . A Social Problem* Commercial Union Insurance Companies, Appendix B (1981).

33. "Baron Challenges Study," *Stockholders & Creditors News Service Re. Johns-Manville Corp.* Edgemont, PA: Andrews Publications (May 7, 1984), pp. 2444-2446.

34. "Briefs: Lloyds Estimates Insurance Costs Between $10 and $30 Billion," *Mealey's Litigation Reporter/Asbestos,* p. 1135 (Sept. 14, 1984).

35. "Manville Path to Chapter 11 Not Paved Simply by Asbestos Suits," *Asbestos Litigation Reporter* (Nov. 26, 1982), pp. 5827-5830.

36. Owens-Corning Fiberglass Corporation, *1989 Annual Report*, p. 35.

37. Labaton, S., "Asbestos Trust Fund of Manville Queried," *New York Times* (May 16, 1990).

38. "Reaction to Plan: Three Committee Members Explain Their Concerns," *Asbestos Litigation Reporter* pp. 11,304-11,308 (Dec. 1985).

39. "Life After Asbestos: Manville Rebuilds, Seeking a New Image," *Wall St. J.* (May 31, 1990). And "Manville Tries to Build New Identity as a Firm Keen on Environment," *Ibid.*

40. Labaton, S., "Courts Tell Manville to Reorganize Fund for Asbestos Claimants," *New York Times* (June 2, 1990).

41. Kotelchuck, D., "Asbestos Compensation: Justice for Whom?" *Health/PAC Bulletin 14(3)*:23-26 (1983). Health Policy Advisory Center, New York.

42. "Asbestos Firms to Pay Y180 Mil. in Compensation," *Japan Times* (July 12, 1986).

43. Millward, D., "New Check on Asbestosis Claim Doctors," *Daily Telegraph* (Dec. 15, 1987).

44. "Quebec Asbestos Mining Association Special Summer Meet-

ing, Jasper, Alberta, Aug. 3-6, 1966/Report of Public Relations Committee."
45. Swetonic, M., "Why Asbestos?" Presentation before the Asbestos Textile Institute (June 7, 1973).
46. Fite, J.F., "Problems and Solutions in the Asbestos Abatement Industry," *Asbestos Abatement Update*, New York: Garland Law Publishing, 1990, pp. 79-139.
47. Spengler, J.D. *et al.*, "Summary on Symposium on Health Effects of Exposure to Asbestos in Buildings" (June 28, 1989).
48. Mossman, B.T. and J.B. Gee, "Asbestos-Related Diseases," *New Engl. J. Med. 320*:1721-1730 (1989).
49. Mossman, B.T., Bignon, J., Corn, M., Seaton, A., and J.B.L. Gee, "Asbestos: Scientific Developments and Implications for Public Policy," *Science 247*:294-301 (1990).
50. Eliasson, O., Letters, *New Engl. J. Med. 322*:130 (1990).
51. Bailey, W.E., "Selikoff Speaks Out on 'Science'," *Asbestos Issues* (Apr. 1990).
52. *Asbestos Control Report* (Mar. 15, Mar. 29, and Apr. 12, 1990).
53. Golden, J.T. (Sheet Metal Workers' International Association), letter to P. Lees, Johns Hopkins School of Hygiene and Public Health (Feb. 2, 1990).
54. Nicholson, W.J., Johnson, E.M., Harington, J.S., Melius, J., and P.J. Landrigan, Letters, *Science 248*:796-799 (1990).
55. Brody, A.R., *Ibid.*, p. 795.
56. Reilly, W.K., "Asbestos Removal," *Science 248*:1064-1065 (1990).
57. Samuels, S.W., Letters, *Science 248*:795-796 (1990).
58. Stevens, W.K., "Scientists Say Risk from Asbestos is Higher than They had Thought," *New York Times* (June 8, 1990).
59. Ives. J.H. *Cross-Cultural, Comparative Study of the Regulation and Administration of Occupational Safety and Health Care Policies in the Workplace: The Chemical Industry in the United States and Great Britain*, doctoral dissertation, University of London School of Economics (1984).
60. Mokhiber, R., *Corporate Crime and Violence*, Sierra Club Books, San Francisco (1988).
61. "Convicted for Dumping," *Chem. Week*, p. 23 (Oct. 14, 1981).
62. *Chemical & Engineering News* (Dec. 7, 1981).
63. "Industrial Bio-Test Sentences," *Chem. Week*, p. 17 (Apr. 18, 1984).
64. Nowinski, P. (U.S. Dept. of Justice), personal communication to the author, 1984.

65. "N.J. Supreme Court to Review Punitive Damages Under Strict Liability," *Asbestos Litigation Reporter,* pp. 8971-8972 (Sept. 21, 1984).

66. Miller, G., Testimony on H.R. 4973, *Corporate Criminal Liability* Hearings before the Subcommittee on Crime, Committee on the Judiciary, U.S. House of Representatives 96th Cong. Ser. No. 71, Washington: Government Printing Office, 1981, pp. 7-35.

67. Mintz, M., "Clergy Support a Bill on Crime by Corporations," *Wash. Post* (Feb. 15, 1980).

68. Mintz, M., "The Executive Mindset," *Multinational Monitor,* pp. 10-16 (June, 1984).

69. Beilock, R.P., "The Economics of Jailing Executives for Violations of Health and Safety Regulations," *J. Consumer Affairs 13*:386-392 (1979).

70. Conyers, J.C. "Nondisclosure of Health and Safety Information: A Criminal Act," *Cong. Record,* p. E-4174 (Oct. 2, 1984).

71. Hammond, E.C., I.J. Selikoff, and H. Seidman, "Asbestos Exposure, Cigarette Smoking, and Death Rates," *Ann. N.Y. Acad. Sci. 330*:473-490 (1979).

72. *Report on Conferences Between Employers and Inspectors Concerning Methods for Suppressing Dust in Asbestos Factories.* London: H.M. Stationery Ofc., 1931, p. 8.

73. Schepers, G.W., "Discussion," *Ann. N.Y. Acad. Sci. 132*:246-247 (1965).

74. Cowton, R. *The Times* (Jan. 20, 1975); in Dalton, A. *Asbestos Killer Dust* London: BSSRS Publ. Ltd., 1979, p. 63.

75. Castleman, B.I. "The Export of Hazardous Factories to Developing Nations," *Internat. J. Health Serv. 9*:569-606 (1979).

76. Castleman, B.I., "Double Standards: Asbestos in India," *New Scientist 89*:522-523 (Feb. 26, 1981).

77. Wyrick, R. "Hazards for Export IV. Asbestos Plant Threatens a Village in India," *Newsday* (Dec. 16, 1981).

78. "Occupational Health and Asbestos," *NACLA Report on the Americas* Vol. 12, New York (1978).

79. Tataryn, L. *Dying for a Living* (Toronto: Deneau and Greenberg, 1979), p. 54.

80. Castleman, B.I., "The 'Double Standard' in Industrial Hazards," *Internat. J. Health Serv. 13*:5-14 (1983).

81. Castleman, B.I., "The Double Standard in Industrial Hazards," *The Export of Hazard* (J. Ives, ed.), Boston: Routledge & Kegan Paul, 1985, pp. 60-89. (revised and expanded version of ref. 80)

82. Van Niekerk, P., "U.S. Steel Holds Interest in Asbestos Dumps," *Rand Daily Mail* (Johannesburg), Sept. 1, 1984.

83. Reiser, P., "Asbestos Warning Labels," memorandum to M. Prus (President, Carey Canada), Apr. 14, 1977. Produced in discovery by Jim Walter Corp.

84. Bagenstosse, A.B. (Vice President, Carey Canada), memorandum to P. Reiser (July 8, 1977).

85. Asbestos International Association. 8th Executive Committee Meeting, Agenda Item 6: Labelling (July 7, 1978).

86. Dahl, J., "Perilous Policy: Canada Encourages Mining of Asbestos, Sells to Third World," *Wall St. J.* (Sept. 12, 1989).

87. *J-M Thermobestos and Magnex HT* product brochures printed by Johns-Manville do Brasil, S.A. (obtained through conventional means in Brazil in 1983). Also, Ed Fenner (Johns-Manville) memoranda, "Caution Label Thermobestos-Brazil" (April 20, 1976) and "Warning Label Thermobestos-Brazil" (May 17, 1976).

88. Berman, D.M., "Asbestos and Health in the Third World: The Case of Brazil," *Internat. J. Health Serv. 16*:253-263 (1986).

89. Rangan, R.K. "Proof of Cancer Among Men in Asbestos Units," *Times of India* (March 27, 1981).

90. Goodwin, W.R. *The Johns-Manville Story* (New York: The Newcomen Society in North America, 1972).

91. Virta, R.L., "Asbestos," Preprint from *1988 Minerals Yearbook* (U.S. Dept. of the Interior, 1989).

92. Société Nationále de l'Amiante advertisement, *Asbestos* (Dec. 1982), p. 17.

93. "Asbestos Mining Industry Review, 1982," *Asbestos* (Jan. 1983).

94. Atherley, G. *et al.*, *Safety in the Use of Asbestos,* International Labor Office, Geneva (1984).

95. Noguiera-Neto, P., letter to B. Castleman (Feb. 6, 1986).

96. Noguiera-Neto, P., letter to B. Castleman (Mar. 12, 1986).

97. Mendes, R., Personal communication to B. Castleman (1990).

98. Mendes Vargas, M.M., Maldonado Torres L., "Aplicacion de Asbesto por Aspersion y Neumoconiosis muy Incapacitante," *Revisita Med. 20*:73-77 (1982).

99. Kamal, A.A.M. *et al.*, "Usage of Personal Protective Devices Among Egyptian Industrial Workers," *Am. J. Indust. Med. 13*:706-716 (1988).

100. *Asbestos: the Dust that Kills,* Centre for Education and Documentation (Bombay), p. 22 (1983).

101. Murray, R. (Consultant in Occupational Health), "Dear Alvaro" letter to Dr. A. Durao (PAHO), Apr. 16, 1985.

102. Harless, K.W., Watanabe, S., and A.D. Renzetti, "The Acute Effects of Chrysotile Asbestos on Lung Function," *Env. Res. 16*:360-72 (1978).

103. Arni, E., letters by fax to B. Castleman (Feb. 2 and 22, 1990); and Comments of the Swiss Eternit Group on the EPA's Notice of Proposed Rulemaking on Asbestos, Washington (June 28, 1986).

104. Cross, A. (Asbestosis Research Council, U.K.), "Practical Methods for the Protection of Men Working with Asbestos Materials in Shipyards," *Safety and Health in Shipbuilding and Ship Repairing*, pp. 93-101. International Labor Office, Geneva (1972).

105. Millette, J.R. *et al.*, "The Need to Control Asbestos Fibers in Potable Water Supply Systems," *Sci. Tot. Env. 18*:91-102 (1981).

106. "Canadian Asbestos/Export and Die?" *The Economist*, pp. 82-83 (Sept. 26, 1987).

107. Cahill, J., "A $30 Million Campaign Aims to Take the Curse Off Asbestos," *Toronto Star* (Mar. 7, 1988).

108. *Asbestos*, Vol. 1 (No. 1), Asbestos Institute, Quebec (1985).

109. Bates, D.V.: Asbestos: Promotion or Prohibition? *Can. Med. Assoc. J. 136*:107-109 (1987).

110. Forget, C., "Dusty Reply," *The Economist*, p. 8 (Dec. 12, 1987).

111. *Proceedings Meeting on Asbestos and Health in Latin America*, pp. 74-75. (M. Mitastein, Ed.) Pan American Health Org., Mexico City (1987).

112. Sentes, R., "Canada's Hazardous Defense of Asbestos," *Financial Times of Canada*, p. 41 (Sept. 25, 1989).

113. Castleman, B., "Health, too, is an Issue in South African Mines," *New York Times* (May 26, 1985).

114. Sluis-Cremer, G.K., Response to questions at conference, "The Third Wave of Asbestos Disease," New York (June 7, 1990).

115. Idris, S.M. Mohd. (President, Consumers Association of Penang), "Re: To Help Stop the Agressive, Unethical Promotion of Asbestos in India and Other Third World Countries," letter and attachments (including "Memorandum on Asbestos—The Killer Dust," to Ministry of Health) to B. Castleman (Apr. 26, 1990).

116. Ählberg, R. (Editor), *Asbestos and Asbestos Substitutes* (Geneva: International Metalworkers Federation Bulletin on Occupational Health and Safety No. 5, 1979).

Appendix 1

THE ASBESTOS MAGAZINE LETTERS OF 1935

This is a series of letters from the "Sumner Simpson papers" between the editor of the trade magazine *Asbestos*, the president of Raybestos-Manhattan (Simpson), and the top lawyer for Johns—Manville (Vandiver Brown). Sumner Simpson's note hand-written at the bottom of the letter from Brown reads: "Mr. Seigle will see Stover and tell him he does not want any publicity." Stover was the publisher of *Asbestos*. W.R. Seigle was a Johns-Manville Vice President.

"ASBESTOS"
Published by
SECRETARIAL SERVICE
16th Floor, Inquirer Bldg.
PHILADELPHIA, PA., U. S. A.

September 25, 1935.

Mr. Sumner Simpson, President,
Raybestos-Manhattan, Inc.,
Bridgeport, Conn.

Dear Sir:

You may recall that we have written you on several occasions concerning the publishing of information, or discussion of, asbestosis and the work which has been, and is being done, to eliminate or at least reduce it.

Always you have requested that for certain obvious reasons we publish nothing, and, naturally your wishes have been respected.

Possibly by this time, however, the reasons for your objection to publicity on this subject have been eliminated, and if so, we would like very much to review the whole matter in "ASBESTOS".

Our thought is that we could either prepare from data which we have in our files, or obtain from Mr. W. A. Godfrey of the Cape Asbestos Company, London, who is much interested in the subject, an article on the work done in England and then follow it with an article written by someone in your organization, as to the work done here.

We understand from Mr. Stover that your North Charleston plant, contains very complete dust control equipment and a description of such equipment, if you approve, would make a very interesting part of the article. Possibly even you could supply a photograph or two showing some part of this dust control equipment.

We await with much interest your reply. If there is no serious objection it would seem to be a most interesting subject for the pages of "ASBESTOS", and possibly a discussion of it in "ASBESTOS" along the right lines, would serve to combat some of the rather undesirable publicity given to it in current newspapers.

Very truly yours,
"ASBESTOS",
A. S. Rossiter, Editor

PLAINTIFF'S EXHIBIT S-13

Bridgeport, Conn.
Oct. 1, 1935

Mr. Vandiver Brown, Attorney,
Johns-Manville Corp.,
22 East 40th St.,
New York City.

My dear Mr. Brown:

Enclosed is a copy of a letter received from Miss Rossiter, of "Asbestos."

As I see it personally, we would be just as well off to say nothing about it until our survey is complete. I think the less said about asbestos, the better off we are, but at the same time, we cannot lose track of the fact that there have been a number of articles on asbestos dust control and asbestosis in the British trade magazines. The magazine "Asbestos" is in business to publish articles affecting the trade and they have been very decent about not re-printing the English articles.

I shall be pleased to have your opinion in the matter.

Very truly yours,

SS-G.

Enc.

President

005[illegible]

Note: Due to the poor reproductive quality of the original copy of this letter, it appears here retyped in the original form and has been inserted on the original paper. — *Author*

Johns-Manville
TWENTY-TWO EAST FORTIETH STREET
NEW YORK, N.Y.

October 3, 1935

Mr. S. Simpson, President,
Raybestos-Manhattan, Inc.,
Bridgeport, Conn.

My dear Mr. Simpson:

I wish to acknowledge receipt of yours of October 1st enclosing copy of the September 25th letter from the editor of the magazine "ASBESTOS". I quite agree with you that our interests are best served by having asbestosis receive the minimum of publicity. Even if we should eventually decide to raise no objection to the publication of an article on asbestosis in the magazine in question, I think we should warn the editors to use American data on the subject rather than English. Dr. Lanza has frequently remarked, to me personally and in some of his papers, that the clinical picture presented in North American localities where there is an asbestos dust hazard is considerably milder than that reported in England and South Africa.

I believe the question raised by Miss Rossiter might well be considered at the committee meeting scheduled for next Tuesday, at which I understand both you and Mr. Judd will be present.

Very truly yours,

Vandiver Brown
Attorney

VB:T

Appendix 2

"During a series of congressional hearings on asbestos last fall, the price of J-M's stock plunged about 20 percent, and it hasn't recovered."

Stephen Solomon, The Asbestos Fallout at Johns-Manville. *Fortune,* 196–206 (May, 1979).

In October of 1978, Congressman George Miller opened a series of hearings on the problem of asbestos disease. At this time, the "Sumner Simpson documents" produced in discovery by Raybestos-Manhattan, Inc. were discussed. Within one month, major news stories appeared in the *Los Angeles Times* (October 23, 1978) and the *Washington Post* (Nov. 12, 1978), which in turn were widely circulated in the U.S. press and in other countries. The price of Johns-Manville stock rapidly plunged from 34 to 24 dollars per share. Two days after the *Washington Post* story, Congressional hearings were held in Honolulu, Hawaii. There, Johns-Manville executives presented their interpretation of the Sumner Simpson Papers and advised the legislators on the subject of comprehensive, equitable, and uniform compensation for occupational diseases.

The testimony of J-M Executive Vice President Francis H. May offered his company's side of the story. His prepared statement is reprinted here in full. Dr. Paul Kotin, Senior Vice President for Health, Safety, and Environment, was not recorded as present at the hearings.

(Source: *Asbestos-Related Occupational Diseases.* Hearings before the Subcommittee on Compensation, Health, and

Safety, U.S. House of Representatives Committee on Education and Labor, conducted November 14, 1978. U.S. Gov't. Printing Ofc. Washington, pp. 637–646, 1979).

PREPARED STATEMENT OF FRANCIS H. MAY, EXECUTIVE VICE PRESIDENT, JOHNS-MANVILLE CORP.

Mr. Chairman, members of the subcommittee, my name is Francis H. May, I am executive vice-president of Johns-Manville Corporation, headquartered in Denver, Colorado. With me this morning are G. Earl Parker, vice-president, General counsel and secretary; Dennis H. Markusson, associate general counsel; and John S. Autry, director of public affairs.

We are pleased to be here today as the subcommittee continues its important work in addressing the issue of asbestos-related occupational disease, and most importantly compensation for occupational illness.

For the past several years our company has been involved in the litigation of asbestos disease related product liability lawsuits. From this experience I think we have gained some insight into the complex nature of the issues presented, the viability of existing methods for addressing these issues, and the present need for innovative measures. It is to these areas that I shall direct my primary remarks this morning.

Following my remarks Mr. Parker will discuss some considerations in legislative approaches to provide uniform, comprehensive and equitable compensation for occupational illness.

Before proceeding further I must first address the growing propensity of some to try legal issues in non-judical forums. While I personally deplore the practice of law by press conference, the issuance of half statements and the calculated use of selected facts—these practices, upon reflection, serve to graphically demonstrate the inability to adequately resolve the complex issues in asbestos products liability cases within the traditional judicial structure.

While I am mindful of Representative Heftel's statement that these hearings are not intended to fix fault or blame—public accusations have been made and a response is appropriate. In recent hearings before this subcommittee attorneys for various plaintiffs made some rather rash statements, and I am sorry to say some of them seem to have been accepted all too quickly at face value.

There seem to have been three basic theses in what I will call the San Francisco accusations:

1. That early knowledge of the biological effects of asbestos in mining, milling and manufacturing operations equates to knowledge that asbestos-containing insulation products could present a hazard.

2. That industry and specifically Johns-Manville failed to respond in a reasonable and responsible manner to developing medical and scientific information.

3. That there existed some conspiracy to manipulate and suppress and that it is somehow related to present litigation.

These theses are categorically false.

While it would be unwarranted for me to comment in these proceedings on every conceivable evidentiary fact I would like to bring some perspective to these accusations.

KNOWLEDGE OF A HAZARD

The issue is not whether asbestos exposure under certain conditions can constitute a possible health hazard. On this there is no longer debate. Nor is the issue the existence in the 1920s and 1930s of medical and scientific information relative to asbestosis among workers exposed to continual and high concentrations of asbestos fiber in mines, mills and manufacturing plants.

The paramount issue in virtually all the litigation including shipyard cases is: When was there adequate medical and scientific knowledge of a possible hazard to workers outside the mines, mills and factories using already manufactured products, notably insulation products containing small amounts of asbestos, to constitute a basis for action? In other words, the issue is reasonable foreseeability.

There was a conscious effort in the material submitted at the San Francisco hearings to imply that by 1930 there existed an abundance of knowledge of a potential health hazard from asbestos. This simply is not true. By 1930 there were but a handful of so-called asbestosis cases reported in the English literature, all from asbestos textile plants.

Indeed, it was not until 1927 that Dr. Cooke in England, reporting on one single case involving a textile worker, coined the term "asbestosis" to describe a type of fibrotic occupational disease.[1,2]

However, by 1930 and based in large part upon the world's first large scale survey undertaken by Dr. Merewether asbestosis was being found with some frequency in the asbestos textile mills of England.[3]

The first major medical work in the United States was the study of asbestos textile factories by Dr. Anthony Lanza which was published by the United States Public Health Service in 1935.[4] This publication was the culmination of research in this country sponsored not by the Public Health Service, but by Johns-Manville and Raybestos-Manhattan. As this article has become a matter of some contention I will remark on it in detail in a few moments.

In 1938 the Public Health Service did another study of the asbestos textile industry, and took a step which was to dramatically impact on asbestos-related occupational disease issues for the next 25 years. The 1938 Dreessen Study established a recommended standard or threshold limit value for asbestos dust exposure of 5 million particles per cubic foot, eight hours per day, forty hours per week for a working lifetime as a safe level of exposure.[5]

It is to be noted that throughout the literature of this period there prevailed in the medical and scientific community a feeling that asbestosis was a limited problem, and that if the dust levels in the factories could be reduced the problem of asbestosis would disappear.[6]

In 1946 the First Epidemiological Study of Insulation Applicators (as opposed to mine, mill or factory workers) was published by Fleischer-Drinker, et al.[7] The study was done in shipyards, and was undertaken on behalf of the Navy. Two significant findings came out of that report; first, that the measured exposures to asbestos dust for the insulation workers were with one exception below what the U.S. Public Health Service/Dreessen, article had established as a "safe level" (5 MPPCF standard) and, second, that pipecovering was deemed to be not a hazardous occupation. That insulation worker exposures were generally below the U.S. Public Health Service standard is a fact subsequently documented by other investigators.[8]

It is appropriate to reflect for a moment on this state of the medical art in the United States in 1946 with reference to insulation workers. At this time we were faced with a U.S. Public Health service standard of 5 MPPCF; actual measured exposures well below that "safe level", and an epidemiological study concluding that insulation work was not a hazardous occupation. Was there, then, in 1946 any basis for action on the grounds that asbestos-containing insulation products constituted an occupational hazard to workers? I think not. This conclusion seems eminently justified by the fact that there were no cries to the contrary from Government, labor, medicine, or academia.

The popular rhetoric now is to assert that the 5 MPPCF standard and the Fleischer-Drinker Report were wrong. Of course they were wrong, but when was this error discovered—certainly not until the landmark 1960s work of Dr. Irving J. Selikoff, a physician well known to this subcommittee.[9] It will be of interest to this subcommittee that in the American Medical Literature there is not a single criticism of the Fleischer-Drinker conclusions or the 5 MPPCF standard until Dr. Selikoff's work.

While attempts are made by learned advocates to extrapolate mining, milling and manufacturing data and apply it to the insulation workers who are the subject of most present lawsuits, the facts simply do not support such an extrapolation. Two quotes from Dr. Selikoff's writings eloquently place the development of knowledge of any insulation worker hazard in proper perspective.

In 1965 he wrote: "We may conclude that asbestosis and its complications are significant hazards among insulation workers in the United States at this time."[10]

In 1970 he concluded: "In the asbestos mining and manufacturing industry, the risk of heavy exposure to the occupational dusts had been recognized for some years. And this primary industry has understood the need to install ventilation systems and other dust control devices to reduce the hazard. Experience had indicated that reduction of dust levels and exposures could result in greatly improved health experience among asbestos factory workers. But the extrapolation of that experience to another classification of workers—specifically those who fabricate and install insulating materials—was a more sophisticated task for clinical medicine and epidemiology."[11]

While I have generally tracked the medical literature with respect of asbestosis the situation is virtually the same as to cancer. Early isolated case reports of lung cancer in association with asbestosis in factory workers were followed by years of uncertainly and scientific disagreement. The 1960s brought general agreement that there was an excess of lung cancer among those workers exposed to asbestos including insulation workers. However, this association has been complicated by the fact that almost all cases of asbestos worker lung cancer involve cigarette smokers, and there remain honest differences as to whether cigarette smoking is the determinant or the modifier of the lung cancer. As to mesothelioma there is no serious difference of agreement that this rare tumor was first associated with asbestos exposure by Dr. Wagner's South African studies published in 1960, and that by the mid-1960s it too had been associated with insulation workers by Dr. Selikoff.[12,13]

This brief review hopefully will serve to give the subcommittee some feel for the "foreseeability-of-hazard" issue which is at the heart of most the past and pending litigation.

This admittedly brief review is not intended to be all inclusive. It does not, for example, attempt to deal with the complex matter of individual case reports, and their effect on the state of the medical art. My purpose in presenting this review is to give the subcommittee some perspective with respect to the medical literature, the concepts of dose, the pitfalls of attempted extrapolations. Only in this way can the subcommittee appreciate and evaluate the complexity of the foreseeability-of-hazard issue which is at the very heart of most of the past and pending litigation, and the continued futility of attempting to deal equitably and effectively with this issue within existing judicial structures.

FAILURE TO ACT

The second San Francisco thesis is the inference that Johns-Manville failed to respond to medical and scientific information of possible asbestos exposure hazards. This subcommittee and its media audience were led to believe that nothing was done, and that lives were sacrificed for profits. While such invective makes for good copy and a rousing jury argument—it—simply is not true.

Johns-Manville's long history of commitment to the resolution of asbestos-related occupational disease problems is unparalleled in industry, labor or government. It is that commitment that brings us here this morning.

Let's turn to some specifics. As you will recall from my earlier testimony, by 1930 the British Medical Literature was suggesting a possible occupational disease hazard of asbestosis in asbestos textile factories. Did Johns-Manville respond? It did indeed. In conjunction with Raybestos-Manhattan Corporation, Johns-Manville commissioned the Metropolitan Life Insurance Company to commence a survey to ascertain the existence of any asbestos disease hazards in North American mining, milling and manufacturing operations. The scope of the Johns-Manville response is eloquently conceded by an adversary, Robert E. Sweeney, Esq., who represents many insulation workers in lawsuits throughout the United States writing in the October 1978 issue of *Trial* magazine he states:

"Alerted by the work of medical and scientific investigators throughout the world, the asbestos industry, led by Johns-Manville, commissioned the Metropolitan Life Insurance

Company in the early 1930s to investigate and determine the relationship of asbestos exposure to the high rate of pulmonary disease encountered among workers in the asbestos mines and factories.

These studies were conducted under the leadership of the medical director of the Metropolitan Life Insurance Company, Dr. Anthony J. Lanza.

The project ran from October 1929 to January 1931. It included study of dust conditions in asbestos mines and mills in Canada and the United States.

Physical examination of asbestos workers included X-rays, films, and studies of dust exhaust systems.

The conclusions of the industry's own research proved that prolonged exposure to asbestos dust caused pulmonary fibrosis and that cases of definite cardiac enlargement were frequently found to be associated with asbestosis.

The study recommended that the industry face seriously the problem of dust control in asbestos plants and sponsor studies on known cases of asbestosis."[14]

Based upon the limited medical and scientific information available in the 1929 to 1930 period one may ask whether this was a responsible and responsive course of action for two corporations to take, and I think the answer is obviously in the affirmative. At this juncture, in 1930, no action on this subject had been undertaken by any agency of the Federal Government. Several more years would pass before the Government first acted.

Johns-Manville undertook immediate and concerted efforts to implement dust control procedures at its mines, mills and manufacturing facilities, and the company has been an acknowledged leader in the development of dust control devices. Since appropriate dust control devices were not available in the marketplace, the company undertook development of in-house dust control engineering expertise and design of dust control devices. Unique applications of fabric filters, as the most effective asbestos dust control device, and which today are universally used, were developed by Johns-Manville.[15]

To give the subcommittee a brief example of the extent of

the company's major commitment, I did a quick historical survey of dust control installations at three Johns-Manville manufacturing facilities. I learned that between 1931 and 1970 approximately 160 major dust control devices were installed at just 3 plants. I stopped my survey at 1970 as I wanted to cover a period when there were no mandatory governmental standards or requirements. In other words, these are 160 voluntary projects. As an aside one might ask where the public health agencies of the Government were during this 30-year period.

In terms of money expended for dust control equipment in Johns-Manville plants, it is conservatively estimated that between 1931 and 1970 $25 to $30 million was spent. If viewed in terms of 1978 dollars this sum would no doubt be four or five times that amount.

In addition to dust control equipment the company has had safety meeting respirator and employee physical examination programs in effect for several decades. (sic)

These programs continue to the present time, and today's worker receives ever increasing amounts of asbestos and health literature.

Because of the dramatic effects of cigarette smoking among individuals occupationally exposed to asbestos Johns-Manville has banned smoking at all asbestos using locations, although this is not required by existing Federal standards. It is noteworthy that unions have forced litigation opposing implementation of this policy at two locations.

With respect to asbestos-containing thermal insulation products, Johns-Manville undertook a voluntary labeling program in September of 1964 contemporaneous with the Selikoff revelations that the 5 MPPCF Public Health Service recommended standard was not a safe exposure level, and that a hazard did in fact exist. Johns-Manville led the industry in caution labeling, and led the Federal Government by 6 years (sic) as it was not until July 1972 that a Federal standard for labeling became effective.

There is an interesting contrast between Johns-Manville labels from 1964 to 1972 and the Federal label mandated in 1972 and still in use today:

Caution—This product contains asbestos fiber.

Inhalation of asbestos in excessive quantities over long periods of time may be harmful.

If dust is created when this product is handled, avoid breathing the dust.

If adequate ventilation control is not possible, wear respirators approved by the U.S. Bureau of Mines for pneumoconiosis-producing dusts. (1964–70 J-M Label.)

Caution—This product contains asbestos fiber.

Avoid breathing the dust. Inhalation of asbestos in excessive quantities over long periods of time may be harmful.

If dust is created when this product is handled, use proper protection.

If proper dust control cannot be provided, respirators approved by the U.S. Bureau of Mines for protection against pneumoconiosis-producing dusts should be worn. (1970–72 J–M label.)

Caution—Contains asbestos fiber avoid creating dust. Breathing asbestos dust may cause serious bodily harm. (1972 to present, Federal OSHA label.)

I think even the most biased observer would concede that the Johns-Manville label voluntarily implementary (sic) in 1964 is far superior to present Federal requirements.

In addition to the warning labels the record is clear that Johns-Manville undertook a variety of other affirmative measures in the 1960s:

1. Seminars were conducted for insulation contractors to explain possible hazards and safe handling techniques.

2. In cooperation with the National Insulation Manufacturers Association and the National Insulation Contractors Association a booklet entitled "Recommended Safe Practices for Handling and Applying Thermal Insulation Products Containing Asbestos" was prepared and circulated to insulation contractors throughout the United States.

3. In cooperation with Mount Sinai Hospital, Dr. Selikoff and the Asbestos Workers Union the "Insulation Industry Hygiene Research Program" was formed. Activities of this organization resulted in material on asbestos and health and

safe work practices going directly to the homes of insulation workers in the form of "green sheets" which were inserted in the union magazine.

4. Substitute thermal insulation products were developed and by 1973 the company ceased production of asbestos-containing insulation materials with the exception of a few accessory items.

In the area of medical research Johns-Manville's extensive support of medical research on the biological effects of asbestos has continued on an ever increasing scale since 1929. (An appendix outlining the numerous projects is attached hereto.)

There was some effort at the San Francisco hearing to cast in a negative light the company's payment of workers' compensation claims to factory workers with asbestos-related illnesses. Johns-Manville has indeed paid workers' compensation to factory workers on asbestos claims. To my knowledge no bona fide claim has ever been contested. In fact, there have been instances where the company has waived available statute of limitations defenses, and allowed the claim.

Johns-Manville's record of voluntary commitment to the resolution of asbestos-related occupational disease problems is clear. Johns-Manville did respond to medical and scientific knowledge in a prompt, reasonable and responsible fashion.

CONSPIRACY

In recent weeks much attention has been focused on some very old correspondence between employees of Johns-Manville and Raybestos-Manhattan. Indeed, this correspondence set much of the tone for this subcommittee's San Francisco hearings. It is a tribute to the plaintiffs' lawyers that they have been able to make so much of so little.

In any objective consideration of this correspondence two factors become paramount, first, the age of the documents, and, second, the nature of the problem being addressed.

The correspondence at issue is more than 40 years old, and was written at a time when the world's body of knowledge concerning possible asbestos-related health problems was in its infancy. It was written at a time when legitimate questions far outnumbered available answers; at a time when any potential hazard from asbestos was thought to be mild compared to other problems such as silicosis; at a time when it was thought any problem was confined to mines, mills and manufacturing plants, and would be readily solved with some additional dust control. An objective review of the entire body of documents confirms these facts, and further indicates consistency with the then state of medical and scientific knowledge. It is inconceivable that reasonable persons would base today's crucial policy judgements on these ancient letters.

The fact that the health issues addressed in this correspondence are entirely different from those in most of the present litigation has been conveniently ignored. Simply stated the correspondence had nothing whatsoever to do with asbestos-containing insulation materials or insulation applicators.

The correspondence relates to possible hazards in mines, mills and manufacturing plants to which Johns-Manville then and thereafter responded with leadership. As indicated in my earlier comments, in the 1930s asbestos-containing insulation materials were not known to present a problem to insulation applicators. Just as Dr. Selikoff has indicated that the mine, mill and factory experience cannot be extrapolated to the insulation worker experience, likewise correspondence relative to factory situations cannot be extrapolated to present cases involving exposure to insulation products.[16]

Some specifics: A document ignored by the plaintiff's attorneys is the minutes of a meeting of January 5, 1934 wherein a decision was made by Johns-Manville and Raybestos-Manhattan to "Have the Metropolitan Life Insurance Company bring up to date the survey with respect to dust conditions in their respective factories." Is this an irresponsible course of conduct? Quite to the contrary, and remember too that at this time the Federal Government had still done nothing.

The January 5, 1934 minutes go on: "The policy of the two companies concerned is that they desire through the operation of this committee and the resulting investigations to obtain, each for itself, the best practice possible for the elimination of dust and the protection of employees."

Subsequent 1934 correspondence confirms the employment of Otto L. Binder to do dust counts, and the purchase of X-ray equipment. Again, hardly irresponsible conduct.

We come now to the review of the galley proofs of Dr. Lanza's 1935 article. This is a significant item because it has generated accusations that Johns-Manville and Raybestos-Manhattan somehow manipulated, dictated and even impeded the development of medical and scientific knowledge in the United States. An examination of facts quickly and vividly uncovers the shallowness and inaccuracy of such accusations:

1. V. Brown to Dr. Lanza, December 10, 1934:

(a) Brown indicates two clerical points where material from the original report was not picked up in the galley proofs. This certainly is not a manipulation of Dr. Lanza's independent conclusions;

(b) The remainder of Brown's comments also relate to clerical omissions or questions of clarity;

(c) Nowhere does Brown suggest substantive alterations.

2. Hobart to Brown, December 15, 1934. Hobart was an attorney in private practice, who apparently was asked to review and comment on the Lanza article:

(a) Hobart suggests deletion of the sentence: "It might well be assumed that similar variables would influence the occurrence of asbestosis." That sentence was not deleted from the article as published.

(b) Hobart refers to the defense of lawsuits. This is a reference to actions arising out of the Manville, N.J. plant at a time before asbestos occupational disease claims were covered in New Jersey by Workers' Compensation.[17]

(c) Hobart next suggested that some material appear in the body of the article rather than in a footnote. In the published article the material remained as a footnote on page 3.

(d) Hobart next suggested deletion of the words: "Was unnecessarily dusty" from a portion of the report with reference to a description of plant E. In reviewing the actual Lanza article it does appear that in the section on dust studies there is no reference to the words "was unnecessarily dusty." However, on page 5 and the top of page 6 of the actual Lanza article it is indicated that at plant E there was excessive dust. Accordingly, it can hardly be argued that the deletion of the words "was unnecessarily dusty" changes in any way the scientific import of the Lanza study.

(e) As did Brown, Hobart points out that the galley omits from conclusion 1 the sentence "Clinically, from this study, it (asbestosis) appears to be of a type milder than silicosis"; which had appeared in the original report. Hobart does add that such an addition should be made to the conclusions only, "If the doctors are satisified that such is the facts." These are hardly the words of a manipulator of medical science.

(f) With respect to conclusion No. 5 Hobart points out that the galley indicated that asbestosis did not add to the mortality in tuberculosis cases, and that such an inference did not seem justified. Dr. Lanza did reword his conclusions so as not to negate the hazard to individuals with tuberculosis. This certainly is clear evidence of openness, objectivity and honesty in the review of the Lanza article.

(g) Hobart criticizes conclusion No. 6 and a reference and inference concerning granite dust, and in the final article we see that Hobart's suggestions were adopted by Lanza. However, this is not a departure from a sound scientific conclusion. It appears that all Hobart was seeking was to avoid an unnecessary parallel being drawn between asbestos and granite dust.

(h) With respect to recommendation No. 4 Hobart asks to have inserted the word "possible" as to future studies of the "possible" effects of asbestosis on the heart and circulation. It is interesting to note that in item No. 4 of Dr. Lanza's recommendations set forth on page 11 of the actual report that Dr. Lanza obviously rejected this suggestion as the word "possible" does not appear prior to the word "effects."

3. Brown and Judd, December 18, 1934. Brown transmits a copy of the galley proofs of the Lanza article to Raybestos-Manhattan.

4. Brown to Lanza, December 21, 1934. Brown returns the galley proofs to Dr. Lanza together with Mr. Hobart's comments. The following is found in this letter:

"I trust that you will give his comments and suggestions, as well as those mentioned in my letter of December 10th, your most serious consideration. I am sure that you understand fully that no one in our organization is suggesting for a moment that you alter by one jot or tittle any scientific facts or inevitable conclusions revealed or justified by your preliminary survey. All we ask is that all of the favorable aspects of the survey be included and that none of the unfavorable be unintentionally pictured in darker tones than the circumstances justify."

5. Brown to Judd, December 24, 1934. A letter indicating that Hobart and Brown had "together canvassed fairly thoroughly the points in the proof to which we could justifiably suggest additions, omissions, or changes in phraseology that will be beneficial from the industry viewpoint. The use of the word "justifiable" is certainly consistent with Brown's letter to Lanza of Decmber 21, 1934, and the entire objective review of the Lanza article.

This then is the entire record of the review of the Lanza article by Raybestos-Manhattan and Johns-Manville. The article was then published by the U.S. Public Health Service, and subject to that Agency's critical review.

Some additional observations are in order with respect to the Lanza article. If Johns-Manville and Raybestos-Manhattan are deemed to have been conspirators, manipulators and suppressors in the 1930s, then they were poor ones, for who interested in suppression or manipulation would promote a study to be published by the U.S. Public Health Service and which recommended:

1. That the industry seriously face the problem of dust control in asbestos plants.

2. That new employees be examined physically, including X-ray examination of the chest, and rejected for employment if they show tuberculosis or pneumoconiosis.

3. That employees be examined physically, preferably every year, but at least every 2 years, this examination to include an X-ray examination of the chest.

4. That the industry sponsor studies on known cases of asbestosis, as well as studies on effects of asbestosis on the heart and circulation.[18]

It would further be a poor suppressor who would have Dr. Lanza in the course of his study work with 11 other physicians including a physician of the U.S. Public Health Service.[18]

Finally, as indicated earlier, all of the recommendations of Dr. Lanza were implemented by Johns-Manville.

I realize my comments with respect to the Lanza article have been quite long and detailed, but it is only through this type of detailed review that the falsity of the quick accusation and self-serving conclusion can be revealed.

There have been other unwarranted and exaggerated statements concerning this correspondence. Clearly, it would neither be possible nor appropriate for me to address each such contention or allegation in this forum. Generally this material can be summarized as indicating a continuing concern and involvment in research as to the possible biological effects of asbestos. Almost all of the correspondence in 1936 and subsequent years relates to industry financed studies undertaken by Dr. Leroy Gardner at the Saranac Laboratories. The correspondence confirms Johns-Manville and Raybestos-Manhattan as taking the lead in the financing of such research, and ultimately obtaining contributions from several other companies.

Rather than speculate further on the import of these statements or strain to apply them to today's issues, I prefer to deal with the truly relevant facts.

I do know that the entire record makes it abundantly clear that Johns-Manville and Raybestos-Manhattan went forward with the first medical research done in this country; I do know that such research was published for all the world to see in the public health reports of the U.S. Public Health Service; I do know that industry continued to finance research; I do know that the findings of such research were consistent with other developing medical information; I do know that these actions were voluntary; I do know that industry's efforts antedated by several years any action by the Federal Government; I do know that Johns-Manville was promoting and has continued to promote basic medical research; and I do know that but for industry's efforts, which I suspect were unparalleled in the 1930s, the state of medical knowledge in this country would have lagged for years. I don't understand the contention that manipulation and suppression and total lack of concern for individuals were basic motives of industry. If that were so why did industry bother to do anything at all? And yet, the record is clear this was not the path chosen.

I would like to turn now to the basic issue faced by this subcommittee: Whether there is a need for legislative action to provide compensation for occupational disease, and in particular, asbestos-related occupational disease.

In seeking an objective resolution of this issue there are several preliminary questions which must first be answered.

Is the assurance of fair compensation for occupational disease a desirable and necessary social objective? Johns-Manville president, John A. McKinney, clearly answered this question in his testimony before the Senate Committee on Human Resources on S. 3060 stating: "Comprehensive, equitable, and uniform compensation for occupational disease is a worthy and proper social goal. On this there can be no debate."[11]

The next question to be answered is whether such a goal can be achieved with existing systems, remedies and mechanisms. From my personal experience I tell you in all sincerity, that absent innovative and decisive action, compensation for asbestos-related occupational disease under present structures will never be comprehensive, equitable or uniform.

At present there are but two means of compensation for occupational disease: Workers' compensation and the products liability lawsuit. At your recent hearings in San Francisco you heard testimony on the inadequacies of workers' compensation. Suffice it to say that at present there are wide disparities in the amount and duration of workers' compensation payments, and in many instances both are woefully inadequate.

Turning to the occupational disease product liability lawsuit, it must be understood at the outset that exposure, disease and causal relationship do not equate to liability, or culpability or fault in the world of civil products liability law. Lack of understanding of this basic fact has created great frustration in the minds of many in consideration of the problems of compensation for occupational disease.

In the products liability lawsuit, for there to be a recovery there must be a determination of liability, culpability, or, if you will, fault. It is an adversary situation, and we must recognize that as presently constituted the American civil adversary system has deliberately chosen to resolve contested matters by the clash of mutally inconsistent and divergent viewpoints. Unfortunately, such a system only frustrates our socially desirable goal of comprehensive, equitable and uniform compensation for occupational disease.

The fly in the ointment is the matter of fault. In the typical case involving an insulation worker with asbestosis the jury must ultimately resolve two issues. First, at what point in time was a hazard to the insulation worker reasonably foreseeable, thus giving rise to a duty to warn? Second, after any such duty arose, were reasonable steps taken toward its satisfaction?

Resolution of these issues, particularly the former, in an asbestos-related occupational disease case is a highly complex exercise. Unlike other types of products liability cases where there is physical evidence such as a broken casting or a ruptured tire to serve as a focal point, in the asbestos case the evidence is far more esoteric. From the body of medical and scientific literature a determination must be made as to when on a reasonable basis there was or should have been knowledge of a hazard to insulation workers. It is an exercise in hindsight.

As the subcommittee will appreciate from my earlier testimony, and other testimony received, the interpretation of the state of the medical art has become in the truest sense of the American adversary system a clash of mutally inconsistent and divergent viewpoints. The clearest evidence that legitimate but divergent viewpoints exist is the fact that each case is individually handled by the courts, and that juries do indeed reach different results. In some cases the plaintiffs prevail while in others the verdict favors the defendants. While such a state of affairs might well be consistent with American judicial tradition we must ask if it is achieving anything toward attainment of the goal of comprehensive, equitable and uniform compensation for occupational disease.

For so long as liability and fault are the cornerstones upon which attempts to resolve the issue of compensation for occupational disease are based, there will, in fact, be no resolution.

Mr. McKinney in his testimony on S.3060, to which I referred earlier, outlined many specific shortcomings of the present product liability system for fairly and equitably dealing with the issue of compensation for occupational disease. That testimony has previously been submitted to this subcommittee, and therefore I will not reiterate the points raised in that testimony. I do urge the subcommittee to consider carefully Mr. McKinney's testimony.

I want to turn briefly to what I will call a concept of collective responsibility. I emphasize collective responsibility—not collective liability or fault. Any equitable resolution of the issue of compensation for occupational disease must include all who, as a matter of basic realities and fairness, are involved. Due to factors such as the insulation from suit provided by workers' compensation laws and variations in state law on contribution, indemnification and joinder, all parties to the equation are not included in present proceedings. For example:

1. What of the employer and his responsibility for health and safety considerations in the workplace of his employees? This is a particularly troublesome question in insulation worker cases where subsequent to knowledge, warnings, and instructions, working conditions with respect to asbestos exposure remained, at best, marginal. Should a product manufacturer rather than the employer be responsible for occupational disease attributable to deficient working conditions? From early discovery in shipyard cases it appears that this may be a particularly acute problem in naval shipyards.

2. What of the Federal government and its public health responsibility? The history of the Government's attention to asbestos-related health issues is one of noninvolvement, erroneous standards, and a constant lagging behind industry and academia.

3. What of other contributing factors to occupational health burdens such as cigarette smoking?

Within a framework of collective responsibility all should share in the comprehensive, equitable and uniform compensation for occupational disease.

The problems of compensation for asbestos-related occupational disease under existing systems are clear. Returning to the original question raised, I submit to the subcommittee that a goal of comprehensive, equitable and uniform compensation for asbestos-related occupational disease cannot be achieved within existing structures, and that legislation is required.

The issues presented at these hearings merit the subcommittee's most serious attention. A great deal rests on your decisions. Personally, I am fearful that if we fail to join together to take dramatic and innovative action the number of lawsuits will continue to grow, millions of dollars will be spent for attorney's fees, court costs and expert witnesses, court backlogs will grow, inconsistent results will continue, and in future years we will look back and regret our failure to resolve the basic question of comprehensive, equitable and uniform compensation for occupational disease. This subcommittee has the opportunity to take innovative, progressive, and effective action. The status quo is no longer acceptable.

[1]Cooke, W. E., "Pulmonary Asbestosis," *British Journal of Medicine* (sic), Vol. II, pp. 1024–25.

[2]It is to be noted that the document entitled "Asbestos, Chronological Highlights" and submitted to the subcommittee in San Francisco is replete with errors. For example, dates are erroneous, the numbers of cases are misstated, and the document implies the existence of workers' compensation laws specifically addressing asbestosis up to 13 years before the term asbestosis was coined.

[3]Merewether, E. R. A., *Report on Effects of Asbestos Dust on the Lungs and Dust Suppression in the Asbestos Industry,* H.M. Stationery Office (1930).

[4]Lanza, A. J., McConnell, W. J. and Fehnel, J. W., "Effects of the Inhalation of Asbestos Dust on the Lungs of Asbestos Workers," *Public Health Reports,* Vol. 50. pp. 1–12 (1935).

[5]Dreessen, W. C., *et al.,* "A Study of Asbestosis in the Asbestos Textile Industry," *Public Health Bulletin No. 241,* (1938).

[6]Dreessen, *ibid.,* Merewether, supra., (1930); Lanza, supra., (1935).

[7]Fleischer, Walter E., Viles, Jr., Frederick J., Gade, Robert L. and Drinker, Philip, "A Health Survey of Pipe Covering Operations in Constructing Naval Vessels", *Journal of Industrial Hygiene and Toxicology,* January 1946.

[8]Selikoff, I., infra., at pg. 142.

[9]Selikoff, I. J., "The Occurrence of Asbestosis Among Insulation Workers in the United States." *Annals New York Academy of Sciences,* 1965.

[10]Ibid., 1965.

[11]Selikoff, I. J., "Partnership for Prevention—The Insulation Industry Hygiene Research Program," *Industrial Medicine,* Vol. 39, No. 4, April 1970.

[12]Wagner, J. C., Sleggs, C. A. and Marchand, Paul, "Diffuse Pleural Mesothelioma and Asbestos Exposure in the North Western Cape Province," *British Journal of Industrial Medicine,* 1960, 17, 260.

[13]Selikoff, I. J., Churg, J. and Hammond, E. C., "Asbestos Exposure and Neoplasia," *Journal American Medical Association,* April 1964.

Selikoff, I.J., Churg, J. and Hammond, E. C., "Relation Between Exposure to Asbestos and Mesothelioma," *the New England Journal of Medicine,* March 1965.

[14]Sweeney, Robert E., "The Asbestosis Time Bomb," *Trial.* October 1978, p. 17. It is to be noted that the cases of disease to which Mr. Sweeney makes reference were in the asbestos textile industry, and among individuals who had experienced long periods of continually heavy exposure to 100 percent raw asbestos fiber.

[15]The world's largest fabric filter is maintained at Johns-Manville's Jeffery Mine in Asbestos, Quebec.

[16]Selikoff, I. J., "Partnership for Prevention—The Insulation Industry Hygiene Research Program," supra.

[17]A settlement of this type claim is referred to in the minutes of a 1933 meeting of the board of directors of Johns-Manville.

[18]Lanza, supra., p. 6, 11.

Appendix 3

There are many examples in this book of the suppression of findings and opinions by health professionals. However, the scientific journals are sometimes also open to criticism for the way they choose what to publish. Conspicuous in this regard is the *Journal of Occupational Medicine,* the "official publication" of the American Occupational Medical Association (AOMA). The author's effort to get this journal to publish a letter on the threat of asbestos in drinking water is illustrative.

(Here follow full texts of letter from BC to JOM 6-13-83 and JOM reply 9-27-83)

June 13, 1983
For Publication

to the *Journal of Occupational Medicine*

Dear Editor:

In response to an inquiry (Occupational Medicine Forum, *JOM 25*: 361, May, 1983) on the health effects of ingested asbestos, the AOMA Committee on Occupational Medical Practice offered the opinion, "there is little evidence to support a health risk problem from asbestos fibers in drinking water."

This opinion is very open to dispute in light of current scientific knowledge. Asbestos is a universally recognized carcinogen, and numerous studies show excessive rates of gastrointestinal cancer and other cancers among workers occupationally exposed to inhaled asbestos. There is little or no basis for expecting that asbestos fibers' carcinogenic properties are altered by taking a ride up the mucociliary escalator and then being swallowed. What basis then could there be for thinking the asbestos fibers are less of a digestive cancer threat if directly swallowed in drinking water than if swallowed after clearance from the lung?

If we accept the idea that one route of swallowed fiber can be presumed an equal GI cancer threat to the other, then we can make estimates of risk as a function of dose. What dose of swallowed asbestos fibers does it take to constitute a "health risk problem"? Here the AOMA Committee may have a different perspective than others in public health concerned with environmental cancer risks to which tens of millions are constantly exposed. What might be an unnoticeably small excess risk for several thousand workers occupationally exposed could still be a major public health threat when the number exposed to the same risk is 10,000 times as great.

The expert panel of the International Agency for Research on Cancer concluded in its 1977 Monograph on asbestos, "At present, it is not possible to assess whether there is a level of exposure in humans below which an increased risk of cancer would not occur." More recently, it has been noted that at least four epidemiological studies of asbestos workers demonstrated a linear dose-response relationship with no evidence of a threshold below which disease does not appear (W.J. Nicholson. *Criteria Document for Swedish Occupational Standards: Asbestos and Inorganic Fibers,* 1981).

Asbestos is widely present at levels exceeding 10 million fibers per liter in U.S. drinking water supplies. And there is every reason to expect that this problem is getting worse, not better. Using EPA dose-response estimates, Millette and his co-workers have calculated that 1,000 cancer deaths per year in the U.S. may be caused by asbestos in drinking water.

The AOMA Committee cited Dr. Millette as an authority

on this subject. Readers who examine the paper by him and his co-workers, entitled "The Need to Control Asbestos Fibers in Potable Water Supply Systems" (*Sci. Total Environment 18*: 91–102, 1981) may come away with a very different opinion from that offered by the Committee. Dr. Millette would no doubt regard it as a public service to provide copies of this paper to interested readers (address in *JOM, op. cit.)*.

Sincerely yours,
Barry I. Castleman

* * *

September 27, 1983

Dear Mr. Castleman:

Your letter-to-the-editor of June 13 was referred to the AOMA Committee on Occupational Medical Practice. After due consideration, the Committee concluded that perhaps its response to the old question about whether there are indeed thresholds for carcinogens in biological studies should have been more equivocal than it was. Rather than "Epidemiological studies . . . have permitted the conclusion that no cancer risk is associated with asbestos fibers in water" probably should have been written "Epidemiological studies . . . do not permit the conclusion that cancer risk is associated with asbestos fibers in water at this time."

Our Editors have decided, based on the Committee report, that publication of your letter-to-the-editor therefore is not indicated.

AUTHOR'S NOTE: The Editor of the *Journal of Occupational Medicine* is Dr. Lloyd Tepper, Corporate Medical Director of Air Products and Chemicals, Inc. The Associate Editor is Dr. Charles Reinhardt, Director of the Haskell Laboratories of E.I. du Pont de Nemours and Company, Inc. Dr. Paul Kotin, retired Senior Vice President for Health, Safety, and Environment of the Johns-Manville Corporation, serves on the editorial board.

A Committee of the National Research Council has estimated that lifetime consumption of drinking water containing 1.4 million asbestos fibers per liter would cause 10 cases of gastrointestinal cancer per 100,000 persons exposed. Similarly, water containing 10 million fibers per liter (a concentration exceeded in 11 percent of U.S. drinking water supplies analyzed by the Environmental Protection Agency) would be expected to cause 91 cases of gastrointestinal cancer per 100,000 exposed persons. Data were considered insufficient to base any estimate of the additional risk of other forms of cancer, notably peritoneal mesothelioma. (Asbestos, *Drinking Water and Health,* Vol. 5, National Academy Press, Washington, D.C., 1983, pp. 123-147)

See also R. Lemen *et. al.*, "Report on Cancer Risks Associated With the Ingestion of Asbestos." *Env. Health Perspectives* 72: 253-265 (1987).

Appendix 4

Chart used in consolidated trial of *Wanda Jenkins et al. v. Raymark et al.* (over 700 plaintiffs) in Marshall, Texas federal court (C.A. No. M-84-193-CA), March, 1986. Plaintiffs charged defendants with a "Conspiracy of Silence."

	GAF Ruberoid	Eagle–Picher	Owens–Corning	Owens–Illinois	Keene	Philip Carey	Pittsburgh Corning	Armstrong	Fibreboard	Raymark	J–M
Asbestos 1930	X				X	X			X	X	X
Metropolitan Life										X	X
Saranac Reports			X	X						X	X
IHF	X	X	X	X			X			X	X
ATI										X	X
7th Saranac (Unpublished)			X	X							X
Contract unit w.c. compensation defendants			X			X		X	X		X
MIMA					X	X			X		X
NIMA	X	X	X		X		X				X

ATI— Asbestos Textile Institute
IHF— Industrial Hygiene Foundation
MIMA—Magnesia Insulation Manufacturers Association
NIMA—National Insulation Manufacturers Association

Appendix 5

THE ANTHONY J. LANZA RESEARCH LABORATORIES: NEW YORK UNIVERSITY'S MONUMENT TO MENDACITY IN INDUSTRIAL MEDICINE

1930—with Dr. Pedley of McGill, Dr. Anthony J. Lanza of Metropolitan Life identifies 42 cases of asbestosis among 195 Quebec miners; results never published, Lanza even wrote in 1939 that asbestos miners don't get asbestosis (*Am J Tuberc*).

1932—Lanza arranges evaluation of X-rays of employees at Johns-Manville NJ plant by US government doctors in Picher (OK) clinic, finds 329 with pneumoconiosis. Histories of workers with asbestosis included watchmen, shipping clerks. Predates reports of bystander disease from asbestosis in the world medical literature. Never published or cited.

1933—Lanza advises Johns-Manville (J-M) Waukegan, IL plant doctor to not post asbestos warning signs because of "the extraordinary legal situation"; J-M sued by about 20 former Waukegan employees alleging asbestosis within months later.

1934—Lanza sends galley proofs on asbestosis study to J-M corporate lawyer Vandiver Brown, who advises editing changes to make asbestosis seem a less serious disease than silicosis. Brown encloses attorney Hobart's letter explaining that J-M hoped to use Lanza's paper as a lobbying tool to prevent adoption of asbestosis as a compensable disease in NJ. Lanza complies, NJ compensation law doesn't include asbestosis until 1945.

1935, 1936, 1940—Lanza papers in *Pub Hlh Rep, JAMA, Minn Med* downplay seriousness of asbestosis in US, influencing other occupational health professionals for years thereafter.

1935—Lanza a central figure in formation of Industrial Hygiene Foundation and later member of its Board of Trustees. IHF performed confidential industrial hygiene and medical surveys for Asbestos Textile Institute (1947) and many other industrial firms. IHF also performed controversial epidemiological study of lung cancer in asbestos miners for Quebec Asbestos Mining Association (1957) and altered final report published in 1958 to delete data on prevalence of lung cancer in asbestos miners who had asbestosis.

1936—Lanza assures Raybestos-Manhattan President that Lanza's former colleague, Public Health Service investigator Dr. Sayers, can be relied upon to not disclose findings of asbestosis to the workers if allowed to conduct medical surveys in R-M plants.

1942—R-M President thanks Lanza for repeated efforts on behalf of R-M in defense of compensation suits over asbestosis.

1946—Following the death of Dr. Leroy Gardner at Saranac Laboratory, Lanza becomes a member of Board of Trustees of Saranac's parent organization, Trudeau Institute (in addition to his regular job at Metropolitan Life). Lanza presses pathologist Kenneth Lynch to write up Gardner's animal experiments with asbestos that had been jointly sponsored by 7 companies. Eulogizing Gardner at the annual IHF meeting, Lanza lauds "honesty" of the Saranac Lab researchers.

1947—Lanza meets with J-M top executives to plan a way to get some of Gardner's research published by the new Saranac Lab director, Dr. Arthur Vorwald. V. Brown stresses the importance of excluding any mention of cancer from asbestos and observes that the contract with Saranac gives asbestos company sponsors editorial control over any publication.

1948—Vorwald draft report analyzed by sponsoring asbestos company executives, who decide unanimously that all references to cancer must be deleted. Lanza, now at New York University, sends the asbestos industry instructions to Vorwald, who then makes the requested changes in a paper published 1951 (the paper was given the Merit in Authorship Award by the Industrial Medical Association).

1949—Lanza tells visiting researcher Dr. Gerrit Schepers he must submit a thesis for completion of his work on pneumoconiosis at NYU. Lanza then provides the "thesis" to J-M executive V. Brown, who demands that Schepers not submit his report to his country's government (S. Africa) or publish his observations on asbestosis/cancer in any manner.

—Lanza and Vorwald attend First National Cancer Conference and go on record as saying their experience provides no evidence that asbestos causes lung cancer.

1950—Lanza, Vorwald, J-M executive Page Woodard, and the lawyer for the Quebec Asbestos Mining Association (QAMA) meet at Saranac, and a confidential animal study is planned to determine whether mice inhaling asbestos develop pulmonary cancer. Interim report at 14 months (5/52) indicates a positive trend in the formation of tumors, no subsequent report ever located.

—Prof. Lanza offers "postgraduate course in compensation medicine" at NYU for physicians in industrial medicine.

1951—Lanza approaches the U.S. Surgeon General, and succeeds in getting an order sent down to Dr. Wilhelm Hueper at

National Cancer Institute (NCI) to cease contact with private and government organizations that had clinical data on industrial agents suspected of causing cancer.

—President of Mutual Chemical lauds Lanza (confidential letter to another chromate manufacturer) for getting Hueper's name and that of NCI removed from authorship of positive cancer epidemiology report on chromate workers—as a result of Lanza's visit to the Surgeon General.

—QAMA lawyer Sabourin lauds Lanza for contributing "greatly" in defending a workers' compensation claim against British-owned Bell Asbestos Mines, "debunking... figures relating to cancer incidence in the British Isles."

1952—Lanza comment published (*Arch Ind Hyg Occ Med*) saying the reason the UK authorities report so much lung cancer with asbestosis is because they look so carefully through lungs of asbestotics and often find tiny tumors (rebutted by WE Smith, who noted the contrast in cancer rates between UK asbestotics and silicotics).

—Neither Vorwald nor Lanza mentions the ongoing animal studies for QAMA at the lengthy discussion of pneumoconiosis and cancer at the Seventh Saranac Symposium (Sept.).

1953—Vorwald fired by Saranac Lab with the active participation of Lanza. Lanza personally intercedes to prevent Vorwald from being hired by a medical school in California. Vorwald consulting in defense of Quebec asbestos disease compensation claims just about ceases entirely.

—Lanza hosts a conference (published in *Arch Indust Hlh*, 1955), where doctors associated with various asbestos companies downplay the seriousness of asbestosis, warn against "doctor-induced disability", etc.

—Lanza hired by Lead Industries Association to oppose New York City Board of Health proposal to require warning lables on lead-based paint containers.

1956—Dr. W.E. Smith fired by Lanza at NYU over Smith's

interest in industrial carcinogens generally and asbestos in particular. Lanza's antagonistic attitudes toward researchers in industrial cancer vividly described in Smith's letter sent to director of NYU/Bellevue and Chancellor of NYU, pleading for reconsideration.

1960—Lanza is succeeded as Director of the Institute of Industrial Medicine at NYU by Norton Nelson, who praises Lanza for "unassailable integrity".

1962—J-M medical director refers insurance claims investigator to Lanza, saying Lanza had just completed a cancer study at a Pennsylvania brake lining plant (where local doctors had reported lung cancer). No trace of any such study by Lanza has been found.

1963—Lanza-edited book, *The Pneumoconioses*, includes a chapter on asbestos by J-M's medical director, denying that there was data to show asbestos mining in Canada caused lung cancer; the word mesothelioma does not appear.

1964—Lanza dies and is honored by NYU.
—Selikoff publishes epidemiological study in *JAMA* showing catastrophic mortality from cancer and asbestosis among asbestos insulators in NY/NJ.

1987-88—NYU asked by Castleman, Harriet Hardy, and Paul Brodeur to rename Lanza Research Laboratories. Replies to Castleman (6/87, 5/88) and Brodeur (4/88) say the matter is under consideration.
—Dr. W.E. Smith compares naming an institute of industrial medicine after Lanza to naming a synagogue after Hilter.

Index

A

Abrams, Herbert K., 79
ACGIH (American Conference of Governmental Industrial Hygienists)
  asbestos industry and, 232-233
  documents of, 613-616
  establishment of, 232
  "Symposium on Threshold Limits" and, 265
  TLVs and, 233-237
Ackerman, Harold, 485
ACL. *See* Asbestos Corporation Limited
Addingley, C. 267
Advisory Committee on Asbestos, 291
Aetna Life Insurance Company, 162-163, 242
Air Hygiene Committee, 89, 90-91, 92-93
Air Hygiene Foundation, 155, 596. *See also* Industrial Hygiene Foundation
Air samplings, 250
Amerada Hess, 523, 697
American Association of Industrial Physicians and Surgeons, 229. *See also* American Occupational Medical Association
American Brake Shoe & Foundry, 56
American Cancer Society, 79
American Chemical Society, 225
American Conference of Governmental Industrial Hygienists. *See* ACGIH
American Industrial Hygiene Association, 265
American Occupational Medical Association, 229, 230, 260
Ames, Edward C., 163, 500, 503, 504
Amosite asbestos insulation, 511, 529-530
Ancel Wheeler v. Norfolk & Western, 567
Anderson, Adelaide, 1
Anderson, H.A., 434
Angrist, A., 44
Annual Convention of the International Association of Industrial Accident Boards and Commissions, 94
Anthony J. Lanza Research Laboratories, 210, 730-733. *See also* Lanza

Archives, 636-639
Armstrong Cork Company. *See also* Armstrong World Industries
  knowledge of, 500
  workers' compensation claims against, 172-185
Armstrong World Industries, Inc., 381, 397-398. *See also* Armstrong Cork Company
Asbestos
  abstracts on, 579
  ban of, 289, 291, 293, 729
  blue, 19
  in Canada, 21-22, 94-97, 197-200
  Canadian government and, 728-733
  cancer tests with, 46-55
  carcinogenicity, 39-40, 70-73, 99-101, 111
  conference on, 1990, 728
  congressional hearings on, 723-725
  cost of in U.S., economic and social, 686-688
  criminal sanctions and, 705-711
  deterioration of, 684
  in developing countries, 700-705
  in drinking water, 269-270, 720-723
  in Egypt, 724
  in Europe, 726-727
  exposure to in U.S., continuing, 679-686
  ILO on, 25, 42, 593-595, 702
  insulation workers' exposure to, 278-289
  legacy of, 674-677
  market expansion for, current, 700-706
  Merewether's articles on, 26-28
  mesothelioma and, 110
  in Mexico, 724
  mortality estimates from, 676-679
  personal responsibility and, 705-712
  population studies of, in insulation workers, 332
  public health measures and, traditional, 711-712
  public health policy and, 698-705
  public opinion and, 698-699
  revenue from, 700
  substitutes, 289, 412-422
  at Turner Brothers Asbestos Company, 75
  U.S. Public Health Service plant surveys on, 244-250, 295
  victims' groups and, 690-691
  white. *See* Chrysotile.
Asbestos air pollution, 424-425, 427-431
Asbestos Corporation Limited (ACL), 198, 427, 533, 540-542
Asbestos disease. *See also* Asbestosis; "Bystander" asbestos disease; Cancer
  in brake repair workers, 443-447, 476-479
  British survey of, 11-17
  cost of in U.S., economic and social, 686-688
  ILO on, 17, 18-19
  proliferation of, worldwide, 713-721

published literature on, 318-319
research on, 569
"signal tumor" of, 438
workers' compensation for, 142-144
Asbestos Diseases Society, 713
Asbestos dust
asbestos fiber fraction of inhaled, 250-252
control measures in Germany, 252-254
Fleischer, Viles, Gade, and Drinker report on, 329-332
U.S. Public Health Service study of, 272
Asbestos fibers
asbestosis and, 262-264
Asbestos Textile Institute on, 252
fraction of inhaled dust and, 250-252
standards for, 275-276
U.S. Public Health Service on, 250-251
Asbestos friction products
ban on, 446-447
bibliography of health hazards of, 447-475
patents for, 406-409
standards for, 447
warning labels on, 445
Asbestos industry
ACGIH and, 232-233
asbestos standards and, 273
Canadian government and, 705-710
cancer and, reaction to research on, 90-94
common law defenses used by, 133-134
damage suits against, 172-175, 187-189, 666-676
"editing" of medical journals by, 148-151
government hearing on (1933), 25
insulation standards and, 358
liability of, 705, 706, 708-709
OSHA and, 273
physicians, 111-112, 229-232
plant surveys in, by U.S. Public Health Service, 244-250, 295
public opinion of, 698-705
Saranac Laboratory contracts with, 141
TLVs and, 266-272
trade groups of, 595-606
warning labels and, 711-712
workers' compensation and, 144
Asbestos Industry Regulations, 240
Asbestos Information Association, 99, 274, 632, 654, 655, 717
Asbestos International Association, 601, 739
Asbestosis
abstracts on, 333
asbestos fibers and, 262-264
asbestos product use and, 320-328
British survey of, 11-17
cancer with, 40-46, 427
cancer without, 289-290
case reports in medical journals, 6-11
cumulative dust exposure and, 247
deaths caused by, 83-84

distinctiveness of, 319
Donnelly's research on, 29
Dunn's research on, 102-103
Factory Inspectorate Report on, 62-63
first case report of, 7
George and Leonard's research on, 159-160
Hawes' research on, 157-158
incidence and degree of, 243
insulation workers and, 320-338
J.A.M.A. on, 62
legal literature on, 337-338
literature on compensability of, 165-168
lung cancers with, 44-45, 79
maturation period of, 13
Mills' report on, 17-18
MPPCF levels and, 242
1930 events, other, 17-23
Nordmann's research on, 41-42, 43
numerical guidelines for, U.S., 260-262
Pedley's research on, 21-22
Pennsylvania study of, 249
publications on, 106-108
recognition of, 19-20, 33, 143
stages of, 31-32
in U.S. Navy shipyards, 193-194
unpublished documentation on, 339
Wood and Gloyne's article on, 29-30, 425-426
workers' compensation for, 167, 202
Asbestosis Research Council, 601
Asbestos magazine letters, 151-153, 719-722
Asbestos plant ventilation systems, 429
Asbestos product use
abstracts on hazards of, 333-337
asbestosis and, 320-328
cancer and, 350
charges in damage suits of, 314-316
defense arguments in damage suits of, 316-318
Fleischer, Viles, Gade, and Drinker report on, 329-332
legal literature on, 337-338
medical literature on, 332-337
population studies of, 332
published literature on, 318-319, 329
unpublished documentation on, 339, 340-349
Asbestos School Hazard Detection and Control Act, 666
Asbestos standards
asbestos dust control measures in Germany, 252-254
asbestos fiber fraction of inhaled dust and, 250-252
asbestos fiber length and, 262-264
asbestos industry and, 273
in Brazil, 702
British, 238-241, 276-278
cancer threat and, 264-266
change proposals for, 290-294
current, 272-276,
degree of exposure vs. degree of disease risk, 241-244
efficacy of current, 290-294
"emergency", 273-274, 294
Johns-Manville and, 263, 273

numerical exposure limits and, 254-257
numerical guidelines for asbestosis and, 260-262
Saranac Laboratory and, 251
social origins of, 223-237
in Sweden, 276-278
TLVs and, 257-260, 266-272
Turner & Newall and, 261
U.S. Public Health Service and, 237, 244-250
Asbestos Textile Institute (ATI)
on asbestos fibers, 252
on cancer, 89, 90-91, 92-93
Conklin's article and, 63
Hueper's work and, 265
survey of plants of, 255-257
on toxic substances, 598-599
Asbestos Victims of America, 691
Asbestos Workers' union, 162, 203, 610
Association of Casualty and Surety Executives, 154
Association to Improve Benefits for Retired Disabled Workers and Their Dependents, 691
ATI. *See* Asbestos Textile Institute
Atlas Asbestos Company Ltd, 556
Audicote, 518-519
Aycock Corporation, 187-188

B

Baader, E.W., 42
Bairnco Corporation, 381, 398
Baldwin-Ehret-Hill. *See* Keene Corporation
Baldwin-Hill. *See* Keene Corporation
Bankruptcy, 205-207, 666, 676
Banner Rock Products Company, 369
Bates, David, 706, 707
Baxter, Mason, 361
Behrens, W., 70-71
Beilock, Richard, 688
Bell Asbestos Mines, 198, 532, 556
Bernard Dugan v. R.V. Aycock Co. et al., 340
Bertogliat, Rose, 163-164
Bethlehem Steel, 141
B.I.O.S. (British Intelligence Objectives Sub-Committee), 362
Boemke, F., 43, 46, 61, 78-79
Boeschenstein, Harold, 504, 580
Bohme, A., 101-102
BOHS (British Occupational Hygiene Society), 276-277
Bonser, G.M., 80
Bowditch, Manfred, 53
Brahdy, Leopold, 169-170
Brake repair workers
asbestos disease in, 443-447, 476-479
bibliography on health hazards of, 447-476
cases of, 476-479
health hazard of, 662
OSHA and, 447, 659
research on, 443-447
Braun, D., 94-96, 97, 536
Brazil's environmental protection agency, 702
British Belting and Asbestos, 267
British Factory Department, 5, 8, 11

British Factory Inspectorate, 62-63, 277, 427
British government documents, 633-636
British Intelligence Objectives Sub-Committee (B.I.O.S.), 362
British Medical Association, 10
British Occupational Hygiene Society (BOHS), 276-277
British Workmen's Compensation Act, 18, 132-133, 146-147
Brown, Vandiver, 53, 54, 55-57, 58, 148-150, 152, 161-162, 256-257, 543-544, 597
Browne, Kevin, 675-676
"Bystander" asbestos disease
  asbestos air pollution and, 427-431
  cancer and, 427
  household-contact asbestos disease and, 432-436
  mesothelioma epidemic and, 431-432
  recognition of, earliest, 424-427
  risk groups of, 424

C

"Cable rash", 433
Calcium silicate insulation, 363-370
"Calidria" asbestos, 528
California Industrial Accident Commission, 174, 501
Campbell, Edward, 174
Canadian Asbestos Information Centre. *See* Asbestos Institute
Canadian government, 705-711
Canadian mining companies
  knowledge of, 532-536
  workers' compensation at, 197-200
Cancer
  abstracts on, 46, 333-337, 575
  additional reports on, 59-62, 70-73, 77-80, 101-108
  asbestos carcinogenicity and, 39-40, 70-73, 99-101
  asbestos causing, 101-108
  asbestos industry reaction to, 90-94
  asbestosis with, 40-46, 427
  asbestosis without, 289-290
  asbestos product use and, 349-350
  asbestos standards and, 255-256
  Asbestos Textile Institute on, 89, 90-91, 92-93
  "bystander" asbestos disease and, 427
  developments in research on, other, 87-90
  discovery of threat of, 40-46
  Doll's study on, 80-84
  doubters of asbestos link to, 97-99
  Factory Inspectorate report on, 62-63
  Industrial Hygiene Foundation Center study of, 94-97
  industry medical experts on, 111-112
  information sources on, 109-110, 585-591

J.A.M.A. on, 59-60
Louvain Symposium on, 77
negative opinions of threat of, 84-87
reviews on environmental, 585-589
Saranac report on, 55-59
Saranac Symposium on, Seventh, 73-77
Saranac tests of, 46-55
Schepers' report on, 65-70
Scientific American articles on, 63
workers' compensation for, 168-172
Wyers' report on, 63-64
Canepa, G., 166
Cape Asbestos, 10-11, 63-64, 671
Carcinogens, 585-589. *See also* Cancer
Carding, 4
Carey Canadian Mines, 513, 694-695
Carolina Asbestos Company, 153-154, 245
Cartier, Paul, 64-65, 72-73, 75-77, 86, 198, 200, 427
Cassiar Asbestos Corporation, 554
Celotex. *See* Philip Carey Manufacturing Company
Certain-teed Products Corporation, 554, 557
Chapter 11, 205-207, 668-673
Chemical Industry Associations, 607-609
Chemical Manufacturers Association, 606
Child labor, 3, 7, 9, 24-25
Children's Bureau (U.S. Department of Labor), 24-25
Chrysotile asbestos, 19, 276-277, 291, 293, 298, 519-520
Churg, S, 105
Coast Insulating Company, 370
Collis, E. C., 4, 425
Colonial Sugar Refinery. *See* CSR
Columbia-Southern Chemical Corporation, 368
Committee on Threshold Limits (ACGIH), 234-235
Company knowledge. *See* specific name of company
Compensation. *See* Workers' compensation
Computerized indexes, 571
Conference on Environmental Carcinogens, 346
Conklin, Groff, 63
Conyers, John, Jr., 688-689
Cook, Warren, 265, 296
Cooke, W. E., 7
Cooper, Clark, 268
Corn, Morton, 512, 680, 682
Corporate compensation, 189-191
Council on Industrial Health, 230
Cryor, Robert, 161-162
CSR, 530-541
Cubic feet per minute (CFM), 248
Cureton, R.J.R., 61
"Cyclone" type dust collectors, 429

D

Damage suits
against asbestos industry, 187-189

attorney fees in, 135
in Australia, 685
in Britain, lack of, 675-676
charges in, 314-316
common law defenses in, 133-134
Congressional bills and, 673-674
cost of, 667
defense arguments in, 316-318
discovery rules and, 483
epidemiology of cancer and, 349-350
Fleischer, Viles, Gade, and Drinker report and, 329-332
interrogatories and, 482-483
in Japan, 675
against Johns-Manville, 145-146, 187-189, 547-548, 667-672
legal/accounting games to counteract, 673-674
legal literature and, 337-349
medical literature and, 332-339
number of, 666-667
partial medical coverage in, 138
population studies of asbestosis in insulation workers and, 332
principle of limited and graduated liability in, 137-138
published literature on asbestos disease and, 318-319, 329
unpublished documentation and, 339, 340-349
in workers' compensation, 144-146

Decisions of the Commisioner under the National Insurance (Industrial Injuries) Acts, 337
Degree of disease risk, 241-244
Dewey, Bradley, 158
Dewey & Almy Chemical Company, 158. *See also* W.R. Grace & Company
Discovery rules, 482-483
Doll, Richard, 40, 80-84, 265, 283, 556-557
Donnelly, J., 29
Dreessen, W.C., 245, 249, 295
Drinker, P., 80, 155, 331
Dugan, Bernard, 188, 547
Dunn, J.E., 102-103
DuPont, 142, 227-228, 657
Dust disease, sources on, 558. *See also* Asbestos disease
Dye industry, 59

E

Eagle-Picher Industries
damage suit against, 189
knowledge of, 513-516
patents of, 398-399
warning labels and, 515
Egbert, D.S., 41
Ehret Magnesia. *See* Keene Corporation
Electricians, 433
Eliasson, O., 681
Ellman, Philip, 25-26
"Emergency standard", 273-274, 294
Encyclopedias, 648-649
Engineering Journals, 610-612

Exfoliated vermiculite insulation, 362-363
Expanded perlite insulation, 370-372
Exposure
  degree of, 241-244
  numerical limits of, 254-257
  in U.S., continuing, 657-664

F

Faciane, Gladys, 189
Factory Inspectorate report, 62-63
Federal Occupational Disease Compensation Act, 206
Fiberglass blanket, 362, 372
Fiberglass pipe insulation, 370
Fibreboard Corporation
  knowledge of, 500-501
  patents of, 367-369, 381, 396-397
  TLVs and, 267
Fibreboard Paper Products, 368. *See* Fibreboard Corporation
Finnamore, Carlo, 559
Fireproofing, 662
First Canadian Cancer Research Conference, 94
Fisher, A.R., 53, 146
Fleischer, Viles, Gade, and Drinker report, 329-332
Fleischer, W.E., 193-194, 252, 288, 331-332
Flintkote Mines, Ltd., 533
Forced Vital Capacity (FVC), 272
Francis, Ronald K., 512

G

GAF Corporation, 530-532
Gardner, Leroy, 46-52, 99, 251, 263, 536
Gatke, Thomas, 58, 62
Gatke Corporation, 56
Gee, J. Bernard, 659-660
General Insulating and Manufacturing Company, 370
General Managers Association, 340, 565
George, Arial W., 158-160
German Industrial Insurance Act, 131-132
Glass fiber insulation, 362
Gloyne, S.R., 21, 26, 29-30, 40, 41, 42, 425, 426
Gray, Roscoe, 242
Greenstone, Samuel, 145
Gross, Paul, 268-269

H

H.K. Porter Company, 519. *See also* Southern Textile Corporation
Haddow, A.C., 9, 10
"Halowax acne", 433
Hamilton, Alice, 135, 139, 225, 583, 620-621
Hamlin, Lloyd, 56
Handy, G.W., 530
Hardy, Harriet L., 51, 71, 264
Hawes, John B., 157
Hektoen, Ludwig, 46, 48
Heler, E., 665-666
Hills, David W., 261
Hinshaw, H.C., 98
Hirth, A.C., 155, 480, 536
Hobart, George, 148-151
Hoffman, F. L., 5-6, 99-100

Holleb, H.B., 44
Homburger, F., 46
Household-contact asbestos disease, 432-436
Huelster, Herman Lee, 516
Hueper, Wilhelm C., 43-45, 60, 70, 85, 88, 90, 94, 96-97, 100-101, 168-169, 170-171, 226, 227, 265, 289, 430-431, 436, 564-565, 585-586
Hurlbut, C.S., 250
Hutchinson, F., 255
Hyatt, Floyd, 173-174
Hyatt v. Armstrong, 338

I

IARC (International Agency for Research on Cancer), 589-591
IHF. *See* Industrial Hygiene Foundation
ILO (International Labor Office)
  on asbestos, 25
  on asbestos disease, 17, 18-19
  "Code of Practice" of, 702
  proceedings of (1972), 288
  on toxic substances, 593-604
Index Medicus, 570
Industrial Hygiene Foundation (IHF)
  cancer study, for Q.A.M.A., 94-97
  Factory Inspectorate report and, 62-63
  formation of, 155, 596
  lung cancer study by, 93
  plant surveys by, 140
  Raybestos-Manhattan and, 489
  on toxic substances, 598-599
  Union Carbide and, 525
Industrial Injuries Advisory Council, 290
Industrial Medical Association, 260. *See also* American Occupational Medical Association
Insulating cements, 373, 404-405
Insulation. *See also* specific types of
  asbestos in, 359
  asbestos substitute patents for, 410-422
  ban on asbestos, 694-695
  calcium silicate, 363-370
  government publications on, 356-358
  hazards of asbestos, 355-356
  insulating cements and, 373-374
  magnesia, 359-363
  other, 370-373
  patents for, 356-358, 380-404
  standards for, 357-358
  warning labels on, 314-315
Insulation workers
  asbestos exposure of, 278-289
  asbestosis hazard among, 320-329
  Canadian, 717
  population studies of, 332
  workers' compensation for, 172-175, 191-193
Insulex Mineral Products Limited, 368
Insurance coverage, 138-140
Insurance literature, 644-648
International Agency for Research on Cancer (IARC), 589-591

International Association of Heat and Frost Insulators and Asbestos Workers, 19, 610
International Conference of Experts on Pneumoconiosis, Third, 337
International Labor Office. *See* ILO
International Union against Cancer, 105
Interrogatories, 482-483
Isselbacher, K.J., 79

J

J.A.M.A. Journal of the American Medical Association, 59-60, 62, 104-105, 230
Jackson, Hugh, 164, 262, 546-548
Jim Walter Corporation, 381. *See also* Philip Carey Manufacturing Company
Johns-Manville Corporation
  asbestos standards and, 263, 273
  case reports on, 10
  Chapter 11 and, 205-207, 668-673
  compensation committee at, 189-191
  damage suits against, 145-146, 187-189, 667-672
  Gardner report and, 51
  knowledge of, 542-549
  patents of, 360, 365-366, 370, 372, 381, 382-389
  medical examinations of employees of, 24, 200
  Saranac Laboratory and, 548
  trust fund of, 669-670
  warning labels and, 314-315
  workers' compensation claims against, 170, 198, 547-548
  workers' compensation story about, 160-162
Johnson, W.G., 661-663
Johnson's Company, 198, 513
Johnstone, Rutherford, 98, 257
Jones, E.R., 154
Joseph Crosfield & Sons Limited, 368
Journal of the American Medical Association. See J.A.M.A.

K

Kalousek patents, 366
Kaylo insulation, 259, 366-367, 492, 499-500, 502
Keal, E.E., 102
Keasbey & Mattison Company, 49, 55-56
Keene Corporation, 521-523, 697
Kelly, W.T., 56-57
Kennaway, E.L., 60
Kennaway, N.M., 60
Kershaw, Nellie, 7
Knopp, Samuel P., 192
Knox, John, 81, 276
Koelsch, F., 42
Konig, J., 77, 102
Kotin, Paul, 111-112, 417

L

Labbe, Alphonse, 198
Labels. *See* Warning labels

Lacomastic Corp. v. Parker, 321
Lady Inspector of Factories, 1-5
Lake Asbestos, 533
Lanza, A.J., 22-23, 30-33, 52-55, 57-58, 64-65, 72, 75, 82, 85-86, 139-140, 145, 148-151, 191-192, 244, 729-733
Lanza's surveys, 148-151
Lead Industries Association, 754
Lawsuits. *See* Damage suits
Le Doux, Burton, 58, 198-199
Lee, D.H.K., 23, 444
Legge, Thomas, 10
LeGrande, Frederick, 188
Lehmann, K.B., 224
Leonard, Ralph D., 158-160
Levin, Morton, 59
Liability
- of asbestos industry, 683-684, 686-687
- corporate criminal, 687-689
- of other industries, 685-686
- personal, 683-689
- principle of limited and graduated, 137-138

Lifland, Burton, 668
Litigation. *See* Damage suits
Livingstone, R., 147-148
Local government documents, 632-633
Lorimer, W., 427
Louvain Symposium, 77
Lung cancer
- with asbestosis, 44-45, 79
- Hueper's research on, 44-45, 545
- Industrial Hygiene Foundation study of, 93
- reports on, 101-108
- uranium miners and, 85

Lynch, Kenneth M., 18, 40, 42, 52-54, 61, 87-88, 93-94

M

Madeksho, L., 515
Magnesia insulation, 359-363
Magnesia Insulation Manufacturer's Association, 599
Mancuso, Thomas, 97, 105, 195-197
Mancuso documents, 194-197
Mann, R.H., 101
Manville Corporation. *See* Johns-Manville Corporation
Manville Personal Injury Settlement Trust
Marinite asbestos, 365
Maryland Medical Board for Occupational Diseases, 138
Mazzocchi, Anthony, 610
McAllister, John D., 502
McCarrell, Ervey O., 174-175
McConnell, W.J., 63
McCord, Carey, 229-230, 511
McDonald, S., 8
McLaughlin, A.I.G., 87, 260
McNeely v. Carolina Asbestos Co., 153-154, 235
Medical boards, 138
Medical coverage, 204
Medical textbooks, 580-585
Meiklejohn, 260-261
Merewether, E.R.A., 8, 11-17, 26-28, 42, 67-68, 74, 151, 239-240, 294
Mesothelioma
- asbestos exposure and, 110

attention on, worldwide, 540
epidemic, 431-432
reports on, 101-108
in South Africa, 710
Metropolitan Life Insurance Company, 22, 30-33, 191-192, 244, 521, 523, 751
Mills, R.G., 17-18
Mineral wool insulation, 369-370
Mintz, Morton, 687-688
Molfino, 332
Moore, Henry, 173
Mossman, Brooke, 690-692
MPPCF (million particles per cubic feet)
for asbestos-containing dust, 239
asbestosis and, 242
in carding process, 244-245
cumulative exposure and, 246-247
as guideline, 249-250
insulation workers and, 317-318
in picking process, 248
Muldon v. Charles S. Woods Co., 338
Murphy, J.J., 51, 287, 288
Murray, H. Montague, 3-4, 6
Murray, Robert, 561, 704

N

National Advisory Cancer Council, 46, 51
National Asbestos Mine, 513
National Cancer Institute, 88-89, 216, 217
National Gypsum Company, 549-554
National Institute for Occupational Safety and Health (NIOSH) documents, 571-575
National Insulation Manufacturers Association, 599-600
National Safety Council, 219, 505, 603-604
National Safety News, 604-606
Newspaper articles, 649-650
New York Academy of Sciences, 298-299, 415
Nicholson, William J., 289, 293, 427, 682
Nicolet, Inc., 363, 395-396
Nicolet Asbestos, Ltd., 533
NIOSHA (National Institute for Occupational Safety and Health) criteria documents, 571-575
Nordmann, M., 41-42, 43
Norfolk & Western, 567
North Carolina Worker's Compensation Act, 153-154
Northwestern Asbestos and Cork Co. v. Industrial Commission, 338
Nueva A.G., 704-705

O

Occupational diseases, 134, 201, 202-203. *See also* specific types of
Occupational Safety and Health Act of 1970, 144, 217, 271, 273, 295

Occupational Safety and Health Administration. *See* OSHA
Ohio State Health Department, 226
Oil, Chemical, and Atomic Workers Union, 610
Oliver, Thomas, 8, 9, 132-133
O'Donnell, W.M., 101
Oregon Shipbuilding Corporation, 331
OSHA (Occupational Safety and Health Administration)
  asbestos industry and, 273
  Bethlehem Steel hearings of, 141
  brake repair workers and, 447, 659
  mortality rate from asbestos-related cancer, 294
  rulemaking by, 290-294, 604-605, 659
Owens-Corning Fiberglas (OCF) Corporation
  fibrous glass studies, 92
  formation of, 349
  knowledge of, 502-503
  patents of, 389-392
  TLVs and, 267
  workers' compensation story about, 162-163
Owens-Illinois, Inc.
  knowledge of, 492-500
  patents of, 366-367, 370, 393-394

P

Pabco Products, Inc. See Fibreboard Corporation
  packings, 661
Panacon. *See* Philip Carey Manufacturing Company
Pan American Health Organization, 703
Pancoast, H.K., 24
Paraffine Companies, Inc. See Fibreboard Corporation
Partial medical coverage, 138
Patents
  Armstrong World Industries, Inc., 381, 397-398
  asbestos friction products, 406-409
  asbestos substitutes, 410-422
  background of, 356-358
  Bairnco Corporation, 381, 399
  Banner Rock Products Company, 369
  calcium silicate insulation, 363-370
  Columbia-Southern Chemical Corporation, 368
  Eagle-Picher Company, 398-399
  Fibreboard Corporation, 367-368, 381, 396-397
  friction elements, 406-409
  independent inventors, 400-406
  insulating cements, 373, 404-405
  Insulex Mineral Products Limited, 368
  Jim Walter Corporation, 381, 394-395
  Johns-Manville, 360, 365-366, 370, 372, 381, 382-389
  Joseph Crosfield & Sons Limited, 368
  magnesia insulation, 359-363
  Nicolet, Inc., 381, 395-396
  other companies, 400-404
  Owens-Corning Fiberglas (OCF) Corporation, 367, 389-392

    Owens-Illinois, Inc., 366-367, 393-394
    Philip Carey Manufacturing Company, 360, 371-372
    PPG Industries, 382, 399
    Raymark Corporation, 382, 400
    searches of, 621-622
    UNR Industries, Inc., 382, 399
Pechstein, Louis A., 195
Pedley, Frank, 21-22, 533-534
Pendergrass, E.P., 24
Pennsylvania Compensation Commission, 136
Pennsylvania study of asbestosis (1935), 249
Peretti, John, 501
Personal injury suits. *See* Damage suits
Perth trial, 560-561
Peto, Julian, 293
Philip Carey Manufacturing Company. *See also* Jim Walter Corporation
    knowledge of, 517-520
    liability potential of, 414
    Mancuso documents and, 194-197
    patents of, 360, 371-372
    warning labels and, 539-540
    workers' compensation claims against, 198-199
    workers' compensation story about, 164-165
Picking process, 248
Pittsburgh-Corning Corporation, 511-513
Pittsburgh Plate Glass Company, 511-512
Pliny, 1, 294
Pollard, M., 529-530
Porter, Robert R., 535
PPG Industries, Inc., 382, 399
Pratt-Thomas, H.R., 87-88
Price, C.W., 11, 13, 15, 16, 17, 151, 239, 294
Price, James, 484-485
Princi, Frank, 260
Prockat, F., 253
Prudential Insurance Company, 5-6
Pulmonary disease, 3-4

Q

Q.A.M.A. (Quebec Asbestos Mining Association)
    Industrial Hygiene Foundation cancer study for, 94-97
    Saranac and, 64, 67-69
    on toxic substances, 601-604
Quebec Asbestos Corporation, 533
Quebec Asbestos Information Service, 676
Quebec Asbestos Mining Association. *See* Q.A.M.A.
Quebec Asbestos Producers Association, 601

R

Railroad companies, 561-567
Rappaport, S.M., 237
Raybestos-Manhattan, Inc. *See also* Raymark Corporation
    asbestos magazine letters and, 151
    Gardner's report and, 50
    knowledge of, 484-492
    plant survey of, 244

Saranac report and, 55-56
workers' compensation claims against, 156, 170
Raymark Corporation, 382, 400. *See also* Raybestos-Manhattan, Inc.
Refinery workers, 226
Resilient Floor Covering Institute, 602
Riley, James Whitcomb, 174
Roach, S.A., 236
Roemer, Charles H., 161-162, 481
Rohl, Arthur, 524
Rombola, G., 90
Rothwell, Richard, 173
Rousseau, L., 60
Ruberoid Company. *See* GAF Corporation
Russell, Albert, 165
Russell Manufacturing Company, 56
Russell Sage Foundation, 134

S

Sabourin, Ivan, 64, 96, 197-198
Saint, Eric, 539
Saita, C., 61
Samuels, Sheldon, 235
Saranac Laboratory for Research on Tuberculosis
animal testing at, 157, 263
Asbestos Corporation Limited and, 541
asbestos industry contracts with, 141
asbestos standards and, 251
cancer tests with asbestos at, 46-55
closing of, 92
occupational chest disease conference of, 87
Q.A.M.A. and, 64, 67-69
report by, 55-59, 64, 67-69
Schepers at, 64
on toxic substances, 600
workers' compensation reviews by, 163-165
Saranac Symposium, Seventh, 73-77, 346, 638
Sayers, I.C., 523-524
Sayers, R.R., 249, 597
Schepers, Gerrit, 64-67, 91-92
Schmoll v. AC&S, et al., 674
Scientific American article, 63
Selikoff, Irving J., 23, 105, 201, 270, 317-318
Shipbuilding and Shiprepairing Regulations, 332
Shoemaker, W.E., 192-193
Shull, J.R., 245, 520
"Signal tumor", 438
Silicosis and Asbestos (Medical Arrangements) Scheme, 241
Simpson, Sumner, 50, 152, 156-157, 192
Smith, K.W., 64, 96, 98-99, 515, 545
Smith, L.W., 63
Smith, Ralph, 411
Smith, W.A., 18, 40, 42, 192-193, 200, 427-428, 429
Smith, W.E., 71-72, 73, 82, 754-755
Smoking, 79, 81, 87, 690
Society for the Prevention of Asbestosis and Industrial Diseases, 691
Soper, W.B., 18
Sorge, A., 43

Southern Asbestos Company, 245. *See also* Southern Textile Corporation
Southern Textile Corporation, 519-521
Sparks, J.V., 20-21
State government documents, 632-633
Stewart, Harold L., 23, 77, 241
Stokinger, Herbert, 265-266, 270, 294
Street, E.W., 147-148
"Sumner Simpson Papers", 484, 489, 543-544
Swartout, John, 175
Szczesniak, Anton, 170

T

Tarlau, E.S., 235-236
Technology indexes, 639-643
Thermal Insulation Contractors Association, 409
Thermobestos, 696
Thermoid Company, 56, 519. *See also* Southern Textile Corporation
Thetford Industrial Clinic, 198, 200
Thetford Mines, 21, 64-65, 72, 95
Thomson, J.G., 432
Threshold Limits Committee (ACGIH), 266
Threshold Limit Values. *See* TLVs
TLVs (Threshold Limit Values)
  ACGIH and, 233-237
  as advisory guidelines, 236-237
  aim of, 237
  and asbestos industry, 266-272
  asbestos standards and, 257-260, 266-272
  British reaction to, 260-261
  criticism of, 266-272
  original listings of, 232, 257
  proposal of, 237
  reaction to, 260-262
  Roach and Rappaport's review of, 236
  Samuels' view on, 235
  Tarlau's editorial on, 235-236
  Turner & Newall and, 267
Torbohn, Edmond, 501
Toxic substances. *See also* specific names of
  archives on, 636-639
  Asbestos International Association on, 601
  Asbestosis Research Council on, 601
  Asbestos Textile Institute on, 598-599
  British publications on, 633-636
  carcinogens and, 585-586
  Chemical Manufacturers Association on, 606
  computerized indexes and, 571
  encyclopedias on, 648-649
  historical background of research on, 569-570
  IARC on, 589-591
  ILO publications on, 593-606
  Indexus Medicus and, 570

Industrial Hygiene Foundation on, 600-601
insurance literature on, 644-648
medical conference proceedings on, 591-593
medical textbooks on, 580-585
National Insulation Manufacturers Association on, 599-600
National Safety Council on, 603-604
National Safety News on, 604-606
newspaper articles on, 649-650
NIOSH criteria documents on, 571-575
other groups on, 606
patent search and, 623-624
Q.A.M.A. on, 601-602
references on, 607-612
reports on, 571-575
Resilient Floor Covering Institute on, 602
reviews on, 586-589
Saranac Laboratory on, 600
technology indexes on, 639-643
trade journals on, 639-643
U.S. government documents on, 612-633
Trade journals, 639-643
Trimble, George, 98
Truan, T., 94, 97
Trudeau, Pierre Elliott, 199
Turner Brothers Asbestos Company, 7, 75, 276-277
Turner & Newall
asbestos standards and, 261
Doll and, 81
Gardner's work and, 49, 555
knowledge of, 554-559
TLVs and, 267

U

U.S. Consumer Product Safety Commission, 629
U.S. Department of Health and Human Services, 612-617
U.S. Department of Justice, 630
U.S. Department of Labor, 24-25, 617-628
U.S. Department of the Interior, 629
U.S. Environmental Protection Agency
ban on asbestos by, 289
brake repair workers and, 446-449
on toxic substances, 630-632
U.S. Mineral Products Company, 314
U.S. Navy, 628-629
U.S. Navy shipyards, 193-194
U.S. Public Health Service
asbestos studies by, 250-251, 272
asbestos standards and, 237, 244-250
documents of, 613-616
health hazard evaluations by, 225, 226
plant surveys by, on asbestos, 244-250, 295
Raybestos-Manhattan employee examination by, 156

U.S. Rubber Company, 267
UNARCO, 509-511
"Unibestos" insulation,
Union Asbestos & Rubber Company, 56, 509-511. *See also* UNARCO
Union Carbide Corporation, 267, 523-525
Unions, 610. *See also* Asbestos Workers' Union.
United Asbestos and Rubber Company, 160-162
United States Gypsum Company (USG), 56, 516-519
UNR Industries, Inc., 382, 399
Uranium miners, 85, 226
USG. *See* United States Gypsum Company

V

Vorwald, Arthur J., 54, 68-69, 85-86, 198, 200, 259-260, 263-264, 636-638

W

W.R. Grace & Company, 526-530
Wagner, J.C., 105, 289
Wake, Benjamin, 526-527
Warning labels
  on asbestos friction products, 445
  asbestos industry and, 695-696
  British, 695-696
  Eagle-Picher Industries and, 514
  on insulation, 314-315
  Philip Carey Manufacturing Company and, 539-540
Warren, Shields, 84-85
Wedler, H.W., 45-46
Weill, Hans, 505
Weiss, A., 78
Wells, John, 267
Welz, A., 44, 46
Wenham, Fred C., 189
Werber, M., 71
White Lung Association, 691
Williams, 250
Windel, T., 253
Wood, W.B., 21, 26, 29-30, 40, 151, 407
Workers' compensation
  against Armstrong Cork Company, 172-185
  for asbestos disease, 142-144
  asbestos industry and, 144
  for asbestosis, 167, 202
  British, 146-148, 675
  in Canadian mining companies, 197-200
  for cancer, 168-172
  Chapter 11 and, 205-207
  consultations on, informal, 191-193
  damage suits in, 144-146
  for disability from asbestosis, 167
  expense of, 136-137
  first claims for, 144-145
  history of, early, 131-142
  industry "editing" of medical publications and, 148-151
  for insulation workers, 172-175, 191-193
  insurance coverage and, 139-140

against Johns-Manville, 170, 198, 547-548
Lanza's survey on, 148-151
laws concerning, 137-139
literature on, 165-168
Mancuso documents and, 194-197
medical boards and, 138
medical profession and, 140-141
1930s, 153-160
obstacles to, 200-205
for occupational diseases, 201
against Philip Carey Manufacturing Company, 198-199
against Raybestos-Manhattan, 156, 170
Saranac Laboratory's reviews of, 163-165
stories of, 160-165
in U.S. Navy shipyards, 193-194
Workers' Compensation Act, 7, 17, 18
Working Group on Asbestos and Cancer, 105-108
Workmen's Compensation Act of 1930, 241
Wright, George, 550-551
Wyer, H., 63-64

Y

Yant, W.P., 258-259

Z

Zannini, 332
Ziem, G., 473, 476